3 EDITION

*S*trategies *of*
Qualitative Inquiry

Norman K. Denzin
University of Illinois at Urbana-Champaign

Yvonna S. Lincoln
Texas A&M University

*E*ditors

SAGE Publications

Los Angeles • London • New Delhi • Singapore

For information:

Sage Publications, Inc.
2455 Teller Road
Thousand Oaks, California 91320
E-mail: order@sagepub.com

Sage Publications India Pvt. Ltd.
B 1/I 1 Mohan Cooperative Industrial Area
Mathura Road, New Delhi 110 044
India

Sage Publications Ltd.
1 Oliver's Yard
55 City Road
London EC1Y 1SP
United Kingdom

Sage Publications Asia-Pacific Pte. Ltd.
33 Pekin Street #02-01
Far East Square
Singapore 048763

Printed in the United States of America

Library of Congress Cataloging-in-Publication Data

Strategies of qualitative inquiry / Norman K. Denzin, Yvonna S. Lincoln [editors].—3rd ed.
      p. cm.
Includes bibliographical references and index.
ISBN 978-1-4129-5756-4 (pbk. : alk. paper)
    1. Social sciences—Methodology. 2. Social sciences—Research—Methodology. I. Denzin, Norman K. II. Lincoln, Yvonna S.

H61.S8823 2008
300.72—dc22   2007031741

This book is printed on acid-free paper.

             10   11   10   9   8   7   6   5   4   3   2

Acquisitions Editor:	Vicki Knight
Associate Editor:	Sean Connelly
Editorial Assistant:	Lauren Habib
Production Editor:	Astrid Virding
Copy Editor:	Gillian Dickens
Typesetter:	C&M Digitals (P) Ltd.
Proofreader:	Tracy Marcynzsyn
Indexer:	Juniee Oneida
Cover Designer:	Candice Harman
Marketing Manager:	Stephanie Adams
Cover Photograph:	C. A. Hoffman

3 EDITION

*S*trategies *of*
Qualitative Inquiry

INTERNATIONAL ADVISORY BOARD

CONTENTS

PREFACE

For nearly four decades, a quiet methodological revolution has been taking place in the social sciences. A blurring of disciplinary boundaries has occurred. The social sciences and humanities have drawn closer together in a mutual focus on an interpretive, qualitative approach to inquiry, research, and theory. Although these trends are not new, the extent to which the "qualitative revolution" has overtaken the social sciences and related professional fields continues to be nothing short of amazing.

Reflecting this revolution, a host of textbooks, journals, research monographs, and readers have been published in recent years. In 1994, we published the first edition of the *Handbook of Qualitative Research* in an attempt to represent the field in its entirety, to take stock of how far it had come and how far it might yet go. The immediate success of the first edition suggested the need to offer the *Handbook* in terms of three separate volumes. So in 1998, we published a three-volume set, *The Landscape of Qualitative Research: Theories and Issues; Strategies of Inquiry;* and *Collecting and Interpreting Qualitative Materials.* In 2003, we offered a new three-volume set, based on the second edition of the handbook.

By 2005, when we published the third edition of the *Handbook,* it was abundantly clear, as it had been in 2000, when we published the second edition of the *Handbook,* that the "field" of qualitative research was still defined primarily by tensions, contradictions, and hesitations. These tensions exist in a less-than-unified arena. We have always believed that the handbook, in its first, second, and third editions, could and would be valuable for solidifying, interpreting, and organizing the field despite the essential differences that characterize it.

The first edition attempted to define the field of qualitative research. The second edition went one step further. Building on themes in the first edition, we asked how the practices of qualitative inquiry could be used to address issues of equity and of social justice. The third edition continues where the second edition ended. The transformations that were taking place in the 1990s continue to gain momentum in the first decade of this new century.

Not surprisingly, this quiet revolution has been met by resistance. In many quarters, a resurgent, scientifically based research paradigm has gained the upper hand. Borrowing from the field of biomedical research, the National Research Council (NRC) has appropriated neo-positivist, evidence-based epistemologies. Calls for mixed-method designs are now common. Interpretive methods are read as being unscientific and unsuitable for use by those who legislate social policy.

Still, the days of a value-free inquiry based on a God's-eye view of reality are judged by many to be over. Today, many agree that all inquiry is moral and political. Experimental, reflexive ways of writing first-person ethnographic texts are now commonplace. There continues to be a pressing need to show how the practices of qualitative research can help change the world in positive ways. So at the beginning of the 21st century, it is necessary to reengage the promise of qualitative research as a form of radical democratic practice.

We have been enormously gratified and heartened by the response to the *Handbook* since its publication. Especially gratifying has been that it has been used and adapted by such a wide variety of scholars and graduate students in precisely the way we had hoped: as a starting point, a springboard for new thought and new work.

▣ THE PAPERBACK PROJECT

The third edition of the *Strategies of Qualitative Inquiry* of the *Handbook of Qualitative Research* is virtually a new volume. Indeed, in the third edition of the *Handbook,* there are 42 new chapters, authors, and/or coauthors. There are 16 totally new chapter topics, including contributions on indigenous inquiry, decolonizing methodologies, critical ethnography, critical humanism and queer theory, performance ethnography, narrative inquiry, arts-based inquiry, online ethnography, analytic methodologies, Foucault's methodologies, talk and text, focus groups and critical pedagogy, relativism, criteria and politics, the poetics of place, cultural and investigative poetics, qualitative evaluation and social policy, social science inquiry in the new millennium, and anthropology of the contemporary. All returning authors have substantially revised their original contributions, in many cases producing totally new and different chapters.

The third edition of the *Handbook of Qualitative Research* continues where the second edition ended. It takes as its theme the necessity to reengage the promise of qualitative research as a generative form of radical democratic practice. This is the agenda of the third edition of the *Landscape* series, as it is for the third edition of the *Handbook*— namely, to show how the discourses of qualitative research can be used to help create and imagine a free democratic society. Each of the chapters in the three-volume set takes up this project, in one way or another.

A handbook, we were told by our publisher, should ideally represent the distillation of knowledge of a field, a benchmark volume that synthesizes an existing literature, helping to define and shape the present and future of that discipline. This mandate organized the third edition. In metaphoric terms, if you were to take one book on qualitative research with you to a desert island or a mountaintop (or for a comprehensive graduate examination), a handbook would be the book.

It was again decided that the part structure of the *Handbook* could serve as a useful point of departure for the organization of the paperbacks. Thus, Volume 1, titled *The Landscape of Qualitative Research: Theories and Issues,* takes a look at the field from a broadly theoretical perspective and is composed of the *Handbook*'s Parts I ("Locating the Field"), II ("Paradigms and Perspectives in Contention"), and VI ("The Future of Qualitative Research"). Volume 2, titled *Strategies of Qualitative Inquiry,* focuses on just that, and consists of Part III of the *Handbook.* Volume 3, titled *Collecting and Interpreting Qualitative Materials,* considers the tasks of collecting, analyzing, and interpreting empirical materials and comprises the *Handbook*'s Parts IV ("Methods of Collecting and Analyzing Empirical Materials") and V ("The Art and Practices of Interpretation, Evaluation, and Presentation").

As with the first and second editions of the Landscape series, we decided that nothing should be cut from the original *Handbook.* Nearly everyone we spoke to who used the *Handbook* had his or her own way of using it, leaning heavily on certain chapters and skipping others altogether. But there was consensus that this reorganization made a great deal of sense both pedagogically and economically. We and Sage are committed to making this iteration of the *Handbook* accessible for classroom use. This commitment is reflected in the size, organization, and price of the paperbacks, as well as in the addition of end-of-book bibliographies.

It also became clear in our conversations with colleagues who used the *Handbook* that the single-volume, hardcover version has a distinct place and value, and Sage will keep the original version available until a revised edition is published.

▣ ORGANIZATION OF THIS VOLUME

Strategies of Qualitative Inquiry isolates the major strategies—historically, the research methods—that researchers can use in conducting concrete qualitative studies. The question of inquiry necessarily begins with the issues surrounding the practice and politics of funded research. This is the topic of the chapter by Julianne Cheek. Questions of inquiry always begin with a socially situated observer. The qualitative researcher begins with a research question, moving then to a paradigm or perspective and then to interpretive practices (or methods) that represent the empirical world. So located, the researcher then addresses a range of methods that can be employed in any study. The history and uses of these strategies are explored extensively in this volume. The chapters move from performance ethnography to case studies, to issues of ethnographic representation, then to ethnomethodology, next to grounded theory strategies, then to testimonios, life histories, participatory action research, and clinical research.

Acknowledgments

Of course, this book would not exist without its authors or the editorial board members for the *Handbook* on which it is based. These individuals were able to offer both long-term, sustained commitments to the project and short-term emergency assistance.

In addition, we would like to thank the following individuals and institutions for their assistance, support, insights, and patience: our respective universities and departments, as well as Aisha Durham, Grant Kien, Li Xiong, James Salvo, David Monje, and our respective graduate students. Without them, we could never have kept this project on course. There are also several people to thank at Sage Publications. We thank Lisa Cuevas Shaw, our editor. This three-volume version of the *Handbook* would not have been possible without Lisa's wisdom, support, humor, and grasp of the field in all its current diversity.

As always, we appreciate the efforts of Chris Klein, vice president of Books Acquisitions and Books Marketing at Sage, along with his staff, for their indefatigable efforts in getting the word out about the *Handbook* to teachers, researchers, and methodologists around the world. We thank Christina Ceisel for her excellent work in the production phase of all three volumes of this project. Astrid Virding was essential in moving this project through production; we are also grateful to the copy editor, Judy Selhorst, and to those whose proofreading and indexing skills were so central to the publication of the *Handbook* on which these volumes are based. Finally, as ever, we thank our spouses, Katherine Ryan and Egon Guba, for their forbearance and constant support.

The idea for this three-volume paperback version of the *Handbook* did not arise in a vacuum, and we are grateful for the feedback we received from countless teachers and students, both informally and in response to our formal survey. We wish especially to thank the following individuals: Bryant Alexander, Tom Barone, Jack Z. Bratich, Susan Chase, Shing-Ling Sarina Chen, Nadine Dolby, Susan Finley, Andrea Fontana, Jaber Gubrium, Stephen Hartnett, Stacy Holman Jones, Steve Jones, Ruthellen Josselson, Luis Miron, Ronald J. Pelias, John Prosser, Johnny Saldaña, Paula Saukko, Thomas Schwandt, Patrick Slattery, and Linda Tuhiwai Smith.

Norman K. Denzin
University of Illinois at Urbana-Champaign

Yvonna S. Lincoln
Texas A&M University

1

INTRODUCTION

The Discipline and Practice of Qualitative Research

Norman K. Denzin and Yvonna S. Lincoln

W riting about scientific research, including qualitative research, from the vantage point of the colonized, a position that she chooses to privilege, Linda Tuhiwai Smith (1999) states that "the term 'research' is inextricably linked to European imperialism and colonialism." She continues, "The word itself is probably one of the dirtiest words in the indigenous world's vocabulary. . . . It is implicated in the worst excesses of colonialism," with the ways in which "knowledge about indigenous peoples was collected, classified, and then represented back to the West" (p. 1). This dirty word stirs up anger, silence, distrust. "It is so powerful that indigenous people even write poetry about research" (p. 1). It is one of colonialism's most sordid legacies.

Sadly, qualitative research, in many if not all of its forms (observation, participation, interviewing, ethnography), serves as a metaphor for colonial knowledge, for power, and for truth. The metaphor works this way. Research, quantitative and qualitative, is scientific. Research provides the foundation for reports about and representations of "the Other." In the colonial context, research becomes an objective way of representing the dark-skinned Other to the white world.

Colonizing nations relied on the human disciplines, especially sociology and anthropology, to produce knowledge about strange and foreign worlds. This close

Authors' Note. We are grateful to many who have helped with this chapter, including Egon Guba, Mitch Allen, David Monje, and Katherine E. Ryan.

involvement with the colonial project contributed, in significant ways, to qualitative research's long and anguished history and to its becoming a dirty word (for reviews, see Foley & Valenzuela, Volume 2, Chapter 9; Tedlock, Chapter 5, this volume). In sociology, the work of the "Chicago school" in the 1920s and 1930s established the importance of qualitative inquiry for the study of human group life. In anthropology during the same period, the discipline-defining studies of Boas, Mead, Benedict, Bateson, Evans-Pritchard, Radcliffe-Brown, and Malinowski charted the outlines of the fieldwork method (see Gupta & Ferguson, 1997; Stocking, 1986, 1989).

The agenda was clear-cut: The observer went to a foreign setting to study the culture, customs, and habits of another human group. Often this was a group that stood in the way of white settlers. Ethnographic reports of these groups where incorporated into colonizing strategies, ways of controlling the foreign, deviant, or troublesome Other. Soon qualitative research would be employed in other social and behavioral science disciplines, including education (especially the work of Dewey), history, political science, business, medicine, nursing, social work, and communications (for criticisms of this tradition, see Smith, 1999; Vidich & Lyman, 2000; see also Rosaldo, 1989, pp. 25–45; Tedlock, Chapter 5, this volume).

By the 1960s, battle lines were drawn within the quantitative and qualitative camps. Quantitative scholars relegated qualitative research to a subordinate status in the scientific arena. In response, qualitative researchers extolled the humanistic virtues of their subjective, interpretive approach to the study of human group life. In the meantime, indigenous peoples found themselves subjected to the indignities of both approaches, as each methodology was used in the name of colonizing powers (see Battiste, 2000; Semali & Kincheloe, 1999).

Vidich and Lyman (1994, 2000) have charted many key features of this painful history. In their now-classic analysis they note, with some irony, that qualitative research in sociology and anthropology was "born out of concern to understand the 'other'" (Vidich & Lyman, 2000, p. 38). Furthermore, this "other" was the exotic Other, a primitive, nonwhite person from a foreign culture judged to be less civilized than ours. Of course, there were colonialists long before there were anthropologists and ethnographers. Nonetheless, there would be no colonial, and now no neocolonial, history were it not for this investigative mentality that turned the dark-skinned Other into the object of the ethnographer's gaze. From the very beginning, qualitative research was implicated in a racist project.[1]

In this introductory chapter, we define the field of qualitative research, then navigate, chart, and review the history of qualitative research in the human disciplines. This will allow us to locate this volume and its contents within their historical moments. (These historical moments are somewhat artificial; they are socially constructed, quasi-historical, and overlapping conventions. Nevertheless, they permit a "performance" of developing ideas. They also facilitate an increasing sensitivity to and sophistication about the pitfalls and promises of ethnography and qualitative research.) We also present a conceptual framework for reading the qualitative research act as a multicultural, gendered process and then provide a brief introduction to the chapters that follow. Returning to the observations of Vidich and Lyman as well as those of hooks, we conclude with a brief discussion of qualitative research and critical race theory (see also Ladson-Billings & Donnor, Volume 1, Chapter 11). We also discuss the threats to qualitative, human subject research from the methodological conservatism movement mentioned briefly in our preface. As we note in the preface, we use the metaphor of the bridge to structure what follows. This volume is intended to serve as a bridge connecting historical moments, politics, the decolonization project, research methods, paradigms, and communities of interpretive scholars.

◙ DEFINITIONAL ISSUES

Qualitative research is a field of inquiry in its own right. It crosscuts disciplines, fields, and subject matters.[2] A complex, interconnected family of terms, concepts, and assumptions surround the term *qualitative research*. These include the traditions associated with foundationalism, positivism, postfoundationalism, postpositivism, poststructuralism, and the many qualitative research perspectives, and/or methods connected to cultural and interpretive studies (the chapters in Volume 1, Part II, take up these paradigms).[3] There are separate and detailed literatures on the many methods and approaches that fall under the category of qualitative research, such as case study, politics and ethics, participatory inquiry, interviewing, participant observation, visual methods, and interpretive analysis.

In North America, qualitative research operates in a complex historical field that crosscuts at least eight historical moments. (We discuss these moments in detail below.) These moments overlap and simultaneously operate in the present.[4] We define them as the *traditional* (1900–1950); the *modernist*, or golden age (1950–1970); *blurred genres* (1970–1986); the *crisis of representation* (1986–1990); the *postmodern*, a period of experimental and new ethnographies (1990–1995); *postexperimental inquiry* (1995–2000); the *methodologically contested present* (2000–2004); and the *fractured future*, which is now (2005–). The future, the eighth moment, confronts the methodological backlash associated with the evidence-based social movement. It is concerned with moral discourse, with the development of sacred textualities. The eighth moment asks that the social sciences and the humanities become sites for critical conversations about democracy, race, gender, class, nation-states, globalization, freedom, and community.[5]

The postmodern and postexperimental moments were defined in part by a concern for literary and rhetorical tropes and the narrative turn, a concern for storytelling, for composing ethnographies in new ways (Bochner & Ellis, 2002; Ellis, 2004; Goodall, 2000; Pelias, 2004; Richardson & Lockridge, 2004; Trujillo, 2004). Laurel

Richardson (1997) observes that this moment was shaped by a new sensibility, by doubt, by a refusal to privilege any method or theory (p. 173). But now at the dawn of this new century we struggle to connect qualitative research to the hopes, needs, goals, and promises of a free democratic society.

Successive waves of epistemological theorizing move across these eight moments. The traditional period is associated with the positivist, foundational paradigm. The modernist or golden age and blurred genres moments are connected to the appearance of postpositivist arguments. At the same time, a variety of new interpretive, qualitative perspectives were taken up, including hermeneutics, structuralism, semiotics, phenomenology, cultural studies, and feminism.[6] In the blurred genres phase, the humanities became central resources for critical, interpretive theory, and the qualitative research project broadly conceived. The researcher became a *bricoleur* (see below), learning how to borrow from many different disciplines.

The blurred genres phase produced the next stage, the crisis of representation. Here researchers struggled with how to locate themselves and their subjects in reflexive texts. A kind of methodological diaspora took place, a two-way exodus. Humanists migrated to the social sciences, searching for new social theory, new ways to study popular culture and its local, ethnographic contexts. Social scientists turned to the humanities, hoping to learn how to do complex structural and poststructural readings of social texts. From the humanities, social scientists also learned how to produce texts that refused to be read in simplistic, linear, incontrovertible terms. The line between text and context blurred. In the postmodern, experimental moment, researchers continued to move away from foundational and quasi-foundational criteria (see Smith & Hodkinson, Volume 3, Chapter 13; Richardson & St. Pierre, Volume 3, Chapter 15). Alternative evaluative criteria were sought, criteria that might prove evocative, moral, critical, and rooted in local understandings.

Any definition of qualitative research must work within this complex historical field. *Qualitative research* means different things in each of these moments. Nonetheless, an initial, generic definition can be offered: Qualitative research is a situated activity that locates the observer in the world. It consists of a set of interpretive, material practices that make the world visible. These practices transform the world. They turn the world into a series of representations, including field notes, interviews, conversations, photographs, recordings, and memos to the self. At this level, qualitative research involves an interpretive, naturalistic approach to the world. This means that qualitative researchers study things in their natural settings, attempting to make sense of, or interpret, phenomena in terms of the meanings people bring to them.[7]

Qualitative research involves the studied use and collection of a variety of empirical materials—case study; personal experience; introspection; life story; interview; artifacts; cultural texts and productions; observational, historical, interactional, and visual texts—that describe routine and problematic moments and meanings in individuals' lives. Accordingly, qualitative researchers deploy a wide range of interconnected interpretive practices, hoping always to get a better understanding of the subject matter at hand. It is understood, however, that each practice makes the world visible in a different way. Hence there is frequently a commitment to using more than one interpretive practice in any study.

The Qualitative Researcher as *Bricoleur* and Quilt Maker

The qualitative researcher may be described using multiple and gendered images: scientist, naturalist, field-worker, journalist, social critic, artist, performer, jazz musician, filmmaker, quilt maker, essayist. The many methodological practices of qualitative research may be viewed as soft science, journalism, ethnography, bricolage, quilt making, or montage. The researcher, in turn, may be seen as a *bricoleur*, as a maker of quilts, or, as in filmmaking, a person who assembles images into montages. (On montage, see Cook, 1981, pp. 171–177; Monaco, 1981, pp. 322–328; and the discussion below. On quilting, see hooks, 1990, pp. 115–122; Wolcott, 1995, pp. 31–33.)

Harper (1987, pp. 9, 74–75, 92), de Certeau (1984, p. xv), Nelson, Treichler, and Grossberg (1992, p. 2), Lévi-Strauss (1966, p. 17), Weinstein and Weinstein (1991, p. 161), and Kincheloe (2001) clarify the meanings of *bricolage* and *bricoleur*.[8] A *bricoleur* makes do by "adapting the *bricoles* of the world. *Bricolage* is 'the poetic making do'" (de Certeau, 1984, p. xv) with "such bricoles—the odds and ends, the bits left over" (Harper, 1987, p. 74). The *bricoleur* is a "Jack of all trades, a kind of professional do-it-yourself" (Lévi-Strauss, 1966, p. 17). In their work, *bricoleurs* define and extend themselves (Harper, 1987, p. 75). Indeed, the *bricoleur's* life story, or biography, "may be thought of as bricolage" (Harper, 1987, p. 92).

There are many kinds of *bricoleurs*—interpretive, narrative, theoretical, political, methodological (see below). The interpretive *bricoleur* produces a bricolage—that is, a pieced-together set of representations that is fitted to the specifics of a complex situation. "The solution (bricolage) which is the result of the *bricoleur's* method is an [emergent] construction" (Weinstein & Weinstein, 1991, p. 161) that changes and takes new forms as the *bricoleur* adds different tools, methods, and techniques of representation and interpretation to the puzzle. Nelson et al. (1992) describe the methodology of cultural studies as "a bricolage. Its choice of practice, that is, is pragmatic, strategic and self-reflexive" (p. 2). This understanding can be applied, with qualifications, to qualitative research.

The qualitative researcher as *bricoleur*, or maker of quilts, uses the aesthetic and material tools of his or her craft, deploying whatever strategies, methods, and empirical materials are at hand (Becker, 1998, p. 2). If the researcher needs to invent, or piece together, new tools or techniques, he or she will do so. Choices regarding which interpretive practices to employ are not necessarily made in advance. As Nelson et al. (1992) note, the "choice of research practices depends upon the questions that are asked, and the questions depend on their context" (p. 2), what is available in the context, and what the researcher can do in that setting.

These interpretive practices involve aesthetic issues, an aesthetics of representation that goes beyond the pragmatic or the practical. Here the concept of *montage* is useful (see Cook, 1981, p. 323; Monaco, 1981, pp. 171–172). Montage is a method of editing cinematic images. In the history of cinematography, montage is most closely associated with the work of Sergei Eisenstein, especially his film *The Battleship Potemkin* (1925). In montage, several different images are juxtaposed to or superimposed on one another to create a picture. In a sense, montage is like *pentimento,* in which something that has been painted out of a picture (an image the painter "repented," or denied) becomes visible again, creating something new. What is new is what had been obscured by a previous image.

Montage and pentimento, like jazz, which is improvisation, create the sense that images, sounds, and understandings are blending together, overlapping, forming a composite, a new creation. The images seem to shape and define one another, and an emotional, gestalt effect is produced. In film montage, images are often combined in a swiftly run sequence that produces a dizzily revolving collection of several images around a central or focused picture or sequence; directors often use such effects to signify the passage of time.

Perhaps the most famous instance of montage in film is the Odessa Steps sequence in *The Battleship Potemkin.* In the climax of the film, the citizens of Odessa are being massacred by czarist troops on the stone steps leading down to the harbor. Eisenstein cuts to a young mother as she pushes her baby in a carriage across the landing in front of the firing troops.[9] Citizens rush past her, jolting the carriage, which she is afraid to push down to the next flight of stairs. The troops are above her, firing at the citizens. She is trapped between the troops and the steps. She screams. A line of rifles points to the sky, the rifle barrels erupting in smoke. The mother's head sways back. The wheels of the carriage teeter on the edge of the steps. The mother's hand clutches the silver buckle of her belt. Below her, people are being beaten by soldiers. Blood drips over the mother's white gloves. The baby's hand reaches out of the carriage. The mother sways back and forth. The troops advance. The mother falls back against the carriage. A woman watches in horror as the rear wheels of the carriage roll off the edge of the landing. With accelerating speed, the carriage bounces down the steps, past dead citizens. The baby is jostled from side to side inside the carriage. The soldiers fire their rifles into a group of wounded citizens. A student screams as the carriage leaps across the steps, tilts, and overturns (Cook, 1981, p. 167).[10]

Montage uses brief images to create a clearly defined sense of urgency and complexity. It invites viewers to construct interpretations that build on one another as a scene unfolds. These interpretations are based on associations among the contrasting images that blend into one another. The underlying assumption of montage is that viewers perceive and interpret the shots in a "montage sequence not *sequentially,* or one at a time, but rather *simultaneously*" (Cook, 1981, p. 172). The viewer puts the sequences together into a meaningful emotional whole, as if at a glance, all at once.

The qualitative researcher who uses montage is like a quilt maker or a jazz improviser. The quilter stitches, edits, and puts slices of reality together. This process creates and brings psychological and emotional unity—a pattern—to an interpretive experience. There are many examples of montage in current qualitative research (see Diversi, 1998; Holman Jones, 1999; Lather & Smithies, 1997; Ronai, 1998; see also Holman Jones, Volume 3, Chapter 7). Using multiple voices, different textual formats, and various typefaces, Lather and Smithies (1997) weave a complex text about AIDS and women who are HIV-positive. Holman Jones (1999) creates a performance text using lyrics from the blues songs sung by Billie Holiday.

In texts based on the metaphors of montage, quilt making, and jazz improvisation, many different things are going on at the same time—different voices, different perspectives, points of views, angles of vision. Like autoethnographic performance texts, works that use montage simultaneously create and enact moral meaning. They move from the personal to the political, from the local to the historical and the cultural. These are dialogical texts. They presume an active audience. They create spaces for give-and-take between reader and writer. They do more than turn the Other into the object of the social science gaze (see Alexander, Chapter 3, this volume; Holman Jones, Volume 3, Chapter 7).

Qualitative research is inherently multimethod in focus (Flick, 2002, pp. 226–227). However, the use of multiple methods, or triangulation, reflects an attempt to secure an in-depth understanding of the phenomenon in question. Objective reality can never be captured. We know a thing only through its representations. Triangulation is not a tool or a strategy of validation, but an alternative to validation (Flick, 2002, p. 227). The combination of multiple methodological practices, empirical materials, perspectives, and observers in a single study is best understood, then, as a strategy that adds rigor, breadth, complexity, richness, and depth to any inquiry (see Flick, 2002, p. 229).

In Chapter 15, Volume 3, Richardson and St. Pierre dispute the usefulness of the concept of triangulation, asserting that the central image for qualitative inquiry should be the crystal, not the triangle. Mixed-genre texts in the postexperimental moment have more than three sides. Like crystals, Eisenstein's montage, the jazz solo, or the pieces in a quilt, the mixed-genre text "combines symmetry and substance with an infinite variety of shapes, substances, transmutations. . . . Crystals grow, change, alter. . . . Crystals are prisms that reflect externalities and refract within themselves, creating different colors, patterns, arrays, casting off in different directions" (Richardson, 2000, p. 934).

In the crystallization process, the writer tells the same tale from different points of view. For example, in *A Thrice-Told Tale* (1992), Margery Wolf uses fiction, field notes, and a scientific article to give three different accounts of the same set of experiences in a native village. Similarly, in her play *Fires in the Mirror* (1993), Anna Deavere Smith presents a series of performance pieces based on interviews with people who were involved in a racial conflict in Crown Heights, Brooklyn, on August 19, 1991. The play has multiple speaking parts, including conversations with gang members, police officers, and anonymous young girls and boys. There is no one "correct" telling of this event. Each telling, like light hitting a crystal, reflects a different perspective on this incident.

Viewed as a crystalline form, as a montage, or as a creative performance around a central theme, triangulation as a form of, or alternative to, validity thus can be extended. Triangulation is the simultaneous display of multiple, refracted realities. Each of the metaphors "works" to create simultaneity rather than the sequential or linear. Readers and audiences are then invited to explore competing visions of the context, to become immersed in and merge with new realities to comprehend.

The methodological *bricoleur* is adept at performing a large number of diverse tasks, ranging from interviewing to intensive self-reflection and introspection. The theoretical *bricoleur* reads widely and is knowledgeable about the many interpretive paradigms (feminism, Marxism, cultural studies, constructivism, queer theory) that can be brought to any particular problem. He or she may not, however, feel that paradigms can be mingled or synthesized. That is, one cannot easily move between paradigms as overarching philosophical systems denoting particular ontologies, epistemologies, and methodologies. They represent belief systems that attach users to particular worldviews. Perspectives, in contrast, are less well-developed systems, and one can move between them more easily. The researcher as *bricoleur*-theorist works between and within competing and overlapping perspectives and paradigms.

The interpretive *bricoleur* understands that research is an interactive process shaped by his or her own personal history, biography, gender, social class, race, and ethnicity, and by those of the people in the setting. The critical *bricoleur* stresses the dialectical and hermeneutic nature of interdisciplinary inquiry, knowing that the boundaries that previously separated traditional disciplines no longer hold (Kincheloe, 2001, p. 683). The political *bricoleur* knows that science is power, for all research findings have political implications. There is no value-free science. This researcher seeks a civic social science based on a politics of hope (Lincoln, 1999). The gendered, narrative *bricoleur* also knows that researchers all tell stories about the worlds they have studied. Thus the narratives, or stories, scientists tell are accounts couched and framed within specific storytelling traditions, often defined as paradigms (e.g., positivism, postpositivism, constructivism).

The product of the interpretive *bricoleur*'s labor is a complex, quiltlike bricolage, a reflexive collage or montage—a set of fluid, interconnected images and representations. This interpretive structure is like a quilt, a performance text, a sequence of representations connecting the parts to the whole.

Qualitative Research as a Site of Multiple Interpretive Practices

Qualitative research, as a set of interpretive activities, privileges no single methodological practice over another. As a site of discussion, or discourse, qualitative research is difficult to define clearly. It has no theory or paradigm that is distinctly its own. As the contributions to Part II of Volume 1, multiple theoretical paradigms claim use of qualitative research methods and strategies, from constructivist to cultural studies, feminism, Marxism, and ethnic models of study. Qualitative research is used in many separate disciplines, as we will discuss below. It does not belong to a single discipline.

Nor does qualitative research have a distinct set of methods or practices that are entirely its own. Qualitative researchers use semiotics, narrative, content, discourse, archival and phonemic analysis, even statistics, tables, graphs, and numbers. They also draw on and utilize the approaches, methods, and techniques of ethnomethodology, phenomenology, hermeneutics, feminism, rhizomatics, deconstructionism, ethnography, interviewing, psychoanalysis, cultural studies, survey research, and participant observation, among others.[11] All of these research practices "can provide important insights and knowledge" (Nelson et al., 1992, p. 2). No specific method or practice can be privileged over any other.

Many of these methods, or research practices, are used in other contexts in the human disciplines. Each bears the traces of its own disciplinary history. Thus there is an extensive history of the uses and meanings of ethnography and ethnology in education (see Ladson-Billings & Donnor, Volume 1, Chapter 11; Kincheloe & McLaren, Volume 1, Chapter 12); of participant observation and ethnography in anthropology (see Foley & Valenzuela, Volume 1, Chapter 9; Tedlock, Chapter 5, this volume; Brady, Volume 3, Chapter 16), sociology (see Holstein & Gubrium, Volume 2, Chapter 6; Fontana & Frey, Chapter 4, this volume; Harper, Chapter 6, this volume), communications (see Alexander, Volume 2, Chapter 3; Holman Jones, Chapter 7, this volume), and cultural studies (see Saukko, Chapter 13); of textual, hermeneutic, feminist, psychoanalytic, arts-based, semiotic, and narrative analysis in cinema and literary studies (see Olesen, Volume 1, Chapter 10; Finley, Volume 3, Chapter 3; Brady, Volume 3, Chapter 16) and of narrative, discourse, and conversational analysis in sociology, medicine, communications, and education (see Miller & Crabtree, Volume 2, Chapter 11; Chase, Volume 3, Chapter 2; Peräkylä, Volume 3, Chapter 11).

The many histories that surround each method or research strategy reveal how multiple uses and meanings are brought to each practice. Textual analyses in literary studies, for example, often treat texts as self-contained systems. On the other hand, a researcher working from a cultural studies or feminist perspective reads a text in terms of its location within a historical moment marked by a particular gender, race, or class ideology. A cultural studies use of ethnography would bring a set of understandings from feminism, postmodernism, and poststructuralism to the project. These understandings would not be shared by mainstream postpositivist sociologists. Similarly, postpositivist and poststructural historians bring different understandings and uses to the methods and findings of historical research (see Tierney, 2000). These tensions and contradictions are all evident in the chapters in this volume.

These separate and multiple uses and meanings of the methods of qualitative research make it difficult for scholars to agree on any essential definition of the field, for it is never just one thing.[12] Still, we must establish a definition for purposes of this discussion. We borrow from, and paraphrase, Nelson et al.'s (1992, p. 4) attempt to define cultural studies:

> Qualitative research is an interdisciplinary, transdisciplinary, and sometimes counterdisci-plinary field. It crosscuts the humanities and the social and physical sciences. Qualitative research is many things at the same time. It is multiparadigmatic in focus. Its practitioners are sensitive to the value of the multimethod approach. They are committed to the natural-istic perspective and to the interpretive understanding of human experience. At the same time, the field is inherently political and shaped by multiple ethical and political positions.
>
> Qualitative research embraces two tensions at the same time. On the one hand, it is drawn to a broad, interpretive, postexperimental, postmodern, feminist, and critical sensi-bility. On the other hand, it is drawn to more narrowly defined positivist, postpositivist, humanistic, and naturalistic conceptions of human experience and its analysis. Further, these tensions can be combined in the same project, bringing both postmodern and natu-ralistic, or both critical and humanistic, perspectives to bear.

This rather awkward statement means that qualitative research, as a set of prac-tices, embraces within its own multiple disciplinary histories constant tensions and contradictions over the project itself, including its methods and the forms its findings and interpretations take. The field sprawls between and cuts across all of the human disciplines, even including, in some cases, the physical sciences. Its practitioners are variously committed to modern, postmodern, and postexperimental sensibilities and the approaches to social research that these sensibilities imply.

Resistances to Qualitative Studies

The academic and disciplinary resistances to qualitative research illustrate the pol-itics embedded in this field of discourse. The challenges to qualitative research are many. As Seale, Gobo, Gubrium, and Silverman (2004) observe, we can best under-stand these criticisms by "distinguish[ing] analytically the political (or external) role of [qualitative] methodology from the procedural (or internal) one" (p. 7). Politics sit-uate methodology within and outside the academy. Procedural issues define how qualitative methodology is used to produce knowledge about the world.

Often, the political and the procedural intersect. Politicians and "hard" scientists sometimes call qualitative researchers journalists or soft scientists. The work of qualita-tive scholars is termed unscientific, or only exploratory, or subjective. It is called criticism rather than theory or science, or it is interpreted politically, as a disguised version of Marxism or secular humanism (see Huber, 1995; see also Denzin, 1997, pp. 258–261).

These political and procedural resistances reflect an uneasy awareness that the inter-pretive traditions of qualitative research commit the researcher to a critique of the posi-tivist or postpositivist project. But the positivist resistance to qualitative research goes beyond the "ever-present desire to maintain a distinction between hard science and soft scholarship" (Carey, 1989, p. 99; see also Smith & Hodkinson, Volume 3, Chapter 13). The experimental (positivist) sciences (physics, chemistry, economics, and psychology, for example) are often seen as the crowning achievements of Western civilization, and in their practices it is assumed that "truth" can transcend opinion and personal bias (Carey, 1989, p. 99; Schwandt, 1997b, p. 309). Qualitative research is seen as an assault on this tradition, whose adherents often retreat into a "value-free objectivist science" (Carey, 1989, p. 104) model to defend their position. They seldom attempt to make explicit, or to critique, the "moral and political commitments in their own contingent work" (Carey, 1989, p. 104; see also Guba & Lincoln, Volume 3, Chapter 8).

Positivists further allege that the so-called new experimental qualitative researchers write fiction, not science, and that these researchers have no way of verifying their truth statements. Ethnographic poetry and fiction signal the death of empirical science, and there is little to be gained by attempting to engage in moral criticism. These critics presume a stable, unchanging reality that can be studied using the empirical methods of objective social science (see Huber, 1995). The province of qualitative research, accordingly, is the world of lived experience, for this is where individual belief and action intersect with culture. Under this model there is no preoccupation with discourse and method as material interpretive practices that constitute representation and description. Thus is the textual, narrative turn rejected by the positivists.

The opposition to positive science by the poststructuralists is seen, then, as an attack on reason and truth. At the same time, the positivist science attack on qualitative research is regarded as an attempt to legislate one version of truth over another.

Politics and Reemergent Scientism

The scientifically based research (SBR) movement initiated in recent years by the National Research Council (NRC) has created a hostile political environment for qualitative research. Connected to the federal legislation known as the No Child Left Behind Act of 2001, SBR embodies a reemergent scientism (Maxwell, 2004), a positivist, evidence-based epistemology. The movement encourages researchers to employ "rigorous, systematic, and objective methodology to obtain reliable and valid knowledge " (Ryan & Hood, 2004, p. 80). The preferred methodology employs well-defined causal models and independent and dependent variables. Researchers examine causal models in the context of randomized controlled experiments, which allow for replication and generalization of their results (Ryan & Hood, 2004, p. 81).

Under such a framework, qualitative research becomes suspect. Qualitative research does not require well-defined variables or causal models. The observations and measurements of qualitative scholars are not based on subjects' random assignment to experimental groups. Qualitative researchers do not generate "hard evidence" using such methods. At best, through case study, interview, and ethnographic methods, researchers can gather descriptive materials that can be tested with experimental methods. The epistemologies of critical race, queer, postcolonial, feminist, and postmodern theories are rendered useless by the SBR perspective, relegated at best to the category of scholarship, not science (Ryan & Hood, 2004, p. 81; St. Pierre, 2004, p. 132).

Critics of the SBR movement are united on the following points. "Bush science" (Lather, 2004, p. 19) and its experimental, evidence-based methodologies represent a racialized, masculinist backlash to the proliferation of qualitative inquiry methods over the past two decades. The movement endorses a narrow view of science (Maxwell, 2004) that celebrates a "neoclassical experimentalism that is a throwback to the Campbell-Stanley era and its dogmatic adherence to an exclusive reliance on quantitative methods" (Howe, 2004, p. 42). The movement represents "nostalgia for a simple and ordered universe of science that never was" (Popkewitz, 2004, p. 62). With its emphasis on only one form of scientific rigor, the NRC ignores the value of using complex historical, contextual, and political criteria to evaluate inquiry (Bloch, 2004).

As Howe (2004) observes, neoclassical experimentalists extol evidence-based "medical research as the model for educational research, particularly the random clinical trial" (p. 48). But dispensing a pill in a random clinical trial is quite unlike "dispensing a curriculum," and the "effects" of an educational experiment cannot be easily measured, unlike a "10-point reduction in diastolic blood pressure" (p. 48; see also Miller & Crabtree, Volume 2, Chapter 11).

Qualitative researchers must learn to think outside the box as they critique the NRC and its methodological guidelines (Atkinson, 2004). They must apply their imaginations and find new ways to define such terms as *randomized design, causal model, policy studies,* and *public science* (Cannella & Lincoln, 2004a, 2004b; Lincoln & Cannella, 2004a, 2004b; Lincoln & Tierney, 2004; Weinstein, 2004). More deeply, qualitative researchers must resist conservative attempts to discredit qualitative inquiry by placing it back inside the box of positivism.

Mixed-Methods Experimentalism

As Howe (2004) notes, the SBR movement finds a place for qualitative methods in mixed-methods experimental designs. In such designs, qualitative methods may be "employed either singly or in combination with quantitative methods, including the use of randomized experimental designs" (p. 49). Mixed-methods designs are direct descendants of classical experimentalism. They presume a methodological hierarchy in which quantitative methods are at the top and qualitative methods are relegated to "a largely auxiliary role in pursuit of the *technocratic* aim of accumulating knowledge of 'what works'" (pp. 53–54).

The mixed-methods movement takes qualitative methods out of their natural home, which is within the critical, interpretive framework (Howe, 2004, p. 54; but see Teddlie & Tashakkori, 2003, p. 15). It divides inquiry into dichotomous categories: exploration versus confirmation. Qualitative work is assigned to the first category, quantitative research to the second (Teddlie & Tashakkori, 2003, p. 15). Like the classic experimental model, it excludes stakeholders from dialogue and active participation in the research process. This weakens its democratic and dialogical dimensions and decreases the likelihood that previously silenced voices will be heard (Howe, 2004, pp. 56–57). As Howe (2004) cautions, it is not just the "'methodological fundamentalists' who have bought into [this] approach. A sizable number of rather influential . . . educational researchers . . . have also signed on. This might be a compromise to the current political climate; it might be a backlash against the perceived excesses of postmodernism; it might be both. It is an ominous development, whatever the explanation" (p. 57).

Pragmatic Criticisms of Antifoundationalism

Seale et al. (2004) contest what they regard as the excesses of an antimethodological, "anything goes," romantic postmodernism that is associated with our project. They assert that too often the approach we value produces "low quality qualitative research and research results that are quite stereotypical and close to common sense" (p. 2). In contrast, they propose a practice-based, pragmatic approach that places research practice at the center. They note that research involves an engagement "with a variety of things and people: research materials . . . social theories, philosophical debates, values, methods, tests . . . research participants" (p. 2). (Actually, this approach is quite close to our own, especially our view of the *bricoleur* and bricolage.) Seale et al.'s situated methodology rejects the antifoundational claim that there are only partial truths, that the dividing line between fact and fiction has broken down (p. 3). These scholars believe that this dividing line has not collapsed, and that qualitative researchers should not accept stories if they do not accord with the best available facts (p. 6).

Oddly, these pragmatic procedural arguments reproduce a variant of the evidence-based model and its criticisms of poststructural, performative sensibilities. They can be used to provide political support for the methodological marginalization of the positions advanced by many of the contributors to this volume.

▣ ▣ ▣

The complex political terrain described above defines the many traditions and strands of qualitative research: the British tradition and its presence in other national contexts; the American pragmatic, naturalistic, and interpretive traditions in sociology, anthropology, communications, and education; the German and French phenomenological, hermeneutic, semiotic, Marxist, structural, and poststructural perspectives; feminist studies, African American studies, Latino studies, queer studies, studies of indigenous and aboriginal cultures. The politics of qualitative research creates a tension that informs each of these traditions. This tension itself is constantly being reexamined and interrogated as qualitative research confronts a changing historical world, new intellectual positions, and its own institutional and academic conditions.

To summarize: Qualitative research is many things to many people. Its essence is twofold: a commitment to some version of the naturalistic, interpretive approach to its subject matter and an ongoing critique of the politics and methods of postpositivism. We turn now to a brief discussion of the major differences between qualitative and quantitative approaches to research. We then discuss ongoing differences and tensions within qualitative inquiry.

▣ QUALITATIVE VERSUS QUANTITATIVE RESEARCH

The word *qualitative* implies an emphasis on the qualities of entities and on processes and meanings that are not experimentally examined or measured (if measured at all) in terms of quantity, amount, intensity, or frequency. Qualitative researchers stress the socially constructed nature of reality, the intimate relationship between the researcher and what is studied, and the situational constraints that shape inquiry. Such researchers emphasize the value-laden nature of inquiry. They seek answers to questions that stress *how* social experience is created and given meaning. In contrast, quantitative studies emphasize the measurement and analysis of causal relationships between variables, not processes. Proponents of such studies claim that their work is done from within a value-free framework.

Research Styles: Doing the Same Things Differently?

Of course, both qualitative and quantitative researchers "think they know something about society worth telling to others, and they use a variety of forms, media and means to communicate their ideas and findings" (Becker, 1986, p. 122). Qualitative research differs from quantitative research in five significant ways (Becker, 1996). These points of difference, discussed in turn below, all involve different ways of addressing the same set of issues. They return always to the politics of research and to who has the power to legislate correct solutions to social problems.

Uses of positivism and postpositivism. First, both perspectives are shaped by the positivist and postpositivist traditions in the physical and social sciences (see the discussion below). These two positivist science traditions hold to naïve and critical realist positions concerning reality and its perception. In the positivist version it is contended that there is a reality out there to be studied, captured, and understood, whereas the postpositivists argue that reality can never be fully apprehended, only approximated (Guba, 1990, p. 22). Postpositivism relies on multiple methods as a way of capturing as much of reality as possible. At the same time, it emphasizes the discovery and verification of theories. Traditional evaluation criteria, such as internal and external validity, are stressed, as is the use of qualitative procedures that lend themselves to structured (sometimes statistical) analysis. Computer-assisted methods of analysis that permit frequency counts, tabulations, and low-level statistical analyses may also be employed.

The positivist and postpositivist traditions linger like long shadows over the qualitative research project. Historically, qualitative research was defined within the positivist paradigm, where qualitative researchers attempted to do good positivist research with less rigorous methods and procedures. Some mid-20th-century qualitative researchers reported participant observation findings in terms of quasi-statistics (e.g., Becker, Geer, Hughes, & Strauss, 1961). As recently as 1998, Strauss and Corbin, two leading proponents of the grounded theory approach to qualitative research, attempted to modify the usual canons of good (positivist) science to fit their own postpositivist conception of rigorous research (but see Charmaz, Chapter 7, this volume; see also Glaser, 1992). Some applied researchers, while claiming to be atheoretical, often fit within the positivist or postpositivist framework by default.

Flick (2002) usefully summarizes the differences between these two approaches to inquiry, noting that the quantitative approach has been used for purposes of isolating "causes and effects . . . operationalizing theoretical relations . . . [and] measuring and . . . quantifying phenomena . . . allowing the generalization of findings" (p. 3). But today doubt is cast on such projects: "Rapid social change and the resulting diversification of life worlds are increasingly confronting social researchers with new social contexts and perspectives. . . . traditional deductive methodologies . . . are failing. . . . thus research is increasingly forced to make use of inductive strategies instead of starting from theories and testing them. . . . knowledge and practice are studied as *local* knowledge and practice" (p. 2).

Spindler and Spindler (1992) summarize their qualitative approach to quantitative materials: "Instrumentation and quantification are simply procedures employed to extend and reinforce certain kinds of data, interpretations and test hypotheses across samples. Both must be kept in their place. One must avoid their premature or overly extensive use as a security mechanism" (p. 69).

Although many qualitative researchers in the postpositivist tradition use statistical measures, methods, and documents as a way of locating a group of subjects within a larger population, they seldom report their findings in terms of the kinds of complex statistical measures or methods to which quantitative researchers are drawn (e.g., path, regression, and log-linear analyses).

Acceptance of postmodern sensibilities. The use of quantitative, positivist methods and assumptions has been rejected by a new generation of qualitative researchers who are attached to poststructural and/or postmodern sensibilities. These researchers argue that positivist methods are but one way of telling stories about societies or social worlds. These methods may be no better or no worse than any other methods; they just tell different kinds of stories.

This tolerant view is not shared by all qualitative researchers (Huber, 1995). Many members of the critical theory, constructivist, poststructural, and postmodern schools of thought reject positivist and postpositivist criteria when evaluating their own work. They see these criteria as irrelevant to their work and contend that such criteria reproduce only a certain kind of science, a science that silences too many voices. These researchers seek alternative methods for evaluating their work, including verisimilitude, emotionality, personal responsibility, an ethic of caring, political praxis, multivoiced texts, and dialogues with subjects. In response, positivists and postpositivists argue that what they do is good science, free of individual bias and subjectivity. As noted above, they see postmodernism and poststructuralism as attacks on reason and truth.

Capturing the individual's point of view. Both qualitative and quantitative researchers are concerned with the individual's point of view. However, qualitative investigators think they can get closer to the actor's perspective through detailed interviewing and observation. They argue that quantitative researchers are seldom able to capture their subjects' perspectives because they have to rely on more remote, inferential empirical methods and materials. Many quantitative researchers regard the empirical materials produced by interpretive methods as unreliable, impressionistic, and not objective.

Examining the constraints of everyday life. Qualitative researchers are more likely to confront and come up against the constraints of the everyday social world. They see this world in action and embed their findings in it. Quantitative researchers abstract from this world and seldom study it directly. They seek a nomothetic or etic science based on probabilities derived from the study of large numbers of randomly selected cases. These kinds of statements stand above and outside the constraints of everyday life. Qualitative researchers, on the other hand, are committed to an emic, idiographic, case-based position that directs attention to the specifics of particular cases.

Securing rich descriptions. Qualitative researchers believe that rich descriptions of the social world are valuable, whereas quantitative researchers, with their etic, nomothetic commitments, are less concerned with such detail. Quantitative researchers are deliberately unconcerned with rich descriptions because such detail interrupts the process of developing generalizations.

▣ ▣ ▣

The five points of difference described above reflect qualitative and quantitative scholars' commitments to different styles of research, different epistemologies, and different forms of representation. Each work tradition is governed by a different set of genres; each has its own classics, its own preferred forms of representation, interpretation, trustworthiness, and textual evaluation (see Becker, 1986, pp. 134–135). Qualitative researchers use ethnographic prose, historical narratives, first-person accounts, still photographs, life histories, fictionalized "facts," and biographical and autobiographical materials, among others. Quantitative researchers use mathematical models, statistical tables, and graphs, and they usually write about their research in impersonal, third-person prose.

▣ TENSIONS WITHIN QUALITATIVE RESEARCH

It is erroneous to presume that all qualitative researchers share the same assumptions about the five points of difference described above. As the following discussion reveals, positivist, postpositivist, and poststructural differences define and shape the discourses of qualitative research. Realists and postpositivists within the interpretive, qualitative research tradition criticize poststructuralists for taking the textual, narrative turn. These critics contend that such work is navel gazing. It produces the conditions "for a dialogue of the deaf between itself and the community" (Silverman, 1997, p. 240). Critics accuse those who attempt to capture the point of view of the interacting subject in the world of naïve humanism, of reproducing "a Romantic impulse which elevates the experiential to the level of the authentic" (Silverman, 1997, p. 248).

Still others assert that those who take the textual, performance turn ignore lived experience. Snow and Morrill (1995) argue that "this performance turn, like the preoccupation with discourse and storytelling, will take us further from the field of social action and the real dramas of everyday life and thus signal the death knell of ethnography as an empirically grounded enterprise" (p. 361). Of course, we disagree.

Critical Realism

For some, there is a third stream, between naïve positivism and poststructuralism. Critical realism is an antipositivist movement in the social sciences closely associated with the works of Roy Bhaskar and Rom Harré (Danermark, Ekström, Jakobsen, & Karlsson, 2002). Critical realists use the word *critical* in a particular way. This is not "Frankfurt school" critical theory, although there are traces of social criticism here and there (see Danermark et al., 2002, p. 201). Instead, *critical* in this context refers to a transcendental realism that rejects methodological individualism and universal claims to truth. Critical realists oppose logical positivist, relativist, and antifoundational epistemologies. Critical realists agree with the positivists that there is a world of events out there that is observable and independent of human consciousness. They hold that knowledge about this world is socially constructed. Society is made up of feeling, thinking human beings, and their interpretations of the world must be studied (Danermark et al., 2002, p. 200). Critical realists reject a correspondence theory of truth. They believe that reality is arranged in levels and that scientific work must go beyond statements of regularity to analysis of the mechanisms, processes, and structures that account for the patterns that are observed.

Still, as postempiricist, antifoundational, critical theorists, we reject much of what the critical realists advocate. Throughout the past century, social science and philosophy have been continually tangled up with one another. Various "isms" and philosophical movements have crisscrossed sociological and educational discourses, from positivism to postpositivism, to analytic and linguistic philosophy, to hermeneutics, structuralism, poststructuralism, Marxism, feminism, and current post-post versions of all of the above. Some have said that the logical positivists steered the social sciences on a rigorous course of self-destruction.

We do not think that critical realism will keep the social science ship afloat. The social sciences are normative disciplines, always already embedded in issues of value, ideology, power, desire, sexism, racism, domination, repression, and control. We want a social science that is committed up front to issues of social justice, equity, nonviolence, peace, and universal human rights. We do not want a social science that says it can address these issues if it wants to. For us, that is no longer an option.

With these differences within and between interpretive traditions in hand, we must now briefly discuss the history of qualitative research. We break this history into eight historical moments, mindful that any history is always somewhat arbitrary and always at least partially a social construction.

▣ THE HISTORY OF QUALITATIVE RESEARCH

The history of qualitative research reveals that the modern social science disciplines have taken as their mission "the analysis and understanding of the patterned conduct and social processes of society" (Vidich & Lyman, 2000, p. 37). The notion that social scientists could carry out this task presupposed that they had the ability to observe this world objectively. Qualitative methods were a major tool of such observations.[13]

Throughout the history of qualitative research, qualitative investigators have defined their work in terms of hopes and values, "religious faiths, occupational and professional ideologies" (Vidich & Lyman, 2000, p. 39). Qualitative research (like all research) has always been judged on the "standard of whether the work communicates or 'says' something to us" (Vidich & Lyman, 2000, p. 39), based on how we conceptualize our reality and our images of the world. *Epistemology* is the word that has historically defined these standards of evaluation. In the contemporary period, as we have argued above, many received discourses on epistemology are now being reevaluated.

Vidich and Lyman's (2000) work on the history of qualitative research covers the following (somewhat) overlapping stages: early ethnography (to the 17th century), colonial ethnography (17th-, 18th-, and 19th-century explorers), the ethnography of the American Indian as "Other" (late-19th- and early 20th-century anthropology), community studies and ethnographies of American immigrants (early 20th century through the 1960s), studies of ethnicity and assimilation (midcentury through the 1980s), and the present, which we call the *eighth moment*.

In each of these eras, researchers were and have been influenced by their political hopes and ideologies, discovering findings in their research that confirmed their prior theories or beliefs. Early ethnographers confirmed the racial and cultural diversity of peoples throughout the globe and attempted to fit this diversity into a theory about the origins of history, the races, and civilizations. Colonial ethnographers, before the professionalization of ethnography in the 20th century, fostered a colonial pluralism that left natives on their own as long as their leaders could be co-opted by the colonial administration.

European ethnographers studied Africans, Asians, and other Third World peoples of color. Early American ethnographers studied the American Indian from the perspective of the conqueror, who saw the lifeworld of the primitive as a window to the prehistoric past. The Calvinist mission to save the Indian was soon transferred to the mission of saving the "hordes" of immigrants who entered the United States with the beginnings of industrialization. Qualitative community studies of the ethnic Other proliferated from the early 1900s to the 1960s and included the work of E. Franklin Frazier, Robert Park, and Robert Redfield and their students, as well as William Foote Whyte, the Lynds, August Hollingshead, Herbert Gans, Stanford Lyman, Arthur Vidich, and Joseph Bensman. The post-1960 ethnicity studies challenged the "melting pot" hypotheses of Park and his followers and corresponded to the emergence of ethnic studies programs that saw Native Americans, Latinos, Asian Americans, and African Americans attempting to take control over the study of their own peoples.

The postmodern and poststructural challenge emerged in the mid-1980s. It questioned the assumptions that had organized this earlier history in each of its colonizing moments. Qualitative research that crosses the "postmodern divide" requires the scholar, Vidich and Lyman (2000) argue, to "abandon all established and preconceived values, theories, perspectives . . . and prejudices as resources for ethnographic study" (p. 60). In this new era the qualitative researcher does more than observe history; he or she plays a part in it. New tales from the field will now be written, and they will reflect the researchers' direct and personal engagement with this historical period.

Vidich and Lyman's analysis covers the full sweep of ethnographic history. Ours is confined to the 20th and 21st centuries and complements many of their divisions. We begin with the early foundational work of the British and French as well as the Chicago, Columbia, Harvard, Berkeley, and British schools of sociology and anthropology. This early foundational period established the norms of classical qualitative and ethnographic research (see Gupta & Ferguson, 1997; Rosaldo, 1989; Stocking, 1989).

▣ THE EIGHT MOMENTS OF QUALITATIVE RESEARCH

As we have noted above, we divide our history of qualitative research in North America in the 20th century and beyond into eight phases, which we describe in turn below.

The Traditional Period

We call the first moment the traditional period (this covers the second and third phases discussed by Vidich & Lyman, 2000). It begins in the early 1900s and continues until World War II. In this period, qualitative researchers wrote "objective," colonizing accounts of field experiences that were reflective of the positivist scientist paradigm. They were concerned with offering valid, reliable, and objective interpretations in their writings. The "Other" whom they studied was alien, foreign, and strange.

Here is Malinowski (1967) discussing his field experiences in New Guinea and the Trobriand Islands in the years 1914–1915 and 1917–1918. He is bartering his way into field data:

> Nothing whatever draws me to ethnographic studies. . . . On the whole the village struck me rather unfavorably. There is a certain disorganization . . . the rowdiness and persistence of the people who laugh and stare and lie discouraged me somewhat. . . . Went to the village hoping to photograph a few stages of the *bara* dance. I handed out half-sticks of tobacco, then watched a few dances; then took pictures—but results were poor. . . . they would not pose long enough for time exposures. At moments I was furious at them, particularly because after I gave them their portions of tobacco they all went away. (quoted in Geertz, 1988, pp. 73–74)

In another work, this lonely, frustrated, isolated field-worker describes his methods in the following words:

> In the field one has to face a chaos of facts. . . . in this crude form they are not scientific facts at all; they are absolutely elusive, and can only be fixed by interpretation. . . . *Only laws and generalizations are scientific facts,* and field work consists only and exclusively in the interpretation of the chaotic social reality, in subordinating it to general rules. (Malinowski, 1916/1948, p. 328; quoted in Geertz, 1988, p. 81)

Malinowski's remarks are provocative. On the one hand they disparage fieldwork, but on the other they speak of it within the glorified language of science, with laws and generalizations fashioned out of this selfsame experience.

During this period the field-worker was lionized, made into a larger-than-life figure who went into the field and returned with stories about strange peoples. Rosaldo (1989) describes this as the period of the Lone Ethnographer, the story of the man-scientist who went off in search of his native in a distant land. There this figure "encountered the object of his quest . . . [and] underwent his rite of passage by enduring the ultimate ordeal of 'fieldwork'" (p. 30). Returning home with his data, the Lone Ethnographer wrote up an objective account of the culture studied. This account was structured by the norms of classical ethnography. This sacred bundle of terms (Rosaldo, 1989, p. 31) organized ethnographic texts around four beliefs and commitments: a commitment to objectivism, a complicity with imperialism, a belief in monumentalism (the ethnography would create a museumlike picture of the culture studied), and a belief in timelessness (what was studied would never change). The Other was an "object" to be archived. This model of the researcher, who could also write complex, dense theories about what was studied, holds to the present day.

The myth of the Lone Ethnographer depicts the birth of classic ethnography. The texts of Malinowski, Radcliffe-Brown, Margaret Mead, and Gregory Bateson are still carefully studied for what they can tell the novice about fieldwork, taking field notes, and writing theory. But today the image of the Lone Ethnographer has been shattered. Many scholars see the works of the classic ethnographers as relics from the colonial past (Rosaldo, 1989, p. 44). Whereas some feel nostalgia for this past, others celebrate its passing. Rosaldo (1989) quotes Cora Du Bois, a retired Harvard anthropology professor, who lamented this passing at a conference in 1980, reflecting on the crisis in anthropology: "[I feel a distance] from the complexity and disarray of what I once found a justifiable and challenging discipline. . . . It has been like moving from a distinguished art museum into a garage sale" (p. 44).

Du Bois regards the classic ethnographies as pieces of timeless artwork contained in a museum. She feels uncomfortable in the chaos of the garage sale. In contrast, Rosaldo (1989) is drawn to this metaphor because "it provides a precise image of the postcolonial situation where cultural artifacts flow between unlikely places, and nothing is sacred, permanent, or sealed off. The image of anthropology as a garage sale depicts our present global situation" (p. 44). Indeed, many valuable treasures may be found in unexpected places, if one is willing to look long and hard. Old standards no longer hold. Ethnographies do not produce timeless truths. The commitment to objectivism is now in doubt. The complicity with imperialism is openly challenged today, and the belief in monumentalism is a thing of the past.

The legacies of this first period begin at the end of the 19th century, when the novel and the social sciences had become distinguished as separate systems of discourse (Clough, 1998, pp. 21–22). However, the Chicago school, with its emphasis on the life story and the "slice-of-life" approach to ethnographic materials, sought to develop an interpretive methodology that maintained the centrality of the narrated-life-history approach. This led to the production of texts that gave the researcher-as-author the power to represent the subject's story. Written under the mantle of straightforward, sentiment-free social realism, these texts used the language of ordinary people. They articulated a social science version of literary naturalism, which often produced the sympathetic illusion that a solution to a social problem had been found. Like the Depression-era juvenile delinquent and other "social problems" films (Roffman & Purdy, 1981), these accounts romanticized the subject. They turned the deviant into a sociological version of a screen hero. These sociological stories, like their film counterparts, usually had happy endings, as they followed individuals through the three stages of the classic morality tale: being in a state of grace, being seduced by evil and falling, and finally achieving redemption through suffering.

Modernist Phase

The modernist phase, or second moment, builds on the canonical works from the traditional period. Social realism, naturalism, and slice-of-life ethnographies are still valued. This phase extended through the postwar years to the 1970s and is still present in the work of many (for reviews, see Wolcott, 1990, 1992, 1995; see also Tedlock, Chapter 5, this volume). In this period many texts sought to formalize qualitative methods (see, e.g., Bogdan & Taylor, 1975; Cicourel, 1964; Filstead, 1970; Glaser & Strauss, 1967; Lofland, 1971, 1995; Lofland & Lofland, 1984, 1995; Taylor & Bogdan, 1998).[14] The modernist ethnographer and sociological participant observer attempted rigorous qualitative studies of important social processes, including deviance and social control in the classroom and society. This was a moment of creative ferment.

A new generation of graduate students across the human disciplines encountered new interpretive theories (ethnomethodology, phenomenology, critical theory, feminism). They were drawn to qualitative research practices that would let them give a voice to society's underclass. Postpositivism functioned as a powerful epistemological paradigm. Researchers attempted to fit Campbell and Stanley's (1963) model of internal and external validity to constructionist and interactionist conceptions of the research act. They returned to the texts of the Chicago school as sources of inspiration (see Denzin, 1970, 1978).

A canonical text from this moment remains *Boys in White* (Becker et al., 1961; see also Becker, 1998). Firmly entrenched in mid-20th-century methodological discourse, this work attempted to make qualitative research as rigorous as its quantitative counterpart. Causal narratives were central to this project. This multimethod work combined open-ended and quasi-structured interviewing with participant observation and the careful analysis of such materials in standardized, statistical form. In his classic article "Problems of Inference and Proof in Participant Observation," Howard S. Becker (1958/1970) describes the use of quasi-statistics:

> Participant observations have occasionally been gathered in standardized form capable of being transformed into legitimate statistical data. But the exigencies of the field usually prevent the collection of data in such a form to meet the assumptions of statistical tests, so that the observer deals in what have been called "quasi-statistics." His conclusions, while implicitly numerical, do not require precise quantification. (p. 31)

In the analysis of data, Becker notes, the qualitative researcher takes a cue from more quantitatively oriented colleagues. The researcher looks for probabilities or support for arguments concerning the likelihood that, or frequency with which, a conclusion in fact applies in a specific situation (see also Becker, 1998, pp. 166–170). Thus did work in the modernist period clothe itself in the language and rhetoric of positivist and postpositivist discourse.

This was the golden age of rigorous qualitative analysis, bracketed in sociology by *Boys in White* (Becker et al., 1961) at one end and *The Discovery of Grounded Theory*

(Glaser & Strauss, 1967) at the other. In education, qualitative research in this period was defined by George and Louise Spindler, Jules Henry, Harry Wolcott, and John Singleton. This form of qualitative research is still present in the work of scholars such as Strauss and Corbin (1998) and Ryan and Bernard (2000).

The "golden age" reinforced the picture of qualitative researchers as cultural romantics. Imbued with Promethean human powers, they valorized villains and outsiders as heroes to mainstream society. They embodied a belief in the contingency of self and society, and held to emancipatory ideals for "which one lives and dies." They put in place a tragic and often ironic view of society and self, and joined a long line of leftist cultural romantics that included Emerson, Marx, James, Dewey, Gramsci, and Martin Luther King, Jr. (West, 1989, chap. 6).

As this moment came to an end, the Vietnam War was everywhere present in American society. In 1969, alongside these political currents, Herbert Blumer and Everett Hughes met with a group of young sociologists called the "Chicago Irregulars" at the American Sociological Association meetings held in San Francisco and shared their memories of the "Chicago years." Lyn Lofland (1980) describes this time as a

> moment of creative ferment—scholarly and political. The San Francisco meetings witnessed not simply the Blumer-Hughes event but a "counter-revolution." . . . a group first came to . . . talk about the problems of being a sociologist and a female. . . . the discipline seemed literally to be bursting with new . . . ideas: labelling theory, ethnomethodology, conflict theory, phenomenology, dramaturgical analysis. (p. 253)

Thus did the modernist phase come to an end.

Blurred Genres

By the beginning of the third phase (1970–1986), which we call the moment of blurred genres, qualitative researchers had a full complement of paradigms, methods, and strategies to employ in their research. Theories ranged from symbolic interactionism to constructivism, naturalistic inquiry, positivism and postpositivism, phenomenology, ethnomethodology, critical theory, neo-Marxist theory, semiotics, structuralism, feminism, and various racial/ethnic paradigms. Applied qualitative research was gaining in stature, and the politics and ethics of qualitative research—implicated as they were in various applications of this work—were topics of considerable concern. Research strategies and formats for reporting research ranged from grounded theory to the case study, to methods of historical, biographical, ethnographic, action, and clinical research. Diverse ways of collecting and analyzing empirical materials were also available, including qualitative interviewing (open-ended and quasi-structured) and observational, visual, personal experience, and documentary methods. Computers were entering the situation, to be fully developed as aids in the analysis of qualitative data in the next decade, along with narrative, content, and semiotic methods of reading interviews and cultural texts.

Two books by Clifford Geertz, *The Interpretation of Cultures* (1973) and *Local Knowledge* (1983), defined the beginning and the end of this moment. In these two works, Geertz argued that the old functional, positivist, behavioral, totalizing approaches to the human disciplines were giving way to a more pluralistic, interpretive, open-ended perspective. This new perspective took cultural representations and their meanings as its points of departure. Calling for "thick description" of particular events, rituals, and customs, Geertz suggested that all anthropological writings are interpretations of interpretations.[15] The observer has no privileged voice in the interpretations that are written. The central task of theory is to make sense out of a local situation.

Geertz went on to propose that the boundaries between the social sciences and the humanities had become blurred. Social scientists were now turning to the humanities for models, theories, and methods of analysis (semiotics, hermeneutics). A form of genre diaspora was occurring: documentaries that read like fiction (Mailer), parables posing as ethnographies (Castañeda), theoretical treatises that look like travelogues (Lévi-Strauss). At the same time, other new approaches were emerging: poststructuralism (Barthes), neopositivism (Philips), neo-Marxism (Althusser), micro-macro descriptivism (Geertz), ritual theories of drama and culture (V. Turner), deconstructionism (Derrida), ethnomethodology (Garfinkel). The golden age of the social sciences was over, and a new age of blurred, interpretive genres was upon us. The essay as an art form was replacing the scientific article. At issue now was the author's presence in the interpretive text (Geertz, 1988). How can the researcher speak with authority in an age when there are no longer any firm rules concerning the text, including the author's place in it, its standards of evaluation, and its subject matter?

The naturalistic, postpositivist, and constructionist paradigms gained power in this period, especially in education, in the works of Harry Wolcott, Frederick Erickson, Egon Guba, Yvonna Lincoln, Robert Stake, and Elliot Eisner. By the end of the 1970s, several qualitative journals were in place, including *Urban Life and Culture* (now *Journal of Contemporary Ethnography*), *Cultural Anthropology, Anthropology and Education Quarterly, Qualitative Sociology,* and *Symbolic Interaction,* as well as the book series *Studies in Symbolic Interaction.*

Crisis of Representation

A profound rupture occurred in the mid-1980s. What we call the fourth moment, or the crisis of representation, appeared with *Anthropology as Cultural Critique* (Marcus & Fischer, 1986), *The Anthropology of Experience* (Turner & Bruner, 1986), *Writing Culture* (Clifford & Marcus, 1986), *Works and Lives* (Geertz, 1988), and *The Predicament of Culture* (Clifford, 1988). These works made research and writing more reflexive and called into question the issues of gender, class, and race. They articulated the consequences of Geertz's "blurred genres" interpretation of the field in the early 1980s.[16]

Qualitative researchers sought new models of truth, method, and representation (Rosaldo, 1989). The erosion of classic norms in anthropology (objectivism, complicity with colonialism, social life structured by fixed rituals and customs, ethnographies as monuments to a culture) was complete (Rosaldo, 1989, pp. 44–45; see also Jackson, 1998, pp. 7–8). Critical theory, feminist theory, and epistemologies of color now competed for attention in this arena. Issues such as validity, reliability, and objectivity, previously believed settled, were once more problematic. Pattern and interpretive theories, as opposed to causal, linear theories, were now more common, as writers continued to challenge older models of truth and meaning (Rosaldo, 1989).

Stoller and Olkes (1987, pp. 227–229) describe how they felt the crisis of representation in their fieldwork among the Songhay of Niger. Stoller observes: "When I began to write anthropological texts, I followed the conventions of my training. I 'gathered data,' and once the 'data' were arranged in neat piles, I 'wrote them up.' In one case I reduced Songhay insults to a series of neat logical formulas" (p. 227). Stoller became dissatisfied with this form of writing, in part because he learned "everyone had lied to me and . . . the data I has so painstakingly collected were worthless. I learned a lesson: Informants routinely lie to their anthropologists" (Stoller & Olkes, 1987, p. 9). This discovery led to a second—that he had, in following the conventions of ethnographic realism, edited himself out of his text. This led Stoller to produce a different type of text, a memoir, in which he became a central character in the story he told. This story, an account of his experiences in the Songhay world, became an analysis of the clash between his world and the world of Songhay sorcery. Thus Stoller's journey represents an attempt to confront the crisis of representation in the fourth moment.

Clough (1998) elaborates this crisis and criticizes those who would argue that new forms of writing represent a way out of the crisis. She argues:

> While many sociologists now commenting on the criticism of ethnography view writing as "downright central to the ethnographic enterprise" [Van Maanen, 1988, p. xi], the problems of writing are still viewed as different from the problems of method or fieldwork itself. Thus the solution usually offered is experiments in writing, that is a self-consciousness about writing. (p. 136)

It is this insistence on the difference between writing and fieldwork that must be analyzed. (Richardson & St. Pierre are quite articulate about this issue in Volume 3, Chapter 15).

In writing, the field-worker makes a claim to moral and scientific authority. This claim allows the realist and experimental ethnographic texts to function as sources of validation for an empirical science. They show that the world of real lived experience can still be captured, if only in the writer's memoirs, or fictional experimentations, or dramatic readings. But these works have the danger of directing attention away from the ways in which the text constructs sexually situated individuals in a field of social difference. They also perpetuate "empirical science's hegemony" (Clough, 1998, p. 8), for these new writing technologies of the subject become the site "for the production of knowledge/power . . . [aligned] with . . . the capital/state axis" (Aronowitz, 1988, p. 300; quoted in Clough, 1998, p. 8). Such experiments come up against, and then back away from, the difference between empirical science and social criticism. Too often they fail to engage fully a new politics of textuality that would "refuse the identity of empirical science" (Clough, 1998, p. 135). This new social criticism "would intervene in the relationship of information economics, nation-state politics, and technologies of mass communication, especially in terms of the empirical sciences" (Clough, 1998, p. 16). This, of course, is the terrain occupied by cultural studies.

In Volume 3, Chapter 15, Richardson and St. Pierre develop the above arguments, viewing writing as a method of inquiry that moves through successive stages of self-reflection. As a series of written representations, the field-worker's texts flow from the field experience, through intermediate works, to later work, and finally to the research text, which is the public presentation of the ethnographic and narrative experience. Thus fieldwork and writing blur into one another. There is, in the final analysis, no dif-ference between writing and fieldwork. These two perspectives inform one another throughout every chapter in this volume. In these ways the crisis of representation moves qualitative research in new and critical directions.

A Triple Crisis

The ethnographer's authority remains under assault today (Behar, 1995, p. 3; Gupta & Ferguson, 1997, p. 16; Jackson, 1998; Ortner, 1997, p. 2). A triple crisis of rep-resentation, legitimation, and praxis confronts qualitative researchers in the human disciplines. Embedded in the discourses of poststructuralism and postmodernism (Vidich & Lyman, 2000; see also Richardson & St. Pierre, Volume 3, Chapter 15), these three crises are coded in multiple terms, variously called and associated with the *crit-ical, interpretive, linguistic, feminist,* and *rhetorical* turns in social theory. These new turns make problematic two key assumptions of qualitative research. The first is that qualitative researchers can no longer directly capture lived experience. Such experi-ence, it is argued, is created in the social text written by the researcher. This is the representational crisis. It confronts the inescapable problem of representation, but does so within a framework that makes the direct link between experience and text problematic.

The second assumption makes problematic the traditional criteria for evaluating and interpreting qualitative research. This is the legitimation crisis. It involves a seri-ous rethinking of such terms as *validity, generalizability,* and *reliability,* terms already retheorized in postpositivist (Hammersley, 1992), constructionist-naturalistic (Guba & Lincoln, 1989, pp. 163–183), feminist (Olesen, Volume 1, Chapter 10), interpretive and performative (Denzin, 1997, 2003), poststructural (Lather, 1993; Lather & Smithies, 1997), and critical discourses (Kincheloe & McLaren, Volume 1, Chapter 12). This crisis asks, How are qualitative studies to be evaluated in the contemporary, poststructural moment? The first two crises shape the third, which asks, Is it possible to effect change in the world if society is only and always a text? Clearly these crises intersect and blur, as do the answers to the questions they generate (see Ladson-Billings, 2000; Schwandt, 2000; Smith & Deemer, 2000).

The fifth moment, the postmodern period of experimental ethnographic writing, struggled to make sense of these crises. New ways of composing ethnography were explored (Ellis & Bochner, 1996). Theories were read as tales from the field. Writers struggled with different ways to represent the "Other," although they were now joined by new representational concerns (Fine, Weis, Weseen, & Wong, 2000; see also Fine & Weis, Volume 1, Chapter 3). Epistemologies from previously silenced groups emerged to offer solutions to these problems. The concept of the aloof observer was abandoned. More action, participatory, and activist-oriented research was on the horizon. The search for grand narratives was being replaced by more local, small-scale theories fitted to specific problems and specific situations.

The sixth moment, postexperimental inquiry (1995–2000), was a period of great excitement, with AltaMira Press, under the direction of Mitch Allen, taking the lead. AltaMira's book series titled *Ethnographic Alternatives*, for which Carolyn Ellis and Arthur Bochner served as series editors, captured this new excitement and brought a host of new authors into the interpretive community. The following description of the series from the publisher reflects its experimental tone: "Ethnographic Alternatives publishes experimental forms of qualitative writing that blur the boundaries between social sciences and humanities. Some volumes in the series . . . experiment with novel forms of expressing lived experience, including literary, poetic, autobiographical, multivoiced, conversational, critical, visual, performative and co-constructed representations."

During this same period, two major new qualitative journals began publication: *Qualitative Inquiry* and *Qualitative Research.* The editors of these journals were committed to publishing the very best new work. The success of these ventures framed the seventh moment, what we are calling the methodologically contested present (2000–2004). As discussed above, this is a period of conflict, great tension, and, in some quarters, retrenchment.

The eighth moment is now, the future (2005–). In this moment scholars, as reviewed above, are confronting the methodological backlash associated with "Bush science" and the evidence-based social movement.

Reading History

We draw several conclusions from this brief history, noting that it is, like all histories, somewhat arbitrary. First, each of the earlier historical moments is still operating in the present, either as legacy or as a set of practices that researchers continue to follow or argue against. The multiple and fractured histories of qualitative research now make it possible for any given researcher to attach a project to a canonical text from any of the above-described historical moments. Multiple criteria of evaluation compete for attention in this field. Second, an embarrassment of choices now characterizes the field of qualitative research. Researchers have never before had so many paradigms, strategies of inquiry, and methods of analysis to draw upon and utilize. Third, we are in a moment of discovery and rediscovery, as new ways of looking, interpreting, arguing, and writing are debated and discussed. Fourth, the qualitative research act can no longer be viewed from within a neutral or objective positivist perspective. Class, race, gender, and ethnicity shape inquiry, making research a multicultural process. Fifth, we are clearly not implying a progress narrative with our history. We are not saying that the cutting edge is located in the present. We are saying that the present is a politically charged space. Complex pressures both within and outside of the qualitative community are working to erase the positive developments of the past 30 years.

▣ QUALITATIVE RESEARCH AS PROCESS

Three interconnected, generic activities define the qualitative research process. They go by a variety of different labels, including *theory, analysis, ontology, epistemology,* and *methodology.* Behind these terms stands the personal biography of the researcher, who speaks from a particular class, gender, racial, cultural, and ethnic community perspective. The gendered, multiculturally situated researcher approaches the world with a set of ideas, a framework (theory, ontology) that specifies a set of questions (epistemology) that he or she then examines in specific ways (methodology, analysis). That is, the researcher collects empirical materials bearing on the question and then analyzes and writes about those materials. Every researcher speaks from within a distinct interpretive community that configures, in its special way, the multicultural, gendered components of the research act.

In this volume we treat these generic activities under five headings, or phases: the researcher and the researched as multicultural subjects, major paradigms and interpretive perspectives, research strategies, methods of collecting and analyzing empirical materials, and the art of interpretation. Behind and within each of these phases stands the biographically situated researcher. This individual enters the research process from inside an interpretive community. This community has its own historical research traditions, which constitute a distinct point of view. This perspective leads the researcher to adopt particular views of the "Other" who is studied. At the same time, the politics and the ethics of research must also be considered, for these concerns permeate every phase of the research process.

▣ THE OTHER AS RESEARCH SUBJECT

Since its early 20th-century birth in modern, interpretive form, qualitative research has been haunted by a double-faced ghost. On the one hand, qualitative researchers have assumed that qualified, competent observers can, with objectivity, clarity, and precision, report on their own observations of the social world, including the experiences of others. Second, researchers have held to the belief in a real subject, or real individual, who is present in the world and able, in some form, to report on his or her experiences. So armed, researchers could blend their own observations with the self-reports provided by subjects through interviews and life story, personal experience, and case study documents.

These two beliefs have led qualitative researchers across disciplines to seek a method that will allow them to record accurately their own observations while also uncovering the meanings their subjects bring to their life experiences. Such a method would rely on the subjective verbal and written expressions of meaning given by the individuals studied as windows into the inner lives of these persons. Since Dilthey (1900/1976), this search for a method has led to a perennial focus in the human disciplines on qualitative, interpretive methods.

Recently, as noted above, this position and its beliefs have come under assault. Poststructuralists and postmodernists have contributed to the understanding that there is no clear window into the inner life of an individual. Any gaze is always filtered through the lenses of language, gender, social class, race, and ethnicity. There are no objective observations, only observations socially situated in the worlds of—and between—the observer and the observed. Subjects, or individuals, are seldom able to give full explanations of their actions or intentions; all they can offer are accounts, or stories, about what they have done and why. No single method can grasp all the subtle variations in ongoing human experience. Consequently, qualitative researchers deploy a wide range of interconnected interpretive methods, always seeking better ways to make more understandable the worlds of experience they have studied.

Table 1.1 depicts the relationships we see among the five phases that define the research process. Behind all but one of these phases stands the biographically situated researcher. These five levels of activity, or practice, work their way through the biography of the researcher. We take them up briefly in order here; we discuss these phases more fully in our introductions to the individual parts of this volume.

Phase 1: The Researcher

Our remarks above indicate the depth and complexity of the traditional and applied qualitative research perspectives into which a socially situated researcher enters. These traditions locate the researcher in history, simultaneously guiding and constraining the work that is done in any specific study. This field has always been characterized by diversity and conflict, and these are its most enduring traditions (see Greenwood & Levin, Volume 1, Chapter 2). As a carrier of this complex and contradictory history, the researcher must also confront the ethics and politics of research (see Fine & Weis, Volume 1, Chapter 3; Smith, Volume 1, Chapter 4; Bishop, Volume 1, Chapter 5; Christians, Volume 1, Chapter 6). Researching the native, the indigenous Other, while claiming to engage in value-free inquiry for the human disciplines is over.

Table 1.1.   The Research Process

Phase 1: The Researcher as a Multicultural Subject

History and research traditions
Conceptions of self and the Other
The ethics and politics of research

Phase 2: Theoretical Paradigms and Perspectives

Positivism, postpositivism
Interpretivism, constructivism, hermeneutics
Feminism(s)
Racialized discourses
Critical theory and Marxist models
Cultural studies models
Queer theory

Phase 3: Research Strategies

Design
Case study
Ethnography, participant observation, performance ethnography
Phenomenology, ethnomethodology
Grounded theory
Life history, *testimonio*
Historical method
Action and applied research
Clinical research

Phase 4: Methods of Collection and Analysis

Interviewing
Observing
Artifacts, documents, and records
Visual methods
Autoethnography
Data management methods
Computer-assisted analysis
Textual analysis
Focus groups
Applied ethnography

Phase 5: The Art, Practices, and Politics of Interpretation and Evaluation

Criteria for judging adequacy
Practices and politics of interpretation
Writing as interpretation
Policy analysis
Evaluation traditions
Applied research

Today researchers struggle to develop situational and transsituational ethics that apply to all forms of the research act and its human-to-human relationships. We no longer have the option of deferring the decolonization project.

Phase 2: Interpretive Paradigms

All qualitative researchers are philosophers in that "universal sense in which all human beings . . . are guided by highly abstract principles" (Bateson, 1972, p. 320). These principles combine beliefs about ontology (What kind of being is the human being? What is the nature of reality?), epistemology (What is the relationship between the inquirer and the known?), and methodology (How do we know the world, or gain knowledge of it?) (see Guba, 1990, p. 18; Lincoln & Guba, 1985, pp. 14–15; see also Guba & Lincoln, Volume 1, Chapter 8). These beliefs shape how the qualitative researcher sees the world and acts in it. The researcher is "bound within a net of epistemological and ontological premises which—regardless of ultimate truth or falsity—become partially self-validating" (Bateson, 1972, p. 314).

The net that contains the researcher's epistemological, ontological, and methodological premises may be termed a *paradigm,* or an interpretive framework, a "basic set of beliefs that guides action" (Guba, 1990, p. 17). All research is interpretive; it is guided by the researcher's set of beliefs and feelings about the world and how it should be understood and studied. Some beliefs may be taken for granted, invisible, only assumed, whereas others are highly problematic and controversial. Each interpretive paradigm makes particular demands on the researcher, including the questions the researcher asks and the interpretations he or she brings to them.

At the most general level, four major interpretive paradigms structure qualitative research: positivist and postpositivist, constructivist-interpretive, critical (Marxist, emancipatory), and feminist-poststructural. These four abstract paradigms become more complicated at the level of concrete specific interpretive communities. At this level it is possible to identify not only the constructivist, but also multiple versions of feminism (Afrocentric and poststructural),[17] as well as specific ethnic, Marxist, and cultural studies paradigms. These perspectives, or paradigms, are examined in Part II of Volume 1.

The paradigms examined in Part II work against and alongside (and some within) the positivist and postpositivist models. They all work within relativist ontologies (multiple constructed realities), interpretive epistemologies (the knower and known interact and shape one another), and interpretive, naturalistic methods.

Table 1.2 presents these paradigms and their assumptions, including their criteria for evaluating research, and the typical form that an interpretive or theoretical statement assumes in each paradigm.[18] These paradigms are explored in considerable detail in the chapters in Volume 1, Part II by Guba and Lincoln (Chapter 8), Olesen (Chapter 10), Ladson-Billings and Donnor (Chapter 11), Kincheloe and McLaren (Chapter 12), Saukko (Chapter 13), and Plummer (Chapter 14). We have discussed the

Table 1.2.   Interpretive Paradigms

Paradigm/Theory	Criteria	Form of Theory	Type of Narration
Positivist/ postpositivist	Internal, external validity	Logical-deductive, grounded	Scientific report
Constructivist	Trustworthiness, credibility, transferability, confirmability	Substantive-formal	Interpretive case studies, ethnographic fiction
Feminist	Afrocentric, lived experience, dialogue, caring, accountability, race, class, gender, reflexivity, praxis, emotion, concrete grounding	Critical, standpoint	Essays, stories, experimental writing
Ethnic	Afrocentric, lived experience, dialogue, caring, accountability, race, class, gender	Standpoint, critical, historical	Essays, fables, dramas
Marxist	Emancipatory theory, falsifiability dialogical, race, class, gender	Critical, historical, economic	Historical, economic, sociocultural analyses
Cultural studies	Cultural practices, praxis, social texts, subjectivities	Social criticism	Cultural theory-as criticism
Queer theory	Reflexivity, deconstruction	Social criticism, historical analysis	Theory as criticism, autobiography

positivist and postpositivist paradigms above. They work from within a realist and critical realist ontology and objective epistemologies, and they rely on experimental, quasi-experimental, survey, and rigorously defined qualitative methodologies. Ryan and Bernard (2000) have developed elements of this paradigm.

The constructivist paradigm assumes a relativist ontology (there are multiple realities), a subjectivist epistemology (knower and respondent cocreate understandings), and a naturalistic (in the natural world) set of methodological procedures. Findings are usually presented in terms of the criteria of grounded theory or pattern theories (see Guba & Lincoln, Volume 1, Chapter 8; Charmaz, Chapter 7, this volume; see also Ryan & Bernard, 2000). Terms such as *credibility, transferability, dependability,* and *confirmability* replace the usual positivist criteria of internal and external validity, reliability, and objectivity.

Feminist, ethnic, Marxist, cultural studies, and queer theory models privilege a materialist-realist ontology; that is, the real world makes a material difference in terms of race, class, and gender. Subjectivist epistemologies and naturalistic methodologies (usually ethnographies) are also employed. Empirical materials and theoretical arguments are evaluated in terms of their emancipatory implications. Criteria from gender and racial communities (e.g., African American) may be applied (emotionality and feeling, caring, personal accountability, dialogue).

Poststructural feminist theories emphasize problems with the social text, its logic, and its inability ever to represent the world of lived experience fully. Positivist and postpositivist criteria of evaluation are replaced by other criteria, including the reflexive, multivoiced text that is grounded in the experiences of oppressed peoples.

The cultural studies and queer theory paradigms are multifocused, with many different strands drawing from Marxism, feminism, and the postmodern sensibility (see Saukko, Volume 1, Chapter 13; Plummer, Volume 1, Chapter 14; Richardson & St. Pierre, Chapter 15). There is a tension between a humanistic cultural studies, which stresses lived experiences (meaning), and a more structural cultural studies project, which stresses the structural and material determinants (race, class, gender) and effects of experience. Of course, there are two sides to every coin, and both sides are needed— indeed, both are critical. The cultural studies and queer theory paradigms use methods strategically—that is, as resources for understanding and for producing resistances to local structures of domination. Scholars may do close textual readings and discourse analyses of cultural texts (see Olesen, Volume 1, Chapter 10; Saukko, Volume 1, Chapter 13; Chase, Volume 3, Chapter 2) as well as local, online, reflexive, and critical ethnographies, open-ended interviewing, and participant observation. The focus is on how race, class, and gender are produced and enacted in historically specific situations.

Paradigm and personal history in hand, focused on a concrete empirical problem to examine, the researcher now moves to the next stage of the research process—namely, working with a specific strategy of inquiry.

Phase 3: Strategies of Inquiry and Interpretive Paradigms

Table 1.1 presents some of the major strategies of inquiry a researcher may use. Phase 3 begins with research design, which, broadly conceived, involves a clear focus on the research question, the purposes of the study, and "what information most appropriately will answer specific research questions, and which strategies are most effective for obtaining it" (LeCompte & Preissle, 1993, p. 30; see also Cheek, Chapter 2, this volume). A research design describes a flexible set of guidelines that connect theoretical paradigms first to strategies of inquiry and second to methods for collecting empirical materials. A research design situates the researcher in the empirical world and connects him or her to specific sites, persons, groups, institutions, and bodies of relevant interpretive material, including documents and archives. A research design also specifies how the investigator will address the two critical issues of representation and legitimation.

A strategy of inquiry comprises a bundle of skills, assumptions, and practices that the researcher employs as he or she moves from paradigm to the empirical world. Strategies of inquiry put paradigms of interpretation into motion. At the same time, strategies of inquiry also connect the researcher to specific methods of collecting and analyzing empirical materials. For example, the case study strategy relies on interviewing, observing, and document analysis. Research strategies implement and anchor paradigms in specific empirical sites or in specific methodological practices, such as making a case an object of study. These strategies include the case study, phenomenological and ethnomethodological techniques, and the use of grounded theory, as well as biographical, autoethnographic, historical, action, and clinical methods. Each of these strategies is connected to a complex literature, and each has a separate history, exemplary works, and preferred ways of putting the strategy into motion.

Phase 4: Methods of Collecting and Analyzing Empirical Materials

Qualitative researchers employ several methods for collecting empirical materials.[19] These methods, which are taken up in Volume 3, Part I (Part IV in the *Handbook*), include interviewing; direct observation; the analysis of artifacts, documents, and cultural records; the use of visual materials; and the use of personal experience. The researcher may also read and analyze interviews or cultural texts in a variety of different ways, including content, narrative, and semiotic strategies. Faced with large amounts of qualitative materials, the investigator seeks ways of managing and interpreting these documents, and here data management methods and computer-assisted models of analysis may be of use.

Phase 5: The Art and Politics of Interpretation and Evaluation

Qualitative research is endlessly creative and interpretive. The researcher does not just leave the field with mountains of empirical materials and then easily write up his or her findings. Qualitative interpretations are constructed. The researcher first creates a field text consisting of field notes and documents from the field, what Roger Sanjek (1990, p. 386) calls "indexing" and David Plath (1990, p. 374) calls "filework." The writer-as-interpreter moves from this text to a research text: notes and interpretations based on the field text. This text is then re-created as a working interpretive document that contains the writer's initial attempts to make sense of what he or she has learned. Finally, the writer produces the public text that comes to the reader. This final tale from the field may assume several forms: confessional, realist, impressionistic, critical, formal, literary, analytic, grounded theory, and so on (see Van Maanen, 1988).

The interpretive practice of making sense of one's findings is both artistic and political. Multiple criteria for evaluating qualitative research now exist, and those that we emphasize stress the situated, relational, and textual structures of the ethnographic experience. There is no single interpretive truth. As we argued earlier, there are multiple interpretive communities, each with its own criteria for evaluating interpretations.

Program evaluation is a major site of qualitative research, and qualitative researchers can influence social policy in important ways. The chapters by Greenwood and Levin (Volume 1, Chapter 2), Kemmis and McTaggart (Chapter 10, this volume), Miller and Crabtree (Chapter 11, this volume), Tedlock (Chapter 5, this volume), Smith and Hodkinson (Volume 3, Chapter 13), and House (Volume 3, Chapter 19) trace and discuss the rich history of applied qualitative research in the social sciences. This is the critical site where theory, method, praxis, action, and policy all come together. Qualitative researchers can isolate target populations, show the immediate effects of certain programs on such groups, and isolate the constraints that operate against policy changes in such settings. Action-oriented and clinically oriented qualitative researchers can also create spaces where those who are studied (the Other) can speak. The evaluator becomes the conduit for making such voices heard.

◫ BRIDGING THE HISTORICAL MOMENTS: WHAT COMES NEXT?

In Volume 3, Chapter 15, Richardson and St. Pierre argue that we are already in the post-"post" period—post-poststructuralism, post-postmodernism, post-postexperimentalism. What this means for interpretive ethnographic practices is still not clear, but it is certain that things will never again be the same. We are in a new age where messy, uncertain, multivoiced texts, cultural criticism, and new experimental works will become more common, as will more reflexive forms of fieldwork, analysis, and intertextual representation. The subject of our final essay in Volume 3 is these sixth, seventh, eighth, and ninth moments. It is true that, as the poet said, the center no longer holds. We can reflect on what should be at the new center.

Thus we come full circle. Returning to our bridge metaphor, the chapters that follow take the researcher back and forth through every phase of the research act. Like a good bridge, the chapters provide for two-way traffic, coming and going between moments, formations, and interpretive communities. Each chapter examines the relevant histories, controversies, and current practices that are associated with each paradigm, strategy, and method. Each chapter also offers projections for the future, where a specific paradigm, strategy, or method will be 10 years from now, deep into the formative years of the 21st century.

In reading the chapters that follow, it is important to remember that the field of qualitative research is defined by a series of tensions, contradictions, and hesitations. These tensions work back and forth between and among the broad, doubting postmodern sensibility; the more certain, more traditional positivist, postpositivist, and naturalistic conceptions of this project; and an increasingly conservative, neoliberal global environment. All of the chapters that follow are caught in and articulate these tensions.

▣ NOTES

1. Recall bell hooks's (1990, p. 127) reading of the famous photo of Stephen Tyler doing fieldwork in India that appears on the cover of *Writing Culture* (Clifford & Marcus, 1986). In the picture, Tyler is seated at some distance from three dark-skinned persons. One, a child, is poking his or her head out of a basket. A woman is hidden in the shadows of the hut. A man, a checkered white-and-black shawl across his shoulder, elbow propped on his knee, hand resting along the side of his face, is staring at Tyler. Tyler is writing in a field journal. A piece of white cloth is attached to his glasses, perhaps shielding him from the sun. This patch of whiteness marks Tyler as the white male writer studying these passive brown and black persons. Indeed, the brown male's gaze signals some desire, or some attachment to Tyler. In contrast, the female's gaze is completely hidden by the shadows and by the words of the book's title, which are printed across her face.

2. Qualitative research has separate and distinguished histories in education, social work, communications, psychology, history, organizational studies, medical science, anthropology, and sociology.

3. Some definitions are in order here. *Positivism* asserts that objective accounts of the real world can be given. *Postpositivism* holds that only partially objective accounts of the world can be produced, for all methods for examining such accounts are flawed. According to *foundationalism,* we can have an ultimate grounding for our knowledge claims about the world, and this involves the use of empiricist and positivist epistemologies (Schwandt, 1997a, p. 103). *Nonfoundationalism* holds that we can make statements about the world without "recourse to ultimate proof or foundations for that knowing" (Schwandt, 1997a, p. 102). *Quasi-foundationalism* holds that we can make certain knowledge claims about the world based on neorealist criteria, including the correspondence concept of truth; there is an independent reality that can be mapped (see Smith & Hodkinson, Volume 3, Chapter 13).

4. Jameson (1991, pp. 3–4) reminds us that any periodization hypothesis is always suspect, even one that rejects linear, stagelike models. It is never clear to what reality a stage refers, and what divides one stage from another is always debatable. Our eight moments are meant to mark discernible shifts in style, genre, epistemology, ethics, politics, and aesthetics.

5. Several scholars have termed this model a *progress narrative* (Alasuutari, 2004, pp. 599–600; Seale et al., 2004, p. 2). Critics assert that we believe that the most recent moment is the most up-to-date, the avant-garde, the cutting edge (Alasuutari, 2004, p. 601). Naturally, we dispute this reading. Teddlie and Tashakkori (2003, pp. 5–8) have modified our historical periods to fit their historical analysis of the major moments in the emergence of the use of mixed methods in social science research in the past century.

6. Some additional definitions are needed here. *Structuralism* holds that any system is made up of a set of oppositional categories embedded in language. *Semiotics* is the science of signs or sign systems—a structuralist project. According to *poststructuralism,* language is an unstable system of referents, thus it is impossible ever to capture completely the meaning of an

action, text, or intention. *Postmodernism* is a contemporary sensibility, developing since World War II, that privileges no single authority, method, or paradigm. *Hermeneutics* is an approach to the analysis of texts that stresses how prior understandings and prejudices shape the interpretive process. *Phenomenology* is a complex system of ideas associated with the works of Husserl, Heidegger, Sartre, Merleau-Ponty, and Alfred Schutz. *Cultural studies* is a complex, interdisciplinary field that merges critical theory, feminism, and poststructuralism.

7. Of course, all settings are natural—that is, places where everyday experiences take place. Qualitative researchers study people doing things together in the places where these things are done (Becker, 1986). There is no field site or natural place where one goes to do this kind of work (see also Gupta & Ferguson, 1997, p. 8). The site is constituted through the researcher's interpretive practices. Historically, analysts have distinguished between experimental (laboratory) and field (natural) research settings, hence the argument that qualitative research is naturalistic. Activity theory erases this distinction (Keller & Keller, 1996, p. 20; Vygotsky, 1978).

8. According to Weinstein and Weinstein (1991), "The meaning of *bricoleur* in French popular speech is 'someone who works with his (or her) hands and uses devious means compared to those of the craftsman.' . . . the *bricoleur* is practical and gets the job done" (p. 161). These authors provide a history of the term, connecting it to the works of the German sociologist and social theorist Georg Simmel and, by implication, Baudelaire. Hammersley (1999) disputes our use of this term. Following Lévi-Strauss, he reads the *bricoleur* as a mythmaker. He suggests that the term be replaced with the notion of the boatbuilder. Hammersley also quarrels with our "moments" model of the history of qualitative research, contending that it implies some sense of progress.

9. Brian De Palma reproduced this baby carriage scene in his 1987 film *The Untouchables*.

10. In the harbor, the muzzles of the *Potemkin*'s two huge guns swing slowly toward the camera. Words on the screen inform us, "The brutal military power answered by guns of the battleship." A final famous three-shot montage sequence shows first a sculpture of a sleeping lion, then a lion rising from his sleep, and finally the lion roaring, symbolizing the rage of the Russian people (Cook, 1981, p. 167). In this sequence Eisenstein uses montage to expand time, creating a psychological duration for this horrible event. By drawing out this sequence, by showing the baby in the carriage, the soldiers firing on the citizens, the blood on the mother's glove, the descending carriage on the steps, he suggests a level of destruction of great magnitude.

11. Here it is relevant to make a distinction between techniques that are used across disciplines and methods that are used within disciplines. Ethnomethodologists, for example, employ their approach as a method, whereas others selectively borrow that method as a technique for their own applications. Harry Wolcott (personal communication, 1993) suggests this distinction. It is also relevant to make distinctions among topic, method, and resource. Methods can be studied as topics of inquiry; that is how a case study gets done. In this ironic, ethnomethodological sense, method is both a resource and a topic of inquiry.

12. Indeed, any attempt to give an essential definition of qualitative research requires a qualitative analysis of the circumstances that produce such a definition.

13. In this sense all research is qualitative, because "the observer is at the center of the research process" (Vidich & Lyman, 2000, p. 39).

14. See Lincoln and Guba (1985) for an extension and elaboration of this tradition in the mid-1980s, and for more recent extensions see Taylor and Bogdan (1998) and Creswell (1998).

15. Greenblatt (1997, pp. 15–18) offers a useful deconstructive reading of the many meanings and practices Geertz brings to the term *thick description*.

16. These works marginalized and minimized the contributions of standpoint feminist theory and research to this discourse (see Behar, 1995, p. 3; Gordon, 1995, p. 432).

17. Olesen (Volume 1, Chapter 10) identifies three strands of feminist research: mainstream empirical, standpoint and cultural studies, and poststructural, postmodern. She places Afrocentric and other models of color under the cultural studies and postmodern categories.

18. These, of course, are our interpretations of these paradigms and interpretive styles.

19. *Empirical materials* is the preferred term for what traditionally have been described as data.

▣ REFERENCES

Alasuutari, P. (2004). The globalization of qualitative research. In C. Seale, G. Gobo, J. F. Gubrium, & D. Silverman (Eds.), *Qualitative research practice* (pp. 595–608). London: Sage.

Aronowitz, S. (1988). *Science as power: Discourse and ideology in modern society.* Minneapolis: University of Minnesota Press.

Atkinson, E. (2004). Thinking outside the box: An exercise in heresy. *Qualitative Inquiry, 10,* 111–129.

Bateson, G. (1972). *Steps to an ecology of mind.* New York: Ballantine.

Battiste, M. (2000). Introduction: Unfolding lessons of colonization. In M. Battiste (Ed.), *Reclaiming indigenous voice and vision* (pp. xvi–xxx). Vancouver: University of British Columbia Press.

Becker, H. S. (1970). Problems of inference and proof in participant observation. In H. S. Becker, *Sociological work: Method and substance.* Chicago: Aldine. (Reprinted from *American Sociological Review, 1958, 23,* 652–660)

Becker, H. S. (1986). *Doing things together.* Evanston, IL: Northwestern University Press.

Becker, H. S. (1996). The epistemology of qualitative research. In R. Jessor, A. Colby, & R. A. Shweder (Eds.), *Ethnography and human development: Context and meaning in social inquiry* (pp. 53–71). Chicago: University of Chicago Press.

Becker, H. S. (1998). *Tricks of the trade: How to think about your research while you're doing it.* Chicago: University of Chicago Press.

Becker, H. S., Geer, B., Hughes, E. C., & Strauss, A. L. (1961). *Boys in white: Student culture in medical school.* Chicago: University of Chicago Press.

Behar, R. (1995). Introduction: Out of exile. In R. Behar & D. A. Gordon (Eds.), *Women writing culture* (pp. 1–29). Berkeley: University of California Press.

Bloch, M. (2004). A discourse that disciplines, governs, and regulates: The National Research Council's report on scientific research in education. *Qualitative Inquiry, 10,* 96–110.

Bochner, A. P., & Ellis, C. (Eds.). (2002). *Ethnographically speaking: Autoethnography, literature, and aesthetics.* Walnut Creek, CA: AltaMira.

Bogdan, R., & Taylor, S. J. (1975). *Introduction to qualitative research methods: A phenomenological approach to the social sciences.* New York: John Wiley.

Campbell, D. T., & Stanley, J. C. (1963). *Experimental and quasi-experimental designs for research.* Chicago: Rand McNally.

Cannella, G. S., & Lincoln, Y. S. (2004a). Dangerous discourses II: Comprehending and counter-ing the redeployment of discourses (and resources) in the generation of liberatory inquiry. *Qualitative Inquiry, 10,* 165–174.

Cannella, G. S., & Lincoln, Y. S. (2004b). Epilogue: Claiming a critical public social science—reconceptualizing and redeploying research. *Qualitative Inquiry, 10,* 298–309.

Carey, J. W. (1989). *Communication as culture: Essays on media and society.* Boston: Unwin Hyman.

Cicourel, A. V. (1964). *Method and measurement in sociology.* New York: Free Press.

Clifford, J. (1988). *The predicament of culture: Twentieth-century ethnography, literature, and art.* Cambridge, MA: Harvard University Press.

Clifford, J., & Marcus, G. E. (Eds.). (1986). *Writing culture: The poetics and politics of ethnogra-phy.* Berkeley: University of California Press.

Clough, P. T. (1998). *The end(s) of ethnography: From realism to social criticism* (2nd ed.). New York: Peter Lang.

Cook, D. A. (1981). *A history of narrative film.* New York: W. W. Norton.

Creswell, J. W. (1998). *Qualitative inquiry and research design: Choosing among five traditions.* Thousand Oaks, CA: Sage.

Danermark, B., Ekström, M., Jakobsen, L., & Karlsson, J. C. (2002). *Explaining society: Critical realism in the social sciences.* London: Routledge.

de Certeau, M. (1984). *The practice of everyday life.* Berkeley: University of California Press.

Denzin, N. K. (1970). *The research act.* Chicago: Aldine.

Denzin, N. K. (1978). *The research act: A theoretical introduction to sociological methods* (2nd ed.). New York: McGraw-Hill.

Denzin, N. K. (1997). *Interpretive ethnography: Ethnographic practices for the 21st century.* Thousand Oaks, CA: Sage.

Denzin, N. K. (2003). *Performance ethnography: Critical pedagogy and the politics of culture.* Thousand Oaks, CA: Sage.

Dilthey, W. L. (1976). *Selected writings.* Cambridge: Cambridge University Press. (Original work published 1900)

Diversi, M. (1998). Glimpses of street life: Representing lived experience through short stories. *Qualitative Inquiry, 4,* 131–137.

Ellis, C. (2004). *The ethnographic I: A methodological novel about autoethnography.* Walnut Creek, CA: AltaMira.

Ellis, C., & Bochner, A. P. (Eds.). (1996). *Composing ethnography: Alternative forms of qualita-tive writing.* Walnut Creek, CA: AltaMira.

Filstead, W. J. (Ed.). (1970). *Qualitative methodology.* Chicago: Markham.

Fine, M., Weis, L., Weseen, S., & Wong, L. (2000). For whom? Qualitative research, representa-tions, and social responsibilities. In N. K. Denzin & Y. S. Lincoln (Eds.), *Handbook of qual-itative research* (2nd ed., pp. 107–131). Thousand Oaks, CA: Sage.

Flick, U. (2002). *An introduction to qualitative research* (2nd ed.). London: Sage.

Geertz, C. (1973). *The interpretation of cultures: Selected essays.* New York: Basic Books.

Geertz, C. (1983). *Local knowledge: Further essays in interpretive anthropology.* New York: Basic Books.

Geertz, C. (1988). *Works and lives: The anthropologist as author.* Stanford, CA: Stanford University Press.

Glaser, B. G. (1992). *Emergence vs. forcing: Basics of grounded theory.* Mill Valley, CA: Sociology Press.

Glaser, B. G., & Strauss, A. L. (1967). *The discovery of grounded theory: Strategies for qualitative research.* Chicago: Aldine.

Goodall, H. L., Jr. (2000). *Writing the new ethnography.* Walnut Creek, CA: AltaMira.

Gordon, D. A. (1995). Culture writing women: Inscribing feminist anthropology. In R. Behar & D. A. Gordon (Eds.), *Women writing culture* (pp. 429–441). Berkeley: University of California Press.

Greenblatt, S. (1997). The touch of the real. In S. B. Ortner (Ed.), The fate of "culture": Geertz and beyond [Special issue]. *Representations, 59,* 14–29.

Guba, E. G. (1990). The alternative paradigm dialog. In E. G. Guba (Ed.), *The paradigm dialog* (pp. 17–30). Newbury Park, CA: Sage.

Guba, E. G., & Lincoln, Y. S. (1989). *Fourth generation evaluation.* Newbury Park, CA: Sage.

Gupta, A., & Ferguson, J. (Eds.). (1997). Discipline and practice: "The field" as site, method, and location in anthropology. In A. Gupta & J. Ferguson (Eds.), *Anthropological locations: Boundaries and grounds of a field science* (pp. 1–46). Berkeley: University of California Press.

Hammersley, M. (1992). *What's wrong with ethnography? Methodological explorations.* London: Routledge.

Hammersley, M. (1999). Not bricolage but boatbuilding: Exploring two metaphors for thinking about ethnography. *Journal of Contemporary Ethnography, 28,* 574–585.

Harper, D. (1987). *Working knowledge: Skill and community in a small shop.* Chicago: University of Chicago Press.

Holman Jones, S. (1999). Torch. *Qualitative Inquiry, 5,* 235–250.

hooks, b. (1990). *Yearning: Race, gender, and cultural politics.* Boston: South End.

Howe, K. R. (2004). A critique of experimentalism. *Qualitative Inquiry, 10,* 42–61.

Huber, J. (1995). Centennial essay: Institutional perspectives on sociology. *American Journal of Sociology, 101,* 194–216.

Jackson, M. (1998). *Minima ethnographica: Intersubjectivity and the anthropological project.* Chicago: University of Chicago Press.

Jameson, F. (1991). *Postmodernism; or, The cultural logic of late capitalism.* Durham, NC: Duke University Press.

Keller, C. M., & Keller, J. D. (1996). *Cognition and tool use: The blacksmith at work.* New York: Cambridge University Press.

Kincheloe, J. L. (2001). Describing the bricolage: Conceptualizing a new rigor in qualitative research. *Qualitative Inquiry, 7,* 679–692.

Ladson-Billings, G. (2000). Socialized discourses and ethnic epistemologies. In N. K. Denzin & Y. S. Lincoln (Eds.), *Handbook of qualitative research* (2nd ed., pp. 257–277). Thousand Oaks, CA: Sage.

Lather, P. (1993). Fertile obsession: Validity after poststructuralism. *Sociological Quarterly, 35,* 673–694.

Lather, P. (2004). This *is* your father's paradigm: Government intrusion and the case of qualitative research in education. *Qualitative Inquiry, 10,* 15–34.

Lather, P., & Smithies, C. (1997). *Troubling the angels: Women living with HIV/AIDS.* Boulder, CO: Westview.

LeCompte, M. D., & Preissle, J. (with Tesch, R.). (1993). *Ethnography and qualitative design in educational research* (2nd ed.). New York: Academic Press.

Lévi-Strauss, C. (1966). *The savage mind* (2nd ed.). Chicago: University of Chicago Press.

Lincoln, Y. S. (1999, June). *Courage, vulnerability and truth.* Keynote address delivered at the conference "Reclaiming Voice II: Ethnographic Inquiry and Qualitative Research in a Postmodern Age," University of California, Irvine.

Lincoln, Y. S., & Cannella, G. S. (2004a). Dangerous discourses: Methodological conservatism and governmental regimes of truth. *Qualitative Inquiry, 10,* 5–14.

Lincoln, Y. S., & Cannella, G. S. (2004b). Qualitative research, power, and the radical Right. *Qualitative Inquiry, 10,* 175–201.

Lincoln, Y. S., & Guba, E. G. (1985). *Naturalistic inquiry.* Beverly Hills, CA: Sage.

Lincoln, Y. S., & Tierney, W. G. (2004). Qualitative research and institutional review boards. *Qualitative Inquiry, 10,* 219–234.

Lofland, J. (1971). *Analyzing social settings.* Belmont, CA: Wadsworth.

Lofland, J. (1995). Analytic ethnography: Features, failings, and futures. *Journal of Contemporary Ethnography, 24,* 30–67.

Lofland, J., & Lofland, L. H. (1984). *Analyzing social settings: A guide to qualitative observation and analysis* (2nd ed.). Belmont, CA: Wadsworth.

Lofland, J., & Lofland, L. H. (1995). *Analyzing social settings: A guide to qualitative observation and analysis* (3rd ed.). Belmont, CA: Wadsworth.

Lofland, L. H. (1980). The 1969 Blumer-Hughes Talk. *Urban Life and Culture, 8,* 248–260.

Malinowski, B. (1948). *Magic, science and religion, and other essays.* New York: Natural History Press. (Original work published 1916)

Malinowski, B. (1967). *A diary in the strict sense of the term* (N. Guterman, Trans.). New York: Harcourt, Brace & World.

Marcus, G. E., & Fischer, M. M. J. (1986). *Anthropology as cultural critique: An experimental moment in the human sciences.* Chicago: University of Chicago Press.

Maxwell, J. A. (2004). Reemergent scientism, postmodernism, and dialogue across differences. *Qualitative Inquiry, 10,* 35–41.

Monaco, J. (1981). *How to read a film: The art, technology, language, history and theory of film* (Rev. ed.). New York: Oxford University Press.

Nelson, C., Treichler, P. A., & Grossberg, L. (1992). Cultural studies: An introduction. In L. Grossberg, C. Nelson, & P. A. Treichler (Eds.), *Cultural studies* (pp. 1–16). New York: Routledge.

Ortner, S. B. (1997). Introduction. In S. B. Ortner (Ed.), The fate of "culture": Geertz and beyond [Special issue]. *Representations, 59,* 1–13.

Pelias, R. J. (2004). *A methodology of the heart: Evoking academic and daily life.* Walnut Creek, CA: AltaMira.

Plath, D. W. (1990). Fieldnotes, filed notes, and the conferring of note. In R. Sanjek (Ed.), *Fieldnotes: The makings of anthropology* (pp. 371–384). Ithaca, NY: Cornell University Press.

Popkewitz, T. S. (2004). Is the National Research Council committee's report on scientific research in education scientific? On trusting the manifesto. *Qualitative Inquiry, 10,* 62–78.

Richardson, L. (1997). *Fields of play: Constructing an academic life.* New Brunswick, NJ: Rutgers University Press.

Richardson, L. (2000). Writing: A method of inquiry. In N. K. Denzin & Y. S. Lincoln (Eds.), *Handbook of qualitative research* (2nd ed., pp. 923–948). Thousand Oaks, CA: Sage.

Richardson, L., & Lockridge, E. (2004). *Travels with Ernest: Crossing the literary/sociological divide.* Walnut Creek, CA: AltaMira.

Roffman, P., & Purdy, J. (1981). *The Hollywood social problem film.* Bloomington: Indiana University Press.

Ronai, C. R. (1998). Sketching with Derrida: An ethnography of a researcher/erotic dancer. *Qualitative Inquiry, 4,* 405–420.

Rosaldo, R. (1989). *Culture and truth: The remaking of social analysis.* Boston: Beacon.

Ryan, G. W., & Bernard, H. R. (2000). Data management and analysis methods. In N. K. Denzin & Y. S. Lincoln (Eds.), *Handbook of qualitative research* (2nd ed., pp. 769–802). Thousand Oaks, CA: Sage.

Ryan, K. E., & Hood, L. K. (2004). Guarding the castle and opening the gates. *Qualitative Inquiry, 10,* 79–95.

St. Pierre, E. A. (2004). Refusing alternatives: A science of contestation. *Qualitative Inquiry, 10,* 130–139.

Sanjek, R. (1990). On ethnographic validity. In R. Sanjek (Ed.), *Fieldnotes: The makings of anthropology* (pp. 385–418). Ithaca, NY: Cornell University Press.

Schwandt, T. A. (1997a). *Qualitative inquiry: A dictionary of terms.* Thousand Oaks, CA: Sage.

Schwandt, T. A. (1997b). Textual gymnastics, ethics and angst. In W. G. Tierney & Y. S. Lincoln (Eds.), *Representation and the text: Re-framing the narrative voice* (pp. 305–311). Albany: State University of New York Press.

Schwandt, T. A. (2000). Three epistemological stances for qualitative inquiry: Interpretivism, hermeneutics, and social constructionism. In N. K. Denzin & Y. S. Lincoln (Eds.), *Handbook of qualitative research* (2nd ed., pp. 189–213). Thousand Oaks, CA: Sage.

Seale, C., Gobo, G., Gubrium, J. F., & Silverman, D. (2004). Introduction: Inside qualitative research. In C. Seale, G. Gobo, J. F. Gubrium, & D. Silverman (Eds.), *Qualitative research practice* (pp. 1–11). London: Sage.

Semali, L. M., & Kincheloe, J. L. (1999). Introduction: What is indigenous knowledge and why should we study it? In L. M. Semali & J. L. Kincheloe (Eds.), *What is indigenous knowledge? Voices from the academy* (pp. 3–57). New York: Falmer.

Silverman, D. (1997). Towards an aesthetics of research. In D. Silverman (Ed.), *Qualitative research: Theory, method and practice* (pp. 239–253). London: Sage.

Smith, A. D. (1993). *Fires in the mirror: Crown Heights, Brooklyn, and other identities.* New York: Anchor.

Smith, J. K., & Deemer, D. K. (2000). The problem of criteria in the age of relativism. In N. K. Denzin & Y. S. Lincoln (Eds.), *Handbook of qualitative research* (2nd ed., pp. 877–896). Thousand Oaks, CA: Sage.

Smith, L. T. (1999). *Decolonizing methodologies: Research and indigenous peoples.* Dunedin, New Zealand: University of Otago Press.

Snow, D., & Morrill, C. (1995). Ironies, puzzles, and contradictions in Denzin and Lincoln's vision of qualitative research. *Journal of Contemporary Ethnography, 22,* 358–362.

Spindler, G., & Spindler, L. (1992). Cultural process and ethnography: An anthropological perspective. In M. D. LeCompte, W. L. Millroy, & J. Preissle (Eds.), *The handbook of qualitative research in education* (pp. 53–92). New York: Academic Press.

Stocking, G. W., Jr. (1986). Anthropology and the science of the irrational: Malinowski's encounter with Freudian psychoanalysis. In G. W. Stocking, Jr. (Ed.), *Malinowski, Rivers, Benedict and others: Essays on culture and personality* (pp. 13–49). Madison: University of Wisconsin Press.

Stocking, G. W., Jr. (1989). The ethnographic sensibility of the 1920s and the dualism of the anthropological tradition. In G. W. Stocking, Jr. (Ed.), *Romantic motives: Essays on anthropological sensibility* (pp. 208–276). Madison: University of Wisconsin Press.

Stoller, P., & Olkes, C. (1987). *In sorcery's shadow: A memoir of apprenticeship among the Songhay of Niger*. Chicago: University of Chicago Press.

Strauss, A. L., & Corbin, J. (1998). *Basics of qualitative research: Techniques and procedures for developing grounded theory* (2nd ed.). Thousand Oaks, CA: Sage.

Taylor, S. J., & Bogdan, R. (1998). *Introduction to qualitative research methods: A guidebook and resource* (3rd ed.). New York: John Wiley.

Teddlie, C., & Tashakkori, A. (2003). Major issues and controversies in the use of mixed methods in the social and behavioral sciences. In A. Tashakkori & C. Teddlie (Eds.), *Handbook of mixed methods in social and behavioral research* (pp. 3–50). Thousand Oaks, CA: Sage.

Tierney, W. G. (2000). Undaunted courage: Life history and the postmodern challenge. In N. K. Denzin & Y. S. Lincoln (Eds.), *Handbook of qualitative research* (2nd ed., pp. 537–553). Thousand Oaks, CA: Sage.

Trujillo, N. (2004). *In search of Naunny's grave: Age, class, gender, and ethnicity in an American family*. Walnut Creek, CA: AltaMira.

Turner, V., & Bruner, E. (Eds.). (1986). *The anthropology of experience*. Urbana: University of Illinois Press.

Van Maanen, J. (1988). *Tales of the field: On writing ethnography*. Chicago: University of Chicago Press.

Vidich, A. J., & Lyman, S. M. (1994). Qualitative methods: Their history in sociology and anthropology. In N. K. Denzin & Y. S. Lincoln (Eds.), *Handbook of qualitative research* (pp. 23–59). Thousand Oaks, CA: Sage.

Vidich, A. J., & Lyman, S. M. (2000). Qualitative methods: Their history in sociology and anthropology. In N. K. Denzin & Y. S. Lincoln (Eds.), *Handbook of qualitative research* (2nd ed., pp. 37–84). Thousand Oaks, CA: Sage.

Vygotsky, L. S. (1978). *Mind in society: The development of higher psychological processes* (M. Cole, V. John-Steiner, S. Scribner, & E. Souberman, Eds.). Cambridge, MA: Harvard University Press.

Weinstein, D., & Weinstein, M. A. (1991). Georg Simmel: Sociological flaneur bricoleur. *Theory, Culture & Society, 8,* 151–168.

Weinstein, M. (2004). Randomized design and the myth of certain knowledge: Guinea pig narratives and cultural critique. *Qualitative Inquiry, 10,* 246–260.

West, C. (1989). *The American evasion of philosophy: A genealogy of pragmatism*. Madison: University of Wisconsin Press.

Wolf, M. A. (1992). *A thrice-told tale: Feminism, postmodernism, and ethnographic responsibility*. Stanford, CA: Stanford University Press.

Wolcott, H. F. (1990). *Writing up qualitative research*. Newbury Park, CA: Sage.

Wolcott, H. F. (1992). Posturing in qualitative inquiry. In M. D. LeCompte, W. L. Millroy, & J. Preissle (Eds.), *The handbook of qualitative research in education* (pp. 3–52). New York: Academic Press.

Wolcott, H. F. (1995). *The art of fieldwork*. Walnut Creek, CA: AltaMira.

2

THE PRACTICE AND POLITICS OF FUNDED QUALITATIVE RESEARCH

Julianne Cheek

◻ 1. Introduction: Connecting Practices and Politics

Funding increasingly is being recognized as an enabler for qualitative research. Part of this recognition has involved debunking the myth that qualitative research is cheap to do (Morse, 2002b). Funded qualitative research can take various forms. For example, the researcher might be granted a certain amount of money to be used directly for salaries, equipment, travel, or other expenses identified as necessary for the conduct of the research. In other cases, support for projects is offered "in kind": The funder may choose to provide the researcher with access to specialist staff or equipment as a means of supporting the research rather than supplying cash. Thus, when we talk about *funded* qualitative research, it is not always money that we are talking about. Funded qualitative research is not a homogeneous category able to be reduced to a single understanding. In the same way that qualitative approaches to research are varied in focus and purpose, so are funded qualitative projects.

Seeking, gaining, and accepting funding for qualitative research is not a neutral, value-free process. Funding does more than enable a qualitative project to proceed. Any form of support for qualitative research will have its unique demands on both the researcher and the research project. In particular, the amount of freedom that researchers have—in terms of both project design and the form that the "products" of the research take—will vary depending on what type of support is received. The amount of funding received also may be used to make statements about the relative worth of an individual researcher and to draw up rank tables of successful researchers and research institutions. Accepting funding aligns researchers with certain organizations and funding bodies. Allocation of funding reflects judgments being made as to what is, and is not, acceptable research or research worthy of being funded. Funding thus involves a series of choices being made, all of which have consequences both for the qualitative research itself and for the qualitative researcher. This chapter is about surfacing these choices, interrogating them, and exploring some of their effects. Such exploration involves scrutiny of the contested nature of research, our identities as qualitative researchers, and the nature of qualitative research itself. It moves the focus clearly onto the connections and interactions between qualitative research, funding, and politics.

The contemporary political climate at the time of writing this chapter is one that can be defined broadly as neo-liberal. Although there is no unitary or absolute form of neo-liberalism, neo-liberal governments, and the political regimes of truth that emanate therefrom, promote "notions of open markets, free trade, the reduction of the public sector, the decrease of state intervention in the economy and the deregulation of markets" (Torres, 2002, p. 368). Neo-liberal thought has permeated every aspect of contemporary Western society, including higher education and the world of research. This is evident from trends such as research increasingly being driven by corporate needs, students being positioned and referred to as consumers, and a climate where "paymasters and administrators accrete authority over academics" (Miller, 2003, p. 897). There has been a perceptible shift by governments in the United States, the United Kingdom, Australia, and elsewhere from an emphasis on the social aspects of government to the economic aspects, with the concomitant transformation of social projects to an enterprise form and ethos emphasizing outcomes in terms of economically driven balance sheets and report cards. As Shore and Wright (1999) point out, universities are just one of the sites where "neo-liberal ideas and practices are displacing the norms and models of good government established by the post-war, welfare state" (p. 558). In such a political climate, research increasingly is viewed as an enterprise and is being colonized by corporate and market derived and sustained understandings and premises.

It is with this political backdrop always in mind that this chapter explores aspects of the practicalities of doing funded qualitative research. I asserted in the previous edition of the *Handbook*, some 5 years ago (Cheek, 2000), that discussions of "doing" funded qualitative research often focus only on the writing of proposals or coming up with research ideas. What precedes proposal development in terms of identifying potential funders, and what follows receipt of funding, largely remains an "untold" story. My reading of the literature suggests that this is still the case. What has changed is that managerial, legal, scientific, and economic discourses (that is, ways of thinking and writing about aspects of reality) (Kress, 1985) have emerged with increasing prominence in terms of shaping and influencing the direction of funded qualitative research, in keeping with the increased influence of neo-liberal–driven agendas. Thus, in this chapter, as in my earlier piece of writing, I focus on identifying and approaching potential funding sources as well as on decisions and choices that arise once funding has been acquired. However, it is now not a matter of changing registers at the end of a chapter (Cheek, 2000) to consider a super-context where the "focus is on larger social issues and forces that impact on the funded qualitative researcher" to introduce a "more critical voice, one that probes, challenges, and tests assumptions about . . . the research market and the concomitant commodification of research" (p. 415). Rather, this register is present throughout—the practice of doing funded qualitative research cannot be separated from the political context in which it operates. Thus, the politics that sits behind many of the practices of funded qualitative research will be explored and will form as much a focus of the chapter as the "doing" of funded qualitative research.

As the author of this text, I am writing from a number of positions. Those that I identify are qualitative researcher, funded researcher, coeditor and associate editor of journals, panel member for a number of granting bodies, and reviewer for a number of granting schemes and journals. Just as I have argued that the intersection of qualitative research and funding creates tensions, so do the intersections of these various subject positions that I occupy at any one point in time. For example, as an individual committed to qualitative research as a legitimate and worthwhile research approach in its own right, and defined in its own right, at times I question my motives in applying for funding. Is the funding to do a project that I believe is important and should be done my driving motivation, or is it more that an opportunity to get funding has arisen and I should pursue that? In other words, what is more important to me—the funding or the project? Myself as researcher or myself as entrepreneur? I find myself on occasion torn between these positions because I, like many other researchers, am buffeted by the political context in which I operate.

An example of such buffeting is that while I am sitting here writing this chapter, I have in front of me an e-mail communication congratulating me for being in "the top 10" researchers in the part of the university in which I am located. At first this might seem innocuous or even a good thing, but a closer examination of the premises for such a ranking raises many important questions and issues. First, the criteria used to rank researchers are related to a narrow range of measures. There is no consideration given to the fact that the amount of funding received may be more a product of how much is needed to do a particular research project than a reflection of the relative ability of the researcher. For example, my research does not require large pieces of equipment worth many hundreds of thousands of dollars. Neither is there any consideration that an effect of such a rating based on individual performance may be to discourage collaboration and mentoring of other researchers, because the grant amount or research outcomes will need to be "split" across individuals in the research team. This applies to publications as well: The skill of slicing material into as many articles as possible may be more desirable than having something to say. Similarly, single-author publications will be more strategic than having to "share" performance. Nor is there any consideration of whether or not it is possible to simply transport the language and techniques of corporate management and neo-liberal enterprise culture, such as "the measurement of 'output' and 'efficiency' through competitive league tables, 'performance indicators' and other statistical indices of 'productivity'" (Shore & Wright, 1999, p. 564) into the university and research context. That it is possible, indeed desirable, to do so is a given—indicative of the pervasive influence of the rationality of neo-liberalism.

Questions that I have been asking myself in the past few months, and again while I am actually writing this chapter, include the following: Is it important to me that I am on the "league table" of the top 10 researchers in my area, or is it more important to me that I challenge the assumptions on which such tables are drawn up? Is it better to critique from within—that is, as a person who does attract relatively large sums of money—or does that involve selling out in order to get into that position in the first place, and thereby assisting in perpetuating the structures that I aim to critique? How do I survive in an academic climate where I, like every other facet of the context, am being reduced to a dollar value worked out according to a series of formulae, a large driver in which is the amount of funding received for research? If the amount of funding is key, then where does that leave qualitative research, as I am not going to need pieces of equipment worth large amounts of dollars? What should my response be when I am invited onto grants as "the qualitative person" or because "we thought it would useful to have a bit of qualitative research in it"? My personal journey and explorations with respect to these types of questions form the text to follow. I am sure that many qualitative researchers either are confronting similar issues, or will be, in the near future. It is important that these stories are told. This chapter is a beginning contribution to such a telling.

In what follows, however, I have deliberately tried to avoid setting up any form of polemic. Thus, I am not arguing for, or against, doing funded qualitative research. Rather, I am exploring what "doing" funded qualitative research might mean for both the researcher and the research. I am viewing funded qualitative research as text, recognizing that any text has embedded within it assumptions about the reality in question and a certain view that is being conveyed to the reader of the text. This is the subtext or "the hidden script" (Sachs, 1996). This chapter attempts to surface and explore the often hidden script that shapes and constructs understandings about funded qualitative research. As such, it should not be read as either for or against funded—or any other type—of research. Rather, it should be read as text itself, text that takes a particular view of funded qualitative research. As with any text, it is up to readers as to how they position themselves with respect to that view.

◩ 2. LOCATING FUNDING: PRACTICES AND POLITICS

Locating funding for qualitative research is a political process. There are two major pathways qualitative researchers can take to locate funding for projects. The first is to have an idea for a project and then to seek out funding sources for that project. The other, which is emerging with increasing emphasis in the area where I work, is to respond to tenders that have been advertised from industry or government for clearly defined and clearly delineated research projects, usually of very short duration. This is sometimes known as tendered research. The reason why this type of research is emerging with more prominence in the area that I work in is that this money is perceived, rightly or wrongly, as easier to win than funding in more traditional granting schemes, in which success rates can be less than 20% and it takes months for decisions to be made by a long (and sometimes cumbersome) process of peer review. Applications for these traditional schemes are very demanding and can take up to 6 months to develop, thereby decreasing the attractiveness of such schemes. In addition, it tends to be easier for institutions, with their increasing enterprise orientation, to make a profit from tendered research, in that researcher time will be paid for (whereas in Australia, many "traditional" funding schemes will not pay the time of the chief investigators) and profit margins can be built in. In fact, in many universities in Australia, it is not possible to put in a tender for research until it has been checked by business development units to ensure that the tender has maximized revenue-generating possibilities. There is thus an overt emphasis on the research being at least as much about revenue generation as about the actual research to be conducted. In more traditional schemes, such profit usually is not possible. In fact, in many of these schemes, projects often are not funded for the full amount applied for, with the researcher left to absorb the shortfall. For example, in some of the grants I hold, the granting body will pay a fixed amount towards the oncosts (the institution's contribution toward payroll tax, worker's compensation, and superannuation) of research personnel. However, in some schemes this is less than the oncosts charged by the institution in which I work. This immediately leaves me with a shortfall in funding in this area before I begin. The cumulative effect of this, across several grants, often means that I am actually working on grants as a research assistant on my own time, on weekends and nights, because I do not have enough funds to cover the research after all the "off the top" costs have been taken out. From a purely financial point of view, this makes tendered research a much more attractive proposition, particularly if institutions offer incentives to individual researchers as rewards for revenue generation.

Does this matter? The short answer is that yes, it does. It has serious implications both for qualitative research itself and for the role that qualitative researchers might find themselves playing in funded research. The type of funding sought affects the type of research that can be done. For example, it is highly unlikely that a government department will tender for projects involving long time frames. This immediately eliminates qualitative approaches requiring longer periods in the field and immersion in the data. My experience is that if a qualitative approach is asked for (and it is still the case in Australia that this is the exception rather than the rule), then it is likely to involve the conduct of an already specified number of workshops, focus groups, or interviews. In other words, tendered research is often more about a qualitative researcher operationalizing someone else's idea, intent, and design than it is about designing research to address an issue that the researchers themselves have identified. Even if the tender is in a particular substantive area of interest, it is unlikely that the emphases in the proposed research will be those of the researcher per se. This does not necessarily mean that the research is not valuable or important, but it does mean that the researcher is positioned differently in relation to the research process. It also has implications for understandings and possible future directions of qualitative research itself. If tendered research becomes more prominent, that may skew the type of qualitative research that gets done.

Another emerging trend that I have noticed in the quest to gain an edge in locating funding is the "tacking on" of a (usually small) qualitative component to large-scale, essentially quantitative studies in funding proposals. On one hand, this is an acknowledgment that there are limitations with measuring, for example, only outcomes and opinions. However, the effect of this "tacking on," paradoxically, can be to marginalize qualitative research even more. Often, the qualitative component of such studies involves the application of a few qualitative techniques, devoid of any theoretical grounding. Carey and Swanson (2003) note that "some applications drop in a focus group with no explanation of why it is being proposed or how the expected information will be used, and no description of the method or analysis plans. Although a similarly inappropriate use of quantitative methods could occur, I [sic] have not seen that scenario" (p. 856). This presents a very real possibility of qualitative research becoming more a technique than a theoretically grounded research approach.

Qualitative research is a way of thinking, not a method. When I am approached to be "the qualitative person" on a funding proposal that needs a "qualitative bit or part," that alerts me to the fact that the research is likely to be compartmentalized into the main study and the qualitative component, which is usually much smaller, with far fewer dollars attached to it, and leaves me with little control over the direction of the project itself. Therefore, I am very careful when considering requests of this type. It is important to determine if the proposal going forward for funding, or the tender being called for, understands qualitative research as more than just a few techniques able to be tacked onto the "real" research. It is important to make a decision as to what that means for me as a researcher and what actions I will take in response. I have experienced being in a project in which more than 90% of a large budget was for the quantitative aspects of the study and the qualitative research was underfunded, not well understood, and undervalued. I will not put myself in that position again. By participating in that situation, however, I was able to change the thinking of members of the team and now enjoy very productive and fruitful relationships with them on other funded projects. This is but one example of the underlying and ongoing tensions that permeate the politics and practice of funded qualitative research. I cannot present a "right way" of acting in the funding process; there is no right or wrong way of acting. Rather, the discussion is designed to raise consciousness about what are often unintended consequences with respect to the positioning of both qualitative research and qualitative researchers in funded proposals and research teams.

An important part of being able to locate funding for qualitative research is to be in a position to know about and identify potential funding sources. Zagury (1997) has identified six categories of potential funding sources. These are local community funds, special purpose foundations, family-sponsored foundations, national foundations, government grants and corporate foundations, and corporate funding. It is important to be aware that there are distinct national differences in types and patterns of funding. Hence, it may well be that in certain countries, some of the above categories of funders are of less significance than in others.

One place to start in identifying potential funders is to obtain publications that list them. One such publication is *The GrantSearch Register of Australian Funding* (Summers, 2003). Watching advertisements in newspapers, particularly in the contract/tender section, is another way of identifying potential funding sources, as is getting on the mailing list of the university research office (for those who work in a university setting). Another useful way of learning about potential funding sources that may not be advertised or appear in any grant register or list is to talk to people who have received funding in areas similar to the proposed research. Thus, regardless of the actual mix of funding sources in any particular country or part of the country (there are regional variations in many nations), it is imperative that researchers "do their homework" with respect to uncovering potential funding sources. In light of the preceding discussion, this homework will involve working out what type of funding to seek or apply for, and how this funding might position both the researcher and the qualitative research itself.

Once potential funders are identified, it is important to get as much information as possible about them. One way of doing this is to obtain copies of funding guidelines and/or annual reports. These documents, among other things, give a good overview of the types of projects potential funders have funded in the past and are likely to fund in the future. From this, researchers can assess whether their proposed research seems to fit the priorities and interests of the funder concerned. If review of documentation from the agency reveals it as a viable potential funder for the research in question, the next step is to approach the agency directly to discuss the research idea. How this is done will vary, depending on the type of sponsor. For example, if the funder calls for proposals on an annual basis, the researcher can initiate contact with the office that deals with these applications, both to acquire information about the process and to introduce both the research and the researcher to the people who are likely to be dealing with the application administratively. Speaking with representatives of the agency gives insight into its processes and practices with respect to the way that funding is allocated. Furthermore, it should be possible to ascertain more information about what types of research have been funded in the past. The agency may even supply reports of completed research and/or copies of proposals that have been funded. This information is invaluable for ascertaining the format and scope expected of a proposal, as well as in assisting in the better formulation of ideas, in language appropriate to the funder in question.

Examination of previously funded research also enables the researcher to better locate the proposed study in terms of work already done in the area. Personal communication with potential funding bodies is thus critical, as it provides insights and advice not readily available elsewhere.

Much of what has been discussed also applies when researchers approach a funding agency that does not have regular funding rounds but instead tends to fund research on a more ad hoc basis. One difference is that it may not be immediately obvious whom to contact in the sponsor's organization. It is important to find the right person, in the right section in the organization, to talk to about the intended research and the possibility of funding for it. In this way, the researcher becomes familiar with the organization, and the organization gets to know the researcher. This is important, as a crucial question in funders' minds is whether they can trust a particular researcher to successfully complete a worthwhile project once money is committed to it. When speaking to a funder's representative, it is important to present a clear, simple idea that is both researchable and likely to produce benefits and outcomes that are valuable from the funder's perspective. Consider submitting a concept paper first, either by post or in person, before making personal contact with a representative of the organization. The concept paper could include any preliminary work done or data already collected. This allows the researcher to address the points identified by Bogdan and Biklen (1998) as being important when initiating contact with funders: "1. What have you done already? 2. What themes, concerns, or topics have emerged in your preliminary work? What analytic questions are you pursuing?" (p. 70).

Accompanying the concept paper should be a statement of the researcher's track record. It is important to demonstrate that there is every likelihood, based on past experience, that the research will be completed on time and within budget. Not only is it important to present the research idea, it also is important to present the researchers themselves. One of the problems facing many researchers is the catch-22 situation of needing a track record to attract funding, while not being able to get the funding needed to build up a track record. One way around this is to join a research team that already has established a track record in the same or a closely related area of research, and to work as part of that team. This has a further benefit of establishing contact with the research expertise that is collectively present. It is an ideal way to learn about the research process in a safe way and can lead to the formation of enduring research relationships between colleagues. Another strategy for building a track record is to acquire some form of seed funding. The process may be less competitive than acquiring grants from larger funding bodies, and the funding may be directed to more novice researchers. Such seed funding, though usually modest in amount, can be enough to begin a small research project that can lead to publications and thus provide a foundation on which other research can be built.

What should be evident by now is that acquiring funding is not a quick or easy process. Much lead time often is needed for planning and for establishing research credentials and rapport with funding sources. Failures are inevitable, and it is difficult not to take these personally. Other researchers can provide valuable advice and support throughout this process. As I pointed out previously, many research textbooks begin and end their discussions of how to acquire funding by talking about proposal writing. This, I believe, is nowhere near enough. What has just been discussed—namely, the strategies that must be employed to get to the point where one can write a proposal for a specific funding agency—is, in my opinion, the actual start of "doing" funded qualitative research. In addition, it is imperative to consider, at every stage of the funding process, the politics behind funding itself and any particular funding bid.

▣ 3. Allocating Funding: Practices and Politics

The next step, after identifying a potential funder, is crafting a proposal to seek funding for the research. I have deliberately used the word "crafting" because proposal writing is a craft requiring a unique set of skills, most of which are learned as a result of practice. Writing a proposal involves shaping and tailoring a research idea to fit the guidelines or application process imposed by the intended funding agency. Each application, even for the same project, will vary depending on the characteristics and requirements of the funder being approached. When a proposal is written for a potential sponsor's consideration, it is written for a particular audience, whose members have assumptions and expectations of the form a proposal should take and the language it should use. Thus, as I have emphasized before, it is important for researchers to know that audience and its expectations.

What follows is not about proposal writing per se. Much already has been written about this. For example, a recent edition of *Qualitative Health Research* (Vol. 3, No. 6, July 2003) was devoted to a discussion of qualitative research proposals. Several excellent articles focused on crafting and developing qualitative proposals, along with some of the politics that sits behind this. In these articles, the authors share their experiences by telling their stories of the development, and at times defense, of their proposals. Here, I will continue to expose aspects of what otherwise may remain hidden with respect to the politics and practice of allocating funding for qualitative research.

Writing a proposal is a political process. Researchers need to consider whether the qualitative approach proposed and the likely outcomes of the research "fit" the agenda of the funding body. It is quite reasonable for those who provide funding for research to ask whether or not the proposed project represents appropriate use of the funds for which they have responsibility. The majority of funders take the allocation of monies very seriously. They must weigh the relative merits, from their point of view, of proposals competing for limited resources. Thus, it is essential for the proposal submitted to be clear in terms of its purpose and rationale. Are the outcomes of the project stated? Are they important, useful, and able to make a difference in people's lives?

Some funding bodies may be a little self-serving in their reasons for funding specific proposals, but on the whole, funders do make genuine efforts to fund worthy research proposals, and most treat the selection process very seriously. Funders who are seeking to let a tender for research, while still wanting to ensure that the research done will meet high standards, have other considerations as well. One of these will be cost. This lies at the heart of the tendering process, which is designed for the funder to test the research marketplace in terms of what their money can buy. Qualitative researchers entering this world need to understand the market-driven parameters of tendered research and position themselves competitively. Offering value for money means not only meeting high standards in the research; it also means considering how much, or little, money needs to be allocated to attain those standards.

The trend for universities in Australia, as elsewhere, is to move more into the world of tenders that once belonged to market researchers and consultants. This has meant that university-based qualitative researchers have had to confront issues that they may have been able to ignore in the past. The inherent quality of research no longer is the only consideration. Indeed, understandings of "quality" themselves may have undergone transformation, with traditional measures such as peer review playing less of a role and other factors assuming more prominence, such as perceived value for money. Thus, some means of acquiring funding are becoming overt forms of selling oneself and one's research skills in the research marketplace. The funder does not fund an idea; rather, a researcher's time and expertise are bought to conduct a piece of defined research the agency or organization wants done. This concept, as I have suggested previously and will return to at the end of the chapter, creates new and different tensions for the funded qualitative researcher. Not the least of these tensions revolves around what research funding is for: either remuneration for selling skills, thereby contributing to university or researcher income, or enabling the conduct of research identified by the researcher as important and needing to be done. Of course, these may not be mutually exclusive, although in my experience one or the other tends to be at the fore in any particular funding situation.

Shaping all application forms or guidelines provided by funders are assumptions, often unwritten and unspoken, about research and the way that research is understood. It is important to excavate these assumptions and understandings, for two reasons. The first is to work out whether the funding body is likely to fund qualitative research. Are the guidelines structured in such a way that it is impossible to "fit" qualitative research into them? As Lidz and Ricci (1990) point out, reviewers and funders, like all of us, have "culturally prescribed ideas about 'real' research" (p. 114). The application form and the way that it is structured provide insight and clues as to the funder's particular culturally prescribed ideas about research. Second, in light of some of the preceding discussion, insights also can be gleaned about the way that qualitative research, if present in a detailed tender brief, is understood. Hence, texts such as funding guidelines, tender briefs, and research grant application forms must be read carefully, not only for what they say and how they say it, but also for what they *do not* say. Such a critical reading enables qualitative researchers to take up an informed political position in relation to a particular funding source.

Another guide to the likely success of qualitative proposals is the composition of the review panel used by the funder. Does it contain people who are expert in qualitative research? Does it allow for the possibility for the committee to seek expert opinion outside the committee itself if a proposal comes in that is not within the methodological expertise of committee members? Morse (2003a), Parahoo (2003), and many others have noted that reviews of research proposals can indicate real ignorance about qualitative research, such as asking for power calculations for sample size. Further, Morse (2003a) notes that sometimes the seeking and/or assumption of "expert" advice about qualitative research can be very limited and somewhat ad hoc. The committee members know someone who uses qualitative research or someone who has done a workshop or short course on qualitative research, and "they use these isolated 'facts' as gold standards" (Morse, 2003a, p. 740). Morse refers to this sort of climate as "denigrative" of qualitative research and calls for agencies to be made more accountable for "decisions based on inaccurate, incorrect, or invalid reviews" (2003a, p. 739). Further, she notes that even if there are qualitative reviewers on panels, they invariably are in the minority, often being a "faint voice" on funding panels (Morse, 2002b, p. 1308). If the practice of averaging all the panel members' scores for a particular proposal is followed, then in many instances, because of the relative lack of expertise in and appreciation for qualitative research among the majority of panel members, it is unlikely that average scores for qualitative proposals will be high enough for these proposals to be recommended for funding.

Once the decision has been made to pursue funding from a particular source, the instructions given for applying for funds must be followed carefully. I have reviewed many research funding applications for which it was evident that instructions were not followed. To improve your project's chances of being funded, follow all instructions, beginning with the basics. When asked to confine the application to a certain page limit or word limit, do so. Similarly, if asked to explain something in a lay person's terms, do so. No one is impressed by impenetrable language. Perhaps most crucial is following instructions meticulously with respect to the detail required about the research budget and the way the funds will be used. Many claims appear in proposals for amounts that are obviously well beyond the funding parameters of the grants program in question. Put simply, the proposal must be tailored to the guides, not the guides to the proposal. One strategy employed by many successful researchers to assist in ensuring that the proposal closely approximates the guidelines is to get colleagues to read the draft proposal and provide critical comments.

A key point to bear in mind is that any research proposal, qualitative or not, must formulate a clear issue or question. The initial idea that provided the impetus for the research must be transformed into a researchable focus. The rest of the proposal must unpack that research question and demonstrate how the approach to be taken will enable it to be answered. The proposed research must be contextualized in terms of what has preceded it. The study must be situated in terms of what others are doing and how this research links to that of others. It must be justified in terms of approach and design, having a clear direction and focus with clearly achievable outcomes in line with the funder's priorities and stated goals. The credentials of the researcher or research team also need to be established. The amount of information given about the research design, analysis, and data collection will be determined in part by the format of the guidelines or application form. The proposal must be written so that the reader can understand clearly from the document what is intended for the study, and why. As the proposal is being written and after it is submitted, it is important to ascertain the deadlines and timelines involved, as well as the procedures followed by the decision-making person or committee. In other words, it is important to gain insight into the process of allocating funds. Such insight prepares the researcher to expect a response in a certain format within a set time, and it informs any necessary follow-up.

When the decision about funding finally is made, there are usually three possible outcomes. First, the request may be approved. In this case, the researcher receives funding, and the research commences as soon as all appropriate permissions, such as ethics clearance, are obtained. Another possible outcome is that the researcher is asked to add or change something, for instance, to supply more information about one or more aspects of the proposal. This should be interpreted as a positive sign. More often than not, it means that the funder is considering the request seriously and feels it has some merit; certain aspects of it, however, need clarification before the funder is willing to commit funds. In another version of this outcome, the researcher may be asked if the study could be conducted with a reduced budget, and if so, how. This is not unusual. Sometimes funders have set amounts to allocate, and if the proposed study is toward the bottom of the list of projects they wish to fund, they may be able to offer only a portion of the funds requested. It is important that researchers think carefully about whether to accept such funding. I believe that funded research should not be attempted without adequate support for the activities necessary to the research. It is very tempting to accept any funding offered, but inadequate funding can lead to all sorts of problems in actually doing research. Clearly, research funding poses issues not only about the wise use of funds but also about the wisdom of whether or not to accept funds in the first place.

The third possible outcome is one that is becoming all too common, given the increasing competition for grants: The request for funding is rejected. If this happens, it is important to get as much feedback as possible. Make an appointment to speak to the chair of the committee or a representative of the trust, foundation, or other organization making the decision. Find out as much as possible. Copies of the reviewers' reports may be made available, and these often contain useful critiques that can be used in preparing the proposal for resubmission or submission to another agency. If these reports cannot be obtained, or in addition to them, a list of the projects that were successful may be available. This list may give insights into whether the idea did in fact match the funding priorities of the funder, and what the funder sought in successful proposals. If no feedback at all is available from the funder, then ask researchers who have been funded to review the unsuccessful proposal and to help in debriefing the process just undergone. Talking it through may reveal things that can be done differently in the next application. However, at all times researchers should be aware of their odds of success. In many grants programs in Australia, for example, the success rate is below 20%. Such low success rates are increasingly the case in most countries as the competition for shrinking funding sources grows relentlessly. It is much more likely for researchers *not* to acquire funding than to be successful. Research proposals take much time and effort to complete, and it is hard to cope with rejection, but it may help to remember that no researcher is alone. By maintaining contact with others and setting in place the strategies outlined so far in this chapter, the chances of success can be maximized.

▣ 4. NAVIGATING ETHICS COMMITTEES: PRACTICES AND POLITICS

Receiving a recommendation for funding is not the end of the review process. Funded qualitative research, like other forms of research, needs to undergo a process of formal ethics review. Ethics committees thus become another layer of decision making as to what research will be, and will not be, funded. Funds may not be released until ethics approval is formally received, or if they are released, the research might not be able to proceed until ethics approval has been given. In the university in which I am located, and in keeping with standard practice in Australia, I cannot conduct research with human participants until I have formal ethics approval from the university's Human Research Ethics Committee, as well as from any relevant ethics committees at the sites where my research is situated. An issue for qualitative researchers relates to the role and function of ethics committees with respect to giving such approval. Lincoln and Tierney (2002) assert that there is evidence in the United States that some qualitative researchers are having problems getting research that has already been funded through the Institutional Review Board (IRB) ethics process. In the United States, IRBs were initiated in 1966 (Riesman, 2002) following an order from the U.S. Surgeon General in response to questionable medical research involving elderly patients being injected with live cancer cells. Further regulations designed to protect human subjects (*sic*) became effective in 1974. Thus, the driving force in the establishment of IRBs was the protection of human subjects. This was in keeping with developments stemming from the Nuremberg Code, promulgated in the aftermath of unethical medical experimentation on prisoners and concentration camp inmates during World War II. Thus, the original focus of IRBs and the context from which they emerged was that of medicine and the scientific discourse that underpins medicine.

Similarly, in the United Kingdom, the Royal College of Physicians in 1967 recommended that all medical research be subject to ethical review, and by 1991 every health district was required to have a Local Research Ethics Committee (LREC), with Multi-centre Research Ethics Committees (MRECs) emerging as a means of helping streamline proposals that otherwise would have to go through numerous LRECs (Ramcharan & Cutcliffe, 2001). In the United Kingdom, as in the United States, the formalizing of ethics requirements and the establishment of ethics committees was derived and driven largely by practices from medical research. This is also the case in Australia. For example, university-based Human Research Ethics Committees are modeled on National Health and Medical Research Council guidelines. These apply to all research involving humans, whether it is health related or not. Thus, ethics committees, and the understandings of research with which they operate, often are influenced by the traditions of medicine and science, including the research methods and understandings of research that these disciplines employ.

To some extent, the emergence of qualitative research, and particularly the emergence of funded qualitative research, has occurred at the same time as the emergence of ethics committees and the formalization of ethics requirements and processes. At times, we see the collision of these surfaces of emergence and the working out of the tensions that emanate therefrom. For example, Lincoln and Tierney (2002), Ramcharan and Cutcliffe (2001), and Riesman (2002) assert that qualitative research may be being treated unfairly, and in fact may be disadvantaged, by some ethics committees. Such claims emanate from concerns that qualitative approaches are rejected on the grounds that they are "unscientific" and not able to be generalized. Research methods increasingly have become the remit of ethics committees. In effect, ethics committees can be more powerful than national peer-reviewed funding committees. Even if national and international peers who are experts in my field and the research approaches I employ recommend a project for funding, ethics committees can reject it on the basis of "poor design"—and, thus, "unethical research"—that will result in no benefit, or even possibly in harm, to research participants.

The focus on the quality of the research design stems from legitimate ethical concerns as to the ability of research to make a difference. For example, the U.K. Royal College of Physicians guidelines make the point "that badly designed research is unethical, because unnecessary disturbances may be caused to those concerned, and the lack of validity of results means they cannot be disseminated for the good of society" (Lacey, 1998, p. 215). The upshot of this is that "LRECs must therefore judge the scientific as well as ethical merit of the research under consideration" (Lacey, 1998, pp. 215–216). However, the key question arises as to what constitutes scientific merit or "good" research design, and who determines this. If scientific merit is reduced to "conventional quantitative methods" (Lacey, 1998, p. 216), then this will work against qualitative research unfairly. As van den Hoonaard (2001) points out, ethical review often is based on "the principles and epistemology of deductive research. . . . [This] tends to erode or hamper the thrust and purpose of qualitative research . . . [and] it is a question of whether it is appropriate to judge the ethical merit of qualitative research using criteria derived from other paradigms of research" (pp. 19, 21). It also begs the question of whether ethics and research design are one and the same or different.

Requirements specified by some ethics committees simply can not apply to qualitative research. If, for example, it is necessary for researchers to state clearly, before research begins, each question that they will ask participants, this makes the emergent design of some qualitative research extremely problematic. As Lincoln and Tierney (2002) point out, the issue here is twofold: failure to obtain permission to conduct qualitative research as well as mandates that these studies should be conducted in a positivist fashion. Further issues arise from the politics between ethics committees themselves. Some ethics committees refuse to accept the ethics approval of other committees. Inconsistencies between the decisions and processes of different ethics committees sometimes arise, with the result that it takes a long time to gain approval. I have been caught in such politics of research with funded projects, with one ethics committee approving my research and another not. This example highlights the inconsistencies that can develop around ethics approvals. If the research concerned is a form of tendered research requiring relatively short turnaround times, this protracted approval process can preclude the research from being funded. It may also create and sustain the perception that qualitative research is problematic, unwieldy, and therefore best avoided by funders.

In light of such issues, a strategy I have used when navigating requirements of ethics committees is to write to the particular ethics committees, explaining how I have filled in the form and why I have done so, especially with respect to not being able to provide certain details of the research until the study is actually under way. I state how the initial approach will be made to participants, and I outline the general principles that will be employed regarding confidentiality and other matters. I also suggest that, if the committee would find it useful, I would be happy to talk about the research and discuss any concerns committee members might have. I have found most (but not all) committees willing to listen and to be quite reasonable. However, when talking with ethics committees who have invited me to their meetings to discuss concerns, I am continually struck by the realization that I constantly have to frame my responses in terms of the understandings of research that the committee brings to the table. The conversation usually is as much a discussion of understandings of research as it is about the ethics of that research. I have had to justify all aspects of the research process, not just those I thought were ethical matters. For example, I have found myself engaging in deep, philosophically derived debates about the nature of knowledge and the way that it is possible to study that knowledge. This was despite the fact that a national funding body had deemed the research in question rigorous enough to be funded. Afterwards, I wondered whether any of the committee had ever had to explain the philosophical basis of the research approaches they were familiar with, and I reached the conclusion that they probably had not. This highlighted to me that dominant understandings of research were in play here and that decisions made were as much about what individuals understood and constructed research to be, as they were about the ethics of the research in question. This suggests that ethics committees and the process of ethical approval are as much discursive constructions as any other text.

As another example, a student of mine agreed to change the word "participant" to "patient" in the consent forms and information sheets that would be given to research participants. This was one of the conditions to be met for ethics approval to be granted. We (student and supervisor) had to think deeply about this, but in the end we considered that it was more important for the research to go forward than to take a stand on this issue. In reality, changing this word did not affect the way we did our research. It was more about the comfort levels of some committee members and that their understanding of the positioning of people entering the hospital was maintained. However, this example does raise an important point: At times, researchers may find themselves asked to modify proposals in a way that appears to compromise the approach they wish to take. In instances like this, they must make what I would argue is a fundamentally ethical decision: Can the research proceed under these conditions? Some readers may argue that what we did in changing the word "participant" to "patient" was an ethical issue, one in which we "sold out" to pragmatics and expediency.

One of the reasons for the initial emergence and subsequent prominence of ethics committees and their power was a rise in lawsuits pertaining to medical research that had gone "wrong." As a consequence, van den Hoonaard agrees with "one qualitative researcher" that "qualitative researchers have become the fall guys for ethical mistakes in medical research" (2001, p. 22). He poses the question of whether the rise of ethics committees constitutes a moral panic involving "exaggeration of harm and risk, orchestration of the panic by elite or powerful special-interest groups, the construction of imaginary deviants, and reliance on diagnostic instruments" (van den Hoonaard, 2001, p. 25). In such a construction, qualitative research could be viewed as deviant, and the rise of prescribed forms of deductive research as diagnostic instruments able to be used to detect "suspect" research. The effect, unintended or otherwise, of ethics committees increasingly positioning themselves as determining what type of research will proceed and which will not is an interesting shift from the original intent of ethics committees to uphold the rights of those being researched, to a focus equally concerned with possible legal ramifications of any research undertaken. Thus, protection as a focus of ethics committees has evolved to be as much about protecting from potential litigation the institutions from which researchers come from and/or in which they do their research, as it is about protecting individual participants from adverse research effects.

Putting another spin on this, Kent (1997) notes that ethics committees sometimes take on proxy decision making for participants, making "assumptions about patient's [sic] welfare which do not correspond to patients' actual feelings and beliefs" (p. 187). An interesting insight into this was provided by a recent experience I had when asking participants to sign a consent form for a nominal group I was conducting as part of funded research. The ethics committee requirement was that all participants must sign this consent form before the group could proceed. This particular nominal group comprised senior government and industry representatives. One of the participants objected to having to sign a consent form, seeing it as a form of coercion and control. I was then in a quandary. Did I ask this person to leave and preclude him from the research, or did I proceed, contravening the legalistic requirement of a signed form? In the end, I was able to talk the person around to signing the form but felt that in so doing, I was being coercive and establishing my control of the process. I felt that the forms and procedures had more to do with legalistic requirements than with ethical concerns. Far from empowering this participant, they actually were a form of control and restriction. This is not to argue against the signing of consent forms or the need for consent. Instead, I suggest that techniques employed to ensure that ethical requirements are met can themselves become apparatuses of power that actually do something other than ensuring the ethics of the research. The danger is that regulations (i.e., forms and processes) *become* the ethics, rather than the ethics of the research itself.

Elsewhere (Cheek, 2000), I have suggested strategies for navigating ethics committees. These include finding out as much as possible about the processes used by the committee and asking to see examples of proposals that have been accepted. These actions supply ideas of both the level of detail and the format that the committee requires. Another suggestion is to speak to others who have applied to the committee in question for ethics approval. Remember that qualitative researchers seeking funding or ethical approval have rights, as do all researchers. These include the right "to have their proposals treated with respect and due consideration" (Kent, 1997, p. 186). Stuart (2001) suggests that how we choose to act with respect to how we approach ethics committees (and we could add funding committees) is in fact an ethical decision. He writes, "Will the research be based on practices that treat people as the objects of research and provide them with limited opportunities to contribute to the production of knowledge, or will it be based on collaborative practices that view people as participants in the production of knowledge?" (Stuart, 2001, p. 38). Similarly, do we massage our research into prescribed forms and formulae, knowing that in this form it will be much more likely to achieve funding and approval, but also knowing that it may use systems and practices that work against qualitative research and leave unresolved some of the issues posed?

These sorts of decisions and weighing of tensions and alternatives are important parts of the politics and practice of funded qualitative research. They challenge us to think deeply about every aspect of what we do. It is not a matter of expediency and learning how to "play" the system. We need to try to work for real change, change that will make a difference to, and differences in, the types of research that are funded and approved. Rowan (2000) observed that when the British Psychological Society decided that it was wrong to call people subjects, because it suggested that they were subjected to the will of the researcher, changing 'subjects' to 'participants' was for many psychologists simply a matter of calling up the 'find and replace' facility on the computer. It was not seen as related to a code of ethics, or requiring any change in them. (p. 103)

This highlights the layers of political action that are required to address deep residual practices that can hinder and even subvert the development of funded qualitative research. Without taking such political action, we run the risk of remaining on the surface and playing the politics of the system rather than changing that politics. As Morse (2003b) points out:

This is a task for all of us to do collectively and systematically, for it involves changes such as broadening research priorities and perspectives on what is considered researchable and what constitutes research. It involves political problems, such as expanding and sharing research funds to new groups of investigators. In this light, the administrative changes involved, such as developing appropriate review criteria, expanding committee membership, and educating other scientists about the principles of qualitative inquiry . . . appear trivial. (p. 849)

To focus only on the mechanism of practices associated with funding, be they proposal writing, peer review, or ethics review, is to run the risk of dealing only "with minor changes within the same basic structure" (Martin, 2000, p. 17). Put another way, it is to focus on "what is" and working within that, rather than on "what might be" in terms of "dramatically different allocation principles and associated consequences" (Martin, 2000, p. 21).

◧ 5. Accepting Funding: Practices and Politics

Accepting funding involves entering into a contractual and intellectual agreement with a funder that has consequences for the research that is undertaken. Thus, a central consideration when thinking about doing funded qualitative research is whether or not to accept funding from a particular funding agency. Would-be researchers must consider the potentially conflicting agendas of funders, participants, and researchers. For example, at the university in which I work, we do not accept funding from the tobacco industry. This is just one example, and there are many more instances of question marks over the ethics of accepting funding from certain industries, agencies, or even governments. Other examples include whether a particular industry is involved in questionable environmental activities or health practices and whether it is a multinational company involved in possible exploitation of developing countries' workforces. Taking money from a sponsor is not a neutral activity; it links the researcher and research inexorably with the values of that funder.

A related set of issues emerges from a consideration of who controls the qualitative research that is funded. It is a fact that once funding is accepted for research, the researcher is not an entirely free agent with respect to the direction and outcome of that research. Depending on the policies and attitudes of the funder, the degree of freedom allowed in carrying out the research (such as changing its direction if the need arises as a result of findings, or talking and writing about the research) may vary considerably. Issues of control must be negotiated carefully in the very early stages of the research, as it is often too late once the project is well under way. Too often, researchers either ignore or are simply unaware of the problems that can arise. Taking funding from someone in order to conduct research is not a neutral act. It implies a relationship with that funder that has certain obligations for both parties. It is important for researchers to discuss with funders all the expectations and assumptions, both spoken and unspoken, that they may have about the research.

As an example, one such expectation relates to what can be said about the research, and by whom. Put another way, this is an issue about who actually owns the data or findings that result from the study, as well as about how those data can be used both during and after the study. Some researchers have found themselves in the situation of not being able to write about the research in the way they want to, if at all. For example, I carried out a funded piece of research, using qualitative approaches, that produced four main findings, each of which was accompanied by a series of recommendations. When I submitted the report, I found that the funding body was willing to act on two of the findings, as it believed they were within the body's statutory remit, but not on the other two. Although this seems reasonable at one level, I was concerned that the remaining two findings were in danger of being lost. The recommendations associated with those findings were important and, in my opinion, required action. I was even more concerned when the funder wanted to alter the report to include only the two findings it believed were relevant to it. Fortunately, a solution was found whereby the report was framed to highlight the findings considered relevant by the funder, while making reference to the other findings as well. In some ways, this may seem like an uneasy compromise, but at least the whole picture was given with respect to the findings. Somewhat naïvely, in retrospect, I had not anticipated the issue arising as to what data and findings should or could be included in a study, or what data, conversely, might be excluded. I am now much more careful to negotiate how the findings of a study will be reported, the use of the data, and my rights to publish the study findings in full, myself, in scholarly literature.

Qualitative approaches to research are premised on an honest and open working relationship between the researcher and the participants in the research. Inevitably, in such studies the researcher spends a great deal of time with participants getting to know aspects of their world and learning about the way they live in that world. At the center of a good working relationship in qualitative research is the development of trust. Furthermore, as qualitative researchers, we all have dealt with issues such as participants feeling threatened by the research and therefore concealing information, or participants who are eager to please us and give us the information they think we want to hear or that they think we need to know. These issues can become even more complicated in the conduct of funded qualitative research. Therefore, when conducting funded research, it is important for researchers to tell participants who is providing the funding and the purposes of that funding. Successful researchers report the importance of making their own relationship to the funder clear. For example, are they acting as paid employees of the funder, or are they independent? Equally crucial to a successful relationship between researchers and participants is to ensure, and to give assurance, that the participants will remain anonymous and that the confidentiality of their individual information will be safeguarded. This is a major concern for some participants, who may believe they will be identified and "punished" in some way by the funder—for example, if they criticize a funder who is their employer. When conducting research in a specific setting among a specified group of people, it may be difficult for researchers to ensure the anonymity of participants. It is crucial for researchers to be clear about this issue and to discuss it with participants, who need to know what will happen to specific information in the project, who will have access to it, and how their rights to confidentiality are being ensured. Individuals may choose not to participate if they have concerns about a particular funder having access to information they have given or if they question the motives for that funding being given in the first place.

If there are any restrictions on what can or cannot be said about the findings of the research and the research undertaking itself, then it is important for researchers to make potential participants aware of this. Part of the constant process of giving feedback to participants must include informing them about any issues that arise about ownership of the research and the way it will be disseminated. All of this is to assist participants in making informed decisions about whether to participate or not, as well as to give them some idea about the uses to which the research is likely to be put. This enables them to be better positioned to follow up the research findings and to have a say in what happens as a result of them. It is a part of valuing all perspectives in the research and of treating participants as more than simply research objects who are subject to a research agenda that has been imposed on them.

A related issue can arise when the findings of a study do not please the funder. What happens if the findings are, or have the potential to be, beneficial to the participants but may displease the sponsor? Who has the say as to whether or not these findings will be published? As Parahoo (1991) points out, "too often those who control the purse tend to act in their own interests when they veto the publication of research. To others this is an abuse of power and office, and a waste of public money" (p. 39). This is a particularly important question if the research involves working with groups that are relatively powerless or disenfranchised. Researchers have found themselves in the position of not being able to publish or otherwise disseminate results in any way because of the contractual arrangements that they have entered into when accepting funds. When finalized, a contract should be checked carefully so that researchers can be sure they are comfortable and can live with the conditions set. Such checking of the contract also pertains to the need for clarity about exactly what will be "delivered" to the funder in return for the funding received. What is it that the researcher is contracting with the funder to provide? This is an important question, raising the possibility of numerous problems arising if the parties involved do not share an understanding. It is easy and tempting for researchers, particularly if they are inexperienced, to underestimate the amount of time and energy needed for a project. Consequently, they may "overcommit" in terms of what they can deliver to the funder. They must consider carefully what it is reasonable to provide for the funding received, then make this explicit to the funder. Time frames should be placed on each deliverable so that both parties are aware of what will be produced and when it can be expected.

As we have seen, obtaining funding creates a research relationship to build during the conduct of the research, namely that between the funder and the researcher. All funding bodies require reports about the progress of funded projects. When communicating and reporting to the funder, which often involves reporting to an individual nominated by the funder, it is important for researchers to be honest and up front. This particularly applies if something has "gone wrong" or if for some reason the research plan has had to be changed. In my experience, funders would much rather find out about these things as they arise than be faced at the end with a project that has not met expectations. The extent of a funding body's involvement in research can vary considerably, ranging from the submission of one or two reports a year to a highly hands-on approach in which a representative of the agency seeks to play an active role in the research undertaken. Whatever approach is adopted, it is important that there is clear communication as to the roles that the researcher and the funder will play in the research. It also is important to clarify that if research is being carried out in which participants will be known to the representative of the agency, then there may have to be restrictions on access to information so as to protect participants' rights to confidentiality. Similarly, if a funder requires that an advisory board be established to provide guidance on the progress and direction of the research, it is important to clarify the parameters within which the board will operate. Such boards can be invaluable in assisting with broad issues pertaining to the substantive focus of the research. Indeed, many experienced researchers, recognizing the value of advisory boards in thinking through aspects of doing the project, interpreting the findings, and considering the routes for dissemination, may constitute such a board regardless of funder requirements. However, clear understandings must be put in place as to what access, if any, the board can have to specific sets of information collected in the study, especially if board members are connected in any way to the study site and/or to participants.

All of this highlights the careful thought that must go into deciding whether to accept money from a particular funder. Funders, just like researchers, have motives for wanting research to be done. Some bodies may be entirely altruistic, others less so. Some funders, particularly in the evaluation area, may be funding research overtly to "vindicate policies and practices" (Parahoo, 1991, p. 37). As Guba and Lincoln (1989) note when writing about evaluation studies, "often evaluation contracts are issued as requests for proposals just as research contracts are; in this way, winning evaluators are often those whose definitions of problems, strategies, and methods exhibit 'fit' with the clients' or funders' values" (p. 124). This is why Bogdan and Biklen (1998) assert that "You can only afford to do evaluation or policy research [or, I would add, any funded form of qualitative research] if you can afford not to do it" (p. 217). It is important to consider whether it is possible to retain integrity and independence as a researcher paid by someone else or provided with the support to do research. Key questions to ask are how much freedom will be lost if someone else is paying and how the researcher feels about this loss of freedom. It is important to remember that although "in the research domain, the notion of mutual interest licenses partnerships between state, college and industry . . . such relationships merit scrutiny rather than an amiable blind faith" (Miller, 2003, p. 899) such as that preached by adherents of neo-liberal thought.

It is important in a research team that team members share similar approaches to the issues that have been raised. This needs to be discussed from the outset of the formation of the team, and it is just as important to the smooth functioning of the team as the particular expertise each team member brings to the project. There must be trust among team members that decisions made will be adhered to. Furthermore, it is important to talk about how decisions will be made in and about the team. Who will control the budget? What happens if there is disagreement about the way the research is proceeding? The involvement of a third party, namely the funder, makes the need to be clear about these issues all the more imperative. Furthermore, the team needs to have clear guidelines about who will communicate with the funder and how. Working with other researchers offers the advantages of having a team that is multiskilled and often multidisciplinary in focus. However, funding increases the need for good communication in the team and clear understandings of each member's role, both in terms of the research itself and in terms of dealing with the funder. Strategies that research teams can employ to assist in the smooth functioning of funded projects include outlining each member's responsibilities, including their contribution to the final report; drawing up timelines for each member to adhere to; upholding each member's access to support and funds; and holding regular meetings to discuss issues among the team members.

Accepting funding for qualitative research affects the nature of relationships between the research participants and the researcher. Funded research also can result in the development of a new set of relationships, especially those between the researcher/research team and the funding agency, along with any other structures the funder may wish to put in place, such as advisory boards. When there is clear communication, these relationships can enhance the research effort and assist its smooth functioning. However, such relationships cannot be taken for granted and need to be worked on actively by all those involved. Their development is another part of the practices and politics of funded qualitative research.

◰ 6. Marketing Research: Practices and Politics

The issues discussed in this chapter have arisen against the backdrop of an emergent view of research as a commodity to be traded on an academic, and increasingly commercially driven, marketplace. The late 1990s saw the emergence of a climate of economic restraint and funding cuts by governments in most Western countries. At the time of writing this chapter, this trend continues, with little likelihood of it being reversed or slowing. Fiscal restraint has greatly affected the availability of funding for research in that many funding agencies, particularly government departments, no longer have the resources to support research to the extent that they once did. At the same time, educational institutions such as universities have experienced cuts to their core funding. One of the consequences of such cuts to university operating budgets has been the imperative for staff to be able to generate income for the institution. In some cases, such income has become part of academics' salaries; in others, this income has been factored into the operating budget of the institution to pay for basic resources needed to continue teaching and research programs.

In Australia, as elsewhere, concomitantly we have seen the emergence of increasing regulation of the university sector, including a rise in the frequency of prescribed reporting of performance indicators. We also have seen the emergence and rise of business development units designed to manage and sell research. In some divisions of universities in Australia, the greatest increase in staffing in the past decade has been in marketing and business development units. As an academic, I increasingly find myself in a world like that described by Brennan (2002), in which research is tendered out by, and oriented to, business, industry, and government. Their agendas feature increasingly short time frames for both conducting and reporting on research. This, of course, mitigates against certain types of qualitative research that are viewed as less efficient and more unwieldy. Qualitative research takes time and is very hands-on. The commercially driven tender and business development environment currently driving much research works against qualitative research. If the sole object of writing a proposal is revenue generation, then the research usually will lack strategic foundation and direction. As Morse (2003b) notes, "inadequate time, clearly, will kill a project or result in a project that has not become all that it could . . . be" (p. 846). If we are not careful, an effect of the emphasis on quick research turnaround and research "deliverables" could be to encourage the rise of an atheoretical set of qualitative techniques designed for expediency and framed by reductionist understandings of what qualitative research is and might do.

The contemporary context in which universities and qualitative researchers operate is one where the "fast capitalist texts" (Brennan, 2002, p. 2) of business and management have entered public discourse, normalizing practices and understandings of funded qualitative research and the purpose of that research. This, in some instances, has created a new imperative for obtaining funding, where the funding rather than the research has become highly prized. Put another way, it is possible that what is becoming important to some university administrations is the amount of funding obtained, rather than the contribution of the research and its associated scholarship to new knowledge and problem solving. In such a climate, there is the potential to privilege funded research over unfunded research. There is also the very real possibility that this environment is viewed as "natural" and "normal." We are bombarded with messages that we have to become more accountable, efficient, and effective, with clear implications that in the past research has been inefficient and/or ineffective and that researchers were unaccountable. But we must pause to ask certain questions: Efficient and effective in terms of what? Accountable to whom and in terms of what? It is a relatively recent phenomenon for research and funding to be so closely tied to the marketplace, and limited understandings of that marketplace at that! For example, in the postwar United States in 1946, Poiri and Conrad (see Bromley, 2002) in the Office of Naval Research were asked to suggest how the federal government could support university-based research without destroying academic freedom and creativity, which were recognized as important and integral to advancing discovery. Bromley (2002) notes that they came up with three fundamental principles: (a) Find the best people in the nation on the basis of peer review; (b) support these individuals in doing whatever they decided they wanted to do, as they are much better judges of how best to use their time and talent than anyone in government; and (c) leave them alone while they are doing it (i.e., minimize reporting and paperwork). Why does this approach seem so "abnormal" to those of us working in academe and/or research in the early 2000s? Is it because the understandings and dominant forms of the fast texts of the market and late capitalism have colonized research and academic cultures to such an extent that we cannot imagine that a situation such as the one Bromley described not only existed but was actively promoted, only a few decades ago?

What this highlights is that at any point in history, certain understandings will be at the fore. Which understandings prevail results from the power of particular groups at any one time to promote their frames of discourse to the exclusion or marginalization of others (Foucault, 1977). If Poiri and Conrad were to make their suggestions now, they would be marginalized, talked about as "dreamers," and told to operate in the "real world" by many administrators. Of course, we may well dispute how Poiri and Conrad defined and operationalized some of their categories, such as "best people" and "peer review," but their assertions are useful for highlighting how far we have moved in terms of the ways of thinking and speaking that are afforded mainframe status in many research texts in the contemporary research context. The discourse of the market is preeminent. An effect of this is changing control over the conditions and activities of researchers, who increasingly are being viewed as workers selling their labor and research products. It is the market, not necessarily peers, that determines the worth of research, and even what research will be done. Furthermore, this marketplace is tightly regulated in terms of the means of obtaining funding, what actually is funded, the way research performance is assessed, and the reporting that researchers must do both about their research and the way that they use their time in general. Such regulation codifies our knowledge, reducing it to key performance indicators such as number of publications or number of research dollars obtained, thereby diverting attention from "more productive and educational uses of our time" (Brennan, 2002, p. 2). Emerging trends show academics, for example, being forced to estimate costs for every activity and being told that activities for which they do not get paid directly should not be undertaken. Mentoring, thinking time, community service, and unfunded research are some of the potential casualties of such reductionist discourse.

So, too, is scholarship. Scholarship increasingly has come to be associated with narrowly defined research outcomes, including the number of journal articles published, funding received, or conference papers presented (Cheek, 2002). These measures inevitably are numeric and relative. Thus, institutional lists of "top" researchers are drawn up on the basis of numeric scores, worked out using complicated formulae designed to convert research, ideas, and scholarship into measurable throughput. What becomes important is the score, not how the score was calculated or the assumptions underlying it. It doesn't matter if a researcher's funding is mostly for an expensive piece of equipment; that researcher will score higher than, and "rank above," a qualitative researcher who may have acquired funding for a number of projects. In these formulae, publications also are converted to points and dollars. Morse (2002a), in keeping with many editors of scholarly journals, bemoans the fact that in submissions to the journal of which she is editor, *Qualitative Health Research*, she sees an increasing prevalence of what she calls atheoretical articles that are "shallow, thin and insignificant . . . it is the worst of qualitative inquiry" (p. 3). Morse describes a form of journal submission that is almost formulaic, "trite," and goes on to assert that "a few comments do not an article make" (Morse, 2002a, p. 4). Why the emergence of such a trend now? Could it be an effect of the imperative to publish and that what counts (literally) is the number of articles, not their content, just as what counts is the amount of research money, and not what it funds?

Historically, there has always been a place for both funded and unfunded research in universities and elsewhere. Some types of research simply have not required funding, yet have been able to produce significant contributions to knowledge for which they have been valued. Furthermore, research serves a variety of purposes. On one hand, it can be carried out to investigate a well-defined issue or problem arising in a specific area or field, and on the other it can be conducted to probe or explore what the issues might be in the first place. Research also can be carried out simply for the pleasure of investigating new and different ways of thinking about aspects of our reality. Some research projects might incorporate all of the above. In other words, just as there are a variety of research approaches and associated techniques, so are there a range of purposes for which research might be carried out. Each research project has its own intended audience, who will relate to the assumptions framing the problem to be investigated as embedded within that piece of research. However, with the imperative for academics to generate income, there has been a subtle, and at times not so subtle, shift in thinking toward valuing research that is funded more highly than research that is not. Given this, the question can be asked as to whether we are seeing the taking hold of what Derrida (1977) terms a binary opposition with respect to funded/unfunded research.

Derrida (1977) holds that any positive representation of a concept in language, such as "funded research," rests on the negative representation of its "opposite," in this case, unfunded research. In a binary opposition, there is always a dominant or prior term, and conversely there is always a subordinate or secondary term. For example, consider such common binary oppositions as masculine/feminine and reason/emotion. In each case, the first named term is given priority over the second, which is often defined in terms of "not" the dominant. However, as noted elsewhere, "the definitional dynamic extends to the primary term as well in that it can only sustain its definition by reference to the secondary term. Thus the definition and status of the primary term is in fact maintained by the negation and opposition of the secondary partner" (Cheek, Shoebridge, Willis, & Zadoroznyj, 1996, p. 189). Derrida (1977) points out that binary oppositions are constructions of certain worldviews; they are not natural givens that can be taken for granted. In the instance of funded/unfunded research, it is important to recognize that there is a binary opposition in operation and to explore both how it has come to be and how it is maintained. An interesting way to commence such an exploration is to reverse the binary pairing and note the effect. What is the effect on the way research is viewed and understood if unfunded research assumes primacy and funded research becomes the secondary or derivative term?

In a climate where funded research assumes ever increasing importance, the power of funding agencies to set research agendas has increased markedly. As Parahoo (1991) noted more than a decade ago, "a successful researcher is sometimes defined by the ability to attract funds, and most researchers know that in order to do so one must submit proposals on subjects which sponsors are prepared to spend money on. This can mean that the real issues that concern practitioners are sometimes ignored" (p. 37). What has changed in the past decade is that it is no longer the case that successful researchers are "sometimes" defined in this way, but rather that they "usually" or "normally" are. We see in play here "new neo-liberal notions of the performing professional" (Shore & Wright, 1999, p. 569). Although it is not unreasonable that sponsors should be able to fund research that is relevant to them, a problem arises if funds are not available for researcher-initiated research that addresses questions that have arisen from the field. If funding alone drives research agendas, then this may infringe on the academic freedom of researchers to pursue topics of importance and interest. As Porter (1997) notes, "pressure is therefore exerted on academics to tailor their work in order to meet the requirements of funders" (p. 655). Creativity may be sacrificed for expediency, in that some research topics will have more currency than others in terms of their likeliness to attract funding. Drawing on Mills (1959), Stoesz (1989) observes that "to the extent that this happens, an enormous problem emerges—social science [read qualitative research] becomes a commodity, the nature of which is defined by the bureaucracies of the corporate and governmental sectors" (p. 122).

The emerging emphasis on funded research, in terms of its ability to produce income for institutions, has in my opinion seen the emergence of research as a commodity to be bought and sold on the research market. Information and data from research projects are seen as a "product" to be traded on this market and sold to the highest bidder. Researchers increasingly find themselves struggling with the often competing demands of research as the generation of new knowledge, against research as a commodity to be traded in the marketplace. Such a struggle is exacerbated by a trend in which the act of winning funding for research is itself viewed as a currency to be traded in the academic marketplace. For example, promotion and tenure committees in many universities are influenced by the amount of funding received as a measure of research success. This has the effect of maintaining the binary opposition of funded/unfunded research, in that performance in terms of funded research is valued, while the absence of funding—that is, unfunded research—is not. The idea of research being perceived as a commodity, along with the trend to privilege funded research over unfunded research, poses some particular dilemmas for qualitative researchers. For instance, it is still true that most funding is attracted by research projects using traditional scientific methods. This means that it is relatively harder to obtain funding for qualitative research. If success in obtaining funding is used, rightly or wrongly, to measure performance and to put a value on research, then there is a real danger that qualitative research could be marginalized because it is not as easy to attract funds using qualitative approaches.

All of this is to bring into sharp focus some fundamental questions with which qualitative researchers need to grapple. These questions relate to the background assumptions about research and research performance that are driving many research agendas and researchers. Assumptions about how research performance is measured and valued need to be exposed. They can then be considered and explored in terms of the effect they have on notions of what research is for and what the nature of a research product should be. Funding is important in that it enables research to be carried out that otherwise would not occur because of resource constraints. It is not funding itself that is the issue here; rather, it is the uses to which the act of gaining funding is being put, apart from enabling a specific piece of research to proceed. I am not arguing against funded qualitative research—far from it! What I am suggesting is that researchers need to think about their own assumptions about funded research and how such assumptions have embedded, within them, many taken-for-granteds about the nature of research and research products in what is increasingly becoming a research marketplace.

▣   7. Practices and Politics Beyond
    the "Find and Replace" Function Key

Doing funded qualitative research is not a neutral and value-free activity. Researchers must constantly examine their motives for doing research and the motives of funding bodies in funding research. This is particularly important in a context in which new forms of neo-liberal rationality are emerging, defining the performance, worth, and mission of research, researchers, and the institutions in which they work. In writing this chapter, I am advocating suspended readings. Such readings suspend notions of funded research and attendant practices and organizations, such as funding panels and ethics committees, in order to take another look at what otherwise become taken-for-granted parts of the funding process. This other look begins by exploring the origins of understandings shaping research, and particularly funded qualitative research, how these understandings are maintained, and what this reveals about the context in which researchers operate. I am not advocating that we replace one set of understandings with another, but rather that we recognize, for what they are, current trends and issues in the politics and practice of funded qualitative research, so that we might best position ourselves in relation to them. Questions we need to ask ourselves include the following: Can we accept and live with the tensions and contradictions posed to us as funded qualitative researchers in the reality in which we live and work every day? What should we defend, and what might we give up? How do we respond to the enterprise culture of neo-liberalism increasingly so pervasive in every aspect of the research process? In all of this, a key question and challenge is how to avoid being always located at the margins, as the "faint voice" (Morse, 2002b, p. 1308) in funding panels or funding received, in order that qualitative research can be viewed as legitimate and mainframe.

There are no easy answers to these questions. The position taken by each of us as individuals will be different. What is important is that this conversation is held and that the inherent political nature of funded qualitative research is surfaced and explored. This chapter has provided a lens to bring into focus issues concerning the regulation and production of forms of knowledge, through practices associated with, and arising from, the funded research process. How qualitative researchers respond to the imperatives that confront them every day, and to the imperatives for political action that emanate from the discussion herein, will go a long way in determining what the future holds for qualitative research itself and its positioning, either mainframe or at the margins. The identities that we individually want as qualitative researchers must be embedded in all facets of our research endeavors, including the seeking, acquisition, and use of funds to support that research. We must avoid atheoretical pragmatic types of qualitative research techniques emerging as synonymous with understandings of funded (or fundable) qualitative research. Instead, it will be increasingly important to promote theoretically and politically robust qualitative research. For me, this is the key challenge facing qualitative research as it becomes "more accepted" into the funding fold. Such acceptance can be a double-edged sword for the unwary and could see a subversion of all that we have worked to establish if we are not on our guard. In all of this, I reiterate that funding itself is not the problem—funding is useful as an enabler of qualitative research. Problems arise if funding becomes the end, rather than the means, and qualitative research (or a variant

Cheek: Funded Research ▣ 73

thereof) is subverted to the expedient end of gaining that funding. The choice is ours, both individually and collectively, as to which of these positions we adopt.

▣ REFERENCES

Bogdan, R. C., & Biklen, S. K. (1998). *Qualitative research in education: An introduction to theory and method.* Boston: Allyn and Bacon.

Brennan, M. (2002). *The politics and practicalities of grassroots research in education.* Retrieved May 15, 2002, from www.staff.vu.edu.au/alnarc/forum/ marie_brennan.html

Bromley, D. A. (2002). Science, technology, and politics. *Technology in Society, 24,* 9–26.

Carey, M. A., & Swanson, J. A. (2003). Funding for qualitative research. *Qualitative Health Research, 13*(6), 852–856.

Cheek, J. (2000). An untold story? Doing funded qualitative research. In N. K. Denzin & Y. S. Lincoln (Eds.), *Handbook of qualitative research* (2nd ed., pp. 401–420). Thousand Oaks, CA: Sage.

Cheek, J. (2002). Advancing what? Qualitative research, scholarship, and the research imperative. *Qualitative Health Research, 12*(8), 1130–1140.

Cheek, J., Shoebridge, J., Willis, E., & Zadoroznyj, M. (1996). *Society and health: Social theory for health workers.* Melbourne: Longman Australia Pty Limited.

Derrida, J. (1977). *Of grammatology.* Baltimore: Johns Hopkins University Press.

Foucault, M. (1977). *Discipline and punish.* London: Penguin.

Guba, G. M., & Lincoln, Y. S. (1989). Ethics and politics: The twin failures of positivist science. In *Fourth generation evaluation* (pp. 117–141). Newbury Park, CA: Sage.

Kent, G. (1997). The views of members of local research ethics committees, researchers and members of the public towards the roles and functions of LRECS. *Journal of Medical Ethics, 23*(3), 186–190.

Kress, G. (1985). *Linguistic processes in socio-cultural practice.* Victoria, New South Wales: Deakin University Press.

Lacey, E. A. (1998). Social and medical research ethics: Is there a difference? *Social Sciences in Health, 4*(4), 211–217.

Lidz, C. W., & Ricci, E. (1990). Funding large-scale qualitative sociology. *Qualitative Sociology, 13*(2), 113–126.

Lincoln, Y. S., & Tierney, W. G. (2002, April). *"What we have here is a failure to communicate . . .": Qualitative research and institutional review boards.* Paper presented at the annual meeting of the American Educational Research Association, New Orleans, LA.

Martin, B. (2000). Research grants: Problems and options. *Australian Universities' Review, 2,* 17–22.

Miller, T. (2003). Governmentality or commodification? US higher education. *Cultural Studies, 17*(6), 897–904.

Mills, C. W. (1959). *The sociological imagination.* New York: Oxford University Press.

Morse, J. (2002a). Editorial. A comment on comments. *Qualitative Health Research, 12*(1), 3–4.

Morse, J. (2002b). Myth #53: Qualitative research is cheap. *Qualitative Health Research, 12*(10), 1307–1308.

Morse, J. (2003a). The adjudication of qualitative proposals. *Qualitative Health Research, 13*(6), 739–742.

Morse, J. (2003b). A review committee's guide for evaluating qualitative proposals. *Qualitative Health Research, 13*(6), 833–851.

Parahoo, K. (1991). Politics and ethics in nursing research. *Nursing Standard, 6*(1), 35–39.

Parahoo, K. (2003). Square pegs in round holes: Reviewing qualitative research proposals. *Journal of Clinical Nursing, 12,* 155–157.

Porter, S. (1997). The degradation of the academic dogma. *Journal of Advanced Nursing, 25,* 655–656.

Ramcharan, P., & Cutcliffe, J. R. (2001). Judging the ethics of qualitative research: Considering the "ethics as process" model. *Health and Social Care in the Community, 9*(6), 358–366.

Riesman, D. (2002, November/December). Reviewing social research. *Change,* pp. 9–10.

Rowan, J. (2000). Research ethics. *International Journal of Psychotherapy, 5*(2), 103–111.

Sachs, L. (1996). Causality, responsibility and blame—core issues in the cultural construction and subtext of prevention. *Sociology of Health and Illness, 18*(5), 632–652.

Shore, C., & Wright, S. (1999). Audit culture and anthropology: Neo-liberalism in British higher education. *Journal of the Royal Anthropological Institute, 5*(4), 557–575.

Stoesz, D. (1989). Provocation on the politics of government funded research: Part 1. *Social Epistemology, 4*(1), 121–123.

Stuart, G. (2001). Are you old enough? Research ethics and young people. *Youth Studies Australia, 20*(4), 34–39.

Summers, J. (2003). *The GrantSearch register of Australian funding.* Perth, WA: GrantSearch.

Torres, C. A. (2002). The state, privatisation and educational policy: A critique of neo-liberalism in Latin America and some ethical and political implications. *Comparative Education, 38*(4), 365–385.

van den Hoonaard, W. C. (2001). Is research-ethics review a moral panic? *Canadian Review of Sociology and Anthropology, 38*(1), 19–36.

Zagury, C. S. (1997). Grant writing: The uncertain road to funding, Part V. From the other side: How reviewers look at proposals. *Alternative Health Practitioner, 3*(1), 25–29.

3

PERFORMANCE ETHNOGRAPHY

The Reenacting and Inciting of Culture

Bryant Keith Alexander

P erformance ethnography is literally the staged re-enactment of ethnographically derived notes. This approach to studying and staging culture works toward lessening the gap between a perceived and actualized sense of self and the other. This is accomplished through the union and practice of two distinct and yet interrelated disciplinary formations—*performance studies* and *ethnography*. Practitioners of performance ethnography acknowledge the fact that culture travels in the stories, practices, and desires of those who engage it. By utilizing an experiential method such as performance ethnography, those who seek understanding of other cultures and lived experiences are offered a body-centered method of knowing, what Dwight Conquergood (1986a) calls a dialogical understanding in which "the act of performance fosters identification between dissimilar ways of being without reducing the other to bland sameness, a projection of the performing self" (p. 30).

Performance studies, in its most procedural sense drawn from its link to communication studies, is interested in what Pelias (1999a) calls "the process of dialogic engagement with one's own and others' aesthetic communication through the means of performance" (p. 15). *Ethnography*, in its most utilitarian sense, is what Spradley and McCurdy (1972) refer to as "the task of describing a particular culture" (p. 3). As a broad-based description of performative praxis, performance ethnography is a *form of cultural exchange* (Jones, 2002), *a performative cross-cultural communication* (Chesebro, 1998), an embodied *critical performative pedagogy* (Giroux, 2001; Pineau, 1998, 2002; Worley, 1998), and a theater form that *establishes emancipatory potential* (Mienczakowski, 1995; Park-Fuller, 2003). Performance ethnography is also a method of *putting the critical sociological and sociopolitical imagination to work in understanding the politics and practices that shape human experience* (Denzin, 2003).

Within the explanatory frame of this chapter title, I make the strong suggestion that performance ethnography *is* and *can be* a strategic method of *inciting culture*. The collaborative power of performance and ethnography utilizes an embodied aesthetic practice coupled with the descriptive knowledge of lives and the conditions of living, to stir up feeling and provoke audiences to a critical social realization and possible response. This social action to which I refer here briefly is not necessarily that which is set into violent motion to overthrow dominant structures of oppression: It is a physical force set against the desire of knowing and being in the world.

The potential for social action resides at the core of how *participants in* and *audiences of* performance ethnography see themselves in relation to others. The potential resides in how they understand the act of performing the lives of others, as synecdoche to the larger politics of representation and identity (i.e., race, culture, class, gender, etc.). The potential lies in revealing issues of who gets to speak and for whom, linked with *the politics of culture* that regulate what elements of culture are featured or suppressed (Whisnant, 1983). The potential resides in how participants choose to maintain or disrupt the perceptual stasis that exists within their *habitudes and habitus*, and how they *might* act toward influencing social awareness of problematic human conditions that may be revealed or explored through performance ethnography.

For some, the notion of *overthrowing structures of oppression* might seem farfetched and beyond the traditional scope of performance ethnography, yet theories and practices in both performance studies and theater arts have been moving steadily toward the social and political goals of employing performance as a tool and method of cultural awareness and social change. Such a charge and application has been made in the particularity of practices in traditional and nontraditional performance arenas, as well as planting the seeds of social activism in the classroom with future theater and performance practitioners. Such attempts seek to frame performance as *a critical reflective and refractive lens* to view the human condition and a form of *reflexive agency* that initiates action. Performance ethnography uses theater to illuminate cultural politics and to instill understanding with the potential to invoke change and have a positive effect on the lived conditions of self and others (Boal, 1979, 1995, 1998; Dolan, 2001a, 2001b; Park-Fuller, 2003; Schutzman & Cohen-Cruz, 1994; Spry, 2001; Van Erven, 1993).

The positioning of audience members as agents in the production of cultural meaning places a mandate, if not a culpability, on audience members to act as social agents. It requires them to both interact with the performance and to engage in the imaginative, yet practical, act of creating new possibilities of human interaction in the manner in which such experience could be translated into their daily lives (Pollock, 1998a). In this sense, the power and potency of performance ethnography resides in the demand that a performance text must not only "awaken moral sensibilities. It must move the other and the self to action" (Denzin, 1997, p. xxi). The power and potential of performance ethnography resides in the empathic and embodied engagement of other ways of knowing that heightens the possibility of acting upon the humanistic impulse to transform the world.

In discussing performance ethnography in the second edition of the *Handbook of Qualitative Research*, Michal M. McCall (2000) did a fine job of focusing attention on the foundational issues of performance ethnography—like tracing a conceptual history of performance through Futurism, Dadaism, Surrealism, and varying experimental forms. She then provided concrete examples of performance ethnography with tips on casting, directing, and staging drawn from a variety of scholar-practitioners (Becker, McCall, & Morris, 1989; Conquergood, 1985, 1988; Denzin, 1997; McCall, 1993; Mienczakowski, 2001; Paget, 1990; Pollock, 1990; Richardson, 1997; Siegel & Conquergood, 1985, 1990; Smith, 1993, 1994). In many ways, this chapter should be used as a companion to McCall's efforts in extending the scope of performance ethnography.

This chapter outlines and details the philosophical contingencies, procedural pragmatics, pedagogical possibilities, and political potentialities of *performance ethnography*. The chapter necessarily pushes and expands the borders and ways of thinking about performance ethnography, yet the basic approach of *field research, data collection, script formulation, and performance* should not be overshadowed by other concerns. The value of performing ethnographic materials from the field may be for pedagogical or representational purposes (Van Maanen, 1995), which might bring additional value that circulates around critical and cultural research, political activism, and social change. In these ways, the chapter serves as a guide to those who seek to understand how performance ethnography is an embodied epistemology and how performance ethnography can become a way of engaging a critical cultural discourse.

▣ I. PRACTICAL MATTERS AND PHILOSOPHICAL CONTINGENCIES

In a literal sense of the aphorism "walking a mile in someone else's shoes," performance ethnography most often entails an embodied experience of the cultural practices of the other. This practice has the intent of allowing the participants in and audience of the performance the opportunity to *come to know culture differently*. In the first portion of this section, I offer a practical pedagogical assignment in performance ethnography. In the subsequent subsections, I use that example as a way of teasing out what I consider to be some of the disciplinary, philosophical, theoretical, and methodological promises and pitfalls of engaging performance ethnography.

A. Performing Ethnography/Performing Street Vendors

In response to a classroom assignment in a 300-level performance studies class, a student group consisting of three men and two women focus on migrant streetside vendors. In the Los Angeles area, there is a large number of mostly immigrant Mexican street vendors, male and female, who stand on the entrances and exits of major interstates and highways selling everything from bagged oranges, cherries, and peanuts to flowers, handmade cultural artifacts, and clothing. The students in this group conduct ethnographic interviews and engage in practical assistance under the guise of participant-observation to get a sense of what that experience is like and a better sense of those who engage these practices.

In their performance, the students each carry a commodity that they sell to the audience. They walk in a choreographed circle around the room hawking their items in a syncopated rhythm that mirrors the persistence of the street vendors, some of whom closely approach vehicles in traffic like the seated students in class, trying to initiate a purchase. At varying points, the circulating caravan stops and a particular student in the character of the vendor takes center stage and shares a personal narrative. The narratives—actual, compiled, and constructed[1]—drawn from the interviews reveal the conditions under which the street vendors labor. They labor under the heat of the day. They encounter police officers who chase them away from certain areas and rude drivers who throw things at them, spit on them, or lure them with the chance of purchase and then speed away. They endure suppliers who overcharge them for their goods or swindle them knowing that most of them are *illegal aliens* and will not press police charges. And they experience the occasional kindness from motorists.

The narratives are delivered through impassioned voices, in Spanish and with Spanish accents, then translated by another vendor (student performer). The narratives reveal the multiple reasons for which the vendors come to this circumstance: Some work to send money back to their families in Mexico or to support their families here in the United States. Some are trapped in a type of slave labor with the coyotes (smugglers of human chattel from Mexico) who helped them cross the border. Others labor because they have no other marketable skills. Through the performance and written reflective essays, the students articulate and claim a new understanding of the lives of *particular others*. The efforts of street vendors are not seen as what is casually assumed or asserted to be their culture, but acts of survival and sustenance grounded in their current predicament and their relation to space, place, and time.

The student performance is a dialogic engagement in which they extend the voices of *the other* into the specialized place of public access, the classroom. The performance serves as product and process, a performative representation of their knowing, a starting point of their understanding, and a method of engaging others in the issues that undergird cultural experience. In this particular example, performance ethnography helps in establishing a critical site, an instance in which embodied experience meets social and theoretical knowing to establish a critical dialogue between researcher-performers and observers (Garoian, 1999, p. 67). It is the specificity of the project, the particularity of the culture represented, and the context of the performance in the classroom that affords the opportunity for close scrutiny.

B. Performance Studies, Performance, and Performativity

Performance studies as a disciplinary formation often defies definition—in the way in which definitions codify and categorize, as well as capture and contain, that which they seek to describe—thereby limiting its reach and scope. Borrowing generously from communication studies, sociology, cultural studies, ethnography, anthropology, and theater, among other areas, performance studies explores and considers a wide range of *human activity as expression*. Richard Schechner (1988) states, "The subjects of performance studies are both what is performance and the performative—and the myriad contact points and overlaps, tensions and loose spots, separating and connecting these categories" (p. 362). In other words, performance pivots on the enacted nature of human activity, the socialized and shifting norms of human sociality, and the active processes of human sense-making.

In the preceding example of the street vendors, performance is engaged as an interpretive event of cultural practice. Performance involves scripts of social discourse constructed with intention and performed by actors in the company of particular audiences. The related concept of *performativity* references the stylized repetition of communicative acts, linguistic and corporeal, that are socially validated and discursively established in the moment of the performance (Butler, 1990a, 1990b, 1993). Through the example, students use these related terms in the range of performance studies to explore the fundamental notion of human behavior as performative—as socially constructed, enacted, emergent, repeatable, and subversive.

Performativity becomes the social and cultural dynamic that extends and exposes the import of repetitive human activity. The students use these constructs to acknowledge and engage the study of human nature as both an issue of *being* and *doing*, to explore social structure and human agency as mutually constituted, and that the recursive nature of cultural play can produce unintended and intended consequences. This allows us to see social action as moments of broader power relations that can be illuminated, interrogated, and intervened, if not transformed (Bhabha, 1994; Diamond, 1996; Langellier, 1999).

One version of performance studies sees its shift or evolution from the study of literary texts through oral interpretation[2] to a broader construction of text as the scope of cultural practice and articulated human expression. This then moves from an exclusive focus on *text to context*[3]—such as analyses of religious rituals, wedding ceremonies, sporting events, and particular cultural practices such as those of the street vendors in the student example. This approach valorizes diverse epistemological paradigms in which the role of artist-actor is expanded to include all social beings *as performers.* The focus of study shifts from an exclusive emphasis on canonical texts to cultural practices in everyday life, especially a focus on historically marginalized groups.

These variations ground performance studies' privileging of three concerns. First is an appreciation for the aesthetic/creative nature of human expression across borders of text, context, and embodied practice.[4] Second is a focus on the body as a site of knowing and showing,[5] hence what Conquergood (1998) distinguishes as "struggles to recuperate the *saying* from the *said*, to put mobility, action, and agency back into play" (p. 31). Third is an interest in ethnography as a critical method of observing and studying the performative nature of cultural practice.

This signals what some have coined as *the cultural turn* in performance studies (Chaney, 1994; Conquergood, 1998; Pollock, 1998d; Strine, 1998), or what Victor Turner (1982) refers to as *the performative and reflexive turn in anthropology.* In such cases, there is an intense focus on the ways in which culture is performance practice, sedimented as norms of sociability. Thus in both the cultural turn in performance studies and the performative and reflexive turn in anthropology, there is a move to *put culture back into motion* (Rosaldo, 1989, p. 91). By performing empirical materials derived through ethnographic practice researchers as performers, and the audiences of such performative research are afforded a more intimate understanding of culture.

In this way, performance becomes not only embodied practice but also explanatory metaphor for human engagement, and performativity becomes the everyday practice of *redoing* what is *done* (Pollock, 1998b). The actual sense of the other is derived through embodied experience of the other's cultural practice. In this way, as Peggy Phelan (1998) states, "Performance and performativity are braided together by virtue of iteration; the copy renders performance authentic and allows the spectator to find in the performer 'presence.' Presence can be had only through the citation of authenticity, through reference to something (we have heard) called 'live'" or have seen called life (p. 10). Hence, in performance ethnography the textual subject becomes the empirical subject, allowing performers and audiences to be brought closer to aspects of cultural being that operate at the real and everyday level of experience (Denzin, 1997, pp. 60–61).

In other words, what happens when ethnography becomes performative, when ethnography becomes performance? What happens to the ethnographic? It reinstates the actualization of everyday cultural performance. It rehydrates the objectified, text-bound description of lives-lived into living embodied forms that offer a greater sense of direct experience and the direct knowing of culture. It reinstates ethnographic bodies to the realm of process, of activity, of doing—negotiating beings, both in the simulated presence of their daily lives as well as within the specified moment of performance.

Using performance as an "explanatory metaphor" involves reconstructing the notion of performance from *theatrical entertainment* to performance as a *method of explaining, exemplifying, projecting, knowing, and sharing meaning.* It involves, as in the example with the students in the street vendor performance, ways of using performance as a means, method, and mode of communication establishing an inter-cultural dialogue. The comparative relationship between the object of reflection and the performative act moves toward an embodied and engaged understanding. Conquergood (1998) tracks *this semantic genealogy* "from performance as *mimesis* to *poiesis* to *kinesis*, performance as imitation, construction, and dynamism" (p. 31).[6]

Performance methodology can be described as a collectivized ensemble of pre-cepts used by those committed to the communicative and pedagogical potential that knowledge—the process of attaining, sharing, and projecting knowing—can be accomplished through doing. What Pineau (1995) refers to as "a deep kinesthetic attunement that allows us to attend to experiential phenomena in an embodied, rather than purely intellectualized way" (p. 46). Hence students and audiences *come to know through doing*, whether this is performing ethnographic notes or performing theory as a means of practical experience in testing hypotheses or displaying knowledge.

The broad-based construction of performance methodology opens up the possibility of engaging performance in strategic ways: *performance as a method of inquiry* or *per-formance as a way of knowing* (Geiger, 1973; Hopkins, 1981; O'Brien, 1987; Wolcott, 1999), *performance as a method of reporting knowledge and ideological critique* (Jackson, 1993, 1998; Nudd, 1995; Park-Fuller & Olsen, 1983; Pineau, 1995; Taylor, 1987), *perfor-mance as a method of critical response* (Alexander, 1999; Conquergood, 1986a, 1986b; Harrison-Pepper, 1999), *performance as an act of publication* (Espinola, 1977), and *per-formance as an interpretive tool* (Jackson, 2000; Merrill, 1999; Pollock, 1998a; Roach, 1993; Román, 1998; Wolf, 2002). In each case, performers use the processes of research, analysis, and synthesis leading toward message rehearsal (intent, content, and form) to culminate in an enactment of thought and knowing. Hence, the process of coming to know and the act of projecting the known are intricately interwoven.

C. Cultural Performance and the Performance of Culture

Another version of performance studies sees its particular origins in the collabora-tive discourses between Richard Schechner (1965, 1977, 1985) and Victor Turner (1982, 1988) in which theater and anthropology inform each other to explore the innate the-atricality of cultural expression and intercultural exploration.[7] My interests in what has been constructed as *cultural performance* have been influenced by them and scholars such as Chesebro (1988), Clifford (1998), Conquergood (1983, 1985, 1986a, 1986b, 1988), E. C. Fine and Speer (1992), Fuoss (1997), Guss (2000), Kirshenblatt-Gimbett (1998), MaCaloon (1984), and Singer (1972), to name a few. It is undergirded with the kernel understanding that *cultural performance* refers to the collective expectations and practices of members of particular communities.

Cultural performance is the method in which we all define community, maintain community membership, negotiate identity, and sometimes subvert the rules of social membership and practice. Hence, echoing Turner (1974), Conquergood (1986a) notes that as human beings we are *homo performans*, in that we socially construct the very world that undergirds our enactments. It is how some have approached the notion of performance as *the presentation of self in everyday life* (Goffman, 1959), *the practice of everyday life* (Certeau, 1984), the critical self-reflexivity of engaging *restored behavior or twice-behaved behavior* (Schechner, 1988), and the tensive enactment of *social dramas* (Turner, 1974, 1980).[8] It is the everydayness of performance in culture that becomes the focus of observation in ethnographic research and thus becomes the source model of reperforming culture in performance ethnography that is the primary focus of this discussion.

Signaling an important element of performance ethnography, Clifford (1988) reminds us that we can better understand cultural identity not by studying the artifacts of museums or libraries, but through observing emergent cultural performances. These emergent cultural performances signify the social and cultural constructs that already are in place and those that are being challenged, subverted, or appropriated. The street vendor project exemplifies the way that performance ethnography mirrors social, cultural, and political practices to publicize the politics in the existence of those social occurrences.

In making the link between cultural performance and performance ethnography, I make the reciprocal yet interrelated distinction between *cultural performance* in everyday life and *the performance of culture* in which there is a documentation and re-creation of cultural forms found through research (Alexander, 2002b). The students in the street vendor performance studied culture and then sought to re-create their understanding in/through performance. This was primarily to better know and understand the culture, but for some it might be a process of rehearsal in becoming a cultural member; a form of practiced *enculturation* as it were, leading toward competency and cultural membership (Samovar & Porter, 1994).

The performance of culture that is presented in performance ethnography is a reflection of an actual culture refracted through the lens of ethnographic practices and situated in performing bodies that (re)present that culture. The intentions of the actualized versus the performed version of culture (by others) are different, yet they may inform each other by sensitizing performers and audiences to alternative cultural systems (Chesebro, 1998, p. 317).

Performance ethnography always simulates the fishbowl conditions under which cultures operate in everyday life. Culture operates both within the confines of its own constructions (power, social relations, time, history, and space) and under the forces of externalized pressure that affect the conditions of its operation. *Performance ethnography as a moral discourse* foregrounds this very delicate balance. The presumed subject of scrutiny in performance ethnography is not exclusive to the particular culture being performed but also applies to the process of engaging cultural performance. Conquergood (1986a) writes:

Performance requires a special doubling of consciousness, reflexive self-awareness. The performer plays neither the role of Self or Other; instead of an I or a You, the performer is essentially, at all times, playing a We. . . . Performance can reconcile the tension between Identity, which banalizes, and Difference, which estranges, the Other. (p. 34)

In this way, performance ethnography becomes a form of *standpoint epistemology*, a situated moment of knowing that positions performers and audiences in the interstices of knowing themselves through and as the other (Denzin, 1997). The moment of performance is both practical place and liminal space, a standpoint from which to view culture.

At this point in offering an overview of practical matters and philosophical contingencies, it is necessary to state that performance ethnography cannot and maybe should not be easily reduced to being (just a) method. Although I know that I am pushing the borders of what some might refer to as *traditional performance ethnography*, I am also asking the question of "Why do we do performance ethnography?" In the rendering of and response to the question, I suggest that most people see performance ethnography as moral discourse. Thus, this chapter asks readers to extend their familiar methodological construction of performance ethnography into a larger view of its promise and possibilities.

Beyond the *practical pedagogical* or the *pleasure of the performative, performance ethnography is moral discourse* in the tradition of all qualitative research. It is situated activity that locates the participants, researchers, and observers in the world—a world in which the implications and complications of being and knowing others can be negotiated in mutually beneficial ways. It consists of a set of interpretive material practices that make culture visible; hence making manifest not only the cultural conditions of living, but also the joint concerns of humanism that can be equally distributed. These practices work to illuminate the world as much as they work to transform the world (Denzin & Lincoln, 1998).

Following a *feminist communitarian model*, performance ethnography "interlocks personal autonomy with communal well-being." It encourages the "morally appropriate action [that] intends community" (Christians, 2000, pp. 144–145). Through performance ethnography, performer-researcher-scholars ask audiences (both objectified onlookers and performers as audience to their own engagement) to position themselves in relation to those being represented in performance. These performances are always *enmeshed in moral matters*; they use performance to illuminate the dynamics of culture that are always and already in practice with and across borders of perceived difference (Conquergood, 1985). They contain a moment of judgment of others and of the self in relation to others, a judgment that affects choice not only in the moment of performance but also in those moments after performance in which the sensuousness of performative experience resonates in the body and mind, seeking its own engagement of meaningful expression.

D. Links and Challenges Between Ethnography and Performance

The selection and manner of presenting particular cultural insights in performance ethnography reveal not only an assumed actuality of the other but also a particular critique and understanding of the other. This *is* and in most cases *is not equal to* the actual experiences of the other. This element of *critique and commentary* that is a cornerstone of performance methodology becomes the cautionary tale and the ethical linchpin in the process of performance ethnography. The staged performance of culture is also an appraisal of culture. It foregrounds aspects of human experience for particular reasons, with particular desired effects—either in the form of direct critique or through the more artistic tropes of parody, metaphor, and analogy.

This begins to reveal the problems and the possibilities of performing the other, for selves always intervene experience and foreground orientation, desire, and intent. For example, when performing the lives and narratives of the street vendors, my students (as researchers and performers) had to reconcile their thoughts and feelings about the street vendors. They had to negotiate the balance between their everyday experiences with street vendors and their social commentary on street vendors, with and against their embodied positionality in performing street vendors. They had to ask the question:

> How as researchers and performers in our reciprocal relationships do we negotiate and help to inform and/or transform the politics of class, notions of work ethic, cultural bias, and issues of pride and propriety? This in relation to what we have come to know about the predicament and conditions of these street vendors through the joint effort of performance and ethnography?

In this sense, all those engaged in performance ethnography must always clearly define themselves in relation to the populations being performed, their intentions in performing, the desired effects of their performance, and the methods engaged in gathering and reporting knowledge. Although this works in tension with what might be constructed as "traditional performance ethnography" used as pedagogical practice or public entertainment, these questions and concerns are necessary relational and political issues about representation that only enhance the pedagogical potency of such endeavors.

Ethical guides for performance ethnography are clearly established within the contributing disciplines of both performance and ethnography (Alcoff, 1991/1992; Bateson, 1993; Chambers, 2000; Christians, 2000; Clifford & Marcus, 1986; M. Fine, Weis, Weseen, & Wong, 2000; Lockford, 1998; Rosaldo, 1989; Sparkes, 2002; B. Tedlock, 2000; D. Tedlock, 1983; Valentine, 1998; Valentine & Valentine, 1992). Here I want to foreground three articulations of *ethical relations in performance/ethnography*. My intention here is to offer a particular perspective on the relationship between ethnographer and cultural community—the relational, representational, and variables of translation in any social text—as well as the binary oppositions involved in the dynamics of being audience to the performance of actual lives.

First, in "Performing as a Moral Act: Ethical Dimensions of the Ethnography of Performance," Dwight Conquergood (1985) charts "four ethical pitfalls, performative stances towards the other that are morally problematic" (p. 4). *The Custodian's Rip-off* is likened to a theft or rape, a search and seizure on the part of the ethnographer, who approaches and appropriates culture without a sense of care. *The Enthusiast's Infatuation* jumps to conclusions, making facile assumptions of performative practice in an attempt to quickly assume identification with the other. *The Skeptic's Cop-out* embodies the sterilized and historically objectified approaches to ethnography in which the ethnographer stands outside or above culture, avoiding personal involvement or encounter with the other—but is readily prepared to cast judgment on cultural practice and identity. *The Curator's Exhibitionism* overly identifies with the other, to the point of exoticizing and romanticizing the other as the noble savage and thereby further dichotomizing the difference between self and other.

Conquergood constructs a fifth stance, *the dialogical stance.* "Dialogical performance is a way of having intimate conversation with other people and cultures. Instead of speaking about them, one speaks to and with them" (1985, p. 10). The dialogical stance negotiates the borders between identity, difference, detachment, and commitment not only to represent the other but also to re-present the other as a means of continuing a dialogue that seeks understanding. "It is a kind of performance that resists conclusions, it is intensely committed to keeping the dialogue between performer and text [performer and cultural members] open and ongoing" (p. 9).

In discussing the nature of ethnography and its links to performance, I have often turned to Van Maanen's (1988) construction, which states: "Ethnographies are documents that pose questions at the margins between two cultures. They necessarily decode one culture while re-coding it for another" (p. 4).[9] Within this statement, I see and understand the interpretive nature of ethnography to the lived practices of others—through a detailed description of culture, knowing, of course, that such a description is always and already inflicted with and processed through the particular experience of the ethnographer—the one who reports. It is also shaped and influenced by the sociological, perceptual, and political issues of the audience—those to whom such findings are reported, with a particular concern regarding *why* the report is being made. One asks *how* subjects and their actions are concretized and isolated from the historicity of experience for the scrutiny of others (see Denzin, 1997, pp. 247–248, and his citing of Fiske, 1994), as well as *what* happens in those moments of translation, those moments of an assumed accuracy in decoding culture and the recoding of such understandings across borders of experience. These are also the challenges of performance, what Judith Hamera (2000) describes as "a very specific technology of translation, a look rebounding between two differently framed [experiences] into language" (p. 147).

Second, Norman Denzin (1997) outlines four paired terms that might be used to examine any social text. I present them here as a way to foreground the relational, the representational, and challenges of translation that are faced in both ethnography and performance—with the specific emphasis on the combined effort/event of performance ethnography. Denzin outlines the four as follows: "(a) the real and its representations in the text [performance], (b) the text and the author [performer], (c) lived experience and its textual [and embodied] representations, and (d) the subject and his or her intentional meanings" (p. 4). I extend the use of the following logics to both the specificity of his emphasis, *interpretive ethnography*, and the more exacting process of performance ethnography.

In the case of performance ethnography, there is a double assumption of the ability to capture and contain culture through language and then to assume and embody culture through the materiality of different bodies; bodies that may have different or even opposing historicity, bodies that are framed and conjoined with bones, muscles, and sinews that have not been sufficiently exercised or exorcised into being over time. Maybe this is the *representational crisis* or a *representational challenge* in performance ethnography, one that is not easily solved, but it can be understood if the conjoined effort of performance/ethnography can be seen as a dialogical engagement. In such an engagement, performance ethnography is not only an act of presenting research findings and representing the other but also a means of extending and expanding on a critical dialogue in and about culture, with researcher-performers embodying the nature of their knowledge and inviting audiences to participate.

In this way, performance ethnography is linked appropriately with the traditions of *interpretive ethnography*—the staging of reflexive ethnographic performances that turn ethnographic and theoretical texts back onto each other, a form of both scholarly production and textual critique committed to the critical social processes of meaning-making and illuminating cultural experience. This is done through descriptive language and embodied engagement, as well as engaging the performance of critical accountability for/of the very processes of its production (Bochner & Ellis, 2002; Denzin, 1997, 1999; Ellis & Bochner, 1996, 2000; McCall, 2000).

Performance and ethnography are both concerned with lessening gaps between the known and the unknown, illuminating and exploring the lived practices of others, and bridging geographical and social distances through vivid description, narration, and embodiment—helping readers/audiences to see possibilities through the visualization of experience. Maybe through theatricalizing experience, the challenge of performance ethnography is to represent culture without claiming culture, to *interrogate and decenter culture—without discarding* culture (Conquergood, 1998). Maybe the challenge is to project the knowing of culture, without dominating the experience of the other, thus creating a "recognizable verisimilitude of setting, character and dialogue" that foregrounds culture and not self (Cohen, 1988, p. 815), while providing the necessary critical processes to tease *out/at* those elements that conjoin and separate the two, for both research/writer/performer and audience.

This would also require that the staging of such a performance must dematerialize the fourth wall of theatrical production that often encourages objectified viewing, creating a more *dialectical theater* (Brecht, 1964; Kershaw, 1999), a *theater of performance* that, while framing the aesthetic event as part entertainment, also reframes *the experience of performance ethnography from entertainment to social and intercultural dialogue.* This dialogue exists between performers and cultural informants, and between the performative experience of the audience in the moment of the doing and how that is extended in the everydayness of their being.

Third, Linda Park-Fuller (2003) offers five problematic aspects of *audiencing*—as the engaged practice of participatory viewing. It is a positionality that further implicates the viewer in performance ethnography and, in her specific case, Playback Theatre. Park-Fuller describes Playback Theatre as "an audience-interactive, improvisational form in which audience members tell stories from their lives and then watch those stories enacted on the spot" (p. 291). Playback Theater is further theorized by Fox (1986), Fox and Heinreich (1999), and Salas (1996). It is grounded in logics of community-based theater (Haedicke & Nellhaus, 2001) and the liberatory, democratic, interactive theater practices of Boal (1979, 1995, 1998) and Wirth (1994). It is further explained through the role of witnessing in performance ethnography (Doyle, 2001). In large, these methods engage performance as reflexive praxis, *praxis* as the relationship between theoretical understandings, a critique of society, and action toward social reform (Freire, 1985). Hence, the five problematic aspects of audiencing that Park-Fuller outlines are the relational dynamics between *empathizing/criticizing, empowering/disempowering, supporting/shaping, resisting/ tweaking,* and *the ritual dance of power,* all of which implicate the representational politics of performing others in light of our own *dense particularity,* which is always dichotomous and fluid (Mohanty, 1989).

Risking a conflation of her significant contributions, I see her primary argument grounded in Wallace Bacon's (1979) use of the term "tensiveness." Park-Fuller seemingly extends his logics from the specific exploration of literary texts, to a broader context of social and cultural performance. Tensiveness refers to those competing impulses that give any performative situation dynamism, a push and pull—but not a tension as in friction or strife, but the actions of those elements and attributes of social relations that either maintain social systems or seek to transform them.

So what appear to be binary opposites in Park-Fuller's construction are really dynamic dyads, necessarily co-present variables, and procedural mandates specifically in Playback Theatre that I apply in general to performance ethnography. In her words, they encourage responsibility: "[A] responsibility to listen to, to respect, and to learn from one another's stories, but also to 'talk back,' to intervene, to unmask the latent stances in stories that can divide the human community, and to redress, through its various rituals, the wrongs suffered in silence as well as in speech or action" (p. 303). In this way, performance ethnography encourages a dialogue and action that extends outside the specified site of performance and into the everyday realm of human social interaction.

▣ II. PROCEDURAL PRAGMATICS AND GENRES OF PERFORMANCE ETHNOGRAPHY

Conquergood (1988) writes that performance always "takes as both its subject matter and method the experiencing body situated in time, place, and history" (p. 187). Hence, the procedural pragmatics and genres of performance ethnography that I outline here are centered in the performing body, yet it is how bodies are situated in performance, the body being performed (self/other) and the source model of information gathered (researcher/performer) in performance ethnography that shifts. According to Soyini Madison (1998), "Performance becomes the vehicle by which we travel to the worlds of Subjects and enter domains of intersubjectivity that problematize how we categorize who is 'us' and who is 'them,' and how we see ourselves with 'other' and different eyes" (p. 282). Hence, performance is a way of coming to know self and other, and self as other.

Within this section, I suggest that the bodies and lived experiences being represented in performance ethnography shift between "the other" and back to "the self," with particular interests in denoting and connoting the ties that bind. I fall short of establishing a specific typology that separates and delineates individual approaches to doing performance ethnography, knowing that the borders of performance ethnography bleed and that the impulse is in staging articulated lived experience, cultural practice, and knowledge of culture.

A. Performing Others in Performance Ethnography

Victor Turner and Edie Turner (1982, 1988), who were mostly interested in teaching culture, provided their students with descriptive "strips of behavior" to develop into "playscripts," thereby performing "ethnography in a kind of instructional theater" (Turner, 1982, p. 41). It was their attempt to have students come to understand the intricacies of embodied cultural practice. The full process of such a pedagogical engagement culminates not only in the experiencing body but also later in the critical reflection on what students come to know through assuming the particular cultural practices that have been mostly outside the range of their everyday experiences. This form of performance ethnography was mostly *student-in-class centered*.

This point of origin provides the theoretical and methodological foundation for the type of work being done in performance studies, beginning with a specific example in the work of Joni Jones. In documenting her own work with performance ethnography, based on her research in Nigeria on the Yoruba deity Osun, Jones (2002) offers an *audience-centered brand of performance ethnography* designed to invite audience members to participate within the performance of a particular cultural formation. Her production of *Searching for Osun* was an installation piece that focused on "aspects of Yoruba life that moved [her] most—dance music, divination, Osun's relationship to children, 'women's work,' and food preparation" (p. 1). The cast of performers assumed archetypal characters in Yoruba life, engaging in particular cultural and relational practices. The invited audience to the performance entered the performance space not as distanced onlookers but as participants.

The audience was invited to engage varying dimensions that shape cultural life—food/eating and dining rituals, movement/music and dance, clothing/the wearing of traditional garb, and listening to storytelling and oral lore. Within her method, as in the work of Boal (1979), Jones created opportunities for audiences to make the move from being spectators to being "spect-actors," active participants who were involved in knowing and shaping their own experience. Hence, the process of coming to know is not only relegated to seeing, but also extended and enriched by fully participating in the experience.

Approaches to performance ethnography also engage *group–field study work.* Such approaches culminate in the public performances of research notes and interviews by those who conducted the research and may involve members of the cultural communities explored (see McCall, 1993; Pollock, 1990). It can be *the result of a single researcher's long-term research* that works at excavating specific political and cultural events. Such examples might operate on a *localized level,* such as restaging the politics leading to a cafeteria workers' strike at the University of North Carolina, Chapel Hill (Madison, 1998), or *an intercultural and interracial level of conflict,* such as in the staged and performance work of Anna Deavere Smith—*Fires in the Mirror: Crown Heights, Brooklyn, and Other Identities* (1993) and *Twilight: Los Angeles, 1992* (1994).

This is historical and culturally based work in which artists use performance to foreground and make commentary on culture. They offer performed elements of historical truisms as a method of illuminating aspects of oppression and the politics of social relations based in race, ethnicity, sex, gender, and class.[10] In describing her project dealing with the cafeteria strike, Madison (1998) writes that "the performance strives to communicate a sense of the Subjects' world in their own words; its hopes to amplify their meanings and intentions to a larger group of listeners and observers" (p. 280). In this way, we also come to understand Deavere Smith's work in searching for the American character in *Fires in the Mirror.*

In her project, Deavere Smith interviewed, and later performed, 19 original portraits of African Americans and Jews (politicians, housewives, activists, authors, parents, etc.) after the racial unrest and rioting in Crown Heights, Brooklyn in 1991. The unrest was sparked by what is considered an accident. (A Hasidic man driving a station wagon swerved on a corner and killed a young African American boy. This was followed by the act of retribution 4 days later in which a young Jewish man was stabbed by a group of young African American men.) Through the buttressing of performed ethnographic interviews and character sketches, Deavere Smith illuminates the seeds and logics of racial contestation that were germinating long before the incident that sparked the fires of riot. Thus, the project provides the audience with a searing portrait of race relations in America that operates on the level of performed visceral response.[11]

In this sense, performance ethnography can also operate on a *globalized level* in which a specific issue of the human condition that crosses national borders is exemplified, such as in Soyini Madison's intentions to stage *Trokosi*, the Ghanaian practice of ostracizing girls who have been sexually abused. The intention of such work would be to present the result of the individual scholar's research in Ghana and her critique of the practices. Staged in Ghana amid the Ghanaian debates over the practices, the performance would serve a critical reflexive praxis, a refractive mirror and argument concerning social practice and cultural investment (Jones, 2002).

This approach to performance ethnography reflects that tradition in which empirical materials are presented in the form of scripts, poems, short stories, and dramas that are staged and presented to diverse audiences. (See Bauman, 1986; Becker et al., 1989; Bochner, 1994; Bruner, 1986; Conquergood, 1985, 1986b, 1989, 1991, 1992; Kapferer, 1986; McCall & Becker, 1990; Mienczakowski, 1992, 1994, 1995; Mienczakowski & Morgan, 1993; Paget, 1990, 1993; Richardson & Lockridge, 1991; Schechner, 1986; Stern & Henderson, 1993.)[12] These approaches work toward the redramatization of cultural life, by rehydrating the lived experiences of others described in ethnographic work, restoring aspects of the dramatic, dynamic, and aesthetic qualities of cultural practice in the moment of presenting research.

B. Performance of (Auto)Ethnography

The intention of performance ethnography could be signaled in the desire to build a *template of sociality* (Hamera, 1999). This construct signals not a projected standard of living but an association of experience gained through performance. It allows audiences to see others in relation to themselves; to come to know, to contemplate on how they came to know, to signal ways of being, and to see possibilities for their social relational orientations and obligations to others. Performance ethnography as template of sociality becomes a *generative (auto)ethnographic* experience that sparks and provides a template on which audiences begin their own processes of critical reflection (Alexander, 2000).

In this sense, although performance ethnography is traditionally thought of in terms of the performance of the cultural other and grounded in *externalized ethnographic practices*, it can also reflect a process of *internalized ethnographic practice* in which a performer uses lived experience and personal history as cultural site, such as in autoethnography (Ellis & Bochner, 2000; Lionnet, 1989; Reed-Danahay, 1997; Spry, 1997, 2001). Such a journey into the self is no less treacherous than crossing the borders and boundaries inhabited by the exotic other. Nor are the potential insights gathered less meaningful in coming to understand the politics of cultural identity in the circulation of social relations. In particular, autoethnography is a method that attempts "quite literally, [to] come to terms with sustaining questions of self and culture" (Neumann, 1996, p. 193). It is a method of navigating the "busy intersections" of race, sex, sexuality, class, and gender that is often constructed as the unitary location of cultural identity sedimented in social practice (Rosaldo, 1989, p. 17).

Using this as an alternative approach, performance ethnography thus can include what has been referred to as *autoperformance*, singularly conceived performances such as autobiography, autoethnography, and performance art (Kirby, 1979). All of these, to varying degrees, have as their concerted effort *a critique of self and society, self in society, and self as resistant and transformative force of society*. Despite the suggested critiques of *solo performance* as a narcissistic act of self-indulgence and narcissism (Gentile, 1989), Françoise Lionnet (1989) sees autoethnography in particular as a form of cultural performance. She states that autoethnography "transcends pedestrian notions of referentiality, for the staging of the event is part of the process of 'passing on,' of elaborating cultural forms, which are not static and inviolable but dynamically involved in the creation of culture itself" (p. 102).

Autoethnography thus engages ethnographical analysis of personally lived experience. The evidenced act of showing in autoethnography is less about reflecting on the self in a public space than about using the public space and performance as an act of critically reflecting culture, an act of *seeing the self see the self through and as the other*. Thus, as a form of performance ethnography, it is designed to engage a locus of embodied reflexivity using lived experience as a specific cultural site that offers social commentary and cultural critique (Alexander, 2002b).

Ellis and Bochner (2000) identify five different exemplars for autoethnography that blend and bleed the borders of individualized cultural identity, intentionality, and its orientation to audience. Briefly stated, in *reflexive ethnographies* researchers critically reflect on lived experience in *a* particular cultural community (which may not be their own), specifying their exact relation to self and a particular society. *Native ethnographies* foreground the experiences of researchers, who reflect on their membership in a historically marginalized or exoticized culture. *Complete-member-researchers/ ethnographies* are those in which a member of a particular culture interprets and reports on the culture for outsiders. *Literary autoethnographies* feature writer/ researchers describing and interpreting their culture for audiences that are not familiar with the writer/researcher's culture. *Personal narratives* as critical autobiographical stories of lived experience offer (public) audiences access to personal experience with the intent of politicizing aspects of human experience and social sense-making.

Kristin Langellier (1989) writes that like most narratives, the personal narrative "does something in the social world . . . [it] participate[s] in the ongoing rhythm of people's lives as a reflection of their social organization and cultural values" (p. 261). In this way, the personal narrative as an exemplar and contributing model of self-storying is a reflection of an individual's critical excavation of lived experience and the categorizing of cultural meaning. This is then shared within a public domain to provide the audience with a meaningful articulation of human experience. The benefit, as Langellier (1998) later writes, resides in the consequences and conditions of the telling, the audience that orients to the story and processes the transgressive and recuperative powers of the performative moment. In writing this, I am not collapsing personal narrative into ethnography, nor bleeding the borders between personal narrative and autoethnography—as much as I foreground the links of exploring lived and living experience (self and other) that is germane to all.

I think that at the core of performance ethnography is the desire not only for an audience to see the performance of culture, but, as Ellis and Bochner (1996) suggest, to engage on some level in a "self-conscious reflexivity" on their own relation to the experience (p. 28). I want to claim and categorize this quality and process in the manner in which Victor Turner (1988) defines "performative reflexivity," as "a condition in which a socio-cultural group, or its most perceptive members acting representatively turn, bend or reflect back upon themselves" (p. 24). Turner's thought on reflexivity is culture and context specific. The inherent reflexive turn of performative experience is precisely its power to transmit as well as to critique culture and self.

In his essay "The Personal: Against the Master Narrative," Fred Corey (1998) outlines what I believe to be a key argument for personal narrative as performance ethnography, specifically in his links between the personal and the cultural. He writes: "The master narrative is an artillery of moral truth, and the personal narrative defixes the truth. The master narrative is a cultural discourse, replete with epistemic implications, and the personal narrative is a mode of 'reverse discourse'" (p. 250).[13] Using Foucault's (1982) construct of *reverse discourse* or *counter discourse*, Corey gives territorial distinction to the personal narrative as moral discourse.

Whereas the master narrative often dictates and speculates on collective identities, the personal narrative "tell[s] about personal, lived experience in a way that assists in the construction of identity, reinforces or challenges private and public belief systems and values, and either resists or reinforces the dominate cultural practices of the community in which the narrative event occurs"[14] (Corey, 1998, p. 250). Although there are multiple constructions of the master narrative, I want to suggest, along with Corey, that the master narrative is the dominant, hegemonic, way of seeing or thinking the world is *or* should be, the narrative that often guides and undergirds social, cultural, and political mandates.

The personal narrative always stands in relation to the master narrative, which is the reflection of culture and our relation to/in culture. Hence, the personal narrative is always a reflection on and excavation of the cultural contexts that give rise to experience. In this sense, personal narratives move from what some might presume to be an insular engagement of personal reflection, to a complex process that implicates the performative nature of cultural identity. Like autoethnography as theorized by Ellis and Bochner (2000), personal narrative places the individual in a dialogue with "history, social structure, and culture, which themselves are dialectically revealed through action, feeling, thought, and language" (p. 739).

▣ III. Links Between Critical Pedagogy
and Critical Performative Pedagogy

Drawing from principles in performance studies and ethnography, the preceding sections have laid the foundational logics for performance ethnography as a social force, a strategic embodied methodology, and a moral discourse. This section further grounds performance ethnography as a critical pedagogical practice designed to democratize the classroom. The section also furthers how these logics expand our understanding of the unifying links between performance, pedagogy, culture, and social reform.

By including these logics, I clearly understand that *while performance ethnography may strive to function as a critical pedagogical strategy, not all performance ethnography would participate within the logic of critical pedagogy.* In this case, I am interested in the theorizing of educational practice "that turns the ethnographic into the performative and the performative into the political" (Denzin, 2003, p. xiii). By drawing on the kernel logic of Turner and Turner (1988), I want to necessarily expand the pedagogical use of performance ethnography from mere *class activity* to an insurgent method of engaging, critiquing, and commenting on culture that is an ongoing activity in educational practice.

A. Critical Pedagogy

In Peter McLaren's extensive body of work, listed here in brief (Giroux & McLaren, 1984, 1994; McLaren, 1985, 1989, 1993, 1994, 1997, 1998, 2000; McLaren & Lankshear, 1994), he, perhaps more than any other educator-scholar, has laid the groundwork for a critical pedagogy. Theorists in critical pedagogy argue that schools are grounded in processes of culture and cultural propagation, and that classrooms have always been sites of cultural inscription that seek to legitimate particular forms. In this sense, critical pedagogy is grounded in the moral imperative of exposing systems of oppression that exist within the very structures of education, the process of schooling, and the overarching logic of perpetuating hierarchies of oppression and liberation through the sanctioning of particularly restrictive performances of self and other.

In *Schooling as a Ritual Performance*, McLaren (1993) grounds his critical vision in a politics of the body, which is my core link between pedagogy and performance ethnography. His concept of enfleshment signals "that meeting place of both the unthought social norms in which meaning is always already in place and the ongoing production of knowledge through particular social, institutional and disciplinary procedures" (p. 275). This work centers his ethnographic project in *the feeling body, the dialogically constituted feeling body*, *the discursive body*, and *the performing body* as sites of social inscription. His work suggests that the body is the site of knowing and feeling, and the site from which transformation is instantiated and initiated. McLaren states, "this means decoupling ourselves from the disciplined mobilizations of everyday life in order to rearticulate the sites of our affective investment so that we can 'reenter the strategic politics of the social formation'"[15] (p. 287). Desire must be inflected into a transformative politics of hope and action. I believe that performance ethnography taps into this kernel logic of experience. McLaren goes on to call for a critically reflexive and embodied performance of resistance and subversion that opens spaces for variation and expression.

B. Critical Performative Pedagogy

Grounded in a performance-based methodology, the practical and theoretical construct of *critical performative pedagogy* is used in diverse yet interlocking ways. For example, performance studies scholar Elyse Pineau (1998, 2002) uses the term to reference a body-centered experiential method of teaching that foregrounds the active-body-knowing. Her conceptualization of critical performative pedagogy, heavily supported with precepts from critical pedagogy, "acknowledge[s] that inequities in power and privilege have a physical impact on our bodies and consequently must be struggled against bodily, through physical action and activism" (2002, p. 53). Her performative methodology engages the body as a primary site of meaning-making, of ideological struggle, and of performative resistance. Hence bodies are put "into action in the classroom" as a means of exercising and engaging a liberatory practice that extends beyond the borders of the classroom into everyday citizenship (2002, p. 53).

Her approach is what cultural studies scholar Lawrence Grossberg (1996) might refer to as *the act of doing*. In particular, performative pedagogy in the classroom is used to illuminate and embody social politics "intervening into contexts and power . . . in order to enable people to act more strategically in ways that may change their context for the better" (p. 143). In this way, critical performative pedagogy is a rehearsal process that practices possibility outside the classroom (Boal, 1985).

Communication and sociology scholar Norman K. Denzin (2003) approaches *critical performance pedagogy* as a cluster of performative and emancipatory strategies. It includes Pineau's construction but extends further into a "civic, publicly responsible autoethnography that addresses the central issues of self, race, gender, society, and democracy" (p. 225). The expanse of his survey includes performance ethnography, autoethnography, performative cultural studies, reflexive critical ethnography, critical race theory, and the broader sociological and ethnographic imagination, all of which are undergirded in his expansion of Freirean (1998, 1999) politics, pedagogies, and possibilities of hope.

These methods are all empowered with the ability to open up spaces of pain to critical reflection on self and society. Hence, they exist in that tensive space of being radical and risky—radical in the sense that they strip away notions of a given human condition, and risky in that our sense of comfort in knowing the world is made bare. They give way to the possibility of knowing the world differently. They open a possibility of hope encouraged by social responsibility, political activism, and engaged participation in a moral science of humanistic discourse. This cluster of performative strategies that he refers to as *critical performance pedagogy* are all centered in the active body doing; the active mind knowing; and an active civic responsibility that collectivizes and promotes democracy and human rights.

Denzin's construction addresses Giroux's (2001) search for a project and the politics of hope when he discusses "strategies of understanding, engagement, and transformation that address the most demanding social problems of our time. Such projects are utopian . . ." (p. 7). Denzin refers to utopian as indicating an ideal state of human social relations but also uses utopian to indicate a particular and practical strategy of gaining insight into cultural others in order to build community. Performance ethnography as the overarching logic of this discussion can be what Jill Dolan (2001b) describes as a *utopian performative*. The theater or the situated site of performance can become a place where "audiences are compelled to gather with others, to see people perform live, hoping perhaps for moments of transformation that might let them reconsider and change the world outside the theatre" (p. 455). Although Dolan is referencing the specific project of theater, I am focusing broadly on performance and then applying it back to the specifics of performance ethnography in which actual lives and actual human conditions are presented for public discussion.

C. Border Pedagogy

In *Postmodern Education: Politics, Culture, and Social Criticism*, Aronowitz and Giroux (1991) discuss the construct of *border pedagogy*. "Border pedagogy offers the opportunity for students to engage the multiple references that constitute different cultural codes, experiences, and languages. This means educating students to read these codes critically, to learn the limits of such codes, including the ones they use to construct their own narratives and histories" (pp. 118–119). I believe this to be core logic of a *student-in-class–centered* approach to performance ethnography. It is a logic that promotes student engagement of actual accounts and descriptions of cultural practice, with the intent for them to come to know culture differently. In more specific terms, Aronowitz and Giroux write that border pedagogy helps students to understand that "[o]ne's class, race, gender, or ethnicity may influence, but does not irrevocably predetermine, how one takes up a particular ideology, reads a particular text, or responds to particular forms of oppression" (p. 121). Hence, there is the potential of seeing the links that bind humanity and not the borders of difference that we presume divide us.

Border pedagogy requires teachers to engage students in the places and ideological spaces of their own experiences as they try to make sense of culture and curriculum— while practicing a voice long subdued and silenced in the classroom. Such a performance-based method demands a new level of engagement that crosses borders between the knowing and the known. Giroux and Shannon (1997) state: "Pedagogy in this context becomes performative through the ways in which various authors [teachers and students] engage diverse cultural texts as a context for theorizing about social issues and wider political considerations" (p. 2).

In these ways, the link between performance and ethnography can move the over-all engagement of education beyond mere *teaching*, that process of organizing and integrating knowledge for the purpose of sharing meaning and mandating under-standing in the confines of the classroom. It can move toward the notion of *pedagogy*, which strategizes purposeful learning with an awareness of the social, cultural, and political contexts in which learning and living take place. Performance ethnography as a particular pedagogical strategy can then move even further to encompass a *critical pedagogy* by revealing, interrogating, and challenging legitimated social and cultural forms and opening spaces for additional voices in a meaningful human discourse. Such an act would always be moving toward becoming a *revolutionary pedagogy* that helps to enact the possibilities of social transformation by bleeding the borders of subjectivity and opening spaces of care (McLaren, 2000).

D. Public Pedagogy

In both Pineau's and Denzin's approaches to critical performative pedagogy, there is a hope that the embodied, reflective, and reflexive process of performative pedagogy becomes what Giroux (2001) constructs as *a public pedagogy*, a process in which the efforts and effects of such critical processes are not limited to the sterilizing confines of the classroom or the realm of self-knowing, but are presented to and enacted in the public sphere so as to transform social life. Giroux writes, "Defined through its perfor-mative functions, public pedagogy is marked by its attentiveness to the interconnec-tions and struggles that take place over knowledge, language, spatial relations, and history. Public pedagogy represents a moral and political practice rather than merely a technical procedure" (p. 12). Public pedagogy expands privatized notions of peda-gogical practices, specifically the in-class strategies used by individual teachers that might mark disciplinary limits and boundaries. In such case, a public pedagogy is framed and conceptualized by a political network of principles in critical pedagogy and cultural studies that link teaching and learning with social change.[16]

Through the performed engagement of a cultural dialogue, performance ethnogra-phy becomes a public pedagogy with several characteristics. It is designed to make public the often privatized, if not secularized, experiences of others. It is designed to begin the painstaking process of deconstructing notions of difference that often regu-late the equal distribution of humanistic concern. It makes present and visible the lived experiences of self and other; giving students, performers, and audiences access to knowledge that, one hopes, will open spaces of possibility.

▣ IV. POLITICAL POTENTIALITIES AND PRACTICAL INTERPRETATIONS OF PERFORMANCE ETHNOGRAPHY

Performance ethnography teases at and illuminates a wide variety of issues that are of particular concern both in performance studies and in ethnography. I have already focused on the issue of representation and the social reconstruction of *other people's lives*, whether as pedagogical method or as political activism. Performance ethnography troubles the issue and illuminates the need for careful consideration and delicate attention to the dramatistic questions of who, what, when, where, and why (Burke, 1957), directed to the actions of others and, more important, directed to our own political intentions. Drawing from the conceptual frames of theorists in performance studies, ethnography, and anthropology, I outline and extend *some* of the more dominant issues that reflect these disciplines as they converge in performance ethnography.

A. Dominating Issues at the Convergence of Performance/Ethnography

Performance ethnography highlights the concern in performance studies with how specific cultural practices shape identity and the concern in ethnography of how identity shapes the practice of cultural performance. Performance ethnography also highlights the role of cultural hegemony in the interpretation of cultural performance (E. C. Fine & Speer, 1992, p. 16). In this case, cultural hegemony is defined as the collectivizing practices of cultural familiars who regulate identity through the actualized embodiment of particular norms as identifying markers of communal, cultural, and political membership.

Performance ethnography as a reifying and magnifying cultural performative act replicates aspects of this quality of cultural performance in at least three ways. First, in the staging and embodiment of "the other" in performance, performance ethnography capitalizes on the observable and replicable behavior of cultural members in a particular context. Second, performance ethnography depends on the integrity of relational and ethical acts of the ethnographer who describes culture and the performer who embodies cultural experience. The questions of *why are particular cultural practices engaged* and *why they are studied through performance* should be scrutinized carefully. In this way, performance ethnography foregrounds the representational politics of performance and ethnography and the ethical issues of responsibility to particular audiences and cultures represented in the texts (Carlson, 1996, p. 15). The question of *what aspects of culture are reenacted in performance for what reason and with what perceptual and literal effects on the culture being represented* also should be critically engaged. Third, performance ethnography calls for a reflexive engagement on the part of the participants—actors/audiences to question what they accept as truth and to examine how their truths are shaped by their perspective both in and of performance, as well as in and of the cultural lives represented through performance (Jones, 2002, p. 1).

Discussing the three stages in the methodological process of performance ethnography, *ethnography into playscript*, *script into performance*, and *performance into meta-ethnography*, Victor Turner (1982) comments on a level of critical reflexivity that implicates the nature of ethnography and performance. He writes, "The reflexivity of performance dissolves the bonds (between body and mentality, unconscious and conscious thinking, species and self) and so creatively democratizes" (p. 100).

Performance ethnography orchestrates an embodied understanding of how notions of the self are always constructed in relation to other, and how we hold those perceptual standards as regulatory devices in maintaining human social relations. As a moral discourse, performance ethnography democratizes human sociality by closing the gaps between the known and the unknown, between self and other, and between the borders and boundaries of differently lived experiences.

B. Interpreting and Evaluating Effective Performance Ethnography

In articulating concerns of interpretation and evaluation, I focus on three areas of emphasis: content, form, and impact. I depend heavily on Laurel Richardson's (2000a) essay, in which she writes: "Ethnography is always situated in human activity, bearing both the strengths and limitations of human perception and feeling" (p. 254). These are palpably felt and realized in the conjoined effort of *performance ethnography*, which is to articulate a vision and understanding of a particular cultural experience, as it resonates and ricochets between self and other and, at times, self as other.

Content

1. Substantive contribution (Richardson, 2000a, p. 254): Does this piece contribute to our understanding of social life? Do the writer/performers demonstrate a deeply grounded (if embedded) human-world understanding and perspective? How has this perspective informed the construction of the text?

The notion of contribution is really an issue of intention. It is based in a series of questions that seek to get to the core of the critical endeavor of the performative engagement. What does the performance seek to accomplish? What does the performance seek to contribute, in terms of knowledge and experience, to the audience? In some very literal ways, the constructed entity of the performance must have a specific purpose with specific goals. What is/are the moral and theoretical arguments in the text? In the case of audience-centered performance ethnography, what aspects of culture do the performers seek to expose to the audience—particular traditions, clothing, food, social expressions, and so on? What critical evaluation (or politicized understanding) of cultural practice do the performers seek to share with the audience, or want the audience to assume? What political movement, emotional response, or engaged temperament does the performance seek to incite?

2. Reflexivity (Richardson, 2000a, p. 254): How did the author/performers come to write/perform this text? How was the information gathered? How has the author/performers' subjectivity been both a producer and product of this text? Is there adequate self-awareness and self-exposure for the audience to make judgments about the point of view? Do author/performers hold themselves accountable to the standards of knowing and telling of the people they have studied?

The performative construction and presentation of ethnography has multiple levels of reflexive accountabilities. First, when the performer is representing the cultural other, there is a *performer-based reflexivity*. This level of reflexivity is a critical self-examination of the performer's intentions, a clear understanding of his or her dense particularity in relation to the performed other, and his or her positionality in relation to the politics of performing the other.

Second, performance ethnography encourages a critical reflection on the *performed population*, gathering a clear understanding of their cultural experience. This turns into a *performer-performed reflexivity* that acknowledges the active process of performative embodiment of the other, the resonant points of juncture and disjunction, and how they work toward and in tension with the intended goal of the overall performative engagement. Such critical engagements seek not only to know the selves engaged in the performance (performer and performed), but also how the performance seeks to encourage a certain critical reflexiveness in the audience as they engage the performative moment. The performance should push the audience to learn and engage previously unspoken and unknown things about culture and communication from the experience of their engagement (Goodall, 2000). This performative learning engagement is specific both to the represented culture and to ways in which such knowledge can be extrapolated to broader issues of social and cultural interaction.

3. Expresses a reality (Richardson, 2000a, p. 254): Does this text present a fleshed out, embodied sense of lived experience? Does it seem "true"—meaning a credible account of a cultural, social, individual, or communal sense of the "real"?

The moment of performance presents a context that opens the way for the performer-ethnographer "to present human social behavior as more, rather than as less, complex, to keep explanations from becoming simplistic or reductionist" (Wolcott, 1999, p. 79). In this regard, Denzin (1992) might suggest that performance ethnography must "reflect back on, be entangled in, and critique this current historical moment and its discontents" (p. 25). For my own purposes, the current historical moment is both the actualized lived conditions and practices of those presented in performance, and also the moment of performance.

Form

4. Aesthetic merit (Richardson, 2000a, p. 254): Does this piece succeed aesthetically? Does the use of creative analytical practice open up the text and invite interpretive responses? Is the text artistically shaped, satisfying, complex, and not boring?

The writing in performance ethnography must be well crafted. This implies craft both in poetic terms, through aesthetic language that invokes the links between felt emotion, critical thought, and understanding; as well as craft in the sense that the language must be clear, effective, evocative, and more than subtly representative of the populations to which it reflects (Pelias, 1999a, 1999b; Spry, 2001). The writing must give the audience to which it is presented access to the world of those it represents in a manner that simulates the visceral response of actual experience.

In the case of using empirical materials gathered from ethnographic interviews, the language that informants speak *speaks the logic of their desire.* Their processed and re-articulated voice must be shaped and placed in context, signaling both the actuality of location in the utterance and the regenerated conditions of its use in performance—bridging space, time, and the channeled embodiment of cultural experience. The crafted language and embodied engagement of performance ethnography must meet the standards of intellectual rigor and aesthetic acumen set by experts and theorists in both performance studies and the social sciences (Denzin, 1997; Spry, 2001). It must have the sensuousness of articulate embodied thought, with the clarity and efficacy of good research grounded in ethical care and thick description.

Impact

5. How does performance ethnography affect the performers (emotionally, intellectually, and politically)? How does performance ethnography affect the audience (emotionally, intellectually, and politically)? What new questions are generated in and through the performance? Does the performance move the performer and audience to try new ways of seeing the world, particular cultures, particular research practices, and ways of knowing the world? Does the performance move the performers and audience to a particular action—extending outside the borders of the immediate performative experience (Richardson, 2000a, p. 254)?

These are not questions of measurement or the validation of effect that often trouble the very personalized and deeply felt responses to performative engagement, yet the strategic purposes of engaging performance ethnography might encourage performers and audience members to reflect upon the nature of their experience. They might suggest that audience members of these performances be offered a forum or venue, such as speaking in post-performance discussion sessions or writing on questionnaires or comment sheets. This helps in further theorizing what audiences bring to and take away from performances. It helps to clarify the effectiveness of performance to engage, inform, ignite, and incite response beyond personalized pleasure or the emotional stirrings of dis-ease (Park-Fuller, 2003).

Furthermore, some form of *engaged discourse* might suggest asking performers and audience members to articulate a shift in their way of thinking and seeing the world. What do they know differently? What will they do differently? How can they literally translate performative experience into knowledge and translate knowledge into doing? In many ways, this possibility extends and reifies the dialogic nature of performance ethnography, into a realized dialogue between the aestheticized recreation of cultural others, the performers who make their presence and voices known in performance, and the diverse audiences with whom they come into contact.

▣ V. Directions in/for Performance Ethnography

Performance ethnography is concerned with embodying aspects of ethnographic description. It is this *practice of engagement* that allows performers, subjects, and audiences (in their reciprocated and intensely bound positionalities) to come to an experiential sense of the variables that affect cultural life. It focuses on the important transformative process of becoming, which signals our agency for empathy and our flexibility in embodying cultural norms. One can hope that the pedagogical, aesthetic, and political processes that inform performance ethnography will continue to bubble to the surface while establishing new ways of engaging, extending, and critically reflecting on the multiple variables that shape and affect cultural knowing.

Soyini Madison's (1998) key construction of *the performance of possibilities* offers both validity and direction for performance ethnography. I knowingly and willingly displace my voice to foreground some of her germinal articulations on this note, knowing that they are most certainly key reminders of the ways in which performance ethnography seeks to open realms of knowing and doing through the joint efforts of performance and ethnography and the necessary political activism that yokes and drives engaged citizenship. (See how Madison furthers these imperatives in her chapter on critical ethnography, Chapter 8, this volume.) Here I reframe her articulations as tenets for a performance of possibilities—not rules, but a set of organizing principles that should guide the future of performance ethnography.

Tenets for a Performance of Possibilities

- The *performance of possibilities* functions as a politically engaged pedagogy that never has to convince a predefined subject—whether empty or full, whether essential or fragmented—to adopt a new position. Rather, the task is to win an already positioned, already invested individual or group to a different set of places, a different organization of *the space of possibilities*.
- The *performance of possibilities* invokes an investment in politics and "the Other," keeping in mind the dynamics of performance, audience, and Subjects while at the same time being wary of both cynics and zealots.

- The *performance of possibilities* takes the stand that performance matters because it does something in the world. What it does for the audience, the Subjects, and those engaged in it must be driven by a thoughtful critique of assumptions and purpose.

- The *performance of possibilities* does not accept being heard and included as its focus, but only as a starting point. Instead, voice is an embodied historical self that constructs and is constructed by a matrix of social and political processes. The aim is to present and represent Subjects as made and makers of meaning, symbol, and history in their fullest sensory and social dimensions. Therefore, the *performance of possibilities* is also a performance of voice wedded to experience.

- The *performance of possibilities* as an interrogative field aims to create or contribute to a discursive space where unjust systems and processes are identified and interrogated. It is where what has been expressed through the illumination of voice and the encounter with subjectivity motivates individuals to some level of informed and strategic action.

- The *performance of possibilities* motivates performers and spectators to appropriate the rhetorical currency they need, from the inner space of the performance to the outer domain of the social world, in order to make a material difference.

- The *performance of possibilities* necessitates creating performances where the intent is largely to invoke interrogation of specific political and social processes so that art is seen as consciously working toward a cultural politics of change that resonates in a progressive and involved citizenship.

- The *performance of possibilities* strives to reinforce to audience members the web of citizenship and the possibilities of their individual selves as agents and change-makers.

- The *performance of possibilities* acknowledges that when audience members begin to witness degrees of tension and incongruity between a Subject's life-world and those processes and systems that challenge and undermine that world, something more and new is learned about how power works.

- The *performance of possibilities* suggests that both performers and audiences can be transformed. They can be themselves and more as they travel between worlds—the spaces that they and others actually inhabit and the spaces of possibility of human liberation.

- The *performance of possibilities* is moral responsibility and artistic excellence that culminates in the active intervention of unfair closures, *remaking* the possibility for new openings that bring the margins to a shared center.

- The *performance of possibilities* does not arrogantly assume that we exclusively are giving voice to the silenced, for we understand they speak and have been speaking in spaces and places often foreign to us.

- The *performance of possibilities* in the new millennium will specialize in the wholly impossible reaching toward light, justice, and enlivening possibilities (Madison, 1998, pp. 276–286).

How might Madison's constructions be made manifest in performance ethnography? How might we move toward a concrete materialization of these possibilities? How might we extend the promises and possibilities of performance ethnography outside a sometimes insular academic endeavor characterized by talk and into a community-based application where doing has meaningful consequences? Those of us working for a critical cultural awareness through performance studies, ethnography, cultural studies, and pedagogical studies understand that the stakes are high, but so is our desire. We understand that the steps that we take leave tracks from where we have been but also establish trails to our direction and for others to follow. Allow me to offer some possible directions for us to travel.

First, issues of critical reflexivity are always at the center of performance ethnography. The act of *seeing the self see the self* signals Joseph Roach's (2002) discussion through Brecht of *defamiliarizing* the self—not defamiliarizing the self by simply stepping into the bodies of others, but by becoming aware of what happens in and as a result of that shift. Performance ethnography would benefit from what K. E. Supriya (2001) calls the *staging of ethnographic reflexivity* in which there is a critical emphasis on seeing the self see the self both in moments of ethnographic practice and in the performance of that knowledge. Such performances might at once confirm the power of performance as a method of knowing and present a clear template for audiences to engage in the process of critical reflection on their experiences in performance ethnography, thus assisting them in developing critical skills that extend beyond the performance moment and can affect the ways in which they move through the world.

In this way, we also heed Langellier's (1998) charge related to performing personal narrative when she writes: "To 'just do it'"—in this case performance ethnography—"without producing knowledge about" *the links between performance, ethnography, and culture* risks exploiting cultural practices for personal gains. Joining Langellier, Elizabeth Bell (2002) yearns for performance theory that *can* help to "account for the material, political consequences of performance . . ." (p. 128). I apply her logic toward building a critical theory of performance ethnography, a theory that *can* help to enlighten us on the revelations gained through performative experience. These revelations might exceed the particularity of method, pedagogical purpose, or even the politics of representation to foreground *the logics of effect and the sociopolitical impacts of performative experience.*

Such a theory would ask and answer the following questions: What do performers and audience members take from the experience of performance ethnography? How, through a performance of translated ethnographic materials, do performers and audiences come to know culture better? In answering these questions, performance ethnography might also be formally linked to Giroux's (2001) desire for a public pedagogy, thereby linking practices that are interdisciplinary, pedagogical, and performance-based with such practices that are designed to further racial, economic, and political democracy, practices that are designed to strike a new balance and expand the individual and social dimensions of citizenship (p. 9).[18]

Second, although performance ethnography often seems interested in reflecting on the experience of and with the cultural other, distinctions are made through perceived characteristics of difference. To what degree would performance ethnography also benefit in illuminating the ways in which "difference" as an ideological and practiced construct is a part of any community? To what degree would performance ethnography benefit in turning its gaze on the specified communities to which ethnographers and performers claim membership, and thereby illuminate the ways in which struggle and strife are present within the everyday life of cultural familiars?

Most recently, my work has moved into what I have constructed as *an integrative and reflexive ethnography of performance* that both captures and extends this logic. This experimental approach is grounded both in Denzin's (1997) construction of *reflexive critique* and in Jones's (1997) use of *performance as a critique of the academy*. It is also informed by Schneider's (2002) notion of a *reflexive/diffractive ethnography*, which charges that ethnographic practices should not only re-inscribe the nature of what already happens in the world, but also move toward instantiating ways of seeing and methods of knowing to transform those practices.

The approach allows me the opportunity to address questions about and responses to staged cultural performance that I encounter in the academic communities in which I claim membership. Although these comments and critiques are "seemingly" directed to a particular product or utterance, the inseparability of product, process, and producer (a member of "minority culture") in relation to the variables that shape the life of the critic (a member of "majority culture") always bleed the borders. These bleeding borders are like semi-permeable membranes between the public and the private, between the professional and the personal, and between the politics of power and propriety that always threaten to hold tension-filled historical social relations in stasis. By incorporating such critiques in a restaging of the performance either in embodied or written form, I stage a critical reflexivity for self and other, thereby further theorizing the mechanisms that undergird both performances in everyday life and how others and I reconstruct and critique those occurrences in the academic and scholarly cultural arena (Alexander, 2004b).

The kernel idea that I am suggesting turns on the following questions. Can performance ethnography be used to turn the tables not only on those constructed as "the other" but also on our collective cultural selves? Can performance ethnography be used to look at the very conditions under which ethnographers, scholars, teachers, and students labor, in order to discover, or rather uncover, the ways in which our talk about oppression and liberation of the other are not always the models that we use in developing and maintaining the communities in which we claim membership? Can we use performance ethnography to critically gaze back on our own practices? Can we use performance ethnography to explore the ways in which the mixed identities in any community (e.g., race, ethnicity, class, sex, sexuality) and the investments we have in maintaining these social identities often clash and rub against each other? These points of contact must be acknowledged and addressed sometime before we begin to cure the world.

In this way, maybe performance ethnography can be used to deconstruct disciplinary formations such as white studies, black studies, queer studies, and the varying machinations of identity politics that both center and decenter the vested interests of varying populations in the larger moral discourse of human interaction. Maybe, in some rather specific ways, under the rubric of *performing theory and embodied writing* (Madison, 1999), we can engage a close ethnographic excavation and performative engagement of these logics that undergird human sociality. Such an engagement might reveal how theoretical and academic logics format and foment particular social tensions and thereby sustain borders of difference, even as they purport to democratize. Examples include the following: (a) how the construction of commodity in white studies and black studies is the signifier for myths of nationality and identity that reconfirm problematic constructions of race, power, and division; (b) how queer studies/ theory performs a resistance to regimes of the normal, and in turn generalizes concerns and experiences within an imagined community where there is still contestation over the very terms "gay" and "queer" as informed through issues of race, class, sexual practice, and desire.

I see my own work moving in these areas when issues of personal survival motivate scholarly production (Alexander, 2002a, 2003, 2004a, 2004b). More often, I am positioning myself as an affected party, as a community member, or as an indigenous ethnographer. Through autoethnography, I am exploring and sometimes exposing my own vulnerability to racial, gender, and cultural critique as a method of both understanding self and other, and self as other, while engaging in performances (written and embodied) that seek to transform the social and cultural conditions under which I live and labor.

Third, performance ethnography needs to develop legs, or walking feet, traveling the distance to particular audiences that might effect change, such as Boal's Legislative Theatre, or to those audiences that need an affective awareness of the issues. Following some of the more radical applications of Theatre of the Oppressed, Playback Theatre, and Community-Based Interactive Theatre(s), performance ethnography as an academic construct cannot sit in the ivory tower and invite audiences to come to it. It must go to those places and spaces where such critical performative intervention is needed to magnify issues, to *dynamize* movement—physical, social, and political (Boal)—and to engage audiences most in need of exercising and practicing voice. In this way, performance ethnography would thus develop projects that "reach outside the academy and are rooted in an ethic of reciprocity and exchange" (Conquergood, 2002, p. 152).

Fourth, in a literal move of *stepping into someone else's voice* and consequently his or her lived experience, maybe performance ethnography continues its direction toward cross-cultural and cross-racial performances by having people perform the narratives of others. The kind of work that is engaged by Olga Davis at the University of Arizona in staging events, leading up to and including the Tulsa Race Riots of 1965, might further spur on this impulse. The work includes her students in a long-term ethnographic research project and challenges them to perform aspects of research, race, resistance, and riots.

In many ways, Davis's pedagogical practice of also having students at the predominantly white university where she teaches perform actual slave narratives embarks on a form of performance ethnography that forces students into realms of historical knowing. They begin to think, as Denzin and Lincoln (1998) write, "historically, interactionally, and structurally." They begin "to make connections among lived experience, larger social, and cultural structures" that are made manifest in the current predicaments of race and culture (p. xi). This approach is centered in the performance of autobiography and the performance of biography, embodying the articulated and documented experiences of others as gathered through ethnographic processes or found texts.[19]

Fifth, we must strengthen the commitment of performance ethnography as a civic-minded moral discourse that encourages what Stephen Hartnett (1998) calls a form of "performative citizenship"—one in which the aesthetics of performance "move[s] beyond hypnotized individuality and voracious commodification to approach something closer to engaged cultural history" (p. 288). This type of cultural history, as both realms of individual/human experience and as shared legacies of pain and possibility, enacts citizenship as productive participation in the realm of human relations. In *Geographies of Learning*, Jill Dolan (2001a) takes on this argument to suggest that the arena and engaged practice of performance can create citizens and engage democracy as a participatory forum in which ideas and possibilities for social equity and justice are shared.

Performance ethnography can help us to understand the lived cultural experiences of others, but it also can help us to claim the joint culpability of history's legacy. It can then help us to strategize possibility, ways in which collective social action might lead to a more compatible human condition.

◙ NOTES

1. See Lockford (1998, 2000) for a helpful discussion on performing constructed narratives or performing *the true in experience* or *the true to experience narrative*.

2. See Bacon (1979), Bacon and Breen (1961), Kleinau and McHughes (1980), and Yordon (1989) as germinal texts.

3. See Stern and Henderson (1993) for a good survey of this approach.

4. This is particularly noted in performance studies' most recent interest in "performative writing" or what Richardson (2000b) calls "creative analytic writing practices" (p. 941). See also Madison (1999), Pollock (1998c), Pelias (1999b), and L. Miller and Pelias (2001).

5. See Carlson (1996), Conquergood (2002), Pelias and VanOosting (1987), Strine, Long, and Hopkins (1990), and Stucky and Wimmer (2002) for more expanded surveys of the evolution of performance studies.

6. Conquergood tracks this movement through the work of Goffman (1959), Austin (1962), Searle (1969), Hymes (1975), Turner (1982), Bauman (1986), Turner and Turner

(1988), and Bhabha (1994). He marks his original construction of this moment in Conquergood (1992).

7. See Phelan and Lane (1998) for the further charting of this trajectory.

8. Turner (1988) defines social dramas as units of aharmonic or disharmonic social processes, a rising in conflict situations. Typically, they have four main phases of public action: (a) breach of regular norm-governed social relations; (b) crisis, during which there is a tendency for the breach to widen; (c) redressive action to resolve certain kinds of crisis or legitimate other modes of resolution; and (d) either reintegration of the disturbed social group or the social recognition and legitimization of irreparable schism between the contesting parties (pp. 74–75).

9. Van Maanen credits Barthes (1972) with the insight.

10. See Coco Fusco's (1994) description of her work with Guillermo Gómez-Peña and texts on the origin and impetus of performance art. Performance art is most often interested in the relationship between performance and identity, especially the visibility of those normally excluded by race, class, gender, or sexuality (see Mifflin, 1992, and T. Miller, Kushner, and McAdams, 2002).

11. In *Twilight: Los Angeles, 1992* (1994), Anna Deavere Smith engages the same process in interviewing and later performing people after the 1992 Los Angeles riots.

12. See Denzin's (1997) outlining of procedural types and texts of performance ethnography (pp. 90–125).

13. Corey cites Foucault (1982) for the construct of "reverse discourse."

14. Here Corey cites Stern and Henderson (1993, p. 35).

15. McLaren is citing Grossberg (1992, p. 394).

16. Giroux cites Raymond Williams (1989, p. 158) to help establish this argument.

17. The following is a summary of thoughts presented by Madison (1998, pp. 276–286).

18. Giroux cites Hall and Held (1990, pp. 8–9).

19. See Pineau (1992) for more detailed distinction between performance of autobiography and autobiographical performance.

▣ REFERENCES

Alcoff, L. (1991/1992). The problem of speaking for others. *Cultural Critique, 20,* 5–32.

Alexander, B. K. (1999). Moving toward a critical poetic response. *Theatre Topics, 9*(2), 107–126.

Alexander, B. K. (2000). Skin flint (or the garbage man's kid): A generative autobiographical performance based on Tami Spry's Tattoo stories. *Text and Performance Quarterly, 20*(1), 97–114.

Alexander, B. K. (2002a). The outsider (or *Invisible Man* all over again): Contesting the absented black gay body in queer theory (with apologies to Ralph Ellison). In W. Wright & S. Kaplan (Eds.), *The image of the outsider: Proceedings of the 2002 Society for the Interdisciplinary Study of Social Imagery conference* (pp. 308–315). Pueblo: University of Southern Colorado.

Alexander, B. K. (2002b). Performing culture and cultural performance in Japan: A critical (auto)ethnographic travelogue. *Theatre Annual: A Journal of Performance Studies, 55,* 1–28.

Alexander, B. K. (2003). Querying queer theory again (*Or queer theory as drag performance*). In G. A. Yep, K. E. Lovaas, & J. P. Elia (Eds.), *Queer theory and communication: From disciplining queers to queering the discipline(s)* (pp. 349–352). New York: Harrington Park Press.

Alexander, B. K. (2004a). Black face/white mask: The performative sustainability of whiteness. *Qualitative Inquiry, 10*(5), 647–672.

Alexander, B. K. (2004b). Passing, cultural performance, and individual agency: Performative reflections on black masculine identity. *Cultural Studies ↔ Critical Methodologies, 4*(3), 377–404.

Aronowitz, S., & Giroux, H. (1991). *Postmodern education: Politics, culture, and social criticism.* Minneapolis: University of Minnesota Press.

Austin, J. L. (1962). *How to do things with words.* London: Oxford University Press.

Bacon, W. A. (1979). *The art of interpretation* (3rd ed.). New York: Holt, Rinehart & Winston.

Bacon, W., & Breen, R. (1961). *Literature for interpretation.* New York: Holt, Rinehart & Winston.

Barthes, R. (1972). *Mythologies.* London: Paladin.

Bateson, M. C. (1993). Joint performance across cultures: Improvisation in a Persian garden. *Text and Performance Quarterly, 13,* 113–121.

Bauman, R. (1986). *Story, performance, event: Contextual studies of oral narratives.* Cambridge, UK: Cambridge University Press.

Becker, H. S., McCall, M. M., & Morris, L. V. (1989). Theatres and communities: Three scenes. *Social Problems, 36,* 93–116.

Bell, E. (2002). When half the world's a stage: A feminist excavation of Richard Schechner's theory of "actuals." *The Theatre Annual: A Journal of Performance Studies, 55,* 112–131.

Bhabha, H. (1994). *The location of culture.* New York: Routledge.

Boal, A. (1979). *Theater of the oppressed* (C. A. McBride & M.-O. Leal McBride, Trans.). New York: Urizen Books.

Boal, A. (1985). *Theatre of the oppressed* (C. A. McBride & M.-O. Leal McBride, Trans.). New York: Theatre Communication Group.

Boal, A. (1995). *The rainbow of desire: The Boal method theatre and therapy* (A. Jackson, Trans.). New York: Routledge.

Boal, A. (1998). *Legislative theatre: Using performance to make politics* (A. Jackson, Trans.). New York: Routledge.

Bochner, A. P. (1994). Perspectives on inquiry II: Theories and stories. In M. Knapp & G. R. Miller (Eds.), *The handbook of interpersonal communication* (pp. 21–41). Thousand Oaks, CA: Sage.

Bochner, A. P., & Ellis, C. (2002). *Ethnographically speaking: Autoethnography, literature, and aesthetics.* Walnut Creek, CA: AltaMira.

Brecht, B. (1964). *Brecht on theatre* (J. Willet, Trans.). New York: Hill.

Bruner, E. M. (1986). Experience and its expressions. In V. M. Turner & E. M. Bruner (Eds.), *The anthropology of experience* (pp. 3–30). Urbana: University of Illinois Press.

Burke, K. (1957). *The philosophy of literary form.* New York: Vintage Books.

Butler, J. (1990a). *Gender trouble: Feminism and the subversion of identity.* New York: Routledge.

Butler, J. (1990b). Performative acts and gender constitution: An essay in phenomenology and feminist theory. In S. E. Case (Ed.), *Performing feminisms: Feminist critical theory and theatre* (pp. 270–282). Baltimore: Johns Hopkins University Press.

Butler, J. (1993). *Bodies that matter: On the discursive limits of sex*. New York: Routledge.

Carlson, M. (1996). *Performance: A critical introduction*. London: Routledge.

Certeau, M. (1984). *The practice of everyday life*. (S. Rendall, Trans.). Berkeley: University of California Press.

Chambers, E. (2000). Applied ethnography. In N. K. Denzin & Y. S. Lincoln (Eds.), *Handbook of qualitative research* (2nd ed., pp. 851–869). Thousand Oaks, CA: Sage.

Chaney, D. (1994). *The cultural turn: Scene-setting essay in modern cultural history*. New York: Routledge.

Chesebro, J. W. (1998). Performance studies as paradox, culture, and manifesto: A future orientation. In S. J. Dailey (Ed.), *The future of performance studies: Visions and revisions* (pp. 310–319). Annandale, VA: National Communication Association.

Christians, C. G. (2000). Ethics and politics in qualitative research. In N. K. Denzin & Y. S. Lincoln (Eds.), *Handbook of qualitative research* (2nd ed., pp. 133–155). Thousand Oaks, CA: Sage.

Clifford, J. (1988). *The predicament of culture: Twentieth- century ethnography, literature, and art*. Cambridge, MA: Harvard University Press.

Clifford, J., & Marcus, G. E. (Eds.). (1986). *Writing culture: The poetics and politics of ethnography: A School of American Research advanced seminar*. Berkeley: University of California Press.

Cohen, R. (1988). Realism. In M. Banham (Ed.), *The Cambridge guide to theatre* (p. 815). Cambridge, UK: Cambridge University Press.

Conquergood, D. (1983). A sense of the other: Interpretation and ethnographic research. In I. Crouch (Ed.), *Proceedings of the seminar/conference on oral tradition* (pp. 148–155). Las Cruces: New Mexico State University.

Conquergood, D. (1985). Performing as a moral act: Ethical dimensions of the ethnography of performance. *Literature in Performance, 5,* 1–13.

Conquergood, D. (1986a). Performance and dialogical understanding: In quest of the other. In J. L. Palmber (Ed.), *Communication as performance* (pp. 30–37). Tempe: Arizona State University Press.

Conquergood, D. (1986b). Performing cultures: Ethnography, epistemology, and ethics. In E. Slembek (Ed.), *Miteinander sprechen and handein: Festschrift fur Hellmut Geissner* (pp. 55–147). Frankfurt: Scriptor.

Conquergood, D. (1988). Health Theatre in a Hmong refugee camp: Performance, communication and culture. *The Drama Review: A Journal of Performance Studies, 32*(3), 174–208.

Conquergood, D. (1989). Poetics, play, process and power: The performance turn in anthropology. *Text and Performance Quarterly, 9,* 82–88.

Conquergood, D. (1991). Rethinking ethnography: Towards a critical cultural politics. *Communication Monographs, 58,* 179–194.

Conquergood, D. (1992). Ethnography, rhetoric and performance. *Quarterly Journal of Speech, 78,* 80–97.

Conquergood, D. (1998). Beyond the text: Toward a performative cultural politics. In S. J. Dailey (Ed.), *The future of performance studies: Visions and revisions* (pp. 25–36). Annandale, VA: National Communication Association.

Conquergood, D. (2002). Performance studies: Interventions and radical research. *The Drama Review: A Journal of Performance Studies, 46*(2), 145–156.

Corey, F. C. (1998). The personal: Against the master narrative. In S. J. Dailey (Ed.), *The future of performance studies: Visions and revisions* (pp. 249–253). Annandale, VA: National Communication Association.

Denzin, N. K. (1992). The many faces of emotionality. In C. Ellis (Ed.), *Investigating subjectivity: Research on lived experience* (pp. 17–30). London: Sage.

Denzin, N. K. (1997). *Interpretive ethnography: Ethnographic practices for the 21st century.* Thousand Oaks, CA: Sage.

Denzin, N. K. (1999). Interpretive ethnography for the next century. *Journal of Contemporary Ethnography, 28*(5), 510–519.

Denzin, N. K. (2003). *Performance ethnography: Critical pedagogy and the politics of culture.* Thousand Oaks, CA: Sage.

Denzin, N. K., & Lincoln, Y. S. (1998). Introduction to this volume. In N. K. Denzin & Y. S. Lincoln (Eds.), *Strategies of qualitative inquiry* (pp. xi–xxii). Thousand Oaks, CA: Sage.

Diamond, E. (1996). Introduction. In E. Diamond (Ed.), *Performances and cultural politics* (pp. 1–12). New York: Routledge.

Dolan, J. (2001a). *Geographies of learning: Theory and practice, activism and performance.* Middletown, CT: Wesleyan University Press.

Dolan, J. (2001b). Performance, utopia, and the "Utopian performative." *Theatre Journal, 53*(3), 455–479.

Doyle, D. M. (2001). The role of witnessing in performance ethnography. *Iowa Journal of Communication, 33*(1/2), 22–37.

Ellis, C., & Bochner, A. P. (1996). *Composing ethnography: Alternative forms of qualitative writing.* Walnut Creek, CA: AltaMira.

Ellis, C., & Bochner, A. P. (2000). Autoethnography, personal narrative, reflexivity: Researcher as subject. In N. K. Denzin & Y. S. Lincoln (Eds.), *Handbook of qualitative research* (2nd ed., pp. 733–768). Thousand Oaks, CA: Sage.

Espinola, J. (1977). Oral interpretation performance: An act of publication. *Western Journal of Speech Communication, 41*(2), 90–97.

Fine, E. C., & Speer, J. H. (1992). Introduction. In E. C. Fine & J. H. Speer (Eds.), *Performance, culture, and identity* (pp. 1–22). Westport, CT: Praeger.

Fine, M., Weis, L., Weseen, S., & Wong, L. (2000). For whom? Qualitative research, representations, and social responsibilities. In N. K. Denzin & Y. S. Lincoln (Eds.), *Handbook of qualitative research* (2nd ed., pp. 107–131). Thousand Oaks, CA: Sage.

Fiske, J. (1994). Audiencing: Cultural practice and cultural studies. In N. K. Denzin & Y. S. Lincoln (Eds.), *Handbook of qualitative research* (pp. 189– 198). Thousand Oaks, CA: Sage.

Foucault, M. (1982). The subject and power. *Critical Inquiry, 8,* 777–795.

Fox, J. (1986). *Acts of service: Spontaneity, commitment, tradition in the nonscripted theatre.* New Paltz, NY: Tusitala.

Fox, J., & Heinreich, D. (Eds.). (1999). *Gathering voices: Essays on playback theatre.* New Paltz, NY: Tusitala

Freire, P. (1985). *The politics of education: Culture, power, and liberation.* New York: Bergin & Garvey.

Freire, P. (1998). *Teachers as cultural workers: Letters to those who dare teach* (D. Macedo, D. Koike, & A. Oliveira, Trans.). Boulder, CO: Westview.

Freire, P. (1999). *Pedagogy of the oppressed.* New York: Continuum.

Fuoss, K. (1997). *Striking performance/performing strikes.* Jackson: University of Mississippi Press.

Fusco, C. (1994). The other history of intercultural performance. *The Drama Review: A Journal of Performance Studies, 38,* 143–167.

Garoian, C. R. (1999). *Performing pedagogy: Towards an art of politics.* New York: SUNY Press.

Geiger, D. (1973). Poetic realizing as knowing. *Quarterly Journal of Speech, 59,* 311–318.

Gentile, J. (1989). *A cast of one: One-person shows from the Chautauqua platform to the Broadway stage.* Urbana: University of Illinois Press.

Giroux, H. A. (2001). Cultural studies as performative politics. *Cultural Studies ↔ Critical Methodologies, 1*(1), 5–23.

Giroux, H. A., & McLaren, P. (1984). *Critical pedagogy, the state and cultural struggle.* New York: SUNY Press.

Giroux, H. A., & McLaren, P. (Eds.). (1994). *Between borders: Pedagogy and the politics of cultural studies.* New York: Routledge.

Giroux, H. A., & Shannon, P. (Eds.). (1997). *Education and cultural studies: Toward a performative practice.* New York: Routledge.

Goffman, E. (1959). *The presentation of self in everyday life.* Garden City, NY: Doubleday.

Goodall, H. L., Jr. (2000). *Writing the new ethnography.* Walnut Creek, CA: AltaMira.

Grossberg, L. (1992). *We gotta get out of this place: Popular conservatism and postmodern culture.* London: Routledge.

Grossberg, L. (1996). Toward a genealogy of the state of cultural studies. In C. Nelson & D. Parameshwar (Eds.), *Disciplinarity and dissent in cultural studies* (pp. 87–107). New York: Routledge.

Guss, D. M. (2000). *The festive state: Race, ethnicity, and nationalism as cultural performance.* Los Angeles: University of California Press.

Haedicke, S. C., & Nellhaus, T. (Eds.). (2001). *Performing democracy: International perspectives on urban community-based performance.* Ann Arbor: University of Michigan Press.

Hall, S., & Held, D. (1990). Citizens and citizenship. In S. Hall & M. Jacques (Eds.), *New times: The changing face of politics in the 1990s* (pp. 173–188). London: Verso.

Hamera, J. (1999). Editor's notes. *Text and Performance Quarterly, 19*(2), 106.

Hamera, J. (2000). The romance of monsters: Theorizing the virtuoso body. *Theatre Topics, 10*(2), 145–153.

Harrison-Pepper, S. (1999). Dramas of persuasion: Performance studies and interdisciplinary education. *Theatre Topics, 9*(2), 141–156.

Hartnett, S. (1998). Democracy is difficult: Poetry, prison, and performative citizenship. In S. J. Dailey (Ed.), *The future of performance studies: Visions and revisions* (pp. 287–297). Annandale, VA: National Communication Association.

Hopkins, M. F. (1981). From page to stage: The burden of proof. *Southern Speech Communication Journal, 47,* 1–9.

Hymes, D. (1975). Breakthrough into performance. In D. Ben-Amos & K. Goldstein (Eds.), *Folklore: Performance and communication* (pp. 11–74). The Hague: Mouton.

Jackson, S. (1993). Ethnography and the audition: Performance as ideological critique. *Text and Performance Quarterly, 13,* 21–43.

Jackson, S. (1998). White noises: In performing white, on writing performance. *The Drama Review: A Journal of Performance Studies, 42*(1), 90–97.

Jackson, S. (2000). *Lines of activity: Performance, historiography, Hull-House domesticity.* Ann Arbor: University of Michigan Press.

Jones, J. (1997). Sista docta: Performance as a critique of the academy. *The Drama Review: A Journal of Performance Studies, 41*(2), 51–67.

Jones, J. (2002). Performance ethnography: The role of embodiment in cultural authenticity. *Theatre Topics, 12*(1), 1–15.

Kapferer, B. (1986). Performance and the structuring of meaning and experience. In V. M. Turner & E. M. Bruner (Eds.), *The anthropology of experience* (pp. 188–203). Urbana: University of Illinois Press.

Kershaw, B. (1999). *The radical in performance: Between Brecht and Baudrillard.* London: Routledge.

Kirby, M. (1979). Autoperformance issues: An introduction. *The Drama Review: A Journal of Performance Studies, 23*(1), 2.

Kirshenblatt-Gimbett, B. (1998). *Destination culture: Tourism, museums, and heritage.* Berkeley: University of California Press.

Kleinau, M. L., & McHughes, J. L. (1980). *Theatres for literatures.* Sherman Oaks, CA: Alfred Publishing.

Langellier, K. M. (1989). Personal narratives: Perspectives on theory and research. *Text and Performance Quarterly, 9,* 243–276.

Langellier, K. M. (1998). Voiceless bodies, bodiless voices: The future of personal narrative performance. In S. J. Dailey (Ed.), *The future of performance studies: Visions and revisions* (pp. 207–213). Annandale, VA: National Communication Association.

Langellier, K. M. (1999). Personal narrative, performance, performativity: Two or three things I know for sure. *Text and Performance Quarterly, 19,* 125–144.

Lionnet, F. (1989). *Autobiographical voices: Race, gender, self-portraiture.* Ithaca, NY: Cornell University Press.

Lockford, L. (1998). Emergent issues in the performance of a border-transgressive narrative. In S. J. Dailey (Ed.), *The future of performance studies: Visions and revisions* (pp. 214–220). Annandale, VA: National Communication Association.

Lockford, L. (2000). An ethnographic ghost story: Adapting "What's a nice commodity like you doing in a spectacle like this?" *Text and Performance Quarterly, 20*(4), 402–415.

MaCaloon, H. R. (1984). *Rites, drama, festival, spectacle: Rehearsals toward a theory of cultural performance.* Philadelphia: Institute for the Study of Human Issues.

Madison, D. S. (1998). Performance, personal narratives, and the politics of possibility. In S. J. Dailey (Ed.), *The future of performance studies: Visions and revisions* (pp. 276–286). Annandale, VA: National Communication Association.

Madison, D. S. (1999). Performing theory/embodied writing. *Text and Performance Quarterly, 19,* 107–124.

McCall, M. M. (1993). *Not "just" a farmer and not just a "farm wife."* Unpublished performance script.

McCall, M. M. (2000). Performance ethnography: A brief history and some advice. In N. K. Denzin & Y. S. Lincoln (Eds.), *Handbook of qualitative research* (2nd ed., pp. 421–433). Thousand Oaks, CA: Sage.

McCall, M., & Becker, H. S. (1990). Performance science. *Social Problems, 32,* 117–132.

McLaren, P. (1985). The ritual dimensions of resistance: Clowning and symbolic inversion. *Journal of Education, 167*(2), 84–97.

McLaren., P. (1989). On ideology and education: Critical pedagogy and the cultural politics of resistance. In H. Giroux & P. McLaren (Eds.), *Critical pedagogy, the state and cultural struggle* (pp. 174–202). Albany: State University of New York Press.

McLaren, P. (1993). *Schooling as a ritual performance: Towards a political economy of educational symbols and gestures.* New York: Routledge.

McLaren, P. (1994). *Life in school: An introduction to critical pedagogy in the foundations of education.* New York: Longman.

McLaren, P. (1997). *Revolutionary multiculturalism: Pedagogies of dissent for the new millennium.* Boulder, CO: Westview.

McLaren, P. (1998). *Life in school: An introduction to critical pedagogy in the foundations of education* (3rd ed.). New York: Longman.

McLaren, P. (2000). *Che Guevara, Paulo Freire, and the pedagogy of revolution.* New York: Rowman & Littlefield.

McLaren, P., & Lankshear, C. (1994). *Politics of liberation: Paths from Freire.* New York: Routledge.

Merrill, L. (1999). *When Romeo was a woman: Charlotte Cushman and her circle of female spectators.* Ann Arbor: University of Michigan.

Mienczakowski, J. (1992). *Synching out loud. A journey into illness.* Brisbane, Australia: Griffith University.

Mienczakowski, J. (1994). Reading and writing research. *NADUE Journal, 18,* 45–54.

Mienczakowski, J. (1995). The theatre of ethnography: The reconstruction of ethnography into theatre with emancipatory potential. *Qualitative Inquiry, 1*(3), 360–375.

Mienczakowski, J. (2001). Ethnodrama: Performed research: Limitations and potential. In P. Atkinson, A. Coffey, S. Delamont, J. Lofland, & L. Lofland (Eds.), *Handbook of ethnography* (pp. 468–476). London: Sage.

Mienczakowski, J., & Morgan, S. (1993). *Busting: The challenge of the drought spirit.* Brisbane, Australia: Griffith University.

Mifflin, M. (1992). Performance art: What is it and where is it going? *Art News, 91*(4), 88–89.

Miller, L., & Pelias, R. (2001). *The green window: Proceedings of the Giant City conference on performative writing.* Carbondale: Southern Illinois University Press.

Miller, T., Kushner, T., & McAdams, D. A. (2002). *Body blows: Six performances.* Madison: University of Wisconsin Press.

Mohanty, S. P. (1989). Us and them: On the philosophical bases of political criticism. *Yale Journal of Criticism, 2*(2), 1–31.

Neumann, M. (1996). Collecting ourselves at the end of the century. In C. Ellis & A. P. Bochner (Eds.), *Composing ethnography: Alternative forms of qualitative writing* (pp. 172–198). Walnut Creek, CA: AltaMira.

Nudd, D. M. (1995). The postmodern heroine(s) of Lardo Weeping. *Text and Performance Quarterly, 15,* 24–43.

O'Brien, J. (1987). Performance as criticism: Discoveries and documentation through enactment. *Communication Studies, 40,* 189–201.

Paget, M. A. (1990). Performing the text. *Journal of Contemporary Ethnography, 19,* 136–155.

Paget, M. A. (1993). *A complex sorrow* (M. L. DeVault, Ed.). Philadelphia: Temple University Press.

Park-Fuller, L. (2003). Audiencing the audience: Playback theatre, performative writing, and social activism. *Text and Performance Quarterly, 23*(3), 288–310.

Park-Fuller, L., & Olsen, T. (1983). Understanding what we know: Yonnondio: From the thirties. *Literature in Performance, 4,* 65–77.

Pelias, R. (1999a). *Performance studies: The interpretation of aesthetic texts* (2nd ed.). Dubuque, IA: Kendall/Hunt.

Pelias, R. (1999b). *Writing performance: Poeticizing the researcher's body.* Carbondale: Southern Illinois University Press.

Pelias, R., & VanOosting, J. (1987). A paradigm for performance studies. *Quarterly Journal of Speech, 73,* 219–231.

Phelan, P. (1998). Introduction. In P. Phelan & J. Lane (Eds.), *The ends of performance* (pp. 1–19). New York: New York University Press.

Phelan, P., & Lane, J. (Eds.). (1998). *The ends of performance.* New York University Press.

Pineau, E. L. (1992). A mirror of her own: Anais Nin's autobiographical performances. *Text and Performance Quarterly, 12,* 97–112.

Pineau, E. L. (1995). Re-casting rehearsal: Making a case for production as research. *Journal of the Illinois Speech and Theatre Association, 46,* 43–52.

Pineau, E. L. (1998). Performance studies across the curriculum: Problems, possibilities, and projections. In S. J. Dailey (Ed.), *The future of performance studies: Visions and revisions* (pp. 128–135). Annandale, VA: National Communication Association.

Pineau, E. (2002). Critical performative pedagogy. In N. Stucky & C. Wimmer (Eds.), *Teaching performance studies* (pp. 41–54). Carbondale: Southern Illinois University Press.

Pollock, D. (1990). Telling the told: Performing *Like a family. Oral History Review, 18,* 1–36.

Pollock, D. (1998a). *Exceptional spaces: Essays in performance and history.* Chapel Hill: University of North Carolina Press.

Pollock, D. (Ed.). (1998b). Introduction. In *Exceptional spaces: Essays in performance and history* (pp. 1–45). Chapel Hill: University of North Carolina Press.

Pollock, D. (1998c). Performing writing. In P. Phelan & J. Lane (Eds.), *The ends of performance* (pp. 73–103). New York: New York University Press.

Pollock, D. (1998d). A response to Dwight Conquergood's essay "Beyond the text: Toward a performative cultural politics." In S. J. Dailey (Ed.), *The future of performance studies: Visions and revisions* (pp. 37–46). Annandale, VA: National Communication Association.

Reed-Danahay, D. E. (Ed.). (1997). *Auto/ethnography: Rewriting the self and the social.* New York: Berg.

Richardson, L. (1997). *Fields of play: Constructing an academic life.* New Brunswick, NJ: Rutgers University Press.

Richardson, L. (2000a). Evaluating ethnography. *Qualitative inquiry, 6*(2), 253–255.

Richardson, L. (2000b). Writing: A method of inquiry. In N. K. Denzin & Y. S. Lincoln (Eds.), *Handbook of qualitative research* (2nd ed., pp. 923–948). Thousand Oaks, CA: Sage.

Richardson, L., & Lockridge, E. (1991). The sea monster: An ethnographic drama. *Symbolic Interaction, 14,* 335–340.

Roach, J. (1993). *The player's passion: Studies in the science of acting.* Ann Arbor: University of Michigan Press.

Roach, J. (2002). Theatre studies/cultural studies/ performance studies: The three unities. In N. Stucky & C. Wimmer (Eds.), *Teaching performance studies* (pp. 33–40). Carbondale: Southern Illinois University Press.

Román, D. (1998). *Acts of intervention: Performance, gay culture, and AIDS.* Bloomington: Indiana University Press.

Rosaldo, R. (1989). *Culture and truth: The remaking of social analysis.* Boston: Beacon.

Salas, J. (1996). *Improvising real life: Personal story in playback theatre* (Rev. ed.). New Paltz, NY: Tusitala.

Samovar, L. A., & Porter, R. E. (1994). *Intercultural communication: A reader.* Belmont, CA: Wadsworth.

Schechner, R. (1965). *Rites and symbols of initiation.* New York: Harper.

Schechner, R. (1977). *Essays on performance theory, 1970–1976.* New York: Drama Book Specialists.

Schechner, R. (1985). *Between theater and anthropology.* Philadelphia: University of Pennsylvania Press.

Schechner, R. (1986). Magnitudes of performance. In V. M. Turner & E. M. Bruner (Eds.), *The anthropology of experience* (pp. 344–369). Urbana: University of Illinois Press.

Schechner, R. (1988). *Performance theory* (Rev. and exp. ed.). New York: Routledge.

Schneider, J. (2002). Reflexive/diffractive ethnography. *Cultural studies ↔ Critical Methodologies, 2,* 460–482.

Schutzman, M., & Cohen-Cruz, J. (Eds.). (1994). *Playing Boal: Theatre, therapy, activism.* New York: Routledge.

Searle, J. (1969). *Speech acts.* New York: Cambridge University Press.

Shor, I. (1992). *Culture wars: School and society in the conservative restoration.* Chicago: University of Chicago Press.

Siegel, T., & Conquergood, D. (Producers & Directors). (1985). *Between two worlds: The Hmong shaman in America* [Video documentary].

Siegel, T., & Conquergood, D. (Producers & Directors). (1990). *The heart broken in half* [Video documentary].

Singer, M. (1972). *When a great tradition modernizes: An anthropological approach to Indian civilization.* New York: Praeger.

Smith, A. D. (1993). *Fires in the mirror: Crown Heights, Brooklyn, and other identities.* Garden City, NY: Anchor.

Smith, A. D. (1994). *Twilight: Los Angeles, 1992.* Garden City, NY: Anchor.

Sparkes, A. C. (2002). Autoethnography: Self-indulgence or something more? In A. P. Bochner & C. Ellis. (Eds.), *Ethnographically speaking: Autoethnography, literature, and aesthetics* (pp. 209–232). Walnut Creek, CA: AltaMira.

Spradley, J. P., & McCurdy, D. W. (1972). *The cultural experience: Ethnography in complex society.* Prospect Heights, IL: Waveland.

Spry, T. (1997). Skins: A daughter's (re)construction of cancer: A performative autobiography. *Text and Performance Quarterly, 17,* 361–365.

Spry, T. (2001). Performing autoethnography: An embodied methodical praxis. *Qualitative Inquiry, 7,* 706–732.

Stern, C. S., & Henderson, B. (1993). *Performance: Texts and contexts.* New York: Longman.

Strine, M. S. (1998). Mapping the "cultural turn" in performance studies. In S. J. Dailey (Ed.), *The future of performance studies: Visions and revisions* (pp. 3–9). Annandale, VA: National Communication Association.

Strine, M., Long, B., & Hopkins, M. F. (1990). Research in interpretation and performance studies. In G. Phillips & J. Wood (Eds.), *Speech communication: Essays to commemorate the seventy-fifth anniversary of the Speech Communication Association* (pp. 181–204). Carbondale: Southern Illinois University Press.

Stucky, N., & Wimmer, C. (2002). *Teaching performance studies.* Carbondale: Southern Illinois University Press.

Supriya, K. E. (2001). Evocation of an enactment in *Apna Ghar:* Performing ethnographic self-reflexivity. *Text and Performance Quarterly, 21,* 225–246.

Taylor, J. (1987). Documenting performance knowledge: Two narrative techniques in Grace Paley's fiction. *Southern Speech Communication Journal, 53,* 67–79.

Tedlock, B. (2000). Ethnography and ethnographic representation. In N. K. Denzin & Y. S. Lincoln (Eds.), *Handbook of qualitative research* (2nd ed., pp. 455–486). Thousand Oaks, CA: Sage.

Tedlock, D. (1983). On the translation of style in oral narrative. In B. Swann (Ed.), *Smoothing the ground: Essays on Native American oral literature* (pp. 57–77). Berkeley: University of California Press.

Turner, V. (1974). *Dramas, fields, and metaphors: Symbolic action in human society.* Ithaca, NY: Cornell University Press.

Turner, V. (1980). Social dramas and stories about them. *Critical Inquiry, 7*(1), 141–168.

Turner, V. (1982). *From ritual to theatre.* New York: Performing Arts Journal Publications.

Turner, V. (1988). *The anthropology of performance.* New York: Performing Arts Journal Publications.

Turner, V., & Turner, E. (1982). Performing ethnography. *The Drama Review: A Journal of Performance Studies, 26,* 33–50.

Turner, V., & Turner, E. (1988). Performance ethnography. In V. Turner, *The anthropology of performance* (pp. 139–155). New York: Performing Arts Journal Publications.

Valentine, K. B. (1998). Ethical issues in the transcription of personal narrative. In S. J. Dailey (Ed.), *The future of performance studies: Visions and revisions* (pp. 221–225). Annandale, VA: National Communication Association.

Valentine, K. B., & Valentine, E. (1992). Performing culture through narration: A Gallegan storyteller. In E. Fine & J. H. Speer (Eds.), *Performance, culture, and identity* (pp. 181–205). New York: Praeger.

Van Erven, E. (1993). *The playful revolution: Theatre and liberation in Asia.* Bloomington: Indiana University Press.

Van Maanen, J. (1988). *Tales of the field: On writing ethnography.* Chicago: University of Chicago Press.

Van Maanen, J. (Ed.). (1995). *Representation in ethnography.* Thousand Oaks, CA: Sage.

Whisnant, D. (1983). *All that is native and fine: The politics of culture in an American region.* Chapel Hill: University of North Carolina Press.

Williams, R. (1989). Adult education and social change. In *What I came to say* (pp. 157–166). London: Hutchinson-Radus.

Wirth, J. (1994). *Interactive acting: Acting, improvisation, and interacting for audience participatory theatre*. Fall Creek, OR: Fall Creek Press.

Wolcott, H. F. (1999). *Ethnography: A way of seeing*. Walnut Creek, CA: AltaMira.

Wolf, S. (2002). *A problem like Maria: Gender and sexuality in the American musical*. Ann Arbor: University of Michigan Press.

Worley, D. (1998). Is critical performative pedagogy practical? In S. J. Dailey (Ed.), *The future of performance studies: Visions and revisions* (pp. 136–144). Annandale, VA: National Communication Association.

Yordon, J. (1989). *Roles in interpretation* (2nd ed.). Dubuque, IA: Wm. C. Brown.

4

QUALITATIVE CASE STUDIES

Robert E. Stake

C ase studies are a common way to do qualitative inquiry. Case study research is neither new nor essentially qualitative. Case study is not a methodological choice but a choice of what is to be studied. If case study research is more humane or in some ways transcendent, it is because the researchers are so, not because of the methods. By whatever methods, we choose to study *the case*. We could study it analytically or holistically, entirely by repeated measures or hermeneutically, organi- cally or culturally, and by mixed methods—but we concentrate, at least for the time being, on the case. The focus in this chapter is a qualitative concentration on the case.

The physician studies the child because the child is ill. The child's symptoms are both qualitative and quantitative. The physician's record of the child is more quantita- tive than qualitative. The social worker studies the child because the child is neglected. The symptoms of neglect are both qualitative and quantitative. The formal record that the social worker keeps is more qualitative than quantitative.[1] In many professional and practical fields, cases are studied and recorded. As a form of research, case study is defined by interest in an individual case, not by the methods of inquiry used.

A majority of researchers doing casework call their studies by some other name. Howard Becker, for example, when asked (Simons, 1980) what he called his own studies, reluctantly said, "Fieldwork," adding that such labels contribute little to the

---

Author's Note. This revision of my chapter in the 2000 second edition of the *Handbook* continues to draw heavily from papers on *What Is a Case?*, edited by Charles Ragin and Howard Becker (1992). Editorial review by Rita Davis, Norman Denzin, and Yvonna Lincoln is herewith acknowledged.

understanding of what researchers do. The name "case study" is emphasized by some of us because it draws attention to the question of what specially can be learned about the single case. That epistemological question is the driving question of this chapter: What can be learned about the single case? I will emphasize designing the study to optimize understanding of the case rather than to generalize beyond it.

For a research community, case study optimizes understanding by pursuing scholarly research questions. It gains credibility by thoroughly triangulating the descriptions and interpretations, not just in a single step but continuously throughout the period of study. For a qualitative research community, case study concentrates on experiential knowledge of the case and close attention to the influence of its social, political, and other contexts. For almost any audience, optimizing understanding of the case requires meticulous attention to its activities. These five requirements—issue choice, triangulation, experiential knowledge, contexts, and activities—will be discussed in this chapter.

◙ THE SINGULAR CASE

A case may be simple or complex. It may be a child or a classroom of children or an event, a happening, such as a mobilization of professionals to study a childhood condition. It is one among others. In any given study, we will concentrate on the one. The time we may spend concentrating our inquiry on the one may be long or short, but while we so concentrate, we are engaged in case study.

Custom has it that not everything is a case. A child may be a case, easy to specify. A doctor may be a case. But *his or her doctoring* probably lacks the specificity, the boundedness, to be called a case. As topics of inquiry, ethnomethodologists study *methods*, such as methods of doctoring, methods of cooking, examining how things get done, and the work and play of people (Garfinkel, 1967). Coming to understand a case usually requires extensive examining of how things get done, but the prime referent in case study is the case, not the methods by which the case operates. An Agency (e.g., nongovernmental organization) may be a case. But the *reasons* for child neglect or the *policies* of dealing with neglectful parents seldom will be considered a case. We think of those topics as generalities rather than specificities. The case is a specific One.[2]

If we are moved to study it, the case is almost certainly going to be a functioning body. The case is a "bounded system" (Flood, as reported in Fals Borda, 1998). In the social sciences and human services, most cases have working parts and purposes; many have a self. Functional or dysfunctional, rational or irrational, the case is a system.

It is common to recognize that certain features are within the system, within the boundaries of the case, and other features outside. In ways, the activity is patterned. Coherence and sequence are there to be found. Some outside features are significant as context. William Goode and Paul Hatt (1952) observed that it is not always easy for the case researcher to say where the child ends and where the environment begins. But boundedness and activity patterns nevertheless are useful concepts for specifying the case (Stake, 1988).

Ultimately, we may be interested in a general phenomenon or a population of cases more than in the individual case, and we cannot understand a given case without knowing about other cases. But while we are studying it, our meager resources are concentrated on trying to understand *its* complexities. Later in this chapter, we will talk about comparing two or more cases. We may simultaneously carry on more than one case study, but each case study is a concentrated inquiry into a single case.

Charles Ragin (1992) has emphasized the question of "What is it a case of?" as if "membership in" or "representation of" something else were the main consideration in case study. He referred to the casework of Michel Wieviorka (1988) on terrorism. Ragin and his coeditor, Howard Becker (1992), were writing for the social scientist seeking theoretical generalization, justifying the study of the particular only if it serves an understanding of grand issues or explanations. They recognized that even in formal experimentation and statistical survey work, there is interest in the illustrative or deviant case. But historians, program evaluators, institutional researchers, and practitioners in all professions are interested in the individual case without necessarily caring what it is a case of. This is intrinsic case study.

Even if my definition of the study of cases were agreed upon,[3] and it is not, the terms "case" and "study" defy full specification (Kemmis, 1980). A case study is both a process of inquiry about the case and the product of that inquiry. Lawrence Stenhouse (1984) advocated calling the product a "case record," and occasionally we shall, but the practice of calling the final report a "case study" is widely established.

Here and there, researchers will call anything they please a case study,[4] but the more the object of study is a specific, unique, bounded system, the greater the usefulness of the epistemological rationales described in this chapter.

To move beyond terminology to method, I introduce Figure 4.1, a sketch of a plan for a case study. This was an early plan made by a small team of early childhood education specialists led by Natalia Sofiy in the Ukraine. The case they chose was a boy in the Step by Step child-centered program for inclusion of children with disability in regular classrooms. They used Figure 4.1 to identify content and tasks, selecting three activities to be observed and noting several interviews needed. The researchers were deeply interested in the case but intended to use the report to illustrate their work throughout the country. With such further purpose, I call their research an *instrumental* case study.

Intrinsic and Instrumental Interest in Cases

I find it useful to identify three types of case study. I call a study an *intrinsic case study* if the study is undertaken because, first and last, one wants better understanding of this particular case. It is not undertaken primarily because the case represents

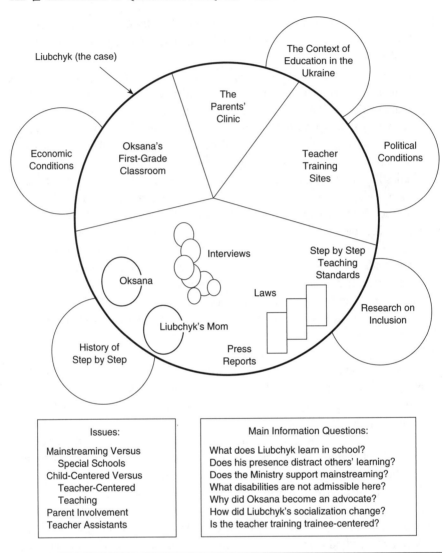

Figure 4.1.   Plan for the Ukraine Case Study

other cases or because it illustrates a particular trait or problem, but instead because, in all its particularity *and* ordinariness, this case itself is of interest. The researcher at least temporarily subordinates other curiosities so that the stories of those "living the case" will be teased out. The purpose is not to come to understand some abstract construct or generic phenomenon, such as literacy or teenage drug use or what a school principal does. The purpose is not theory building—though at other times the researcher may do just that. Study is undertaken because of an intrinsic interest in, for example, this particular child, clinic, conference, or curriculum. Books illustrating intrinsic case study include the following:

The Education of Henry Adams (1918), an autobiography,

God's Choice (1986) by Alan Peshkin,

Bread and Dreams (1982) by Barry MacDonald, Clem Adelman, Saville Kushner, and Rob Walker,[5]

An Aberdeenshire Village Propaganda (1889) by Robert Smith, and

The Swedish School System (1984) by Britta Stenholm.

I use the term *instrumental case study* if a particular case is examined mainly to provide insight into an issue or to redraw a generalization. The case is of secondary interest, it plays a supportive role, and it facilitates our understanding of something else. The case still is looked at in depth, its contexts scrutinized and its ordinary activities detailed, but all because this helps us pursue the external interest. The case may be seen as typical of other cases or not. (In a later section, I will discuss when typicality is important.) Here the choice of case is made to advance understanding of that other interest. We simultaneously have several interests, particular and general. There is no hard-and-fast line distinguishing intrinsic case study from instrumental, but rather a zone of combined purpose. Writings illustrating instrumental case study include the following:

"Campus Response to a Student Gunman" (1995) by Kelly Asmussen and John Creswell,

Boys in White (1961) by Howard Becker, Blanche Geer, Everett Hughes, and Anselm Strauss,

On the Border of Opportunity: Education, Community, and Language at the U.S.-Mexico Line (1998) by Marleen Pugach, and

"A Nonreader Becomes a Reader: A Case Study of Literacy Acquisition by a Severely Disabled Reader" (1994) by Sandra McCormick.

When there is even less interest in one particular case, a number of cases may be studied jointly in order to investigate a phenomenon, population, or general condition. I call this *multiple case study* or *collective case study.*[6] It is instrumental study extended to several cases. Individual cases in the collection may or may not be known in advance to manifest some common characteristic. They may be similar or dissimilar, with redundancy and variety each important. They are chosen because it is believed that understanding them will lead to better understanding, and perhaps better theorizing, about a still larger collection of cases. Illustrations of collective case study include the following:

Teachers' Work (1985) by Robert Connell,

"Researching Practice Settings" (of medical clinics) by Benjamin Crabtree and William Miller in their edited volume *Doing Qualitative Research* (1999),

Savage Inequalities (1991) by Jonathan Kozol,

Bold Ventures: Patterns Among U.S. Innovations in Science and Mathematics Education (1997) edited by Senta Raisin and Edward Britton, and

"The Dark Side of Organizations" (1999) by Diane Vaughan.

Reports and authors often do not fit neatly into the three categories. I see these three as useful for thinking about purpose. Alan Peshkin responded to my classification of his book *God's Choice* (1986) by saying "I mean to present my case so that it can be read with interest in the case itself, but I always have another agenda—to learn from the case about some class of things. Some of what that will be remains an emergent matter for a long time" (personal communication).

For this fine work, for 3 years Peshkin studied at a single school, Bethany Baptist Academy. Until the final chapter, he did not tell the reader about matters of importance to him, particularly unfair treatment of ethnic minorities. The first order of business was to understand the case. The immediate, if not ultimate, interest was intrinsic. The methods Peshkin used centered on the case, only later taking up his abiding concern for community, freedom, and survival.

Other typologies of case study have been offered. Harrison White (1992) categorized social science casework according to three purposes: case studies for identity, explanation, or control. Historians and political scientists regularly examine a singular episode or movement or era, such as Norman Gottwald (1979) did in his study of the emergence of Jewish identity. I choose to call these studies case studies when the episode or relationship—however complex, impacting, and bounded—is easily thought of as organic and systemic, heavy with purpose and self.

It is good to recognize that there is a common form of case study used in teaching to illustrate a point, a condition, a category—something important for instruction (Kennedy, 1979). For decades, professors in law schools and business schools have paraded cases in this manner. For staff development and management training, such reports constitute the articles of the *Journal of Case Research*, a key publication of the North American Case Research Association. Used for instruction and consultation, they come from pedagogically oriented instrumental case study.

Biography has its own history. William Tierney (2000) noted that, like case study, biography calls for special attention to chronological structures and to procedures for the protection of human subjects. Similarly, television documentaries, many of them easily classifiable as case studies, require their own methods. In law, the *case* has a special definition: The practice of law itself could be called case study. The work of ethnographers, critical theorists, institutional demographers, and many others has conceptual and stylistic patterns that not only amplify the taxonomy but also extend the foundation for case study research in the social sciences and social services. My purpose here in categorization is not taxonomic but to emphasize variation in concern for and methodological orientation to *the case*, thus focusing on three types: intrinsic, instrumental, and collective.

Seeking the Particular More Than the Ordinary

Case researchers seek out both what is common and what is particular about the case, but the end product of the research regularly portrays more of the uncommon (Stouffer, 1941), drawing all at once from

1. the nature of the case, particularly its activity and functioning;

2. its historical background;

3. its physical setting;

4. other contexts, such as economic, political, legal, and aesthetic;

5. other cases through which this case is recognized; and

6. those informants through whom the case can be known.

To study the case, to probe its particularity, qualitative case researchers gather data on all the above.

Case uniqueness traditionally has not been a choice ingredient of scientific theory. Case study research has been constrained even by qualitative methodologists, who grant less than full regard to study of the particular (Denzin, 1989; Glaser & Strauss, 1967; Herriott & Firestone, 1983; Yin, 1984). These and other social scientists have written about case study as if intrinsic study of a particular case were not as important as studies intended to obtain generalizations pertaining to a population of cases.[7] Some have emphasized case study as typification of other cases, as exploration leading up to generalization-producing studies, or as an occasional early step in theory building. At least as I see it, case study method has been too little honored as the intrinsic study of a valued particular, as it is in biography, institutional self-study, program evaluation, therapeutic practice, and many lines of work. In the 1994 first edition of this *Handbook*, I wrote, "insistence on the ultimacy of theory building appears to be diminishing in qualitative social science" (p. 238), but now I am not so sure.

Still, even intrinsic case study can be seen as a small step toward grand generalization (Campbell, 1975; Flyvbjerg, 2001; Vaughan, 1992), especially in a case that runs counter to a rule. But generalization should not be emphasized in all research (Feagin et al., 1991; Simons, 1980). Damage occurs when the commitment to generalize or to theorize runs so strong that the researcher's attention is drawn away from features important for understanding the case itself.[8] The case study researcher faces a strategic decision in deciding how much and how long the complexities of the case should be studied. Not everything about the case can be understood—so how much needs to be? Each researcher has choices to make.

Organizing Around Issues

A case study has (as has research of all kinds) some form of conceptual structure. Even an intrinsic case study is organized around a small number of research questions. Issues are not information questions, such as "Who initiated their advocacy of regional forestry planning?" or "How was their hiring policy announced?" The issues or themes are questions such as "In what ways did their changes in hiring policy require a change in performance standards?" or "Did the addiction therapy, originally developed for male clients, need reconceptualization for women?"

Issues are complex, situated, problematic relationships. They pull attention both to ordinary experience and also to the disciplines of knowledge, such as sociology, economics, ethics, or literary criticism. Seeking a different purview from that of most designers of experiments and testers of hypotheses, qualitative case researchers orient to complexities connecting ordinary practice in natural habitats to a few abstractions and concerns of the academic disciplines. This broader purview is applied to the single case, leaving it as the focus, yet generalization and proof (Becker, 1992) linger in the mind of the researcher. A tension exists.[9]

The two issues used as examples two paragraphs back were written for a particular case. A more general question would be "Does a change in hiring policy away from affirmative action require change in performance standards?" or "Does addiction therapy originally developed for male clients need reconceptualization for women?" Whether stated for generalization or for particularization, these organizing themes should serve to deepen understanding of the specific case.

Starting with a topical concern, researchers pose *foreshadowed problems*,[10] concentrate on issue-related observations, interpret patterns of data, and reform the issues as assertions. One transformation experienced in my work in program evaluation is illustrated in Figure 4.2, with an issue for a hypothetical case study of a music education program.

The selection of key issues is crucial. Researchers follow their preference for or obligation to intrinsic or instrumental study. They ask, "Which issue questions bring out our concerns? Which would be the dominant theme?" To maximize understanding of the case, they ask, "Which issues seek out compelling uniquenesses?" For an evaluation study, they ask, "Which issues help reveal merits and shortcomings?" Some researchers raise social justice issues (House & Howe, 1999). In general, they ask, "Which issues facilitate the planning and activities of inquiry?" Issues are chosen partly in terms of what can be learned within the opportunities for study. They will be chosen differently depending on the purpose of the study, and differently by different researchers. One might say a personal contract is drawn between researcher and

1. Topical Issue: The goals of the music education program.

2. Foreshadowed Problem: The majority of the community supports the present emphasis on band, chorus, and performances, but a few teachers and community leaders prefer a more intellectual emphasis, for example, history, literature, and critical review of music.

3. Issue Under Development: What are the pros and cons of having this teaching staff teach music theory and music as a discipline in courses required of everyone?

4. Assertion: As a whole, this community was opposed to providing the extra funding required to provide intellectually based school music.

Figure 4.2.   An Example of Issue Evolution in a Study

phenomenon. Researchers ask, "What can be learned *here* that a reader needs to know?"

The issues used to organize the study may or may not be the ones used to report the case to others. Some cases will be structured by need for information, raising little debate. For example, what led to the change in operating policy? or "Has performance quality been dropping?" Issues often serve to draw attention to important functioning of the case in a situation of stress, as well as to tease out more of its interaction with contexts.

Contexts

The case to be studied is a complex entity located in a milieu or situation embedded in a number of contexts or backgrounds. Historical context is almost always of interest, but so are cultural and physical contexts. Other contexts often of interest are the social, economic, political, ethical, and aesthetic.

The case is singular, but it has subsections (e.g., production, marketing, sales departments), groups (e.g., patients, nurses, administrators), occasions (e.g., work days, holidays, days near holidays), dimensions, and domains—many so well-populated that they need to be sampled. Each of these may have its own contexts, and the contexts may go a long way toward making relationships understandable. Qualitative case study calls for the examination of these complexities. Yvonna Lincoln and Egon Guba (2000) pointed out that much qualitative research is based on a view that social phenomena, human dilemmas, and the nature of cases are situational, revealing experiential happenings of many kinds.

Qualitative researchers sometimes are oriented toward *causal explanation* of events (Becker, 1992) but more often tend to perceive events as Tolstoy did in *War and Peace*—multiply sequenced, multiply contextual, and coincidental more than causal. Many find the search for cause as simplistic. They describe instead the sequence and coincidence of events, interrelated and contextually bound, purposive but questionably determinative. They favor inquiry designs for describing the diverse activities of the case. Doing case studies does not require examination of diverse issues and contexts, but that is the way that most qualitative researchers do them.

▣ THE STUDY

Perhaps the simplest rule for method in qualitative casework is this: "Place your best intellect into the thick of what is going on." The brainwork ostensibly is observational, but more critically, it is *reflective*.[11] In being ever-reflective, the researcher is committed to pondering the impressions, deliberating on recollections and records—but not necessarily following the conceptualizations of theorists, actors, or audiences (Carr & Kemmis, 1986). Local meanings are important, foreshadowed meanings are important, and readers' consequential meanings are important. In Figure 4.1, activities in the first-grade classrooms, parents' clinic, and teacher training sites are to be described and interpreted. The case researcher digs into meanings, working to relate them to contexts and experience. In each instance, the work is reflective.[12]

If we typify qualitative casework, we see data sometimes precoded but continuously interpreted, on first encounter and again and again. Records and tabulations are perused not only for classification and pattern recognition but also for "criss-crossed" reflection (Spiro, Vispoel, Schmitz, Samarapungavan, & Boerger, 1987). An observation is interpreted against one issue, perspective, or utility, then interpreted against others. Qualitative case study is characterized by researchers spending extended time on site, personally in contact with activities and operations of the case, reflecting, and revising descriptions and meanings of what is going on. Naturalistic, ethnographic, phenomenological caseworkers seek to see what is natural in happenings, in settings, in expressions of value.

Reflecting upon case literature, I find case study methods written about largely by people who hold that the research should contribute to scientific generalization. The bulk of case study work, however, is done by people who have *intrinsic* interest in the case. Their intrinsic case study designs draw these researchers toward understandings of what is important about that case within its own world, which is not the same as the world of researchers and theorists. Intrinsic designs aim to develop what is perceived to be the case's own issues, contexts, and interpretations, its "thick description." In contrast, the methods of instrumental case study draw the researcher toward illustrating how the concerns of researchers and theorists are manifest in the case. Because the critical issues are more likely to be known in advance and to follow disciplinary expectations, such a design can take greater advantage of already-developed instruments and preconceived coding schemes.[13]

In intrinsic case study, researchers do not avoid generalization—they cannot. Certainly, they generalize to happenings of their case at times still to come and in other situations. They expect their readers to comprehend their interpretations but to arrive, as well, at their own. Thus, the methods for case work actually used are to learn enough about the case to encapsulate complex meanings into a finite report but to describe the case in sufficient descriptive narrative so that readers can experience these happenings vicariously and draw their own conclusions.

Case Selection

Perhaps the most unusual aspect of case study in the social sciences and human services is the selection of cases to study. Intrinsic casework regularly begins with cases already identified. The doctor, the social worker, and the program evaluator receive their cases; they seldom choose them. The cases are of prominent interest before formal study begins. Instrumental and collective casework regularly requires cases to be chosen. Achieving the greatest understanding of the critical phenomena depends on choosing the case well (Patton, 1990; Vaughan, 1992; Yin, 1989). Suppose we are trying to understand the behavior of people who take hostages and we decide to probe the phenomenon using a case study. Hostage taking does not happen often; in the entire world, there are few cases to choose. Current options, let us imagine, boil down to a bank robber, an airline hijacker, an estranged father who kidnapped his own child, and a Shiite Muslim group. We want to generalize about hostage-taking behavior, yet we realize that each of these cases, each sample of one, weakly *represents* the larger group of interest.

When one designs a study in the manner advocated by Michael Huberman and Matthew Miles (1994) and Gery Ryan and Russell Bernard (2000) in the second edition of the *Handbook*, nothing is more important than making a representative selection of cases. For this design, formal sampling is needed. The cases are expected to represent some population of cases. The phenomenon of interest observable in the case represents the phenomenon writ large. For Miles and Huberman, Yin, and Malinowski, the main work was science, an enterprise to achieve the best possible explanations of phenomena (von Wright, 1971). In the beginning, phenomena are given; the cases are opportunities to study the phenomena. But even in the larger collective case studies, the sample size usually is much too small to warrant random selection. For qualitative fieldwork, we draw a purposive sample, building in variety and acknowledging opportunities for intensive study.[14]

The phenomenon on the table is hostage taking. We want to improve our understanding of hostage taking, to fit it into what we know about criminology, conflict resolution, human relations—that is, various *abstract dimensions*.[15] We recognize a large population of hypothetical cases and a small subpopulation of accessible cases. We want to generalize about hostage taking without special interest in any of those cases available for study. On representational grounds, the epistemological opportunity seems small, but we are optimistic that we can learn some important things from almost any case. We choose one case or a small number of exemplars. Hostages usually are strangers who happen to be available to the hostage taker. We might rule out studying a father who takes his own child as hostage. Such kidnappings actually may be more common, but we rule out the father. We are more interested in hostage taking accompanying a criminal act, hostage taking in order to escape. The researcher examines various interests in the phenomenon, selecting a case of some typicality but leaning toward those cases that seem to offer *opportunity to learn.* My choice would be to choose that case from which we feel we can learn the most.[16] That may mean taking the one most accessible or the one we can spend the most time with. Potential for learning is a different and sometimes superior criterion to representativeness. Sometimes it is better to learn a lot from an atypical case than a little from a seemingly typical case.

Another illustration: Suppose we are interested in the attractiveness of interactive (the visitor manipulates, gets feedback) displays in children's museums. We have resources to study four museums, to do a collective study of four cases. It is likely that we would set up a typology, perhaps of (a) museum types, namely art, science, and history; (b) city types, namely large and very large; and (c) program types, namely exhibitory and participative. With this typology, we could create a matrix of 12 cells. Examples probably cannot be found for all 12 cells, but resources do not allow studying 12 anyway. With four to be studied, we are likely to start out thinking we should have one art, one history, and two science museums (because interactive displays are more common in science museums); two located in large; and two in very large cities; and two each of the program types. But when we look at existing cases, the logistics, the potential reception, the resources, and additional characteristics of relevance, we move toward choosing four museums to study that offer variety (falling short of structured representation) across the attributes, the four that give us the best opportunities to learn about interactive displays.[17] Any best possible selection of four museums from a balanced design would not give us compelling representation of museums as a whole, and certainly not a statistical basis for generalizing about interactions between interactivity and site characteristics. Several desirable types usually have to be omitted. Even for collective case studies, selection by sampling of attributes should not be the highest priority. Balance and variety are important; opportunity to learn is often more important.

The same process of selection will occur as part of intrinsic case study. Even though the case is decided in advance (usually), there are subsequent choices to make about persons, places, and events to observe. They are *cases within the case*—embedded cases or mini-cases. In Figure 4.1, two mini-cases were anticipated, one of the teacher Oksana and one of Liubchyk's mother. Later, a third mini-case was added, that of a clinic created by parents. Here again, training, experience, and intuition help us to make a good selection. The Step by Step early childhood program in the Ukraine (Figure 4.1) aimed to get children with disability ready for the regular classroom, avoiding segregated special education, the usual assignment.[18] The sponsors chose to study a child in the school with the most developed activity. Selecting the child was influenced largely by the activity of his parents, two teachers, a social worker, and the principal. With time short, the researchers needed to select other parents, teachers, and community leaders to interview. Which of them would add most to the portrayal?

Or suppose that we are studying a program for placing computers in the homes of fourth graders for scholastic purposes. The cases—that is, the school sites—already have been selected. Although there is a certain coordination of activity, each participating researcher has one case study to develop. A principal issue has to do with impact on the family, because certain expectations of computer use accompany placement in the home. (The computer should be available for word processing, record keeping, and games by family members, but certain times should be set aside for fourth-grade homework.) At one site, 50 homes now have computers. The researcher can get certain information from every home, but the budget allows observation in only a small number of homes. Which homes should be selected? Just as in the collective case study, the researcher notes attributes of interest, among them perhaps gender of the fourth grader, presence of siblings, family structure, home discipline, previous use of computers, and other technology in the home. The researcher discusses these characteristics with informants, gets recommendations, visits several homes, and obtains attribute data. The choice is made, ensuring variety but not necessarily representativeness, without strong argument for typicality, again weighted by considerations of access and even by hospitality, for the time is short and perhaps too little can be learned from inhospitable parents. Here, too, the primary criterion is opportunity to learn.

Interactivity

Usually we want to learn what the selected case does—its activity, its functioning. We will observe what we can, ask others for their observations, and gather artifacts of that functioning. For example, the department being studied provides services, manages itself and responds to management by external authorities, observes rules, adapts to constraints, seeks opportunities, and changes staffing. Describing and interpreting these activities constitutes a large part of many case studies.

These activities are expected to be influenced by contexts, so contexts need to be described, even if evidence of influence is not found. Staffing, for example, may be affected by the political context, particularly union activity and some form of "old boy network." Public announcement of services may be affected by historical and physical contexts. Budgets have an economic context. Qualitative researchers have strong expectations that the reality perceived by people inside and outside the case will be social, cultural, situational, and contextual—and they want the interactivity of functions and contexts as well described as possible.

Quantitative researchers study the differences among main effects, such as the different influences of rural and urban settings and the different performances of boys and girls, comparing subpopulations. Demographics and gender are common "main effects." Programmatic treatment is another common main effect, with researchers comparing subsequent performance of those receiving different kinds or levels of treatment. Even if all possible comparisons are made, some performance differences remain unexplained. A typical treatment might be personally accommodated work conditions. Suppose urban females respond differently to such a treatment. This would show up in the analysis of variance as an interaction effect. And suppose a particular city girl, Carmen, consistently responds differently from other city girls. Her pattern of behavior is unlikely to be discerned by quantitative analysis but may be spotted easily by case study. And on further analysis, her pattern of behavior may be useful for the interpretation of the functioning of several subgroups. As cases respond differently to complex situations, the interactivity of main effects and settings can be expected to require the particularistic scrutiny of case study.[19]

Data Gathering

Naturalistic, ethnographic, phenomenological caseworkers also seek what is *ordinary* in happenings, in settings, in expressions of value. Herbert Blumer (1969, p. 149) called for us to accept, develop, and use the distinctive expression (of the particular case) in order to detect and study the common. What details of life the researchers are unable to see for themselves is obtained by interviewing people who did see them or by finding documents recording them. Part IV of the *Handbook* deals extensively with the methods of qualitative research, particularly observation, interview, coding, data management, and interpretation. These pertain, of course, to qualitative case study.

Documenting the unusual and the ordinary takes lots of time—for planning, gaining access, data gathering, analysis, and write-up. In many studies, there are no clear stages: Issue development continues to the end of the study, and write-up begins with preliminary observations. A speculative, page-allocating outline for the report helps anticipate how issues will be handled and how the case will become visible. For many researchers, to set out upon an unstructured, open-ended study is a calamity in the making. A plan is essential, but the caseworker needs to anticipate the need to recognize and develop late-emerging issues. Many qualitative fieldworkers invest little in instrument construction, partly because tailored (not standardized) questions are needed for most data sources. The budget may be consumed quickly by devising and field-testing instruments to pursue what turns out to be too many foreshadowing questions, with some of them maturing, some dying, and some moving to new levels of complexity. Even the ordinary is too complicated to be mastered in the time available.

When the case is too large for one researcher to know well or for a collective case study, *teaming* is an important option. Case research requires integrated, holistic comprehension of the case, but in the larger studies, no one individual can handle the complexity. Coding can be a great help, if the team is experienced in the process and with each other. But learning a detailed analytic coding system within the study period often is too great a burden (L. M. Smith & Dwyer, 1979), reducing observations to simple categories, eating up the on-site time. Often sites, key groups or actors, and issues should be assigned to a single team member, including junior members. The case's parts to be studied and the research issues need to be pared down to what can be comprehended by the collection of team members. It is better to negotiate the parts to be studied, as well as the parts not, and to do an in-depth study of a few key issues. Each team member writes up his or her parts; other team members need to read and critique these write-ups. Usually, the team leader needs to write the synthesis, getting critiques from the team, data sources, and selected skeptical friends.

Triangulation

With reporting and reading both "ill-structured" and "socially constructed," it is not surprising to find researcher tolerance for ambiguity and championing of multiple perspectives. Still, I have yet to meet case researchers unconcerned about clarity of their own perception and validity of their own communication. Even if meanings do not transfer intact but instead squeeze into the conceptual space of the reader, there is no less urgency for researchers to assure that their sense of situation, observation, reporting, and reading stay within some limits of correspondence. However accuracy is construed, researchers don't want to be inaccurate, caught without confirmation. Counterintuitive though it may be, the author has some responsibility for the validity of the readers' interpretations (Messick, 1989). Joseph Maxwell (1992) has spoken of the need for thinking of validity separately for descriptions, interpretations, theories, generalizations, and evaluative judgments.

To reduce the likelihood of misinterpretation, various procedures are employed, two of the most common being redundancy of data gathering and procedural challenges to explanations (Denzin, 1989; Goetz & LeCompte, 1984). For qualitative casework, these procedures generally are called *triangulation*.[20] Triangulation has been generally considered a process of using multiple perceptions to clarify meaning, verifying the repeatability of an observation or interpretation.[21]

But acknowledging that no observations or interpretations are perfectly repeatable,[22] triangulation serves also to clarify meaning by identifying different ways the case is being seen (Flick, 1998; Silverman, 1993). The qualitative researcher is interested in diversity of perception, even the multiple realities within which people live. Triangulation helps to identify different realities.

▣ LEARNING FROM THE PARTICULAR CASE

The researcher is a teacher using at least two pedagogical methods (Eisner, 1985). Teaching *didactically*, the researcher teaches what he or she has learned. Arranging for what educationists call *discovery learning*, the researcher provides material for readers to learn, on their own, especially things about which readers may know better than the researcher.

What can one learn from a single case? David Hamilton (1980), Stephen Kemmis (1980), Lawrence Stenhouse (1979), and Robert Yin (1989) are among those who have advanced the epistemology of the particular.[23] Even Donald Campbell (1975), the prophet of scientific generalization, contributed. How we learn from the singular case is related to how the case is like and unlike other cases we do know, mostly by comparison.[24] It is intuition that persuades both researcher and reader that what is known about one case may very well be true about a similar case (Smith, 1978).

Experiential Knowledge

From case reports, we convey and draw forth the essence of qualitative understanding—that is, experiential knowledge (Geertz, 1983; Polanyi, 1962; Rumelhart & Ortony, 1977; von Wright, 1971). Case study facilitates the conveying of experience of actors and stakeholders as well as the experience of studying the case. It can enhance the reader's experience with the case. It does this largely with narratives and situational descriptions of case activity, personal relationship, and group interpretation.

Experiential descriptions and assertions are relatively easily assimilated by readers into memory and use. When the researcher's narrative provides opportunity for *vicarious experience*, readers extend their perceptions of happenings. Naturalistic, ethnographic case materials, at least to some extent, parallel actual experience, feeding into the most fundamental processes of awareness and understanding. Deborah Trumbull and I called these processes *naturalistic generalization* (Stake & Trumbull, 1982). That is, people make some generalizations entirely from personal or vicarious experience. Enduring meanings come from encounter, and they are modified and reinforced by repeated encounter.

In ordinary living, this occurs seldom to the individual alone and more often in the presence of others. In a social process, together people bend, spin, consolidate, and enrich their understandings. We come to know what has happened partly in terms of what others reveal as their experience. The case researcher emerges from one social experience, the observation, to choreograph another, the report. Knowledge is socially constructed—or so we constructivists believe (see Schwandt, 2000)—and through their experiential and contextual accounts, case study researchers assist readers in the construction of knowledge.

Case researchers greatly rely on subjective data, such as the testimony of participants and the judgments of witnesses. Many critical observations and interview data are subjective. Most case study is the empirical study of human activity. The major questions are not questions of opinion or feeling, but of the sensory experience. And the answers come back, of course, with description and interpretation, opinion and feeling, all mixed together. When the researchers are not there to experience the activity for themselves, they have to ask those who did experience it. To make empirical data more objective and less subjective, the researcher uses replicative, falsification, and triangulating methods. Good case study research follows disciplined practices of analysis and triangulation to tease out what deserves to be called experiential knowledge from what is opinion and preference (Stake, 2004).

Understanding the case as personal experience depends on whether or not it can be embraced intellectually by a single researcher (or a small case study team). When the case is something like a person or a small Agency or a legislative session, a researcher who is given enough time and access can become personally knowledgeable about the activities and spaces, the relationships and contexts, of the case, as modeled in Figure 4.1. Possibly with the help of a few others, he or she can become experientially acquainted with the case. The case then is *embraceable*. Through observation, enumeration, and talk, the researcher can personally come to perceive the nature of the case. When the researcher can see and inquire about the case personally, with or without scales and rubrics, that researcher can come to understand the case in the most expected and respected ways. But when the researcher finds the case obscured, extending into too-distant regions or beyond his or her comprehension, and thus beyond personal encounter, that researcher conceptualizes the case differently. The case is likely to become overly abstract, a construct of criteria. Whether or not they want to, researchers then depersonalize the assignment, rely more on instruments and protocols, and accept simplistic reporting from people who themselves lack direct personal experience. Even if the researcher has extensive personal contact with parts of the case, that contact fails to reach too many extremities and complexities. This is a case beyond personal embrace, beyond experiential knowing.

Knowledge Transfer From Researcher to Reader

Both researcher and reader bring their conceptual structures to a case. In the literature, these structures have been called many things, including *advanced organizers* (Ausubel & Fitzgerald, 1961), *schemata* (Anderson, 1977), and an *unfolding of realization* (Bohm, 1985). Some such frameworks for thought are unconscious. Communication is facilitated by carefully crafted structures. Thought itself, conversation surely, and writing especially draw phrases into paragraphs and append labels onto constructs. Meanings aggregate or attenuate. Associations become relationships; relationships become theory (Robinson, 1951). Generalization can be an unconscious process for both researcher and reader.

In private and personal ways, ideas are structured, highlighted, subordinated, connected, embedded *in* contexts, embedded *with* illustration, and laced with favor and doubt. However moved to share ideas case researchers might be, however clever and elaborated their writings, they will, like others, pass along to readers some of their personal meanings of events and relationships—and fail to pass along others. They know that readers, too, will add and subtract, invent and shape—reconstructing the knowledge in ways that leave it differently connected and more likely to be personally useful.

A researcher's knowledge of the case faces hazardous passage from writing to reading. The writer seeks ways of safeguarding the trip. As reading begins, the case slowly joins the company of cases previously known to the reader. Conceptually for the reader, the new case cannot be but some variation of cases already known. A new case without commonality cannot be understood, yet a new case without distinction will not be noticed. Researchers cannot know well which cases their readers already know or their readers' peculiarities of mind. They seek ways to protect and substantiate the transfer of knowledge.

Qualitative researchers recognize a need to accommodate the readers' preexisting knowledge. Although everyone deals with this need every day and draws upon a lifetime of experience, we know precious little about how new experience merges with old. According to Rand Spiro and colleagues (1987), most personal experience is *ill-structured*, neither pedagogically nor epistemologically neat. It follows that a well-structured, propositional presentation often will not be the better way to *transfer* experiential knowledge. The reader has a certain *cognitive flexibility*, the readiness to assemble a situation-relative schema from the knowledge fragments of a new encounter. The Spiro group (1987) contended that

> the best way to learn and instruct in order to attain the goal of cognitive flexibility in knowledge representation for future application is by a method of case-based presentations which treats a content domain as a landscape that is explored by "criss-crossing" it in many directions, by reexamining each case "site" in the varying contexts of different neighboring cases, and by using a variety of abstract dimensions for comparing cases. (p. 178)

Knowledge transfer remains difficult to understand. Even less understood is how a small aspect of the case may be found by many readers to modify an existing understanding about cases in general, even when the case is not typical.[25] In a ghetto school (Stake, 1995), I observed a teacher with *one* set of rules for classroom decorum— except that for Adam, a nearly expelled, indomitable youngster, a more liberal set had to be continuously invented. Reading my account, teachers from very different schools agreed with two seemingly contradictory statements: "Yes, you have to be strict with the rules" and "Yes, sometimes you have to bend the rules." They recognized in the report an unusual but generalizable circumstance. People find in case reports certain insights into the human condition, even while being well aware of the atypicality of the case. They may be *too* quick to accept the insight. The case researcher needs to provide grounds for validating both the observation and the generalization.

▣ STORYTELLING[26]

Some say we should just let the case "tell its own story" (Carter, 1993; Coles, 1989). The story a case tells of itself may or may not be useful. The researcher should draw out such stories, partly by explaining issues and by referring to other stories, but it is risky to leave it to the case actors to select the stories to be conveyed. Is the purpose to convey the storyteller's perception or to develop the researcher's perception of the case? Given expectations of the client, other stakeholders, and readers, either emphasis may be more appropriate. One cannot know at the outset what issues, perceptions, or theory will be useful. Case researchers usually enter the scene expecting, even knowing, that certain events, problems, and relationships will be important; yet they discover that some of them, this time, will be of little consequence (Parlett & Hamilton, 1976; L. M. Smith, 1994). Case content evolves even in the last phases of writing.

Even when empathic and respectful of each person's realities, the researcher decides what the case's "own story" is, or at least what will be included in the report. More will be pursued than was volunteered, and less will be reported than was learned. Even though the competent researcher will be guided by what the case indicates is most important, and even though patrons and other researchers will advise, that which is necessary for an understanding of the case will be decided by the researcher.[27] It may be the case's own story, but the report will be the researcher's dressing of the case's own story. This is not to dismiss the aim of finding the story that best represents the case, but instead to remind the reader that, usually, criteria of representation ultimately are decided by the researcher.

Many a researcher would like to tell the whole story but of course cannot; the whole story exceeds anyone's knowing and anyone's telling. Even those inclined to tell all find strong the obligation to winnow and consolidate. The qualitative researcher, like the single-issue researcher, must choose between telling lots and telling little. John van Maanen (1988) identified seven choices of presentation: realistic, impressionistic, confessional, critical, formal, literary, and jointly told. He added criteria for selecting the content. Some criteria are set by funding agencies, prospective readers, rhetorical convention, the researcher's career pattern, or the prospect of publication. Some criteria are set by a notion of what represents the case most fully, most appreciably for the hospitality received, or most comprehensibly. These are subjective choices not unlike those that all researchers make in choosing what to study. Some are made while designing the case study, but some continue to be made throughout the study and until the final hours.

Reporting a case seldom takes the traditional form of telling a story: introduction of characters followed by the revelation and resolution of problems. Many sponsors of research and many a researcher want a report that looks like traditional social science, running from statement of problem to review of literature, data collection, analysis, and conclusions. The case can be portrayed in many ways.

Many researchers, early in a study, try to form an idea of what the final report might look like. In Figure 4.3, the topics of 16 sections of an anticipated 45-page report have been sequenced in the left column, with guesses of page limits provided for each. This is the plan of the researchers from the Ukraine, Natalia Sofiy and Svitlana Efimova, with Liubchyk as their case. Liubchyk would have been sent to a special school for children of disability, but thanks to a diligent mother and an inclusion-oriented principal, he was "mainstreamed" in Mrs. Oxama's regular kindergarten. Strategically, Liubchyk is used as a pivot for examining the recent mainstreaming

Issues appearing

insertions	topic sections	pages	pages of context	questionnaire info	inclusion	teacher training	child-centered educ.	democratic play	program sustainability	choice vs. standard	minor topics	quotes, impressions
D, C, 3	Liubchyk	5		X		X					1. Teacher selection	A. Black today, green tommorrow
F, 1	Oksana	3	1	X	X	X			X		2. child protection	B. Director not bureaucrat
4	Tchr tng, Lviv	3	1	X	X	X					3. child view of disability	C. L's view of time & mgmt
	Press conf, Lviv	2		X			X				4. tchr view of disability	D. Body contact
	Tchr tng, Kiev	2			X						5. nature of disability	E. tchr staffing or potholes
	Tchr tng, Ukr.	2	2	X	X						6. role of church	F. Oksana's activity centers
3	Liubchyk	3		X	X						7. teacher unions	G. parents voted support
	His parents	2		X	X						8. European Union TACIS	H. psycholog'l assessment
	Parent Org's	2	2	X							9. Chernobyl effects	I. aggression, affection
B, 9	LEA, Lviv	3	1								10. special ed alternatives	
	Ministry	2	2	X		X	X				11. preparing parents	
2, 8	SbS Ukraine	2	2	X		X	X		X			
10	Interpretation: Alt. ed. policy	4				X						
	Interpretation: Teacher training	4		X		X						
E, 5	Interpretation: Inclusion	4			X							
A	Liubchyk	2		X								
		45	11									

Figure 4.3. Plan for Assembling the Ukraine Final Report

thrust in the Ukraine. As seen in column headings, the most important issue was inclusion, followed by teacher training and child-centered education, then three other concerns. Where these issues may be developed in the report is predicted in the figure. In the last two columns, the researchers listed singular moments and quotations for placement in the sections. By forecasting the order and size of the parts of the story, one can lessen the chances of gathering much too much of any kind of data.

Comparisons

A researcher will report his or her case as a case, knowing it will be compared to others. Researchers differ as to how much they set up comparative cases and acknowledge the reader's own cases. Most naturalistic, ethnographic, phenomenological researchers will concentrate on describing the present case in sufficient detail so that the reader can make good comparisons. Sometimes the researcher will point out comparisons that might be made. Many quantitative and evaluation case researchers will try to provide some comparisons, sometimes by presenting one or more reference cases, sometimes providing statistical norms for reference groups from which a hypothetical reference case can be imagined. Both the quantitative and the qualitative approaches provide narrow grounds for strict comparison of cases, even though a tradition of grand comparison exists within comparative anthropology and related disciplines (Ragin, 1987; Sjoberg, Williams, Vaughan, & Sjoberg, 1991; Tobin, 1989).

I see formally designed comparison as actually competing with learning about and from the particular case. Comparison is a grand epistemological strategy, a powerful conceptual mechanism, fixing attention upon one or a few attributes. Thus, it obscures any case knowledge that fails to facilitate comparison. Comparative description is the opposite of what Geertz (1973) called "thick description." Thick description of the music program, for example, might include conflicting perceptions of the staffing, recent program changes, the charisma of the choral director, the working relationship with a church organist, faculty interest in a critical vote of the school board, and the lack of student interest in taking up the clarinet. In these particularities lie the vitality, trauma, and uniqueness of the case. Comparison might be made on any of these characteristics but tends to be made on more general variables traditionally noted in the organization of music programs (e.g., repertoire, staffing, budget, tour policy). With concentration on the bases for comparison, uniquenesses and complexities will be glossed over. A research design featuring comparison substitutes (a) *the comparison* for (b) *the case* as the focus of the study.

Regardless of the type of case study—intrinsic, instrumental, or collective—readers often learn little from control or reference cases chosen only for comparison. When there are multiple cases of intrinsic interest, then of course it can be useful to compare them.[28] But often, there is but one case of intrinsic interest, if any at all. Readers with intrinsic interest in the case learn more about it directly from the description; they do not ignore comparisons with other cases but also do not concentrate on comparisons. Readers examining instrumental case studies are shown how the phenomenon exists within particular cases. As to reliability, differences between measures, such as how much the group changed, are fundamentally more unreliable than simple measurements. Similarly, conclusions about measured differences between any two cases are less to be trusted than are conclusions about a single case. Nevertheless, illustration of how a phenomenon occurs in the circumstances of several exemplars can provide valued and trustworthy knowledge.

Many are the ways of conceptualizing cases to maximize learning from a case. The case is expected to be something that functions, that operates; the study is the observation of operations (Kemmis, 1980). There is something to be described and interpreted. The conceptions of most naturalistic, holistic, ethnographic, phenomenological case studies need accurate description and subjective, yet disciplined, interpretation; a respect for and curiosity about culturally different perceptions of phenomena; and empathic representation of local settings—all blending (perhaps clumped) within a constructivist epistemology.

▣ ETHICS

Ethical considerations for qualitative research are reviewed by Clifford Christians in Chapter 6 of this *Handbook* (and elsewhere by authors such as Coles, 1997, and Graue and Walsh, 1998). Case studies often deal with matters that are of public interest but for which there is neither public nor scholarly *right to know*. Funding, scholarly intent, or Institutional Review Board authorization does not constitute license to invade the privacy of others. The value of the best research is not likely to outweigh injury to a person exposed. Qualitative researchers are guests in the private spaces of the world. Their manners should be good and their code of ethics strict.

Along with much qualitative work, case study research shares an intense interest in personal views and circumstances. Those whose lives and expressions are portrayed risk exposure and embarrassment, as well as loss of standing, employment, and self-esteem. Something of a contract exists between researcher and the researched:[29] a disclosing and protective covenant, usually informal but best not silent, a moral obligation (Schwandt, 1993). Risks to well-being cannot be inventoried but should be exemplified. Issues of observation and reportage should be discussed in advance. Limits to access should be suggested and agreements heeded. It is important (but never sufficient) for targeted persons to receive drafts of the write-up revealing how they are presented, quoted, and interpreted; the researcher should listen well to these persons' responses for signs of concern. It is important that great caution be exercised to minimize risks to participants in the case. Even with good advance information from the researcher about the study, the researched cannot be expected to protect themselves against the risks inherent in participation. Rules for protection of human subjects should be followed (yet protested when they serve little more than to protect the researcher's institution from litigation). The researcher should go beyond those rules, avoid low-priority probing of sensitive issues, and draw in advisers and reviewers to help extend the protective system.

Ethical problems arise (both inside and outside the research topics) with nondisclosure of malfeasance and immorality. When rules for a study are set that prevent the researcher from "whistle-blowing" or the exercise of compassion, a problem exists. Where an expectation has been raised that propriety is being examined and no mention is made of a serious impropriety that has been observed, the report is deceptive. Breach of ethics is seldom a simple matter; often, it occurs when two contradictory standards apply, such as withholding full disclosure (as per the contract) in order to protect a good but vulnerable agency (Mabry, 1999). Ongoing and summative review procedures are needed, with impetus from the researcher's conscience, from stakeholders, and from the research community.

▣ SUMMARY

Major conceptual responsibilities of the qualitative case researcher include the following:

a. Bounding the case, conceptualizing the object of study;
b. Selecting phenomena, themes, or issues (i.e., the research questions to emphasize);
c. Seeking patterns of data to develop the issues;
d. Triangulating key observations and bases for interpretation;
e. Selecting alternative interpretations to pursue; and
f. Developing assertions or generalizations about the case.

Except for (a), the steps are similar to those of other qualitative researchers. The more intrinsic the interest of the researcher in the case, the more the focus of study will be on the case's idiosyncrasy, its particular context, issues, and story. Some major stylistic options for case researchers are the following:

a. How much to make the report a story,
b. How much to compare with other cases,
c. How much to formalize generalizations or leave such generalizing to readers,
d. How much description of the researcher to include in the report, and
e. Whether or not and how much to protect anonymity.

Case study is a part of scientific methodology, but its purpose is not limited to the advance of science. Populations of cases can be represented poorly by single cases or samples of a very few cases, and such small samples of cases can provide questionable grounds for advancing grand generalization. Yet, "Because more than one theoretical notion may be guiding an analysis, confirmation, fuller specification, and contradiction all may result from one case study" (Vaughan, 1992, p. 175). For example, we lose confidence in the generalization that a child of separated parents is better off placed with the mother than with the father when we find a single instance of resulting injury. Case studies are of value in refining theory, suggesting complexities for further investigation as well as helping to establish the limits of generalizability.

Case study also can be a disciplined force in setting public policy and in reflecting on human experience. Vicarious experience is an important basis for refining action options and expectations. Formal epistemology needs further development, but somehow people draw, from the description of an individual case, implications for other cases—not always correctly, but with a confidence shared by people of dissimilar views.

The purpose of a case report is not to represent the world, but to represent the case. Criteria for conducting the kind of research that leads to valid generalization need modification to fit the search for effective particularization. The utility of case research to practitioners and policy makers is in its extension of experience. The methods of qualitative case study are largely the methods of disciplining personal and particularized experience.

▣ NOTES

1. Many case studies are both qualitative and quantitative. In search of fundamental pursuits common to both qualitative and quantitative research, Robert Yin (1992) analyzed three well-crafted research efforts: (a) a quantitative investigation to resolve disputed authorship of the Federalist Papers, (b) a qualitative study of Soviet intent at the time of the Cuban missile crisis, and (c) his own studies of the recognizability of human faces. He found four common commitments: to bring expert knowledge to bear upon the phenomena studied, to round up all the relevant data, to examine rival interpretations, and to ponder and probe the degree to which the findings have implications elsewhere. These commitments are as important in case research as in any other type.

2. Another specific one for targeting a qualitative study is the event or instance. Events and instances are bounded, complex, and related to issues, but they lack the organic systemacity of most cases. Media instances have been studied by John Fiske (1994) and Norman Denzin (1999). Conversation analysis is a related approach (Psathas, 1995; Silverman, 2000).

3. Definition of the case is not independent of interpretive paradigm or methods of inquiry. Seen from different worldviews and in different situations, the "same" case *is* different. And however we originally define the case, the working definition changes as we study. And the definition of the case changes in different ways under different methods of study. The case of Theodore Roosevelt was not just differently portrayed but was differently defined as biographer Edmund Morris (1979) presented him, one chapter at a time, as "the Dude from New York," "the Dear Old Beloved Brother," "the Snake in the Grass," "the Rough Rider," "the Most Famous Man in America," and so on.

4. The history of case study, like the history of curiosity and common sense, is found throughout the library. Peeps at that history can be found in Robert Bogdan and Sara Bicklin (1982), John Creswell (1998), Sara Delamont (1992), Joe Feagin, Anthony Orum, and Gideon Sjoberg (1991), Robert Stake (1978), Harrison White (1992), and throughout the *Handbook*.

5. *Bread and Dreams* is a program evaluation report. Most evaluations are intrinsic case studies (see Mabry, 1998).

6. Collective case study is essentially what Robert Herriott and William Firestone (1983) called "multisite qualitative research." Multisite program evaluation is another common example. A number of German sociologists, such as Martin Kohli and Fritz Schütze, have used collective case studies with Strauss's grounded theory approach.

7. In a thoughtful review of an early draft of this chapter, Orlando Fals Borda urged abandoning the effort to promote intrinsic casework and the study of particularity. In persisting here, I think it important to support disciplined and scholarly study that has few scientific aspirations.

8. In 1922, Bronislaw Malinowski wrote, "One of the first conditions of acceptable Ethnographic work certainly is that it should deal with the totality of all social, cultural and psychological aspects of the community . . ." (1922/1984, p. xvi). There is a good spirit there, although totalities defy the acuity of the eye and the longevity of the watch.

9. Generalization from collective case study has been discussed by Herriott and Firestone (1983), John and Lyn Lofland (1984), Miles and Huberman (1994), and again by Firestone (1993).

10. Malinowski claimed that we could distinguish between arriving with closed minds and arriving with an idea of what to look for. He wrote:

> Good training in theory, and acquaintance with its latest results, is not identical with being burdened with "preconceived ideas." If a man sets out on an expedition, determined to prove certain hypotheses, if he is incapable of changing his views constantly and casting them off ungrudgingly under the pressure of evidence, needless to say his work will be worthless. But the more problems he brings with him into the field, the more he is in the habit of moulding his theories according to facts, and of seeing facts in their bearing upon theory, the better he is equipped for the work. Preconceived ideas are pernicious in any scientific work, but *foreshadowed problems* are the main endowment of a scientific thinker, and these problems are first revealed to the observer by his theoretical studies. (1922/1984, p. 9)

11. I would prefer to call it *interpretive* to emphasize the production of meanings, but ethnographers have used that term to mean "learn the special views of actors, the local meanings" (see Erickson, 1986; Schwandt, 2000).

12. Ethnographic use of the term *reflective* sometimes limits attention to the need for self-challenging the researcher's etic issues, frame of reference, and cultural bias (Tedlock, Chapter 5, this volume). That challenge is important but, following Donald Schön (1983), I refer to a general frame of mind when I call qualitative case work *reflective*. (Issues "brought in" are called *emic* issues; those found during field study are called *etic*.)

13. Coding is the method of connecting data, issues, interpretations, data sources, and report writing (Miles & Huberman, 1994). In small studies, this means careful labeling and sorting into file folders or computer files. Many entries are filed into more than one file. If the file becomes too bulky, subfiles need to be created. Too many files spoils the soup. In larger studies with files to be used by several team members, a formal coding system needs to be developed, possibly using a computer program such as *Ethnograph*, *ATLAS-ti*, or *Hyper-RESEARCH*.

14. Michael Patton (1990), Anselm Strauss and Juliet Corbin (1990), and William Firestone (1993) have discussed successive selection of cases over time.

15. As indicated in a previous section, I call them issues. Mary Kennedy (1979) called them "relevant attributes." Spiro et al. (1987) called them "abstract dimensions." Malinowski (1922/1984) called them "theories." In contemporary case research, these will be our "working theories" more than the "grand theories" of the disciplines.

16. If my emphasis is on learning about both the individual case and the phenomenon, I might do two studies, one a case study and the other a study of the phenomenon, giving close attention to an array of instances of hostage taking.

17. Firestone (1993) advised maximizing diversity and "to be as like the population of interest as possible" (p. 18).

18. The project is ongoing, and no report is yet available. The Step by Step program is described in Hansen, Kaufmann, and Saifer (n.d.).

19. For a number of years, psychologists Lee Cronbach and Richard Snow (1977) studied aptitude-treatment interactions. They hoped to find general rules by which teachers could adapt instruction to personal learning styles. At deeper and deeper levels of interaction they found significance, leading not to prespecifying teaching methods for individuals but supporting the conclusion that differentiated consistencies of response by individuals are to be expected in complex situations.

20. Laurel Richardson and Elizabeth St. Pierre speak similarly of *crystallization* in Chapter 15 in Volume 3.

21. Creative use of "member checking," submitting drafts for review by data sources, is one of the most needed forms of validation of qualitative research (Glesne & Peshkin, 1992; Lincoln & Guba, 1985).

22. Or that a reality exists outside the observers.

23. Among the earlier philosophers of science providing groundwork for qualitative contributions to theory elaboration were Herbert Blumer, Barney Glaser, Bronislaw Malinowski, and Robert Merton.

24. Yet, in the words of Charles Ragin, "variable oriented comparative work (e.g., quantitative cross-national research) as compared with case oriented comparative work disembodies and obscures cases" (Ragin & Becker, 1992, p. 5).

25. Sociologists have used the term "micro/macro" to refer to the leap from understanding individual cases or parts to understanding the system as a whole. Even without an adequate epistemological map, sociologists do leap, and so do our readers (Collins, 1981).

26. Storytelling as representative of culture and as sociological text emerges from many traditions, but nowhere more than from oral history and folklore. It is becoming more disciplined in a line of work called narrative inquiry (Clandenin & Connelly, 1999; Ellis & Bochner, 1996; Heron, 1996; Lockridge, 1988; Richardson, 1997). The *Journal of Narrative and Life History* includes studies using such methods.

27. It may appear that I claim here that participatory action research is problematic. Joint responsibility for design, data gathering, and interpretation is possible, often commendable. It is important that readers know when the values of the study have been so shaped.

28. Evaluation studies comparing an innovative program to a control case regularly fail to make the comparison credible. No matter how well studied, the control case too weakly represents cases presently known by the reader. By comprehensively describing the program case, the researcher may help the reader draw naturalistic generalizations.

29. A special obligation exists to protect those with limited resources. Those who comply with the researcher's requests, who contribute in some way to the making of the case, should not thereby be hurt—usually. When continuing breaches of ethics or morality are discovered, or when they are the reason for the study, the researcher must take some ameliorative action. Exposé and critique are legitimate within case study, but luring self-indictment out of a respondent is no more legitimate in research than in the law.

▣ REFERENCES

Adams, H. (1918). *The education of Henry Adams: An autobiography.* Boston: Houghton Mifflin.

Anderson, R. C. (1977). The notion of schema and the educational enterprise. In R. C. Anderson, R. J. Spiro, & W. E. Montague (Eds.), *Schooling and the acquisition of knowledge* (pp. 415–431). Hillsdale, NJ: Lawrence Erlbaum.

Asmussen, K. J., & Creswell, J. W. (1995). Campus response to a student gunman. *Journal of Higher Education, 66,* 575–591.

Ausubel, D. P., & Fitzgerald, D. (1961). Meaningful learning and retention: Interpersonal cognitive variables. *Review of Educational Research, 31,* 500–510.

Becker, H. S. (1992). Cases, causes, conjunctures, stories, and imagery. In C. C. Ragin & H. S. Becker (Eds.), *What is a case? Exploring the foundations of social inquiry* (pp. 205–216). Cambridge, UK: Cambridge University Press.

Becker, H. S., Geer, B., Hughes, E. C., & Strauss, A. L. (1961). *Boys in white: Student culture in medical school.* Chicago: University of Chicago Press.

Blumer, H. (1969). *Symbolic interactionism: Perspective and method.* Englewood Cliffs, NJ: Prentice-Hall.

Bogdan, R. C., & Biklen, S. K. (1982). *Qualitative research for education: An introduction to theory and methods.* Boston: Allyn & Bacon.

Bohm, D. (1985). *Unfolding meaning: A weekend of dialogue with David Bohm.* New York: Routledge.

Campbell, D. T. (1975). Degrees of freedom and case study. *Comparative Political Studies, 8,* 178–193.

Carr, W. L., & Kemmis, S. (1986). *Becoming critical: Education, knowledge and action research.* London: Falmer.

Carter, K. (1993). The place of story in the study of teaching and teacher education. *Educational Researcher, 22,* 5–12.

Clandenin, J., & Connelly, M. (1999). *Narrative inquiry.* San Francisco: Jossey-Bass.

Coles, R. (1989). *The call of stories: Teaching and the moral imagination.* Boston: Houghton Mifflin.

Coles, R. (1997). *Doing documentary work.* Oxford, UK: Oxford University Press.

Collins, R. (1981). On the microfoundations of macrosociology. *American Journal of Sociology, 86,* 984–1014.

Connell, R. W. (1985). *Teachers' work.* Sydney: George Allen & Unwin.

Crabtree, B. F., & Miller, W. L. (1999). Researching practice settings: A case study approach. In B. F. Crabtree & W. L. Miller (Eds.), *Doing qualitative research* (2nd ed., pp. 293–312). Thousand Oaks, CA: Sage.

Creswell, J. W. (1998). *Qualitative inquiry and research design: Choosing among five traditions.* Thousand Oaks, CA: Sage.

Cronbach, L. J., & Snow, R. E. (1977). *Aptitudes and instructional methods: A handbook for research on interactions.* New York: Irvington.

Delamont, S. (1992). *Fieldwork in educational settings: Methods, pitfalls and perspectives.* London: Falmer.

Denzin, N. K. (1989). *The research act* (3rd ed.). Englewood Cliffs, NJ: Prentice Hall.

Denzin, N. K. (1999). Cybertalk and the method of instances. In S. Jones (Ed.), *Doing Internet research: Critical issues and methods for examining the Net* (pp. 107–126). Thousand Oaks, CA: Sage.

Eisner, E. (Ed.). (1985). *Learning and teaching the ways of knowing* [84th yearbook of the National Society for the Study of Education]. Chicago: University of Chicago Press.

Ellis, C., & Bochner, A. P. (Eds.). (1996). *Composing ethnography.* Walnut Creek, CA: AltaMira.

Erickson, F. (1986). Qualitative methods in research on teaching. In M. C. Wittrock (Ed.), *Handbook of research on teaching* (3rd ed., pp. 119–161). New York: Macmillan.

Fals Borda, O. (Ed.). (1998). *People's participation: Challenges ahead.* New York: Apex.

Feagin, J. R., Orum, A. M., & Sjoberg, G. (1991). *A case for the case study.* Chapel Hill: University of North Carolina Press.

Firestone, W. A. (1993). Alternative arguments for generalizing from data as applied to qualitative research. *Educational Researcher, 22*(4), 16–23.

Fiske, J. (1994). Audiencing: Cultural practice and cultural studies. In N. K. Denzin & Y. S. Lincoln (Eds.), *Handbook of qualitative research* (pp. 359–378). Thousand Oaks, CA: Sage.

Flick, U. (1998). *An introduction to qualitative research: Theory, method and applications.* London: Sage.

Flyvbjerg, B. (2001). *Making social science matter.* Cambridge, UK: Cambridge University Press.

Garfinkel, H. (1967). *Studies in ethnomethodology.* New York: Prentice Hall.

Geertz, C. (1973). Thick description: Toward an interpretive theory of culture. In C. Geertz, *The interpretation of cultures* (pp. 3–30). New York: Basic Books.

Geertz, C. (1983). *Local knowledge: Further essays in interpretive anthropology.* New York: Basic Books.

Glaser, B. G., & Strauss, A. L. (1967). *The discovery of grounded theory: Strategies for qualitative research.* Chicago: Aldine.

Glesne, C., & Peshkin, A. (1992). *Becoming qualitative researchers: An introduction.* White Plains, NY: Longman.

Goetz, J. P., & LeCompte, M. D. (1984). *Ethnography and qualitative design in educational research.* New York: Academic Press.

Goode, W. J., & Hatt, P. K. (1952). The case study. In W. J. Goode & P. K. Hatt, *Methods of social research* (pp. 330–340). New York: McGraw-Hill.

Gottwald, N. K. (1979). *The tribes of Jahweh: A sociology of the religion of liberated Israel, 1250–1050 B.C.E.* Maryknoll, NY: Orbis Books.

Graue, M. E., & Walsh, D. J. (1998). *Studying children in context: Theories, methods, ethics.* Newbury Park, CA: Sage.

Hamilton, D. (1980). Some contrasting assumptions about case study research and survey analysis. In H. Simons (Ed.), *Towards a science of the singular* (pp. 76–92). Norwich, UK: University of East Anglia, Centre for Applied Research in Education.

Hansen, K. A., Kaufmann, R. K., & Saifer, S. (no date). *Education and the culture of democracy: Early childhood practice.* (Available from New York: Open Society Institute, 888 Seventh Ave., New York, NY 10106)

Heron, J. (1996). *Co-operative inquiry: Research into the human condition.* London: Sage.

Herriott, R. E., & Firestone, W. A. (1983). Multisite qualitative policy research: Optimizing description and generalizability. *Educational Researcher, 12*(2), 14–19.

House, E. R., & Howe, K. R. (1999). *Values in evaluation and social research*. Thousand Oaks, CA: Sage.

Huberman, A. M., & Miles, M. B. (1994). Data management and analysis methods. In N. K. Denzin & Y. S. Lincoln (Eds.), *Handbook of qualitative research* (pp. 428–445). Thousand Oaks, CA: Sage.

Kemmis, S. (1980). The imagination of the case and the invention of the study. In H. Simons (Ed.), *Towards a science of the singular* (pp. 93–142). Norwich, UK: University of East Anglia, Centre for Applied Research in Education.

Kennedy, M. M. (1979). Generalizing from single case studies. *Evaluation Quarterly, 3*, 661–678.

Kozol, J. (1991). *Savage inequalities*. New York: Harper.

Lincoln, Y. S., & Guba, E. G. (1985). *Naturalistic inquiry*. Beverly Hills, CA: Sage.

Lincoln, Y. S., & Guba, E. G. (2000). Paradigmatic controversies, contradictions, and emerging confluences. In N. K. Denzin & Y. S. Lincoln (Eds.), *Handbook of qualitative research* (pp. 163–188). Thousand Oaks, CA: Sage.

Lockridge, E. (1988). Faithful in her fashion: Catherine Barkley, the invisible Hemingway heroine. *Journal of Narrative Technique, 18*(2), 170–178.

Lofland, L. J., & Lofland, L. H. (1984). *Analyzing social settings: A guide to qualitative observation and analysis* (2nd ed.). Belmont, CA: Wadsworth.

Mabry, L. (1998). Case study methods. In H. J. Walberg & A. J. Reynolds (Eds.), *Advances in educational productivity: Vol. 7. Evaluation research for educational productivity* (pp. 155–170). Greenwich, CT: JAI.

Mabry, L. (1999). Circumstantial ethics. *American Journal of Evaluation, 20,* 199–212.

MacDonald, B., Adelman, C., Kushner, S., & Walker, R. (1982). *Bread and dreams: A case study in bilingual schooling in the U.S.A.* Norwich, UK: University of East Anglia, Centre for Applied Research in Education.

Malinowski, B. (1984). *Argonauts of the western Pacific*. Prospect Heights, IL: Waveland. (Original work published 1922)

Maxwell, J. A. (1992). Understanding and validity in qualitative research. *Harvard Educational Review, 63,* 279–300.

McCormick, S. (1994). A nonreader becomes a reader: A case study of literacy acquisition by a severely disabled reader. *Reading Research Quarterly, 29*(2), 157–176.

Messick, S. (1989). Validity. In R. L. Linn (Ed.), *Educational measurement* (3rd ed., pp. 13–103). New York: Macmillan.

Miles, M. B., & Huberman, A. M. (1994). *Qualitative data analysis* (2nd ed.). Thousand Oaks, CA: Sage.

Morris, E. (1979). *The rise of Theodore Roosevelt*. New York: Coward, McCann & Geognegan.

Parlett, M., & Hamilton, D. (1976). Evaluation as illumination: A new approach to the study of innovative programmes. In G. V Glass (Ed.), *Evaluation studies review annual* (Vol. 1, pp. 141–157). Beverly Hills, CA: Sage.

Patton, M. Q. (1990). *Qualitative evaluation and research methods* (2nd ed.). Newbury Park, CA: Sage.

Peshkin, A. (1986). *God's choice*. Chicago: University of Chicago Press.

Polanyi, M. (1962). *Personal knowledge: Towards a post-critical philosophy*. Chicago: University of Chicago Press.

Pugach, M. (1998). *On the border of opportunity: Education, community, and language at the U.S.-Mexico line.* Mahwah, NJ: Erlbaum.

Psathas, G. (1995). *Conversation analysis.* Thousand Oaks, CA: Sage.

Ragin, C. C. (1987). *The comparative method.* Berkeley: University of California Press.

Ragin, C. C. (1992). Cases of "What is a case?" In C. C. Ragin & H. S. Becker (Eds.), *What is a case? Exploring the foundations of social inquiry* (pp. 1–18). Cambridge, UK: Cambridge University Press.

Ragin, C. C., & Becker, H. S. (Eds.). (1992). *What is a case? Exploring the foundations of social inquiry.* Cambridge, UK: Cambridge University Press.

Raisin, S., & Britton, E. D. (1997). *Bold ventures: Patterns among U. S. innovations in science and mathematics education.* Dordrecht, the Netherlands: Kluwer Academic.

Richardson, L. (1997). *Fields of play.* New Brunswick, NJ: Rutgers University Press.

Robinson, W. S. (1951). The logical structure of analytic induction. *American Sociological Review, 16,* 812–818.

Rumelhart, D. E., H.Ortony, A. (1977). The representation of knowledge in memory. In R. C. Anderson, R. J. Spiro, & W. E. Montague (Eds.), *Schooling and the acquisition of knowledge* (pp. 99–135). Hillsdale, NJ: Erlbaum.

Ryan, G. W., & Bernard, H. R. (2000). Data analysis and management methods. In N. K. Denzin & Y. S. Lincoln (Eds.), *Handbook of qualitative research* (2nd ed., pp. 769–802). Newbury Park, CA: Sage.

Schön, D. (1983). *The reflective practitioner: How professionals think in action.* New York: Basic Books.

Schwandt, T. A. (1993). Theory for the moral sciences: Crisis of identity and purpose. In G. Mills & D. J. Flinders (Eds.), *Theory and concepts in qualitative research* (pp. 5–23). New York: Teachers College Press.

Schwandt, T. A. (2000). Three epistemological stances for qualitative inquiry: Interpretivism, hermeneutics, and social constructionism. In N. K. Denzin & Y. S. Lincoln (Eds.), *Handbook of qualitative research* (2nd ed., pp. 189–213). Newbury Park, CA: Sage.

Silverman, D. (1993). *Interpreting qualitative data.* London: Sage.

Silverman, D. (2000). Analyzing talk and text. In N. K. Denzin & Y. S. Lincoln (Eds.), *Handbook of qualitative research* (2nd ed., pp. 821–834). Newbury Park, CA: Sage.

Simons, H. (Ed.). (1980). *Towards a science of the singular.* Norwich, UK: University of East Anglia, Centre for Applied Research in Education.

Sjoberg, G., Williams, N., Vaughan, T. R., & Sjoberg, A. (1991). The case approach in social research: Basic methodological issues. In J. R. Feagin, A. M. Orum, & G. Sjoberg (Eds.), *A case for the case study* (pp. 27–79). Chapel Hill: University of North Carolina Press.

Smith, L. M. (1978). An evolving logic of participant observation, educational ethnography and other case studies. In L. Shulman (Ed.), *Review of Research in Education, 6* (pp. 316–377). Chicago: Peacock Press.

Smith, L. M. (1994). Biographical method. In N. K. Denzin & Y. S. Lincoln (Eds.), *Handbook of qualitative research* (pp. 286–305). Thousand Oaks, CA: Sage.

Smith, L. M., & Dwyer, D. (1979). *Federal policy in action: A case study of an urban education project.* Washington, DC: National Institute of Education.

Smith, R. (1889). *An Aberdeenshire Village Propaganda: Forty years ago.* Edinburgh: David Douglas.

Spiro, R. J., Vispoel, W. P., Schmitz, J. G., Samarapungavan, A., & Boerger, A. E. (1987). Knowledge acquisition for application: Cognitive flexibility and transfer in complex content domains. In B. C. Britton (Ed.), *Executive control processes* (pp. 177–199). Hillsdale, NJ: Lawrence Erlbaum.

Stake, R. E. (1978). The case study method of social inquiry. *Educational Researcher, 7*(2), 5–8.

Stake, R. E. (1988). Case study methods in educational research: Seeking sweet water. In R. M. Jaeger (Ed.), *Complementary methods for research in education* (pp. 253–278). Washington, DC: American Educational Research Association.

Stake, R. E. (1995). *The art of case study research.* Thousand Oaks, CA: Sage.

Stake, R. E. (2004). *Standards-based and responsive evaluation.* Thousand Oaks, CA: Sage.

Stake, R. E., & Trumbull, D. J. (1982). Naturalistic generalizations. *Review Journal of Philosophy and Social Science, 7,* 1–12.

Stenholm, B. (1984). *The Swedish school system.* Stockholm: The Swedish Institute.

Stenhouse, L. (1979). *The study of samples and the study of cases.* Presidential address to the annual conference of the British Educational Research Association.

Stenhouse, L. (1984). Library access, library use and user education in academic sixth forms: An autobiographical account. In R. G. Burgess (Ed.), *The research process in educational settings: Ten case studies* (pp. 211–234). London: Falmer.

Stouffer, S. A. (1941). Notes on the case-study and the unique case. *Sociometry, 4,* 349–357.

Strauss, A. L., & Corbin, J. (1990). *Basics of qualitative research: Grounded theory procedures and techniques.* Newbury Park, CA: Sage.

Tierney, W. (2000). Undaunted courage: Life history and the postmodern challenge. In N. K. Denzin & Y. S. Lincoln (Eds.), *Handbook of qualitative research* (pp. 537–554). Thousand Oaks, CA: Sage.

Tobin, J. (1989). *Preschool in three cultures.* New Haven, CT: Yale University Press.

van Maanen, J. (1988). *Tales of the field: On writing ethnography.* Chicago: University of Chicago Press.

Vaughan, D. (1992). Theory elaboration: The heuristics of case analysis. In C. C. Ragin & H. S. Becker (Eds.), *What is a case? Exploring the foundations of social inquiry* (pp. 173–202). Cambridge, UK: Cambridge University Press.

Vaughan, D. (1999). The dark side of organizations: Mistake, misconduct and disaster. *Annual Review of Sociology, 25,* 271–305.

von Wright, G. H. (1971). *Explanation and understanding.* London: Routledge & Kegan Paul.

White, H. C. (1992). Cases are for identity, for explanation, or for control. In C. C. Ragin & H. S. Becker (Eds.), *What is a case? Exploring the foundations of social inquiry* (pp. 83–104). Cambridge, UK: Cambridge University Press.

Wieviorka, M. (1988). *Sociétés et terrorisme.* Paris: Fayard.

Yin, R. K. (1984). *Case study research: Design and methods* (Applied Social Research Methods, Vol. 5). Beverly Hills, CA: Sage.

Yin, R. K. (1989). *Case study research: Design and methods* (2nd ed.). Newbury Park, CA: Sage.

Yin, R. K. (1992, November). *Evaluation: A singular craft.* Paper presented at the annual meeting of the American Evaluation Association, Seattle, WA.

5

THE OBSERVATION OF PARTICIPATION AND THE EMERGENCE OF PUBLIC ETHNOGRAPHY

Barbara Tedlock

P articipant observation was created during the late 19th century as an ethnographic field method for the study of small, homogeneous cultures.
Ethnographers were expected to live in a society for an extended period of time
(2 years, ideally), actively participate in the daily life of its members, and carefully
observe their joys and sufferings as a way of obtaining material for social scientific
study. This method was widely believed to produce documentary information that not
only was "true" but also reflected the native's own point of view about reality.[1]

The privileging of participant observation as a scientific method encouraged
ethnographers to demonstrate their observational skills in scholarly monographs and
their social participation in personal memoirs. This dualistic approach split public
(monographs) from private (memoirs) and objective (ethnographic) from subjective
(autobiographical) realms of experience. The opposition created what seems, from a
21st-century perspective, not only improbable but also morally suspect.[2]

More recently, ethnographers have modified participant observation by undertaking "the observation of participation" (B. Tedlock, 1991, 2000). During this activity, they reflect on and critically engage with their own participation within the
ethnographic frame. A new genre, known as "autoethnography," emerged from this
practice. Authors working in the genre attempt to heal the split between public and
private realms by connecting the autobiographical impulse (the gaze inward) with

the ethnographic impulse (the gaze outward). Autoethnography at its best is a cultural performance that transcends self-referentiality by engaging with cultural forms that are directly involved in the creation of culture. The issue becomes not so much distance, objectivity, and neutrality as closeness, subjectivity, and engagement. This change in approach emphasizes relational over autonomous patterns, interconnectedness over independence, translucence over transparency, and dialogue and performance over monologue and reading.[3]

Such once-taboo subjects as admitting one's fear of physical violence as well as one's intimate encounters in the field are now not only inscribed but also described and performed as social science data.[4] The philosophical underpinnings of this discourse lie in the domains of critical, feminist, poststructuralist, and postmodern theories, with their comparative, interruptive, non-universalistic modes of analysis. Social science in this environment has given up on simple data collection and instead "offers re-readings of representations in every form of information processing, empirical science, literature, film, television, and computer simulation" (Clough, 1992, p. 137).

◙ PUBLIC ENGAGEMENT

Early anthropology in the United States included a tradition of social criticism and public engagement. As a result, most articles and books of that time could be read, understood, and enjoyed by any educated person. Scholars such as Franz Boas, Ruth Benedict, and Margaret Mead shaped public opinion through their voluminous writing, public speaking, and calls for social and political action. Boas spent most of his career battling against the racist confusion of physical and cultural human attributes. His student Ruth Benedict, in her best-selling book *Patterns of Culture* (1934), promoted the notion of "culture" as not just those art events that found their way into the women's pages of the newspapers of her era, but a people's entire way of life. In so doing, she humanized non-elite and non-Western peoples—they too have culture—and delegitimated evolutionary ideas concerning hierarchies of peoples. Margaret Mead, in *Coming of Age in Samoa* (1928), contested the notion that adolescence was necessarily a period of strain. Later, in *Sex and Temperament in Three Primitive Societies* (1935), she argued against the dominant Western sexual ideology of her time, which claimed that men were naturally aggressive while women were naturally passive.[5]

By the 1950s, however, as academic culture in the United States felt the chill wind of the McCarthy era, many researchers no longer dared to address their work to the general public. Instead, they withdrew into small professional groups where they addressed one another. As they did so, they elaborated ever more elegant apolitical theoretical paradigms: functionalism, culture and personality, structuralism, componential analysis, and semiotics. In time, social and political disengagement became entrenched in academia and a strong taboo against any form of social criticism of hegemonic institutions or practices arose. It would not be until the mid-1960s that the critical function of ethnography in the United States would reappear. Stanley Diamond coined the term "critical anthropology" in 1963 and subsequently clarified its socially engaged nature in his journal *Dialectical Anthropology.*[6]

This rekindling of public engagement took place in the context of the civil rights movement, opposition to the war in Vietnam and other U.S. interventions in the Third World, the writings of the California branch of the Frankfurt School, and the research of educational revisionists. As a more general research paradigm, this renewed public and critical engagement was known as "critical theory." Scholars working within the paradigm saw it as a way to free academic work from capitalist domination and to help schools and other institutions to become places where people might be socially empowered rather than subjugated.[7]

One way critical theory was put into practice was through the production of plays addressing the economic and political plight of impoverished working people and peasants. In the mid-1960s, popular theater groups such as Bread and Puppet in the United States and *Teatro Campesino* in Mexico began working together as egalitarian collectives, producing free theater for the masses. The goal of such theater groups in Latin America was to politically transform the peasants' view of themselves as independent rural farmers to that of exploited, underpaid workers.

Paulo Freire theorized that this empowerment process, which he called *conscientization*, takes place whenever people recognize and act upon their own ideas rather than consuming the ideas of others. In *Pedagogy of the Oppressed* (1973), he described how the process of *conscientization* occurs by means of dialogue, during which people share information on institutional injustices and challenge powerful interests so as to change their own everyday realities. Grassroots participatory research grew out of this environment and became a strategy for groups lacking resources and power to work together to achieve political empowerment.[8]

As participatory research and grassroots theater became important movements in Latin America, university students and intellectuals, in their rush for solidarity with the masses, reduced cultural differences to class differences. What they failed to realize was that indigenous peoples live on the margins of capitalist society mainly for reasons of linguistic and religious differences, rather than simply because of economic disenfranchisement (Taylor, 2003, p. 198).

Peru's leading theater collective, *Grupo Cultural Yuyachkani*, has worked to avoid this politically naïve stance by making visible a combined multilingual and multiethnic epistemology. This predominantly "white," Spanish-speaking group is deeply involved with the local indigenous and mestizo populations as well as with transcultural Andean-Spanish ways of knowing and remembering. The Quechua part of their name, Yuyachkani, which means "I am thinking," "I am remembering," and "I am your thought," highlights their recognition of the complexity of Peru's social memory. It consists not only of archival memory existing in written texts but also, and perhaps more importantly, of embodied memory transmitted in performance. The group attempts to make its urban audiences able to recognize the many different ways of being "Peruvian," and in so doing it insists on creating a community of witnesses through its performances (Taylor, 2001).

There exists a similar history of popular theater in Africa (Coplan, 1986). In Ghana, for example, Concert Party Theatre combined oral and vernacular forms in such a way as to be simultaneously accessible to both illiterate and educated people (Cole, 2001). As in Latin America, intellectuals in Africa initially disapproved of popular theater for what they saw as its lack of social or political radicalism. They had been unaware of the political nature of the performances, which, instead of voicing criticism in a direct and obvious narrative form, subtly imbedded political subversion within the doing of the performance itself. The actors' self-positioning as "preachers," and the audiences' endorsement of this in their search for "lessons," created a new theater form that was neither mimetic nor spectacular, neither realist nor classical. Rather, it was a discourse of example. As such, it was both socially and politically engaged.[9]

Concert Party Theatre transformed the authorizing fiction of colonialism, "civilization," into a humorous practice rather than allowing it a fixed ontological status (cf. Bakhtin, 1984). This suggests that in order to discover the social, cultural, and political significance of popular theater, one must analyze the poetry of action. West African concert artists chose elements from local, national, continental, diasporic, European, and American sources and poetically reshaped them, producing an altogether new and powerful form of popular politics.

▣ PERFORMANCE ETHNOGRAPHY

Performance is everywhere in life: from simple gestures to melodramas and macrodramas. Because dramatic performances can communicate engaged political and theoretical analysis, together with nuanced emotional portraits of human beings, they have gained acceptance by a number of documentarians. Plays and other performances become vibrant forms of ethnography that combine political, critical, and expressive actions centering on lived experiences locally and globally. A number of ethnographers have served as producers, actors, and dramaturges.[10]

There are two main types of performance ethnography that directly link anthropological and theatrical thought. One considers human behavior as performance, and the other considers performance as human interaction. Edith and Victor Turner suggested that every socioeconomic formation has its own cultural-aesthetic mirror in which it achieves self-reflexivity. Their goal was to aid students in understanding how people in a multitude of cultures experience their own social lives. To that end, they staged a Virginia wedding, the midwinter ceremony of the Mohawk, an Ndembu girl's puberty ceremony, and the Kwakiutl Hamatsa ceremony.[11]

Because culture is emergent in human interaction rather than located deep inside individual brains or hearts, or loosely attached to external material objects or impersonal social structures, dramas are a powerful way to both shape and show cultural construction in action. Because of this subjunctive quality, plays create and enact moral texts that communicate vibrant emotional portraits of human beings, together with an empathic response and deeply engaged political analysis (Cole, 1985).

Playwriting and production (as contrasted with writing short stories or novels) provide checks on flights of the imagination, because dramatic performance demands that the vision be embodied. Public performances encourage authors and performers to think concretely about what can be observed rather than dwelling on inner thoughts. Actors communicate, by means of gesture and other bodily forms, an understandable and believable mimetic reality for their spectators. Such performances operate on a feedback principle of approximating reality by checking the details and then refining the representation in a reiterative or "closed loop" approach. In contrast, novels and theatrical dramas, although they may be ethnographically informed, operate on a more "open" principle.

Because of these and other characteristics, popular theater, with its egalitarian "by the people, for the people" ethos, serves as an imitation of aspects of the sensible world, and thus is a form of cultural mimesis or representation. Milton Singer (1972) introduced the notion of "cultural performance" as an important institution embodying key aspects of cultural traditions. Since then, popular theater, especially improvisation, has been studied as cultural performance in many places. Popular theaters in Iran and Indonesia, as examples, are extemporized around minimal plots. The actors ad lib among themselves and dialogue with the audience.[12]

Music, song, dance, storytelling, puppetry, and other theatrical forms often are embraced as forms of political analysis, catharsis, and group healing by indigenous peoples who have experienced ethnic, cultural, and social displacement; grinding poverty; and horrendous acts of violence. Basotho migrant laborers, for example, respond to their social situation with highly evocative word music, creating a "cultural shield" against dependency, expropriation, and the dehumanizing relations of race and class in South Africa (Coplan, 1994). Women living in the *favelas*, or urban shanty-towns, of Brazil create absurdist and black-humor modes of storytelling in the face of poverty, trauma, and tragedy. These stories aesthetically define and emotionally release the alienation and frustration caused by years of severe economic deprivation and social desperation (Goldstein, 2003). In so doing, they produce a commentary in which the actors, who are also their own authors, refuse the surplus of knowledge that typifies an authoritative author. These actor-authors, with the help of their audience members, create multiple comic subplots. As a result of this contingent situation, each performance is unique and unrepeatable.

An indigenous theater group in Mozambique produced a play in Maputo that opened with an attack on a market woman who was brutally killed and transformed into a spirit. A ceremony was then performed that included healing stories, songs, ritual bathing, and the holding and stroking of victims of violence as one would a frightened child. According to the group, the key purpose for writing and performing the drama was to mobilize women into a sex strike until the killing stopped (Nordstrum, 1997).

In Chiapas, Mexico, during the late 1980s, a group of Mayan farmers who had served for many years as informants to foreign ethnographers founded a theater company called *Lo'il Maxil*, or "Monkey Business" (Breslin, 1992). Their goal was to produce dramas that could showcase Mayan history and culture. From its inception, anthropologist Robert Laughlin worked as a dramaturge for the group. An early play they produced was titled *Herencia fatal*, "fatal inheritance" (Sna Jtz'ibajom, 1996). It concerned two brothers who killed their sister in a dispute over land. Such disputes are still a common problem in rural Mexico and Guatemala, where siblings often end up in court due to a lack of adequate available agricultural land upon which to support their families.

The play opened with a curing ceremony showing a shaman at work. During the premiere in San Cristóbal, an initiated shaman, who also was a member of the troupe, sat backstage with the cast. In the middle of the performance, he suddenly jumped up and walked around to the front of the curtain in order to see if the shamanic healing was properly performed. Because this scene was an important part of the play's verisimilitude, it had to be absolutely true to life. If it were not, then the mostly Mayan audience would not connect with the cultural continuity message provided by the example of traditional healing. In the face of enormous historical injustices, in which the majority of the land is owned by absentee landholders, healing rituals allow Mayans a space for resistance and recuperation. This was accomplished in the play by revealing the ongoing colonial imperialism at the heart of Mayan social problems.

This and other plays have continued to be produced in dozens of rural Mayan hamlets, as well as in the large, multiethnic cities of Mexico and the United States (Laughlin, 1994, 1995). At the end of each performance, the cast and audience conduct a dialogue. Ideas for ways to improve the production as a work of art, cultural document, and political critique are aired, and changes are included in future performances. This type of feedback loop is at the heart of Bertholt Brecht's (1964) distinction between "traditional" and "epic" theater. Traditional theater is monologic, and as a result the spectators are unable to influence what happens on the stage because it is art and they represent life. Epic theater is dialogic, and as a result the audience undergoes a process of learning something about their lives. Popular theater consisting of ethnographically derived plays, also called "ethnodramas" (Mienczakowski, 1995, 1996), is located within the tradition of epic theater.

Another instructive example of ethnodrama is the Zuni play *Ma'l Okyattsik an Denihalowilli:we*, "Gifts from Salt Woman." It was written, sponsored, and performed several times in the 1990s by the theater group known as *Idiwanan An Chawe* or "Children of the Middle Place." This bilingual play, exploring the physical and spiritual care of Zuni Salt Lake, raised important issues about the United States government's continuing violation of Zuni sovereignty. The tribe sponsored a number of public performances in the pueblo as well as a cross-country tour. After each performance, the director, playwright, actors, dancers, singers, and audience members conversed about the meaning and interpretation of the play. In collaboration with the Appalachian group Roadside Theater, they also produced a bicultural play titled *Corn Mountain/ Pine Mountain: Following the Seasons*, or *Dowa Yalanne/Ashek'ya Yalanne Debikwayinan Idulohha*. The performers included 3 Zuni and 3 Appalachian storytellers wearing modern dress and 16 traditionally dressed Zuni dancers and singers. Instead of underscoring cultural differences, of which there were many, they focused on the similarity of their reciprocal caring relationships with humans, animals, and mountains (Cocke, Porterfield, & Wemytewa, 2002).

Ethnodramas also have been used to address urban and institutional social issues. A performance piece centering on schizophrenia, titled *Syncing Out Loud: A Journey into Illness*, was presented in several residential psychiatric settings in Australia. The play was written by sociologists and performed by a group of professional actors and nursing students as a psychotherapeutic strategy intended to instruct both students and patients (Cox, 1989). Each performance was followed by an open forum that not only built communicative consensus but also revealed elements of the performance that were inaccurate and disenfranchising. As a result of this public performance-editing strategy, the script remained open ended and constantly evolving (Mienczakowski, 1996).

What happens when an ethnodrama is not handled in this manner was revealed in a play called *Talabot*, performed in 1988 by the Danish theatre group Odin Teatret (Hastrup, 1992). The central character was a Danish woman ethnographer, Kirsten Hastrup. She wrote a detailed autobiography for use by the cast in performing her life. The other characters—Knud Rasmussen (the Danish Polar explorer), Che Guevara (the Latin American revolutionary), and Antonin Artaud (the French surrealist poet)—were chosen to mirror specific elements in her life. Kirsten had read about Rasmussen's arctic explorations as a child, which is what lured her into anthropology. Che Guevara chose revolution to empower the weak, while Kirsten chose ethnography to defend weaker cultures. Antonin Artaud juxtaposed theater and the plague, and in so doing he mirrored Kirsten's own madness after her fieldwork, when she was caught in a spider's web of competing realities. The ethnographer also had a twin in the play, a trickster figure who, like herself, served as a mirror promising not to lie but never telling the whole truth either, a classic ethnographic dilemma (Crapanzano, 1986).

Kirsten's initial response to seeing the play staged was the feeling of shock and betrayal at "having been fieldworked upon" (Hastrup, 1995, p. 144). In analyzing her own discomfort, she noticed that exaggeration of her biography, accomplished through the use of masculine heroes, created schizophrenia in her self concept. As a result, she found she could neither fully identify with, nor fully distance herself from, the staged Kirsten. "She was neither my double nor an other. She restored my biography in an original way, being not-me and not-not-me at the same time. I was not represented, I was performed" (Hastrup, 1995, p. 141). When the theater troupe left Denmark for performances in Italy, she felt that they were running away with the meaning of her life, with her soul, and in so doing they had stripped her of her concept of a self. The pain this caused made her understand the informant's loss at the departure of the ethnographer, who for a brief time had encouraged her to see who she was for another.

Because Hastrup learned something about herself as a spectator, the play might be described as falling within the Brechtian category of "epic theater." However, because the director failed to include her responses and observations in his subsequent performances, the play operated in a traditional theatrical mode, revealing a fictive attitude toward reality. Thus, even though the play was ethnographically researched, it was not an ethnodrama in the epic mode, because it did not operate within a closed-loop feedback model of refining the details again and again until it became closer and closer to the reality of her life.

▣ Public Ethnography

At about the same time as the development of ethnodrama, a few publishing houses and professional associations began to encourage social scientists to communicate openly with nonspecialist audiences. One of the earliest and the most successful of these efforts was that of Jean Malaurie, who established the French series *Terre Humaine* at the publishing house Plon in Paris. Over the years, *Terre Humaine* developed an enormous public audience for its passionate and politically engaged narrative portraiture. This distinguished run of accessible narrative ethnographies and biographies is now more than 80 titles in length.[13]

A similar opening up of anthropology occurred in Britain and the United States. In 1985, The Royal Anthropological Institute, located in London, launched a new journal titled *Anthropology Today*. This bimonthly publication was designed to appeal to people working in neighboring disciplines, including other social sciences, education, film, health, development, refugee studies, and relief aid (Benthall, 1996). It has focused on still photography, ethnographic films, fieldwork dilemmas, native anthropology, globalization, and the role of anthropologists in development.

The American Anthropological Association also assumed a central role in stimulating a broader mission for the discipline of anthropology. The flagship journal of the association, the *American Anthropologist*, under the editorship of Barbara and Dennis Tedlock (1993–1998) included many more well-written, illustrated, passionate, moral, and politically engaged essays than ever before in its hundred-year history. The association also invited a group of scholars to its headquarters to discuss "Disorder in U.S. Society." On this occasion, Roy Rappaport (1995) suggested that engaged ethnography ought to both critique and enlighten members of one's own society. This stimulated the

Center for Community Partnership at the University of Pennsylvania to initiate discussions of strategies for encouraging researching and writing about socially relevant topics. The center labeled its undertaking "public interest anthropology."[14]

More recently, a sociological collective at the University of California, Berkeley, undertook a project involving finely tuned participant observation within local political struggles worldwide. They documented many newly emerging social issues, including the privatization of nursing homes, the medicalization of breast cancer, and the dumping of toxic waste. Their work, which showed how ethnography could have a global reach and relevance, consisted of directly engaged fieldwork that was both conceptually rich and empirically concrete. In their edited volume, *Global Ethnography: Forces, Connections, and Imaginations in a Postmodern World* (Burawoy et al., 2000), they demonstrated how globalization impacted the daily lives of Kerala nurses, Irish software programmers, and Brazilian feminists, among dozens of other groups. In this work, we see clearly how researchers can weave back and forth within the storied lives of others, creating an engaged narrative grounded within a specific community that is, in turn, located within an international mosaic of global forces. In so doing, the veil of scientific professionalism that surrounded and protected social inquiry during the McCarthy era was pulled aside, revealing how private joys and troubles create and blend with larger national and international public issues.

As one group of progressive colleagues in anthropology focused their critical gaze within the borders of the United States, another group of progressive colleagues in the social sciences focused their critical gaze outside the United States. The School of American Research, located in Santa Fe, New Mexico, valorized both of these directions for anthropologists when in 2003 it split the prestigious J. I. Staley Prize between Reyna Rapp (1999) for her book on amniocentesis in the United States and Lawrence Cohen (1998) for his book on Alzheimer's disease in India. Rapp's ethnography centered on the moral conflicts women face when they choose to abort fetuses because of information gained by genetic testing. Cohen centered on the culturally and historically located description and embodiment of the anxiety surrounding aging. These authors not only are excellent researchers and writers but also are deeply implicated in and passionate about their topics. I consider their ethnographies, together with ethnodrama, as important forms of "public ethnography."

By public ethnography, I mean the type of research and writing that directly engages with the critical social issues of our time, including such topics as health and healing, human rights and cultural survival, environmentalism, violence, war, genocide, immigration, poverty, racism, equality, justice, and peace. Authors of such works passionately inscribe, translate, and perform their research in order to present it to the general public. They also use the observation of their own participation to understand and artistically portray the pleasures and sorrows of daily life at home as well as in many out-of-the-way places. In so doing, they emotionally engage, educate, and move the public to action.[15]

Public ethnography, as I conceive it, is both a theory and a practice. It straddles the domains of lived experience and recollected memory of time spent interacting in the field, on one hand, with time spent alone in reflection, interpretation, and analysis, on the other. As a revolutionary theory and a powerful pedagogical strategy, it creates a location within which new possibilities for describing and changing the world co-occur.

In an attempt to fulfill these new mandates, ethnographers are once again engaging with the general public. They are penning op-ed pieces in newspapers and writing magazine essays, popular books, short stories, and novels. They are also creating dramas, poems, performance pieces, films, videos, websites, and CD-ROMs. These various ethnographic stagings are deeply "enmeshed in moral matters" (Conquergood, 1985, p. 2). Experimental theater, personal narratives, filmmaking, and documentary photography produce mimetic parallels through which the subjective is made present and available to its performers and witnesses. This is true for both indigenous and outsider ethnographers, producers, and performers.

Three recent books beautifully document public ethnography in action. Paul Farmer's *Pathologies of Power: Health, Human Rights, and the New War on the Poor* (2003) illustrates the way in which racism and gender inequality in the United States create disease and death. He passionately argues that health care should be a basic human right. Aihwa Ong, in her ethnography *Buddha Is Hiding: Refugees, Citizenship, the New America* (2003), documents the way in which Cambodian refugees become citizens through a combination of being-made and self-making. Along the way, she raises important questions about the meaning of citizenship in an age of rapid globalization.

David Anderson and Eeva Berglund, in their edited volume *Ethnographies of Conservation: Environmentalism and the Distribution of Privilege* (2003), reveal that conservation efforts not only fail to protect environments but also disempower already underprivileged groups. The authors make visible these marginalized peoples, examine how projects to protect landscapes are linked to myths of state identity and national progress, and show how conservation creates privileged enclaves for consumption while restricting local people's engagement with their environment. Drawing on the tradition of critical theory, they shed light on overlooked aspects of environmentalism, and as a result they were challenged by a powerful conservation organization that hinted at litigation if they published their critique. This extreme reaction to their project helped them to realize that their efforts "had moved the anthropological gaze toward relatively powerful organizations without giving these organizations the right of veto" (Berglund & Anderson, 2003, p. 15). To avoid a lawsuit but still publish their research, they edited their contributions so as to conceal all personal and organizational identities.

As scholars and activists produce more public ethnography, they will move ever further into the political arena. As they are read and listened to, they will encounter legal and other attempts to silence them. Such is the price of what Michael Fischer (2003, p. 2) has called "moral entrepreneurship," the directing of attention to matters about which something ought and might be done. This is a price that many researchers will pay happily in return for the chance to practice ethnography that makes a difference both at home and abroad.

We have moved far from the Enlightenment goals of "value-free" social science based on a rationalist presumption of canonical ethics; we have entered into the arena of postcolonial social science, with its focus on morally engaged research. This new ethical framework presumes that the public sphere consists of a mosaic of communities with a pluralism of identities and worldviews. Researchers and participants are united by a set of ethical values in which personal autonomy and communal well-being are interlocked. Undertaking research in alliance with indigenous, disabled, and other marginalized peoples empowers diverse cultural expressions and creates a vibrant discourse in the service of respect, freedom, equality, and justice. This new ethnography is deeply rooted in ideas of kindness, neighborliness, and a shared moral good. Within this politically engaged environment, social science projects serve the communities in which they are carried out, rather than serving external communities of educators, policy makers, military personnel, and financiers.[16]

▣ CONCLUSION

The observation of participation produces a combination of cognitive and emotional information that ethnographers can use to create engaged ethnodramas and other forms of public ethnography. Such performances and books address important social issues in a humanistic, self-reflexive manner, engaging both the hearts and the minds of their audiences. The public ethnographies currently being written, published, and performed today are robust examples of humanistic concerns and moral entrepreneurship in action. They will engage and embolden a whole new generation of scholars in many disciplines to tackle the ethical dilemmas stemming from ongoing developments in environmentalism, biotechnology, and information databases. There is much public ethnography yet to be done.

▣ NOTES

1. The replacement of armchair ethnography by experientially gained knowledge of other cultures was pioneered by Matilda Cox Stevenson, Alice Fletcher, Franz Boas, and Frank Hamilton Cushing (B. Tedlock, 2000, p. 456). This new type of research was claimed as a formal method later by Bronislaw Malinowski (Firth, 1985). Malinowski also claimed that anthropology was concerned with understanding other cultures from the "native's point of view" (1922, p. 25). For a discussion of the history and practice of participant observation, see B. Tedlock (2000).

2. This split between monographs and memoirs is illustrated by the books of Jean-Paul Dumont (1976, 1978).

3. For discussions of the genre of autoethnography, see Strathern (1987), Lionnet (1989), Deck (1990), Friedman (1990), B. Tedlock (1991), Okely and Callaway (1992), Pratt (1994), Van Maanen (1995), Ellis and Bochner (1996, 2000), Clough (1997), Harrington (1997), and Reed-Danahay (1997).

4. Examples of works touching on these topics include Cesara (1982), Weston (1991, 1998), Scheper-Hughes (1992), Kleinman and Copp (1993), Newton (1993), Wade (1993), Blackwood (1995), Bolton (1995), Dubisch (1995), Grindal and Salomone (1995), Kulick (1995), Kulick and Willson (1995), Lewin (1995), Nordstrum and Robben (1995), Shokeid (1995), Behar (1996), Daniel (1996), Kennedy and Davis (1996), Lewin and Leap (1996), Wafer (1996), Zulaika and Douglass (1996), Willson (1997), Lee-Treweek and Linkogle (2000), Theidon (2001), Wolcott (2002), Gusterson (2003), and Wax (2003).

5. A recent long essay in *The New Yorker* (Pierpont, 2004) profiled the public legacy of Boas as well as his students. See also the book on race by Benedict (1945).

6. See Diamond (1974) and Gailey (1992). Stanley Diamond founded the international journal *Dialectical Anthropology* in 1975. From its inception, it has had an important critical role in critiquing the discipline of anthropology: its intellectual leaders, paradigms, and representations.

7. See Marcuse (1964), Leacock (1969), Freire (1973), Bowles and Gintis (1976), Brodkey (1987), and Giroux (1988).

8. Participatory research, also known as "participatory action research," is closely associated with critical performance ethnography, liberation theory, neo-Marxism, and human rights activism. See Oliveira and Darcy (1975); Fals Borda and Rahman (1991); Whyte (1991); Marika, Ngurruwutthun, and White (1992); Park et al. (1993); Heron and Reason (1997); Cohen-Cruz (1998); Kemmis and McTaggart (2000); and Haedicke (2001).

9. For discussions of this new type of postcolonial politically engaged theater in Africa, see Desai (1990), Mlama (1991), Mda (1993), Kerr (1995), Idoko (1997), and Barber (2000).

10. For examples and discussions of performance ethnography, see Kuper (1970), Garner and Turnbull (1979), Grindal and Shepard (1986), Turner (1988), Turnbull in Higgins and Cannan (1984), D. Tedlock (1986, 1998, 2003), Conquergood (1989), McCall and Becker (1990), Richardson and Lockridge (1991), Hastrup (1992, 1995), Mienczakowski and Morgan (1993), Smith (1993), Allen and Garner (1994), Laughlin (1994), Bynum (1995), Isbell (1995), Kondo (1995), Mienczakowski (1995, 1996), Schevill and Gordon (1996), Cole (2001), Wolcott (2002), and Chatterjee (2003).

11. See Turner and Turner (1982), Schechner (1983, 1985), Schechner and Appel (1990), Turner (1988), Beeman (1993), and Bouvier (1994) for discussions of theatrical anthropology. This research is very different from Eugenio Barba's "theater anthropology," which is concerned with cross-cultural actor training (Barba & Savarese, 1991). For an analysis of Iranian popular theater, see Beeman (1979, 1981).

12. Ethnographic descriptions and discussions of Indonesian popular theater include those of Belo (1960), Peacock (1978), Wallis (1979), Keeler (1987), and Hobart (2002). Balinese popular theater can be observed in a classic documentary film by Bateson, Belo, and Mead (1952).

13. See Balandier (1987), Malaurie (1993), Descola (1996), and Aurégan (2001) for discussions about the nature and impact of the series. For a recent title in this series, see B. Tedlock (2004).

14. Participants in the development and discussion of this activist paradigm within anthropology include Peggy Sanday (1976, 2003), James Peacock (1995, 1997), Anne Francis Okongwa and Joan P. Mencher (2000), and Julia Paley (2002), among others.

15. Some examples of advocacy and engaged ethnographic research include Bello, Cunningham, and Rav (1994); Curtis and McClellan (1995); Mullings (1995); Buck (1996); Dehavenon (1996); Seavey (1996); Zulaika and Douglass (1996); Harrison (1997); Cummins (1998); Thornton (1998); Brosius (1999); Fairweather (1999); Lyons and Lawrence (1999); Kim, Irwin, Millen, and Gershman (2000); Howitt (2001); McClusky (2001); Lamphere (2002); Gusterson (2003); Siegel (2003); Battiste and Youngblood Henderson (2004); Frommer (2004); Griffiths (2004); McIntosh (2004); Stevenson (2004); and B. Tedlock (2005). Electronically available reports and other information are becoming more and more important for researchers working in these rapidly developing areas. See, for example, both "New Issues in Refugee Research" and the monthly Refugee Livelihoods e-mail digest at www.unhcr.ch. See also the portal called "Forced Migration Online" at www.forcedmigration.org. and www.secure .migrationexpert.com.

16. For more information about, and models of, this morally engaged turn within the social sciences, see Harrison (1991), Denzin (1997), Frank (2000), and Chatterjii (2004). This is rapidly becoming a visible social movement. At the American Anthropological Association meeting in November, 2003, in Chicago, a coalition called the Justice Action Network of Anthropologists (JANA) was founded. Its membership list currently consists of more than 250 anthropologists from Canada, the United States, the United Kingdom, Australia, South Korea, Costa Rica, Mexico, and the Netherlands.

▣ REFERENCES

Allen, C., & Garner, N. (1994). *Condor qatay* [Play]. Produced and performed by the Department of Theatre and Dance, George Washington University, Dorothy Betts Marvin Theater, March 31–April 3.

Anderson, D. G., & Berglund, E. (Eds.). (1993). *Ethnographies of conservation: Environmentalism and the distribution of privilege.* New York: Berghahn Books.

Aurégan, P. (2001). *Des récits et des homes. Terre Humaine: un autre regard sur les sciences de l'homme.* Paris: Nathan/HER.

Bakhtin, M. (1984). *Rabelais and his world* (H. Iwolsky, Trans.). Bloomington: Indiana University Press.

Balandier, G. (1987). "Terre Humaine" as a literary movement. *Anthropology Today, 3,* 1–2.

Barba, E., & Savarese, N. (1991). *A dictionary of theatre anthropology: The secret art of the performer.* London: Routledge.

Barber, K. (2000). *The generation of plays: Yoruba popular life in theater.* Bloomington: Indiana University Press.

Bateson, G., Belo, J., & Mead, M. (1952). *Trance and dance in Bali* [Motion picture]. New York: New York University Film Library.

Battiste, M., & Youngblood Henderson, S. (2000). *Protecting indigenous knowledge and heritage: A global challenge.* Saskatoon, Saskatchewan: Purich.

Beeman, W. O. (1979). Cultural dimensions of performance conventions in Iranian Ta'ziyeh. In P. J. Chelkowski (Ed.), *Ta'ziyeh: Ritual and drama in Iran.* New York: New York University Press.

Beeman, W. O. (1981). Why do they laugh? An Interactional approach to humor in traditional Iranian improvisatory theatre. *Journal of American Folklore, 94*(374), 506–526.

Beeman, W. O. (1993). The anthropology of theater and spectacle. *Annual Reviews in Anthropology, 22,* 369–393.

Behar, R. (1996). *The vulnerable observer: Anthropology that breaks your heart.* Boston: Beacon.

Bello, W., Cunningham, S., & Rav, B. (1994). *Dark victory: The United States, structural adjustment, and global poverty.* London: Pluto.

Belo, J. (1960). *Trance in Bali.* New York: Columbia University Press.

Benedict, R. (1934). *Patterns of culture.* Boston: Houghton Mifflin.

Benedict, R. (1945). *Race: Science and politics.* New York: Viking.

Benthall, J. (1996). Enlarging the context of anthropology: The case of *Anthropology Today.* In J. MacClancy & C. McDonaugh (Eds.), *Popularizing anthropology* (pp. 135–141). London: Routledge.

Berglund, E., & Anderson, D. G. (1993). Introduction: Towards an ethnography of ecological underprivilege. In D. G. Anderson & E. Berglund (Eds.), *Ethnographies of conservation: Environmentalism and the distribution of privilege* (pp. 1–15). New York: Berghahn Books.

Blackwood, E. (1995). Falling in love with an-Other lesbian: Reflections on identity in fieldwork. In D. Kulick & M. Willson (Eds.), *Taboo: Sex, identity and erotic subjectivity in anthropological fieldwork* (pp. 51–75). London: Routledge.

Bolton, R. (1995). Tricks, friends, and lovers: Erotic encounters in the field. In D. Kulick & M. Willson (Eds.), *Taboo: Sex, identity and erotic subjectivity in anthropological fieldwork* (pp. 140–167). New York: Routledge.

Bouvier, H. (1994). Special issue on anthropology and theatre [Special issue]. *Theatre Research International, 19.*

Bowles, S., & Gintis, H. (Eds.). (1976). *Schooling in capitalist America.* New York: Basic Books.

Brecht, B. (1964). *Brecht on theater* (J. Willett, Ed.). New York: Hill & Wang.

Breslin, P. (1992, August). Coping with change: The Maya discover the play's the thing. *Smithsonian,* pp. 79–87.

Brodkey, L. (1987). Writing critical ethnographic narratives. *Anthropology and Education Quarterly, 18,* 67–76.

Brosius, P. J. (1999). Analyses and interventions: Anthropological engagements with environmentalism. *Current Anthropology, 40*(3), 277–309.

Buck, P. (1996). Sacrificing human rights on the altar of morality: White desperation, far right, and punitive social welfare reform. *Urban Anthropology, 25*(2), 195–210.

Burawoy, M., Blum, J. A., George, S., Gill, Z., Gowan, T., Haney, L., et al. (2000). *Global ethnography: Forces, connections, and imaginations in a postmodern world.* Berkeley: University of California Press.

Bynum, B. (1995, December). *My heart is still aching* [Play]. Performed at the American Anthropological Association Meeting in Atlanta, GA.

Cesara, M. [pseudonym of K. Poewe]. (1982). *Reflections of a woman anthropologist: No hiding place.* London: Academic Press.

Chatterjee, P. (2003). Staging "A time for tea": Theater and poetry in writing the plantation. *XCP (Cross Cultural Poetics), 12,* 72–78.

Chatterjii, A. (2004). Anthropology and cultural survival: On representations of indigenousness. *Anthropology News, 45*(3), 7–8.

Clough, P. T. (1992). *The end(s) of ethnography: From realism to social criticism.* Newbury Park, CA: Sage.

Clough, P. T. (1997). Autotelecommunication and autoethnography: A reading of Carolyn Ellis's *Final negotiations. Sociological Quarterly, 38,* 95–110.

Cocke, D., Porterfield, D., & Wemytewa, E. (2002). *Journeys home: Revealing a Zuni-Appalachia collaboration.* Zuni, NM: A:shiwi Publishing.

Cohen, L. (1998). *No aging in India: Alzheimer's, the bad family, and other modern things.* Berkeley: University of California Press.

Cohen-Cruz, J. (Ed.). (1998). *Radical street performance: An international anthology.* New York: Routledge.

Cole, C. M. (2001). *Ghana's concert party theatre.* Bloomington: Indiana University Press.

Conquergood, D. (1985). Performing as a moral act: Ethical dimensions of the ethnography of performance. *Literature in Performance, 5,* 1–13.

Conquergood, D. (1989). Poetics, play, process and power: The performance turn in anthropology. *Text and Performance Quarterly, 9,* 81–88.

Coplan, D. (1986). Ideology and tradition in South African black popular theater. *Journal of American Folklore, 99,* 151–176.

Coplan, D. (1994). *In the time of cannibals: The word music of South Africa's Basotho migrants.* Chicago: University of Chicago Press.

Cox, H. (1989). Drama in the arts lab. *Australian Nurses Journal, 19*(1), 14–15.

Crapanzano, V. (1986). Hermes' dilemma: The masking of subversion in ethnographic description. In J. Clifford & G. Marcus (Eds.), *Writing culture: The poetics and politics of ethnography* (pp. 51–76). Berkeley: University of California Press.

Cummins, J. (1998). Organic agriculture and the threat of genetic engineering. *Third World Resurgence, 93,* 6–7.

Curtis, K., & McClellan, S. (1995). Falling through the safety net: Poverty, food assistance and shopping constraints in an American city. *Urban Anthropology, 24,* 93–135.

Daniel, E. V. (1996). *Charred lullabies: Chapters in an anthropology of violence.* Princeton, NJ: Princeton University Press.

Deck, A. (1990). Autoethnography: Zora Neale Hurston, Noni Jabavu, and cross-disciplinary discourse. *Black American Literature Forum, 24,* 237–256.

Dehavenon, A. (1996). *From bad to worse at the emergency assistance unit: How New York City tried to stop sheltering homeless families in 1996.* New York: Action Research Project.

Denzin, N. K. (1997). *Interpretive ethnography: Ethnographic practices for the 21st century.* Thousand Oaks, CA: Sage.

Desai, G. (1990). Theater as praxis: Discursive strategies in African popular theater. *African Studies Review, 33*(1), 65–92.

Descola, P. (1996). A *bricoleur's* workshop: Writing *Les lances du créspuscule.* In J. MacClancy & C. McDonaugh (Eds.), *Popularizing anthropology* (pp. 208–224). London: Routledge.

Diamond, S. (1974). *In search of the primitive: A critique of civilization.* New Brunswick, NJ: Transaction Books.

Dubisch, J. (1995). Lovers in the field: Sex, dominance, and the female anthropologist. In D. Kulick & M. Willson (Eds.), *Taboo: Sex, identity and erotic subjectivity in anthropological fieldwork* (pp. 29–50). London: Routledge.

Dumont, J.-P. (1976). *Under the rainbow: Nature and supernature among the Panaré Indians.* Austin: University of Texas Press.

Dumont, J.-P. (1978). *The headman and I: Ambiguity and ambivalence in the fieldworking experience.* Austin: University of Texas Press.

Ellis, C., & Bochner, A. P. (Eds.). (1996). *Composing ethnography: Alternative forms of qualitative writing.* Walnut Creek, CA: AltaMira.

Ellis, C., & Bochner, A. P. (2000). Autoethnography, personal narrative, reflexivity. In N. K. Denzin & Y. S. Lincoln (Eds.). *Handbook of qualitative research* (2nd ed., pp. 733–768). Thousand Oaks, CA: Sage.

Fairweather, J. R. (1999). Understanding how farmers choose between organic and conventional production: Results from New Zealand and policy implications. *Agriculture and Human Values, 16*(1), 51–63.

Fals Borda, O., & Rahman, M. A. (Eds.). (1991). *Action and knowledge: Breaking the monopoly with participatory action-research.* New York: Apex.

Farmer, P. (2003). *Pathologies of power: Health, human rights, and the new war on the poor.* Berkeley: University of California Press.

Firth, R. (1985). Degrees of *intelligibility.* In J. Overing (Ed.), *Reason and morality* (pp. 29–46). London: Tavistock.

Fischer, M. J. (2003). *Emergent forms of life and the anthropological voice.* Durham, NC: Duke University Press.

Frank, G. (2000). *Venus on wheels: Two decades of dialogue on disability, biography, and being female in America.* Berkeley: University of California Press.

Freire, P. (1973). *Pedagogy of the oppressed.* New York: Seabury.

Friedman, N. (1990). Autobiographical sociology. *American Sociologist, 21,* 60–66.

Frommer, C. (2004). Protecting traditional medicinal knowledge. *Cultural Survival, 27*(4), 83–87.

Gailey, C. W. (1992). Introduction: Civilization and culture in the work of Stanley Diamond. In C. W. Gailey (Ed.), *Dialectical anthropology: Essays in honor of Stanley Diamond* (pp. 1–25). Gainesville: University Press of Florida.

Garner, N. C., & Turnbull, C. M. (1979). *Anthropology, drama, and the human experience.* Washington, DC: George Washington University.

Giroux, H. (1988). Critical theory and the politics of culture and voice: Rethinking the discourse of educational research. In R. Sherman & R. Webb (Eds.), *Qualitative research in education: Focus and methods* (pp. 190–210). New York: Falmer.

Goldstein, D. M. (2003). *Laughter out of place: Race, class, violence, and sexuality in a Rio shantytown.* Berkeley: University of California Press.

Griffiths, T. (2004). Help or hindrance? The global environment facility, biodiversity conservation, and indigenous peoples. *Cultural Survival, 28*(1), 28–31.

Grindal, B., & Salomone, F. (Eds.). (1995). *Bridges to humanity: Narratives on anthropology and friendship.* Prospect Heights, IL: Waveland.

Grindal, B., & Shepard, W. H. (1986, November). *Redneck girl* [Play].

Gusterson, H. (2003). Anthropology and the military: 1968, 2003, and beyond? *Anthropology Today, 19*(3), 25–26.

Haedicke, S. C. (2001). Theater for the next generation: The Living Stage Theatre Company's program for teen mothers. In S. C. Haedicke & E. Nellhaus (Eds.), *Performing democracy: International pe spectives on urban community-based performance* (pp. 269–280). Ann Arbor: University of Michigan Press.

Harrington, W. (1997). *Intimate journalism: The art and craft of reporting everyday life.* Thousand Oaks, CA: Sage.

Harrison, F. V. (1991). Ethnography as politics. In F. V. Harrison (Ed.), *Decolonizing anthropology: Moving further toward an anthropology for liberation* (pp. 88–109). Washington, DC: Association of Black Anthropologists, American Anthropological Association.

Harrison, F. V. (1997). The gendered politics and violence of structural adjustment: View from Jamaica. In L. Lamphere, H. Ragoné, & P. Zavella (Eds.), *Situated lives—gender and culture in everyday life* (pp. 451–468). New York: Routledge.

Hastrup, K. (1992). Out of anthropology: The anthropologist as an object of dramatic representation. *Cultural Anthropology,7*, 327–345.

Hastrup, K. (1995). *A passage to anthropology: Between experience and theory.* London: Routledge.

Heron, J., & Reason, P. (1997). A participatory inquiry paradigm. *Qualitative Inquiry, 3*, 274–294.

Higgins, C., & Cannan, D. (1984). *The Ik* [Play]. Woodstock, IL: The Dramatic Publishing Company.

Hobart, M. (2002). Live or dead? Televising theater in Bali. In F. D. Ginsburg, L. Abu-Lughod, & B. Larkin (Eds.), *Media worlds: Anthropology on new terrain* (pp. 370–382). Berkeley: University of California Press.

Howitt, R. (2001). *Rethinking resource management: Justice, sustainability, and indigenous peoples.* New York: Routledge.

Idoko, E. F. (1997). "Residual" forms: Viable tools for community development through drama—the "Tandari" experiment. *Borno Museum Society Newsletter, 30–31*, 27–36.

Isbell, B. J. (1995). Women's voices: Lima 1975. In D. Tedlock & B. Mannheim (Eds.), *The dialogic emergence of culture* (pp. 54–74). Urbana: University of Illinois Press.

Keeler, W. (1987). *Javanese shadow plays: Javanese selves.* Princeton, NJ: Princeton University Press.

Kemmis, S., & McTaggart, R. (2000). Participatory action research. In N. K. Denzin & Y. S. Lincoln (Eds.), *Handbook of qualitative research* (2nd ed., pp. 567–605). Thousand Oaks, CA: Sage.

Kennedy, E. L., & Davis, M. D. (1996). *Boots of leather, slippers of gold: The history of a lesbian community.* London: Routledge.

Kerr, D. (1995). *African popular theatre.* London: James Currey.

Kim, J. Y., Irwin, A., Millen, J., & Gershman, J. (2000). *Dying for growth: Global inequality and the health of the poor.* Monroe, ME: Common Courage.

Kleinman, S., & Copp, M. A. (Eds.). (1993). *Emotions and fieldwork.* Newbury Park, CA: Sage.

Kondo, D. (1995). Bad girls: Theater, women of color, and the politics of representation. In R. Behar & D. Gordon (Eds.), *Women writing culture* (pp. 49–64), Berkeley: University of California Press.

Kulick, D. (1995). The sexual life of anthropologists: Erotic subjectivity and ethnographic work. In D. Kulick & M. Willson (Eds.), *Taboo: Sex, identity and erotic subjectivity in anthropological fieldwork* (pp. 1–28). London: Routledge.

Kulick, D., & Willson, M. (Eds.). (1995). *Taboo: Sex, identity and erotic subjectivity in anthropological fieldwork.* London: Routledge.

Kuper, H. (1970). *A witch in my heart: A play set in Swaziland in the 1930s.* London: Oxford University Press.

Lamphere, L. (2002). *Structuring diversity: Ethnographic perspectives on the new immigration.* Chicago: University of Chicago Press.

Laughlin, R. M. (1994, March). *From all for all* [Play]. Performed March 24 at the conference "La sabiduria Maya ah idzatil: The wisdom of the Maya," Gainesville, FL.

Laughlin, R. M. (1995). From all for all: A Tzotzil-Tzeltal tragicomedy. *American Anthropologist, 97*(3), 528–542.

Leacock, E. (1969). *Teaching and learning in city schools: A comparative study.* New York: Basic Books.

Lee-Treweek, G., & Linkogle, S. (Eds.). (2000). *Danger in the field: Ethics and risk in social research.* London: Routledge.

Lewin, E. (1995). Writing lesbian ethnography. In R. Behar & D. Gordon (Eds.), *Women writing culture* (pp. 322–335). Berkeley: University of California Press.

Lewin, E., & Leap, W. L. (Eds.). (1996). *Out in the field: Reflections of lesbian and gay anthropologists.* Urbana: University of Illinois Press.

Lionnet, F. (1989). Autoethnography: The an-archic style of *Dust tracks on a* road. In F. Lionnet (Ed.), *Autobiographical voices: Race, gender, self-portraiture* (pp. 97–129). Ithaca, NY: Cornell University Press.

Lyons, K., & Lawrence, G. (1999). Alternative knowledges, organic agriculture, and the biotechnology debate. *Culture and Agriculture, 21*(2), 1–12.

Malaurie, J. (1993). *Le livre Terre Humaine* (Vol. 1). Paris: Plon.

Malinowski, B. (1922). *Argonauts of the western Pacific.* London: Routledge.

Marcuse, H. (1964). *One dimensional man: Studies in ideology of advanced industrial society.* New York: Houghton Mifflin.

Marika, R., Ngurruwutthun, D., & White, L. (1992). Always together, Yaka gäna: Participatory research at Yirrkala as part of the development of Yolngu education. *Convergence, 25*(1), 23–39.

McCall, M., & Becker, H. S. (1990). Performance science. *Social Problems, 32,* 117–132.

McClusky, L. J. (2001). *Here our culture is hard: Stories of domestic violence from a Mayan community in Belize.* Austin: University of Texas Press.

McIntosh, I. S. (2004). Seeking environmental and social justice. *Cultural Survival, 28*(1), 5.

Mda, Z. (1993). *When people play people: Development communication through theatre.* London: Zed Books.

Mead, M. (1928). *Coming of age in Samoa.* Harmondsworth, UK: Penguin.

Mead, M. (1935). *Sex and temperament in three primitive societies.* Harmondsworth, UK: Penguin.

Mienczakowski, J. (1995). The theatre of ethnography: The reconstruction of ethnography into theatre with emancipatory potential. *Qualitative Inquiry, 1*(3), 360–375.

Mienczakowski, J. (1996). An ethnographic act: The construction of consensual theatre. In C. Ellis & A. P. Bochner (Eds.), *Composing ethnography: Alternative forms of qualitative writing* (pp. 244–264). Walnut Creek, CA: AltaMira.

Mienczakowski, J., & Morgan, S. (1993). *Busting: The challenge of the drought spirit* [Play]. Brisbane, Australia: Griffith University Reprographics.

Mlama, P. M. (1991). *Culture and development: The popular theatre approach in Africa.* Uppsala, Sweden: Scandinavian Institute of African Studies.

Mullings, L. (1995). Households headed by women: The politics of race, class and gender. In S. D. Ginsburg & R. Rapp (Eds.), *Conceiving the new world order: The global politics of reproduction* (pp. 122–139). Berkeley: University of California Press.

Newton, E. (1993). My best informant's dress: The erotic equation in fieldwork. *Cultural Anthropology, 8*, 3–23.

Nordstrum, C. (1997). *A different kind of war story.* Philadelphia: University of Pennsylvania Press.

Nordstrum, C., & Robben, A. C. (Eds.). (1995). *Fieldwork under fire: Contemporary studies of violence and survival.* Berkeley: University of California Press.

Okely, J., & Callaway, H. (Eds.). (1992). *Anthropology and autobiography.* London: Routledge.

Okongwa, A. F., & Mencher, J. P. (2000). Anthropology of public policy: Shifting terrains. *Annual Review of Anthropology, 29*, 107–124.

Oliveira, R., & Darcy, M. (1975). *The militant observer: A sociological alternative.* Geneva: IDAC.

Ong, A. (2003). *Buddha is hiding: Refugees, citizenship, the new America.* Berkeley: University of California Press.

Paley, J. (2002). Toward an anthropology of democracy. *Annual Review of Anthropology, 31*, 469–496.

Park, P., et al. (Eds.). (1993). *Voices of change: Participatory research in the United States and Canada.* Toronto, Canada: OISE.

Peacock, J. L. (1978). Symbolic reversal and social history: Transvestites and clowns of Java. In B. Babcock (Ed.), *The reversible world: Symbolic inversion in art and society* (pp. 209–224). Ithaca, NY: Cornell University Press.

Peacock, J. L. (1995). American cultural values: Disorders and challenges. In S. Forman (Ed.), *Diagnosing America: Anthropology and public engagement* (pp. 23–50). Ann Arbor: University of Michigan Press.

Peacock, J. L. (1997). The future of anthropology. *American Anthropologist, 99*(1), 9–17.

Pierpont, C. R. (2004, March 8). The measure of America: How a rebel anthropologist waged war on racism. *The New Yorker*, pp. 48–63.

Pratt, M. L. (1994). Transculturation and autoethnography: Peru 1615/1980. In F. Barker, P. Hulme, & M. Iverson (Eds.), *Colonial discourse/postcolonial theory* (pp. 24–46). Manchester, UK: Manchester University Press.

Rapp, R. (1999). *Testing women, testing the fetus: The social impact of amniocentesis in America.* New York: Routledge.

Rappaport, R. (1995). Disorders of our own. In S. Forman (Ed.), *Diagnosing America: Anthropology and public engagement* (pp. 235–294). Ann Arbor: University of Michigan Press.

Reed-Danahay, D. E. (1997). *Auto-ethnography: Rewriting the self and the social.* Oxford, UK: Berg.

Richardson, L., & Lockridge, E. (1991). The sea monster: An ethnographic drama. *Symbolic Interaction, 14*, 335–340.

Sanday, P. (1976). *Anthropology and the public interest: Fieldwork and theory.* New York: Academic Press.

Sanday, P. (2003, November). *Public interest anthropology: A model for engaged social science.* Paper prepared for the Public Interest Anthropology Workshop, Chicago.

Schechner, R. (1983). Points of contact between anthropological and theatrical thought. *South Asian Anthropologist, 4*(1), 9–30.

Schechner, R. (1985). *Between theater and anthropology.* Philadelphia: University of Pennsylvania Press.

Schechner, R. & Appel, W. (Eds.). (1990). *By means of performance.* Cambridge, UK: Cambridge University Press.

Scheper-Hughes, N. (1992). *Death without weeping: The violence of everyday life in Brazil.* Berkeley: University of California Press.

Schevill, J., & Gordon, A. (1996). *The myth of the docile woman* [Play]. San Francisco, CA: California On Stage.

Seavey, D. (1996). *Back to basics: Women's poverty and welfare reform.* Washington, DC: Center for Research on Women.

Shokeid, M. (1995). *A gay synagogue in New York.* New York: Columbia University Press.

Siegel, S. (2003, December). *Conservation at all costs: How industry backed environmentalism creates violent conflict among indigenous peoples.* Corporate Watch. Retrieved from www .corpwatch.org/

Singer, M. (1972). *When a great tradition modernizes.* London: Pall Mall.

Smith, A. D. (1993). *Fires in the mirror: Crown Heights, Brooklyn, and other identities.* [Play]. Garden City, NY: Anchor.

Sna Jtz'ibajom (1996). *Xcha'kuxesel ak'ob elav ta slumal batz'i viniketik ta Chyapa. Renacimiento del teatro Maya en Chiapas* (2 vols.). San Cristóbal, Mexico: La Casa del Escritor.

Stevenson, M. G. (2004). Decolonizing co-management in northern Canada. *Cultural Survival, 28*(1), 68–71.

Strathern, M. (1987). The limits of auto-anthropology. In A. Jackson (Ed.), *Anthropology at home* (pp. 59–67). London, UK: Tavistock.

Taylor, D. (2001). Yuyachkani: Remembering community. In S. C. Haedicke & E. Nellhaus (Eds.), *Performing democracy: International perspectives on urban community-based performance* (pp. 310–325). Ann Arbor: University of Michigan Press.

Taylor, D. (2003). *The archive and the repertoire: Performing cultural memory in the Americas.* Durham, NC: Duke University Press.

Tedlock, B. (1991). From participant observation to the observation of participation: The emergence of narrative ethnography. *Journal of Anthropological Research, 47,* 69–94.

Tedlock, B. (2000). Ethnography and ethnographic representation. In N. K. Denzin & Y. S. Lincoln (Eds.), *Handbook of qualitative research* (2nd ed., pp. 455–484). Thousand Oaks, CA: Sage.

Tedlock, B. (2004). *Rituels et pouvoirs, les Indiens Zuñis Nouveau-Mexique.* Paris: Editions Plon, Collection Terre Humaine.

Tedlock, B. (2005). Struggles between nation states and native peoples over herbal medicines and indigenous crops. In K. Torjesen & D. Champagne (Eds.), *Indigenous peoples and the modern state* (pp. 43–59). Walnut Creek, CA: AltaMira.

Tedlock, D. (1986). The translator or why the crocodile was not disillusioned: A play in one act. *Translation Review, 20,* 6–8.

Tedlock, D. (1998, April). *Man of Rabinal: The Mayan dance of the trumpets of sacrifice* [Play]. Produced and performed in the Katharine Cornell Theater, State University of New York at Buffalo.

Tedlock, D. (2003). *Rabinal Achi: A Mayan drama of war and sacrifice.* New York: Oxford University Press.

Theidon, K. (2001). Terror's talk—fieldwork and war. *Dialectical Anthropology, 26*(1), 19–35.

Thornton, T. (1998). Crisis in the last frontier: The Alaskan subsistence debate. *Cultural Survival, 22*(3), 29–34.

Turner, V. (1988). *The anthropology of performance.* New York: PAJ Publications.

Turner, V., & Turner, E. (1982). Performing ethnography. *Drama Review, 26*(2), 33–50.

Van Maanen, J. (1995). An end to innocence: The ethnography of ethnography. In J. Van Maanen (Ed.). *Representation in ethnography* (pp. 1–35). Thousand Oaks, CA: Sage.

Wade, P. (1993). Sexuality and masculinity among Colombian blacks. In D. Bell, P. Caplan, & W. J. Karim (Eds.), *Gendered fields: Women, men and ethnography* (pp. 199–214). London: Routledge.

Wafer, J. (1996). Out of the closet and into print: Sexual identity in the textual field. In E. Lewin & W. L. Leap (Eds.), *Out in the field: Reflections of lesbian and gay anthropologists* (pp. 262–273). Urbana: University of Illinois Press.

Wallis, R. (1979). Balinese theater: Coping with old and new. *Papers in International Studies: Southeast Asia Series, 52,* 37–47.

Wax, M. L. (2003). Wartime dilemmas of an ethical anthropology. *Anthropology Today, 19*(3), 23–24.

Weston, K. (1991). *Families we choose: Lesbians, gays, kinship.* New York: Columbia University Press.

Weston, K. (1998). *Long slow burn: Sexuality and social science.* London: Routledge.

Whyte, W. F. (Ed.). (1991). *Participatory action research.* London: Sage.

Willson, M. (1997). Playing the dance, dancing the game: Race, sex and stereotype in anthropological fieldwork. *Ethnos, 62*(3–4), 24–48.

Wolcott, H, F. (2002). *Sneaky Kid and its aftermath: Ethics and intimacy in fieldwork.* Walnut Creek, CA: AltaMira.

Zulaika, J., & Douglass, W. A. (1996). *Terror and taboo: The follies, fables, and faces of terrorism.* New York: Routledge.

6

INTERPRETIVE PRACTICE AND SOCIAL ACTION

James A. Holstein and Jaber F. Gubrium

Qualitative inquiry's analytic pendulum is constantly in motion. There have been times when naturalism was on the upswing, when the richly detailed description of social worlds was the goal. At other times, analysis has shifted toward the processes by which these worlds and their experiences are socially constructed. The pendulum has even doubled back on itself as postmodern sensibilities refocus the analytic project on itself, viewing it as a source of social reality in its own right (see Gubrium & Holstein, 1997). Although it can be unsettling, the oscillation invariably clears new space for growth.

This chapter capitalizes on a momentum that is currently building among qualitative researchers interested in the practical accomplishment of meaning and its relation to social action. As social constructionist analysis expands, diversifies, and claims an increasingly prominent place on the qualitative scene, analysts are drawing new inspiration from ingenious "misreadings" and innovative admixtures of canonical sources. Recently, ethnomethodological sensibilities have been appropriated to the constructionist move (see Gubrium & Holstein, 1997; Holstein & Gubrium, 2000), heightening and broadening its analytic acuity. At the same time, yet riding a different current in the discursive and linguistic flow of the social sciences, poststructuralist discourse analysis has suffused constructionism with cultural, institutional, and historical concerns. This chapter outlines one attempt to explore and extend the discursive and interactional terrain that is emerging at the intersection of ethnomethodology and Foucauldian discourse analysis.

For some time, qualitative researchers have been interested in documenting the processes by which social reality is constructed, managed, and sustained. Alfred Schutz's

(1962, 1964, 1967, 1970) social phenomenology, Peter Berger and Thomas Luckmann's (1966) social constructionism, and process-oriented strains of symbolic interactionism (e.g., Blumer, 1969; Hewitt, 1997; Weigert, 1981) all have contributed to the constructionist project, but ethnomethodology arguably has been the most analytically radical and empirically productive in specifying the actual procedures through which social order is accomplished (see Garfinkel, 1967; Heritage, 1984; Maynard & Clayman, 1991; Mehan & Wood, 1975; Pollner 1987, 1991).[1] The analytic emphasis throughout has been on the question of *how* social reality is constructed, with ethnomethodology taking the lead in documenting the mechanisms by which this is accomplished in everyday life.

Recently, a new set of concerns has emerged in relation to ethnomethodology, reflecting a heretofore suspended interest in *what* is being accomplished, under *what* conditions, and out of *what* resources. Older naturalistic questions are being resurrected, but with a more analytically sophisticated, empirically sensitive mien, and with a view toward social action. Analyses of reality construction are now re-engaging questions concerning the broad cultural and the institutional contexts of meaning-making and social order. The emerging empirical horizons, while still centered on processes of social accomplishment, are increasingly viewed in terms of "interpretive practice"—the constellation of procedures, conditions, and resources through which reality is apprehended, understood, organized, and conveyed in everyday life (Gubrium & Holstein, 1997; Holstein, 1993; Holstein & Gubrium, 2000). Interpretive practice engages both the *hows* and the *whats* of social reality; it is centered in both how people methodically construct their experiences and their worlds, and in the configurations of meaning and institutional life that inform and shape their reality-constituting activity. A growing attention to both the *hows* and the *whats* of the social construction process echoes Karl Marx's (1956) adage that people actively construct their worlds but not completely on, or in, their own terms. The dual concern not only makes it possible to understand the construction process but also foregrounds the realities themselves that enter into and are produced by the process.

The new set of concerns converges on the issue of social action. Strict attention to the *hows* of the construction process informs us of the mechanisms by which social forms are brought into being in everyday life. But this tells us little about the shape and distribution of these realities in their own right. The possibility, for example, that family troubles will be constructed a particular way at some time and place, and differently in another, is glossed over for the construction process. The *whats* of social reality are outshone by attending exclusively to the *hows* of its construction. It's the times and places of these *whats*—the *whens* and the *wheres*—that locate the concrete, yet constructed, realities that challenge us. Attending to the latter offers a basis for making particular choices and taking action. Although an approach that emphasizes the *hows* of the construction process rests on the assumption that social life is not set in stone but is a product of practical choices, there is a need to attend carefully to the choices in tow as well as imminent possibilities. The latter moves interpretive practice into the realm of politics.

▣ FOUNDATIONAL MATTERS

Interpretive practice has diverse conceptual bases. These range from Schutz's development of a social phenomenology, to the related empirical concerns embodied in ethnomethodological programs of research developed in the wake of Harold Garfinkel's (1967) early studies and later work on talk in interaction (see Sacks, 1992; Silverman, 1998), and to the contemporaneous studies of institutional and historical discourses presented by Michel Foucault (see Dreyfus & Rabinow, 1982). Let us consider these in turn as they point us toward more recent developments.

Phenomenological Background

Edmund Husserl's (1970) philosophical phenomenology provides the point of departure for Schutz and other social phenomenologists. Concerned with the experiential underpinnings of knowledge, Husserl argues that the relation between perception and its objects is not passive. Rather, human consciousness actively constitutes objects of experience. Consciousness, in other words, is always consciousness-of-something. It does not stand alone, over and above experience, more or less immaculately perceiving and conceiving objects and events, but, instead, exists always already—from the start—as a constitutive part of what it is conscious of. Although the term "construction" came into fashion much later, we might say that consciousness constructs as much as it perceives the world. Husserl's project is to investigate the structures of consciousness that make it possible to apprehend an empirical world.

Schutz (1962, 1964, 1967, 1970) turns Husserl's philosophical project toward the ways in which ordinary members of society attend to their everyday lives, introducing a set of tenets that aligns with ethnomethodological sensibilities. He argues that the social sciences should focus on the ways that the life world—the world every individual takes for granted—is experienced by its members. Schutz cautions that "the safeguarding of [this] subjective point of view is the only but sufficient guarantee that the world of social reality will not be replaced by a fictional non-existing world constructed by the scientific observer" (1970, p. 8). From this perspective, the scientific observer deals with how the social world is made meaningful. Her focus is on *how* members of the social world apprehend and act upon the objects of their experience as if they were things separate and distinct from themselves. Emile Durkheim's (1961, 1964) formulation of a sociology based on the emergence of categories *sui generis*, separate and distinct from individual thought and action, resonates with this aim.

This is a radical departure from the assumptions underlying what Schutz calls "the natural attitude," which is the stance that takes the world to be principally "out there," so to speak, categorically distinct from acts of perception or interpretation. In the natural attitude, it is assumed that the life world exists before members are present and that it will be there after they depart. Schutz's recommendation for studying members' attention to this life world is to first "bracket" it for analytic purposes. That is, the analyst temporarily sets aside belief in its reality in order to bring its apprehension into focus. This makes it possible to view the constitutive processes—the *hows*—by which a separate and distinct empirical world becomes an objective reality for its members. Ontological judgments about the nature and essence of things and events are suspended temporarily so that the observer can focus on the ways that members of the life world subjectively constitute the objects and events they take to be real, that is, to exist independently of their attention to, and presence in, the world.

Schutz's orientation to the subjectivity of the life world pointed him to the common-sense knowledge that members use to "objectify" (make into objects) its social forms. He noted that individuals approach the life world with a stock of knowledge composed of ordinary constructs and categories that are social in origin. These images, folk theories, beliefs, values, and attitudes are applied to aspects of experience, thus making them meaningful and giving them a semblance of everyday familiarity. The stock of knowledge produces a world with which members already seem to be acquainted. In part, this is because of the categorical manner by which knowledge of particular objects and events is articulated. The myriad phenomena of everyday life are subsumed under a delimited number of shared constructs (or types). These "typifications" make it possible to account rationally for experience, rendering various things and sundry occurrences recognizable as particular types of objects or events. Typification, in other words, organizes the flux of life into apprehensible form, making it meaningful. In turn, as experience is given shape, the stock of knowledge is itself elaborated and altered in practice.

Ordinary language is the *modus operandi*. In the natural attitude, the meaning of a word is taken principally to be what it references or stands for in the real world, following a correspondence theory of meaning. In this framework, the leading task of language is to convey accurate information. Viewed as a process of typification, however, words and categories are the constitutive building blocks of the social world. Typification through ordinary language use creates the sense among users that the life world is familiarly organized and substantial, simultaneously giving it shape and meaning. Individuals who interact with one another do so in an environment that is concurrently constructed and experienced in fundamentally the same terms by all parties, even though mistakes may be made in its particular apprehensions. Taking for granted that we intersubjectively share the same reality, we assume further that we can understand each other in its terms. Intersubjectivity is thus a social accomplishment, a set of understandings sustained in and through the shared assumptions of interaction and recurrently sustained in processes of typification.

Ethnomethodological Formulations

Although indebted to Schutz, ethnomethodology is not a mere extension of his social phenomenological program. Ethnomethodology addresses the problem of order by combining a "phenomenological sensibility" (Maynard & Clayman, 1991) with a paramount concern for everyday social practice (Garfinkel, 1967). From an ethnomethodological standpoint, the social world's facticity is accomplished by way of members' constitutive interactional work, the mechanics of which produces and maintains the accountable circumstances of their lives.[2] In a manner of speaking, ethnomethodologists focus on how members actually "do" social life, aiming in particular to document the mechanisms by which they concretely construct and sustain social entities, such as gender, self, or family, for example.

Although Garfinkel's studies were phenomenologically informed, his overall project responded more directly to his teacher Talcott Parsons's theory of action (Heritage, 1984; Lynch, 1993). According to Parsons, social order was made possible through socially integrating systems of norms and values, a view that left little room for the everyday production of social order. Garfinkel sought an alternative to this approach, which in his judgment portrayed actors as "cultural dopes" who automatically put into place the effects of external social forces and internalized moral imperatives. Garfinkel's (1952) response was a vision of social order built from the socially contingent, practical reasoning of ordinary members of society, which, contrastingly, foregrounded their cultural acuity. He viewed members as possessing ordinary linguistic and interactional skills through which the accountable features of everyday life were produced. This approach deeply implicated members in the production of social order. Rather than more or less playing out moral directives, Garfinkel conceptualized members of society as actively using them, thus *working* to give their world a sense of orderliness. Indeed, ethnomethodology's focus became members' integral "methods" for accomplishing everyday reality.

The empirical investigation of members' methods takes its point of departure from phenomenological bracketing. Adopting the parallel policy of "ethnomethodological indifference" (Garfinkel & Sacks, 1970), the investigator temporarily suspends all commitments to a priori or privileged versions of the social world, focusing instead on how members accomplish a sense of social order. Social realities such as crime or mental illness are not taken for granted; instead, belief in them is suspended temporarily in order to make visible how they become realities for those concerned. This brings into view the ordinary constitutive work that produces the locally unchallenged appearance of stable realities. This policy vigorously resists judgmental characterizations of the correctness of members' activities. Contrary to the common sociological tendency to ironicize and criticize commonsense formulations from the standpoint of ostensibly correct sociological views, ethnomethodology takes members' practical reasoning for what it is—circumstantially adequate ways of interpersonally orienting to and interpreting the world at hand. The abiding guideline is succinctly conveyed by Melvin Pollner (personal communication): "Don't argue with the members!"

Ethnomethodologists have examined many facets of social order. One aim has been to document how recognizable structures of behavior, systems of motivation, or causal ties between motivations and social structures are evidenced in members' practical reasoning (Zimmerman & Wieder, 1970). Whereas conventional sociology orients to rules, norms, and shared meanings as exogenous explanations for members' actions, ethnomethodology turns this around to consider how members themselves orient to and use rules, norms, and shared meanings to account for the regularity of their actions. Ethnomethodology sets aside the idea that actions are externally rule-governed or internally motivated in order to observe how members themselves establish and sustain social regularities. The appearance of action as being the consequence of a rule is treated as just that—the *appearance* of action as compliant or noncompliant. In "accounting" for their actions by prospectively invoking rules or retrospectively offering rule-motivated explanations for action, members convey a sense of structure and order, and, in the process, cast their actions as rational, coherent, precedented, and reproducible for all practical purposes (Zimmerman, 1970).

For example, a juror in the midst of deliberations may account for her opinion by saying that the judge's instructions on how to consider the case in question compel her to think as she does. She actively uses the judge's instructions to make sense of her opinion, thereby giving it the semblance of rationality, legality, and correctness because it was formed "according to the rule" invoked (Holstein, 1983). In contrast, another juror might account for his opinion by saying that it was serving the interests of justice, citing a value or moral principle in explanation (Maynard & Manzo, 1993). From an ethnomethodological standpoint, the rationality or correctness of these opinions and the reasoning involved is not at issue. Instead, the focus is on the *hows* involved—the use of instructions, values, moral principles, and other accounts to construct a sense of coherence in social action, in this case a shared understanding among jurors of what led them to form their opinions and reach a verdict.

The accountable display of social order forms ethnomethodology's analytic horizon. Rather than assuming a priori that members share meanings and definitions of situations, ethnomethodologists consider how members achieve them by applying a native capacity to "artfully" account for their actions, rendering them orderly. Social order is not externally imposed by proverbial social forces, nor is it the expression of more or less socialized members of society; instead, ethnomethodologists view it as locally produced by way of the practices of mundane reason (Pollner, 1987). If social order is accomplished in and through its practices, then social worlds and circumstances are self-generating. Members, as we put it earlier, are continually "doing" social life in the very actions they take to communicate and make sense of it. Their language games, to borrow from Ludwig Wittgenstein (1958), virtually constitute their everyday realities; in this sense, the games themselves are "forms of life."

This implicates two properties of ordinary social action. First, all actions and objects are "indexical"; they depend upon (or "index") context (see Holstein & Gubrium, 2004). Objects and events have equivocal or indeterminate meanings without a discernible context. It is through contextualization that practical meaning is derived. Second, the circumstances that provide meaningful contexts are themselves self-generating. Each reference to, or account for, an action—such as the juror's comment that she is expressly following the judge's directives—establishes a context (in this case, of procedural dutifulness) for evaluating the self-same and related actions of the juror herself and the actions of others. The account establishes a particular context, which in turn becomes a basis for making her own and others' actions accountable. Having established this context, the juror can then virtually turn around and account for her actions by saying, for example, "That's why I feel as I do," in effect parlaying the context she has constructed for her actions into something recognizable and reasonable (accountable), if not ultimately acceptable. Practical reasoning, in other words, is simultaneously in and about the settings to which it orients and that it describes. Social order and its practical realities are thus "reflexive." Accounts or descriptions of a setting constitute that setting, while they are simultaneously being shaped by the contexts they constitute.

Ethnomethodological research is keenly attuned to naturally occurring talk and social interaction, orienting to them as constitutive elements of the settings studied (see J. M. Atkinson & Drew, 1979; Maynard, 1984, 1989; Mehan & Wood, 1975; Sacks, 1972). This has taken different empirical directions, in part depending on whether the interactive meanings or the structure of talk is emphasized. Ethnographic studies tend to focus on locally crafted meanings and the settings within which social interaction constitutes the practical realities in question. Such studies consider the situated content of talk in relation to local meaning-making (see Gubrium, 1992; Holstein, 1993; Lynch & Bogen, 1996; Miller, 1991; Pollner, 1987; Wieder, 1988). They combine attention to how social order is built up in everyday communication with detailed descriptions of place settings as those settings and their local understandings and perspectives mediate the meaning of what is said in the course of social interaction. The texts produced from such studies are highly descriptive of everyday life, with both conversational extracts from the settings and ethnographic accounts of interaction being used to convey the methodical production of the subject matter in question. To the extent the analysis of talk in relation to social interaction and setting is undertaken, this tends to take the form of (non-Foucauldian) discourse analysis, or DA, which more or less critically orients to how talk, conversation, and other communicative processes are used to make meaning (see Potter, 1996, 1997; Potter & Wetherell 1987; Wodak, 2004).

Studies that emphasize the structure of talk itself examine the conversational "machinery" through which meaning emerges. The focus here is on the sequential, utterance-by-utterance, socially structuring features of talk or "talk-in-interaction," the now familiar bailiwick of conversation analysis, or CA (see Heritage, 1984; Sacks, Schegloff, & Jefferson, 1974; Silverman, 1998; Zimmerman, 1988). The analyses produced from such studies are detailed explications of the communicative processes by which speakers methodically and sequentially construct their concerns in conversational practice. These analyses are often bereft of ethnographic detail except for brief lead-ins that describe place settings, and the analytic sense conveyed is that biographical and social particulars can be understood as artifacts of the unfolding conversational machinery, although the analysis of what is called "institutional talk" or "talk at work" has struck a greater balance with place settings in this regard (see, for example, Drew & Heritage, 1992). Although some contend that CA's connection to eth- nomethodology is tenuous because of this lack of concern with ethnographic detail (P. Atkinson, 1988; Lynch, 1993; Lynch & Bogen, 1994; for counterarguments see Maynard & Clayman, 1991, and ten Have, 1990), CA clearly shares ethnomethodol- ogy's interest in the local and methodical construction of social action (Maynard & Clayman, 1991).

John Heritage (1984) summarizes the fundamentals of conversation analysis in three premises. First, interaction is sequentially organized, and this may be observed in the regularities of ordinary conversation. All aspects of interaction can be found to exhibit stable and identifiable features, which are independent of speakers' indi- vidual characteristics. This sets the stage for the analysis of talk as structured in and through social interaction, not by internal sources such as motives or by external determinants such as social status. Second, social interaction is contextually oriented in that talk is simultaneously productive of, and reflects, the circumstances of its pro- duction. This premise highlights both the local conditioning and the local construc- tiveness of talk and interaction, exhibiting the dual properties of indexicality and reflexivity noted earlier. Third, these properties characterize all social interaction, so that no form of talk or interactive detail can be dismissed as irrelevant.

Conversation analysis has come under fire from ethnomethodologists who argue that the in situ details of everyday life are ignored at the risk of reducing social life to recorded talk and conversational sequencing. Michael Lynch, for example, has drawn a parallel between CA and molecular biology, which, proverbially speaking, tends to miss the forest for the trees, in this case the molecules. On one hand, this serves to underscore Lynch's claims about CA's basic formalism and scientism. On the other, it projects the image of conversation as a relatively predictable set of socially structured techniques through which orderly social activities are assembled. Conversation analysts, according to Lynch, attempt to describe "a simple order of structural elements and rules for combining them, and thus they undertake a reductionist program not unlike molecular biology" (1993, p. 259), which attempts to deconstruct DNA for its molecu- lar structures and rules of combination, glossing over the distinct forms of life in tow.

As a "molecular sociology" (Lynch, 1993), CA focuses on the normative, sequential "machinery" of conversation that constitutes social action. This machinery in many ways inverts conventional understandings of human agency, substituting the demands of a moral order of conversation for psychological and motivational imper- atives. Although this does not strip participants of all agency, it does place them in the midst of a "liberal economy" of conversational rights and obligations (Lynch, 1993) that tests ethnomethodological tolerance for deterministic formulations.

In contrast to what Lynch and David Bogen (1994) have labeled the "enriched pos- itivism" of CA, Garfinkel, Lynch, and others have elaborated what they refer to as a "postanalytic" ethnomethodology that is less inclined to universalistic generalizations regarding the enduring structures or machinery of social interaction (see Garfinkel, 1988; Lynch, 1993; Lynch & Bogen, 1996). This program of research centers on the highly localized competencies that constitute specific domains of everyday "work," especially the (bench)work of astronomers (Garfinkel, Lynch, & Livingston, 1981), biologists and neurologists (Lynch, 1985), and mathematicians (Livingston, 1986). The aim is to document the *haecceity*—the "just thisness"—of social practices within circumscribed domains of knowledge and activity (Lynch, 1993). The practical details of the real-time work of these activities are viewed as an *incarnate* feature of the knowledges they produce. It is impossible to separate the knowledges from the highly particularized occasions of their production. The approach is theoretically minimalist in that it resists a priori conceptualization or categorization, especially historical time, while advocating detailed descriptive studies of the specific, local practices that manifest order and render it accountable (Bogen & Lynch, 1993).

Despite their success at displaying a panoply of social accomplishment practices, CA and postanalytic ethnomethodology in their separate ways tend to disregard an important balance in the conceptualizations of talk, setting, and social interaction that was evident in Garfinkel's early work and Harvey Sacks's (1992) pioneering lectures on conversational practice (see Silverman, 1998). Neither Garfinkel nor Sacks envisioned the machinery of conversation as productive of recognizable social forms in its own right. Attention to the constitutive *hows* of social realities were balanced with an eye to the meaningful *whats*. Settings, cultural understandings, and their everyday mediations were viewed as reflexively interwoven with talk and social interaction. Sacks, in particular, understood culture to be a matter of practice, something that served as a resource for discerning the possible linkages of utterances and exchanges. Whether they wrote of (Garfinkel's) "good organizational reasons" or (Sacks's) "membership categorization devices," both initially avoided the reduction of social practice to highly localized or momentary *haecceities* of any kind.

As such, some of the original promise of ethnomethodology has been short-circuited as CA and postanalytic ethnomethodology have increasingly restricted their investigations to the relation between social practices and the immediate accounts of those practices. If the entire goal of postanalytic and CA projects is describing the accounting practices by which descriptions are made intelligible in the immediate circumstances of their production, then constructionists would need to formulate a new project that retains ethnomethodology's interactional sensibilities while extending its scope to both the constitutive and constituted *whats* of everyday life. Michel Foucault, among others, is a valuable resource for such a project.

Foucauldian Discourse Analysis

Whereas ethnomethodology engages the accomplishment of everyday life at the interactional level, Foucault has undertaken a parallel project in a different empirical register. Appearing on the analytic stage during the early 1960s, at about the same time ethnomethodologists did, Foucault considers how historically and culturally located systems of power/knowledge construct subjects and their worlds. Foucauldians refer to these systems as "discourses," emphasizing that they are not merely bodies of ideas, ideologies, or other symbolic formulations, but are also working attitudes, modes of address, terms of reference, and courses of action suffused into social practices. Foucault (1972, p. 48) himself explains that discourses are not "a mere intersection of things and words: an obscure web of things, and a manifest, visible, colored chain of words." Rather, they are "practices that systematically form the objects [and subjects] of which they speak" (p. 49). Even the design of buildings such as prisons reveals the social logic that specifies ways of interpreting persons and the physical and social landscapes they occupy (Foucault, 1979).

Like the ethnomethodological perspective on social interaction, Foucault views discourse as socially reflexive, both constitutive and meaningfully descriptive of the world and its subjects. For Foucault, however, the accent is as much on the constructive *whats* that discourse constitutes as it is on the *hows* of discursive technology. Although this represents a swing in the analytic pendulum toward the culturally "natural," Foucault's treatment of discourse as social practice suggests, in particular, the importance of understanding the practices of subjectivity. If he offers a vision of subjects and objects constituted through discourse, he also allows for an unwittingly active subject who simultaneously shapes and puts discourse to work (Best & Kellner, 1991). As Foucault (1988) explains:

> If now I am interested . . . in the way in which the subject constitutes himself in an active fashion, by the practices of the self, these practices are nevertheless not something that the individual invents by himself. They are patterns that he finds in his culture and which are proposed, suggested and imposed on him by his culture, his society and his social group. (p. 11)

This parallels ethnomethodology's interest in documenting the accomplishment of order in the everyday practice of talk and social interaction. Foucault is particularly concerned with social locations or institutional sites—the asylum, the hospital, and the prison, for example—that specify the practical operation of discourses, linking the discourse of particular subjectivities with the construction of lived experience. As in ethnomethodology, there is an interest in the constitutive quality of systems of discourse; it is an orientation to practice that views social worlds and their subjectivities as always already embedded and embodied in its discursive conventions.

Several commentators have pointed to the parallel between what Foucault (1988) refers to as systems of "power/knowledge" (or discourses) and ethnomethodology's formulation of the constitutive power of language use (P. Atkinson, 1995; Gubrium & Holstein, 1997; Heritage, 1997; Miller, 1997b; Potter, 1996; Prior, 1997; Silverman, 1993). The correspondence suggests that what Foucault documents historically as "discourses-in-practice" in varied institutional or cultural sites may be likened to what ethnomethodology traces as "discursive practice" in varied forms of social inter-action.[3] We will continue to apply these terms—discourses-in-practice and discursive practice—throughout the chapter to emphasize the parallel, as well as the possibili-ties for critical awareness and social action that it suggests.

Although ethnomethodologists and Foucauldians draw upon different intellectual traditions and work in distinct empirical registers, we want to emphasize their respec-tive concerns with social practice: They both attend to the reflexivity of discourse. Neither discursive practice nor discourse-in-practice is viewed as being caused or explained by external social forces or internal motives. Rather, they are taken to be the working mechanism of social life itself, as actually known or performed in time and place. For both, "power" lies in the articulation of distinctive forms of social life as such, not in the application of particular resources by some to affect the lives of others. Although discourses-in-practice are represented by "regimens/regimes" or lived pat-terns of action that broadly (historically and institutionally) "discipline" or encom-pass their adherents' lives, and discursive practice is manifest in patterns of talk and interaction that constitute everyday life, the practices refer in common to the lived "doing," or ongoing accomplishment, of social worlds.

For Foucault, power operates in and through discourse as the other face of knowl-edge, thus the term "power/knowledge." Discourse not only puts words to work, it also gives them their meaning, constructs perceptions, and formulates understanding and ongoing courses of interaction. The "work" entailed simultaneously and reflexively constitutes the realities that words are taken otherwise to merely reference or specify. To deploy a particular discourse of subjectivity is not simply a matter of representing a subject; in practice, it simultaneously constitutes the kinds of subjects that are meaningfully embedded in the discourse itself. For example, to articulate the dis-course of medicine in today's world automatically generates the roles of professional healer and patient, each of whose actions in turn articulate the application and recep-tion of technologies of healing served by the dominance of scientific knowledge. The taken-for-grantedness of this socially encompassing discourse makes challenges to this way of "thinking" (or speaking) seem oddly misplaced. Even the weak "power-fully" participate in the discourse that defines them as weak. This is a kind of knowledge-in-practice, and it is powerful because it not only represents but also ineluctably puts into practice what is known and shared. Language is not just more or less correlated with what it represents, but is always already a "form of life," to again put it in Wittgenstein's (1958) terms. If ethnomethodologists tend to emphasize *how* members use everyday methods to account for their activities and their worlds, Foucault makes us aware of the related conditions of possibility for *what* the results are likely to be. For example, in a Western postindustrial world, to seriously think of medicine and voodoo as equally viable paradigms for understanding sickness and healing would seem idiosyncratic, if not amusing or preposterous, in most conventional situations. The power of medical discourse partially lies in its ability to be "seen but unnoticed," in its ability to appear as *the* only possibility while other possibilities are outside the plausible realm.

Both ethnomethodology's and Foucault's approach to empirical material are "analytics," not theoretical frameworks in the traditional sense. Conventionally understood, theory purports to explain the state of the matters in question. It provides answers to *why* concerns, such as why the suicide rate is rising or why individuals are suffering depression. Ethnomethodology and the Foucauldian project, in contrast, aim to answer how it is that individual experience comes to be understood in particular terms such as these. They are pretheoretical in this sense, respectively seeking to arrive at an understanding of how the subject matter of theory comes into existence in the first place, and of what the subject of theory might possibly become. The parallel lies in the common goal of documenting the practiced bases of such realities.

Still, this remains a parallel. Because Foucault's project (and most Foucauldian projects) operates in a historical register, real-time talk and social interaction are understandably missing from chosen bodies of empirical material. Although Foucault himself points to sharp turns in the discursive formations that both form and inform the shifting realities of varied institutional spheres, contrasting extant social forms with the "birth" of new ones, he provides little or no sense of the *everyday* technology by which this is achieved (see P. Atkinson, 1995; Holstein & Gubrium, 2000). Certainly, he elaborates the broad birth of new technologies, such as the emergence of new regimes of surveillance in medicine and modern criminal justice systems (Foucault, 1965, 1979), but he doesn't provide us with a view of how these operate in social interaction. Neither do latter-day Foucauldians—such as Nikolas Rose (1990), who informatively documents the birth and rise of the technical apparatus for "governing the soul" that forms a private self—offer much insight into the everyday processes through which such regimes are accomplished. These *hows*, in other words, are largely missing from their analyses.

Conversely, ethnomethodology's commitment to documenting the real-time, interactive processes by which reality is built up into accountable structures precludes a broader perspective on constitutive resources, possibilities, and limitations. Such *whats*, so to speak, are largely absent in adherents' work. It is one thing to show in interactive detail that our everyday encounters with reality are ongoing accomplishments, but is quite another matter to derive an understanding of what the general parameters of those everyday encounters might be. The machinery of talk-in-interaction tells us little about the massive resources that are taken up in, and that guide, the operation of conversation, or about the consequences of producing particular results and not others, each of which is an important ingredient of practice. Members speak their worlds and their subjectivities, but they also articulate particular forms of life as they do so. What Foucauldian considerations offer ethnomethodology in this regard is an analytic sensitivity to the discursive opportunities and possibilities at work in talk and social interaction, but without making it necessary to take these up as external templates for the everyday production of social order.

▣ AN ANALYTICS OF INTERPRETIVE PRACTICE

The analytics of interpretive practice has benefited from drawing together eth-nomethodological and Foucauldian sensibilities. This is not simply another attempt at bridging the so-called macro-micro divide. That debate usually centers on the question of how to conceptualize the relationship between preexisting larger and smaller social forms, the assumption being that these are categorically distinct and separately discernible. Issues raised in the debate perpetuate the distinction between, say, social systems, on one hand, and social interaction, on the other. In contrast, those who consider ethnomethodology and Foucauldian analytics to be parallel operations focus their attention instead on the interactional, institutional, and cultural variabilities of socially constituting discursive practice or discourses- in-practice, as the case might be. They are concerned with how the social construction process is shaped across various domains of everyday life, not in how separate theories of macro and micro domains can be linked together for a fuller account of social organization. Doctrinaire accounts of Garfinkel, Sacks, Foucault, and others may continue to sustain a variety of distinct projects, but these projects are not likely to inform one another; nor will they lead to profitable "conversations" between dogmatic practitioners who insist on viewing themselves as speaking different analytic languages.[4] In our view, what is required is a new, hybridized analytics of reality construction at the crossroads of institutions, culture, and social interaction—an analytics that "misreads" and co-opts useful insights from established traditions in order to appreciate the possible complementarity of analytic idioms, without losing sight of their distinctive utilities, limitations, and contributions.

▣ BEYOND ETHNOMETHODOLOGY

Some conversation analysts have edged in this direction by analyzing the sequential machinery of talk-in-interaction as it is patterned by institutional context, bringing a greater concern for the *whats* of social life into the picture. Their studies of "talk at work" aim to specify how the "simplest systematics" of ordinary conversation (Sacks, Schegloff, & Jefferson, 1974) is shaped in various ways by the reflexively constructed speech environments of particular interactional regimes (see Boden & Zimmerman, 1991; Drew & Heritage, 1992). Ethnomethodologically oriented ethnographers approach the problem from another direction by asking how institutions and their respective representational cultures are brought into being, managed, and sustained in and through members' social interaction (or "reality work") (see P. Atkinson, 1995; Dingwall, Eekelaar, & Murray, 1983; Emerson, 1969; Emerson & Messinger, 1977; Gubrium, 1992; Holstein, 1993; Mehan, 1979; Miller, 1991, 1997a). Self-consciously Foucauldian ethnographers, too, have drawn links between everyday discursive practice and discourses-in-practice to document in local detail how the formulation of everyday texts such as psychiatric case records or coroners' reports reproduce institutional discourses (see Prior, 1997).

In their own fashions, these efforts consider both the *hows* and the *whats* of reality construction. But this is analytically risky business. Asking *how* questions without having an integral way of getting an analytic handle on *what* questions makes concern with the *whats* arbitrary. Although talk-in-interaction is locally "artful," as Garfinkel (1967) puts it, not just anything goes. On the other hand, if we swing too far analytically in the direction of contextual or cultural imperatives, we end up with the cultural, institutional, or judgmental "dopes" that Garfinkel (1967) decried.

The admonition that "not just anything goes" has been taken seriously, but cautiously, by both ethnomethodologists and conversation analysts as they have sought to carefully document the practical contours of interaction in the varied circumstances in which it unfolds. Systematic attention to everyday reasoning and to the sequential organization of conversations have made it clear that outcomes are constructed in the interactional apparatuses within which their antecedents are made topical. But this is a very delimited approach to the constitutive *whats* of social construction, one that lacks a broad view of the institutional and cultural discourses that serve as resources for what is likely to be constructed, when, and where in everyday life.

To broaden and enrich ethnomethodology's analytic scope and repertoire, we have extended its reach into the institutional and cultural *whats* that come into play in social interaction. This needn't be a historical extension, as was Foucault's metier, although that certainly should not be ruled out. Rather, we appeal to a "cautious" (and self-conscious) naturalism that addresses the practical and sited production of everyday life (Gubrium, 1993) and that, as will be seen, provides a integral basis for critically, not just descriptively, attending to ongoing talk and social interaction. The analytics of interpretive practice is such an effort. It centers on the interplay, not the synthesis, of discursive practice and discourses-in-practice, the tandem projects of ethnomethodology and Foucauldian discourse analysis. This analytics assiduously avoids theorizing social forms, lest the discursive practices associated with the construction of these forms be taken for granted. By the same token, it concertedly keeps institutional or cultural discourses in view, lest they be dissolved into localized displays of practical reasoning or forms of sequential organization for talk-in-interaction. First and foremost, an analytics of interpretive practice takes us, in real time, to the "going concerns" of everyday life, as Everett Hughes (1984) liked to call social institutions. There, we can focus on how members artfully put distinct discourses to work as they constitute their subjectivities and related social worlds.

The emphasis on the interplay between the *hows* and *whats* of interpretive practice is paramount. Interplay connotes a dynamic relationship. We assiduously avoid analytically privileging either discursive practice or discourses-in-practice. Putting it in ethnomethodological terms, the aim of an analytics of interpretive practice is to document the interplay between the practical reasoning and interactive machinery entailed in constructing a sense of everyday reality, on one hand, and the institutional conditions, resources, and related discourses that substantively nourish and interpretively mediate interaction, on the other. Putting it in Foucauldian terms, the goal is to describe the interplay between institutional discourses and the "dividing practices" that constitute local subjectivities and their worlds of experience (Foucault, 1965). The symmetry of real-world practice requires that we give equal treatment to both its articulative and its substantive engagements.

Qualitative researchers are increasingly focusing on these two sides of interpretive practice, looking to both the artful processes and the substantive conditions of meaning-making and social order. Douglas Maynard (1989), for example, notes that most ethnographers traditionally have asked "How do participants see things?" whereas ethnomethodologically informed discourse studies have asked "How do participants do things?" Although his own work typically begins with the later question, Maynard cautions us not to ignore the former. He explains that, in the interest of studying how members *do* things, ethnomethodological studies have tended to de-emphasize factors that condition their actions. Recognizing that "external social structure is used as a resource for social interaction at the same time as it is constituted within it," Maynard suggests that ethnographic and discourse studies can be mutually informative, allowing researchers to better document the ways in which the "structure of interaction, while being a local production, simultaneously enacts matters whose origins are externally initiated" (1989, p. 139). "In addition to knowing how people 'see' their workaday worlds," writes Maynard (p. 144), researchers should try to understand how people "discover and exhibit features of these worlds so that they can be 'seen.'"

Expressing similar interests and concerns, Hugh Mehan has developed a discourse-oriented program of "constitutive ethnography" that puts "structure and structuring activities on an equal footing by showing *how* the social facts of the world emerge from structuring work to become external and constraining" (1979, p. 18, emphasis in the original). Mehan examines "contrastive" instances of interpretation in order to describe both the "distal" and the "proximate" features of the reality-constituting work people do "within institutional, cultural, and historical contexts" (1979, pp. 73, 81).

Beginning from similar ethnomethodological and discourse analytic footings, David Silverman (1993) likewise attends to the institutional venues of talk and social construction (also see Silverman, 1985, 1997). Seeking a mode of qualitative inquiry that exhibits both constitutive and contextual sensibilities, he suggests that discourse studies that consider the varied institutional contexts of talk bring a new perspective to qualitative inquiry. Working in the same vein, Gale Miller (1991, 1997b) has proposed "ethnographies of institutional discourse" that serve to document "the ways in which setting members use discursive resources in organizing their practical actions, and how members' actions are constrained by the resources available in the settings"

(Miller, 1991, p. 280). This approach makes explicit overtures to both conversation analysis and Foucauldian discourse analysis.

Miller's (1997a) ethnography of the discourses characterizing a therapy agency is instructive, especially as it sheds light on the everyday production of the client in therapy. His 12-year ethnographic study of Northland Clinic, an internationally prominent center of "brief therapy," recounts a marked shift in client subjectivity that accompanied a conscious alteration of treatment philosophy. When Miller began his fieldwork, Northland employed "ecosystemic brief therapy," which emphasized the social contexts of clients' lives and problems. In this therapeutic environment, clients' subjectivity was linked with the systems of social relationships that were taken to form and fuel their problems. The approach required the staff to discern the state of these systems and to intervene so as to alter their dynamics and thereby effect change. Miller notes that this approach was informed by a "modern" discourse of the reality of the problems in question.

Several years into the fieldwork, Northland shifted to a more "postmodern" approach, articulating intervention in an everyday linguistic and constructivist discourse. Therapists began to apply what was called "solution-focused brief therapy," which meant viewing troubles as ways of talking about everyday life. This prompted the staff to orient to the therapy process as a set of language games, expressly appropriating Wittgenstein's sense of the term. The idea here was that troubles were as much constructions—ways of talking or forms of life—as they were real difficulties for the clients in question. This transformed clients' institutional subjectivity from being relatively passive agents of systems of personal troubles and negative stories, to being active problem solvers with the potential to formulate positive stories about themselves and design helpful solutions. As an everyday language of solutions, not a discourse of problems, became the basis of intervention, the narrative identity of clients was transformed to reveal entirely different selves. Changes in the therapy agency were articulations of transformations of both the discourse-in-practice and related discursive practices. This resulted in the construction of distinctly different "clients" and "problems" (subsequently "solutions"). Emphasizing both the *hows* and *whats* of the agency's changing interpretive practices provides both the researcher and those researched an awareness of the alternative ways client troubles can be construed and the kinds of action that can be taken to deal with them in the process.

Dorothy Smith (1987, 1990) has been quite explicit in addressing a version of the interplay between the *whats* and *hows* of social life from a feminist point of view, pointing to the critical consciousness made possible by the perspective. Hers has been an analytics initially informed by ethnomethodological and, increasingly, Foucauldian sensibilities. Moving beyond ethnomethodology, she calls for what she refers to as a "dialectics of discourse and the everyday" (1990, p. 202). Stressing the "play and interplay" of discourse, Smith articulates her view of women's "active" placement in their worlds.

It is easy to misconstrue the discourse as having an overriding power to determine the values and interpretation of women's appearances in local settings, and see this power as essentially at the disposal of the fashion industry and media. But women are active, skilled, make choices, consider, are not fooled or foolish. Within discourse there is play and interplay. (p. 202)

Philosopher Calvin Schrag (1997) similarly emphasizes the advantage of the strategy of analytic interplay over theoretical integration. Schrag puts this in the context of the need to guard against reducing what we refer to as discursive practice to mere speech acts or talk-in-interaction, on one hand, or supplanting the local artfulness of social interaction with its institutional discourses, on the other. Considering the self after postmodernity, Schrag echoes our own aim to keep both the constructive *whats* and *hows* in balance at the forefront of an analytics, lest the study of lived experience neglect or overemphasize one or the other.

We must stand guard to secure the space of discourse as temporalized event of speaking *between* the objectification of speech acts and language on the one hand and the abstractions and reifications in the structuralist designs of narratology on the other hand. The event of discourse as a saying of something by someone to someone is threatened from both "below" and "above"—from below in terms of a tendency toward an ontology of elementarism fixated on the isolable, constitutive elements of speech acts and linguistic units . . . and from above in the sense of a predilection toward an abstract holism of narratological structures that leave the event of discourse behind. Only by sticking to the terrain of the "between" will the subject as the who of discourse and the who of narrative remain visible. It is on this terrain, which we will later come to call the terrain of lived-experience, that we are able to observe the august event of a self understanding itself through the twin moments of discourse and narration. (pp. 22–23)

We echo Schrag's warning against integrating an analytics of discursive practice with an analytics of discourse-in-practice. To integrate one with the other is to reduce the empirical purview of a common enterprise. Reducing the analytics of discourse-in-practice into discursive practice risks losing the lessons of attending to institutional differences and cultural configurations as they mediate, and are not "just talked into being" through, social interaction. Conversely, figuring discursive practice as the mere residue of institutional discourse risks a totalized marginalization of local artfulness.

Analytic Bracketing

Rather than attempting synthesis or integration, we view an analytics of interpretive practice as more like a skilled juggling act, alternately concentrating on the myriad *hows* and *whats* of everyday life. This requires a new form of bracketing to capture the interplay between discursive practice and discourses-in-practice. We've called this technique of oscillating indifference to the realities of everyday life "analytic bracketing" (see Gubrium & Holstein, 1997).

Recall that ethnomethodology's interest in the *hows* by which realities are constructed requires a studied, temporary indifference to those realities. Like phenomenologists, ethnomethodologists begin their analysis by setting aside belief in the real in order to bring into view the everyday practices by which subjects, objects, and events come to have a sense of being observable, rational, and orderly for those concerned. The ethnomethodological project moves forward from there, documenting how discursive practice constitutes social structures by identifying the particular mechanisms at play. As Wittgenstein (1958, p. 19) might put it, language is "taken off holiday" in order to make visible how language works to construct the objects it is otherwise viewed as principally describing.

Analytic bracketing works somewhat differently. It is employed throughout analysis, not just at the start. As analysis proceeds, the observer intermittently orients to everyday realities as both the *products* of members reality-constructing procedures and as *resources* from which realities are constituted. At one moment, the analyst may be indifferent to the structures of everyday life in order to document their production through discursive practice. In the next analytic move, he or she brackets discursive practice in order to assess the local availability, distribution, and/or regulation of resources for reality construction. In Wittgensteinian terms, this translates into attending to both language-at-work and language-on-holiday, alternating considerations of how languages games, in particular institutional discourses, operate in everyday life and what games are likely to come into play at particular times and places. In Foucauldian terms, it leads to alternating considerations of discourses-in-practice, on one hand, and the locally fine-grained documentation of related discursive practices, on the other.

Analytic bracketing amounts to an orienting procedure for alternately focusing on the *whats*, then the *hows*, of interpretive practice (or vice versa) in order to assemble both a contextually scenic and a contextually constructive picture of everyday language-in-use. The objective is to move back and forth between discursive practice and discourses-in-practice, documenting each in turn, and making informative references to the other in the process. Either discursive machinery or available discourses becomes the provisional phenomenon, while interest in the other is temporarily deferred, but not forgotten. The constant interplay between the analysis of these two sides of interpretive practice mirrors the lived interplay between social interaction, its immediate surroundings, and its going concerns.

Because discursive practice and discourses-in-practice are mutually constitutive, one cannot argue that analysis should begin or end with either one, although there are predilections in this regard. As those who are ethnographically oriented are wont to do, Smith (1987, 1990), for example, advocates beginning "where people are"; we take her to mean that this refers to where people are located in the institutional landscape of everyday life. Conversely, conversation analysts insist on beginning with discursive practice, even while a variety of unanalyzed *whats* typically informs their efforts.[5]

Wherever one starts, neither the cultural and institutional details of discourse nor its interpolations in social interaction predetermines the other. If we set aside the need for an indisputable resolution to the question of which comes first or last, or has priority, we can designate a suitable point of departure and proceed from there, so long as we keep firmly in mind that the interplay within interpretive practice requires that we move back and forth analytically between its facets. Because we don't want to reify the components, we continuously remind ourselves that the analytic task centers on the dialectics of two fields of play, not the reproduction of one by the other.

Although we advocate no rule for where to begin, we needn't fret that the overall task is impossible or logically incoherent. Maynard (1998, p. 344), for example, compares analytic bracketing to "wanting to ride trains that are going in different directions, initially hopping on one and then somehow jumping to the other." He asks, "How do you jump from one train to another when they are going in different directions?" The question is, in fact, merely an elaboration of the issue of how one brackets in the first place, which is, of course, the basis for Maynard's and other ethnomethodologists' and conversation analysts' own projects. The answer is simple: Knowledge of the *principle* of bracketing (and unbracketing) makes it possible. Those who bracket the life world or treat it indifferently, as the case might be, readily set reality aside every time they get to work on their respective corpuses of empirical material. It becomes as routine as rising in the morning, having breakfast, and going to the workplace.[6] On the other hand, the desire to operationalize bracketing of any kind, analytic bracketing included, into explicitly codified and sequenced procedural moves would turn bracketing into a set of recipe-like, analytic directives, something surely to be avoided. We would assume that no one, except the most recalcitrant operationalist, would want to substitute a recipe book for an analytics.[7]

Analytic bracketing, however, is far from undisciplined: It has distinct procedural implications. As we have noted, the primary directive is to alternately examine both sides of interpretive practice. Researchers engaging in analytic bracketing must constantly turn their attention in more than one direction. This has resulted in new methodological hybrids. Some analysts undertake a more content-oriented form of discourse analysis (see Potter, 1996; Potter & Wetherell, 1987). Others develop methods of "constitutive ethnography" (Mehan, 1979), the "ethnography of practice" (Gubrium, 1988), or other discursively sensitive ethnographic approaches (see Holstein, 1993; Miller, 1991, 1997a). The distinguishing feature of such studies is their disciplined focus on both discourse-in-practice and discursive practice.

The dual focus should remind us that, in describing the constitutive role of discourses-in-practice, we must take care not to appropriate these naïvely into our analysis. We must sustain ethnomethodology's desire to distinguish between members' resources and our own. As a result, as we consider discourses-in-practice, we must attend to how they mediate, not determine, members' socially constructive activities. Analytic bracketing is always substantively temporary. It resists full-blown attention to discourses as systems of power/knowledge, separate from how they operate in lived experience. It also is enduringly empirical in that it does not take the everyday operation of discourses for granted as the truths of a setting *tout court*.[8]

Working Against Totalization

Centered at the crossroads of discursive practice and discourses-in-practice, an analytics of interpretive practice works against totalization. It offers breathing room for choice and action. It restrains the propensity of a Foucauldian analytics to view all interpretations as artifacts of particular regimes of power/knowledge. Writing in relation to the broad sweep of his "histories of the present," Foucault was inclined to overemphasize the predominance of discourses in constructing the horizons of meaning at particular times or places, conveying the sense that discourses fully detail the nuances of everyday life. A more interactionally sensitive analytics of discourse—one tied to discursive practice—resists this tendency.

Because interpretive practice is mediated by discourse through institutional functioning, we discern the operation of power/knowledge in the separate going concerns of everyday life. Yet, what one institutional site brings to bear is not necessarily what another puts into practice. Institutions constitute distinct, yet sometimes overlapping, realities. Whereas one may deploy a gaze that confers agency or subjectivity upon individuals, for example, another may constitute subjectivity along different lines, such as the family systems that are called into question as subjects and agents of troubles in family therapy (see Gubrium, 1992; Miller, 1997a).

Still, if interpretive practice is complex and fluid, it is not socially arbitrary. In the practice of everyday life, discourse is articulated in myriad sites and is socially variegated; actors methodically build up their shared realities in diverse, locally nuanced, and biographically informed terms. Although this produces considerable slippage in how discourses do their work, it is far removed from the uniform hegemonic regimes of power/knowledge presented in some Foucauldian readings. Social organization nonetheless is evident in the going concerns referenced by participants, to which they hold their talk and interaction accountable.

An analytics of interpretive practice must deal with the perennial question of what realities and/or subjectivities are being constructed in the myriad sites of everyday life. In practice, diverse articulations of discourse intersect, collide, and work against the construction of common or uniform subjects, agents, and social realities. Interpretations shift in relation to the institutional and cultural markers they reference, which, in turn, fluctuate with respect to the varied settings in which social interaction unfolds. Discourses-in-practice refract one another as they are methodically adapted to practical exigencies, local discursive practice serving up variation and innovation in the process (see Abu-Lughod, 1991, 1993; Chase, 1995; Narayan & George, 2002).

From How *and* What *to* Why

Traditionally, qualitative inquiry has concerned itself with *what* and *how* questions. *Why* questions have been the hallmark of quantitative sociology, which seeks to explain and ostensibly predict behavior. Qualitative researchers typically approach *why* questions cautiously. Explanation is a tricky business, one that qualitative inquiry embraces discreetly in light of its appreciation for *interpretive elasticity*. It is one thing to describe what is going on and how things or events take shape, but the question of why things happen the way they do can lead to inferential leaps and empirical speculations that propel qualitative analysis far from its stock-in-trade. The challenge is to respond to *why* question in ways that are empirically and conceptually consonant with qualitative inquiry's traditional concerns.

Our approach to interpretive practice provides a limited basis for raising particular kinds of *why* questions in the context of qualitative inquiry. In order to pursue *why* questions, one needs to designate a domain of explanation for that which is to be explained. The familiar distinction in sociology between macrosociological and microsociological domains, for instance, specifies two kinds of explanatory footing. Most commonly, macrosociological variables are used as footing for explaining microsociological phenomena, for example, using the rural/urban or the traditional/modern distinction to explain qualities of face-to-face relationships. Parsons's (1951) social system framework was once a leading model of this kind of explanation, applying macro-level systemic variables as explanations for functioning and variation in individual lives and actions.

One way for qualitative inquiry to approach *why* questions without hazarding its traditional analytic interests is to proceed from the *whats* and *hows* of social life. Provisional explanatory footing can be found at the junction of concerns for what is going on in everyday life in relation to how that is constructed, centered in the space we have located interpretive practice. Bracketing the *whats*, footing for explaining the constructive nuances of social patterns can be found in discursive practice. Bracketing the *hows*, footing for explaining the delimited patterns of meaning consequent to social construction processes can be found in discourses-in-practice.

The interplay between discourses-in-practice and discursive practice is a source of two kinds of answer for why things are organized as they are in everyday life. One kind stems from the explanatory footings of discursive practice, directing us to the artful talk and interaction that designs and designates the local contours of our social worlds. From such footings, we learn why discourses are not templates for action. Their articulation is subject to the everyday contingencies of discursive practice. Discourses-in-practice are talked into action, so to speak; they do not dictate what is said and done from the outside or from the inside, as if they were separate and distinct sources of influence. To answer why social structures are as circumstantially nuanced as they are, one can bracket the constitutive *whats* of the matter in order to reveal how recognizable activities and systems of meaning are constituted in particular domains of everyday life. Discursive practice, in other words, provides the footing for answering why recognizable constellations of social order take on locally distinctive shapes.

We may also answer limited *why* questions that are related to discursive practice, questions such as why discursive actions unfold in specific directions or why they have particular consequences. Answers emerge when we bracket the constitutive work that shapes who and what we are and what it is that we do. By itself, the machinery of conversation gives us few clues as to when, where, or what particular patterns of meaning or action will be artfully produced and managed. The machinery is like a galloping horse, but we have little or no sense of when it began to run, where it's headed, what indeed it is up to, and what might happen when it gets there. Is it racing, fleeing, playing polo, delivering the mail, or what? Each of these possibilities requires a discourse to set its course and to tell us what messages it might be conveying. This can inform us in delimited ways of why the machinery of speech environments is organized and propelled in the ways it is. Discourse-in-practice provides the footing for answering why discursive practice proceeds in the direction it does, toward what end, in pursuit of what goals, and in relation to what meanings.

◩ SUSTAINING A CRITICAL CONSCIOUSNESS

The interplay of discourse-in-practice and discursive practice sustains an integral critical consciousness for qualitative inquiry, which is a necessary basis for related social action. Each component of interpretive practice serves as *endogenous* grounds for raising serious questions relating to the empirical assumptions of ongoing inquiry. Critical consciousness is built into this framework; it is not external to it. Indeed, it's the other face of analytic bracketing. If, for purposes of broadening our knowledge of everyday life, analytic bracketing provides a means of combining attention to constitutive *hows* with substantive *whats*, it simultaneously enjoins us to continuously pay attention to what we may be shortchanging in the service of one of these questions or the other. The continuing enterprise of analytic bracketing doesn't keep us comfortably ensconced throughout the research process in a domain of indifference to the lived realities of experience, as a priori bracketing does. Nor does analytic bracketing keep us comfortably engaged in the unrepentant naturalism of documenting the world of everyday life the way it really is. Rather, it continuously jerks us out of the analytic lethargies of both endeavors.

When questions of discourse-in-practice take the stage, there are grounds for problematizing or politicizing the sum and substance of what otherwise can be too facilely viewed as arbitrarily or individualistically constructed, managed, and sustained. The persistent urgency of *what* questions cautions us not to assume that interpersonal agency, artfulness, or the machinery of social interaction is the whole story. The urgency prompts us to inquire into the broader sources of matters that are built up across time and circumstance in discursive practice, the contemporaneous conditions that inform and shape the construction process, and the personal and interpersonal consequences for those involved of having constituted their world in the way they have. Although the view toward interpretive practice doesn't orient naturalistically to the "real world," neither does it take everyday life as built from the ground up in talk-in-interaction on each and every conversational or narrative occasion. The political consequence of this is an analytic framework that turns to matters of social organization and control, implicating a reality that doesn't rest completely on the machinery of talk or the constructive quality of social interaction. It turns us to wider contexts in search of other sources of change or stability.

When discursive practice commands the spotlight, there is a basis for critically challenging the representational hegemony of taken-for-granted realities. The continual urgency of *how* questions warns us not to assume that the world as it now is, is the world that must be (cf. Freire's [1970] strategy of *conscientização*). The warning prompts us to "unsettle" realities in search of their construction to reveal the constitutive processes that produce and sustain particular realities as the processes are engaged, not for time immemorial. Critically framed, the *how* concerns of interpretive practice caution us to remember that the everyday realities of our lives—whether they are being normal, abnormal, law abiding, criminal, male, female, young, or old—are realities we *do*. Having done them, they can be undone. We can move on to do realities, producing and reproducing, time and again, the world we inhabit. Politically, this presents the recognition that, in the world we live in, we could enact alternate possibilities or alternative directions, which the apparent organization of our lives might appear to make seem impossible. If we make visible the constructive fluidity and malleability of social forms, we also reveal a potential for change (see Gubrium & Holstein, 1990, 1994, 1995, 1997; Holstein & Gubrium, 2000).

The critical consciousness of this perspective deploys the continuous imperative to take issue with discourse or discursive practice when either one is foregrounded, thus turning the analytics on itself as it pursues its goals. Reflexively framed, the interplay of discourse and discursive practice transforms analytic bracketing into critical bracketing, offering a basis not only for documenting interpretive practice, but also for critically commenting on its own constructions, putting the analytic pendulum in motion in relation to itself.

Social Action

The critical consciousness that is endogenous to interpretive practice can be taken outside the context of research and analysis. Further attending to the substance of the social realities at stake in a realm of everyday life can specify the *whats* into *whens* and *wheres*. Further attending to what is at stake in the construction process can lead us to identify the times when and the places where those concerned construct particular social forms in the ways they do. Knowing this provides interested parties, such as family members and troubled individuals, not just social researchers, with knowledge of the alternative constructions available to them for assembling themselves and their experiences in particular ways. They are provided distinct bases for action in the context of various discourses, as Foucauldians might put it, to construct their lives so that preferred solutions come into play. This works against totalization in the world of action.

For example, Gubrium's (1992) comparative field study of two family therapy programs focused on both the *hows* and the *whats* of the process by which therapists and family members constructed family troubles. His material shows how participants in both programs went about assembling the knowledge and approaches available to them into explicit pictures of domestic disorder and equally straightforward designs for turning disorder into orderly, or functional, family lives. The *hows*, or mechanisms of the process, were similar in the two programs, including cataloging and classifying particular experiences into reflexively constructed categories recognizable to all. The *whats*, however, were distinct. In one of the facilities, an outpatient program called "Westside House," family troubles were interpreted and clinically categorized as the dysfunctions of a hierarchical family system. In the other facility, an inpatient program located at what Gubrium called "Fairview Hospital," troubles took on an emotional cast, hierarchy being displaced by mutual disclosure and democratic communication centered on individual members' feelings. What was constructed in these two locations was distinct and had contrasting consequences for the family members' lives, even though the construction process was similar.

The social action consequences follow directly from the identification and documentation of constructed differences. Comparing what is constructed at Westside House with what is constructed at Fairview Hospital provides a modicum of choice for anyone seeking solutions—in this case, to family troubles. Westside House is a discursive environment that privileges authority and downplays individual feelings, whereas Fairview Hospital is a discursive environment in which feelings and clear communication loom forth as a basis for healing familial wounds. Broadening the comparative perspective to include other discursive environments of family construction adds to the concrete choices for constructing both what these families are and solutions for what they could be (see Miller, 2001).

Taken into the world of everyday life, this provides those concerned—stakeholders such as troubled sons and daughters and distressed mothers and fathers—with evidence of the possible solutions available for understanding constructions of what troubles them as well as alternative ways of resolving those troubles. This moves beyond single solutions by providing evidence of the varied ways that troubles can be assembled into concrete realities. The *hows* and the *whats*, respectively, show that stakeholders have a choice in how their troubles will be construed as well as the options for construing them in particular ways. From related knowledge of when and where options present themselves, action can be organized toward preferred possibilities.

Although social researchers themselves aren't obliged to take a critical consciousness into the outside world, a critical consciousness does obligate them to document, publish, and make broadly available the possibilities for constructing everyday life. It is in this spirit, which stems in many ways from C. Wright Mills's (1959) call for a publicly oriented critical consciousness, that we have offered the framework of interpretive practice for public consumption and social action.

▣ NOTES

1. Some self-proclaimed ethnomethodologists, however, would reject the notion that ethnomethodology is in any sense a "constructionist" or "constructivist" enterprise (see Lynch, 1993). Some reviews of the ethnomethodological canon also clearly imply that constructionism is anathema to the ethnomethodological project (see Maynard, 1998; Maynard & Clayman, 1991).

2. Although clearly reflecting Garfinkel's pioneering contributions, this characterization of the ethnomethodological project is perhaps closer to the version conveyed in the work of Melvin Pollner (1987, 1991) and D. Lawrence Wieder (1988) than to some of the more recent "postanalytic" or conversation analytic forms of ethnomethodology. Indeed, Garfinkel (1988), Lynch (1993), and others might object to how we ourselves portray ethnomethodology. We would contend, however, that there is much to be gained from a studied "misreading" of the ethnomethodological "classics," a practice that Garfinkel himself advocates for the sociological classics more generally (see Lynch, 1993). With the figurative "death of the author" (Barthes, 1977), those attached to doctrinaire readings of the canon should have little grounds for argument.

3. Other ethnomethodologists have drawn upon Foucault, but without necessarily endorsing these affinities or parallels. Lynch (1993), for example, writes that Foucault's studies can be relevant to ethnomethodological investigations in a "restricted and 'literal' way" (p. 131), and he resists the generalization of discursive regimes across highly occasioned "language games." See McHoul (1986) and Lynch and Bogen (1996) for exemplary ethnomethodological appropriations of Foucauldian insights.

4. There is still considerable doctrinaire sentiment for maintaining "hard-headed, rigorous investigation in one idiom" while recognizing its possible "incommensurability" with others (Maynard, 1998, p. 345). The benefit, according to Maynard (1998, p. 345), would be "strongly reliable understanding in a particular domain of social life, and it need not imply narrowness, fragmentation, limitation, or isolation." Our sense is that such conversations do produce fragmentation and isolation (see Hill and Crittenden [1968] for a vivid example of nonproductive conversation deriving from incompatible analytic idioms), resulting in the stale reproduction of knowledge and, of course, the equally stale representation of the empirical world. In our view, reliability has never been a strong enough incentive to ignore the potential validities of new analytic horizons.

5. The CA argument for this point of departure is that ostensibly distinct patterns of talk and interaction are constitutive of particular settings, and therefore must be the point of departure. This is tricky, though. CA's practitioners routinely designate and describe particular institutional contexts *before* the analysis of the conversations that those conversations are said to reveal. CA would have us believe that setting, as a distinct context for talk and interaction, would

be visibly (hearably) constituted *in the machinery of talk* itself (see Schegloff, 1991). This would mean that no scene-setting would be necessary (or even need to be provided) for the production of the discursive context to be apparent. One wonders if what is demonstrated in these studies could have been produced in the unlikely event that no prior knowledge of the setting had been available, or if prior knowledge were rigorously bracketed.

CA studies always admit to being about conversation in *some* context. Even the myriad studies of telephone interaction make that discursive context available to readers *before* the analysis begins. Indeed, titles of research reports literally announce institutional context at the start. For example, one of Heritage's (1985) chapters is titled "Analyzing News Interviews: Aspects of the Production of Talk for an 'Overhearing' Audience." Immediately, the reader knows and, in a manner of speaking, is prepared to get the gist of, what conversation is "doing" in what follows. In a word, the *productivity* of talk relies as much on this analytically underrecognized start as on what the analysis proper aims to show. In such studies, context inevitably sneaks in the front door, in titles and "incidental" stage setting. Apparently, analysts fail to recognize that some measure of discursive context is being imported to assist in the explanation of how context is indigenously constructed.

Strictly speaking, the researcher cannot hope to attribute institutional patterns completely to the machinery of conversation. Nor can she completely disattend to discourse-in-practice and meaning while describing the sequential flow of conversation. Analytically, one must at some point reappropriate institutions and external cultural understandings in order to know what is artfully and methodically going on in that talk and interaction. Centered as analytic bracketing is on both sides of interpretive practice, there is concerted warrant for the continual return of the analytic gaze to discourse-in-practice.

6. There are other useful metaphors for describing how analytic bracketing changes the focus from discourse-in-practice to discursive practice. One can liken the operation to shifting gears while driving a motor vehicle equipped with a manual transmission. One mode of analysis may prove quite productive, but eventually it will strain against the resistance engendered by its own temporary analytic orientation. When the analyst notes that the analytic "engine" is laboring under, or being constrained by, the restraints of what it is currently "geared" to accomplish, she can decide to virtually "shift" analytic "gears" in order to gain further purchase on the aspects of interpretive interplay that were previously bracketed. Just as there can be no prescription for shifting gears while driving (i.e., one can never specify in advance at what speed one should shift up or down), changing analytic brackets always remains an artful enterprise, awaiting the empirical circumstances it encounters. Its timing cannot be prespecified. Like shifts in gears while driving, changes are not arbitrary or undisciplined; rather, they respond to the analytic challenges at hand in a principled, if not predetermined, fashion.

7. This may be the very thing Lynch (1993) decries with respect to conversation analysts who attempt to formalize and professionalize CA as a "scientific" discipline.

8. Some critics (see Denzin, 1998) have worried that analytic bracketing represents a selective objectivism, a form of "ontological gerrymandering." These, of course, have become fighting words among constructionists. But we should soberly recall that Steve Woolgar and Dorothy Pawluch (1985) have suggested that carving out some sort of analytic footing may be a pervasive and unavoidable feature of any sociological commentary. Our own constant attention to the *interplay* between discourse-in-practice and discursive practice—as they are understood and used by members—continually reminds us of their reflexive relationship.

Gerrymanderers stand their separate ground and unreflexively deconstruct; analytic bracketing, in contrast, encourages a continual and methodical deconstruction of empirical groundings themselves. This may produce a less-than-tidy picture, but it also is designed to keep reification at bay and ungrounded signification under control.

▣ REFERENCES

Abu-Lughod, L. (1991). Writing against culture. In R. Fox (Ed.), *Recapturing anthropology* (pp. 137–162). Santa Fe, NM: SAR Press.

Abu-Lughod, L. (1993). *Writing women's worlds: Bedouin stories.* Berkeley: University of California Press.

Atkinson, J. M., & Drew, P. (1979). *Order in court.* Atlantic Highlands, NJ: Humanities Press.

Atkinson, P. (1988). Ethnomethodology: A critical review. *Annual Review of Sociology, 14,* 441–465.

Atkinson, P. (1995). *Medical talk and medical work.* London: Sage.

Barthes, R. (1977). *Image, music, text.* New York: Hill & Wang.

Berger, P. L., & Luckmann, T. (1966). *The social construction of reality.* New York: Doubleday.

Best, S., & Kellner, D. (1991). *Postmodern theory: Critical interrogations.* New York: Guilford.

Blumer, H. (1969). *Symbolic interactionism.* Englewood Cliffs, NJ: Prentice-Hall.

Boden, D., & Zimmerman, D. (Eds.). (1991). *Talk and social structure.* Cambridge, UK: Polity.

Bogen, D., & Lynch, M. (1993). Do we need a general theory of social problems? In J. Holstein & G. Miller (Eds.), *Reconsidering social constructionism: Debates in social problems theory* (pp. 213–237). Hawthorne, NY: Aldine de Gruyter.

Chase, S. E. (1995). *Ambiguous empowerment: The work narratives of women school superintendents.* Amherst: University of Massachusetts Press.

Denzin, N. K. (1998). The new ethnography. *Journal of Contemporary Ethnography, 27,* 405–415.

Dingwall, R., Eekelaar, J., & Murray, T. (1983). *The protection of children: State intervention and family life.* Oxford, UK: Blackwell.

Drew, P., & Heritage, J. (Eds.). (1992). *Talk at work.* Cambridge, UK: Cambridge University Press.

Dreyfus, H. L., & Rabinow, P. (1982). *Michel Foucault: Beyond structuralism and hermeneutics.* Chicago: University of Chicago Press.

Durkheim, E. (1961). *The elementary forms of the religious life.* New York: Collier-Macmillan.

Durkheim, E. (1964). *The rules of sociological method.* New York: Free Press.

Emerson, R. M. (1969). *Judging delinquents.* Chicago: Aldine.

Emerson, R. M., & Messinger, S. (1977). The micro- politics of trouble. *Social Problems, 25,* 121–134.

Foucault, M. (1965). *Madness and civilization.* New York: Random House.

Foucault, M. (1972). *The archaeology of knowledge.* New York: Pantheon.

Foucault, M. (1979). *Discipline and punish.* New York: Vintage.

Foucault, M. (1988). The ethic of care for the self as a practice of freedom. In J. Bernauer & G. Rasmussen (Eds.), *The final Foucault* (pp. 1–20). Cambridge: MIT Press.

Freire, P. (1970). *Pedagogy of the oppressed.* New York: Continuum.

Garfinkel, H. (1952). *The perception of the other: A study in social order.* Unpublished doctoral dissertation, Harvard University.

Garfinkel, H. (1967). *Studies in ethnomethodology.* Englewood Cliffs, NJ: Prentice Hall.

Garfinkel, H. (1988). Evidence for locally produced, naturally accountable phenomena of order*, logic, reason, meaning, method, etc. in and as of the essential quiddity of immortal ordinary society, (I of IV): An announcement of studies. *Sociological Theory, 6,* 103–109.

Garfinkel, H., Lynch, M., & Livingston, E. (1981). The work of a discovering science construed with materials from the optically discovered pulsar. *Philosophy of the Social Sciences, 11,* 131–158.

Garfinkel, H., & Sacks, H. (1970). On the formal structures of practical actions. In J. C. McKinney & E. A. Tiryakian (Eds.), *Theoretical sociology* (pp. 338–366). New York: Appleton-Century-Crofts.

Gubrium, J. F. (1988). *Analyzing field reality.* Newbury Park, CA: Sage.

Gubrium, J. F. (1992). *Out of control: Family therapy and domestic disorder.* Newbury Park, CA: Sage.

Gubrium, J. F. (1993). For a cautious naturalism. In J. Holstein & G. Miller (Eds.), *Reconsidering social constructionism* (pp. 89–101). New York: Aldine de Gruyter.

Gubrium, J. F., & Holstein, J. A. (1990). *What is family?* Mountain View, CA: Mayfield.

Gubrium, J. F., & Holstein, J. A. (1994). *Constructing the life course.* Dix Hills, NY: General Hall.

Gubrium, J. F., & Holstein, J. A. (1995). Life course malleability: Biographical work and deprivatization. *Sociological Inquiry, 65,* 207–223.

Gubrium, J. F., & Holstein, J. A. (1997). *The new language of qualitative method.* New York: Oxford University Press.

Heritage, J. (1984). *Garfinkel and ethnomethodology.* Cambridge, UK: Polity.

Heritage, J. (1985). Analyzing news interviews: Aspects of the production of talk for an overhearing audience. In T. A. van Dijk (Ed.), *Handbook of discourse analysis* (Vol. 3, pp. 95–119). New York: Academic Press.

Heritage, J. (1997). Conversation analysis and institutional talk: Analyzing data. In D. Silverman (Ed.), *Qualitative research: Theory, method and practice* (pp. 161–182). London: Sage.

Hewitt, J. P. (1997). *Self and society.* Boston: Allyn & Bacon.

Hill, R. J., & Crittenden, K. S. (1968). *Proceedings of the Purdue Symposium on Ethnomethodology.* West Lafayette, IN: Purdue Research Foundation.

Holstein, J. A. (1983). Jurors' use of judges' instructions. *Sociological Methods and Research, 11,* 501–518.

Holstein, J. A. (1993). *Court-ordered insanity: Interpretive practice and involuntary commitment.* Hawthorne, NY: Aldine de Gruyter.

Holstein, J. A., & Gubrium, J. F. (2000). *The self we live by: Narrative identity in a postmodern world.* New York: Oxford University Press.

Holstein, J. A., & Gubrium, J. F. (2004). Context: working it up, down, and across. In C. Seale, G. Gobo, J. F. Gubrium, & D. Silverman (Eds.), *Qualitative research practice* (pp. 297–311). London: Sage.

Hughes, E. C. (1984). Going concerns: The study of American institutions. In D. Riesman & H. Becker (Eds.), *The sociological eye* (pp. 52–64). New Brunswick, NJ: Transaction Books.

Husserl, E. (1970). *Logical investigation.* New York: Humanities Press.

Livingston, E. (1986). *The ethnomethodological foundations of mathematics.* London: Routledge and Kegan Paul.

Lynch, M. (1985). *Art and artifact in laboratory science.* London: Routledge and Kegan Paul.

Lynch, M. (1993). *Scientific practice and ordinary action.* Cambridge, UK: Cambridge University Press.

Lynch, M., & Bogen, D. (1994). Harvey Sacks' primitive natural science. *Theory, Culture, and Society, 11,* 65–104.

Lynch, M., & Bogen, D. (1996). *The spectacle of history.* Durham, NC: Duke University Press.

Marx, K. (1956). *Selected writings in sociology and social philosophy* (T. Bottomore, Ed.). New York: McGraw-Hill.

Maynard, D. W. (1984). *Inside plea bargaining.* New York: Plenum.

Maynard, D. W. (1989). On the ethnography and analysis of discourse in institutional settings. In J. Holstein & G. Miller (Eds.), *Perspectives on social problems* (Vol. 1, pp. 127–146). Greenwich, CT: JAI.

Maynard, D. W. (1998). On qualitative inquiry and extramodernity. *Contemporary Sociology, 27,* 343–345.

Maynard, D. W., & Clayman, S. E. (1991). The diversity of ethnomethodology. *Annual Review of Sociology, 17,* 385–418.

Maynard, D. W., & Manzo, J. (1993). On the sociology of justice. *Sociological Theory, 11,* 171–193.

McHoul, A. (1986). The getting of sexuality: Foucault, Garfinkel, and the analysis of sexual discourse. *Theory, Culture, and Society, 3,* 65–79.

Mehan, H. (1979). *Learning lessons: Social organization in the classroom.* Cambridge, MA: Harvard University Press.

Mehan, H., & Wood, H. (1975). *The reality of ethnomethodology.* New York: Wiley.

Miller, G. (1991). *Enforcing the work ethic.* Albany: SUNY Press.

Miller, G. (1997a). *Becoming miracle workers: Language and meaning in brief therapy.* New York: Aldine de Gruyter.

Miller, G. (1997b). Building bridges: The possibility of analytic dialogue between ethnography, conversation analysis, and Foucault. In D. Silverman (Ed.), *Qualitative research: Theory, method and practice* (pp. 24–44). London: Sage.

Miller, G. (2001). Changing the subject: Self-construction in brief therapy. In J. F. Gubrium & J. A. Holstein (Eds.), *Institutional selves: Troubled identities in a postmodern world* (pp. 64–83). New York: Oxford University Press.

Mills, C. W. (1959). *The sociological imagination.* New York: Grove Press.

Narayan, K., & George, K. M. (2002). Personal and folk narrative as culture representation. In J. F. Gubrium & J. A. Holstein (Eds.), *Handbook of interview research* (pp. 815–832). Thousand Oaks, CA: Sage.

Parsons, T. (1951). *The social system.* New York: Free Press.

Pollner, M. (1987). *Mundane reason.* Cambridge, UK: Cambridge University Press.

Pollner, M. (1991). Left of ethnomethodology: The rise and decline of radical reflexivity. *American Sociological Review, 56,* 370–380.

Potter, J. (1996). *Representing reality: Discourse, rhetoric, and social construction.* London: Sage.

Potter, J. (1997). Discourse analysis as a way of analyzing naturally-occurring talk. In D. Silverman (Ed.), *Qualitative research: Theory, method and practice* (pp. 144–160). London: Sage.

Potter, J., & Wetherell, M. (1987). *Discourse and social psychology.* London: Sage.

Prior, L. (1997). Following in Foucault's footsteps: Text and context in qualitative research. In D. Silverman (Ed.), *Qualitative research: Theory, method and practice* (pp. 63–79). London: Sage.

Rose, N. (1990). *Governing the soul: The shaping of the private self.* New York: Routledge.

Sacks, H. (1972). An initial investigation of the usability of conversational data for doing sociology. In D. Sudnow (Ed.), *Studies in social interaction* (pp. 31–74). New York: Free Press.

Sacks, H. (1992). *Lectures on conversation* (Vols. 1 & 2). Oxford, UK: Blackwell.

Sacks, H., Schegloff, E., & Jefferson, G. (1974). A simplest systematics for the organization of turn-taking for conversation. *Language, 50,* 696–735.

Schegloff, E. A. (1991). Reflections on talk and social structure. In D. Boden & D. Zimmerman (Eds.), *Talk and social structure* (pp. 44–70). Cambridge, UK: Polity.

Schrag, C. O. (1997). *The self after postmodernity.* New Haven, CT: Yale University Press.

Schutz, A. (1962). *The problem of social reality.* The Hague: Martinus Nijhoff.

Schutz, A. (1964). *Studies in social theory.* The Hague: Martinus Nijhoff.

Schutz, A. (1967). *The phenomenology of the social world.* Evanston, IL: Northwestern University Press.

Schutz, A. (1970). *On phenomenology and social relations.* Chicago: University of Chicago Press.

Silverman, D. (1985). *Qualitative methodology and sociology.* Aldershot, UK: Gower.

Silverman, D. (1993). *Interpretive qualitative data.* London: Sage.

Silverman, D. (Ed.). (1997). *Qualitative research: Theory, method and practice.* London: Sage.

Silverman, D. (1998). *Harvey Sacks: Conversation analysis and social science.* New York: Oxford University Press.

Smith, D. E. (1987). *The everyday world as problematic.* Boston: Northeastern University Press.

Smith, D. E. (1990). *Texts, facts, and femininity.* London: Routledge.

ten Have, P. (1990). Methodological issues in conversation analysis. *Bulletin de Methodologie Sociologique, 27,* 23–51.

Weigert, A. J. (1981). *Sociology of everyday life.* New York: Longman.

Wieder, D. L. (1988). *Language and social reality.* Washington, DC: University Press of America.

Wittgenstein, L. (1958). *Philosophical investigations.* New York: Macmillan.

Wodak, R. (2004). Critical discourse analysis. In C. Seale, G. Gobo, J. F. Gubrium, & D. Silverman (Ed.), *Qualitative research practice* (pp. 197–214). London: Sage.

Woolgar, S., & Pawluch, D. (1985). Ontological gerrymandering. *Social Problems, 32,* 214–227.

Zimmerman, D. H. (1970). The practicalities of rule use. In J. Douglas (Ed.), *Understanding everyday life* (pp. 221–238). Chicago: Aldine.

Zimmerman, D. H. (1988). On conversation: The conversation analytic perspective. In J. A. Anderson (Ed.), *Communication yearbook 11* (pp. 406–432). Beverly Hills, CA: Sage.

Zimmerman, D. H., & Wieder, D. L. (1970). Ethnomethodology and the problem of order. In J. Douglas (Ed.), *Understanding everyday life* (pp. 285–295). Chicago: Aldine.

7

GROUNDED THEORY IN THE 21ST CENTURY

Applications for Advancing Social Justice Studies

Kathy Charmaz

G rounded theory methods of the 20th century offer rich possibilities for advancing qualitative research in the 21st century. Social justice inquiry is one area among many in which researchers can fruitfully apply grounded theory methods that Barney G. Glaser and Anselm L. Strauss (1967) created. In keeping with the theme for the current *Handbook* of advancing constructive social critique and change through qualitative research, this chapter opens discussion about applying grounded theory methods to the substantive area(s) of social justice. Inquiry in this area assumes focusing on and furthering equitable distribution of resources, fairness, and eradication of oppression (Feagin, 1999).[1]

Author's Note. I thank Adele E. Clarke, Norman K. Denzin, Udo Kelle, Anne Marie McLauglin, and Janice Morse for their comments on an earlier version of this chapter. I also appreciate having the views of the following members of the Sonoma State University Faculty Writing Program: Karin Enstam, Scott Miller, Tom Rosin, Josephine Schallehn, and Thaine Stearns. I presented brief excerpts from earlier drafts in a keynote address, "Reclaiming Traditions and Re-forming Trends in Qualitative Research," at the Qualitative Research Conference, Carleton University, Ottawa, Canada, May 22, 2003, and in a presentation, "Suffering and the Self: Meanings of Loss in Chronic Illness," at the Sociology Department, University of California, Los Angeles, January 9, 2004.

The term "grounded theory" refers both to a method of inquiry and to the product of inquiry. However, researchers commonly use the term to mean a specific mode of analysis (see Charmaz, 2003a). Essentially, grounded theory methods are a set of flexible analytic guidelines that enable researchers to focus their data collection and to build inductive middle-range theories through successive levels of data analysis and conceptual development. A major strength of grounded theory methods is that they provide tools for analyzing processes, and these tools hold much potential for studying social justice issues. A grounded theory approach encourages researchers to remain close to their studied worlds and to develop an integrated set of theoretical concepts from their empirical materials that not only synthesize and interpret them but also show processual relationships.

Grounded theory methods consist of simultaneous data collection and analysis, with each informing and focusing the other throughout the research process.[2] As grounded theorists, we begin our analyses early to help us focus further data collection.[3] In turn, we use these focused data to refine our emerging analyses. Grounded theory entails developing increasingly abstract ideas about research participants' meanings, actions, and worlds and seeking specific data to fill out, refine, and check the emerging conceptual categories. Our work results in an analytic interpretation of participants' worlds and of the processes constituting how these worlds are constructed. Thus, we can use the processual emphasis in grounded theory to analyze relationships between human agency and social structure that pose theoretical and practical concerns in social justice studies. Grounded theorists portray their understandings of research participants' actions and meanings, offer abstract interpretations of empirical relationships, and create conditional statements about the implications of their analyses.

Applying grounded theory methods to the substantive area of social justice produces reciprocal benefits. The critical stance in social justice in combination with the analytic focus of grounded theory broadens and sharpens the scope of inquiry. Such efforts locate subjective and collective experience in larger structures and increase understanding of how these structures work (see also Clarke, 2003, 2005; Maines, 2001, 2003). Grounded theory can supply analytic tools to move social justice studies beyond description, while keeping them anchored in their respective empirical worlds.[4] Not only are justice and injustice abstract concepts, but they are, moreover, *enacted processes*, made real through actions performed again and again. Grounded theorists can offer integrated theoretical statements about the conditions under which injustice or justice develops, changes, or continues. How might we move in this direction? Which traditions provide starting points?

CONSTRUCTIVIST RE-VISIONS OF GROUNDED THEORY

To develop a grounded theory for the 21st century that advances social justice inquiry, we must build upon its constructionist elements rather than objectivist leanings. In the past, most major statements of grounded theory methods minimized what numerous critics (see, for example, Atkinson, Coffey, & Delamont, 2003; Bryant, 2002, 2003; Coffey, Holbrook, & Atkinson, 1996; Silverman, 2000) find lacking: interpretive, constructionist inquiry. Answering this criticism means building on the Chicago school roots in grounded theory consistent with my constructivist statement in the second edition of the handbook (Charmaz, 2000a).[5] Currently, the Chicago school antecedents of grounded theory are growing faint and risk being lost. Contemporary grounded theorists may not realize how this tradition influences their work or may not act from its premises at all. Thus, we need to review, renew, and revitalize links to the Chicago school as grounded theory develops in the 21st century.

Building on the Chicago heritage supports the development of grounded theory in directions that can serve inquiry in the area of social justice. Both grounded theory methods and social justice inquiry fit pragmatist emphases on process, change, and probabilistic outcomes.[6] The pragmatist conception of emergence recognizes that the reality of the present differs from the past from which it develops (Strauss, 1964). Novel aspects of experience give rise to new interpretations and actions. This view of emergence can sensitize social justice researchers to study change in new ways, and grounded theory methods can give them the tools for studying it. Thus, we must revisit and reclaim Chicago school pragmatist and fieldwork traditions and develop their implications for social justice and democratic process.[7] To do so, we must move further into a constructionist social science and make the positivist roots of grounded theory problematic.

For many researchers, grounded theory methods provided a template for doing qualitative research stamped with positivist approval. Glaser's (see, especially, Glaser, 1978, 1992) strong foundation in mid-20th-century positivism gave grounded theory its original objectivist cast with its emphases in logic, analytic procedures, comparative methods, and conceptual development and assumptions of an external but discernible world, unbiased observer, and discovered theory. Strauss's versions of grounded theory emphasized meaning, action, and process, consistent with his intellectual roots in pragmatism and symbolic interactionism. These roots seem shrunken in his methodological treatises with Juliet Corbin (Strauss & Corbin, 1990, 1998) but grow robust in other works (see, for example, Corbin & Strauss, 1988; Strauss, 1993). Like Glaser, Strauss and Corbin also advanced positivistic procedures, although different ones. They introduced new technical procedures and made verification an explicit goal, thus bringing grounded theory closer to positivist ideals.[8] In divergent ways, Strauss and Corbin's works as well as Glaser's treatises draw upon objectivist assumptions founded in positivism.

Since then, a growing number of scholars have aimed to move grounded theory in new directions away from its positivist past. I share their goal and aim to build on the constructivist elements in grounded theory and to reaffirm its Chicago school antecedents. To date, scholars have questioned the epistemologies of both Glaser's and Strauss and Corbin's versions of grounded theory. We challenge earlier assumptions about objectivity, the world as an external reality, relations between the viewer and viewed, the nature of data, and authors' representations of research participants. Instead, we view positivist givens as social constructions to question and alter. Thus, when we adopt any positivist principle or procedure, we attempt to do so knowingly and to make our rationales explicit. In the second edition of the handbook (Charmaz, 2000a), I argued for building on the pragmatist underpinnings in grounded theory and developing it as a social constructionist method. Clive Seale (1999) contends that we can retain grounded theory methods without adhering to a naïve realist episte-mology. Antony Bryant (2002, 2003) calls for re-grounding grounded theory in an epistemology that takes recent methodological developments into account, and Adele E. Clarke (2003, 2005) aims to integrate postmodern sensibilities with grounded theory and to provide new analytic tools for discerning and conceptualizing subtle empirical relationships. These moves by grounded theorists reflect shifts in approaches to quali-tative research.[9]

A constructivist grounded theory (Charmaz, 1990, 2000a, 2003b; Charmaz & Mitchell, 2001) adopts grounded theory guidelines as tools but does not subscribe to the objectivist, positivist assumptions in its earlier formulations. A constructivist approach emphasizes the studied phenomenon rather than the methods of studying it. Constructivist grounded theorists take a reflexive stance on modes of knowing and representing studied life. That means giving close attention to empirical realities and our collected renderings of them—and locating oneself in these realities. It does not assume that data simply await discovery in an external world or that methodological procedures will correct limited views of the studied world. Nor does it assume that impartial observers enter the research scene without an interpretive frame of refer-ence. Instead, what observers see and hear depends upon their prior interpretive frames, biographies, and interests as well as the research context, their relationships with research participants, concrete field experiences, and modes of generating and recording empirical materials. No qualitative method rests on pure induction—the questions we ask of the empirical world frame what we know of it. In short, we share in constructing what we define as data. Similarly, our conceptual categories arise through our interpretations *of* data rather than emanating *from* them or from our methodologi-cal practices (cf. Glaser, 2002). Thus, our theoretical analyses are interpretive renderings of a reality, not objective reportings of it.

Whether informed by Glaser (1978, 1992, 1998, 2002) or Strauss and Corbin (1990, 1998), many researchers adopted positivist grounded theory as a template. The con-structivist position recasts this template by challenging its objectivist underpin-nings. We can use a constructivist template to inform social justice research in the 21st century. Clearly, much research in the area of social justice is objectivist and flows from standard positivist methodologies. A constructivist grounded theory offers another alternative: a systematic approach to social justice inquiry that fosters integrating sub-jective experience with social conditions in our analyses.

An interest in social justice means attentiveness to ideas and actions concerning fairness, equity, equality, democratic process, status, hierarchy, and individual and collective rights and obligations. It signifies thinking about being human and about creating good societies and a better world. It prompts reassessment of our roles as national and world citizens. It means exploring tensions between complicity and consciousness, choice and constraint, indifference and compassion, inclusion and exclusion, poverty and privilege, and barriers and opportunities. It also means taking a critical stance toward actions, organizations, and social institutions. Social justice studies require looking at both realities and ideals. Thus, contested meanings of "shoulds" and "oughts" come into play. Unlike positivists of the past, social justice researchers openly bring their shoulds and oughts into the discourse of inquiry.

◙ Reexamining Grounded Theory of the Past

In the 20th century, grounded theory methods offered guidelines and legitimacy for conducting research. Glaser and Strauss (1967) established qualitative research as valuable in its own right and argued that it proceeds from a different logic than quantitative research. Although researchers did not always understand grounded theory methods and seldom followed them beyond a step or two, they widely cited and acclaimed these methods because they legitimized and codified a previously implicit process. Grounded theory methods offered explicit strategies, procedural rigor, and seeming objectivity. As Karen Locke (1996) notes, many researchers still use grounded theory methods for "a rhetoric of justification as opposed to a rhetoric of explication" (p. 244; see also Charmaz, 1983; Silverman, 2000).

All analyses come from particular standpoints, including those emerging in the research process. Grounded theory studies emerge from wrestling with data, making comparisons, developing categories, engaging in theoretical sampling, and integrating an analysis. But *how* we conduct all these activities does not occur in a social vacuum. Rather, the entire research process is interactive; in this sense, we bring past interactions and current interests into our research, and we interact with our empirical materials and emerging ideas as well as, perhaps, granting agencies, institutional review boards, and community agencies and groups, along with research participants and colleagues. Neither data nor ideas are mere objects that we passively observe and compile (see also Holstein & Gubrium, 1995).

Glaser (2002) treats data as something separate from the researcher and implies that they are untouched by the competent researcher's interpretations. If, perchance, researchers somehow interpret their data, then according to Glaser, these data are "rendered objective" by looking at many cases. Looking at many cases strengthens a researcher's grasp of the empirical world and helps in discerning variation in the studied phenomenon. However, researchers may elevate their own assumptions and interpretations to "objective" status if they do not make them explicit.

No analysis is neutral—despite research analysts' claims of neutrality. We do not come to our studies uninitiated (see also Denzin, 1994; Morse, 1999; Schwandt, 1994, 2000). What we know shapes, but does not necessarily determine, what we "find." Moreover, *each* stage of inquiry is constructed through social processes. If we treat these processes as unproblematic, we may not recognize how they are constructed. Social justice researchers likely understand their starting assumptions; other researchers may not—including grounded theorists.[10] As social scientists, we *define* what we record as data, yet how we define data outlines how we represent them in our works. Such definitional decisions—whether implicit or explicit—reflect moral choices that, in turn, spawn subsequent moral decisions and actions.[11]

Rather than abandoning the traditional positivist quest for empirical detail, I argue that we advance it—*without the cloak of neutrality and passivity enshrouding midcentury positivism.* Gathering rich empirical materials is the first step. Recording these data systematically prompts us to pursue leads that we might otherwise ignore or not realize. Through making systematic recordings, we also gain comparative materials to pinpoint contextual conditions and to explore links between levels of analysis. By seeking empirical answers to emerging theoretical questions, we learn about the worlds we enter and can increase the cogency of our subsequent analyses. Hence, data need to be informed by our theoretical sensitivity. Data alone are insufficient; they must be telling and must answer theoretical questions.

Without theoretical scrutiny, direction, and development, data culminate in mundane descriptions (see also Silverman, 2000). The value of the product then becomes debatable, and critics treat earlier studies as reified representations of the limits of the method itself rather than how it was used (Charmaz, 2000a). Burawoy (1991) categorizes the products of grounded theory as empirical generalizations. Moreover, he claims that the method does not consider power in micro contexts and that "it represses the broader macro forces that both limit change and create domination in the micro sphere" (p. 282). I disagree. Simply because earlier authors did not address power or macro forces does not mean that grounded theory methods cannot. In contrast to Burawoy's claims, I argue that we should use grounded theory methods in precisely these areas to gain fresh insights in social justice inquiry.

Critics of grounded theory commonly miss four crucial points: (a) theorizing is an activity; (b) grounded theory methods provide a way to proceed with this activity; (c) the research problem and the researcher's unfolding interests shape the *content* of this activity, not the method; and (d) the products of theorizing reflect how researchers acted on these points. As Dan E. Miller (2000) argues, the ironic issue is that researchers have done so little grounded theory, despite their claims to use it. Its potential for developing theory remains untapped, as does its potential for studying power and inequality.

Social justice studies require data that diverse audiences agree represent the empirical world and that researchers have given a fair assessment. I do not mean that we reify, objectify, and universalize these data. Instead, I mean that we must start by gathering thorough empirical materials precisely because social justice research may provoke controversy and contested conclusions. Thus, we need to identify clear boundaries and limits of our data. Locating the data strengthens the foundation for making theoretical insights and for providing evidence for evaluative claims. Critics can then evaluate an author's argument on its merits. The better they can see direct connections between the evidence and points in the argument, the more this argument will persuade them. The lingering hegemony of positivism still makes controversial research suspect, as Fine, Weis, Weseen, and Wong (2000) observe. Therefore, the data for such studies must be unassailable.

A strong empirical foundation is the first step in achieving credibility—for both social justice researchers and grounded theorists. Despite reliance on data-driven interpretations, the rush to "theorize"—or perhaps to publish—has led some grounded theorists to an unfortunate neglect of thorough data collection, which has persisted since Lofland and Lofland (1984) first noted it. Glaser (1992, 2002) discounts quests for accurate data and dismisses full description as distinguishing conventional qualitative data analysis from grounded theory. However, leading studies with implications for social justice and policy have had solid empirical foundations (see, for example, Duneire, 1992; Glaser & Strauss, 1965; Goffman, 1961; Mitchell, 2002; Snow & Anderson, 1993). Grounded theory studies that lack empirical vitality cannot support a rationale for major social change—or even minor policy recommendations. The stronger the social justice arguments derived from a study, particularly controversial ones, the greater the need for a robust empirical foundation with compelling evidence.

▣ USING GROUNDED THEORY TO STUDY SOCIAL JUSTICE ISSUES

Initial Reflections

Both the steps and the logic of grounded theory can advance social justice research. Grounded theorists insist that researchers define what is happening in the setting (Glaser, 1978; Glaser & Strauss, 1967). Sensitivity to social justice issues fosters defining latent processes as well as explicit actions. Grounded theory tools for studying action—collective as well as individual action—can make social justice analysis more precise and predictive. By focusing the data gathering, a researcher can seek new information to examine questions concerning equality, fairness, rights, and legitimacy.[12] The grounded theory openness to empirical leads spurs the researcher to pursue emergent questions and thus shifts the direction of inquiry.

A social justice researcher can use grounded theory to anchor agendas for future action, practice, and policies in the *analysis* by making explicit connections between the theorized antecedents, current conditions, and consequences of major processes. Social justice research, particularly participatory action research (Kemmis & McTaggart, 2000), proceeds from researchers' and participants' joint efforts and commitments to change practices. Because it arises in settings and situations in which people have taken a reflexive stance on their practices, they already have tools to conduct systematic research on their practices in relation to subjective experience, social actions, and social structures. Hence, adopting constructivist grounded theory would foster their efforts to articulate clear links between practices and each level and, thus, to strengthen their arguments for change.

Other researchers need to weigh whether, when, how, and to what extent to bring research participants into the process. Although well intended, doing so may create a series of knotty problems in concrete situations.[13] Janice Morse (1998) finds that the consequences of bringing participants into research decisions include keeping the analytic level low, overstating the views of participants who clamored for more space in the narrative, and compromising the analysis. Moreover, Morse (1998) notes that qualitative analyses differ from participants' descriptive accounts and may reveal paradoxes and processes of which participants are unaware.

Adopting grounded theory strategies in social justice research results in putting ideas and perspectives to empirical tests. Any extant concept must earn its way into the analysis (Glaser, 1978). Thus, we cannot import a set of concepts such as hegemony and domination and paste them on the realities in the field. Instead, we can treat them as sensitizing concepts, to be explored in the field settings (Blumer, 1969; van den Hoonaard, 1997). Then we can define if, when, how, to what extent, and under which conditions these concepts become relevant to the study (Charmaz, 2000b). We need to treat concepts as problematic and look for their characteristics as lived and understood, not as given in textbooks. Contemporary anthropologists, for example, remain alert to issues of cultural imperialism. Most sociologists attend to agency, power, status, and hierarchy.

Grounded theory studies can show how inequalities are played out at interactional and organizational levels. True, race, class, and gender—and age and disability—are everywhere. But how do members of various groups define them?[14] How and when do these status variables affect action in the scene? Researchers must define how, when, and to what extent participants *construct* and *enact* power, privilege, and inequality. Robert Prus (1996) makes a similar point in his book *Symbolic Interaction and Ethnographic Research*. Race, class, gender, age, and disability are social constructions with contested definitions that are continually reconstituted (see, for example, Olesen, Volume 1, Chapter 10). Using them as static variables, as though they have uncontested definitions that explain data and social processes *before* or *without* looking, undermines their potential power. Taking their meanings as given also undermines using grounded theory to develop fresh insights and ideas. Adopting my alternative tack involves juxtaposing participants' definitions against academic or sociological notions. In turn, researchers themselves must be reflexive about how they represent participants' constructions and enactments.

What new dimensions will social justice foci bring to research? Societal and global concerns are fundamental to a critical perspective. Thus, these studies situate the studied phenomenon in relation to larger units. How and where does it fit? For example, a study of sales interactions could look not only at the immediate interaction and how salespeople handle it but also at the organizational context and perhaps the corporate world, and its global reach, in which these interactions occur. Like many qualitative researchers, grounded theorists often separate the studied interactions from their situated contexts. Thus, a social justice focus brings in more structure and, in turn, a grounded theory treatment of that structure results in a dynamic, processual analysis of its enactment. Similarly, social justice research often takes into account the historical evolution of the current situation, and a grounded theory analysis of this evolution can yield new insights and, perhaps, alternative understandings. For that matter, researchers can develop grounded theories from analyses of pertinent historical materials in their realm of inquiry (see, for example, Clarke, 1998; Star, 1989).

Critical inquiry attends to contradictions between myths and realities, rhetoric and practice, and ends and means. Grounded theorists have the tools to discern and analyze contradictions revealed in the empirical world. We can examine what people *say* and compare it to what they *do* (Deutscher, Pestello, & Pestello, 1993). Focusing on words or deeds are ways of representing people; however, observed contradictions between the two may indicate crucial priorities and practices. To date, grounded theorists have emphasized the *overt*—usually overt statements—more than the tacit, the liminal, and the implicit. With critical inquiry, we can put our data to new tests and create new connections in our theories.

▣ Social Justice Emphases: Resources, Hierarchies, and Policies and Practices

A social justice focus can sensitize us to look at both large collectivities and individual experiences in new ways. Several emphases stand out: *resources, hierarchies*, and *policies and practices*. First, present, partial, or absent resources—whether economic, social, or personal—influence interactions and outcomes. Such resources include information, control over meanings, access to networks, and determination of outcomes. Thus, information and power are crucial resources. As Martha Nussbaum (1999) argues, needs for resources vary among people, vary at different times, and vary according to capabilities. Elders with disabling conditions need more resources than other people do or than they themselves needed in earlier years. What are the resources in the empirical worlds we study? What do they mean to actors in the field? Which resources, if any, are taken for granted? By whom? Who controls the resources?

Who needs them? According to which and whose criteria of need? To what extent do varied capabilities enter the discussion? Are resources available? If so, to whom? How, if at all, are resources shared, hoarded, concealed, or distributed? How did the current situation arise? What are the implications of having control over resources and of handling them, as observed in the setting(s)?

Second, any social entity has hierarchies—often several. What are they? How did they evolve? At what costs and benefits to involved actors? Which purported and actual purposes do these hierarchies serve? Who benefits from them? Under which conditions? How are the hierarchies related to power and oppression? How, if at all, do definitions of race, class, gender, and age cluster in specific hierarchies and/or at particular hierarchical levels? Which moral justifications support the observed hierarchies? Who promulgates these justifications? How do they circulate? How do these hierarchies affect social actions at macro, meso, and micro social levels? How and when do the hierarchies change?

Third, the consequences of social policies and practices are made real in collective and individual life. Here we have the convergence of structure and process. What are the rules—both tacit and explicit? Who writes or enforces them? How? Whose interests do the rules reflect? From whose standpoint? Do the rules and routine practices negatively affect certain groups or categories of individuals? If so, are they aware of them? What are the implications of their relative awareness or lack of it? To what extent and when do various participants support the rules and the policies and practices that flow from them? When are they contested? When do they meet resistance? Who resists, and which risks might resistance pose?

By asking these questions, I aim to stimulate thinking and to suggest diverse ways that critical inquiry and grounded theory research may join. The potential of advancing such endeavors already has been indicated by symbolic interactionists who point the way to demonstrating micro consequences of structural inequalities (L. Anderson & Snow, 2000; Scheff, 2003; Schwalbe et al., 2000). Combining critical inquiry and grounded theory furthers these efforts.

◫ Working With Grounded Theory

Studying the Data

The following interview stories provide the backdrop for introducing how grounded theory guidelines can illuminate social justice concerns. My research is social psychological; however, grounded theory methods hold untapped potential for innovative studies at the organizational, societal, and global levels of analysis. The examples below offer a glimpse of the kinds of initial comparisons I make.[15] I began studying the experience of chronic illness with interests in meanings of self and time. Such social psychological topics can reveal hidden effects of inequality and difference on the self and social life that emerge in research participants' many stories of their experiences.

Both grounded theory and critical inquiry are inherently comparative methods. In earlier renderings, I treated the excerpt of Christine Danforth below as a story of suffering and Marty Gordon's initial tale as a shocking significant event that marked a turning point in her life. The first step of grounded theory analysis is to study the data. Grounded theorists ask: What is happening? and What are people doing? A fresh look at the accounts below can suggest new leads to pursue and raise new questions.

At the time of the following statement, Christine was a 43-year-old single woman who had systemic lupus erythematosus, Sjögren's syndrome, diabetes, and serious back injuries. I had first met her 7 years earlier, when her multiple disabilities were less visible, although intrusive and worrisome. Since then, her health had declined, and she had had several long stretches of living on meager disability payments. Christine described her recent episode:

I got the sores that are in my mouth, got in my throat and closed my throat up, so I couldn't eat or drink. And then my potassium dropped down to 2.0. I was on the verge of cardiac arrest. . . . That time when I went in they gave me 72 bottles of pure potassium, burned all my veins out.

I asked, "What does that mean, that it burned your veins out?"

She said, "It hurts really bad; it's just because it's so strong and they can't dilute it with anything. They said usually what they do is they dilute with something like a numbing effect, but because I was 2.0, which is right on cardiac arrest that they couldn't do it, they had to get it in fast."

I asked, "Did you realize that you were that sick?"

She said, "Well, I called the doctor several times saying, 'I can't swallow.' I had to walk around and drool on a rag. They finally made an appointment, and I got there and I waited about a half hour. The lady said that there was an emergency and said that I'd have to come back tomorrow. And I said, 'I can't.' I said, 'As soon as I stand up, I'm going to pass out.' And she said, 'Well there's nothing we can do.' . . . And then this other nurse came in just as I got up and passed out, so then they took me to emergency. . . . And it took them 12 hours to— they knew when I went in there to admit me, but it took them 12 hours to get me into a room. I sat on a gurney. And they just kept fluid in me until they got me to a room.

Later in the interview, Christine explained,

[When the sores] go to my throat, it makes it really hard to eat or drink, which makes you dehydrated. After that first time . . . when I called her it had been 3 days since I'd ate or drank anything . . . and by the time I got an appointment, it was, I believe, six or seven days, without food or water.

Imagine Christine walking slowly and determinedly up the short sidewalk to my house. See her bent knees and lowered head, as she takes deliberate steps. Christine looks weary and sad, her face as laden with care as her body is burdened by pain and pounds. Always large, she is heavier than I have ever seen her, startlingly so.

Christine has a limited education; she can hardly read. Think of her trying to make her case for immediate treatment—without an advocate. Christine can voice righteous indignation, despite the fatigue and pain that saps her spirit and drains her energy. She can barely get through her stressful workday, yet she must work as many hours as possible because she earns so little. The low pay means that Christine suffers directly from cutbacks at the agency where she works. Her apartment provides respite, but few comforts. It has no heat —she cannot afford it. Christine does not eat well. Nutritious food is an unobtainable luxury; cooking is too strenuous, and cleanup is beyond imagination. She tells me that her apartment is filled with pictures and ceramic statues of cats as well as stacks of things to sort. Maneuverable space has shrunk to aisles cutting through the piles. Christine seldom cleans house—no energy for that. I've never been to her apartment; it embarrasses her too much to have visitors. Christine would love to adopt a kitten but cats are not permitted. Her eyes glaze with tears when my skittish cat allows her to pet him.

Christine has become more immobile and now uses a motorized scooter, which she says has saved her from total disability. But since using the scooter and approaching midlife, she also has gained one hundred pounds and needs a better vehicle to transport the scooter. Christine has little social life by now; her friends from high school and her bowling days have busy family and work lives. When she first became ill, Christine had some nasty encounters with several of those friends who accused her of feigning illness. She feels her isolation keenly, although all she can handle after work is resting on the couch. Her relationship with her elderly mother has never been close; she disapproves of her brother, who has moved back in with their mother and is taking drugs. One continuing light in Christine's life is her recently married niece, who just had a baby.

The years have grown gray with hardships and troubles. Christine has few resources—economic, social, or personal. Yet she perseveres in her struggle to remain independent and employed. She believes that if she lost this job, she would never get another one. Her recent weight gain adds one more reason for the shame she feels about her body.

Christine suffers from chronic illness and its spiraling consequences. Her physical distress, her anger and frustration about her life, her sadness, shame, and uncertainty all cause her to suffer. Christine talks some about pain and much about how difficult disability and lack of money make her life. She has not mentioned the word "suffering." Like many other chronically ill people, Christine resists describing herself in a way that might undermine her worth and elicit moral judgments. Yet she has tales to tell of her turmoil and troubles. (Charmaz, 1999, pp. 362–363)

The following interview account of Marty Gordon's situation contrasts with Christine's story. Marty received care from the same health facility as Christine and also had a life-threatening condition that confounded ordinary treatment and management. However, Marty's relationship to staff there and the content and quality of her life differed dramatically from Christine's.

When I first met Marty Gordon in 1988, she was a 59-year-old woman with a diagnosis of rapidly progressing pulmonary fibrosis. A hospitalization for extensive tests led to the diagnosis of Marty's condition. She had moved to a new area after her husband, Gary, retired as a school superintendent, and she herself retired early from her teaching and grant-writing post at a high school. Marty said that she and Gary were "very, very close." They had had no children, although Gary had a son by an earlier marriage and she, a beloved niece.

Pure retirement lasted about 3 months before they became bored. Subsequently, Marty became a part-time real estate agent and Gary worked in sales at a local winery. Not only did working bring new interests into their lives, but it also helped pay their hefty health insurance costs. They had not realized that their retirement benefits would not cover a health insurance plan. They both found much pleasure in their new lives and in their luxurious home high in the hills overlooking the city. Marty seemed to remain almost as busy as she was before retiring. While working full-time, she had entertained her husband's professional associates, had run a catering business, and had created special meals to keep Gary's diabetes and heart condition under control. She had taken much pride—and still did—in keeping up her perfectly appointed house and in keeping her weight down through regular exercise. For years, she had arisen at 5 each morning to swim an hour before going to work, then stopped at church afterward to say her rosaries.

When I first met Marty, she told the following tale about her first hospitalization:

> The doctor came in to tell me, "Uh, it didn't look good and that this was a—could be a rapidly"—and it appeared that mine was really going rapidly and that it might be about six weeks. Whoa! That blew my mind. It really did. . . . Right after that—I'm a Catholic—right after that, a poor little volunteer lady came in and said, "Mrs. Gordon?" And the doctor had said, "Mrs. Gordon?" "Yeah, OK." And then he told me. She said, "I'm from St. Mary's Church." I said, "Jesus, Mary, and Joseph, they've got the funeral already." And it really just—then I began to see humor in it, but I was scared. . . .
>
> This was the point when—[I decided], "If this is going to happen OK, but I'm not going to let it happen." . . . And I think probably that was the turning point when I said I wouldn't accept it. You know, I will not accept that uhm, death sentence, or whatever you want to call it. (Charmaz, 1991, p. 215)

However, from that point on, Marty had Gary promise her that she would die first. She needed him to take care of her when she could no longer care for herself; moreover, she could not bear the thought of living without him. During the next 5 years, Marty made considerable gains, despite frequent pain, fatigue, and shortness of breath. One Sunday evening, when Gary came home from a wine-pouring and Marty saw his ashen face, she insisted, "We're going to emergency." He had had a second heart attack, followed by a quadruple bypass surgery. Marty said, "He sure is a lot better now. And, of course, *I was very angry with him.* I said to him, 'You can never leave me. *I tell you, I'll sue you!*' [She explained to me.] Because we've had a deal for a long time." When telling me about her own health, she recounted this conversation with her surgeon:

> I come in for an appointment and I had just played 18 holes of golf, and so he said, "I think we misdiagnosed you." And I said, "Well, why do you think that?" And he said, "You're just going over, you're surpassing everything." So I said, "Well, that doesn't necessarily mean a diagnosis is wrong." I said, "Are you going to give me credit for anything?" And he said, "Well, what do you mean?" I said, "You have to have a medical answer, you can't have an answer that I worked very hard, on my whole body and my mind, to get, you know, the integral part of myself, and that maybe that might be helping? And the fact that I don't touch fats and I don't do this and I do exercise? *That's not helping, huh?*" So he said, "Well, I guess so." And I said,

"Well, do you want to take out my lungs again and see?" I said, "You took them out [already]." So he acknowledged, he said, "Yeah, it's just that it's so unusual." And maybe not accepting something, you know, denial is one thing, but not *excepting* is another thing.

Marty strove to be the exception to her dismal prognosis—she insisted on being an exception. She made great efforts to keep herself and her husband alive, functioning, and enjoying life. By confronting her doctor and challenging *his* definition of her, Marty rejected his narrow, medicalized definition of her. She implied that he was *denying her wellness*. Thus, she enacted a dramatic reversal of the conventional scenario of a doctor accusing the patient of denying her illness. Marty fought feelings of self-pity and sometimes talked about suffering and self-pity interchangeably. When she reflected on how she kept going, she said:

> I do, do really think that, if you sit down, and I mean, literally sit down, because it's hard to get up, you do start feeling sorry for yourself. And I'm saying, "Oh, God if I could only get up without hurting." And I've begun to feel, once in a while, I get this little sorry for myself thing, that if I could have a day without pain, I wonder what I'd do? *Probably nothing.* Because I wouldn't push myself and I'd get less done.
> I asked, "How so?"
> Marty replied, "My whole thing is faith and attitude. You've just got to have it. I feel so sorry for people who give in. But maybe that's why . . . you've got to have some people die. [Otherwise they'd] be hanging around forever."

Marty had fortitude—and attitude. Marty intended to live—by will and grit. Dying? The prospect of dying undermined her belief in individual control and thus conflicted with her self-concept.

▣ INTEGRATING GROUNDED THEORY WITH SOCIAL JUSTICE RESEARCH

What do these stories indicate? What might they suggest about social justice? How do grounded theory methods foster making sense of them? Both women have serious debilitating conditions with multiple harrowing episodes that make their lives uncertain. Both are courageous and forthright, are aware of their conditions, and aim to remain productive and autonomous.

Coding is the first step in taking an analytic stance toward the data. The initial coding phase in grounded theory forces the researcher to define the action in the data statement. In the figures illustrating coding (Figures 7.1–7.3), my codes reflect standard grounded theory practice. The codes are active, immediate, and short. They focus on defining action, explicating implicit assumptions, and seeing processes. By engaging in line-by-line coding, the researcher makes a close study of the data and lays the foundation for synthesizing it.

Coding gives a researcher analytic scaffolding on which to build. Because researchers study their empirical materials closely, they can define both new leads from them and gaps in them. Each piece of data—whether an interview, a field note, a case study, a personal account, or a document—can inform earlier data. Thus, should a researcher discover a lead through developing a code in one interview, he or she can go back through earlier interviews and take a fresh look as to whether this code sheds light on earlier data. Researchers can give their data multiple readings and renderings. Interests in social justice, for example, would lead a researcher to note points of struggle and conflict and to look for how participants defined and acted in such moments.

Grounded theory is a comparative method in which the researcher compares data with data, data with categories, and category with category. Comparing these two women's lives illuminates their several similarities and striking contrasts between their personal, social, and material resources. I offer these comparisons here for heuristic purposes only, to clarify points of convergence and divergence. Both women shared a keen interest in retaining autonomy, and both were aware that illness and disability raised the specter of difference, disconnection, and degradation. Nonetheless, Marty Gordon enjoyed much greater economic security, choices, privileges, and opportunities throughout her life than did Christine Danforth. Marty's quick wit, articulate voice, organizational skills, and diligence constituted a strong set of capabilities that served her well in dealing with failing health.

Poverty and lack of skills had always constrained Christine's life and curtailed her choices. They also diminished her feelings of self-worth and moral status, that is, the extent of virtue or vice attributed to a person by others and self (Charmaz, in press). Then illness shrunk her limited autonomy, and her moral status plummeted further. Christine lived under a cloud of nagging desperation. The anger she felt earlier about being disabled, deprived, and disconnected had dissipated into a lingering sadness and shame. Clearly, Christine has far fewer resources than Marty. She also has had fewer opportunities to develop capabilities throughout her life that could help her to manage her current situation.

Marty struggled periodically with daily routines, but she exerted control over her life and her world. Her struggles resided at another level; she fought against becoming inactive and sinking into self-pity. She treated both her body and her mind as objects to work on and to improve, as projects. Marty worked with physicians, if they agreed on her terms. Although she had grown weaker and had pronounced breathing problems, she believed living at all testified to her success. For long years, Marty kept her illness contained, or at least mostly out of view. Her proactive stance toward her body and her high level of involvements sustained her moral status. Whatever social diminishment of moral status she experienced derived more from age than from suffering.

The kinds of insights that grounded theory methods can net social justice research vary according to level, scope, and objectives of the study. Through comparing the

Recognizing illness spiral Recounting symptom progression Approaching crisis	I got the sores that are in my mouth, got in my throat and closed my throat up, so I couldn't eat or drink. And then my potassium dropped down to 2.0. I was on the verge of cardiac arrest. . . . That time when I went in they gave me 72 bottles of pure potassium, burned all my veins out. I asked, "What does that mean, that it burned your veins out?"
Suffering the effects of treatment Receiving rapid treatment Forfeiting comfort for speed	She said, "It hurts really bad; it's just because it's so strong and they can't dilute it with anything. They said usually what they do is they dilute with something like a numbing effect, but because I was 2.0, which is right on cardiac arrest that they couldn't do it, they had to get it in fast." I asked, "Did you realize that you were that sick? She said,
Seeking help Remaining persistent Explaining symptoms Encountering bureaucratic dismissal Experiencing turning point Explaining severity Receiving second refusal Collapsing Prolonging the ordeal— fitting into organizational time	"Well, I called the doctor several times saying, 'I can't swallow.' I had to walk around and drool on a rag. They finally made an appointment, and I got there and I waited about a half hour. The lady said that there was an emergency and said that I'd have to come back tomorrow. And I said, 'I can't.' I said, 'As soon as I stand up, I'm going to pass out.' And she said, 'Well there's nothing we can do.' . . . And then this other nurse came in just as I got up and passed out, so then they took me to emergency. . . . And it took them 12 hours to—they knew when I went in there to admit me, but it took them 12 hours to get me into a room. I sat on a gurney. And they just kept fluid in me until they got me to a room. Later in the interview, Christine explained:
Explaining symptoms Awareness of complications Enduring the wait Suffering induced by organization	[When the sores] go to my throat, it makes it really hard to eat or drink, which makes you dehydrated. After that first time . . . when I called her it had been three days since I'd ate or drank anything . . . and by the time I got an appointment, it was, I believe, six or seven days, without food or water.

Figure 7.1.   Initial Coding—Christine Danforth

Receiving bad news Facing death Suffering diagnostic shock Identifying religion Recounting the identifying moment Finding humor Feeling frightened	The doctor came in to tell me, "Uh, it didn't look good and that this was a—could be a rapidly"—and it appeared that mine was really going rapidly and that it might be about six weeks. Whoa! That blew my mind. It really did. . . . Right after that—I'm a Catholic—right after that, a poor little volunteer lady came in and said, "Mrs. Gordon?" And the doctor had said, "Mrs. Gordon?" "Yeah, OK." And then he told me. She said, "I'm from St. Mary's Church." I said, "Jesus, Mary, and Joseph, they've got the funeral already." And it really just—then I began to see humor in it, but I was scared. . . .
Accepting the present but not the prognosis Insisting on controlling the illness Turning point— Refusing the death sentence	This was the point when—[I decided], "If this is going to happen OK, but I'm not going to let it happen." . . . And I think probably that was the turning point when I said I wouldn't accept it. You know, I will not accept that uhm, death sentence, or whatever you want to call it.

Figure 7.2. Initial Coding—Marty Gordon

stories above, we gain some sense of structural and organizational sources of suffering and their differential effects on individuals. The comparisons suggest how research participants' relative resources and capabilities became apparent through studying inductive data.

The comparisons also lead to ideas about structure. Most policy research emphasizes *access* to health care. Comparing these two interviews indicates differential treatment *within* a health care organization. In addition, the comparisons raise questions about rhetoric and realities of receiving care. Marty Gordon credited her "faith and attitude" for managing her illness; however, her lifestyle, income, supportive relationships, and quick wit also helped to buffer her losses. But might not her attitude and advantages be dialectic and mutually reinforcing? Could not her advantages have also fostered her faith and attitude? Each person brings a past to the present. When invoking a similar logic, the residues of the past—limited family support, poor education, undiagnosed learning problems, and lack of skills—complicated and magnified Christine Danforth's troubles with chronic

	Christine Danforth	Marty Gordon
Awareness of illness	Predicting symptom intensification Recognizing illness spiral Lack of control over escalating symptoms Experiencing stigma	Learning and experimenting Becoming an expert Realizing the potential of stigma
Developing a stance toward illness	Remaining persistent Monitoring progression of symptoms Seeking help	Suffering initial diagnostic shock Feeling frightened Taking control Refusing death sentence Making deals Challenging physician's view Attacking physician's assumptions Discrediting physician's opinion Rejecting medical model Working on body and mind Following strict regimen Swaying physician's view Believing in her own perceptions Seeing self as an exception
Material resources	Fighting to keep the job Having a health plan Struggling to handle basic expenses Eking out a life—Juggling to pay the rent; Relying on an old car	Working part-time for extras Having a health plan Having solid retirement income Enjoying comfortable lifestyle with travel and amenities
Personal resources	Persevering despite multiple obstacles Defending self Recognizing injustice Abiding sense of shame about educational deficits and poverty Hating her appearance Trying to endure life Feeling excluded from organizational worlds	Preserving autonomy Forging partnerships with professionals Trusting herself Having a good education Assuming the right to control her life Believing in individual power Finding strength through faith Possessing a sense of entitlement Aiming to enjoy life Having decades of experience with organizations and professionals
Social resources	Living in a hostile world Taking delight in her niece Retreating from cruel accusations Suffering loneliness Realizing the fragility of her existence Foreseeing no future help	Taking refuge in a close marriage Having strong support, multiple involvements Maintaining powerful images of positive and negative role models Knowing she could obtain help, if needed
Strategies for managing life	Minimizing visibility of deficits Avoiding disclosure of illness Limiting activities	Obtaining husband's promise Avoiding disclosure of illness Controlling self-pity Remaining active Maintaining religious faith

Figure 7.3.   Comparing Life Situations

illness and in negotiating care. The structure of Christine's life led to her increasing isolation and decreasing moral status. Might not her anger and sadness have followed? From Marty and Christine's stories, we can discern hidden advantages of high social class status as well as hidden injuries of low status (Sennett & Cobb, 1973).

Last, coding practices can help us to see *our* assumptions, as well as those of our research participants. Rather than raising our codes to a level of objectivity, we can raise questions about how and why we developed certain codes.[16] Another way to break open our assumptions is to ask colleagues and, perhaps, research participants themselves to engage in the coding. When they bring divergent experience to the coding, their responses to the data may call for scrutiny of our own.

▣ RECLAIMING CHICAGO SCHOOL TRADITIONS

Marty Gordon and Christine Danforth's situations and statements above indicate the construction of their views and actions. Note that at certain points, they each struggle with obdurate social structures that take on tangible meaning in their stories of crucial interactions. To make further sense of situations and stories like these and to interpret the social justice issues with them, I have called for reclaiming Chicago school underpinnings in grounded theory. These underpinnings will move grounded theory more completely into constructionist social science. What are these underpinnings? What does reclaiming them entail? On which assumptions does Chicago school sociology rest? Why are they significant for both the development of grounded theory methods and social justice inquiry?

In brief, the Chicago school assumes human agency, attends to language and interpretation, views social processes as open-ended and emergent, studies action, and addresses temporality. This school emphasizes the significance of language for selfhood and social life and understands that human worlds consist of meaningful objects. In this view, subjective meanings emerge from experience, and they change as experience changes (Reynolds, 2003a). Thus, the Chicago school assumes dynamic, reciprocal relationships between interpretation and action, and it views social life as people fitting together diverse forms of conduct (Blumer, 1979, p. 22).[17] Because social life is interactive and emergent, a certain amount of indeterminacy characterizes it (Strauss & Fisher, 1979a, 1979b). How might we use Chicago school sociology now to inform contemporary grounded theory studies and social justice inquiry? Where might it lead us? What moral direction might it give?

Both pragmatist philosophy and Chicago school ethnography foster openness to the world and curiosity about it. The Meadian concept of role-taking assumes empathetic understanding of research participants and their worlds. To achieve this understanding, we must know how people define their situations and act on them. Social justice researchers can turn this point into a potent tool for discovering if, when, and to what extent people's meanings and actions contradict their economic or political interests— and whether and to what extent they are aware of such contradictions (see, for example, Kleinman, 1996). Thus, seeking these definitions and actions can make critical inquiry more complex and powerful. Knowing them can alert the researcher to points of actual or potential conflict and change—or compliance. Similarly, learning what things mean to people makes what they do with them comprehensible—at least from their world-view. Conversely, how people act toward things in their worlds indicates their relative significance. Such considerations prompt the researcher to construct an inductive analysis rather than, say, impose structural concepts on the scene.

Although Chicago school sociology has been viewed as microscopic, it also holds implications for the meso and macro levels that social justice researchers aim to engage. A refocused grounded theory would aid and refine connections with these levels. Horowitz (2001) shows how extending Mead's (1934) notion of "generalized other" takes his social psychology of the self to larger social entities and addresses expanding democratic participation of previously excluded groups. Her argument is two-pronged: (a) the development of a critical self is prerequisite for democracy and (b) groups that achieve self-regulation gain empowerment.

The naturalistic inquiry inherent in Chicago school tradition means studying what people in specific social worlds do over time and gaining intimate familiarity with the topic (Blumer, 1969; Lofland & Lofland, 1984, 1995). Hence, to reclaim the Chicago tradition, we must first: *Establish intimate familiarity with the setting(s) and the events occurring within it—as well as with the research participants.*[18] This point may seem obvious; however, much qualitative research, including grounded theory studies, skate the surface rather than plumb the depths of studied life.

An emphasis on action and process leads to considerations of time. The pragmatist treatment of social constructions of past, present, and future could direct social justice researchers to look at timing, pacing, and temporal rhythms. These concerns could alert us to new forms of control and organization. In addition, understanding timing and sequencing can shed light on the success or failure of collective action. Thus, attending to temporality affords us new knowledge of the worlds we study.

Chicago fieldwork traditions have long emphasized situated analyses embedded in social, economic, and occasionally political contexts, as evident in urban ethnographies (see, for example, E. Anderson, 2003; Horowitz, 1983; Suttles, 1968; Venkatesh, 2000). Numerous grounded theory studies have not taken account of the context in which the studied research problem or process exists. Combining Chicago intellectual traditions with social justice sensitivities would correct tendencies toward decontextualized—and, by extension, objectified—grounded theory analyses.

Looking at data with a Chicago school lens entails focusing on meaning and process at both the subjective and social levels. Like many other people with chronic illness, the women above are aware of the pejorative moral meanings of illness and suffering and sensed the diminished status of those who suffer. When I asked Marty Gordon how her condition affected her job, she said, "I never let it show there. *Never.* Never give cause for anybody either to be sorry for you or want to get rid of you." Although Christine Danforth hated her job, she viewed it as her lifeline and feared losing it. After telling me about receiving written ultimatums from her supervisor, she said:

> Nobody else is going to hire me. . . . An able body can't get one [job], how am I going to get one? So if I'm dyslexic, you know, those people don't even know what it is, let alone how to deal with it. I wouldn't be able to get a job as a receptionist because I can't read and write like most people, so I'm there for life.

Christine Danforth's employers knew the names of her medical diagnoses, but they did not understand her symptoms and their effects in daily life. Christine's story took an ironic twist. She worked for an advocacy agency that served people with disabilities. Several staff members who challenged her work and worth had serious physical disabilities themselves. Christine also discovered that her supervisors had imposed rules on her that they allowed other staff to ignore. Thus, the situation forced Christine to deal with multiple moral contradictions. She suffered the consequences of presumably enlightened disability advocates reproducing negative societal judgments of her moral worth. Tales of such injustice inform stories of suffering.

These examples suggest the second step to reclaiming the Chicago tradition: *Focus on meanings and processes.* This step includes addressing subjective, situational, and social levels. By piecing together many research participants' statements, I developed a moral hierarchy of suffering. Suffering here is much more than pain; it defines self and situation—and ultimately does so in moral terms that support inequities. Suffering takes into account stigma and social definitions of human worth. Hence, suffering includes the lived experience of stigma, reduced autonomy, and loss of control of the defining images of self. As a result, suffering magnifies difference, forces social disconnection, elicits shame, and increases as inequalities mount.[19]

Meanings of suffering, however, vary and are processual. As researchers, we must find the range of meanings and learn how people form them. Figure 7.4 shows how suffering takes on moral status and assumes hierarchical form. In addition, it suggests how suffering intersects with institutional traditions and structural conditions that enforce difference. In keeping with a grounded theory perspective, any attributes taken as status variables must earn their way into the analysis rather than be assumed. Note that I added resources and capabilities as potential markers of difference as their significance became clear in the data.[20] Figure 7.4 implies how larger social justice issues can emerge in open-ended, inductive research. In this case, these issues concern access, equitable treatment, and inherent human worth in health care.

The figure reflects an abstract statement of how individual experience and social structure come together in emergent action. The figure derives from inductive and comparative analyses of meaning and action, consistent with Chicago school sociology. When we compare individual accounts, we can see that Marty Gordon and Christine

Danforth develop their stance toward illness from different starting places and different experiences, yet they both are active in forming their definitions. The Chicago school concept of human nature has long contrasted with much of structural social science. We not only assume human agency but also study it and its consequences. People are active, creative beings who *act*, not merely behave. They attempt to solve problems in their lives and worlds. As researchers, we need to learn how, when, and why participants act. Thus, the third step in reclaiming Chicago traditions follows: *Engage*

HIERARCHY of MORAL STATUS in SUFFERING

HIGH MORAL STATUS—VALIDATED MORAL CLAIMS

MEDICAL EMERGENCY

INVOLUNTARY ONSET

BLAMELESSNESS FOR CONDITION

"APPROPRIATE" APPEARANCE AND DEMEANOR

SUSTAINED MORAL STATUS—ACCEPTED MORAL CLAIMS

CHRONIC ILLNESS

NEGOTIATED DEMANDS

PRESENT OR PAST POWER & RECIPROCITIES

Diminished Moral Status—Questionable Moral Claims

CHRONIC TROUBLE

BLAME FOR CONDITION AND COMPLICATIONS

"INAPPROPRIATE/REPUGNANT" APPEARANCE AND/OR DEMEANOR

PERSONAL VALUE

worth less

worth less

Worth Less

WORTHLESS

Institutional Traditions   **Structural Conditions**

Difference—class, race, gender, age, sexual preference, resources, capabilities

---

Figure 7.4.   Hierarchy of Moral Status in Suffering

Source: Adapted and expanded from Charmaz (1999), "Stories of Suffering: Subjects' Stories and Research Narratives," *Qualitative Health Research, 9,* 362–382.

in a close study of action. The Chicago emphasis on process becomes evident here. What do research participants see as routine? What do they define as problems? In Marty Gordon's case, the problems disrupted her life and could kill her. She had good reason for wanting to oversee her care. At one point, she described her conversation with Monica, her lung specialist, about ending treatment with prednisone:

> I've had a couple of setbacks. . . . The first time I went off it [prednisone], my breathing capacity cut right in half, so she said, "No." And I make deals with her. . . . So I'm going to Ireland and she said, "Okay, I want you to double it now, go back up while you're traveling, and then we'll talk about it. But no deals, and don't be stupid." So when I came back I said, "Let's try it again."

But when Marty came back from Ireland, she had complications. She described what happened while she was playing golf:

> I wound up in emergency Easter Sunday because I thought . . . I pulled a muscle. . . . But they thought it was a pulmonary embolism. . . . They said, "Well, with your condition we have to take an X ray, a lung X ray." And he [physician] said, "Oh, I don't like what I see here." And I said, "Look, you're not the doctor that looks at that all the time, don't get nervous, it's been there." So he said, "No, there's a lot more scar tissue than your other X ray." And I said, "Yeah, well that's par for the course, from what I understand." And he said, "But there's a hole there I don't like to see." I said, "Look, it's a pulled muscle. *Give me the Motrin.*" [At the time of this interview, Motrin was a prescription drug.] And finally he said, ". . . Maybe it is a pulled muscle." So she [Monica, her lung specialist] called me the next day and she said, "Okay, let's slow down on this going down on the prednisone, too many side things are happening, so we're going slower." And I think it will work. . . . I'm still playing golf and still working.

Marty Gordon's recounted conversations attest to her efforts to remain autonomous. She insisted on being the leading actor in her life and on shaping its quality. From the beginning, she had remained active in her care and unabashed in her willingness to challenge her physicians and to work with them—on her terms.

Agency does not occur in isolation; it always arises within a social context already shaped by language, meaning, and modes of interaction. This point leads us to the next step in reclaiming the Chicago tradition: *Discover and detail the social context within which action occurs.* A dual focus on action and context can permit social justice researchers to make nuanced explanations of behavior. What people think, feel, and do must be analyzed within the relevant social contexts, which, in turn, people construct through action and interaction. Individuals take into account the actions of those around them as they themselves act. Interaction depends on fitting lines of action together, to use Herbert Blumer's term (Blumer, 1969, 1979). We sense how Marty Gordon and Monica fit lines of actions together to quell her symptoms. Marty crafted an enduring professional partnership with Monica that has eased her way through an increasingly less accessible health care organization for more than 10 years. Knowing that others are or will be involved shapes how people respond to their situations. The more participants create a shared focus and establish a joint goal, the more they will build a shared past and projected future. Marty and Monica shared the goal of keeping Marty alive and of reducing her symptoms while minimizing medication side effects. They built a history of more than a decade, and to this day they project a shared future.

The women in these two stories grapple with the issues that confront them and thus affect the social context in which they live. Marty had a voice and made herself heard; Christine tried but met resistance. She lacked advocates, social skills, and a shared professional discourse to enlist providers as allies, which commonly occurs when class and culture divide providers and patients. The construction of social context may be more discernible in Marty's statements than in other kinds of interviews. In Christine's attempt to obtain care, she related the sequence and timing of events. We see that she received care only because she became a medical emergency, and we learn how earlier refusals and delays increased her misery.

These interview statements contain words and phrases that tell and hint of meaning. Marty Gordon talks about "making deals," "working hard," "not excepting," "wallowing," and "pushing myself." Christine Danforth contrasts herself with an "able body" and recounts how the sequence of events affected her actions. The fifth step in reclaiming the Chicago school tradition follows this dictum: *Pay attention to language.* Language shapes meaning and influences action. In turn, actions and experiences shape meanings. Marty's interview excerpts suggest how she uses words to make her meanings real and tries to make her meanings stick in interaction. Chicago school sociology assumes reciprocal and dynamic relations between interpretation and action. We interpret what happens around and to us and shape our actions accordingly, particularly when something interrupts our routines and causes us to rethink our situations.

In addition to the points outlined above, Chicago school scholars have generated other concepts that can fruitfully inform initial directions in social justice research and can sensitize the researcher's empirical observations. Among these concepts are Glaser and Strauss's (1965) concept of awareness contexts, Scott and Lyman's (1968) idea of accounts, Mills's (1990) notion of vocabularies of motive, Goffman's (1959) metaphor of the theater, and Hochschild's (1983) depiction of emotion work and feeling rules. Establishing who knows what, and when they know it, can provide a crucial focus for studying interaction in social justice research. Both the powerful and the powerless may be forced to give accounts that justify or excuse their actions. People describe their motives in vocabularies in situated social, cultural, historical, and economic contexts. Viewing life as theater can alert social justice researchers to main actors, minor characters and audiences, acts and scenes, roles and scripts, and front-stage impressions and backstage realities. Different kinds of emotion work and feeling rules reflect the settings in which they arise. Expressed emotions and stifled feelings stem from rules and enacted hierarchies of power and advantage that less privileged actors may unwittingly support and reproduce (see, for example, Lively, 2001).

◙ RETHINKING OUR LANGUAGE

Just as we must attend to how our research participants' language shapes meaning, we must attend to our own language and make *it* problematic. I mention a few key terms that we qualitative researchers assume and adopt. These terms have served as guiding metaphors or, more comprehensively, as organizing concepts for entire studies. Perhaps ironically, Chicago school sociologists and their followers have promulgated most of these terms. Researchers have made them part of their taken-for-granted lexicon and, I believe, imposed them too readily on our studied phenomena. The logic of both the earlier Chicago school and grounded theory means developing our concepts *from* our analyses of empirical realities, rather than applying concepts *to* them. If we adopt extant concepts, they must earn their way into the analysis through their usefulness (Glaser, 1978). Then we can extend and strengthen them (see, for example, Mamo, 1999; Timmermans, 1994).

Two major concepts carry images of tactical manipulations by a calculating social actor: strategies and negotiations. Despite what we social scientists say, much of human behavior does not reflect explicit *strategies*. Subsuming ordinary actions under the rubric of "strategies" implies explicit tactical schemes when, in fact, an actor's intentions may not have been so clear to him or her, much less to this actor's audience. Rather than strategies, much of what people do reflects their taken-for-granted habitual actions. These actions become routine and scarcely recognized unless disrupted by change or challenge. Note that in the long lists of codes comparing Christine Danforth's and Marty Gordon's situations, I list many actions but few strategies.

When looking for taken-for-granted actions in our research, John Dewey's (1922) central ideas about habit, if not the term itself, can prove helpful to attend to participants' assumptions and taken-for-granted practices, which may not always be in their own interests. Like Snow's (2001) point that much of life is routine and proceeds without explicit interpretation, Dewey (1922) views habits as patterned predispositions that enable individuals to respond to their situations with economy of thought and action: People can act while focusing attention elsewhere (see also Clark, 2000; Cutchin, 2000). Thus, habits include those taken-for-granted modes of thinking, feeling, and acting that people invoke without reflection (Dewey, 1922; Hewitt, 1994). The habits of a lifetime enabled Marty Gordon to maintain hope and to manage her illness. Christine's habits let her eke by but also increased her isolation and physical problems.

Like the concept of strategies, negotiation also imparts a strategic character to interaction. Negotiation is an apt term to describe Marty Gordon's "deals" and disputes with her practitioners. At least from her view, contests did emerge, and bargaining could bring them to effective closure. Then interaction could proceed from the negotiated agreement. Marty brought not only her resolve to her negotiations, but also years of skills and fearlessness in dealing with professionals, a partnership with her primary physician, a network of supportive others, and the ability to pay for nutritious food, conveniences, and a good health plan. Little negotiation may proceed when a person has few such resources and great suffering, as Christine Danforth's story suggests.

Although the concept of negotiations may apply in Marty Gordon's case, we have stretched its applicability, as if it reflected most interactions. It does not. Much of social life proceeds as people either unconsciously adapt their response to another person or interpret what the other person says, means, or does and then they subsequently respond to it (Blumer, 1979). Interaction can alter views, temper emotions, modify intentions, and change actions—all without negotiation. The strategic quality of negotiation may be limited or absent during much sociability. People can be persuasive without attempting to negotiate. Negotiation assumes actors who are explicitly aware of the content and structure of the ensuing interaction. Negotiation also assumes that participants' interactional goals conflict or need realignment if future mutual endeavors are to occur. For that matter, the term assumes that all participants have sufficient power to make their voices heard, if not also to affect outcomes. Judith Howard (2003) states, "The term 'negotiation' implies that the interacting parties have equal opportunities to control the social identities presented, that they come to the bargaining table with equal resources and together develop a joint definition of the situation" (p. 10). Nonetheless, much negotiation ensues when the parties involved do not have equal resources, and much foment may occur about enforcing definitions of social identities, despite unequal positions. For negotiations to occur, each party must be involved with the other to complete joint actions that matter to both, likely for different reasons.

The problems of applying these concepts and of importing their meanings and metaphors on our data extend beyond the concepts above. These problems also occur with applying the concepts of "career," "work," or "trajectory," which we could examine with the same logic. However, the current social scientific emphasis on stories merits scrutiny here.

▣ METAPHORS OF STORIES AND MEANINGS OF SILENCES

The term "story" might once have been a metaphor for varied qualitative data such as interview statements, field note descriptions, or documents. However, we cease to use the term "story" as metaphor and have come to view it as concrete reality, rather than a construction we place on these data. With several exceptions (e.g., Charmaz, 2002, in press; Frank, 1997), social scientists have treated the notion of "story" as unproblematic. We have questioned whose story we tell, how we tell it, and how we represent those who tell us their stories, but not the idea of a story itself or whether our materials fit the term "story." The reliance on qualitative interviews in grounded theory studies (Creswell, 1997), as well as in other qualitative approaches, such as narrative analysis, furthered this focus on stories. In addition, the topics themselves of intensive interviews foster producing a story.

Limiting data collection to interviews, as is common in grounded theory research, delimits the theory we can develop. In social justice studies, we must be cautious about which narrative frame we impose on our research, and when and how we do it. The frame itself can prove consequential. The story frame assumes a linear logic and boundaries of temporality that we might over- or underdraw.[21]

Part of my argument about stories concerns silences. In earlier works (Charmaz, 2002, in press), I have emphasized silences at the individual level of analysis; they are also significant at the organizational, social worlds, and societal levels. Clarke (2003, 2005) provides a new grounded theory tool, situational mapping, for showing action and inaction, voices and silences, at varied levels of analysis. She observes that silences reveal absent organizational alignments. Thus, mapping those silences, in their relation to active alignments, can render invisible social structure visible. Invisible aspects of social structure and process are precisely what critical inquiry needs to tackle.[22]

Silences pose significant meanings and telling data in any research that deals with moral choices, ethical dilemmas, and just social policies. Silence signifies absence and sometimes reflects a lack of awareness or inability to express thoughts and feelings. However, silence speaks to power arrangements. It also can mean attempts to control information, to avoid redirecting actions, and, at times, to impart tacit messages. The "right" to speak may mirror hierarchies of power: *Only those who have power dare to speak*. All others are silenced (see, for example, Freire, 1970). Then, too, the powerless may retreat into silence as a last refuge. At one point, Christine Danforth felt that her life was out of control. She described being silenced by devastating events and by an aggressive psychiatrist, and she stopped talking. In all these ways, silence is part of language, meaning, *and* action.

Making stories problematic and attending to silences offers new possibilities for understanding social life for both social justice and grounded theory research. What people in power do not say is often more telling than what they do say. We must note those who choose to remain silent, as well as those who have been silenced. Treating both stories and silences with a critical eye and comparing them with actions and inaction provides empirical underpinnings for any emerging grounded theory. Subsequently, the constructed theory will gain usefulness in its explanatory and predictive power.

▣ ESTABLISHING EVALUATION CRITERIA

Using grounded theory for social justice studies requires revisiting the criteria for evaluating them. Glaser and Strauss's (1967; Glaser, 1978) criteria for assessing grounded theory studies include fit, workability, relevance, and modifiability. Thus, the theory must fit the empirical world it purports to analyze, provide a workable understanding and explanation of this world, address problems and processes in it, and allow for variation and change that make the core theory useful over time. The criterion of modifiability allows for refinements of the theory that simultaneously make it more precise and enduring.

Providing cogent explanations stating how the study meets high standards will advance social justice inquiry and reduce unmerited dismissals of it. However, few grounded theorists provide a model. They seldom offer explicit discussions about how their studies *meet* the above or other criteria, although they often provide statements on the logic of their decisions (cf. S. I. Miller & Fredericks, 1999). In the past, some grounded theorists have claimed achieving a theoretical grounding with limited empirical material. Increasingly, researchers justify the type, relative depth, and extent of their data collection and analysis on *one* criterion: saturation of categories. They issue a claim of saturation and end their data collection (Flick, 1998; Morse, 1995; Silverman, 2000). But what does saturation mean? To whom? Janice Morse (1995), who initiated the critique of saturation, accepts defining it as "data adequacy" and adds that it is "operationalized as collecting data until no new information is obtained" (p. 147). Often, researchers invoke the criterion of saturation to justify small samples—very small samples with thin data. Such justifications diminish the credibility of grounded theory. Any social justice study that makes questionable claims of saturation risks being seen as suspect.

Claims of saturation often reflect rationalization more than reason, and these claims raise questions. What stands as a category?[23] Is it conceptual? Is it useful? Developed? By whose criteria? All these questions add up to the big question: *What stands as adequate research*? Expanded criteria that include the Chicago school's rigorous study of context and action makes any grounded theory study more credible and advances the claims of social justice researchers. Then we can augment our criteria by going beyond "saturation" and ask if our empirical detail also achieves Christians's (2000) and Denzin's (1989) criterion of "interpretive sufficiency," which takes into account cultural complexity and multiple interpretations of life.

To reopen explicit discussion of criteria for grounded theory studies, and particularly those in social justice research, I offer the following criteria.

Criteria for Grounded Theory Studies in Social Justice Inquiry

Credibility

- Has the researcher achieved intimate familiarity with the setting or topic?
- Are the data sufficient to merit the researcher's claims? Consider the range, number, and depth of observations contained in the data.
- Has the researcher made systematic comparisons between observations and between categories?

- Do the categories cover a wide range of empirical observations?
- Are there strong logical links between the gathered data and the researcher's argument and analysis?
- Has the researcher provided enough evidence for his or her claims to allow the reader to form an independent assessment—and *agree* with the researcher's claims?

Originality

- Are the categories fresh? Do they offer new insights?
- Does the analysis provide a new conceptual rendering of the data?
- What is the social and theoretical significance of the work?
- How does the work challenge, extend, or refine current ideas, concepts, and practices?

Resonance

- Do the categories portray the fullness of the studied experience?
- Has the researcher revealed liminal and taken-for-granted meanings?
- Has the researcher drawn links between larger collectivities and individual lives, when the data so indicate?
- Do the analytic interpretations make sense to members and offer them deeper insights about their lives and worlds?

Usefulness

- Does the analysis offer interpretations that people can use in their everyday worlds?
- Do the analytic categories speak to generic processes?
- Have these generic processes been examined for hidden social justice implications?
- Can the analysis spark further research in other substantive areas?
- How does the work contribute to making a better society?

A strong combination of originality and credibility increases resonance, usefulness, and the subsequent value of the contribution. The criteria above account for the empirical study and development of the theory. They say little about how the researcher writes the narrative or what makes it compelling. Other criteria speak to the aesthetics of the writing. Our written works derive from aesthetic principles and rhetorical devices—in addition to theoretical statements and scientific rationales. The act of writing is intuitive, inventive, and interpretive, not merely a reporting of acts and facts, or, in the case of grounded theory, causes, conditions, categories, and consequences. Writing leads to further discoveries and deeper insights; it furthers inquiry. Rather than claiming silent authorship hidden behind a scientific facade, grounded theorists—as well as proponents of social justice—should claim audible voices in their writings (see Charmaz & Mitchell, 1996; Mitchell & Charmaz, 1996). For grounded theorists, an audible voice brings the writer's self into the words while illuminating intersubjective worlds. Such evocative writing sparks the reader's imagined involvement in the scenes portrayed and those beyond. In this sense, Laurel Richardson's (2000) criteria for the evocative texts of "creative analytic practice ethnography" also apply here. These criteria consist of the narrative's substantive contribution, aesthetic merit, reflexivity, impact, and expression of a reality (p. 937).

A grounded theory born from reasoned reflections and principled convictions that conveys a reality makes a substantive contribution. Add aesthetic merit and analytic impact, and then its influence may spread to larger audiences. Through reclaiming Chicago traditions, conducting inquiry to make a difference in the world, and creating evocative narratives, we will not be silenced. We will have stories to tell and theories to proclaim.

🔳 SUMMARY AND CONCLUSIONS

A turn toward qualitative social justice studies promotes combining critical inquiry and grounded theory in novel and productive ways. An interpretive, constructivist ground theory supports this turn by building on its Chicago school antecedents. Grounded theory can sharpen the analytic edge of social justice studies. Simultaneously, the critical inquiry inherent in social justice research can enlarge the focus and deepen the significance of grounded theory analyses. Combining the two approaches enhances the power of each.

A grounded theory informed by critical inquiry demands going deeper into the phenomenon itself and its situated location in the world than perhaps most grounded theory studies have in the past. This approach does not mean departing from grounded theory guidelines. It does not mean investigative reporting. Grounded theory details process and context—and goes into the social world and setting far beyond one investigative story. Grounded theory contains tools to study how processes become institutionalized practices. Such attention to the processes that constitute structure can keep grounded theory from dissolving into fragmented small studies.

With the exception of those studies that rely on historical documents, grounded theory studies typically give little scrutiny to the past and sometimes blur inequalities with other experiences or overlook them entirely. Studying social justice issues means paying greater attention to inequality and its social and historical contexts. Too much of qualitative research today minimizes current *social* context, much less historical evolution. Relying on interview studies on focused topics may preclude attention to context—particularly when our research participants take the context of their lives for granted and do not speak of it. Hence, the mode of inquiry itself limits what researchers may learn. Clearly, interviewing is the method of choice for certain topics, but empirical qualitative research suffers if it becomes synonymous with interview studies.

Like snapshots, interviews provide a picture taken during a moment in time. Interviewers gain a view of research participants' concerns as they present them, rather than as events unfold. Multiple visits over time combined with the intimacy of intensive interviewing do provide a deeper view of life than one-shot structured or informational interviews can provide. However, anyone's retelling of events may differ markedly from an ethnographer's recording of them. In addition, as noted above, what people say may not be what they do (Deutscher et al., 1993). At that, what an interviewer asks and hears or an ethnographer records depends in part on the overall context, the immediate situation, *and* his or her training and theoretical proclivities.

At its best, grounded theory provides methods to explicate an empirical process in ways that prompt seeing beyond it. By sticking closely to the leads and explicating the relevant process, the researcher can go deeper into meaning and action than given in words. Thus, the focused inquiry of grounded theory, with its progressive inductive analysis, moves the work theoretically and covers more empirical observations than other approaches. In this way, a focused grounded theory portrays a picture of the whole.

◨ Notes

1. Such emphases often start with pressing social problems, collective concerns, and impassioned voices. In contrast, Rawls's (1971) emphasis on fairness begins from a distanced position of theorizing individual rights and risks from the standpoint of the rational actor under hypothetical conditions. Conceptions of social justice must take into account both collective goods and individual rights and must recognize that definitions both of rationality and of "rational" actors are situated in time, space, and culture—and both can change. To foster justice, Nussbaum (2000, p. 234) argues that promoting a collective good must not subordinate the ends of some individuals over others. She observes that women suffer when a collective good is promoted without taking into account the internal power and opportunity hierarchies within a group.

2. For descriptions of grounded theory guidelines, see Charmaz (2000a, 2003b), Glaser (1978, 1992), and Strauss and Corbin (1990, 1998).

3. I use the term "data" throughout for two reasons: It symbolizes (a) a fund of empirical materials that we systematically collect and assemble to acquire knowledge about a topic and (b) an acknowledgment that qualitative resources hold equal significance for studying empirical reality as quantitative measures, although they differ in kind.

4. In this way, integrating a critical stance offers a corrective to narrow and limited studies conducted as grounded theory studies. Neither a narrow focus nor limited empirical material is part of the method itself. We cannot blur how earlier researchers have used grounded theory with the guidelines in the method. Although social justice inquiry suggests substantive fields, it also assumes questions and concerns about power, privilege, and hierarchy that some grounded theorists may not yet have entertained.

5. Chicago school sociology shaped an enduring tradition of qualitative research in sociology, of which grounded theory remains a part. What stands as "the" Chicago school varies depending on who defines it (Abbott, 1999; L. H. Lofland, 1980). In my view, the Chicago school theoretical heritage goes back to the early years of the 20th century, in the

works, for example, of Charles Horton Cooley (1902), John Dewey (1922), George Herbert Mead (1932, 1934), and Charles S. Peirce (Hartshorne & Weiss, 1931–1935). In research practice, the Chicago school sparked study of the city and spawned urban ethnographies (see, for example, Park & Burgess, 1925; Shaw, 1930; Thomas & Znaniecki, 1927; Thrasher, 1927). Chicago sociologists often held naïve and partial views but many sensed the injustices arising in the social problems of the city, and Abbott (1999) notes that Albion Small attacked capitalism. Nonetheless, some Chicago school sociologists reinforced inequities in their own bailiwicks (Deegan, 1995). Mid-century ethnographers and qualitative researchers built on their Chicago school intellectual heritage and created what scholars have called a second Chicago school (G. A. Fine, 1995). For recent renderings of the Chicago school, see Abbott (1999), G. A. Fine (1995), Musolf (2003), and Reynolds (2003a, 2003b). Chicago school sociology emphasizes the contextual backdrop of observed scenes and their situated nature in time, place, and relationships. Despite the partial emergence of grounded theory from both theoretical and methodological Chicago school roots, Glaser (2002) disavows the pragmatist, constructionist elements in grounded theory.

6. Symbolic interactionism provides an open-ended theoretical perspective from which grounded theory researchers can start. This perspective is neither inherently prescriptive nor microsociological. Barbara Ballis Lal (2001) not only suggests the contemporary usefulness of early Chicago school symbolic interactionist ideas for studying race and ethnicity but also notes their implications for current political action and social policy. David Maines (2001) demonstrates that symbolic interactionist emphases on agency, action, and negotiated order have long had macrosociological import. He shows that the discipline of sociology has incorrectly—and ironically—compartmentalized symbolic interactionism while increasingly becoming more interactionist in its assumptions and directions.

7. In particular, the Chicago school provides antecedents for attending to social reform, as in Jane Addams's (1919) work at Hull-House and Mead and Dewey's interests in democratic process. The field research founded in Chicago school sociology has been called into question at various historical junctures from Marxist and postmodernist perspectives (see, for example, Burawoy, Blum, et al., 1991; Burawoy, Gamson, et al., 2002; Clough, 1992; Denzin, 1992; Wacquant, 2002). Criticisms of Chicago school sociology have suggested that grounded theory represents the most codified and realist statement of Chicago school methodology (Van Maanen, 1988).

8. Strauss and Corbin's (1990, 1998) emphasis on technical procedures has been met with chagrin by a number of researchers (Glaser, 1992; Melia, 1996; Stern, 1994). In his 1987 handbook *Qualitative Analysis for Social Scientists*, Strauss mentions axial coding and verification, which depart from earlier versions of grounded theory, and he and Juliet Corbin (1990, 1998) develop them in their coauthored texts.

9. My critique mirrors a much larger trend. Lincoln and Guba (2000) find that the movement away from positivism pervades the social sciences. They state that the turn toward interpretive, postmodern, and critical theorizing makes most studies vulnerable to criticism (p. 163).

10. Grounded theory provides tools that researchers can—and do—use from any philosophical perspective—or political agenda. Studies of worker involvement, for example, may start from addressing employees' concerns or management's aim to increase corporate profits.

11. Tedlock (2000) states, "Ethnographers' lives are embedded within their field experiences in such a way that all their interactions involve moral choices" (p. 455). Ethnography may

represent one end of a continuum. Nevertheless, does not grounded theory research also involve moral choices?

12. Feminist research suggests ways to proceed. DeVault (1999) and Olesen (2000) provide excellent overviews of and debates in feminist research.

13. Issues of exploitation arise when participants work without pay or recognition. Feminist researchers often recommend having participants read drafts of materials, yet even reading drafts may be too much when research participants are struggling with losses, although they may have requested to see the researcher's writings in progress. When research participants express interest, I share early drafts, but I try to reduce participants' potential feelings of obligation to finish reading them. Morse (1998) agrees with sharing results but not the conduct of inquiry.

14. Schwalbe et al. (2000) and Harris (2001) make important moves in this analytic direction.

15. The first two interview excerpts appear in earlier published accounts. I include them so that readers interested in seeing how I used them in social psychological accounts may obtain them. Subsequent interview statements have not been published. The data are part of an evolving study of 170 interviews of chronically ill persons. A subset of research participants that includes these two women have been interviewed multiple times.

16. Further specifics of grounded theory guidelines are available in Charmaz (2000a, 2003b, Charmaz & Mitchell, 2001), Glaser (1978, 1992, 2001), Strauss, (1987), and Strauss and Corbin (1990, 1998).

17. I realize that presenting the Chicago school as a unified perspective is something of a historical gloss because differences are discernible between the early pragmatists as well as among the sociologists who followed them. Furthermore, a strong quantitative tradition developed at the University of Chicago (see Bulmer, 1984).

18. See Lofland and Lofland (1984, 1995) for an emphasis on describing the research setting. Lincoln and Guba (1985) offer a sound rationale for naturalistic inquiry as well as good ideas for conducting it. When the data consist of extant texts such as documents, films, or texts, then the researcher may need to seek multiple empirical sources.

19. See Scheff (2003) for a discussion of relationships between shame and society.

20. Grounded theory methods can inform traditional quantitative research, although these approaches seldom have been used together. Hypotheses can be drawn from Figure 7.4, such as that the greater the definitions of an individual's difference, the more rapid his or her tumble down the moral hierarchy of suffering. Quantitative researchers could pursue such hypotheses.

21. And as I have pointed out with individual accounts (Charmaz, 2002), raw experience may fit neither narrative logic nor the comprehensible content of a story.

22. Clarke's (2003, 2004) concept of implicated actors can be particularly useful to analyze voices and silences in social justice discourses.

23. See Dey (1999) for an extensive discussion on constructing categories in the early grounded theory works.

References

Abbott, A. (1999). *Department & discipline: Chicago sociology at one hundred.* Chicago: University of Chicago Press.

Addams, J. (1919). *Twenty years at Hull-House.* New York: Macmillan.

Anderson, E. (2003). Jelly's place: An ethnographic memoir. *Symbolic Interaction, 26,* 217–237.

Anderson, L., & Snow, D. A. (2001). Inequality and the self: Exploring connections from an interactionist perspective. *Symbolic Interaction, 24,* 396–406.

Atkinson, P., Coffey, A., & Delamont, S. (2003). *Key themes in qualitative research: Continuities and changes.* New York: Rowman and Littlefield.

Blumer, H. (1969). *Symbolic interactionism.* Englewood Cliffs, NJ: Prentice-Hall.

Blumer, H. (1979). Comments on "George Herbert Mead and the Chicago tradition of sociology." *Symbolic Interaction, 2*(2), 21–22.

Bryant, A. (2002). Regrounding grounded theory. *The Journal of Information Technology Theory and Application, 4,* 25–42.

Bryant, A. (2003). A constructive/ist response to Glaser. *Forum Qualitative Sozialforschung/ Forum: Qualitative Social Research, 4.* Retrieved from www.qualitative-research.net/fqs-texte/ 1-03/1-bryant-e-htm

Bulmer, M. (1984). *The Chicago school of sociology: Institutionalization, diversity, and the rise of sociology.* Chicago: University of Chicago Press.

Burawoy, M (1991). Reconstructing social theories. In M. Burawoy, J. Gamson, J. Schiffman, A. Burton, A. A. Ferguson, L. Salzinger, L., et al. (Eds.), *Ethnography unbound : Power and resistance in the modern metropolis* (pp. 8–28). Berkeley: University of California Press.

Burawoy, M., Blum, J. A., George, S., Gill, Z., Gowan, T., Haney, L., et al. (2000). *Global ethnography: Forces, connections, and imaginations in a postmodern world.* Berkeley: University of California Press.

Burawoy, M., Gamson, J., Schiffman, J., Burton, A., Ferguson, A. A., Salzinger, L., et al. (1991). *Ethnography unbound: Power and resistance in the modern metropolis.* Berkeley: University of California Press.

Charmaz, K. (1983). The grounded theory method: An explication and interpretation. In R. M. Emerson (Ed.), *Contemporary field research* (pp. 109–126). Boston: Little, Brown.

Charmaz, K. (1990). Discovering chronic illness: Using grounded theory. *Social Science and Medicine, 30,* 1161–1172.

Charmaz, K. (1991). *Good days, bad days: The self in chronic illness and time.* New Brunswick, NJ: Rutgers University Press.

Charmaz, K. (1999). Stories of suffering: Subjects' stories and research narratives. *Qualitative Health Research, 9,* 362–382.

Charmaz, K. (2000a). Constructivist and objectivist grounded theory. In N. K. Denzin & Y. S. Lincoln (Eds.), *Handbook of qualitative research* (2nd ed., pp. 509–535). Thousand Oaks, CA: Sage.

Charmaz, K.(2000b). Looking backward, moving forward: Expanding sociological horizons in the twenty-first century. *Sociological Perspectives, 43,* 527–549.

Charmaz, K. (2002). Stories and silences: Disclosures and self in chronic illness. *Qualitative Inquiry, 8,* 302–328.

Charmaz, K. (2003a). Grounded theory. In M. Lewis-Beck, A. E. Bryman, & T. F. Liao (Eds.), *The Sage encyclopedia of social science research methods* (pp. 440–444). Thousand Oaks, CA: Sage.

Charmaz, K. (2003b). Grounded theory. In J. A. Smith (Ed.), *Qualitative psychology: A practical guide to research methods* (pp. 81–110). London: Sage.

Charmaz, K. (in press). Stories and silences: Disclosures and self in chronic illness. In D. Brashers & D. Goldstein (Eds.), *Health communication*. New York: Lawrence Erlbaum.

Charmaz, K., & Mitchell, R. G. (1996). The myth of silent authorship: Self, substance, and style in ethnographic writing. *Symbolic Interaction, 19*(4), 285–302.

Charmaz, K., & Mitchell, R. G. (2001). Grounded theory in ethnography. In P. Atkinson, A. Coffey, S. Delamont, J. Lofland, & L. H. Lofland (Eds.), *Handbook of ethnography* (pp. 160–174). London: Sage.

Christians, C. G. (2000). Ethics and politics in qualitative research. In N. K. Denzin & Y. S. Lincoln (Eds.), *Handbook of qualitative research* (2nd ed., pp. 133–155). Thousand Oaks, CA: Sage.

Clark, F. A. (2000). The concepts of habit and routine: A preliminary theoretical synthesis. *The Occupational Therapy Journal of Research, 20*, 123S–138S.

Clarke, A. E. (1998). *Disciplining reproduction: Modernity, American life sciences and the "problem of sex."* Berkeley: University of California Press.

Clarke, A. E. (2003). Situational analyses: Grounded theory mapping after the postmodern turn. *Symbolic Interaction, 26*, 553–576.

Clarke, A. E. (2004). *Situational analysis: Grounded theory after the postmodern turn.* Thousand Oaks, CA: Sage.

Clough, P. T. (1992). *The end(s) of ethnography: From realism to social criticism.* Newbury Park, CA: Sage.

Coffey, A., Holbrook, P., & Atkinson, P. (1996). Qualitative data analysis: Technologies and representations. *Sociological Research Online, 1*(1). Retrieved from www.socresonline.org.uk/1/1/4.html

Cooley, C. H. (1902). *Human nature and the social order.* New York: Scribner's.

Corbin, J. M., & Strauss, A. (1988). *Unending care and work.* San Francisco: Jossey-Bass.

Creswell, J. W. (1997). *Qualitative inquiry and research design.* Thousand Oaks, CA: Sage.

Cutchin, M. P. (2000). Retention of rural physicians: Place integration and the triumph of habit. *The Occupational Therapy Journal of Research, 20*, 106S–111S.

Deegan, M. J. (1995). The second sex and the Chicago school: Women's accounts, knowledge, and work, 1945–1960. In G. A. Fine (Ed.), *A second Chicago school?* (pp. 322–364). Chicago: University of Chicago Press.

Denzin, N. K. (1989). *Interpretive biography.* Newbury Park, CA: Sage.

Denzin, N. K. (1992). *Symbolic interactionism and cultural studies: The politics of interpretation.* Oxford, UK: Basil Blackwell.

Denzin, N. K. (1994). The art and politics of interpretation. In N. K. Denzin & Y. S. Lincoln (Eds.), *Handbook of qualitative research* (pp. 500–515). Thousand Oaks, CA: Sage.

Deutscher, I., Pestello, R., & Pestello, H. F. (1993). *Sentiments and acts.* New York: Aldine de Gruyter.

DeVault, M. L. (1999). *Liberating method: Feminism and social research.* Philadelphia: Temple University Press.

Dewey, J. (1922). *Human nature and conduct.* New York: Modern Library.

Dey, I. (1999). *Grounding grounded theory.* San Diego: Academic Press.

Duneire, M. (1992). *Slim's table: Race, respectability, and masculinity.* Chicago: University of Chicago Press.

Feagin, J. R. (1999). Social justice and sociology: Agendas for the twenty-first century. *American Sociological Review, 66*, 1–20.

Fine, G. A. (Ed.). (1995). *A second Chicago school? The development of a postwar American sociology.* Chicago: University of Chicago Press.

Fine, M., Weis, L., Weseen, S., & Wong, L. (2000). For whom? Qualitative research, representations, and social responsibilities. In N. K. Denzin & Y. S. Lincoln (Eds.), *Handbook of qualitative research* (2nd ed., pp. 107–131). Thousand Oaks, CA: Sage.

Flick, U. (1998). *An introduction to qualitative research.* Thousand Oaks, CA: Sage.

Frank, A. W. (1997). Enacting illness stories: When, what, and why. In H. L. Nelson (Ed.), *Stories and their limits: Narrative approaches to bioethics* (pp. 31–49). New York: Routledge.

Freire, P. (1970). *The pedagogy of the oppressed* (M. B. Ramos, Trans.). New York: Herder and Herder.

Glaser, B. G. (1978). *Theoretical sensitivity.* Mill Valley, CA: Sociology Press.

Glaser, B. G. (1992). *Basics of grounded theory analysis.* Mill Valley, CA: Sociology Press.

Glaser B. G. (1998). *Doing grounded theory: Issues and discussions.* Mill Valley, CA: Sociology Press.

Glaser, B. G. (2001). *Conceptualization contrasted with description.* Mill Valley, CA: Sociology Press.

Glaser, B. G. (2002). Constructivist grounded theory? *Forum Qualitative Sozialforschung/Forum: Qualitative Social Research, 3*(3). Retrieved from www.qualitative-research.net/fqs-texte/3-02/3-02glaser-e-htm

Glaser, B. G., & Strauss, A. L. (1965). *Awareness of dying.* Chicago: Aldine.

Glaser, B. G., & Strauss, A. L. (1967). *The discovery of grounded theory.* Chicago: Aldine.

Goffman, E. (1959). *The presentation of self in everyday life.* Garden City, NY: Doubleday.

Goffman, E. (1961). *Asylums.* Garden City, NY: Doubleday.

Harris, S. R. (2001). What can interactionism contribute to the study of inequality? The case of marriage and beyond. *Symbolic Interaction, 24,* 455–480.

Hartshorne, C., & Weiss, P. (Eds.). (1931–1935). *Collected papers of Charles Saunders Peirce* (Vols. 1–6). Cambridge, MA: Harvard University Press.

Hewitt, J. P. (1994). *Self and society: A symbolic interactionist social psychology* (6th ed.). Boston: Allyn & Bacon.

Hochschild, A. (1983). *The managed heart: Commercialization of human feeling.* Berkeley: University of California Press.

Holstein, J. A., & Gubrium, J. F. (1995). *The active interview.* Thousand Oaks, CA: Sage.

Horowitz, R. (1983). *Honor and the American dream: Culture and identity in a Chicano community.* New Brunswick, NJ: Rutgers University Press.

Horowitz, R. (2001). Inequalities, democracy, and fieldwork in the Chicago schools of yesterday and today. *Symbolic Interaction, 24,* 481–504.

Howard, J. A. (2003). Tensions of social justice. *Sociological Perspectives, 46,* 1–20.

Kemmis, S., & McTaggart, R. (2000). Participatory action research. In N. K. Denzin & Y. S. Lincoln (Eds.), *Handbook of qualitative research* (2nd ed., pp. 567–605). Thousand Oaks, CA: Sage.

Kleinman, S. (1996). *Opposing ambitions: Gender and identity in an alternative organization.* Chicago: University of Chicago Press.

Lal, B. B. (2001). Individual agency and collective determinism: Changing perspectives on race and ethnicities in cities, the Chicago school 1918–1958. In J. Mucha, D. Kaesler, & W. Winclawski (Eds.), *Mirrors and windows: Essays in the history of sociology* (pp. 183–196). Torun: International Sociological Association.

Lincoln, Y. S., & Guba, E. G. (1985). *Naturalistic inquiry.* Beverly Hills, CA: Sage.

Lincoln, Y. S., & Guba, E. G. (2000). Paradigmatic controversies, contradictions, and emerging confluences. In N. K. Denzin & Y. S. Lincoln (Eds.), *Handbook of Qualitative Research* (2nd ed., pp. 163–188). Thousand Oaks, CA: Sage.

Lively, K. (2001). Occupational claims to professionalism: The case of paralegals. *Symbolic Interaction, 24,* 343–365.

Locke, K. (1996). Rewriting *The Discovery of Grounded Theory* after 25 years? *Journal of Management Inquiry, 5,* 239–245.

Lofland, J., & Lofland, L. H. (1984). *Analyzing social settings* (2nd ed.). Belmont, CA: Wadsworth.

Lofland, J., & Lofland, L. H. (1995). *Analyzing social settings* (3rd ed.). Belmont, CA: Wadsworth.

Lofland, L. H. (1980). Reminiscences of classic Chicago. *Urban Life, 9,* 251–281.

Maines, D. R. (2001). *The faultline of consciousness: A view of interactionism in sociology.* New York: Aldine de Gruyter.

Maines, D. R.(2003). Interactionism's place. *Symbolic Interaction, 26,* 5–18.

Mamo, L. (1999). Death and dying: Confluences of emotion and awareness. *Sociology of Health and Illness, 21,* 13–26.

Mead, G. H. (1932). *Philosophy of the present.* LaSalle, IL: Open Court.

Mead, G. H. (1934). *Mind, self and society.* Chicago: University of Chicago Press.

Melia, K. M. (1996). Rediscovering Glaser. *Qualitative Health Research, 6,* 368–378.

Miller, D. E. (2000). Mathematical dimensions of qualitative research. *Symbolic Interaction, 23,* 399–402.

Miller, S. I., & Fredericks, M. (1999). How does grounded theory explain? *Qualitative Health Research, 9,* 538–551.

Mills, C. W. (1990). Situated actions and vocabularies of motive. In D. Brissett & C. Edgley (Eds.), *Life as theatre* (2nd ed., pp. 207–218). New York: Aldine de Gruyter.

Mitchell, R. G., Jr. (2002). *Dancing to Armageddon: Survivalism and chaos in modern times.* Chicago: University of Chicago Press.

Mitchell, R. G., & Charmaz, K. (1996). Telling tales, writing stories. *Journal of Contemporary Ethnography, 25,* 144–166.

Morse, J. M. (1995). The significance of saturation. *Qualitative Health Research, 5,* 147–149.

Morse, J. M. (1998). Validity by committee. *Qualitative Health Research, 8,* 443–445.

Morse, J. M. (1999). The armchair walkthrough. *Qualitative Health Research, 9,* 435–436.

Musolf, G. R. (2003). The Chicago school. In L. T. Reynolds & N. J. Herman-Kinney (Eds.), *Handbook of symbolic interactionism* (pp. 91–117). Walnut Creek, CA: AltaMira.

Nussbaum, M. C. (1999). *Sex and social justice.* New York: Oxford University Press.

Nussbaum, M. C. (2000). Women's capabilities and social justice. *Journal of Human Development, 1,* 219–247.

Olesen, V. L. (2000). Feminisms and qualitative research at and into the millennium. In N. K. Denzin & Y. S. Lincoln (Eds.), *Handbook of qualitative research* (2nd ed., pp. 215–255). Thousand Oaks, CA: Sage.

Park, R. E., & Burgess, E. W. (1925). *The city.* Chicago: University of Chicago Press.

Prus, R. (1996). *Symbolic interaction and ethnographic research: Intersubjectivity and the study of human lived experience.* Albany: State University of New York Press.

Rawls, J. (1971). *A theory of justice.* Cambridge, MA: Belknap Press of Harvard University Press.

Reynolds, L. T. (2003a). Early representatives. In L. T. Reynolds & N. J. Herman-Kinney (Eds.), *Handbook of symbolic interactionism* (pp. 59–81). Walnut Creek, CA: AltaMira.

Reynolds, L. T. (2003b). Intellectual precursors. In L. T. Reynolds & N. J. Herman-Kinney (Eds.), *Handbook of symbolic interactionism* (pp. 39–58). Walnut Creek, CA: AltaMira.

Richardson, L. (2000). Writing: A method of inquiry. In N. K. Denzin & Y. S. Lincoln (Eds.), *Handbook of qualitative research* (2nd ed., pp. 923–948). Thousand Oaks, CA: Sage.

Scheff, T. J. (2003). Shame in self and society. *Symbolic Interaction, 26,* 239–262.

Schwalbe, M. S., Goodwin, S., Holden, D., Schrock, D., Thompson, S., & Wolkomir, M. (2000). Generic processes in the reproduction of inequality: An interactionist analysis. *Social Forces, 79,* 419–452.

Schwandt, T. A. (1994). Constructivist, interpretivist approaches to human inquiry. In N. K. Denzin & Y. S. Lincoln (Eds.), *Handbook of qualitative research* (pp. 118–137). Thousand Oaks, CA: Sage.

Schwandt, T. A. (2000). Three epistemological stances for qualitative inquiry: Interpretivism, hermeneutics, and social constructionism. In N. K. Denzin & Y. S. Lincoln (Eds.), *Handbook of qualitative research* (2nd ed., pp. 189–213). Thousand Oaks, CA: Sage.

Scott, M., & Lyman, S. M. (1968). Accounts. *American Sociological Review, 33,* 46–62.

Seale, C. (1999). *The quality of qualitative research.* London: Sage.

Sennett, R., & Cobb, J. (1973). *The hidden injuries of class.* New York: Vintage.

Shaw, C. (1930). *The jack-roller.* Chicago: University of Chicago Press.

Silverman, D. (2000). *Doing qualitative research: A practical handbook.* London: Sage.

Snow, D. (2001). Extending and broadening Blumer's conceptualization of symbolic interactionism. *Symbolic Interaction, 24,* 367–377.

Snow, D., & Anderson, L. (1993). *Down on their luck: A study of homeless street people.* Berkeley: University of California Press.

Star, S. L. (1989). *Regions of the mind: Brain research and the quest for scientific certainty.* Stanford, CA: Stanford University Press.

Stern, P. N. (1994). Eroding grounded theory. In J. Morse (Ed.), *Critical issues in qualitative research methods* (pp. 212–223). Thousand Oaks, CA: Sage.

Strauss, A. L. (Ed.). (1964). *George Herbert Mead on social psychology.* Chicago: University of Chicago Press.

Strauss, A. L. (1987). *Qualitative analysis for social scientists.* New York: Cambridge University Press.

Strauss, A. L. (1993). *Continual permutations of action.* New York: Aldine de Gruyter.

Strauss, A., & Corbin, J. (1990). *Basics of qualitative research: Grounded theory procedures and techniques.* Newbury Park, CA: Sage.

Strauss, A., & Corbin, J. (1998). *Basics of qualitative research: Grounded theory procedures and techniques* (2nd ed.). Thousand Oaks, CA: Sage.

Strauss, A., & Fisher, B. (1979a). George Herbert Mead and the Chicago tradition of sociology, Part 1. *Symbolic Interaction, 2*(1), 9–26.

Strauss, A., & Fisher, B. (1979b). George Herbert Mead and the Chicago tradition of sociology, Part 2. *Symbolic Interaction, 2*(2), 9–19.

Suttles, G. (1968). *Social order of the slum.* Chicago: University of Chicago Press.

Tedlock, B. (2000). Ethnography and ethnographic representation. In N. K. Y. S. Lincoln (Eds.), *Handbook of qualitative research* (2nd ed., pp. 455–486) Oaks, CA: Sage.

Thomas, W. I., & Znaniecki, F. (1927). *The Polish peasant in America.* New York: Knopf.

Thrasher, F. (1927). *The gang.* Chicago: University of Chicago Press.

Timmermans, S. (1994). Dying of awareness: The theory of awareness contexts revisited. *Sociology of Health and Illness, 17,* 322–339.

van den Hoonaard, W. C. (1997). *Working with sensitizing concepts: Analytical field research.* Thousand Oaks, CA: Sage.

Van Maanen, J. (1988). *Tales of the field.* Chicago: University of Chicago Press.

Venkatesh, S. (2000). *American project: The rise and fall of a modern ghetto.* Cambridge, MA: Harvard University Press.

Wacquant, L. (2002). Scrutinizing the street: Poverty, morality, and the pitfalls of urban ethnography. *American Journal of Sociology, 107,* 1468–1534.

CRITICAL ETHNOGRAPHY AS STREET PERFORMANCE

Reflections of Home, Race, Murder, and Justice

D. Soyini Madison

W hat does it mean to be at home? How does leaving home affect home and being-at-home?

Home is here, not a particular place that one simply inhabits, but more than one place: there are too many homes to allow place to secure the roots or routes of one's destination. It is not simply that the subject does not belong anywhere. The journey between homes provides the subject with the contours of a space of belonging, but a space that expresses the very logic of an interval, the passing through of the subject between apparently fixed moments of departure and arrival. (Ahmed, 2000, p. 76)

▣ THE AIRPORT: DEPARTING HOME/ARRIVING HOME

When my plane was about to land at Kotoka International Airport in Ghana, West Africa, in March of 2000, I had been away from Africa for nearly a month. I had gone home to the United States to see my son and my daughter after more than 2 years of fieldwork in Ghana. I was leaving home to come home. For the last 2 years, airports on both sides of the Atlantic marked physical and symbolic junctures of the departure and arrival of home (Ahmed, 2000). Airports had become rhizomes of perennial beginnings and endings, of a marked liminality that delineated what it meant to depart one life and arrive in another. Airports became the synecdoche for a black Diaspora citizenship and for a politics of mobility.

During 14 hours of travel, I departed home in order to arrive home, and, in the sentiment of Alice Walker, to do the work my soul must do (Walker, 1974), in Ghana, by doing the work of performance and by making a performance that, hopefully, mattered. As I gathered my belongings to leave the plane, I realized it was my last year in Africa. I was in the final stage of my fieldwork—the culminating stage. This was the year I would stage the performance, thereby making my fieldwork public and its purpose known.

It was upon entering the airport and waiting for my friend and fellow Fulbright sister, Lisa Aubrey, to pick me up that I began to feel the full weight of this final arrival. This was it. There was no turning back. It was time to transform 2 years of fieldwork data on poverty and indigenous human rights activism into a public performance, a public performance for the purpose of advocacy and change. The performance would depict a debate raging within a community of Ghanaians, one side representing the human rights of women and girls, and the other side representing the preservation of traditional religious practices. The former believed that traditional religion must be changed for the freedom and development of their people, while the latter believed that traditional religion must be preserved for the sustenance and protection of their people. The performance would represent these opposing claims, but it would do more—it would implicate the corporate, capitalist economy and the consequences of poverty on human rights abuses in the global South.

I. Performance of Possibility

As I walked through the airport, thoughts of the performance and its purpose took hold. This performance was going to be about the work of Ghanaian human rights activists and the work they were doing in their own country, and it had to be powerful and true and absolutely urgent because bodies were on the line. These people were changing the lives of women and girls by re-imagining the discourse of rights, by mobilizing their communities, and by changing the law. Moreover, Ghanaians did this for themselves under the forces of wretched poverty and global inequity. The performance had to unveil the labor of these activists working in their local communities, AND it had to unveil the devastation of global forces that impeded and burdened their victories. This performance aimed to expose the hidden, clarify the oblique, and articulate the possible. It would be a performance of possibility (Madison, 1998) that aimed to create and contribute to a discursive space where unjust systems and processes are identified and interrogated. Social critic Anna Marie Smith (1998) states:

> Dissemination of democratic discourse to new and needed areas of the social is the first step toward change. . . . One becomes radicalized when one finds a compelling discourse to speak. (p. 8)

I hoped the performance would provide such a discourse through the descriptions and narratives of those Ghanaian rights activists who told me their stories. Staging their struggles for human rights and the mandate for economic justice through the illuminating frame of performance promised this dissemination of democratic discourse. I hoped the performance would offer its audience another way to speak of rights and the origins of poverty that would then un-nestle another possibility of informed and strategic action. In other words, the significance of the performance for the subjects of my fieldwork is for those who bear witness to their stories to interrogate actively and purposefully those processes that limit their health and freedom. I do not mean to imply that one performance can bring down a revolution, but one performance can be revolutionary in enlightening citizens to the possibilities that grate against injustice. One performance may or may not change someone's world, but, as James Scott reminds us, acts of resistance amass, rather like snowflakes on a steep mountainside, and can set off an avalanche. Everyday forms of resistance give way to collective defiance (Scott, 1990, p. 192). In the performance of possibilities, the expectation is for the performers and spectators to appropriate the rhetorical currency they need, from the inner space of the performance to the outer domain of the social world, to make a material difference (Madison, 1998).

Performance scholar Diana Taylor reminds us that when confronted with certain "truths," theater has the power to illuminate not only what we see and how we see it, but how we can reject the reality of what we see and know to be true (Taylor, 1997). I believe more and more that a performance of possibility is always a harbinger of and a confrontation with the truth.

II. The Unexpected in the Present Tense: The Murder of Amadou Diallo

I see Lisa at the baggage claim. How on Earth did she actually get inside the airport! Those hard-core guards don't let anyone come inside the airport unless they're traveling. This woman is a wonder, with her combination of striking beauty, unabashed willfulness, irreverence for rules, and extraordinary intellect. She always averts the expected, the predictable, the required. I won't even ask her how she might have charmed the guards to get through this blockade of an airport, while throngs of others are waiting outside to greet friends and relations.

"Lisa!" I shout, so happy to see my friend.

"Soyiiiineeee!" she calls out with excitement in her Louisiana accent. "How was the flight?"

"The flight was fine. I have just been so worried about getting this performance ready. This is all on top of the fatigue of not sleeping for 2 days trying to get back here."

"Oh Soyini, girrrrl, the performance will be wonderful and you will be fine. Besides, you don't have time to be tired."

"Why?" I asked curiously. "What's happening?"

"We must organize a protest march on the American embassy for Amadou!"

"Lisa, it is all so awful and so redundant."

Lisa's voice tightens. "Does a blackman's life, a poor blackman's life, mean anything in the U.S.?"

The march was Lisa's idea, and I knew that she would be stalwart in mobilizing people of conscience to stand up and speak out against the murder of Amadou Diallo and the miscarriage of justice that followed. Still, I was so exhausted I could hardly speak.

"Lisa, are we meeting tonight?"

"Yes, we're all meeting at Flavors Pub in Osu tonight. This will be our second meeting. I need you there to help organize. We don't have much time. We need to mount the protest for next week!"

I'm stunned. "Next week?"

"Yes, next week. We need to get the letters and petitions to Washington within 2 weeks for a retrial. Are you too tired, Soyini? Can you make it, because we may be up all night."

I take a deep, uneasy breath, not so much from fatigue but from the contradiction. I am in the home of my heart, Africa, reflecting back on a 400-year-old rage for the home of my birth, the United States. The ideology of liberal democracy in the United States is, for some, a model for the world, yet its democratic principles partner with racial injustice with flagrant consistency. Racism in America is no moribund phenomenon; whatever or however its forms of disguise, it is alive and still hurting people. I will protest here, in my African home, for what was done there, in my American home, to a blackman born on this continent. I say to Lisa, "Let's go."

▣ ▣ ▣

[African] Americans organizing protest activities in Ghana against the United States government posed interesting political and social contractual questions regarding citizen's rights, state responsibility, and democracy in an international context. For instance, in what ways can citizens lawfully exercise their constitutional rights to hold institutions of government accountable for their actions when those citizens reside outside of the country of their birth and citizenship? Additionally, how do we ensure that protests comply to laws of both the land of citizenship and the land of residence? Furthermore, how can we operate within the confines of both sets of laws and still maintain the passion, outrage and fervor of our demands? (Aubrey, 2001, p. 1)

Africanist and political science professor Lisa Aubrey wrote these words for *In Salute of Hero Amadou Diallo: African Americans Organize Amadou Diallo Protest Activities in Accra, Ghana in 2000: Lesson for Democracy in the United States and in Ghana.*

◫ THE STREET PERFORMANCE: BLACKNESS AND OUTSIDE BELONGING

There are more people here at the march than we expected. We've worked very hard, and we've pulled it off. The teach-ins, the awareness sessions, the petitions, the letter writing campaign, and the international solidarity day for Mumia Abu Jamal each were essential and dynamic projects in our organizing efforts for this march, the Amadou Diallo march. Each of these activities was a success, now culminating in this day. I look at all these people gathered here: They are a blend of races and ethnicities, expatriates from Europe, Asia, Africa, and the Americas living in Ghana from all over the world and coming to voice their indignation over the death of a young, innocent black man in New York City who was murdered by four plainclothes police officers as he was entering his residence in the Bronx. The police officers fired 41 bullets at Amadou Diallo; 19 of those bullets entered his body after he had fallen to the ground. The police were looking for a criminal, a young black man they thought was Amadou. They asked him if they could have a word with him. Amadou reached for his wallet to show his identification; then, the bullets came, and they kept coming. He did not have a weapon. The officers were brought to trial. A jury of eight white men and four black women acquitted the four white police officers. I wonder, if all the officers had been black, would Amadou's life have been spared? It is a troubling thought, but I don't think it would have made a difference. Blackness is a universal signifier of fear, danger, and threat across color lines; the meanings play out in the destruction of too many black men in American cities by those powerful and powerless with guns.

Here we all stand, together, on this day, March 8, 2000, remembering Amadou and demanding justice. And here I stand, African American, between two homes—one majority white, the other majority black. I stand here thinking about this thing called race that wrestles between Africa and America and that is complicated by the category "African American."

Performance scholar Joni Jones writes:

Just what is an African American in Africa? My inability to answer this question uprooted a heretofore, fundamental aspect of my identity, a part of the self I took for granted in the United States as a part of my cultural identity. In my mind, my dreadlocks, West African inspired clothing, and blackness of tongue meant something powerful in the United States, while for the Yoruba, these artifacts of identity elicited puzzlement, amusement, and sometimes disdain. I did not feel that my self, the self I had constructed on U.S. soil, was visible. Indeed, I felt out of my self. (1996, p. 133)

I Remember: A Digression

I remember, during my first days in Ghana, I went to visit Lisa. I was looking for her flat; I couldn't figure out which apartment was hers. A Ghanaian living on the first floor of her building saw that I was lost. He knew that I was looking for Lisa, so referring to her, he asked, "Are you looking for the white girl upstairs?"

I was taken aback by his description. Lisa is honey brown, with natural hair and West African–inspired clothing and blackness of tongue. How could he mistake Lisa for a white woman!

"No," I said, unsettled and insulted. "I am not looking for a white girl, I am looking for Lisa Aubrey and we are both African Americans."

The man pointed to her apartment and then just shook his head and chuckled under his breath, "Abruni."

I trembled. He had just called me a foreigner, a white person.

Black people are dying and catching hell in the United States, and that man called me Abruni! I belong to blackness as much as this man! I am reminded of cultural critic Elspeth Probyn: "If you have to think about belonging, perhaps you are already outside. Instead of presuming a common locus, I want to consider the ways in which the very longing to belong embarrasses its taken-for-granted nature" (1996, pp. 8–9).

For many black Americans, at profound moments, belonging requires a fixed political ground. Understanding that ultimately we belong in different categories and to different communities and that our belonging may be annunciated at different stages of political and social progressions (or regressions), beyond all this, "African American" as signifier and as signified is nonetheless a relatively stable reality of belonging to blackness in the United States, however complicated that belonging may be. I experience belonging within the racialization of blackness in the United States not as a longing from an outside identity to enter into an inside identity. I am always already inside. Even when I'm not thinking about it, am I ever not a black person? Granted, I experience black belonging on American soil as a space of flux and ambiguity constituting multiple identities; however, this belonging remains a discursive and material association with specific bodies based on historical, social, and political arrangements that are regulated through law, culture, and the everyday. As this belonging is discursively instituted and materially experienced, my black body is further evidence that I am not white and that I belong to the category of blackness.

Black people can or cannot and will or will not choose to be slippery and equivocal about their racial identity and belonging. But for many black people in the United States, embracing this belonging, however it is articulated or whatever the level of its consistency, becomes a matter of saving one's life and one's sanity. This kind of belonging falls beyond intellectual or philosophical pondering; it is psychological and physical protection.

I never questioned the fact of my blackness. It is as much a part of me as my skin, my nose, my mouth, my hair, and my speech, all the while with an understanding that it is beyond appearances. When Anna Julia Cooper said, "When and where I enter, my race enters with me," she was acknowledging the ubiquity of race as it is internally felt and externally constructed (Giddings, 1996). The ever-present fact of race looms within the multilayered realms of blackness in the United States and within a web of projections both colored and white, both hostile and admiring, where race/blackness often precedes being. In Ghana, West Africa, the words "white girl upstairs" disrupted my reality of belonging (that I've always known) to its very core. I was reminded that geography might be one of the greatest determiners of them all. Perhaps geography is destiny after all.

My personhood, for Lisa's neighbor, was outside blackness. I was outside belonging (Probyn, 1996). I represented something else to him. At that moment, it was representation that eclipsed any notion of belonging. I was not a black woman, but the representation of a white one, the representation of a white, advanced country. The neighbor certainly understood that I was not white like Julia Roberts is white. I was not white by phenotype, but by country. Although he may have understood that I was of African descent, it did not matter. Nation and global order took primacy over racial identification. In that instant, I represented an individual of American descent, not African descent. I live in an advanced country; he lives in the developing world. This fact of economy eclipsed blackness within the U.S. context or any unity around Diaspora blackness that I might fantasize.

Belonging may be the effect of identity, but representation became a framework for meaning in the white girl upstairs (Hall, 1997). And if representation embodies meaning, my meaning was now constructed as not black, as not belonging. And if one of the things that culture is based on is the production and exchange of meanings, and if one of the ways we give things meaning is by how we produce them and how we represent them or how they appear to us, in that moment the white girl upstairs became the classic encounter between cultural insider and cultural outsider. At that moment, insider/outsider was deeply inscribed and poignantly reversed. I was the outsider, and belonging was reversed. That race is socially made became an understatement at the sound of "white girl." We are reminded repeatedly (and for good reason) that race is constructed, reconstructed, and deconstructed depending on locale, history, and power, but immediate experience sometimes penetrates deeper. Would he have called Lisa white if she had been a man and if I had been a man? Would he have said, "the white boy upstairs"? If I had been a white American woman, would he have referred to race at all? Would he have said, "you mean the lady upstairs?"

I personalize my experiences in the field to engage ironically with a vulnerability toward universal questions and human unease. Race as personally experienced in the ethnographic then, when I became subject and object of the Other's gaze, brings me to the ethnographic now, writing. I theorize from the starting point of the personal and from my own racial dislocation between, within, and outside belonging in Africa. Race, in the moment—"white girl upstairs"—meant that this (re)construction of who I am is tied to where I live and where I travel, as well as politicized perspectives on wealth, opportunity, and technology, specifically as they are perceived by those in the global South, the developing world. That blackness is contingent—relative to African Americans, NOT on being of African descent but on being American citizens—is for many Africans taken for granted, while for many black Americans it is disheartening. Blackness is tied to slavery, terror, and discrimination, as it is also tied to a culture and past that are generative, free, and prosperous. However, in that ethnographic then, all these layers were displaced in recognition of my American citizenship that is complicated because I am of African descent.

III. Street Performance and Diaspora Identity

We are marching down the streets of Accra. This is less a protest march and more a street performance, or is it more a protest march because it is a street performance?

We had all planned to meet at the Labonne Coffee Shop in town and then march in silence to the American embassy; upon reaching the embassy, we would begin our program of speeches and testimonies. But the silence has surrendered to the sheer energy of our collective will. We are all caught in the drama and the urgency of our indignation, which cannot be stilled by silence, not here on this continent of drums, poetry, and dance, always dance, because this coming together has evolved into a precious praise song mightily strung together by the antiquity of dark-skinned motion. The march is a performance of movement made into a variance of sounds, symbolic rhythms, and lyrical incantations of mourning and politics. The onlookers in our path join our chorus of steps. They sing and chant with us. They see the black and white T-shirts we are wearing, the word "Diallo" written in black letters across the front and the numbers "19 of 41" written across our backs. We pick up more and more people on our way. This march is becoming a carnival of contestation of the highest order, of purposeful action (Conquergood, 2002). We are all together, absorbed spontaneously in the communitas and flow of this assemblage of movement and this alchemy of collective will. There is no white girl upstairs here; there is only, in this heightened moment, communal energy. On this path of street performance and protest, for this brief moment in time, all of us belong to each other for performance and because of it, and some of us, for justice and because of it. More and more come to join the march. We are stepping and singing; we are meeting new friends; we are learning about the particularity of a lost life; we are enacting our urgency for justice. Reggae singer Shasha Marley raises his voice and calls. We respond. He calls again, and we respond again in the reverie of Ghanaian high life.

Anthropologist Victor Turner (1982) writes:

> Is there any of us who has not known this moment when the mood, style, or fit of spontaneous communitas is upon us, we place a high value on personal honesty, openness, and lack of pretensions or pretentiousness. We feel that it is important to relate directly to another person as he presents himself in the here and now, free from the culturally defined

encumbrances of his role, status, reputation, class, caste, sex, or other structural niche. Individuals who interact with one another in the mode of spontaneous communitas become totally absorbed into a single synchronized, fluid event. It has something magical about it. (pp. 47–48)

The magic of our inspired oneness summoned by the dramatic sounds and motions of street performance displaced "white girl upstairs," at least today and with a possibility for tomorrow, into a Diaspora consciousness, a black Atlantic identity, that would demand that African peoples on the continent and in the United States understand Amadou's death as an allegory for political action on both sides of the ocean. Describing that day, I turn again to Lisa's article and her words:

African American individuals in Ghana who took the initiative of organizing protest activities were supported by many Pan-African and other humanitarian communities that believe in justice, fairness, equality, and democracy. Individuals, community organizations, non-governmental organizations (NGOs), businesses, especially private radio stations, offered untiring support for the Diallo protest activities. Among the supporters were the African American Association of Ghana, One-Africa, the Brotherhood, members of the Ghana legal profession and the Ghana Bar Association, other concerned Ghanaians, Liberian refugees in Ghana, the W.E.B. Dubois Center, the Embassy of Guinea, the Commission on Human Rights and Administrative Justice (CHRAJ, a quasi governmental organization of Ghana), the Student and Workers Solidarity Committee, Musicians of Ghana (MUSIGA) and Ghanaian and American students from the University of Ghana, Legon. (Aubrey, 2001, pp. 1–2)

Now, the march has grown to even greater numbers. Amadou Diallo's memory is reaching out like a hand gesturing for another to hold and to remember. Manifest through performance, the gesture is exquisite, evolving into a celebratory embrace.

We finally reach the American embassy. We form a large circle in front of the building. As the circle forms, we begin lighting our candles. Lisa begins the ceremony by recounting the night of Amadou's death. She concludes her presentation by speaking eloquently on the nature of democracy and descent. Her words are a call to action for free speech, for collective action, and for the U.S. Department of Justice to intervene and bring federal civil rights charges against the acquitted police officers.

After Lisa ends her presentation, I begin to speak. I am speaking of the power of mourning: mourning the hope of Amadou Diallo, who was so like so many immigrants, who strive most of their lives to come to the land of opportunity, wealth, and happiness, and discover that when they finally arrive, they must confront the ominous inequality and violence of race in America. I close by recovering what it means to mourn, not only as loss but also as evocation. Our mourning evokes social activism. I am reminded of rights activists who have fought across national borders and their urgent cry: "Don't mourn, organize!"

The ceremony is drawing to an end. The written statement we crafted, demanding a retrial and that civil charges be brought against the four police officers, is given to the director of the embassy. She receives the statement with the promise that the embassy would look into the matter and take action, as its officers also believe in justice.

▣ NOVEMBER 15, 2002, NORTH CAROLINA, U.S.A.

And the Hate Goes On La, La, La, La, La

A retrial was not ordered. The acquittal of the four police officers was granted without further interference by the justice system. When I first began preparing this chapter, 2 years after our protest march, I went to the Internet to search for new developments relating to the Diallo case. I discovered that there was an Amadou Diallo Web site. I opened the site and, to my surprise, although the murder of Diallo was on February 4, 1999, nearly 3 years prior, there was a posting for that very day, November 15, 2002. What follows are samples of the most recent exchange over a 3-day period from when I first discovered the site. These verbatim exchanges (including spelling and grammar) represent the sentiment of most of the entries sent to the Amadou Diallo home page. I have chosen to include only three that were the least offensive.

Name: Nigger God Killer

Date: Tuesday, November 12, 2002, at 20:44:06

Comments: Phuck you Nigger God you stupid fucking worthless faggot ass nigger! Someone should kill your worthless cocksucking faggot nigger ass! Kill all niggers! White Power!

Name: Aryan

Date: Thursday, November 12, 2002, at 20:47:22

Comments: Amadou Diallo is a worthless nigger; the cops should have blown this nigger brains out. The only good nigger is a dead nigger. Heil Hitler! Deutschesland Uber Alles! Ein Reich, Ein volk, Ein Fuhrer! Seig heil!

Name: All niggers and niggerlovers must die!

Date: Friday, November 15, 2002, at 01:44:51

Comments: I totally agree with you Aryan. The cops should have not only blown Amadou Diallo's brains out, but have also blown out his whole family's brains. allus true white people (excluding kikes, wiggers, and faggots, because they're niggerloving white race traitors) should blow every nigger on this earth's brains out. if niggerkilling and niggerloverkilling was legalized I'd be killing tons and tons of niggers and niggerloving white race traitor kikes, wiggers, and faggots everyday.

And the hate goes on, even after death. We are in an era when many still relegate such racism to bygone days. The messages from the Internet notwithstanding, and given that the murder of Amadou Diallo met no justice, what good did our street protest do? People still hate, and more people of color have died since 1999 at the hands of murderous authority. What is the value of such performances when what we aim for is not achieved? What effect did our performance march have in the light of these despicable and violent words?

IV. Conclusion

Just like a bell cannot be unrung, our street performance cannot be undone. It is remembered, and it has produced friends, allies, and comrades, as it has also inspired imagination. The promise of a performance of possibility is that it not only creates alliances while it names and marks injustice, but it also enacts a force beyond ideology; it enacts and imagines the vast possibilities of collective hopes and dreams coming into fruition, of actually being lived. In the words of performance scholar Janelle Reinelt, "performance can overrun ideology's containment" (1996, p. 3). Why, then, did our street performance matter?

The performance made public international injustice committed on an American city street. It brought that injustice beyond its particular location by extending the arena of public viewing and awareness across national boundaries to invoke and materialize a transborder participatory call for justice, generating a street performance that embodied a dialogue with authority (Gunner, 1994). Therefore, in this more expanded performative participation, a re-visioning of ingrained social arrangements relating to authority and violence, class and power, as well as freedom of speech and social change, were called into question by the voices and action of those situated within the context of globalization from below (Brecher, Costello, & Smith, 2002; Cohen-Cruz, 1998).

The march evolved into a street performance that made spirited actors out of passive observers. Engaged action motivated by performative intervention, a performance of possibility was required for the call and the response, for the testimonies, the dialogue, and the demand upon the American embassy. Moreover, it is the emotionally charged animation drawn from the body in motion, within the heightened moments of performative intervention, that unleashes a palpable defiance that dissolves apathy (Conquergood, 2002; Denzin, 2003; Madison, 1999). The performance evoked spontaneous communitas that offers the alchemy of human connection, conjoinment, and intersubjectivity to the power and ubiquity of memory. We remember how this communion felt for us and for each other, together. It was made even more powerfully human because it was publicly performed. I echo the sentiment of social activist Ernesto J. Cortes, Jr., that there is a dimension of our humanity that emerges only when we engage in public discourse.

The street performance, empowered by communitas and the humanizing dynamics of public discourse, provided us with the gift of remembering (Pollock, 1999). The street performance became a method and a means for the dissemination of discourse relative to rights, justice, and change, and, moreover, for transborder participatory democracy (Brecher et al., 2002). The march was a local and a dramatic point of inter-rogation of U.S. foreign policy relative to democracy assistance programs that demand that other nations in the world make their state institutions accountable and fair (Aubrey, 2001, p. 2). Lisa Aubrey states: "By organizing the protest activities, African Americans were forcing the U.S. to look into the mirror for the very transparency and probity it aims to cultivate and extract from other governments" (p. 2). The street per-formance honored the local in speaking truth to power (Marable, 1996) and became a communicative instrument in the public interrogation of injustice that resulted in the enactment of collective memory and mourning.

Finally, the street performance opens the possibility for another strategy for glob-alization from below. Globalization from above is making poor people poorer and rich people richer. Brecher, Costello, and Smith, in their powerfully concise book *Globali-zation From Below*, state:

> The ultimate source of power is not the command of those at the top, but the acquiescence of those at the bottom. . . . In response to globalization from above, movements are emerg-ing all over the world in social locations that are marginal to the dominant power centers. These are linking up by means of networks that cut across national borders. They are beginning to develop a sense of solidarity, a common belief system, and a common pro-gram. They are utilizing these networks to impose new norms on corporations, govern-ments, and international institutions. (pp. 23, 26)

The street performance is another illustration of the communicative function and political effectiveness of performance in mobilizing communities for change. It serves as an added example of the potential of street performance as a platform for subaltern voices and cross-border access and networks.

Several years have passed since our march on the American embassy in Ghana, and I still relive in my memory the words and chants from several of our Ghanaian friends who were responsible for turning a protest march into a street performance: Shasha chanted, "We are One Love"; Akosua kept repeating, "We prove today that we are sis-ters"; Helen asserted, "We are all African people"; and, as the march came to an end, Kweku said, "An ocean cannot divide our blood."

I remember the resounding force of the drummers and how our steps marked the rhythms of the drums along the road to the embassy under the hot sun, the blazing heat, and the many accented voices filled with song, chant, banter, and laughter. In Shasha's words and in the words of many other Ghanaians who performed that day, we were living in the communitas of one love.

But after the march, and beyond the path of the marchers, Lisa and I still remain the white girls upstairs. However, on that particular day, the magic of performance evoked a politics that was lived in the flesh and on the ground and that demanded social justice, a politics that is now remembered and recounted for the possibilities of another way of being.

◨ REFERENCES

Ahmed, S. (2000). *Strange encounters: Embodied others in post-coloniality.* New York: Routledge.

Aubrey, L. (2001). *In salute of hero Amadou Diallo: African Americans organize Amadou Diallo protest activities in Accra, Ghana in 2000: Lesson for democracy in the United States and in Ghana.* Retrieved from www.ohio.edu/tonguna/winter/2001/lisa-aubrey.htm

Brecher, B., Costello, T., & Smith, B. (2002). *Globalization from below.* Cambridge, UK: South End.

Cohen-Cruz, J. (Ed.). (1998). *Radical street performance: An international anthology.* New York: Routledge.

Conquergood, D. (2002). Performance studies: Interventions and radical research. *The Drama Review, 46*(2), 145–156.

Denzin, N. (2003). *Performance ethnography: Critical pedagogy and the politics of culture.* Thousand Oaks, CA: Sage.

Giddings, P. (1996). *When and where I enter: The impact of black women on race and sex in America.* New York: William Morrow.

Gunner, L. (Ed.). (1994). *Politics and performance: Theatre, poetry, and song in southern Africa.* Johannesburg : Witwatersrand University Press.

Hall, S. (1997). *Representation: Cultural representations and signifying practices.* London: Sage.

Jones, J. L. (1996). The self as other: Creating the role of Joni the Ethnographer for Broken Circles. *Text and Performance Quarterly, 16,* 131–145.

Madison, S. (1998). Performance, personal narratives, and the politics of possibility: The future of performance studies. In S. J. Daily (Ed.), *Visions and revisions* (pp. 276–286). Washington, DC: National Communication Association.

Madison, D. S. (1999). Performing theory/embodied writing. *Text and Performance Quarterly, 19,* 107–124.

Marable, M. (1996). *Speaking truth to power.* Boulder, CO: Westview.

Pollock, D. (1999). *Telling bodies, performing birth.* New York: Columbia University Press.

Probyn, E. (1996). *Outside belonging.* New York: Routledge.

Reinelt, J. (1996). *Crucibles of crisis: Performing social change.* Ann Arbor: University of Michigan Press.

Scott, J. (1990). *Domination and the arts of resistance.* New Haven, CT: Yale University Press.

Smith, A. (1998). *Laclau and Mouffe: The radical democratic imaginary.* New York: Routledge.

Taylor, D. (1997). *Disappearing acts: Spectacles of gender and nationalism in Argentina's "Dirty War."* Durham, NC: Duke University Press.

Turner, V. (1982). *From ritual to theatre: The human seriousness of play.* New York: Performing Art Journal Publications.

Walker, A. (1974). *In search of our mothers' gardens.* New York: Harcourt, Brace & Company.

9

TESTIMONIO, SUBALTERNITY, AND NARRATIVE AUTHORITY

John Beverley

I n a justly famous essay, Richard Rorty (1985) distinguishes between what he calls the "desire for solidarity" and the "desire for objectivity" as cognitive modes:

> There are two principal ways in which reflective human beings try, by placing their lives in a larger context, to give sense to those lives. The first is by telling the story of their contribution to a community. This community may be the actual historical one in which they live, or another actual one, distant in time or place, or a quite imaginary one, consisting perhaps of a dozen heroes and heroines selected from history or fiction or both. The second way is to describe themselves as standing in an immediate relation to a nonhuman reality. This relation is immediate in the sense that it does not derive from a relation between such a reality and their tribe, or their nation, or their imagined band of comrades. I shall say that stories of the former kind exemplify the desire for solidarity, and that stories of the latter kind exemplify the desire for objectivity. (p. 3)[1]

The question of *testimonio*—testimonial narrative—has come prominently onto the agenda of the human and social sciences in recent years in part because *testimonio* intertwines the "desire for objectivity" and "the desire for solidarity" in its very situation of production, circulation, and reception.

Testimonio is by nature a demotic and heterogeneous form, so any formal definition of it is bound to be too limiting.[2] But the following might serve provisionally: A
testimonio is a novel or novella-length narrative, produced in the form of a printed
text, told in the first person by a narrator who is also the real protagonist or witness of
the events she or he recounts. Its unit of narration is usually a "life" or a significant life
experience. Because in many cases the direct narrator is someone who is either func-
tionally illiterate or, if literate, not a professional writer, the production of a *testimonio*
generally involves the tape recording and then the transcription and editing of an oral
account by an interlocutor who is a journalist, ethnographer, or literary author.

Although one of the antecedents of *testimonio* is undoubtedly the ethnographic life
history of the *Children of Sánchez* sort, *testimonio* is not exactly commensurable with the
category of life history (or oral history). In the life history, it is the intention of the
interlocutor-recorder (the ethnographer or journalist) that is paramount; in *testimonio,* by contrast, it is the intention of the direct narrator, who *uses* (in a pragmatic
sense) the possibility the ethnographic interlocutor offers to bring his or her situation
to the attention of an audience—the bourgeois public sphere—to which he or she
would normally not have access because of the very conditions of subalternity to
which the *testimonio* bears witness.[3] *Testimonio* is not intended, in other words, as a
reenactment of the anthropological function of the native informant. In René Jara's
(1986, p. 3) phrase, it is rather a *narración de urgencia*—an "emergency" narrative—
involving a problem of repression, poverty, marginality, exploitation, or simply survival that is implicated in the act of narration itself. In general, *testimonio* could be
said to coincide with the feminist slogan "The personal is the political." The contemporary appeal of *testimonio* for educated, middle-class, transnational publics is perhaps related to the importance given in various forms of 1960s counterculture to oral
testimony as a form of personal and/or collective catharsis and liberation in (for
example) the consciousness-raising sessions of the early women's movement, the
practice of "speaking bitterness" in the Chinese Cultural Revolution, or psychotherapeutic encounter groups.

The predominant formal aspect of the *testimonio* is the voice that speaks to the
reader through the text in the form of an "I" that demands to be recognized, that wants
or needs to stake a claim on our attention. Eliana Rivero (1984–1985) notes that "the
act of speaking faithfully recorded on the tape, transcribed and then 'written,' remains
in the *testimonio* punctuated by a repeated series of interlocutive and conversational
markers . . . which constantly put the reader on the alert, so to speak: True? Are you
following me? OK? So?" (pp. 220–221, my translation). The result, she argues, is a
"snaillike" discourse (*discurso encaracolado*) that keeps turning in on itself and that in
the process invokes the complicity of the reader through the medium of his or her
counterpart in the text, the direct interlocutor. This presence of the voice, which the
reader is meant to experience as the voice of a *real* rather than a fictional person, is the
mark of a desire not to be silenced or defeated, to impose oneself on an institution of

power and privilege from the position of the excluded, the marginal, the subaltern—hence the insistence on the importance of personal name or identity evident sometimes in titles of *testimonios,* such as *I, Rigoberta Menchú* (even more strongly in the Spanish: *Me llamo Rigoberta Menchú y así me nació la conciencia*), *I'm a Juvenile Delinquent* (*Soy un delincuente*), and *Let Me Speak* (*Si me permiten hablar*).

This insistence suggests an affinity between testimony and autobiography (and related forms, such as the autobiographical *bildungsroman,* the memoir, and the diary). Like autobiography, *testimonio* is an affirmation of the authority of personal experience, but, unlike autobiography, it cannot affirm a self-identity that is separate from the subaltern group or class situation that it narrates. *Testimonio* involves an erasure of the function and thus also of the textual presence of the "author" that is so powerfully present in all major forms of Western literary and academic writing.[4] By contrast, in autobiography or the autobiographical *bildungsroman,* the very possibility of "writing one's life" implies necessarily that the narrator is no longer in the situation of marginality and subalternity that his or her narrative describes, but now has attained precisely the cultural status of an author (and, generally speaking, middle- or upper-class economic status). Put another way, the transition from storyteller to author implies a parallel transition from *gemeinschaft* to *gesellschaft,* from a culture of primary and secondary orality to writing, from a traditional group identity to the privatized, modern identity that forms the subject of liberal political and economic theory.

The metonymic character of testimonial discourse—the sense that the voice that is addressing us is a part that stands for a larger whole—is a crucial aspect of what literary critics would call the convention of the form: the narrative contract with the reader it establishes. Because it does not require or establish a hierarchy of narrative authority, *testimonio* is a fundamentally democratic and egalitarian narrative form. It implies that *any* life so narrated can have a symbolic and cognitive value. Each individual *testimonio* evokes an absent polyphony of other voices, other possible lives and experiences (one common formal variation on the first-person singular *testimonio* is the polyphonic *testimonio* made up of accounts by different participants in the same event).

If the novel is a closed form, in the sense that both the story and the characters it involves end with the end of the text, in *testimonio,* by contrast, the distinctions between text and history, representation and real life, public and private spheres, objectivity and solidarity (to recall Rorty's alternatives) are transgressed. It is, to borrow Umberto Eco's expression, an "open work." The narrator in *testimonio* is an actual person who continues living and acting in an actual social space and time, which also continue. *Testimonio* can never create the illusion—fundamental to formalist methods of textual analysis—of the text as autonomous, set against and above the practical domain of everyday life and struggle. The emergence of *testimonios,* for the form to have become more and more popular in recent years, means that there are experiences in the world today (there always have been) that cannot be expressed adequately in the dominant forms of historical, ethnographic, or literary representation, that would be betrayed or misrepresented by these forms.

Because of its reliance on voice, *testimonio* implies in particular a challenge to the loss of the authority of orality in the context of processes of cultural modernization that privilege literacy and literature as a norm of expression. The inequalities and contradictions of gender, class, race, ethnicity, nationality, and cultural authority that determine the "urgent" situation of the testimonial narrator may also reproduce themselves in the relation of the narrator to the interlocutor, especially when (as is generally the case) that narrator requires to produce the *testimonio* a "lettered" interlocutor from a different ethnic and/or class background in order first to elicit and record the narrative, and then to transform it into a printed text and see to its publication and circulation as such. But it is equally important to understand that the testimonial narrator is not the subaltern as such either; rather, she or he functions as an organic intellectual (in Antonio Gramsci's sense of this term) of the subaltern, who speaks to the hegemony by means of a metonymy of self in the name and in the place of the subaltern.

By the same token, the presence of subaltern voice in the *testimonio* is in part a literary illusion—something akin to what the Russian formalists called *skaz*: the textual simulacrum of direct oral expression. We are dealing here, in other words, not with reality itself but with what semioticians call a "reality effect" that has been produced by both the testimonial narrator—using popular speech and the devices of oral storytelling—and the interlocutor-compiler, who, according to hegemonic norms of narrative form and expression, transcribes, edits, and makes a story out of the narrator's discourse. Elzbieta Sklodowska (1982) cautions in this regard that it would be naïve to assume a direct homology between text and history (in *testimonio*).

> The discourse of a witness cannot be a reflection of his or her experience, but rather a refraction determined by the vicissitudes of memory, intention, ideology. The intention and the ideology of the author-editor further superimposes the original text, creating more ambiguities, silences, and absences in the process of selecting and editing the material in a way consonant with norms of literary form. Thus, although the testimonio uses a series of devices to gain a sense of veracity and authenticity—among them the point of view of the first-person witness-narrator—the play between fiction and history reappears inexorably as a problem. (p. 379, my translation; see also Sklodowska, 1996)

The point is well-taken, but perhaps overstated. Like the identification of *testimonio* with life history (which Sklodowska shares), it concedes agency to the interlocutor-editor of the testimonial text rather than to its direct narrator. It would be better to say that what is at stake in *testimonio* is the *particular* nature of the reality effect it produces. Because of its character as a narrative told in the first person to an actual interlocutor, *testimonio* interpellates the reader in a way that literary fiction or third-person journalism or ethnographic writing does not. The word *testimonio* carries the connotation in Spanish of the act of testifying or bearing witness in a legal or religious sense. Conversely, the situation of the reader of *testimonio* is akin to that of a jury member in a courtroom. *Something* is asked of us by *testimonio*, in other words. In this sense, *testimonio* might be seen as a kind of speech act that sets up special ethical and epistemological demands. (When we are addressed directly by an actual person, in such a way as to make a demand on our attention and capacity for judgment, we are under an obligation to respond in some way or other; we can act or not on that obligation, but we cannot ignore it.)

What *testimonio* asks of its readers is in effect what Rorty means by solidarity— that is, the capacity to identify their own identities, expectations, and values with those of another. To understand how this happens is to understand how *testimonio* works ideologically as discourse, rather than what it *is*.

In one of the most powerful sections of her famous *testimonio I, Rigoberta Menchú* (Menchú, 1984), which has come to be something like a paradigm of the genre, Menchú describes the torture and execution of her brother Petrocinio by elements of the Guatemalan army in the plaza of a small highland town called Chajul, which is the site of an annual pilgrimage by worshippers of the local saint. Here is part of that account:

> After he'd finished talking the officer ordered the squad to take away those who'd been "punished," naked and swollen as they were. They dragged them along, they could no longer walk. Dragged them to this place, where they lined them up all together within sight of everyone. The officer called to the worst of the criminals—the *Kaibiles*, who wear different clothes from other soldiers. They're the ones with the most training, the most power. Well, he called the *Kaibiles* and they poured petrol over each of the tortured. The captain said, "This isn't the last of their punishments, there's another one yet. This is what we've done with all the subversives we catch, because they have to die by violence. And if this doesn't teach you a lesson, this is what'll happen to you too. The problem is that the Indians let themselves be led by the communists. Since no-one's told the Indians anything, they go along with the communists." He was trying to convince the people but at the same time he was insulting them by what he said. Anyway, they [the soldiers] lined up the tortured and poured petrol on them; and then the soldiers set fire to each one of them. Many of them begged for mercy. Some of them screamed, many of them leapt but uttered no sound—of course, that was because their breathing was cut off. But—and to me this was incredible— many of the people had weapons with them, the ones who'd been on their way to work had machetes, others had nothing in their hands, but when they saw the army setting fire to the victims, everyone wanted to strike back, to risk their lives doing it, despite all the soldiers' arms. . . . Faced with its own cowardice, the army itself realized that the whole people were prepared to fight. You could see that even the children were enraged, but they didn't know how to express their rage. (pp. 178–179)

This passage is undoubtedly compelling and powerful. It invites the reader into the situation it describes through the medium of the eyewitness narrator, and it is the sharing of the experience through the medium of Menchú's account that constitutes the possibility of solidarity. But "what if much of Rigoberta's story is not true?" anthropologist David Stoll (1999, p. viii) asks. On the basis of interviews in the area where the massacre was supposed to have occurred, Stoll concludes that the killing of Menchú's brother did not happen in exactly this way, that Menchú could not have been a direct witness to the event as her account suggests, and that therefore this account, along with other details of her *testimonio*, amounts to, in Stoll's words, a "mythic inflation" (pp. 63–70, 232). It would be more accurate to say that what Stoll is able to show is that *some* rather than "much" of Menchú's story is not true. He does not contest the fact of the murder of Menchú's brother by the army, and he stipulates that "there is no doubt about the most important points [in her story]: that a dictatorship massacred thousands of indigenous peasants, that the victims included half of Rigoberta's immediate family, that she fled to Mexico to save her life, and that she joined a revolutionary movement to liberate her country" (p. viii). But he does argue that the inaccuracies or omissions in her narrative make her less than a reliable spokesperson for the interests and beliefs of the people for whom she claims to speak. In response to Stoll, Menchú herself has publicly conceded that she grafted elements of other people's experiences and stories onto her own account. In particular, she has admitted that she was not herself present at the massacre of her brother and his companions in Chajul, and that the account of the event quoted in part above came instead from her mother, who (Menchú claims) was there. She says that this and similar interpolations were a way of making her story a collective one, rather than a personal autobiography. But the point remains: If the epistemological and ethical authority of testimonial narratives depends on the assumption that they are based on personal experience and direct witness, then it might appear that, as Stoll puts it, "*I, Rigoberta Menchú* does not belong in the genre of which it is the most famous example, because it is not the eyewitness account it purports to be" (p. 242).

In a way, however, the argument between Menchú and Stoll is not so much about what really happened as it is about who has the authority to narrate. (Stoll's quarrel with Menchú and *testimonio* is a *political* quarrel that masquerades as an epistemological one.) That question, rather than the question of "what really happened," is crucial to an understanding of how *testimonio* works. What seems to bother Stoll above all is that Menchú *has* an agenda. He wants her to be in effect a native informant who will lend herself to *his* purposes (of ethnographic information gathering and evaluation), but she is instead functioning in her narrative as an organic intellectual, concerned with producing a text of local history— that is, with elaborating hegemony.

The basic idea of Gayatri Spivak's famous, but notoriously difficult, essay "Can the Subaltern Speak?" (1988) might be reformulated in this way: If the subaltern could speak—that is, speak in a way that really *matters* to us, that we would feel compelled to listen to—then it would not be subaltern. Spivak is trying to show that behind the gesture of the ethnographer or solidarity activist committed to the cause of the subaltern in allowing or enabling the subaltern to speak is the trace of the construction of an other who is available to speak to us (with whom we *can* speak or with whom we would feel comfortable speaking), thus neutralizing the force of the reality of difference and antagonism to which our own relatively privileged position in the global system might give rise. She is saying that one of the things being subaltern means is not mattering, not being worth listening to, or not being understood when one is "heard."

By contrast, Stoll's argument with Rigoberta Menchú is precisely with how her *testimonio* comes to matter. He is bothered by the way it was used by academics and solidarity activists to mobilize international support for the Guatemalan armed struggle in the 1980s, long after (in Stoll's view) that movement had lost whatever support it may have initially enjoyed among the indigenous peasants for whom Menchú claims to speak. That issue—"how outsiders were using Rigoberta's story to justify continuing a war at the expense of peasants who did not support it" (Stoll, 1999, p. 241)—is the main problem for Stoll, rather than the inaccuracies or omissions themselves. From Stoll's viewpoint, by making Menchú's story seem (in her own words) "the story of all poor Guatemalans"—that is, by its participating in the very metonymic logic of *testimonio*—*I, Rigoberta Menchú* misrepresents a more complex and ideologically contradictory situation among the indigenous peasants. It reflects back to the reader not the subaltern as such, but a narcissistic image of what the subaltern *should be*:

> Books like *I, Rigoberta Menchú* will be exalted because they tell academics what they want to hear. . . . What makes *I, Rigoberta Menchú* so attractive in universities is what makes it misleading about the struggle for survival in Guatemala. We think we are getting closer to understanding Guatemalan peasants when actually we are being borne away by the mystifications wrapped up in an iconic figure. (Stoll, 1999, p. 227)

In one sense, of course, there is a coincidence between Spivak's concern with the production in metropolitan ethnographic and literary discourse of what she calls a "domesticated Other" and Stoll's concern with the conversion of Menchú into an icon of academic political correctness. But Stoll's argument is also explicitly *with* Spivak, as a representative of the very kind of "postmodern scholarship" that would privilege a text like *I, Rigoberta Menchú*, even to the extent of wanting to deconstruct its metaphysics of presence. Thus, Stoll states, for example:

> Following the thinking of literary theorists such as Edward Said and Gayatri Spivak, anthropologists have become very interested in problems of narrative, voice, and representation, especially the problem of how we misrepresent voices other than our own. In reaction, some anthropologists argue that the resulting fascination with texts threatens the claim of anthropology to be a science, by replacing hypothesis, evidence, and generalization with stylish forms of introspection. (p. 247)

Or this: "Under the influence of postmodernism (which has undermined confidence in a single set of facts) and identity politics (which demands acceptance of claims to victimhood), scholars are increasingly hesitant to challenge certain kinds of rhetoric" (p. 244). Or "With postmodern critiques of representation and authority, many scholars are tempted to abandon the task of verification, especially when they construe the narrator as a victim worthy of their support" (p. 274).

Where Spivak is concerned with the way in which hegemonic literary or scientific representation effaces the effective presence and agency of the subaltern, Stoll's case against Menchú is precisely that: a way of, so to speak, *resubalternizing* a narrative that aspired to (and to some extent achieved) cultural authority. In the process of constructing her narrative and articulating herself as a political icon around its circulation, Menchú is becoming not-subaltern, in the sense that she is functioning as what Spivak calls a subject of history. Her *testimonio* is a *performative* rather than simply descriptive or denotative discourse. Her narrative choices, and silences and evasions, entail that there are versions of "what really happened" that she does not or cannot represent without relativizing the authority of her own account.

It goes without saying that in any social situation, indeed even within a given class or group identity, it is always possible to find a variety of points of view or ways of telling that reflect contradictory, or simply differing, agendas and interests. "Obviously," Stoll (1999) observes:

> Rigoberta is a legitimate Mayan voice. So are all the young Mayas who want to move to Los Angeles or Houston. So is the man with a large family who owns three worn-out acres and wants me to buy him a chain saw so he can cut down the last forest more quickly. Any of these people can be picked to make misleading generalizations about Mayas. (p. 247)

The presence of these other voices makes Guatemalan indigenous communities—indeed even Menchú's own immediate family—seem irremediably driven by internal rivalries, contradictions, and disagreements.

But to insist on this is, in a way, to deny the possibility of subaltern agency as such, because a hegemonic project by definition points to a possibility of collective will and action that depends precisely on the transformation of the conditions of cultural and political disenfranchisement, alienation, and oppression that underlie these rivalries and contradictions. The appeal to diversity ("any of these people") leaves intact the authority of the outside observer (the ethnographer or social scientist) who is alone in the position of being able to both hear and sort through all the various conflicting testimonies.

The concern about the connection between *testimonio* and identity politics that Stoll evinces is predicated on the fact that multicultural rights claims carry with them what Canadian philosopher Charles Taylor (1994) has called a "presumption of equal worth" (and *I, Rigoberta Menchú* is, among other things, a strong argument for seeing the nature of American societies as irrevocably multicultural and ethnically heterogeneous). That presumption in turn implies an epistemological relativism that coincides with the postmodernist critique of the Enlightenment paradigm of scientific objectivity. If there is no one universal standard for truth, then claims about truth are contextual: They have to do with how people construct different understandings of the world and historical memory from the same sets of facts in situations of gender, ethnic, and class inequality, exploitation, and repression. The truth claims for a testimonial narrative like *I, Rigoberta Menchú* depend on conferring on the form a special kind of epistemological authority as embodying subaltern voice and experience. Against the authority of that voice—and, in particular, against the assumption that it can represent adequately a collective subject ("all poor Guatemalans")—Stoll wants to affirm the authority of the fact-gathering and -testing procedures of anthropology and journalism, in which accounts like Menchú's will be treated simply as ethnographic data that must be processed by more objective techniques of assessment, which, by definition, are not available to the direct narrator. In the final analysis, what Stoll is able to present as evidence against the validity of Menchú's account are, precisely, *other testimonios*: other voices, narratives, points of view, in which, it will come as no surprise, he can find something *he* wants to hear.

We know something about the nature of this problem. There is not, outside the realm of human discourse itself, a level of facticity that can guarantee the truth of this or that representation, given that society itself is not an essence prior to representation, but rather the consequence of struggles to represent and over-representation. That is the deeper meaning of Walter Benjamin's aphorism "Even the dead are not safe": Even the historical memory of the past is conjectural, relative, perishable. *Testimonio* is both an art and a strategy of subaltern memory.

We would create yet another version of the native informant of classical anthropology if we were to grant testimonial narrators like Rigoberta Menchú only the possibility of being witnesses, and not the power to create their own narrative authority and negotiate its conditions of truth and representativity. This would amount to saying that the subaltern can of course speak, but only through *us*, through our institutionally sanctioned authority and pretended objectivity as intellectuals, which give us the power to decide what counts in the narrator's raw material. But it is precisely that institutionally sanctioned authority and objectivity that, in a less benevolent form, but still claiming to speak from the place of truth, the subaltern must confront every day in the forms of war, economic exploitation, development schemes, obligatory acculturation, police and military repression, destruction of habitat, forced sterilization, and the like.[5]

There is a question of agency here. What *testimonio* obliges us to confront is not only the subaltern as a (self-)represented victim, but also as the agent—in that very act of representation—of a transformative project that aspires to become hegemonic in its own right. In terms of this project, which is not our own in any immediate sense and which may in fact imply structurally a contradiction with our own position of relative privilege and authority in the global system, the testimonial text is a *means* rather than an end in itself. Menchú and the persons who collaborated with her in the creation of *I, Rigoberta Menchú* certainly were aware that the text would be an important tool in human rights and solidarity work that might have a positive effect on the genocidal conditions the text itself describes. But *her* interest in the text is not to have it become an object for us, our means of getting the "whole truth"—*toda la realidad*—of her experience. It is rather to act tactically in a way she hopes and expects will advance the interests of the community and social groups and classes her *testimonio* represents: "poor" (in her own description) Guatemalans. That is as it should be, however, because it is not only *our* desires and purposes that count in relation to *testimonio.*

This seems obvious enough, but it is a hard lesson to absorb fully, because it forces us to, in Spivak's phrase, "unlearn privilege." Unlearning privilege means recognizing that it is not the intention of subaltern cultural practice simply to signify its subalternity to us. If that is what *testimonio* does, then critics like Sklodowska are right in seeing it as a form of the status quo, a kind of postmodernist *costumbrismo.* The force of a *testimonio* such as *I, Rigoberta Menchú* is to displace the centrality of intellectuals and what they recognize as culture—including history, literature, journalism, and ethnographic writing. Like any testimonial narrator (like anybody), Menchú is of course also an intellectual, but in a sense she is clearly different from what Gramsci meant by a traditional intellectual—that is, someone who meets the standards and carries the authority of humanistic and/or scientific high culture. The concern with the question of subaltern agency and authority in *testimonio* depends, rather, on the suspicion that intellectuals and writing practices are themselves complicit in maintaining relations of domination and subalternity.

The question is relevant to the claim made by Dinesh D'Souza (1991) in the debate over the Stanford Western Culture undergraduate requirement (which centered on the adoption of *I, Rigoberta Menchú* as a text in one of the course sections) that *I, Rigoberta Menchú* is not good or great literature. D'Souza writes, "To celebrate the works of the oppressed, apart from the standard of merit by which other art and history and literature is judged, is to romanticize their suffering, to pretend that it is naturally creative, and to give it an aesthetic status that is not shared or appreciated by those who actually endure the oppression" (p. 87). It could be argued that *I, Rigoberta Menchú* is one of the most powerful works of *literature* produced in Latin America in the past several decades, but there is also some point in seeing it as a provocation in the academy, as D'Souza feels it to be. The subaltern, by definition, is a social position that is not, and cannot be, adequately represented in the human sciences or the university, if only because the human sciences and the university are among the institutional constellations of power/knowledge that create and sustain subalternity. This is not, however, to draw a line between the world of the academy and the subaltern, because the point of *testimonio* is, in the first place, to intervene in that world—that is, in a place where the subaltern is not. In its very situation of enunciation, which juxtaposes radically the subject positions of the narrator and interlocutor, *testimonio* is involved in and constructed out of the opposing terms of a master/slave dialectic: metropolis/periphery, nation/region, European/indigenous, creole/mestizo, elite/popular, urban/rural, intellectual/manual, male/female, "lettered"/illiterate or semiliterate. *Testimonio* is no more capable of transcending these oppositions than are more purely literary or scientific forms of writing or narrative; that would require something like a cultural revolution that would abolish or invert the conditions that produce relations of subordination, exploitation, and inequality in the first place. But *testimonio* does involve a new way of articulating these oppositions and a new, collaborative model for the relationship between the intelligentsia and the popular classes.

To return to Rorty's point about the "desire for solidarity," a good part of the appeal of *testimonio* must lie in the fact that it both represents symbolically and enacts in its production and reception a relation of solidarity between ourselves—as members of the professional middle class and practitioners of the human sciences—and subaltern social subjects. *Testimonio* gives voice to a previously anonymous and voiceless popular-democratic subject, but in such a way that the intellectual or professional is interpellated, in his or her function as interlocutor/reader of the testimonial account, as being in alliance with (and to some extent dependent on) this subject, without at the same time losing his or her identity as an intellectual.

If first-generation *testimonio*s such as *I, Rigoberta Menchú* effaced textually in the manner of the ethnographic life story (except in their introductory presentations) the presence of the interlocutor, it is becoming increasingly common in what is sometimes called the "new ethnography" to put the interlocutor into the account, to make the dynamic of interaction and negotiation between interlocutor and narrator part of what *testimonio* testifies to. Ruth Behar's *Translated Woman: Crossing the Border with Esperanza's Story* (1993), for example, is often mentioned as a model for the sort of ethnographic text in which the authority (and identity) of the ethnographer is counterpointed against the voice and authority of the subject whose life history the ethnographer is concerned with eliciting. In a similar vein, Philippe Bourgois's innovative ethnography of Puerto Rican crack dealers in East Harlem, *In Search of Respect* (1995), often pits the values of the investigator—Bourgois—against those of the dealers he befriends and whose stories and conversations he transcribes and reproduces in his text. In *Event, Metaphor, Memory: Chauri Chaura, 1922–1992* (1995), the subaltern studies historian Shahid Amin is concerned with retrieving the "local memory" of an uprising in 1922 in a small town in northern India in the course of which peasants surrounded and burned down a police station, leading to the deaths of 23 policemen. But he is also concerned with finding ways to incorporate formally the narratives that embody that memory into his own history of the event, thus abandoning the usual stance of the historian as omniscient narrator and making the heterogeneous voices of the community itself the historian(s).

These ways of constructing testimonial material (obviously, the examples could be multiplied many times over) make visible that what happens in *testimonio* is not only the textual staging of a "domesticated Other," to recall Spivak's telling objection, but the confrontation through the text of one person (the reader and/or immediate interlocutor) with another (the direct narrator or narrators) at the level of a *possible* solidarity. In this sense, *testimonio* also embodies a new possibility of political agency (it is essentially that possibility to which Stoll objects). But that possibility—a postmodernist form of Popular Front–style alliance politics, if you will—is necessarily built on the recognition of and respect for the radical incommensurability of the situation of the parties involved. More than empathic liberal guilt or political correctness, what *testimonio* seeks to elicit is *coalition*. As Doris Sommer (1996) puts it succinctly, *testimonio* "is an invitation to a tête-à-tête, not to a heart to heart" (p. 143).

▣ Bibliographic Note

Margaret Randall, who has organized testimonial workshops in Cuba and Nicaragua (and who has herself edited a number of *testimonio*s on the roles of women in the Cuban and Nicaraguan revolutions), is the author of a very good, albeit hard to find, handbook on how to prepare a *testimonio* titled *Testimonios: A Guide to Oral History* (1985). The first significant academic discussion of *testimonio* that I am aware of was published in the 1986 collection *Testimonio y literatura,* edited by René Jara and Hernán Vidal at the University of Minnesota's Institute for the Study of Ideologies and Literature. The most comprehensive representation of the debate around *testimonio* in the literary humanities in the ensuing decade or so is the collection edited by Georg Gugelberger titled *The Real Thing: Testimonial Discourse and Latin America* (1996), which incorporates two earlier collections: one by Gugelberger and Michael Kearney for a special issue of *Latin American Perspectives* (vols. 18–19, 1991), and the other by myself and Hugo Achugar titled *La voz del otro: Testimonio, subalternidad, y verdad narrativa,* which appeared as a special issue of *Revista de Crítica Literaria Latinoamericana* (1992). The initial literary "manifesto" of *testimonio* was the essay by the Cuban novelist-ethnographer Miguel Barnet (apropos his own *Biography of a Runaway Slave*), "La novela-*testimonio*: Socioliteratura" (1986), originally published in the late 1960s in the Cuban journal *Unión.* On the academic incorporation of *testimonio* and its consequences for pedagogy, see Carey-Webb and Benz (1996). Jara and Vidal's (1986) collection happened to coincide with the famous collection on ethnographic authority and writing practices edited by James Clifford and George Marcus, *Writing Culture* (1986), which exercised a wide influence in the fields of anthropology and history. One should note also in this respect the pertinence of the work of the South Asian Subaltern Studies Group (see, e.g., Guha, 1997; Guha & Spivak, 1988) and of the Latin American Subaltern Studies Group (see Rabasa, Sanjinés, & Carr, 1994/1996). For both social scientists and literary critics, a touchstone for conceptualizing *testimonio* should be Walter Benjamin's great essays, "The Storyteller" and "Theses on the Philosophy of History" (see Benjamin, 1969).

⬚ NOTES

1. Rorty's (1985) distinction may recall for some readers Marvin Harris's well-known distinction between *emic* and *etic* accounts (where the former are personal or collective "stories" and the latter are representations given by a supposedly objective observer based on empirical evidence).

2. Widely different sorts of narrative texts could in given circumstances function as *testimonios*: confession, court testimony, oral history, memoir, autobiography, autobiographical novel, chronicle, confession, life story, *novela-testimonio,* "nonfiction novel" (Truman Capote), or "literature of fact" (Roque Dalton).

3. Mary Louise Pratt (1986) describes the *testimonio* usefully in this respect as "autoethnography."

4. In Miguel Barnet's (1986) phrase, the author has been replaced in *testimonio* by the function of a "compiler" (*compilador*) or "activator" (*gestante*), somewhat on the model of the film producer.

5. Lacan (1977, pp. 310–311) writes:

> Any statement of authority has no other guarantee than its very enunciation, and it is pointless for it to seek another signifier, which could not appear outside this locus in any way. Which is what I mean when I say that no metalanguage can be spoken, or, more aphoristically, that there is no Other of the Other. And when the Legislator (he who claims to lay down the Law) presents himself to fill the gap, he does so as an impostor.

⬚ REFERENCES

Amin, S. (1995). *Event, metaphor, memory: Chauri Chaura 1922–1992.* Berkeley: University of California Press.

Barnet, M. (1986). La novela-*testimonio:* Socioliteratura. In R. Jara & H. Vidal (Eds.), *Testimonio y literatura* (pp. 280–301). Minneapolis: University of Minnesota, Institute for the Study of Ideologies and Literatures.

Behar, R. (1993). *Translated woman: Crossing the border with Esperanza's story.* Boston: Beacon.

Benjamin, W. (1969). *Illuminations* (H. Zohn, Trans.). New York: Schocken.

Beverley, J., & Achugar, H. (Eds.). (1992). *La voz del otro: Testimonio, subalternidad, y verdad narrativa* [Special issue]. *Revista de Crítica Literaria Latinoamericana, 36.*

Bourgois, P. (1995). *In search of respect.* Cambridge, UK: Cambridge University Press.

Carey-Webb, A., & Benz, S. (Eds.). (1996). *Teaching and testimony.* Albany: State University of New York Press.

Clifford, J., & Marcus, G. E. (Eds.). (1986). *Writing culture: The poetics and politics of ethnography.* Berkeley: University of California Press.

D'Souza, D. (1991). *Illiberal education.* New York: Free Press.

Gugelberger, G. M. (Ed.). (1996). *The real thing: Testimonial discourse and Latin America.* Durham, NC: Duke University Press.

Gugelberger, G. M., & Kearney, M. (Eds.). (1991). [Special issue]. *Latin American Perspectives, 18–19.*

Guha, R. (Ed.). (1997). *A subaltern studies reader.* Minneapolis: University of Minnesota Press.

Guha, R., & Spivak, G. C. (Eds.). (1988). *Selected subaltern studies.,* New York: Oxford University Press.

Jara, R. (1986). Prólogo. In R. Jara & H. Vidal (Eds.), *Testimonio y literatura* (pp. 1–3). Minneapolis: University of Minnesota, Institute for the Study of Ideologies and Literatures.

Jara, R., & Vidal, H. (Eds.). (1986). *Testimonio y literatura.* Minneapolis: University of Minnesota, Institute for the Study of Ideologies and Literatures.

Lacan, J. A. (1977). *Écrits: A selection.* New York: W. W. Norton.

Menchú, R. (1984). *I, Rigoberta Menchú: An Indian woman in Guatemala* (E. Burgos-Debray, Ed.; A. Wright, Trans.). London: Verso.

Pratt, M. L. (1986). Fieldwork in common places. In J. Clifford & G. E. Marcus (Eds.), *Writing culture: The poetics and politics of ethnography* (pp. 27–50). Berkeley: University of California Press.

Rabasa, J., Sanjinés, J., & Carr, R. (Eds.). (1996). Subaltern studies in the Americas [Special issue]. *Dispositio/n, 19*(46). (Contributions written in 1994)

Randall, M. (1985). *Testimonios: A guide to oral history.* Toronto: Participatory Research Group.

Rivero, E. (1984–1985). Testimonio y conversaciones como discurso literario: Cuba y Nicaragua. *Literature and Contemporary Revolutionary Culture, 1,* 218–228.

Rorty, R. (1985). Solidarity or objectivity? In J. Rajchman & C. West (Eds.), *Postanalytic philosophy* (pp. 3–19). New York: Columbia University Press.

Sklodowska, E. (1982). La forma testimonial y la novelística de Miguel Barnet. *Revista/Review Interamericana, 12,* 368–380.

Sklodowska, E. (1996). Spanish American testimonial novel: Some afterthoughts. In G. M. Gugelberger (Ed.), *The real thing: Testimonial discourse and Latin America* (pp. 84–100). Durham, NC: Duke University Press.

Sommer, D. (1996). No secrets. In G. M. Gugelberger (Ed.), *The real thing: Testimonial discourse and Latin America* (pp. 130–160). Durham, NC: Duke University Press.

Spivak, G. C. (1988). Can the subaltern speak? In C. Nelson & L. Grossberg (Eds.), *Marxism and the interpretation of culture* (pp. 280–316). Urbana: University of Illinois Press.

Stoll, D. (1999). *Rigoberta Menchú and the story of all poor Guatemalans.* Boulder, CO: Westview.

Taylor, C. (1994). The politics of recognition. In C. Taylor, K. A. Appiah, J. Habermas, S. C. Rockefeller, M. Walzer, & S. Wolf, *Multiculturalism: Examining the politics of recognition* (A. Gutmann, Ed.). Princeton, NJ: Princeton University Press.

10

PARTICIPATORY ACTION RESEARCH

Communicative Action and the Public Sphere

Stephen Kemmis and Robin McTaggart

P articipatory action research has an extensive history in many fields of social practice. Our aim in this chapter is to develop the view of participatory action research that has shaped our own theory and practice during recent years. We begin with a short overview of the evolution of our own thinking and the influence of several generations of action research. In our chapter on "Participatory Action Research" for the second edition of the *Handbook*, we identified several key approaches to action research, the sites and settings where they are most frequently used, several criticisms that have been advanced for each, and key sources to explore them (Kemmis & McTaggart, 2000). The approaches identified were a somewhat eclectic mix—participatory research, classroom action research, action learning, action science, soft systems approaches, and industrial action research. We summarize those approaches again here but do not reiterate our views of them in this chapter. We acknowledge the influence of each approach on the field and as stimulus to reflection on our own ideas and practices.

For our current purposes, we proceed to develop a comprehensive view of social practice and reflect on aspects of our own work that we term "myths, misinterpretations, and mistakes" to move toward reconceptualizing research itself as a social practice. Thinking about research as a social practice leads us to an exploration of Habermas's notion of the public sphere as a way of extending the theory and practice

271

of action research. We hope that this argument shows more clearly how participatory action research differs from other forms of social inquiry, integrating more clearly its political and methodological intentions. We anticipate that this argument will provide direction for a new generation of participatory action research, and we trust that it will strengthen the theory and practice of participatory action research in the many fields and settings that draw on its intellectually and morally rich traditions, ideas, and challenges.

▣ THE FAMILY OF ACTION RESEARCH

Action research began with an idea attributed to social psychologist Kurt Lewin. It first found expression in the work of the Tavistock Institute of Human Relations in the United Kingdom (Rapaport, 1970), where Lewin had visited in 1933 and 1936 and had maintained contact for many years. Lewin's (1946, 1952) own earliest publications on action research related to community action programs in the United States during the 1940s. However, it is worth noting that Altrichter and Gstettner (1997) argued that there were earlier, more "actionist" approaches to action research in community development practiced by H. G. Moreno, for example, working with prostitutes in Vienna at the turn of the 20th century. Nevertheless, it was Lewin's work and reputation that gave impetus to the action research movements in many different disciplines. Stephen Corey initiated action research in education in the United States soon after Lewin's work was published (Corey, 1949, 1953). However, efforts to reinterpret and justify action research in terms of the prevailing positivistic ideology in the United States led to a temporary decline in its development there (Kemmis, 1981).

A second generation of action research, building on a British tradition of action research in organizational development championed by researchers at the Tavistock Institute (Rapaport, 1970), began in Britain with the Ford Teaching Project directed by John Elliott and Clem Adelman (Elliott & Adelman, 1973). Recognition in Australia of the "practical" character of the British initiative led to calls for more explicitly "critical" and "emancipatory" action research (Carr & Kemmis, 1986). The critical impulse in Australian action research was paralleled by similar advocacies in Europe (Brock-Utne, 1980). These advocacies and efforts for their realization were called the third generation of action research. A fourth generation of action research emerged in the connection between critical emancipatory action research and participatory action research that had developed in the context of social movements in the developing world, championed by people such as Paulo Freire, Orlando Fals Borda, Rajesh Tandon, Anisur Rahman, and Marja-Liisa Swantz as well as by North American and British workers in adult education and literacy, community development, and development studies such as Budd Hall, Myles Horton, Robert Chambers, and John Gaventa. Two key themes were

(a) the development of theoretical arguments for more "actionist" approaches to action research and (b) the need for participatory action researchers to make links with broad social movements.

Participatory Research

Participatory research is an alternative philosophy of social research (and social life [*vivéncia*]) often associated with social transformation in the Third World. It has roots in liberation theology and neo-Marxist approaches to community development (e.g., in Latin America) but also has rather liberal origins in human rights activism (e.g., in Asia). Three particular attributes are often used to distinguish participatory research from conventional research: shared ownership of research projects, community-based analysis of social problems, and an orientation toward community action. Given its commitment to social, economic, and political development responsive to the needs and opinions of ordinary people, proponents of participatory research have highlighted the politics of conventional social research, arguing that orthodox social science, despite its claim to value neutrality, normally serves the ideological function of justifying the position and interests of the wealthy and powerful (Fals Borda & Rahman, 1991; Forester, Pitt, & Welsh, 1993; Freire, 1982; Greenwood & Levin, 2000, 2001; Hall, Gillette, & Tandon, 1982; Horton, Kohl, & Kohl, 1990; McGuire, 1987; McTaggart, 1997; Oliveira & Darcy, 1975; Park, Brydon-Miller, Hall, & Jackson, 1993).

Critical Action Research

Critical action research expresses a commitment to bring together broad social analysis—the self-reflective collective self-study of practice, the way in which language is used, organization and power in a local situation, and action to improve things. Critical action research is strongly represented in the literatures of educational action research, and there it emerges from dissatisfactions with classroom action research that typically does not take a broad view of the role of the relationship between education and social change. It has a strong commitment to participation as well as to the social analyses in the critical social science tradition that reveal the disempowerment and injustice created in industrialized societies. During recent times, critical action research has also attempted to take account of disadvantage attributable to gender and ethnicity as well as to social class, its initial point of reference (Carr & Kemmis, 1986; Fay, 1987; Henry, 1991; Kemmis, 1991; Marika, Ngurruwutthun, & White, 1992; McTaggart, 1991a, 1991b, 1997; Zuber-Skerritt, 1996).

Classroom Action Research

Classroom action research typically involves the use of qualitative interpretive modes of inquiry and data collection by teachers (often with help from academics) with a view to teachers making judgments about how to improve their own practices. The practice of classroom action research has a long tradition but has swung in and out of favor, principally because the theoretical work that justified it lagged behind the progressive educational movements that breathed life into it at certain historical moments (McTaggart, 1991a; Noffke, 1990, 1997). Primacy is given to teachers' self-understandings and judgments. The emphasis is "practical," that is, on the interpretations that teachers and students are making and acting on in the situation. In other words, classroom action research is not just practical idealistically, in a utopian way, or just about how interpretations might be different "in theory"; it is also practical in Aristotle's sense of practical reasoning about how to act rightly and properly in a situation with which one is confronted. If university researchers are involved, their role is a service role to the teachers. Such university researchers are often advocates for "teachers' knowledge" and may disavow or seek to diminish the relevance of more theoretical discourses such as critical theory (Dadds, 1995; Elliott, 1976–1977; Sagor, 1992; Stenhouse, 1975; Weiner, 1989).

Action Learning

Action learning has its origins in the work of advocate Reg Revans, who saw traditional approaches to management inquiry as unhelpful in solving the problems of organizations. Revans's early work with colliery managers attempting to improve workplace safety marks a significant turning point for the role of professors, engaging them directly in management problems in organizations.

The fundamental idea of action learning is to bring people together to learn from each other's experiences. There is emphasis on studying one's own situation, clarifying what the organization is trying to achieve, and working to remove obstacles. Key aspirations are organizational efficacy and efficiency, although advocates of action learning affirm the moral purpose and content of their own work and of the managers they seek to engage in the process (Clark, 1972; Pedler, 1991; Revans, 1980, 1982).

Action Science

Action science emphasizes the study of practice in organizational settings as a source of new understandings and improved practice. The field of action science systematically builds the relationship between academic organizational psychology and practical problems as they are experienced in organizations. It identifies two aspects of professional knowledge: (a) the formal knowledge that all competent members of the profession are thought to share and into which professionals are inducted during their initial training and (b) the professional knowledge of interpretation and enactment. A distinction is also made between the professional's "espoused theory" and "theories in use," and "gaps" between these are used as points of reference for change. A key factor in analyzing these gaps between theory and practice is helping the professional to unmask the "cover-ups" that are put in place, especially when participants are feeling anxious or threatened. The approach aspires to the development of the "reflective practitioner" (Argyris, 1990; Argyris & Schön, 1974, 1978; Argyris, Putnam, & McLain Smith, 1985; Reason, 1988; Schön, 1983, 1987, 1991).

Soft Systems Approaches

Soft systems approaches have their origins in organizations that use so-called "hard systems" of engineering, especially for industrial production. Soft systems methodology is the human "systems" analogy for systems engineering that has developed as the science of product and information flow. It is defined as oppositional to positivistic science with its emphasis on hypothesis testing. The researcher (typically an outside consultant) assumes a role as discussion partner or trainer in a real problem situation. The researcher works with participants to generate some (systems) models of the situation and uses the models to question the situation and to suggest a revised course of action (Checkland, 1981; Checkland & Scholes, 1990; Davies & Ledington, 1991; Flood & Jackson, 1991; Jackson, 1991; Kolb, 1984).

Industrial Action Research

Industrial action research has an extended history, dating back to the post-Lewinian influence in organizational psychology and organizational development in the Tavistock Institute of Human Relations in Britain and the Research Center for Group Dynamics in the United States. It is typically consultant driven, with very strong advocacies for collaboration between social scientists and members of different levels of the organization. The work is often couched in the language of workplace democratization, but more recent explorations have aspired more explicitly to the democratization of the research act itself, following the theory and practice of the participatory research movement. Especially in its more recent manifestations, industrial action research is differentiated from action science and its emphasis on cognition taking a preferred focus on reflection and the need for broader organizational and social change. Some advocacies have used critical theory as a resource to express aspirations for more participatory forms of work and evaluation, but more typically the style is somewhat humanistic and individualistic rather than critical. Emphases on social systems in organizations, such as improving organizational effectiveness and employee relations, are common. Also, the Lewinian aspiration to learn from trying to bring about change is a strong theme (Bravette, 1996; Elden, 1983; Emery & Thorsrud, 1976; Emery, Thorsrud, & Trist, 1969; Foster, 1972; Levin, 1985; Pasmore & Friedlander, 1982; Sandkull, 1980; Torbert, 1991; Warmington, 1980; Whyte, 1989, 1991).

▣ The Emergence of Critical Participatory Action Research

Until the late 1990s, the hallmark of the action research field was eclecticism. Although the Lewinian idea was often used as a first point of legitimation, quite different rationales and practices had emerged in different disciplines. The sequestering of much literature under disciplinary rubrics meant that there was little dialogue between groups of different practitioners and advocates. Increases in visibility and popularity of the approaches rapidly changed this. There were large increases in scale and attendance at the world congresses on participatory action research as well as burgeoning interest at international sociological conferences. Action research reemerged as an influential approach in the United States (Greenwood & Levin, 2000, 2001). New associations between researchers and a vast literature of critique of modernity and its insinuation of capitalist, neocapitalist, and postcapitalist state and social systems into social life created both the impetus for and the possibility of dialogue. The historical and geographical distribution of action research approaches around the world and their interrelationships were better understood.

Critical participatory action research emerged as part of this dialogue. It aimed to provide a frame of reference for comprehension and critique of itself and its predecessors and to offer a way of working that addressed rampant individualism, disenchantment, and the dominance of instrumental reason—the key features of the "malaise of modernity" (Taylor, 1991). Critical participatory action research, as we now understand it, also creates a way of reinterpreting our own views of action research as they develop practically, theoretically, and pedagogically over time (e.g., Carr & Kemmis, 1986; Kemmis & McTaggart, 1988a, 1988b, 2000; McTaggart, 1991a). Before we revisit some of the myths, misinterpretations, and mistakes associated with our work over three decades, we present a summary of what we have regarded as the key features of participatory action research. We do this to identify some key principles as markers of progress, but we then look back at our own experience to develop what might potentially be seen as the rationale for a new generation of critical participatory action research.

Key Features of Participatory Action Research

Although the process of participatory action research is only poorly described in terms of a mechanical sequence of steps, it is generally thought to involve a spiral of self-reflective cycles of the following:

- *Planning* a change
- *Acting* and *observing* the process and consequences of the change
- *Reflecting* on these processes and consequences
- *Replanning*
- *Acting* and *observing again*
- *Reflecting again,* and so on . . .

Figure 10.1 presents this spiral of self-reflection in diagrammatic form. In reality, the process might not be as neat as this spiral of self-contained cycles of planning, acting and observing, and reflecting suggests. The stages overlap, and initial plans quickly become obsolete in the light of learning from experience. In reality, the process is likely to be more fluid, open, and responsive. The criterion of success is not whether participants have followed the steps faithfully but rather whether they have a strong and authentic sense of development and evolution in their *practices,* their *understandings* of their practices, and the *situations* in which they practice.

Each of the steps outlined in the spiral of self-reflection is best undertaken collaboratively by coparticipants in the participatory action research process. Not all theorists of action research place this emphasis on collaboration; they argue that action research is frequently a solitary process of systematic self-reflection. We concede that it is often so; nevertheless, we hold that participatory action research is best conceptualized in collaborative terms. Participatory action research is itself a social—and educational—process. The "subjects" of participatory action research undertake their research as a social practice. Moreover, the "object" of participatory action research is social; participatory action research is directed toward studying, reframing, and reconstructing social practices. *If practices are constituted in social interaction between people, changing practices is a social process.* To be sure, one person may change so that others are obliged to react or respond differently to that individual's changed behavior, but the willing and committed involvement of those whose interactions constitute the practice is necessary, in the end, to secure and legitimate the change. Participatory action research offers an opportunity to create forums in which people can join one another as coparticipants in the struggle to remake the practices in which they interact—forums in which rationality and democracy can be pursued together without an artificial separation ultimately hostile to both. In his book *Between Facts and Norms,* Jürgen Habermas described this process in terms of "opening communicative space" (Habermas, 1996), a theme to which we return later.

At its best, then, participatory action research is a social process of collaborative learning realized by groups of people who join together in changing the practices through which they interact in a shared social world in which, for better or worse, we live with the consequences of one another's actions.

It should also be stressed that participatory action research involves the investigation of *actual* practices and not *abstract* practices. It involves learning about the real, material, concrete, and particular practices of particular people in particular places. Although, of course, it is not possible to suspend the inevitable abstraction that occurs whenever we use language to name, describe, interpret, and evaluate things, participatory action research differs from other forms of research in being more obstinate about its focus on changing particular practitioners' particular practices. Participatory action researchers may be interested in practices in general or in the abstract, but their principal concern is in changing practices in "the here and

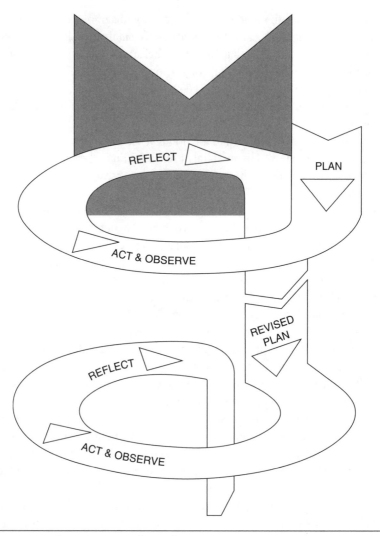

Figure 10.1. The Action Research Spiral

now." In our view, participatory action researchers do not need to apologize for see-ing their work as mundane and mired in history; on the contrary, by doing so, they may avoid some of the philosophical and practical dangers of the idealism that sug-gests that a more abstract view of practice might make it possible to transcend or rise above history and to avoid the delusions of the view that it is possible to find a safe haven in abstract propositions that construe but do not themselves constitute practice. Participatory action research is a learning process whose fruits are the real and material changes in the following:

- What people do
- How people interact with the world and with others
- What people mean and what they value
- The discourses in which people understand and interpret their world

Through participatory action research, people can come to understand that—and how—their social and educational practices are located in, and are the product of, particular material, social, and historical circumstances that *produced* them and by which they are *reproduced* in everyday social interaction in a particular setting. By understanding their practices as the product of particular circumstances, participatory action researchers become alert to clues about how it may be possible to *transform* the practices they are producing and reproducing through their current ways of working. If their current practices are the product of one particular set of intentions, conditions, and circumstances, other (or transformed) practices may be produced and reproduced under other (or transformed) intentions, conditions, and circumstances.

Focusing on practices in a concrete and specific way makes them accessible for reflection, discussion, and reconstruction as products of past circumstances that are capable of being modified in and for present and future circumstances. While recognizing that the real space–time realization of every practice is transient and evanescent, and that it can be conceptualized only in the inevitably abstract (but comfortingly imprecise) terms that language provides, participatory action researchers aim to understand their own particular practices as they emerge in their own particular circumstances without reducing them to the ghostly status of the general, the abstract, or the ideal—or, perhaps one should say, the unreal.

If participatory action research is understood in such terms, then through their investigations, participatory action researchers may want to become especially sensitive to the ways in which their particular practices are *social practices* of material, symbolic, and social

- communication,
- production, and
- social organization,

which shape and are shaped by *social structures* in

- the cultural/symbolic realm,
- the economic realm, and
- the sociopolitical realm,

which shape and are shaped by the *social media* of

- language/discourses,
- work, and
- power,

which largely shape, but also can be shaped by, participants' *knowledge* expressed in their

- understandings,
- skills, and
- values,

which, in turn, shape and are shaped by their *social practices* of material, symbolic, and social

- communication,
- production, and
- social organization, and so on.

These relationships are represented diagrammatically in Figure 10.2.

Participatory action researchers might consider, for example, how their acts of communication, production, and social organization are intertwined and interrelated in the real and particular practices that connect them to others in the real situations in which they find themselves (e.g., communities, neighborhoods, families, schools, hospitals, other workplaces). They consider how, by collaboratively changing the ways in which they participate with others in these practices, they can change the *practices* themselves, their *understandings* of these practices, and the *situations* in which they live and work.

For many people, the image of the spiral of cycles of self-reflection (planning, acting and observing, reflecting, replanning, etc.) has become the dominant feature of action research as an approach. In our view, participatory action research has seven other key features that are at least as important as the self-reflective spiral.

1. *Participatory action research is a social process.* Participatory action research deliberately explores *the relationship between the realms of the individual and the social.* It recognizes that "no individuation is possible without socialization, and no socialization is possible without individuation" (Habermas, 1992b, p. 26), and that the processes of individuation and socialization continue to shape individuals and social relationships in all of the settings in which we find ourselves. Participatory action research is a process followed in research in settings such as those of education and community development, when people—individually and collectively—try to understand how they are formed and reformed as individuals, and in relation to one another in a

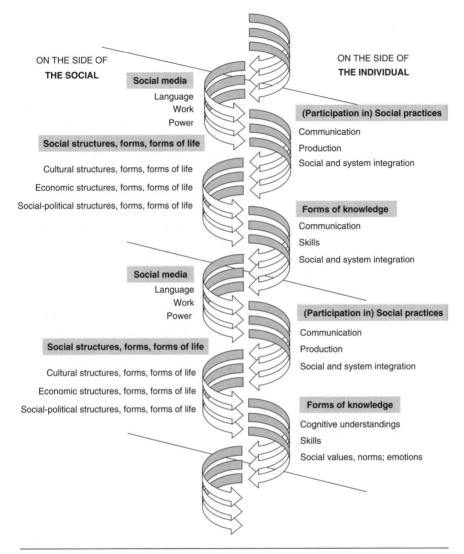

Figure 10.2. Recursive Relationships of Social Mediation That Action Research Aims to Transform

variety of settings, for example, when teachers work together (or with students) to improve processes of teaching and learning in the classroom.

2. *Participatory action research is participatory.* Participatory action research engages people in examining their *knowledge* (understandings, skills, and values) and interpretive categories (the ways in which they interpret themselves and their action in the social and material world). It is a process in which all individuals in a group try to get a

handle on the ways in which their knowledge shapes their sense of identity and agency and to reflect critically on how their current knowledge frames and constrains their action. It is also participatory in the sense that people can only do action research "on" themselves, either individually or collectively. It is *not* research done "on" others.

3. *Participatory action research is practical and collaborative.* Participatory action research engages people in examining the *social practices* that link them with others in social interaction. It is a process in which people explore their practices of communication, production, and social organization and try to explore how to improve their interactions by changing the acts that constitute them, that is, to reduce the extent to which participants experience these interactions (and their longer-term consequences) as irrational, unproductive (or inefficient), unjust, and/or unsatisfying (alienating). Participatory researchers aim to work together in reconstructing their social interactions by reconstructing the acts that constitute them.

4. *Participatory action research is emancipatory.* Participatory action research aims to help people recover, and release themselves from, the constraints of irrational, unproductive, unjust, and unsatisfying *social structures* that limit their self-development and self-determination. It is a process in which people explore the ways in which their practices are shaped and constrained by wider social (cultural, economic, and political) structures and consider whether they can intervene to release themselves from these constraints—or, if they cannot, how best to work within and around them to minimize the extent to which they contribute to irrationality, lack of productivity (inefficiency), injustice, and dissatisfactions (alienation) as people whose work and lives contribute to the structuring of a shared social life.

5. *Participatory action research is critical.* Participatory action research aims to help people recover, and release themselves from, the constraints embedded in the *social media* through which they interact—their language (discourses), their modes of work, and the social relationships of power (in which they experience affiliation and difference, inclusion and exclusion—relationships in which, grammatically speaking, they interact with others in the third, second, or first person). It is a process in which people deliberately set out to contest and reconstitute irrational, unproductive (or inefficient), unjust, and/or unsatisfying (alienating) ways of interpreting and describing their world (e.g., language, discourses), ways of working (work), and ways of relating to others (power).

6. *Participatory action research is reflexive (e.g., recursive, dialectical).* Participatory action research aims to help people to investigate reality in order to change it (Fals Borda, 1979) and (we might add) to change reality in order to investigate it. In particular, it is a deliberate process through which people aim to transform their practices through a spiral of cycles of critical and self-critical action and reflection. As

Figure 10.2 (presented earlier) aims to show, it is a deliberate social process designed to help collaborating groups of people to transform their world so as to learn more about the nature of the recursive relationships among the following:

- Their (individual and social) *practices* (the work)
- Their *knowledge of their practices* (the workers)
- The *social structures* that shape and constrain their practices (the workplace)
- The *social media* in which their practices are expressed (the discourses in which their work is represented and misrepresented)

In our view, this is what theorizing practice means. Participatory action research does not, however, take an armchair view of theorizing; rather, it is a process of learning, with others, by doing—changing the ways in which we interact in a shared social world.

7. *Participatory action research aims to transform both theory and practice.* Participatory action research does not regard either theory or practice as preeminent in the relationship between theory and practice; rather, it aims to articulate and develop each in relation to the other through critical reasoning about both theory and practice and their consequences. It does not aim to develop forms of theory that can stand above and beyond practice, as if practice could be controlled and determined without regard to the particulars of the practical situations that confront practitioners in their ordinary lives and work. Nor does it aim to develop forms of practice that might be regarded as self-justifying, as if practice could be judged in the absence of theoretical frameworks that give them their value and significance and that provide substantive criteria for exploring the extent to which practices and their consequences turn out to be irrational, unjust, alienating, or unsatisfying for the people involved in and affected by them. Thus, participatory action research involves "reaching out" from the specifics of particular situations, as understood by the people within them, to explore the potential of different perspectives, theories, and discourses that might help to illuminate particular practices and practical settings as a basis for developing critical insights and ideas about how things might be transformed. Equally, it involves "reaching in" from the standpoints provided by different perspectives, theories, and discourses to explore the extent to which they provide practitioners themselves with a critical grasp of the problems and issues they actually confront in specific local situations. Thus, participatory action research aims to transform *both* practitioners' theories and practices *and* the theories and practices of others whose perspectives and practices may help to shape the conditions of life and work in particular local settings. In this way, participatory action research aims to connect the local and the global and to live out the slogan that the personal is political.

These seven features summarize some of the principal features of participatory action research as we see it. It is a particular partisan view. There are writers on action research who prefer to move immediately from a general description of the action research process (especially the self-reflective spiral) to questions of methodology and research technique—a discussion of the ways and means of collecting data in different social and educational settings. This is a somewhat methodologically driven view of action research; it suggests that research methods are what makes action research "research." This is not to argue that participatory action researchers should not be capable of conducting sound research; rather, it is to emphasize that sound research must respect much more than the canons of method.

▣ MYTHS, MISINTERPRETATIONS, AND MISTAKES IN CRITICAL PARTICIPATORY ACTION RESEARCH

The critical view of participatory action research that we developed over the more than two decades since 1981 emerged in a practice that involved some successes; however, from the perspective of our current understandings, it also engendered some failures. Sometimes we, as well as some of our colleagues, mythologized or overstated the power of action research as an agent of individual and social change. Sometimes we misinterpreted our own experience and the ways in which substantive and methodological literatures might be useful pedagogically. Sometimes others misinterpreted our views, occasionally even despite our stout disavowal. The repeated reference to the action research spiral as "*the method* of action research" continues to frustrate us. We also made some mistakes. These myths, misinterpretations, and mistakes clustered around four key foci:

- Exaggerated assumptions about how *empowerment* might be achieved through action research
- Confusions about the role of those helping others to learn how to conduct action research, the problem of *facilitation,* and the illusion of neutrality
- The falsity of a supposed *research–activism dualism,* with research seen as dispassionate, informed, and rational and with activism seen as passionate, intuitive, and weakly theorized
- Understatement of the *role of the collective* and how it might be conceptualized in conducting the research and in formulating action in the "project" and in its engagement with the "public sphere" in all facets of institutional and social life

We present these reflections on our practices here and return to them later from a different theoretical perspective.

Empowerment

In our earliest work on action research, we argued that self-reflection on efforts to bring about change that was disciplined by group planning and reflection of observations would give participants a greater sense of control of their work. Sometimes we overstated our claims; we were victims of our own enthusiasm and persuasion. This was not always unconscious. We faced the dilemma of the advocate; that is, rhetoric can help lead to changes in reality. Our aspirations were often picked up by others, and the result left action research advocates vulnerable to charges of hyperbole or naïveté in real settings where individual and collective change often proved to be extremely difficult to effect.

It is true that an increased understanding of social situations through action materially changes individual power, authority, and control over people's work. However, it is equally true that such change is often technical and constrained, invoking concepts such as "efficiency." Authentic change, and the empowerment that drives it and derives from it, requires political sustenance by some kind of collective, too easily construed as an "action group" that defined itself by opposition to, and distinctiveness from, a wider social or public realm. Nevertheless, it was a mistake not to emphasize sufficiently that power comes from collective commitment and a methodology that invites the democratization of the objectification of experience and the disciplining of subjectivity. A question remains as to whether this was an adequate conceptualization of "empowerment," the way in which to achieve it, or indeed who or what empowerment was for.

The Role of the Facilitator of Action Research

We were troubled by the concept of "facilitation" as early as 1981 at the Australian National Seminar on Action Research (Brown, Henry, Henry, & McTaggart, 1988). Too often the facilitator lapsed into the role of "process consultant" with pretensions or aspirations to expertise about a "method" of action research, a role quite inconsistent with the commitment to participate in the personal and social changes in practice that had brought participants together. Despite efforts to contain the concept then, and to disavow its utility and outline its dangers later, it was a mistake to perpetuate the use of a term that already carried connotations of neutrality. Although the role of university researchers in action research is always somewhat problematic and an important object of critique, conceptualizing facilitation as a neutral or merely technical activity denies the social responsibility of the facilitator in making or assisting social change (McTaggart, 2002). The emphasis on techniques of facilitation also overplayed the importance of academic researchers and implicitly differentiated the work of theoreticians and practitioners, academics and workers, and community developers and peasant workers. Preoccupation with neutrality sustained the positivistic myth of the researcher as detached secretary to the universe and focused attention on the social practices (and research practices) of "the other." This in turn helped to make action research look like research for amateurs.

University professors often play an active role in action research. In the education field, for example, they are often teacher educators as well as researchers. Teacher education is just one "subpractice" of *education* as a social practice and, of course, is not practiced exclusively by university professors. In education, there are also curriculum practices, policy and administration practices, and research and evaluation practices. There is also a variety of student learning practices and community and parent participation practices that help to constitute the practice of education. Similarly, in action research for community development in some parts of the world, outside researchers have often been indispensable advocates and *animateurs* of change and not just technical advisers. It is clear to us that some of these *animateurs* have been heroes in social transformation, and we must acknowledge that many have lost their lives because of their work with dispossessed and disempowered people and communities, struggling with them for justice and democracy against repressive social and economic conditions.

Apart from these moral and political reasons against seeing facilitation as a merely technical role, there are reasons of epistemology. Emphasis on facilitation as a neutral role blinds one to the manifoldness of practice, that is, to the constitution of practice through the knowledge of individuals and a range of extraindividual features, including its social, discursive, moral, and political aspects as well as its historical formation such as the way in which it is shaped and reshaped in traditions of practice (Kemmis, 2004). Seeing facilitation in neutral terms also blinds one to the way in which practice is constituted as a "multiple reality" that is perceived differently by different participants in and observers of practice (e.g., professionals, clients, clients' families and friends, interested observers). Thus, seeing the role of facilitation as a neutral role obscures key aspects of practices and impedes critique of the way in which practices may sustain and daily reconstitute social realities whose character and consequences can be unjust, irrational, unproductive, and unsatisfactory for some of the people involved in or affected by them.

This leads us to the nub of a problem. What is the shared conceptual space that allows the intrication of these subpractices of broad social practices, such as education, health, agriculture, and transportation, to become the object of critique and the subject of enhancement? To understand how these subpractices are constitutive of lived social realities requires what Freire called *conscientization,* that is, the development of an informed critical perspective on social life among ordinary people or, to put it another way, the development of a critical theory of social life by the people who participate in it.

The Research–Activism Dualism

We find significant understatement of the role of theory and theory building in the literature of action research. The causes of this are complex. On the one hand, they include the difficulties associated with group members introducing theoretical concepts and experience of similar cases that are too difficult or confronting for other participants (McTaggart & Garbutcheon-Singh, 1986). On the other hand, they include the difficulties of ignoring or oversimplifying pertinent theoretical resources without which participants may be obliged to construe their own problems or concerns as if in a vacuum, isolating them from useful intellectual and discursive resources and sometimes leaving them vulnerable to charges of mere navel gazing. This is compounded by thinking in terms of a theory–action (thinking–activism) dualism. Thinking about unsatisfactory conditions is less confronting than actually changing them, and some take refuge in the view that political action is somehow less rational than thinking or talking about change. We reject this dualism; on the contrary, our experience suggests that there should be both more theory and more action in action research. Political activism should be theoretically informed just like any other social practice. Although action research is often incremental in the sense that it encourages growth and development in participants' expertise, support, commitment, confidence, knowledge of the situation, and understanding of what is prudent (i.e., changed thinking), it also encourages growth and development in participants' capacity for action, including direct and substantial collective action that is well justified by the demands of local conditions, circumstances, and consequences.

The Role of the Collective

The idea of the action research *group* is typically credited to Lewin immediately after World War II, although it may be that Moreno pioneered the practice a generation earlier (Altrichter & Gstettner, 1997). It was Lewin who argued the potency of "group commitment" in bringing about changes in social practices. In more recent views of action research, the "collective" is seen as supporting three important functions. First, it is seen as an expression of the democratization of scientific practice. Instead of deferring to the pronouncements of professional experts, a local scientific community is established to use principles of scientific inquiry to enhance and create richer local understandings. We have referred to this process as the "objectification of experience." Two further roles of the collective are expressed in the idea of the "disciplining of subjectivity," where subjectivity refers to an *affective* aspect, the emotional reactions of participants, and an aspect of political *agency*. In the affective aspect of subjectivity, the action research process creates opportunities for feelings to be made accessible and explored. At the same time, it creates opportunities for the way in which people feel about their situations to be examined for deeper causes and meanings and for participants to differentiate serious and abiding concerns from transient or peripheral reactions to immediate difficulties. Again, this work is not simply the preserve of the scientific or professional specialist group therapist or facilitator; on the contrary, in participatory action research, it must be part of a social process of transformation (of selves as well as situations) that is comprehensible to participants. Participants play a supportive role, but the collective has a disciplining function, helping to clarify thinking and providing a context where affect as well as cognitive questions can be justified. People come to realize that some feelings are superficial, misdirected, unfair, and overreactions. Other feelings are focused, strengthened, and nurtured as they are revealed, articulated, thought through, and reflected on. This is introspective in part, but its aim is refined action.

Political agency is a corollary of heightened understanding and motivation. As affect becomes mobilized and organized, and as experience is more clearly objectified and understood, both knowledge and feeling become articulated and disciplined by the collective toward prudent action. Individual action is increasingly informed and planned with the support and wisdom of others directly participating in related action in a situation. The collective provides critical support for the development of personal political agency and critical mass for a commitment to change. Through these interactions, new forms of practical consciousness emerge. In other words, both the action and research aspects of action research *require* participation as well as the disciplining effect of a collective.

The extension of action research collectives to include "critical friends," to build alliances with broader social movements, and to extend membership across institutional hierarchies has been a way of enhancing the understanding and political efficacy of individuals and groups. However, the problem of how to create the conditions of learning for participants persists. People not only are hemmed in by material institutional conditions, they frequently are trapped in institutional discourses that channel, deter, or muffle critique. How do we create (or re-create) new possibilities for what Fals Borda (1988) called *vivéncia,* through the revitalization of the public sphere, and also promote decolonization of lifeworlds that have become saturated with the bureaucratic discourses, routinized practices, and institutionalized forms of social relationships characteristic of social systems that see the world only through the prism of organization and not the human and humane living of social lives? This is an issue that we have now come to interpret through the notion of public discourse in public spheres and the idea of research as a social practice.

▣ PARTICIPATORY ACTION RESEARCH AND THE STUDY OF PRACTICE

In our chapter on participatory action research for the second edition of the *Handbook,* we outlined five traditions in the study of practice. We argued that *research on practice* is itself a practice and that the practice of research on practice has historically taken, and continues to take, different forms. Different practitioners of research on practice see it more from the perspective of the *individual* and/or the *social* and more from an *"objective"* perspective and/or a *"subjective"* perspective. They use different research methods and techniques that reflect these epistemological and ontological choices, that is, choices about what it means to *know* a practice (the epistemological choice) and about what a practice *is* and thus how it manifests itself in reality (the ontological choice). If research on practice is *methodologically defined,* however, researchers may obscure, even from themselves, the epistemological and ontological choices that underpin their choices of methods. As ways of "seeing" practice, research methods both illuminate and obscure what the research and the researcher can see. As Ludwig

Wittgenstein noticed, this may involve a "conjuring trick" that obscures the very thing we hoped to see:

> How does the philosophical problem about mental processes and states and about behaviourism arise? The first step is the one that altogether escapes notice. We talk of processes and states and leave their nature undecided. Sometime perhaps we shall know more about them—we think. But that is just what commits us to a particular way of looking at the matter. For we have a definite concept of what it means to learn to know a process better. (The decisive movement in the conjuring trick has been made, and it was the very one that we thought quite innocent.) And now the analogy which was to make us understand our thoughts falls to pieces. So we have to deny the yet uncomprehended process in the yet unexplored medium. And now it looks as if we had denied mental processes. And naturally we don't want to deny them. (Wittgenstein, 1958, p. 103)

We conclude, therefore, that it is risky to proceed in a discussion of research on practice principally *from* research methods and techniques—risky because the methods we choose may inadvertently have "committed us to a particular way of seeing the matter."

In our chapter in the second edition of the *Handbook,* we depicted the relationships among five broad traditions in the study of practice. Table 23.1 summarizes these traditions.

We argued that these different approaches to the study of practice involved different kinds of relationships between *the researcher* and *the researched.* Essentially, we argued that "objective" approaches tended to see practice from the perspective of an outsider in the *third person;* that "subjective" approaches tended to see practice from the perspective of an insider in the *second person;* and that the reflexive dialectical perspective of critical social science tended to see practice from the perspective of the insider group, whose members' interconnected activities constitute and reconstitute their own social practices, in the *first person* (plural). This last perspective on practice is the one taken by participant-researchers in participatory action research.

In terms of these five aspects of practice and the five traditions in the study of practice, it seems to us that a methodologically driven view of participatory action research finds itself mired in the assumptions about practice to which one or another of the different traditions of research on practice is committed. Depending on which of these sets of presuppositions it adopts, it may find itself unable to approach (the study of) practice in a sufficiently rich and multifaceted way, that is, in terms that recognize different aspects of practice and do justice to its social, historical, and discursive construction.

If participatory action research is to explore practice in terms of each of the five aspects outlined in our chapter in the second edition of the *Handbook,* it will need to consider how different traditions in the study of practice, and different research methods and techniques, can provide *multiple* resources for the task. It must also avoid accepting the assumptions and limitations of particular methods and techniques. For example, the participatory action researcher may legitimately eschew the narrow empiricism of those approaches that attempt to construe practice entirely "objectively," as if it were possible to exclude consideration of participants' subjective intentions, meanings, values, and interpretive categories from an understanding of practice or as if it were possible to exclude consideration of the frameworks of language, discourse, and tradition by which people in different groups construe their practices. It does not follow from this that quantitative approaches are never relevant in participatory action research; on the contrary, they may be—but without the constraints of empiricism and objectivism that many quantitative researchers put on these methods and techniques. Indeed, when quantitative researchers use questionnaires to convert participants' views into numerical data, they tacitly concede that practice cannot be understood without taking participants' views into account. Participatory researchers will differ from one-sidedly quantitative researchers in the ways in which they collect and use such data because participatory action researchers will regard them as crude approximations of the ways in which participants understand themselves and not (as empiricistic, objectivistic, quantitative researchers may assert) as more rigorous (e.g., valid, reliable) because they are scaled.

On the other hand, the participatory action researcher will differ from the one-sidedly qualitative approach that asserts that action can be understood only from a qualitative perspective, for example, through close clinical or phenomenological analysis of an individual's views or close analysis of the discourses and traditions that shape the way in which a particular practice is understood by participants. The participatory action researcher will also want to explore how changing "objective" circumstances (e.g., performances, events, effects, patterns of interaction, rules, roles, system functioning) shape and are shaped by the "subjective" conditions of participants' perspectives.

In our view, questions of research methods should not be regarded as unimportant, but (in contrast with the methodologically driven view) we would want to assert that what makes participatory action research "research" is not the machinery of research techniques but rather an abiding concern with the relationships between social and educational theory and practice. In our view, before questions about what kinds of research methods are appropriate can be decided, it is necessary to decide what kinds of things "practice" and "theory" are, for only then can we decide what kinds of data or evidence might be relevant in describing practice and what kinds of analyses might be relevant in interpreting and evaluating people's real practices in the real situations in which they work. On this view of participatory action research, a central question is how practices are to be understood "in the field," as it were, so that they become available for more systematic theorizing. Having arrived at a general view of what it means to understand (theorize) practice in the field, it becomes possible to work out what kinds of evidence, and hence what kinds of research methods and techniques, might be appropriate for advancing our understanding of practice at any particular time.

The theoretical scheme depicted in Figure 10.2 takes a view of what theorizing a practice might be like—locating practice within frameworks of participants' knowledge, in relation to social structures, and in terms of social media. By adopting a more encompassing view of practice like the one outlined in Table 10.1, we may be able to understand and theorize it more richly, and in more complex ways, so that powerful social dynamics (e.g., the tensions and interconnections between system and lifeworld [Habermas 1984, 1987b]) can be construed and reconstituted through a critical social practice such as participatory action research.

Table 10.1.   Relationships Among Different Traditions in the Study of Practice

Perspective	*The Individual*	*The Social*	*Both: Reflexive–dialectical view of individual–social relations and connections*
Objective	(1) Practice as individual behavior, seen in terms of performances, events, and effects: Behaviorist and most cognitivist approaches in psychology	(2) Practice as social interaction (e.g., ritual, system-structured): Structure-functionalist and social systems approaches	
Subjective	(3) Practice as intentional action, shaped by meaning and values: Psychological *verstehen* (empathetic understanding) and most constructivist approaches	(4) Practice as socially structured, shaped by discourses, tradition: Interpretive, aesthetic-historical *verstehen* (empathetic understanding), and poststructuralist approaches	
Both: Reflexive–dialectical view of subjective–objective relations and connections			(5) Practice as socially and historically constituted and as reconstituted by human agency and social action: Critical methods; dialectical analysis (multiple methods)

The participants in participatory action research understand practice from *both* its individual and its social aspects and understand it *both* objectively and subjectively. They view practice as constructed and reconstructed *historically* both in terms of the *discourses* in which practices are described and understood and in terms of socially and historically constructed *actions and their consequences.* Moreover, they view practice as constituted and reconstituted in *human and social action* that projects a living past through the lived present into a future where the people involved and affected will live with the consequences of actions taken.

This view of practice as *projected through history by action* applies not only to the "first-level" practices that are the object and subject of participants' interests (e.g., the practices of economic life in a village aiming at community development) but also to the practice of research itself. Participants in participatory action research understand their research practices as *meta-practices* that help to construct and reconstruct the first-level practices they are investigating. For example, participants in a participatory action research project on practices of community development (the first-level practices) understand their research practices as among the meta-practices that shape their practices of community development. Practices of management, administration, and social integration are also meta-practices shaping their practices of community development. However, unlike those other meta-practices, the meta-practice of participatory action research is deliberately and systematically reflexive. It is both outwardly directed and inwardly (self-)directed. It aims to change community development practitioners, community development practices, and the practice situations of community development through practices of research that are also malleable and developmental and that, through collaborative processes of communication and learning, change the practitioners, practices, and practice situations of the research. Like other practices, the practices of participatory action research are projected through history by action. They are meta-practices that aim to transform the world so that other first-level transformations become possible, that is, transformations in people's ways of thinking and talking, ways of doing things, and ways of relating to one another.

This view of *research practices* as specifically located in time (history) and social space has implications that are explored later in this chapter. In the process of participatory action research, the same people are involved in two parallel, reflexively related sets of practices. On the one hand, they are the practitioners of community development (to use our earlier example); on the other hand, they are the practitioners of the meta-practice of participatory action research. They are *both practitioners and researchers* in, say, community development, the development of primary health care, or school–community relations. They understand their research as "engaged research" (Bourdieu & Wacquant, 1992) through which they, as researchers, aim to *transform* practices of community development, primary health care, or school–community relations. But they also understand their research practices as constructed and open to reconstruction. They do not regard the research process as the application of fixed and preformed research techniques to the particular "applied" problem with which they are concerned. On the contrary, they regard their research practices as a matter of borrowing, constructing, and reconstructing research methods and techniques to throw light on the nature, processes, and consequences of the particular object they are studying (whether community development practices, primary health care practices, or practices of school–community relations). And this means that participatory action researchers are embarked on a process of transforming themselves as researchers, transforming their research practices, and transforming the practice settings of their research.

In our chapter in the second edition of the *Handbook*, we also argued for a view of research that we termed "symposium research," that is, research drawing on the multiple disciplinary perspectives of different traditions in social science theorizing and multiple research methods that illuminate different aspects of practices. We believe that this approach will increasingly come to characterize participatory action research inquiries. That is, we expect that as participatory action research becomes more sophisticated in its scope and intentions, it will draw on transdisciplinary theoretical resources (e.g., relevant psychological and sociological theories) and multiple research methods and techniques that will allow participant-researchers to gain insight into the formation and transformation of their practices in context. For example, we expect to see more participatory action research using research techniques characteristic of all five of the traditions depicted in Table 10.1. These methods and techniques are presented in Table 10.2.

In the current edition of the *Handbook*, we argue that the nature of the social relationships involved in participatory action research—and the proper politics of participatory action research—can be more clearly understood from the perspective of Habermas's (1984, 1987a) *theory of communicative action* and, in particular, his later commentary on the nature of the *public sphere*, as outlined in *Between Facts and Norms* (Habermas, 1996, chap. 8).

▣ THE POLITICS OF PARTICIPATORY ACTION RESEARCH: COMMUNICATIVE ACTION AND THE PUBLIC SPHERE

In his book *Theory of Communicative Action*, and especially the second volume, Habermas (1984, 1987b) described communicative action as what people do when they engage in communication of a particular—and widespread—kind, with three particular features. It is communication in which people consciously and deliberately aim

1. to reach *intersubjective agreement* as a basis for

2. *mutual understanding* so as to

3. reach an *unforced consensus about what to do* in the particular practical situation in which they find themselves.

Communicative action is the kind of action that people take when they interrupt what they are doing (Kemmis, 1998) to ask four particular kinds of questions (the four validity claims):

- Whether their understandings of what they are doing *make sense* to them and to others (are *comprehensible*)
- Whether these understandings are *true* (in the sense of being *accurate* in accordance with what else is known)
- Whether these understandings are *sincerely held and stated* (authentic)
- Whether these understandings are *morally right and appropriate* under the circumstances in which they find themselves

In *Between Facts and Norms*, Habermas (1996) added a fourth feature to the original list of three features of communicative action. He noticed something obvious that previously had been overlooked, namely that communicative action also *opens communicative space* between people. He gave this fourth feature of communicative action special attention because he considered that opening space for communicative action produces two particular and simultaneous effects. First, it builds *solidarity* between the people who open their understandings to one another in this kind of communication. Second, it underwrites the understandings and decisions that people reach with *legitimacy*. In a world where communications are frequently cynical, and where people feel alienated from public decisions and even from the political processes of their world, legitimacy is hard-won. More important for our purposes here, however, Habermas's argument is that *legitimacy is guaranteed only through communicative action,* that is, when people are free to choose—authentically and for themselves, individually and in the context of mutual participation—to decide *for themselves* the following:

- What is comprehensible to *them* (whether in fact they understand what others are saying)
- What is true in the light of *their own* knowledge (both their individual knowledge and the shared knowledge represented in the discourse used by members)
- What participants *themselves* regard as sincerely and truthfully stated (individually and in terms of their joint commitment to understanding)
- What participants *themselves* regard as morally right and appropriate in terms of their individual and mutual judgment about what it is right, proper, and prudent to do under the circumstances in which they find themselves

What is projected here is not an ideal against which actual communications and utterances are to be judged; rather, it is something that Habermas believes we normally take for granted about utterances—unless they are deliberately distorted or challenged. In ordinary speech, we may or may not regard any particular utterance as suspect on the grounds of any or all of the four validity claims; whether any particular utterance will be regarded as suspect or needing closer critical examination will depend on "who is saying what about what to whom in what context." On the

Table 10.2.   Methods and Techniques Characteristic of Different Approaches to the Study of Practice

Perspective	The Individual	The Social	Both: Reflexive–dialectical view of individual–social relations and connections
Objective	(1) Practice as individual behavior: Quantitative and correlational–experimental methods; psychometric and observational techniques, tests, and interaction schedules	(2) Practice as social and systems behavior: Quantitative and correlational–experimental methods; observational techniques, sociometrics, systems analysis, and social ecology	
Subjective	(3) Practice as intentional action: Qualitative and interpretive methods; clinical analysis, interview, questionnaire, diaries, journals, self-report, and introspection	(4) Practice as socially structured, shaped by discourses and tradition: Qualitative, interpretive, and historical methods; discourse analysis and document analysis	
Both: Reflexive–dialectical view of subjective–objective relations and connections			(5) Practice as socially and historically constituted and as reconstituted by human agency and social action: Critical methods; dialectical analysis (multiple methods)

other hand, when we move into the mode of *communicative action,* we acknowledge at the outset that we must strive for intersubjective agreement, mutual understanding, and unforced consensus about what to do in this particular situation because we already know that one or all four of the validity claims must be regarded as problematic—by *us* here and now, for our situation, and in relation to what to do in practice about the matter at hand. That is, the validity claims do not function merely as *procedural* ideals for critiquing speech; they also function as bases for, or underpinnings of, the *substantive* claims we need to explore to reach mutual agreement, understanding, and consensus about what to do in the *particular* concrete situation in which a particular group of people in a shared socially, discursively, and historically structured specific communicative space are deliberating together.

What we notice here, to reiterate, is that the process of recovering and critiquing validity claims is not merely an abstract ideal or principle but also an invocation of critique and critical self-awareness in *concrete* and *practical* decision making. In a situation where we are genuinely acting collaboratively with others, and where practical reason is genuinely called for, we are obliged, as it were, to "retreat" to a meta-level of critique—communicative action—because it is *not* self-evident what should be done. Perhaps we simply do not comprehend what is being talked about or we are not sure that we understand it correctly. Perhaps we are unsure of the truth or accuracy of the facts on which our decisions might be based. Perhaps we fear that deliberate deception or accidental self-deception may lead us astray. Perhaps we are not sure what it is morally right and appropriate to do in this practical situation in which our actions will, as always, be judged by their historical consequences (and their differential consequences for different people and groups). In any of these cases, we need to consider how to approach the practical decision before us, and we must gather our shared understandings to do so. In such cases, we interrupt what we are doing to move into the mode of communicative action. In some such cases, we may also move into the slower, more concretely practical, and more concretely critical mode of participatory action research, aiming deliberately and collaboratively to investigate the world in order to transform it, as Fals Borda observed, and to transform the world in order to investigate it. We take a problematic view of our own action in history and use our action in history as a "probe" with which to investigate reflexively our own action and its place as cause and effect in the unfolding history of our world.

Participatory Action Research and Communicative Space

In our view, *participatory action research opens communicative space* between participants. The process of participatory action research is one of *mutual inquiry* aimed at reaching intersubjective agreement, mutual understanding of a situation, unforced consensus about what to do, and a sense that what people achieve together will be *legitimate* not only for themselves but also for every reasonable person (a universal claim). Participatory action research aims to create circumstances in which people can search together collaboratively for more comprehensible, true, authentic, and morally right and appropriate ways of understanding and acting in the world. It aims to create circumstances in which *collaborative social action* in history is not justified by appeal to authority (and still less to coercive force); rather, as Habermas put it, it is justified by the force of better argument.

To make these points is to notice three things about the social relations engendered through the process of action research. First, it is to notice that certain relationships are appropriate in the *research* element of the term "participatory action research." It is to notice that the social practice of this kind of research is *a practice directed deliberately toward discovering, investigating, and attaining* intersubjective agreement, mutual understanding, and unforced consensus about what to do. It is aimed at testing, developing, and retesting agreements, understandings, and decisions against the criteria of mutual comprehensibility, truth, truthfulness (e.g., sincerity, authenticity), and moral rightness and appropriateness. In our view, *participatory action research projects communicative action into the field of action and the making of history.* It does so in a deliberately critical and reflexive way; that is, it aims to change both our unfolding history and ourselves as makers of our unfolding history. As science, participatory action research is *not* to be understood as the kind of science that gathers knowledge as a precursor to and resource for controlling the unfolding of events (the technical knowledge–constitutive interest characteristic of positivistic social science [Habermas, 1972]). Nor is it to be understood as the kind of science directed toward educating the person to be a wiser and more prudent actor in as yet unspecified situations and circumstances (the practical knowledge–constitutive interest characteristic of hermeneutics and interpretive social science [Habermas, 1972]). Participatory action research is to be understood as a collaborative practice of critique, performed in and through a collaborative practice of research that aims to change the researchers themselves as well as the social world they inhabit (the emancipatory knowledge–constitutive interest characteristic of critical social science [Carr & Kemmis, 1986; Habermas, 1972]).

Second, it is to notice that similar relationships are appropriate in the *action* element of participatory action research. It is to notice that the decisions on which action is based must first have withstood the tests of the research element and must then withstand the tests of wisdom and prudence—that people are willing to, and indeed can, reasonably live with the consequences of the decisions they make, and the actions they take, and the actions that follow from these decisions. This is to notice that participatory action research generates not only a collaborative sense of agency but also a collaborative sense of the *legitimacy* of the decisions people make, and the actions they take, together.

Third, it is to notice that participatory action research involves relationships of *participation* as a central and defining feature and not as a kind of instrumental or contingent value tacked on to the term. In many views of action research, including some of our earliest advocacies for it, the idea of "participation" was thought to refer to an action research group whose members had reached an agreement to research and act together on some shared topic or problem. This view caused us to think in terms of "insiders" and "outsiders" to the group and to the action research process. Such a view carries resonances of discussions of the role of the avant-garde in making the revolution. It suggests that the action research group constitutes itself *against* established authorities or ways of working, as if it were the role of the group to show how things can and should be done better despite the constraints and exigencies of taken-for-granted ways of doing things.

The idea of participation as central to participatory action research is not so easily enclosed and encapsulated. The notion of *inclusion* evoked in participatory action research should not, in our view, be regarded as static or fixed. Participatory action research should, in principle, create circumstances in which all of those involved in and affected by the processes of research and action (all of those involved in thought and action as well as theory and practice) about the topic have a right to speak and act in transforming things for the better. It is to say that, in the case of, for example, a participatory action research project about education, it is not only teachers who have the task of improving the social practices of schooling but also students and many others (e.g., parents, school communities, employers of graduates). It is to say that, in projects concerned with community development, not only lobby groups of concerned citizens but also local government agencies and many others will have a share in the consequences of actions taken and, thus, a right to be heard in the formation of programs of action.

In reality, of course, not all involved and affected people will participate in any particular participatory action research project. Some may resist involvement, some might not be interested because their commitments are elsewhere, and some might not have the means to join and contribute to the project as it unfolds. The point is that a participatory action research project that aims to transform existing ways of understanding, existing social practices, and existing situations must also transform other people and agencies who might not "naturally" be participants in the processes of doing the research and taking action. *In principle,* participatory action research issues an invitation to previously or naturally uninvolved people, as well as a self-constituted action research group, to participate in a common process of *communicative action for transformation.* Not all will accept the invitation, but it is incumbent on those who do participate to take into account those others' understandings, perspectives, and interests—even if the decision is to oppose them in the service of a broader public interest.

Participatory Action Research and the Critique of the "Social Macro-Subject"

As these comments suggest, participatory action research does not—or need not—valorize a particular *group* as the carrier of legitimate political action. In his critique of the "social macro-subject" in *The Philosophical Discourse of Modernity* and *Between Facts and Norms,* Habermas (1987a, 1996) argued that political theory has frequently been led astray by the notion that a state or an organization can be autonomous and self-regulating in any clear sense. The circumstances of late modernity are such, he argued, that it is simplistic and mistaken to imagine that the machinery of government or management is unified and capable of self-regulation in any simple sense of "self." Governments and the machinery of government, and managements and the machinery of contemporary organizations, are nowadays so complex, multifaceted, and (often) internally contradictory as "systems" that they do not operate in any autonomous way, let alone in any way that could be regarded as self-regulating in relation to the publics they aim to govern or manage. They are not unified systems but rather complex sets of subsystems having transactions of various kinds with one another economically (in the steering medium of money) and administratively (in the steering medium of power). *Between Facts and Norms* is a critique of contemporary theories of law and government that are based on concrete, historically outmoded notions of governmentality that presume a single, more or less unified body politic that is regulated by law and a constitution. Such theories presume that governments can encapsulate and impose order on a social body as a unified whole across many dimensions of social, political, cultural, and individual life or lives. Many of those who inhabit the competing subsystems of contemporary government and management in fact acknowledge that no such simple steering is possible; on the contrary, steering takes place—to the extent that it can happen at all—through an indeterminate array of established practices, structures, systems of influence, bargaining, and coercive powers.

The same is true of participatory action research groups. When they conceive of themselves as closed and self-regulating, they may lose contact with social reality. In fact, participatory action research groups are internally diverse, they generally have no unified "center" or core from which their power and authority can emanate, and they frequently have little capacity to achieve their own ends if they must contend with the will of other powers and orders. Moreover, participatory action research groups connect and interact with various kinds of external people, groups, and agencies. In terms of thought and action, and of theory and practice, they arise and act out of, and back into, the wider social reality that they aim to transform.

The most morally, practically, and politically compelling view of participatory action research is one that sees participatory action research as a practice through which people can create networks of communication, that is, sites for the practice of communicative action. It offers the prospect of opening communicative space in public spheres of the kind that Habermas described. Based on such a view, participatory action research aims to engender practical critiques of existing states of affairs, the development of critical perspectives, and the shared formation of emancipatory commitments, that is, commitments to overcome distorted ways of understanding the world, distorted practices, and distorted social arrangements and situations. (By "distorted" here, we mean understandings, practices, and situations whose consequences are unsatisfying, ineffective, or unjust for some or all of those involved and affected.)

Communicative Action and Exploratory Action

Participatory action research creates a communicative space in which communicative action is fostered among participants and in which problems and issues can be thematized for critical exploration aimed at overcoming felt dissatisfactions (Fay, 1987), irrationality, and injustice. It also fosters a kind of "playfulness" about action—what to do. At its best, it creates opportunities for participants to adopt a thoughtful but highly exploratory view of what to do, knowing that their practice can and will be "corrected" in the light of what they learn from their careful observation of the processes and consequences of their action as it unfolds. This seems to us to involve a new kind of understanding of the notion of communicative action. It is not just "reflection" or "reflective practice" (e.g., as advocated by Schön, 1983, 1987, 1991) but also action taken with the principal purpose of learning from experience by careful observation of its processes and consequences. It is deliberately designed as an *exploration* of ways of doing things in this particular situation at this particular historical moment. It is designed to be *exploratory action*.

Participatory action research is scientific and reflective in the sense in which John Dewey described "scientific method." Writing in *Democracy and Education,* Dewey (1916) described the essentials of reflection—and scientific method—as follows:

> They are, first, that the pupil has a genuine situation of experience—that there be a continuous activity in which he is interested for its own sake; secondly, that a genuine problem develop within this situation as a stimulus to thought; third, that he possess the information and make the observations needed to deal with it; fourth, that suggested solutions occur to him which he shall be responsible for developing in an orderly way; fifth, that he shall have the opportunity and occasion to test his ideas by application, to make their meaning clear, and to discover for himself their validity. (p. 192)

For Dewey, experience and intelligent action were linked in a cycle. Education, like science, was to aim not just at filling the minds of students but also at helping them to take their place in a democratic society ceaselessly reconstructing and transforming the world through action. Intelligent action was always experimental and exploratory, conducted with an eye to learning and as an opportunity to learn from unfolding experience.

In our view, participatory action research is an elaboration of this idea. It is exploratory action that parallels and builds on the notion of communicative action. It does more than conduct its reflection in the rear-view mirror, as it were, looking backward at what has happened to learn from it. It also generates and conducts action in an exploratory and experimental manner, with actions themselves standing as practical hypotheses or speculations to be tested as their consequences emerge and unfold.

▣ CONSTITUTING PUBLIC SPHERES FOR COMMUNICATIVE ACTION THROUGH PARTICIPATORY ACTION RESEARCH

Baynes (1995), writing on Habermas and democracy, quoted Habermas on the *public sphere:*

> [Deliberative politics] is bound to the demanding communicative presuppositions of political arenas that do not coincide with the institutionalized will-formation in parliamentary bodies but extend equally to the political public sphere and to its cultural context and social basis. A deliberative practice of self-determination can develop only in the interplay between, on the one hand, the parliamentary will-formation institutionalized in legal procedures and programmed to reach decisions and, on the other, political opinion-building in informal circles of political communication. (p. 316)[1]

Baynes (1995) described Habermas's conceptualization of the "strong publics" of parliamentary and legal subsystems and the "weak publics" of the "public sphere ranging from private associations to the mass media located in 'civil society' ... [which] assume responsibility for identifying and interpreting social problems" (pp. 216–217). Baynes added that, in this connection, Habermas "also describes the task of an opinion-forming public sphere as that of laying siege to the formally organized political system by encircling it with reasons without, however, attempting to overthrow or replace it" (p. 217).

In practice, this has been the kind of task that many action researchers, and especially participatory action researchers, have set for themselves—surrounding established institutions, laws, policies, and administrative arrangements (e.g., government departments) with *reasons* that, on the one hand, respond to contemporary crises or problems experienced "in the field" (in civil society) and, on the other, provide a rationale for changing current structures, policies, practices, procedures, or other arrangements that are implicit in causing or maintaining these crises or problems. In response to crises or problems experienced in particular places, participatory action researchers are frequently involved in community development projects and initiatives of various kinds, including community education, community economic development, raising political consciousness, and responding to "green" issues. In one sense, they see themselves as oppositional, that is, as protesting current structures and functions of economic and administrative systems. In another sense, although sometimes they are confrontational in their tactics, they frequently aim not to *overthrow* established authority or structures but rather to get them to *transform* their ways of working so that problems and crises can be overcome. As Baynes observed, their aim is to besiege authorities with *reasons* and not to destroy them. We might also say, however, that some of the reasons that participatory action researchers employ are the fruits of their practical experience in making change. They create *concrete contradictions* between established or current ways of doing things, on the one hand, and alternative ways that are developed through their investigations. They read and contrast the nature and consequences of existing ways of doing things with these alternative ways, aiming to show that irrationalities, injustices, and dissatisfactions associated with the former can be overcome *in practice* by the latter.

As we indicated earlier, the approach that participatory action researchers take to identified problems or crises is *to conduct research* as a basis for informing themselves and others about the problems or crises and to explore ways in which the problems or crises might be overcome. Their stock in trade is communicative action both internally, by opening dialogue within the group of researcher-participants, and externally, by opening dialogue with the powers-that-be about the nature of the problems or crises that participants experience in their own lives and about ways of changing social structures and practices to ease or overcome these problems or crises. Sometimes advocates of participatory action research (including ourselves) have misstated the nature of this oppositional role—seeing themselves as simply opposed to established *authorities* rather than as opposed to particular *structures* or established *practices*. We recognize that in our own earlier advocacies, the language of "emancipation" was always ambiguous, permitting or encouraging the idea that the emancipation we sought was from the structures and systems of the state itself rather than, or as much as, emancipation from the real objects of our critique—self-deception, ideology, irrationality, and/or injustice (as our more judicious formulations described it).

Habermas's critique of the social macro-subject suggests that our formulation of the action group as a kind of avant-garde was always too wooden and rigid. It encouraged the notion that there were "insiders" and "outsiders" and that the insiders could be not only self-regulating and relatively autonomous but also effective in confronting a more or less unitary, self-regulating, and autonomous state or existing authority. That is, it seemed to presume an integrated (unconflicted) "core" and an integrated (unconflicted) political object to be changed as a consequence of the investigations undertaken by the action group. In reality, we saw action groups characterized by contradictions, contests, and conflicts within that were interacting with contradictory, contested, and conflict-ridden social structures without. Alliances shifted and changed both inside action groups and in the relations of members with structures and authorities in the wider social context of which they were a part. Indeed, many participatory action research projects came into existence *because* established structures and authorities wanted to explore possibilities for change in existing ways of doing things, even though the new ways would be in a contradictory relationship with the usual ways of operating.

This way of understanding participatory action research groups is more open-textured and fluid than our earlier advocacies suggested. In those advocacies, we imagined action groups as more tightly knotted, better integrated, and more "solid" than the way in which we see them now. Now we recognize the more open and fluid connections between "members" of action groups and between members and others in the wider social context in which their investigations take place.

Public Spheres

In *Between Facts and Norms,* Habermas (1996, chap. 8) outlined the kinds of conditions under which people can engage in communicative action in the contexts of social action and social movements. He set out to describe the nature of what he called *public spheres.* (Note that he did not refer solely to "the public sphere," which is an abstraction; rather, he referred to "public spheres," which are concrete and practical contexts for communication.) The public spheres that Habermas had in mind are *not* the kinds of communicative spaces of most of our social and political communication. Communication in very many political contexts (especially in the sense of *realpolitik*) is frequently distorted and disfigured by interest-based bargaining, that is, by people speaking and acting in ways that are guided by their own (self-)interests (even if they are shared political interests) in the service of their own (shared) particular goals and ends. We return to this in our discussion of participatory action research and communicative space later.

From Habermas's (1996, chap. 8) discussion in *Between Facts and Norms,* we identified 10 key features of public spheres as he defined them. In what follows, drawing on other recent work (Kemmis, 2004; Kemmis & Brennan Kemmis, 2003), we describe each of these features and then briefly indicate how critical participatory action research projects might exemplify each feature. From Kemmis and Brennan Kemmis (2003), we also present comments indicating how two kinds of social action projects displayed some of the characteristics of public discourses in public spheres, that is, how participatory action research work can create more open and fluid relationships than can the closed and somewhat mechanical notions sometimes associated with action research groups and methodologically driven characterizations of their work. To use this illustration, it is necessary to give a brief introduction to these examples. The first is an example of a participatory action research project in Yirrkala, Australia, during the late 1980s and 1990s. The second is an example of a large educational congress held in the Argentine Republic in 2003.

Example 1: The Yirrkala Ganma Education Project. During the late 1980s and 1990s, in the far north of Australia in the community of Yirrkala, North East Arnhem Land, Northern Territory, the Yolngu indigenous people wanted to change their schools.[2] They wanted to make their schools more appropriate for Yolngu children. Mandawuy Yunupingu, then deputy principal at the school and later lead singer of the pop group Yothu Yindi, wrote about the problem this way:

Yolngu children have difficulties in learning areas of Balanda [white man's] knowledge. This is not because Yolngu cannot think, it is because the curriculum in the schools is not relevant for Yolngu children, and often these curriculum documents are developed by Balanda who are ethnocentric in their values. The way that Balanda people have institutionalised their way of living is through maintaining the social reproduction process where children are sent to school and they are taught to do things in a particular way. Often the things that they learn favour [the interests of] the rich and powerful, because when they leave school [and go to work] the control of the workforce is in the hands of the middle class and the upper class.

An appropriate curriculum for Yolngu is one that is located in the Aboriginal world which can enable the children to cross over into the Balanda world. [It allows] for identification of bits of Balanda knowledge that are consistent with the Yolngu way of learning. (Yunupingu, 1991, p. 102)

The Yolngu teachers, together with other teachers and with the help of their community, began a journey of participatory action research. Working together, they changed the white man's world of schooling. Of course, sometimes there were conflicts and disagreements, but they worked through them in the Yolngu way—toward consensus. They had help but no money to conduct their research.

Their research was not research about schools and schooling *in general;* rather, their participatory action research was about how schooling was done in *their* schools. As Yunupingu (1991) put it,

So here is a fundamental difference compared with traditional research about Yolngu education: We start with Yolngu knowledge and work out what comes from Yolngu minds as of central importance, not the other way [a]round. (pp. 102–103)

Throughout the process, the teachers were guided by their own collaborative research into their problems and practices. They gathered stories from the old people. They gathered information about how the school worked and did not work for them. They made changes and watched what happened. They thought carefully about the consequences of the changes they made, and then they made still further changes on the basis of the evidence they had gathered.

Through their shared journey of participatory action research, the school and the community discovered how to limit the culturally corrosive effects of the white man's way of schooling, and they learned to respect *both* Yolngu ways and the white man's ways. At first, the teachers called the new form of schooling "both ways education." Later, drawing on a sacred story from their own tradition, they called it "Ganma education."

Writing about his hopes for the Ganma research that the community conducted to develop the ideas and practices of Ganma education, Yunupingu (1991) observed,

I am hoping the Ganma research will become critical educational research, that it will empower Yolngu, that it will emphasize emancipatory aspects, and that it will take a side— just as the Balanda research has always taken a side but never revealed this, always claiming to be neutral and objective. My aim in Ganma is to help, to change, to shift the balance of power.

Ganma research is also critical in the processes we use. Our critical community of action researchers working together, reflecting, sharing, and thinking includes important Yolngu elders, the Yolngu action group [teachers in the school], Balanda teachers, and a Balanda researcher to help with the process. Of course, she is involved too; she cares about our problems, [and] she has a stake in finding solutions—this too is different from the traditional role of a researcher. (p. 103) . . .

It is, I must stress, important to locate Ganma in our broader development plans . . . in the overall context of Aboriginalisation and control into which Ganma must fit. (p. 104)

Together, the teachers and the community found new ways in which to think about schools and schooling, that is, new ways in which to think about the work of teaching and learning and about their community and its future. Their collaborative participatory action research changed not only the school but also the people themselves.

We give a little more information about the communicative relationships established in the project as we describe 10 features of public spheres as discussed by Habermas.

Example 2: The Córdoba Educational Congress. In October 2003, some 8,000 teachers gathered in Córdoba, Argentina, for the Congreso Internacional de Educación (Congreso V Nacional y III Internacional).[3] We want to show that the congress opened a shared communicative space to explore the nature, conditions, and possibilities for change in the social realities of education in Latin America. When participants opened this communicative space, they created open-eyed and open-minded social relationships in which participants were jointly committed to gaining a critical and self-critical grasp on their social realities and the possibilities for changing the educational practices of their schools and universities and for overcoming the injustice, inequity, irrationality, and suffering endemic in the societies in which they live. Although we are not claiming that the case perfectly realizes the ideal type of the public sphere, it seems to us that the participants in the Córdoba congress created the kind of social arena that is appropriately described as a public sphere. Moreover, the congress is also to be understood as one of many key moments in a broad social and educational movement at which participants reported on particular projects of different kinds (many of them participatory action research projects), seeing these particular projects as contributions to the historical, social, and political process of transforming education in various countries in South America.

The 10 features of public spheres we mentioned earlier are as follows:

1. Public spheres are *constituted as actual networks of communication among actual participants.* We should not think of public spheres as entirely abstract, that is, as if there were just one public sphere. In reality, *there are many public spheres.*

Understood in this way, participatory action research groups and projects might be seen as open-textured networks established for communication and exploration of social problems or issues and as having relationships with other networks and organizations in which members also participate.

The Yirrkala Ganma project involved a particular group of people in and around the schools and community at that time. It was a somewhat fluid group that was focused on a group of indigenous teachers at the school together with community elders and other community members—parents and others—and students at the schools. It also involved nonindigenous teachers and coresearchers who acted as critical friends to the project. The network of actual communications among these people constituted the project as a public sphere.

The Córdoba congress brought together some 8,000 teachers, students, education officials, and invited experts in various fields. For the 3 days of the congress, they constituted an overlapping set of networks of communication that could be regarded as a large but highly interconnected and thematized set of conversations about contemporary educational conditions and educational practices in Latin America. They were exploring the question of how current educational practices and institutions continued to contribute to and reproduce inequitable social relations in those countries and how transformed educational practices and institutions might contribute to transforming those inequitable social conditions.

2. Public spheres are *self-constituted.* They are formed by people who get together *voluntarily.* They are also *relatively autonomous;* that is, they are outside formal systems such as the administrative systems of the state. They are also outside the formal systems of influence that mediate between civil society and the state such as the organizations that represent particular interests (e.g., a farmers' lobby). They are composed of people who want to explore particular problems or issues, that is, around particular themes for discussion. Communicative spaces or communication networks organized as part of the communicative apparatus of the economic or administrative subsystems of government or business would *not* normally qualify as public spheres.

Participatory action research groups come into existence around themes or topics that participants want to investigate, and they make a shared commitment to collaborating in action and research in the interests of transformation. They constitute themselves as a group or project for the purpose of mutual critical inquiry aimed at practical transformation of existing ways of doing things (practices/work), existing understandings (which guide them as practitioners/workers), and existing situations (practice settings/workplaces).

The Yirrkala Ganma project was formed by people who wanted to get together to work on changing the schools in their community. They participated voluntarily. They were relatively autonomous in the sense that their activities were based in the schools but were not "owned" by the schools, and their activities were based in the community but were not "owned" by any community organization. The project was held together by a common commitment to communication and exploration of the possibilities for changing the schools to enact the Ganma (both ways) vision of Yolngu schooling for Yolngu students and communities.

People attended the Córdoba congress voluntarily. Despite the usual complex arrangements for people to fund their attendance and sponsorship of students and others who could not afford to attend (approximately 800 of the 8,000 attendees received scholarships to subsidize their attendance), the congress remained autonomous of particular schools, education systems, and states. The administrative apparatus of the congress was not "owned" by any organization or state, although its core administrative staff members were based at the Dr. Alejandro Carbó Normal School. The congress was coordinated by a committee of educators based in Córdoba and was advised by an academic committee composed of people from many significant Argentinean education organizations (e.g., the Provincial Teachers' Union, universities, the National Academy of Sciences based in Córdoba). Arguably, however, the structuring of the congress as a self-financing economic enterprise (as distinct from its connection with a broader social and educational movement) jeopardized the extent to which it might properly be described as a public sphere.

3. Public spheres frequently come into existence in response to *legitimation deficits;* that is, they frequently come into existence because potential participants do not feel that existing laws, policies, practices, or situations are legitimate. In such cases, participants do not feel that they would necessarily have come to the decision to do things the ways they are now being done. Their communication is aimed at exploring ways in which to overcome these legitimation deficits by finding alternative ways of doing things that will attract their informed consent and commitment.

Participatory action research groups and projects frequently come into existence because existing ways of working are regarded as lacking legitimacy in the sense that they do not (or no longer) command respect or because they cannot be regarded as authentic for participants, either individually or collectively.

The Yirrkala Ganma project came into existence because of prolonged and profound dissatisfaction with the nature and consequences of the white man's way of schooling for Yolngu students, including the sense that current ways of doing schooling were culturally corrosive for Yolngu students and communities. As indicated earlier, Yolngu teachers and community members wanted to find alternative ways of schooling that would be more inclusive, engaging, and enabling for Yolngu students and that would help to develop the community under Yolngu control.

The people attending the Córdoba congress generally shared the view that current forms of education in Latin America serve the interests of a kind of society that does not meet the needs of most citizens, that is, that current forms of schooling are not legitimate in terms of the interests of the majority of students and their families. They wanted to explore alternative ways of doing education that might better serve the interests of the people of Latin America (hence the theme for the congress, "Education: A Commitment With the Nation").

4. Public spheres are constituted for *communicative action* and for *public discourse*. Usually they involve face-to-face communication, but they could be constituted in other ways (e.g., via e-mail, via the World Wide Web). Public discourse in public spheres has a similar orientation to communicative action in that it is oriented toward intersubjective agreement, mutual understanding, and unforced consensus about what to do. Thus, communicative spaces organized for essentially instrumental or functional purposes—to command, to influence, to exercise control over things— would *not* ordinarily qualify as public spheres.

Participatory action research projects and groups constitute themselves for communication oriented toward intersubjective agreement, mutual understanding, and unforced consensus about what to do. They create communication networks aimed at achieving communicative action and at projecting communicative action into practical inquiries aimed at transformation of social practices, practitioners' understandings of their practices, and the situations and circumstances in which they practice.

The Yirrkala Ganma project was created with the principal aim of creating a shared communicative space in which people could think, talk, and act together openly and with a commitment to making a difference in the way in which schooling was enacted in their community. Communications in the project were mostly face-to-face, but there was also much written communication as people worked on various ideas and subprojects within the overall framework of the Ganma project. They spent many hours in reaching intersubjective agreement on the ideas that framed their thinking about education, in reaching mutual understanding about the conceptual framework in which their current situation was to be understood and about the Ganma conceptual framework that would help to guide their thinking as they developed new forms of schooling, and in determining ways in which to move forward based on unforced consensus about how to proceed. Although it might appear that they had an instrumental approach and a clear goal in mind—the development of an improved form of schooling—it should be emphasized that their task was not merely instrumental. It was not instrumental because they had no clear idea at the beginning about what form this new kind of schooling would take; both their goal and the means to achieve it needed to be critically developed through their communicative action and public discourse.

In the Córdoba congress, people came together to explore ways of conceptualizing a reconstructed view of schooling and education for Latin America at this critical moment in the history of many of its nations. The point of the congress was to share ideas about how the current situation should be understood and how it was formed and to consider ideas, issues, obstacles, and possible ways in which to move forward toward forms of education and schooling that might, on the one hand, overcome some of the problems of the past and, on the other, help to shape forms of education and schooling that would be more appropriate to the changed world of the present and future. Participants at the congress presented and debated ideas; they explored social, cultural, political, educational, and economic problems and issues; they considered the achievements of programs and approaches that offered alternative "solutions" to these problems and issues; and they aimed to reach critically informed views about how education and schooling might be transformed to overcome the problems and address the issues they identified in the sense that they aimed to reach practical decisions about what might be done in their own settings when participants returned home from the congress.

5. Public spheres aim to be *inclusive.* To the extent that communication among participants is *exclusive,* doubt may arise as to whether a sphere is in fact a "public" sphere. Public spheres are attempts to create communicative spaces that include not only the parties most obviously interested in and affected by decisions but also people and groups peripheral to (or routinely excluded from) discussions in relation to the topics around which they form. Thus, essentially private or privileged groups, organizations, and communicative networks do *not* qualify as public spheres.

Participatory action research projects and groups aim to include not only practitioners (e.g., teachers, community development workers) but also others involved in and affected by their practices (e.g., students, families, clients).

The Yirrkala Ganma project aimed to include as many of the people who were (and are) involved in and affected by schooling in the community as was possible. It reached out from the school to involve the community and community elders, it included nonindigenous teachers as well as indigenous teachers, and it involved students and their families as well as teachers in the school. It was not exclusive in the sense that its assertion of Yolngu control excluded Balanda (nonindigenous) people; still, it invited Balanda teachers, advisers, and others to join the common commitment of Yolngu people in their search for improved forms of education and schooling that would meet the needs and aspirations of Yolngu people and their communities more genuinely.

The Córdoba congress aimed to be broadly inclusive. It was a congress that was described by its coordinator, María Nieves Díaz Carballo, as "by teachers for teachers"; nevertheless, it included many others involved in and affected by education and schooling in Latin America—students, education officials, invited experts, representatives of a range of government and nongovernment organizations, and others. It aimed to include all of these different kinds of people as friends and contributors to a common cause—creating new forms of education and schooling better suited to the needs of the present and future in Latin America and the world.

6. As part of their inclusive character, public spheres tend to involve communication in *ordinary language.* In public spheres, people deliberately seek to break down the barriers and hierarchies formed by the use of specialist discourses and the modes of address characteristic of bureaucracies that presume a ranking of the importance of speakers and what they say in terms of their positional authority (or lack thereof). Public spheres also tend to have only the weakest of distinctions between insiders and

outsiders (they have relatively permeable boundaries and changing "memberships") and between people who are relatively disinterested and those whose (self-)interests are significantly affected by the topics under discussion. Thus, the communicative apparatuses of many government and business organizations, and of organizations that rely on the specialist expertise of some participants for their operations, do *not* ordinarily qualify as public spheres.

While drawing on the resources and discourses of theory and policy in their investigations, participatory action researchers aim to achieve mutual comprehension and create discourse communities that allow all participants to have a voice and play a part in reaching consensus about what to do. By necessity, they use language that all can use rather than relying on the specialist discourses of social science that might exclude some from the shared task of understanding and transforming shared everyday lives and a shared lifeworld.

In the Yirrkala Ganma project, much of the communication about the project not only was in ordinary language but was also conducted in the language of the community, that is, *Yolngu-matha*. This not only was a deliberate shift from the language in which Balanda schooling was usually discussed in the community (English and some specialist educational discourse) but also was a shift to engage and use the conceptual frameworks of the community and Yolngu culture. On the other hand, the modes of address of the Yolngu culture require respect for elders and specialist forms of language for "inside" matters (secret/sacred, for the initiated) versus "outside" matters (secular, for the uninitiated), so many discussions of the Ganma conceptual framework required participants to respect these distinctions and the levels of initiation of speakers and hearers.

At the Córdoba congress, many speakers used specialist educational (and other) discourses to discuss their work or ideas, but much of the discussion took place in language that was deliberately intended to be inclusive and engaging for participants, that is, to share ideas and open up participants for debate without assuming that hearers were fluent in specialist discourses for understanding either the sociopolitical context of education in Latin America or the technical aspects of contemporary education in Latin American countries. More particularly, the languages used at the congress, including translations from English and Portuguese, were inclusive because they were directed specifically toward fostering the shared commitment of participants about the need for change and the obstacles and possibilities ahead if participants wanted to join the shared project of reconstructing education in Argentina and elsewhere. Specialist discourses were used to deal with specific topics (e.g., in philosophy, in social theory, in curriculum), but the conversations about those topics soon shifted register to ensure that ideas were accessible to any interested participants.

7. Public spheres presuppose *communicative freedom*. In public spheres, participants are free to occupy (or not occupy) the particular discursive roles of speaker, listener, and observer, and they are free to withdraw from the communicative space of the discussion. Participation and nonparticipation are voluntary. Thus, communicative

spaces and networks generally characterized by obligations or duties to lead, follow, direct, obey, remain silent, or remain outside the group could *not* be characterized as public spheres.

Participatory action research projects and groups constitute themselves to "open communicative space" among participants. They constitute themselves to give participants the right and opportunity to speak and be heard, to listen, or to walk away from the project or group. Contrary to some of our earlier views, they are not closed and self-referential groups in which participants are (or can be) bound to some "party line" in the sense of a "correct" way of seeing things. Moreover, they constitute themselves deliberately for *critical* and *self-critical* conversation and decision making that aims to open up existing ways of saying and seeing things, that is, to play with the relationships between the actual and the possible.

In the Yirrkala Ganma project, participants were free to occupy the different roles of speaker, listener, and observer or to withdraw from discussions. In any particular discussion, some may have occupied one or another of these roles to a greater extent, but over the life of the project, people generally occupied the range of these roles at one time or another. As indicated earlier, some people continued to occupy privileged positions as speakers (e.g., on matters of inside knowledge), but they also occupied roles as listeners in many other situations, responding with their specialist knowledge whenever and wherever it was appropriate to do so. In general, however, the prolonged discussions and debates about giving form to the idea of the Ganma (both ways) curriculum was conducted in ways that enabled participants to gather a shared sense of what it was and could be and how it might be realized in practice. The discussions were consistently open and critical in the sense that all participants wanted to reach shared understandings and agreements about the limitations of Balanda education for Yolngu children and communities and about the possibilities for realizing a different and improved form of education for Yolngu children and their community.

The Córdoba congress engendered conditions of communicative freedom. Although the congress program and timetable privileged particular participants as speakers at particular times, the vast conversation of the congress, within and outside its formal sessions and in both formal and informal communication, presupposed the freedom of participants to speak in, listen to, observe, and withdraw from particular discussions. Conversations were open and critical, inviting participants to explore ideas and possibilities for change together.

8. The communicative networks of public spheres generate *communicative power;* that is, the positions and viewpoints developed through discussion will command the respect of participants not by virtue of obligation but rather by the power of mutual understanding and consensus. Thus, communication in public spheres creates legitimacy in the strongest sense, that is, the shared belief among participants that they freely and authentically consent to the decisions they reach. Thus, systems of

command or influence, where decisions are formed on the basis of obedience or self-interests, would *not* ordinarily qualify as public spheres.

Participatory action research projects and groups allow participants to develop understandings of, reasons for, and shared commitment to transformed ways of doing things. They encourage exploration and investigation of social practices, understandings, and situations. By the very act of doing so, they generate more authentic understandings among participants and a shared sense of the legitimacy of the decisions they make.

Over the life of the Yirrkala Ganma project, and in the continuing work arising from it, participants developed the strongest sense that the new way of thinking about education and schooling that they were developing was timely, appropriate, true to their circumstances, and generative for Yolngu children and their community. They were clearly conscious that their shared viewpoint, as well as their conceptual framework, contrasted markedly with taken-for-granted assumptions and presuppositions about schooling in Australia, including many taken-for-granted (Balanda) ideas about indigenous education. The communicative power developed through the project sustained participants in their commitment to these new ways of schooling despite the occasional resistances they experienced when the Northern Territory education authorities found that community proposals were counter to, or exceptions to, usual ways of operating in the system. (It is a tribute to many nonindigenous people in the Northern Territory who worked with Yirrkala Community Schools and the associated Homelands Centre Schools that they generally took a constructive and supportive view of the community's proposals even when the proposals fell outside established practice. The obvious and deep commitment of the Yolngu teachers and community to the tasks of the project, the support of credible external coresearchers, and the long-term nature of the project encouraged many nonindigenous system staff members to give the project "the benefit of the doubt" as an educational project that had the possibility to succeed in indigenous education where many previous proposals and plans developed by nonindigenous people had failed.)

The Córdoba congress was infused by a growing sense of shared conviction and shared commitment about the need and possibilities for change in education in Argentina and elsewhere in Latin America. On the other hand, the impetus and momentum of the developing sense of shared conviction may have been more fragile and transitory because the congress was just a few days long (although building on the momentum from previous congresses and other work that participants were doing toward the same transformative ends). Seen against the broader sweep of education and educational change in education in Latin America, however, it is clear that the congress was drawing on, refreshing, and redirecting long-standing reserves of critical educational progressivism in the hearts, minds, and work of many people who attended.

The shared conviction that new ways of working in education are necessary generated a powerful and nearly tangible sense of *solidarity* among participants in the congress—a powerful and lasting shared commitment to pursuing the directions suggested by the discussions and debates in which they had participated. It also generated an enduring sense of the *legitimacy* of decisions made by participants in the light of shared exploration of their situations, shared deliberation, and shared decision making.

9. Public spheres do not affect social systems (e.g., government, administration) *directly;* their impact on systems is *indirect.* In public spheres, participants aim to change the climate of debate, the ways in which things are thought about and how situations are understood. They aim to generate a sense that alternative ways of doing things are possible and feasible and to show that some of these alternative ways actually work or that the new ways do indeed resolve problems, overcome dissatisfactions, or address issues. Groups organized primarily to pursue the particular interests of particular groups by direct intervention with government or administrative systems would *not* ordinarily qualify as public spheres. Similarly, groups organized in ways that usually serve the particular interests of particular groups, even though this may happen in a concealed or "accidental" way (as frequently happens with news media), do *not* ordinarily qualify as public spheres.

Participatory action research projects and groups rarely have the power to legislate or compel change, even among their own members. It is only by the force of better argument, transmitted to authorities who must decide for themselves what to do, that they influence existing structures and procedures. They frequently establish themselves, and are permitted to establish themselves, at the margins of those structures and procedures, that is, in spaces constituted for exploration and investigation and for trying out alternative ways of doing things. They are frequently listened to because they have been deliberately allowed to explore this marginal space, with the tacit understanding that what they learn may be of benefit to others and to existing systems and structures. Although they may understand themselves as oppositional or even "outlaw" (in a metaphorical sense), they are frequently acting with the knowledge and encouragement of institutional authorities who recognize that changes might be needed.

As already indicated, the Yirrkala Ganma project was based in the schools but was not an official project of the school system or education system, and it was based in the community but was not an official project of any community organization. The schools and the Northern Territory education system, as well as various community organizations, knew of the existence of the project and were generally supportive. The work of the project was not an improvement or development project undertaken by any of these organizations, nor did the project "speak" directly to these organizations from within the functions and operations of the systems as systems. On the contrary, the project aimed to change the way in which these systems and organizations thought about and organized education in the community. In particular, it aimed to change the conceptual frameworks and discourses in which Yolngu education was understood and the activities that constituted it. In a sense, the transformations produced by the project were initially "tolerated" by these systems and organizations as exceptions to usual ways of operating. Over time, through the indirect influence of showing that alternative ways of doing things could work, the systems began to accept them—even though the alternative ways were at odds with practice elsewhere. The project changed the climate of discussion and the nature of the discourse about what constitutes good education for Yolngu children and communities. Because similar experiments were going on elsewhere around Australia (e.g., with the involvement of staff members from Deakin University, the University of Melbourne, and Batchelor College), there was a sense within education systems that the new experiment should be permitted to proceed in the hope (increasingly fulfilled) that the new ways of working might prove to be more effective in indigenous schools in indigenous communities where education had frequently produced less satisfactory outcomes than in nonindigenous schools and for nonindigenous students and communities. In a variety of small but significant ways, education systems began to accept the discourses of "both ways" education (realized differently in different places) and to encourage different practices of "both ways" education in indigenous communities and schools with large enrollments of indigenous students.

The Córdoba congress operated outside the functional frameworks of education and state systems and aimed to change the ways in which education and schooling were understood and practiced indirectly rather than directly. No state agency sponsor controlled the congress; as indicated earlier, it is a congress created and maintained by its organizers "by teachers for teachers." On the other hand, state officials (e.g., the minister of education for the Province of Córdoba [Amelia López], the Argentinean federal minister of education [Daniel Filmus]) addressed the congress and encouraged participants in their efforts to think freshly about the educational problems and issues being confronted in schools and in Argentina. The size, success, and generativity of previous congresses was well known (the 2003 congress was the fifth national congress and third international congress held in Córdoba), and it is reasonable to assume that representatives of the state would want to endorse the congress even if some of the ideas and practices being debated and developed by participants were at the periphery of, or even contrary to, state initiatives in education and schooling. Of course it is also true that many of the ideas and practices discussed at the congress, such as those concerned with social justice in education, were generally in the spirit of state initiatives, although most congress participants appeared to take an actively and constructively critical view of the forms and consequences of contemporary state initiatives in schooling.

10. Public spheres frequently arise in practice through, or in relation to, the communication networks associated with *social movements,* that is, where voluntary groupings of participants arise in response to a legitimation deficit or a shared sense that a social problem has arisen and needs to be addressed. Nevertheless, the public spheres created by some organizations (e.g., Amnesty International) can be long-standing and

well organized and can involve notions of (paid) membership and shared objectives. On the other hand, many organizations (e.g., political parties, private interest groups) do *not* ordinarily qualify as public spheres for reasons already outlined in relation to other items on this list and also because they are part of the social order rather than social movements.

Participatory action research groups and projects often arise in relation to broad social movements such as the women's movement, the green movement, peace movements, the civil rights movement, and other movements for social transformation. They frequently arise to explore alternative ways of doing things in settings where the impact of those movements is otherwise unclear or uncertain (e.g., in the conduct of teaching and learning in schools, in the conduct of social welfare by family and social welfare agencies, in the conduct of catchment management by groups of landholders). They draw on the resources of those social movements and feed back into the broader movements, both in terms of the general political potency of the movements and in terms of understanding how the objectives and methods of those movements play out in the particular kinds of situations and settings (e.g., village life, schooling, welfare practice) being investigated.

As some of the statements of Yunupingu (1991) quoted earlier suggest, the Yirrkala Ganma project was an expression of several important contemporary indigenous social movements in Australia, particularly the land rights movement, the movement for Aboriginal self-determination and control, and (for Australians generally) the movement for reconciliation between indigenous and nonindigenous Australians. Arguably, some of the ideas developed in the Ganma project have had a far wider currency than might have been expected, for example, through the songs and music of Yunupingu's pop group, Yothu Yindi, which have resolutely and consistently advocated mutual recognition and respect between indigenous and nonindigenous Australians and have educated and encouraged nonindigenous Australians to understand and respect indigenous people, knowledge, communities, and cultures. The Ganma project was a manifestation of these indigenous rights movements at the local level and in the particular setting of schools and was also a powerful intellectual contribution to shaping the wider movements. On the one hand, the project named and explained ways in which schooling was culturally corrosive for indigenous peoples; on the other hand, it showed that it was possible to create and give rational justifications of alternative, culturally supportive ways of doing schooling and education for indigenous people and in indigenous communities.

In the Córdoba congress, there was a strong sense of connection to a broad social movement for change in Latin American education and societies. Endemic corruption, ill-considered economic adventures, antidemocratic practices, the denial of human rights, and entrenched social inequity in a number of Latin American countries were opposed and critiqued by many progressive people, including many teachers and education professionals, and there was (and is) a hunger for alternative forms of education that might prevent the tragic inheritance of previous regimes (e.g., escalating national debt, fiscal crises, impoverishment, the collapse of services) from being passed on to rising generations of students and citizens. The negative/critical and positive/constructive aspects of the education movement represented in and by the congress are connected to a wider social movement for change, but they are also a particular and specific source of intellectual, cultural, social, political, and economic ideas and practices that make a distinctive contribution to the shape and dynamics of the wider movement. The congress itself is now something of a rallying point for progressive and critical teachers and education professionals, but it remains determinedly and politely independent of the state and commercial sponsors that might seek to exercise control over or through it. Its organizers are convinced that their best chance to change the climate of thinking about education and society is to remain independent of the state machinery of social order and to strive only for an indirect role in change by having a diffuse role in changing things "by the force of better argument" rather than striving to create change through the administrative power available through the machinery of the state or (worse) through any kind of coercive force. The congress also expressed, not only in its written materials but also in its climate and culture, a profound sense of passion, hope, and joy; participants clearly regard it as an opportunity to celebrate possibilities and achievements in creating new forms of education aimed at making (and speaking and writing into existence) a better future.

These 10 features of public spheres describe a space for social interaction in which people strive for intersubjective agreement, mutual understanding, and unforced consensus about what to do and in which legitimacy arises. These are the conditions under which participants regard decisions, perspectives, and points of view reached in open discussion as compelling for—and even binding on—themselves. Such conditions are very different from many other forms of communication, for example, the kind of functional communication characteristic of social systems (which aims to achieve particular ends by the most efficient means) and most interest-based bargaining (which aims to maximize or optimize self-interests rather than to make the best and most appropriate decision for all concerned).

These conditions are ones under which practical reasoning and exploratory action by a community of practice are possible—theorizing, research, and collective action aimed at changing practices, understandings of practices, and the settings and situations in which practice occurs. They are conditions under which a loose affiliation of people can gather to address a common theme based on contemporary problems or issues, aiming to inform themselves about the core practical question of "what is to be done?" in relation to the formation and transformation of practice, practitioners, and the settings in which practice occurs at particular times and in particular places.

As already suggested, such communities of practice sometimes come into existence when advocacy groups believe that problems or issues arise in relation to a program, policy, or practice and that change is needed. An example would be the kind of collaboration that occurs when a group of mental health service clients meet with mental health service providers and professionals to explore ways in which to improve mental health service delivery at a particular site. Another example would be the project work of groups of teachers and students who conduct participatory action research investigations into problems and issues in schooling. Another would be the kind of citizens' action campaign that sometimes emerges in relation to issues of community well-being and development or environmental or public health issues. This approach to the transformation of practice understands that changing practices is not just a matter of changing the ideas of practitioners alone; it also is a matter of changing the social, cultural, discursive, and material conditions under which the practice occurs, including changing the ideas and actions of those who are the clients of professional practices and the ideas and actions of the wider community involved in and affected by the practice. This approach to changing practice, through fostering public discourse in public spheres, is also the approach to evaluation advocated by Niemi and Kemmis (1999) under the rubric of "communicative evaluation" (see also Ryan, 2003).

▣ MYTHS, MISINTERPRETATIONS, AND MISTAKES REVISITED

In the light of the Habermasian notions of *system and lifeworld* (explored in our chapter in the second edition of the *Handbook*), *the critique of the social macro-subject,* and the notion of *public spheres* developed in *Between Facts and Norms,* we can throw new light on the myths, misinterpretations, and mistakes about critical participatory action research identified earlier in this chapter. The following comments present a necessarily brief summary of some of the ways in which our understandings of these topics have evolved during recent years.

Empowerment

In the light of the Habermasian theory of system and lifeworld, we came to understand the notion of empowerment neither solely in lifeworld terms (in terms of the lifeworld processes of cultural, social, and personal reproduction and transformation and their effects) nor solely in systems terms (in terms of changing systems structures or functioning or through effects produced by the steering media of money and administrative power of organizations and institutions). Exploring practices, our understandings of them, and the settings in which we worked from *both* lifeworld and system perspectives gave us richer critical insight into how processes of social formation and transformation occur in the contexts of particular projects. Increasingly, we came to understand empowerment not only as a lifeworld process of cultural, social, and personal development and transformation but also as implying that protagonists experienced themselves as working both in and against system structures and functions to produce effects intended to be read in changed systems structures and functioning. From this stereoscopic view, system structures and functions are not only sources of constraint but also sources of possibility, and lifeworld processes of cultural, social, and personal reproduction and transformation are not only sources of possibility but also sources of constraint on change. Thus, in real-world settings inevitably constructed by both, the notion of empowerment plays across the conceptual boundary between lifeworld and system, and it now seems likely that one would say that empowerment had occurred only when transformations were evident in both lifeworld and system aspects of a situation.

In the light of Habermas's critique of the social macro-subject, we increasingly recognized that the notion of empowerment is not to be understood solely in terms of closed organizations achieving self-regulation (by analogy with the sovereignty of states) as a process of achieving autonomy and self-determination, whether at the level of individual selves or at the level of some collective (understood as a macro-"self"). It turns out that neither individual actors nor states can be entirely and coherently autonomous and self-regulating. Their parts do not form unified and coherent wholes but rather must be understood in terms of notions such as difference, contradiction, and conflict as much as unity, coherence, and independence. In the face of internal and external differentiation, perhaps ideas such as dialogue, interdependence and complementarity are the positives for which one might hope. Despite its rhetorical power and its apparent political necessity, the concept of empowerment does not in reality produce autonomous and independent self-regulation; rather, it produces only a capacity for individuals, groups, and states to interact more coherently with one another in the ceaseless processes of social reproduction and transformation. At its best, it names a process in which people, groups, and states engage one another more authentically and with greater recognition and respect for difference in making decisions that they will regard as legitimate because they have participated in them openly and freely, more genuinely committed to mutual understanding, intersubjective agreement, and consensus about what to do.

In the light of Habermas's commentary on the public sphere, the basis for empowerment is not to be understood in terms of activism justified by ideological position taking; rather, the basis for empowerment is the communicative power developed in public spheres through communicative action and public discourse. On this view, the aim of empowerment is rational and just decisions and actions that will be regarded as legitimate by those involved and affected.

The Role of the Facilitator

In the light of the Habermasian theory of system and lifeworld, we came to understand that facilitation is not to be understood solely in system terms as a specialized role with specialized functions, nor is it to be understood solely in lifeworld terms as a process of promoting the reproduction and transformation of cultures, social relationships, and identities. Instead, it is to be understood as a process to be critically explored from both perspectives. The question of facilitation usually arises when there is an asymmetrical relationship of knowledge or power between a person expecting or expected to do "facilitation" and people expecting or expected to be "facilitated" in the process of doing a project. It is naïve to believe that such asymmetries will disappear; sometimes help *is* needed. At the same time, it must be recognized that those asymmetries can be troublesome and that there is little solace in the idea that they can be made "safe" because the facilitator aims to be "neutral." On the other hand, it is naïve to believe that the person who is asked for help, or to be a facilitator, will be an entirely "equal" coparticipant along with others, as if the difference were invisible. Indeed, the facilitator *can* be a coparticipant, but one with some special expertise that may be helpful to the group in its endeavors. The theory of system and lifeworld allows us to see the doubleness of the role in terms of a specialist role and functions in critical tension with processes of cultural, social, and personal reproduction and transformation that aspire to achieving self-expression, self-realization, and self-determination (recognizing that the individual or collective self in each case is not a unified, coherent, autonomous, responsible, and independent whole entirely capable of self-regulation). The stereoscopic view afforded by the theory of system and lifeworld provides conceptual resources for critical enactment and evaluation of the role of the facilitator in practice.

In the light of Habermas's critique of the social macro-subject, we no longer understand the people involved in collaborative participatory action research projects as a closed group with a fixed membership; rather, we understand them as an open and inclusive network in which the facilitator can be a contributing coparticipant, albeit with particular knowledge or expertise that can be of help to the group. Moreover, at different times, different participants in some groups can and do take the facilitator role in relation to different parts of the action being undertaken and in relation to the participatory action research process.

In the light of Habermas's commentary on the public sphere, the facilitator should not be understood as an external agent offering technical guidance to members of an action group but rather should be understood as someone aiming to establish or support a collaborative enterprise in which people can engage in exploratory action as participants in a public sphere constituted for communicative action and public discourse in response to legitimation deficits.

The Research–Action Dualism

In the light of the Habermasian theory of system and lifeworld, action in participatory action research should not be understood as separated from research in a technical division of labor mirrored in a social division of labor between participants and researchers. Instead, research and action converge *in* communicative action aimed at practical and critical decisions about what to do in the extended form of exploratory action, that is, practices of action and research jointly projected through history by action. Equally, however, we do not understand the research and action elements of participatory action research as the "natural" realization of the lifeworld processes of cultural, social, and personal reproduction and transformation. In participatory action research, systems categories of structure, functions, goals, roles, and rules are relevant when a group works on a "project" (implying some measure of rational–purposive or strategic action). Here again, participatory action research crosses and recrosses the conceptual boundaries between system and lifeworld aspects of the life of the project, and the stereoscopic view afforded by the theory of system and lifeworld offers critical resources for exploring and evaluating the extent to which the project might become nothing but a rational–purposive project and the extent to which it risks dissolving into the lifeworld processes of the group conducting it. Both the research element and the action element of the project have system and lifeworld aspects, and both elements are candidates for critical exploration and evaluation from the perspectives of system and lifeworld. Indeed, we might now conclude that it is the commitment to conducting this critique, in relation to the action, the research, and the relationship between them, that is the hallmark of critical participatory action research.

In the light of Habermas's critique of the social macro-subject, research and action are to be understood not in terms of steering functions for an individual or for a closed group (e.g., to steer the group by exercising administrative power) but rather as mutually constitutive processes that *create* affiliations and collaborative action among people involved in and affected by particular kinds of decisions and actions.

In the light of Habermas's commentary on the public sphere, research and action are to be understood not as separate functions but rather as different moments in a unified process of struggle characteristic of social movements—struggles against irrationality, injustice, and unsatisfying social conditions and ways of life (a unification of research for action that recalls the insight that all social movements are also educational movements). In the light of Habermas's (1996, chap. 8) description of the public sphere in *Between Facts and Norms,* we now conclude that the impulse to undertake participatory action research is an impulse to subject practice—social action—to deliberate and continuing critique by making action deliberately exploratory and arranging things so that it will be possible to learn from what happens and to make the process of learning a collective process to be pursued through public discourse in a public sphere constituted for that purpose.

The Role of the Collective

In the light of the Habermasian theory of system and lifeworld, the collective is not to be understood either solely in systems terms, as an organization or institution, or solely in lifeworld terms, as a social group constituted in face-to-face social relationships. Instead, it must be critically explored from *both* perspectives and as constituted by processes associated with each (on the systems side: steering media; on the lifeworld side: cultural reproduction and transformation, social reproduction and transformation, and the formation and transformation of individual identities and capabilities).

In the light of Habermas's critique of the social macro-subject, the collective should be understood not as a closed group with fixed membership—a coherent, unified, autonomous, independent, and self-regulating whole—but rather as internally diverse, differentiated, and sometimes inconsistent and contradictory. Nor does a participatory action research group stand in the position of an avant-garde in relation to other people and groups in the setting in which the research occurs, but it retains its connections with those others, just as it retains responsibility for the consequences of its actions as they are experienced in those wider communities in which they take place.

In the light of Habermas's commentary on the public sphere, the collective formed by a participatory action research project should be understood not as a closed and exclusive group constituted to perform the particular organizational roles and functions associated with a project but rather as an open and inclusive space constituted to create conditions of communicative freedom and, thus, to create communicative action and public discourse aimed at addressing problems and issues of irrationality, injustice, and dissatisfaction experienced by particular groups at particular times. In our view, some of the most interesting participatory action research projects are those directly connected with wider social movements (e.g., green issues; issues of peace, race, or gender), but it should not go unnoticed that many participatory action research projects constitute themselves in ways that are very like social movements in relation to local issues, although often with wider ramifications, for example, by addressing issues about the effects of hyperrationalization of practices in local settings that frequently have much more widespread relevance. For example, around the world there are hundreds—probably thousands—of different kinds of action research projects being conducted by teachers to explore the potential and limitations of various innovative forms of teaching and learning that address the alienating effects of state regulation of curriculum, teaching, and assessment at every level of schooling. The multiplication of such projects suggests that there is a social movement under way aimed at recovering or revitalizing education in the face of the very widespread colonization of the lifeworld of teaching and learning by the imperatives of increasingly muscular and intrusive administrative systems regulating and controlling the processes of schooling. These projects in education are paralleled by similar action research projects in welfare, health, community development, and other fields. Taken together, despite their differences, they make an eloquent statement of refusal and reconstruction in the face of a version of corporate and public administration that places the imperative of institutional control above the moral and substantive imperatives and virtues traditionally associated with the practice of these professions.

▣ REIMAGINING CRITICAL PARTICIPATORY ACTION RESEARCH

The view of critical participatory action research we have advanced in this chapter is somewhat different from the view of it that we held in the past. Two decades ago, our primary aim was to envisage and enact a well-justified form of research to be conducted by teachers and other professional practitioners into their own practices, their under-standings of their practices, and the situations in which they practiced. Despite our critique of established ways of thinking about social and educational research, certain remnant elements of conventional perceptions of research continued to survive in the forms of research we advocated, for example, ideas about theory, knowledge, and the cen-trality of the researcher in the advancement of knowledge.

Two decades ago, we hoped for advances in theory through action research that would somehow be similar to the kinds of theory conventionally produced or extended in the social and educational research of that time. We expected that practi-tioners would also develop and extend their own theories of education, but we were perhaps less clear about what the nature and form of those theories would be. We had admired Lawrence Stenhouse's definition of research as "systematic enquiry made public" (Stenhouse, 1975) but had given less thought to how those theories might emerge in a literature of practitioner research. Now we have a clearer idea that some-times the theories that motivate, guide, and inform practitioners' action are frequently in the form of *collective understandings* that elude easy codification in the forms con-ventionally used in learned journals and books. They accumulate in conversations, archives of evidence, and the shared knowledge of *communities of practice.*

Two decades ago, although we had regarded "knowledge" as a problematic category and had distinguished between the private knowledge of individuals and the collec-tive knowledge of research fields and traditions, we probably valued the knowledge outcomes of research over the practical outcomes of participant research—the effects of participant research in changing social and educational practices, understandings of those practices, and the situations and settings of practice. Now we have a clearer idea that the outcomes of participatory action research are written in histories—the histories of practitioners, communities, the people with whom they interact, and (again) communities of practice. And we see that the outcomes of participatory action research are to be read in terms of historical consequences for participants and others involved and affected by the action people have taken, judged not only against the cri-terion of truth but also against the criteria of wisdom and prudence, that is, whether people were better off in terms of the consequences they experienced. We can ask whether their understandings of their situations are less irrational (or ideologically skewed) than before, whether their action is less unproductive and unsatisfying for those involved, or whether the social relations between people in the situation are less inequitable or unjust than before. The product of participatory action research is not just knowledge but also different histories than might have existed if participants had not intervened to transform their practices, understandings, and situations and, thus, transformed the histories that otherwise seemed likely to come into being. We look for the products of participatory action research in *collective action* and the making and remaking of *collective histories.*

Two decades ago, we were excited by participatory research that connected with social movements and made changes in particular kinds of professional practices (e.g., nursing, education, community development, welfare), but we were less aware than we are now that this kind of engagement with social movements is a two-way street. Social movements can be expressed and realized in the settings of professional practice (e.g., the powerful connections made between the women's movement and health or education or between green issues and education or community development), but social movements also take strength and direction from participatory studies that explore and critically investigate issues in the particular contexts of different kinds of social practices. Social movements set agendas around the broad themes that are their focus, but studies of particular practices and local settings also show how differently those broad themes must be understood in terms of issues identified in in-depth local investigations. Now we have a clearer understanding not only that participatory action research expresses the spirit of its time in terms of giving life to social movements in local settings or in relation to particular themes (e.g., gender, indigenous rights) but also that local investigations into locally felt dissatisfactions, disquiets, or concerns also open up themes of broader interest, sometimes linking to existing social movements but also bringing into existence new movements for transformation in professional fields and in the civil life of communities. Now, in judging the long-term success of participatory action research projects, we are more likely to ask about the extent to which they have fed *collective capacities for transformation* locally and in the widening sphere of social life locally, regionally, nationally, and even internationally, as has happened in the history of participatory action research as it has contributed to the development of *people's collective communicative power.*

Most particularly, two decades ago we valorized the researcher. According to conventional views of research, researchers were the people at the center of the research act—heroes in the quiet adventures of building knowledge and theory. We encouraged participant research that would make "ordinary" practitioners local heroes of knowledge building and theory building and collaborative research that would make heroic teams of researching practitioners who produced new understandings in their communities and communities of practice. Increasingly, in those days, we saw research "collectives" as key activist groups that would make and change history. We continue to advocate this view of participatory research as making history by making exploratory changes. Now, however, our critiques of the research–action dualism, and our changing views of the facilitator and the research collective, encourage us to believe that critical participatory action research needs *animateurs* but that it also thrives in *public spheres* in which people can take a variety of roles as researchers, questioners, interlocutors, and interested observers. And if we reject the heroic view of history as being "made" by individuals—great men or great women—then we must see the real transformations of history as transformations made by ordinary people working together in the light of emerging themes, issues, and problems (e.g., via social movements). We now see a central task of participatory action research as including widening groups of people in the task of making their own history, often in the face of established ways of doing things and often to overcome problems caused by living with the consequences of the histories others make for us—often the consequences of new ways of doing things that were intended to improve things but that turned out to have unexpected, unanticipated, and untoward consequences for those whom the new ways were intended to help. As we hope we have shown, Habermas's description of public discourse in public spheres gives us another way in which to think about who can do "research" and what research might be like if it is conceptualized as exploratory action aimed at nurturing and feeding public discourse in public spheres. Now we are less inclined to think in terms of heroes of knowledge building or even of heroes of history making; we are more inclined to think in terms of people working together to develop a greater collective capacity to change the circumstances of their own lives in terms of *collective capacity building.*

Now, more so than two decades ago, we are excited by notions of collective understanding, collective research, communicative power, and collective capacity. We are interested in describing and identifying conditions under which people can investigate their own professional fields or community circumstances to develop communicative power and strengthen their collective capacity. In "projects" and movements aimed at collective capacity building, we see people securing new ways of working on the basis of *collective commitment.* We see them achieving new ways of working and new ways of being that have *legitimacy* because their decisions are made in conditions like those we described in the last section—the conditions of public discourse in public spheres. Now, more so than two decades ago, we see participatory action research as a process of sustained *collective deliberation* coupled with sustained *collective investigation* of a topic, a problem, an issue, a concern, or a theme that allows people to explore possibilities in action, judging them by their consequences in history and moving with a measure of tentativeness and prudence (in some cases with great courage in the face of violence and coercion) but also with the support that comes with *solidarity.*

This account of what we now value as outcomes and consequences of participatory action research—well-justified and agreed-on collective action that reduces the world's stock of irrationality, injustice, inequity, dissatisfaction, and unproductive ways of doing things—may seem a far cry from the kind of justification for much social and educational research. Perhaps more modestly, that research makes few claims to changing history for the better and promises only improved knowledge and theories that *may* contribute to clearer understanding and improved policy and practice. That is not necessarily the way it is used, of course; sometimes "scientific" theories or findings are used to justify social programs, policies, and practices of breathtaking foolhardiness. Our advocacy of critical participatory research is intended partly as an antidote to such foolhardiness but also to insist, in an age of hyperrationality and the technologization of everything, that people can still, gaps and miscues notwithstanding, have a hope of knowing what they are doing and doing what they think is right and, more particularly, doing less of what they think will have untoward consequences for themselves and others. Perhaps this is to take too "activist" a view of participatory action research and to give up on the conventional understanding that people should wait for experts and theorists to tell them what will work best—what will be best for them.

In 1957, in the *Journal of Educational Sociology*, Harold Hodgkinson presented a critique of action research that he regarded as "a symptom of the times in which we live" (Hodgkinson, 1957, p. 152). Against Arthur Foshay, whom he quoted as saying, "Cooperative action research is an approach to making what we do consistent with what we believe" (which we would argue fails to acknowledge the power of action research to put our ideas to the test and correct what we believe), Hodgkinson retorted,

> This is simply not so. Action research merely focuses attention on the doing and eliminates most of the necessity for believing. We are living in a "doing" age, and action research allows people the privilege of "doing" something. This method could easily become an end in itself. (p. 153)

Hodgkinson (1957) believed that action research would produce "teachers who spend much of their time measuring and figuring, playing with what Dylan Thomas would call 'easy hobby games for little engineers'" (p. 153). He held out for the great scientific generalizations, based on sound empirical and statistical methods that would provide a secure scientific basis for what teachers could or should do.

Those other approaches to research have produced some justifications for improved ways of working in education, social work, community development, and other spheres of social action. They will continue to do so. But they will always create a problem of putting the scientist as "expert" in the position of mediator, that is, mediating between the knowledge and action and the theory and practice of practitioners and ordinary people. They will always create disjunctions between what scientific communities and policymakers believe to be prudent courses of action and the courses of action that people would (and will) choose for themselves, knowing the consequences of their actions and practices for the people with whom they work. For two decades, we have insisted that *practitioners'* interpretive categories (not just how they think about their work but also how they think about their world) must be taken into account in deciding what, when, whether, and how research should be conducted into professional practice and community life. Critical participatory action research is an expression of this impulse, and it has proved, in hundreds of studies, to be a means by which people have transformed their worlds. Sometimes, perhaps, things have *not* turned out for the better, but many times people have concluded that their participatory action research work has changed their circumstances for the better and avoided untoward consequences that they otherwise would have had to endure. This has been true in rebuilding education in South Africa, in literacy campaigns in Nicaragua, in developments in nursing practice in Australia, in improving classroom teaching in the United Kingdom, in community development in the Philippines, in farms in Sri Lanka, in community governance in India, in improving water supplies in Bangladesh, and in hundreds of other settings around the world. These are not "easy hobby games for little engineers," as Hodgkinson might have it, but rather matters of great human and social significance. These people might not have changed the world, but they have changed their worlds. Is that not the same thing? They might not have changed everything everywhere, but they have improved things for particular people in particular places and in many other places where their stories have traveled. We do not think that it is too immodest an aspiration to judge participatory action research in terms of historical consequences. Indeed, perhaps we judge too much social and educational science against too low a bar. We are used to expecting too little help from it, and our expectations have been met. Under such circumstances, we believe, people would be wise to conduct their own research into their own practices and situations. Under such circumstances, there continues to be a need for critical participatory action research.

◨ NOTES

1. The quotation is from page 334 of the German edition of Habermas's (1992a) *Faktizität und Geltung* (Between Facts and Norms).
2. This description is adapted from Kemmis and Brennan Kemmis (2003).
3. This description is adapted from Kemmis (2004).

◨ REFERENCES

Altrichter, H., & Gstettner, P. (1997). Action research: A closed chapter in the history of German social science? In R. McTaggart (Ed.), *Participatory action research: International contexts and consequences* (pp. 45–78). Albany: State University of New York Press.

Argyris, C. (1990). *Overcoming organisational defences: Facilitating organisational learning.* Boston: Allyn & Bacon.

Argyris, C., Putnam, R., & McLain Smith, D. (1985). *Action science.* San Francisco: Jossey–Bass.

Argyris, C., & Schön, D. A. (1974). *Theory in practice: Increasing professional effectiveness.* San Francisco: Jossey–Bass.

Argyris, C., & Schön, D. A. (1978). *Organisational learning: A theory of action perspective.* Reading, MA: Addison-Wesley.

Baynes, K. (1995). Democracy and the *Rechsstaat: Habermas's Faktizität und Geltung.* In S. K. White (Ed.), *The Cambridge companion to Habermas* (pp. 201–232). Cambridge, UK: Cambridge University Press.

Bourdieu, P., & Wacquant, L. J. D. (1992). *An invitation to reflexive sociology.* Cambridge, UK: Polity.

Bravette, G. (1996). Reflection on a black woman's management learning. *Women in Management Review, 11*(3), 3–11.

Brock-Utne, B. (1980, Summer). What is educational action research? *Classroom Action Research Network Bulletin*, No. 4, pp. 10–15.

Brown, L., Henry, C., Henry, J., & McTaggart, R. (1988). Action research: Notes on the national seminar. In S. Kemmis & R. McTaggart (Eds.), *The action research reader* (3rd ed., pp. 337–352). Geelong, Australia: Deakin University Press.

Carr, W., & Kemmis, S. (1986). *Becoming critical: Education, knowledge, and action research.* London: Falmer.

Checkland, P. (1981). *Systems thinking, systems practice.* Chichester, UK: Wiley.

Checkland, P., & Scholes, J. (1990). *Soft systems methodology in action.* Chichester, UK: Wiley.

Clark, P. A. (1972). *Action research and organisational change.* London: Harper & Row.

Corey, S. M. (1949). Action research, fundamental research, and educational practices. *Teachers College Record, 50,* 509–514.

Corey, S. M. (1953). *Action research to improve school practices.* New York: Columbia University, Teachers College Press.

Dadds, M. (1995). *Passionate enquiry and school development: A story about teacher action research.* London: Falmer.

Davies, L., & Ledington, P. (1991). *Information in action: Soft systems methodology.* Basingstoke, UK: Macmillan.

Dewey, J. (1916). *Education and democracy.* New York: Macmillan.

Elden, M. (1983). Participatory research at work. *Journal of Occupational Behavior, 4*(1), 21–34.

Elliott, J. (1976–1977). Developing hypotheses about classrooms from teachers' practical constructs: An account of the work of the Ford Teaching Project. *Interchange, 7*(2), 2–22. Reprinted in Kemmis, S., & McTaggart, R. (Eds.). (1988). *The action research reader* (pp. 195–213). Geelong, Australia: Deakin University Press.

Elliott, J., & Adelman, C. (1973). Reflecting where the action is: The design of the Ford Teaching Project. *Education for Teaching, 92,* 8–20.

Emery, F. E., & Thorsrud, E. (1976). *Democracy at work: The report of the Norwegian Industrial Democracy Program.* Leiden, Netherlands: M. Nijhoff.

Emery, F. E., Thorsrud, E., & Trist, E. (1969). *Form and content in industrial democracy: Some experiences from Norway and other European countries.* London: Tavistock.

Fals Borda, O. (1979). Investigating reality in order to transform it: The Colombian experience. *Dialectical Anthropology, 4,* 33–55.

Fals Borda, O. (1988). *Knowledge and people's power.* New Delhi: Indian Social Institute.

Fals Borda, O., & Rahman, M. (1991). *Action and knowledge: Breaking the monopoly with participatory action research.* New York: Apex Press.

Fay, B. (1987). *Critical social science: Liberation and its limits.* Cambridge, UK: Polity.

Flood, R. L., & Jackson, M. C. (1991). *Creative problem solving: Total systems intervention.* Chichester, UK: Wiley.

Forester, J., Pitt, J., & Welsh, J. (Eds.). (1993). *Profiles of participatory action researchers.* Ithaca, NY: Cornell University, Department of Urban and Regional Planning.

Foster, M. (1972). An introduction to the theory and practice of action research in work organizations. *Human Relations, 25,* 529–566.

Freire, P. (1982). Creating alternative research methods: Learning to do it by doing it. In B. Hall, A. Gillette, & R. Tandon (Eds.), *Creating knowledge: A monopoly?* (pp. 29–37). New Delhi: Society for Participatory Research in Asia. Reprinted in Kemmis, S., & McTaggart, R.

(Eds.). (1988). *The action research reader* (pp. 291–313). Geelong, Australia: Deakin University Press.

Greenwood, D., & Levin, M. (2000). Reconstructing the relationships between universities and society through action research. In N. Denzin & Y. Lincoln (Eds.), *Handbook of qualitative research* (2nd ed., pp. 85–106). Thousand Oaks, CA: Sage.

Greenwood, D., & Levin, M. (2001). Pragmatic action research and the struggle to transform universities into learning communities. In P. Reason & H. Bradbury (Eds.), *Handbook of action research* (pp. 103–113). London: Sage.

Habermas, J. (1972). *Knowledge and human interests* (J. J. Shapiro, Trans.). London: Heinemann.

Habermas, J. (1984). *Theory of communicative action,* Vol. 1: *Reason and the rationalization of society* (T. McCarthy, Trans.). Boston: Beacon.

Habermas, J. (1987a). *The philosophical discourse of modernity: Twelve lectures* (F. G. Lawrence, Trans.). Cambridge: MIT Press.

Habermas, J. (1987b). *Theory of communicative action,* Vol. 2: *Lifeworld and system: A critique of functionalist reason* (T. McCarthy, Trans.). Boston: Beacon.

Habermas, J. (1992a). *Faktizität und Geltung* (Between facts and norms). Frankfurt, Germany: Suhrkamp.

Habermas, J. (1992b). *Postmetaphysical thinking: Philosophical essays* (W. M. Hohengarten, Trans.). Cambridge: MIT Press.

Habermas, J. (1996). *Between Facts and Norms* (trans. William Rehg). Cambridge, Massachusetts: MIT Press.

Hall, B., Gillette, A., & Tandon, R. (1982). *Creating knowledge: A monopoly?* New Delhi: Society for Participatory Research in Asia.

Henry, C. (1991). If action research were tennis. In O. Zuber-Skerritt (Ed.), *Action learning for improved performance.* Brisbane, Australia: Aebis Publishing.

Hodgkinson, H. (1957). Action research: A critique. *Journal of Educational Sociology, 31*(4), 137–153.

Horton, M., with Kohl, J., & Kohl, H. (1990). *The long haul.* New York: Doubleday.

Jackson, M. C. (1991). *Systems methodology for the management sciences.* New York: Plenum.

Kemmis, S. (1981). Action research in prospect and retrospect. In S. Kemmis, C. Henry, C. Hook, & R. McTaggart (Eds.), *The action research reader* (pp. 11–31). Geelong, Australia: Deakin University Press.

Kemmis, S. (1991). Action research and post-modernisms. *Curriculum Perspectives, 11*(4), 59–66.

Kemmis, S. (1998). Interrupt and say: Is it worth doing? An interview with Stephen Kemmis. *Lifelong Learning in Europe, 3*(3).

Kemmis, S. (2004, March). *Knowing practice: Searching for saliences.* Paper presented at the "Participant Knowledge and Knowing Practice" conference, Umeå, Sweden.

Kemmis, S., & Brennan Kemmis, R. (2003, October). *Making and writing the history of the future together: Exploratory action in participatory action research.* Paper presented at the Congreso Internacional de Educación, Córdoba, Argentina.

Kemmis, S., & McTaggart, R. (1988a). *The action research planner* (3rd ed.). Geelong, Australia: Deakin University Press.

Kemmis, S., & McTaggart, R. (1988b). *The action research reader* (3rd ed.). Geelong, Australia: Deakin University Press.

Kemmis, S., & McTaggart, R. (2000). Participatory action research. In N. Denzin & Y. Lincoln (Eds.), *Handbook of qualitative research* (2nd ed., pp. 567–605). Thousand Oaks, CA: Sage.

Kolb, D. (1984). *Experiential learning: Experience as the source of learning and development.* Englewood Cliffs, NJ: Prentice Hall.

Levin, M. (1985). *Participatory action research in Norway.* Trondheim, Norway: ORAL.

Lewin, K. (1946). Action research and minority problems. *Journal of Social Issues, 2,* 34–46.

Lewin, K. (1952). Group decision and social change. In T. M. Newcomb & E. E. Hartley (Eds.), *Readings in social psychology* (pp. 459–473). New York: Holt.

Marika, R., Ngurruwutthun, D., & White, L. (1992). Always together, Yaka gäna: Participatory research at Yirrkala as part of the development of Yolngu education. *Convergence, 25*(1), 23–39.

McGuire, P. (1987). *Doing participatory research: A feminist approach.* Amherst: University of Massachusetts, Center for International Education.

McTaggart, R. (1991a). *Action research: A short modern history.* Geelong, Australia: Deakin University Press.

McTaggart, R. (1991b). Western institutional impediments to Aboriginal education. *Journal of Curriculum Studies, 23,* 297–325.

McTaggart, R. (Ed.). (1997). *Participatory action research: International contexts and consequences.* Albany: State University of New York Press.

McTaggart, R. (2002). The mission of the scholar in action research. In M. P. Wolfe & C. R. Pryor (Eds.), *The mission of the scholar: Research and practice* (pp. 1–16). London: Peter Lang.

McTaggart, R., & Garbutcheon-Singh, M. (1986). New directions in action research. *Curriculum Perspectives, 6*(2), 42–46.

Niemi, H., & Kemmis, S. (1999). Communicative evaluation: Evaluation at the crossroads. *Lifelong Learning in Europe, 4*(1), 55–64.

Noffke, S. E. (1990). *Action research: A multidimensional analysis.* Unpublished PhD thesis, University of Wisconsin–Madison.

Noffke, S. E. (1997). Themes and tensions in U.S. action research: Towards historical analysis. In S. Hollinsworth (Ed.), *International action research: A casebook for educational reform* (pp. 2–16). London: Falmer.

Oliveira, R., & Darcy, M. (1975). *The militant observer: A sociological alternative.* Geneva: Institute d'Action Cultural.

Park, P., Brydon-Miller, M., Hall, B., & Jackson, T. (Eds.). (1993). *Voices of change: Participatory research in the United States and Canada.* Toronto: OISE Press.

Pasmore, W., & Friedlander, F. (1982). An action research program for increasing employee involvement in problem-solving. *Administrative Science Quarterly, 27,* 342–362.

Pedler, M. (Ed.). (1991). *Action learning in practice.* Aldershot, UK: Gower.

Rapaport, R. N. (1970). Three dilemmas in action research. *Human Relations, 23,* 499–513.

Reason, P. (Ed.). (1988). *Human inquiry in action: Developments in new paradigm research.* London: Sage.

Revans, R. W. (1980). *Action learning: New techniques for management.* London: Blond & Briggs.

Revans, R. W. (1982). *The origins and growth of action learning.* Lund, Sweden: Studentlitteratur.

Ryan, K. E. (2003, November). *Serving public interests in educational accountability.* Paper presented at the meeting of the American Evaluation Association, Reno, NV.

Sagor, R. (1992). *How to conduct collaborative action research.* Alexandria, VA: Association for Supervision and Curriculum Development.

Sandkull, B. (1980). Practice of industry: Mis-management of people. *Human Systems Management, 1,* 159–167.

Schön, D. A. (1983). *The reflective practitioner: How professionals think in action.* New York: Basic Books.

Schön, D. A. (1987). *Educating the reflective practitioner.* San Francisco: Jossey–Bass.

Schön, D. A. (Ed.). (1991). *The reflective turn: Case studies in and on educational practice.* New York: Columbia University, Teachers College Press.

Stenhouse, L. (1975). *An introduction to curriculum research and development.* London: Heinemann Educational.

Taylor. C. (1991). *The malaise of modernity.* Concord, Ontario: House of Anansi.

Torbert, W. R. (1991). *The power of balance: Transforming self, society, and scientific inquiry.* Newbury Park, CA: Sage.

Warmington, A. (1980). Action research: Its methods and its implications. *Journal of Applied Systems Analysis, 7,* 23–39.

Weiner, G. (1989). Professional self-knowledge versus social justice: A critical analysis of the teacher– researcher movement. *British Educational Research Journal, 15*(1), 41–51.

Whyte, W. F. (1989). Introduction to action research for the twenty-first century: Participation, reflection, and practice. *American Behavioral Scientist, 32,* 502–512.

Whyte, W. F. (Ed.). (1991). *Participatory action research.* Newbury Park, CA: Sage.

Wittgenstein, L. (1958). *Philosophical investigations* (2nd ed., G. E. M. Anscombe, Trans.). Oxford, UK: Basil Blackwell.

Yunupingu, M. (1991). A plan for Ganma research. In R. Bunbury, W. Hastings, J. Henry, & R. McTaggart (Eds.), *Aboriginal pedagogy: Aboriginal teachers speak out* (pp. 98–106). Geelong, Australia: Deakin University Press.

Zuber-Skerritt, O. (Ed.). (1996). *New directions in action research.* London: Falmer.

11

CLINICAL RESEARCH

William L. Miller and Benjamin F. Crabtree

*Under a sky the color of pea soup she is looking at her work grow-
ing away there actively, thickly like grapevines or pole beans as
things grow in the real world, slowly enough.*

—Opening stanza of Marge Piercy's "The Seven of Pentacles"

A tornado approaches the fields of our dreams. How well has our clinical research prepared the ground for the coming whirlwind? Jocelyn arrives to consult with her primary care clinician. For 3 years, the 50-year-old Jocelyn notices some burning pain "around my heart" shortly after meals and when she lies down for extended periods. This pain is frequently associated with a "sour taste in my mouth." On the morning of her visit, shortly after her fourth cup of coffee, she stands by the grill at work nearly doubled over by the pain. She can tolerate the suffering no longer. By nearly everyone's account, the clinical encounter that follows is a success. Her doctor quickly diagnoses gastroesophageal reflux disease (GERD) and prescribes Nexium, the "purple pill." The whole visit takes only 6 minutes and helps the doctor to meet his productivity quota. Jocelyn, knowing about the pill from television commercials, is worried about the diagnosis but pleased with the simple solution. AstraZeneca, which produces Nexium, is delighted. The office staff and practice group manager are happy, and Jocelyn's employer at the fast-food restaurant is glad that Jocelyn has very little time lost from work. Clinical researchers, proud of their randomized controlled trials demonstrating the effectiveness of esomeprazole (the generic name for Nexium), feel vindicated. So, where's the tornado? If you are a clinical researcher, are you worrying about the standardized simplicity of this story?

GERD is the disease label affixed to a symptom complex associated with the experience of heartburn. GERD is related to the reflux of gastric acid (important for immunity and digestion) into the esophagus because of the inappropriate relaxation or leakage of the lower esophageal sphincter (LES) that separates the stomach from the esophagus. The healthy stomach has a protective coating of mucous shielding it from acid, whereas the esophagus does not and often produces alerting symptoms such as heartburn in the presence of acid. Proton pump inhibitors (PPIs) such as Nexium block the cellular pumps that produce normal acid in the stomach and, by nearly eliminating the acid, prevent heartburn (but not the reflux of acid-free stomach juices). Reflux results from multiple factors that weaken the LES, relax it inappropriately, or create excessive pressure on it. These factors include overeating, bedtime snacking, wearing tight clothing or tight clip-on earrings, rapid eating, being obese (especially with large abdominal girth), experiencing emotional stress, and using several common drugs, caffeine, tobacco, and/or alcohol—in summary, an acquisitive, materialistic consumer lifestyle. These factors are named and chided in a PPI commercial where a patient celebrates being liberated from the agony of lifestyle change simply by taking the right pill. She is now free to continue whatever lifestyle she wishes and no longer needs to wonder what else her body is trying to communicate through the symptom of heartburn. She is learning to ignore the questions that emerge from her own experiences and to pay more attention to consumer-oriented answers and corporation-generated questions. These are questions of instrumental rationality that are eagerly and extravagantly funded by government-sponsored research institutions and the medical technology and pharmaceutical industries and that are most commonly addressed by current clinical research.

One by one, islands of rock, with a solitary person standing on each, loom into view as the surf pounds below. Each voice urgently proclaims, "I didn't know!" As the hidden camera fades back, the islands merge together, each person appearing securely confident—protected by the purple pill—and the erosive raging of the sea below now controlled. The war against the terrorism of stomach acid pouring across its boundary into the esophagus has been won. Millions of television viewers, including Jocelyn, watch this AstraZeneca commercial about its newest PPI, Nexium. What didn't they know? The veiled threat is that GERD could lead to Barrett's esophagus and then to adenocarcinoma, even though this connection is rare and uncertain and there is no evidence that taking PPIs prevents it (Conio et al., 2003). Thousands of physicians, fed by AstraZeneca representatives, have their offices cluttered with tablets, pens, and trinkets labeled "Nexium" and have their drug cabinets stocked with Nexium samples. How well has our clinical research prepared Jocelyn and her clinician, as well as everyone else, for this global corporate tornado? On their desks or computer screens appear article reprints of clinical research exclaiming the effectiveness of esomeprazole

(Nexium) in controlling the symptoms of heartburn (Johnson et al., 2001; Talley et al., 2002) but none about what it means.

Sickness pervades the landscape. Suburban sprawl contributes to obesity and the epidemic of diabetes (Perdue, Stone, & Gostin, 2003). Millions of socioeconomically impoverished people are dying or dead from AIDS, tuberculosis, and malaria because economically colonized countries lack access to care and the necessary medicines despite supporting the profits of global pharmaceutical corporations (Farmer, 2001; Kim, Millen, Irwin, & Gershman, 2000). Sustainable ways of living across our globe are disrupted and replaced by capitalist market economies. People who were once self-sufficient are now bound to wage labor and assured the freedom to choose soft drinks. Greatly reduced is their freedom to choose a local vocation and way of life (Coote, 1996; Douthwaite, 1999). Water, air, forests, soil, and the ecologies of which they are a part are deteriorating (Gardner, 2003). The acid of Western civilization's quest for domination is pouring across its boundaries, scorching the land, and consuming the earth's diversity. The proposed solutions are even more technology and business as usual, a global purple pill for global GERD. Part of what is going on here is the complex interactions of an expectant and frightened public, the myopic arrogance of military and economic power, and many (often well-intentioned) individuals trapped in their own and the dominant culture's webs of denial (Jensen, 2002). Welcome to the clinical research space.

Meanwhile, amid a Middle Atlantic landscape of small farms, sprawling suburbs, crowded urban streets, and rigid walls of private property, Jocelyn is taking the purple pill every day. She is confused and worried. Although free of heartburn symptoms, nothing else has changed in her life. The heartburn began about 1 year after her daughter's infant child died in an auto accident and 6 months after starting a new job in a fast-food restaurant. Over that year, Jocelyn resumed smoking, gained 30 pounds, and was drinking more coffee. The heartburn was getting worse despite taking many over-the-counter medicines. During this same time, she worried about her son serving in the U.S. Army in Iraq and about the threat of terrorism. Is it possible that parts of this story are related to her symptoms? To the global issues noted? What does the new diagnosis of GERD mean to Jocelyn? What and whose questions were addressed in her encounter? What and whose questions were missing? Poor, frightened, and 50 years old, she knows that something is wrong. Where is the meaning in her embodied embedded lived experiences? Her life, composed of memories, children, career, lovers, and anticipated hopes, appears shredded; she fears that no one is listening. Now she is noticing some low back pain. Her doctors hide their fears and lose their empathy behind the latest tests and the newest drugs and clinical trial protocols. Working for "HamsterCare," they are exhausted turning their wheels of productivity (Morrison, 2000). They feel tired, overregulated, angry at the continued emphasis on cost cutting and efficiency and on the threat of malpractice, and inadequate in the face of death, but they conceal their emotions behind a wall of professional "objectivity." The clinicians also struggle to mediate guidelines, multiple languages of specialization, ambiguities of new technological visions of the body, their own clinical knowledge and experience, and patient values and idiosyncrasies. Meanwhile, marketing researchers for AstraZeneca are conducting focus groups to learn more effective ways of convincing adults and physicians of Nexium's value. But these are stories rarely known by the "public." These stories are hidden, if known at all, by conscious concealment and by the forces of unconscious cultural preference. The story told is that GERD is dangerous to you and that Nexium is the safe and effective product fix. The ecological, social, and spiritual consequences are invisible.

This is a typical tale in clinical medical research. *Suffering and normality are standardized, commoditized, and marketed.* The suffering related to heartburn is framed as a threat, that is, a universal need for some marketable product that restores control. The story is framed as a "restitution" narrative (Frank, 1995). Everyone has something wrong with him or her; normal now means inadequate in moral and standardized ways such as the recent guidelines creating the new disease of prehypertension (Chobanian et al., 2003) and the guidelines on obesity that make most U.S. adults overweight or obese (National Heart, Lung, and Blood Institute, 1998). The complexities, multiplicities, and individualities of suffering and normality are subsumed within this technological and commercial frame. This is the tornado! Important voices, questions, and evidence are missing. Knowing the efficacy of the drug—the internal validity—is sufficient to approve using all means necessary to convince all people to "choose" the pill as a requirement for a safe and healthy life. It is assumed that there is a real material world that is, in principle, knowable through scientific methodology, especially the randomized controlled trial, and nothing should stand in the way of pursuing this truth. Outside the swirl of this neorealist tornado, there is so much silence. Jocelyn's experience of taking a daily pill that labels her self and body as endangered is missing. The voices of her family members are missing. Relationships and moral discourse are missing. The place and role of power are missing. Feeling, spirituality, and ecology are missing. Depth and context are reduced, simplified, or eliminated, and relationships are isolated and alienated. What hope is there after the tornado passes?

This is the clinical research space we have witnessed above ground—clinical research too often working on behalf of the dominant cultural tornado of global corporate capitalism. There are alternatives! The stories of interest and hope for clinical researchers are in what is missing and how the stories are framed. We imagine clinical research spaces where Jocelyn and the many communities of patients and neighbors, clinicians, and researchers meet together and seek transformation. The suffering related to heartburn is framed as broken-ness calling for reconnection, generosity, and love. The story is framed as a movement from "chaos" to "quest" narrative (Frank, 1995). We imagine at least two different and deeply connected research spaces. One is at ground level, visible, helpful, and growing and healing within the dominant culture, at the places where the questions of embodied and embedded lived experience meet clinical reality and current institutional structures and processes. Here, using a more participatory and mixed methods approach guided by the questions of lived experience, the ground is tended and weeded and opportunities for planting seeds and nurturing healthier plants are identified and enacted. This is the quest toward transformation that assumes that even the oppressors are oppressed. We do not believe that this will be enough. The tornado already creates wastelands based on ethnicity, color, class, gender, and sexuality, and it ravishes the life-sustaining soul of our one earth—the soil, water, air, and intricate web of interdependent species. The tornado often leaves us in chaos, with no clear storyline apparent; there is only the hope of each other. We propose a second space below ground—out of reach of the tornado. Within the burrows and entanglements of garden soil, clinician/patient, qualitative/quantitative, academy/practice, very different ways, cultures, and technologies of knowing can meet, converse, and create a "solidarity" clinical research for the future that serves nascent institutional forms. This chapter explores both of these spaces and conversations.

The *Handbook* celebrates the qualitative research community's conversations—the internal discourse about our identity, what we do, and the faith and hope for our own growth and transformation that is sustained there. The opportunity to translate this conversation into both an expanded and a new alternative clinical research space was never better or more urgent. Historical calls for a shift away from a strictly positivist position and for seeking greater methodological diversity, including the use of qualitative research methods (e.g., Freymann, 1989; McWhinney, 1986, 1989; Waitzkin, 1991), are being answered. Qualitative clinical research is finding its way into funding agency agendas, especially in primary health and medical care and nursing. Patients[1] and clinicians are increasingly invited into research conversations. Methods are also evolving; they are beginning to separate from their parent traditions (e.g., ethnography, phenomenology, grounded theory) and generating new hybrids in the clinical research space. Unfortunately, this success is also leading to powerful efforts from within the dominant paradigm to co-opt qualitative methods despite a small and articulate resistance (Morse, Swanson, & Kuzel, 2001). This is most evident in the development of checklists for ensuring validity of qualitative studies (Barbour, 2001). Versions of this chapter in earlier editions of the *Handbook* were solely about continuing and accelerating this successful flow, that is, the exploration and conversations at ground level. We no longer believe this to be sufficient. Our own recent experiences at working within the toxic embrace of the dominant paradigm and its forces of elite corporate globalization alert us to the additional need for work below ground preparing for after the tornado passes.

The understandings of clinical research presented here are grounded in the authors' own stories. Our rhizomes are deeply embedded within the nexus of applied anthropology and the practice of primary health care, particularly family medicine. Both authors have appointments in departments of family medicine and are trained in anthropology. Our social science roots were fed by the development of clinically applied anthropology during the 1970s (Chrisman, 1977; Chrisman & Maretzki, 1982; Fabrega, 1976, 1979; Foster, 1974; Foster & Anderson, 1978; Polgar, 1962) and were nurtured by the later work of Kleinman (1988, 1992, 1995; see also Kleinman, Eisenberg, & Good, 1978), the Goods (Good, 1994; Good & Good, 1981), Lock (1982, 1986, 1993), the Peltos (Pelto & Pelto, 1978, 1990), and Young (1982a, 1982b). These roots are currently challenged by the poststructuralist debate (Burawoy et al., 1991; Clifford & Marcus, 1986; Haraway, 1993; Jackson, 1989) and critical theory (Baer, 1993; Morsy, 1996; Singer, 1995). One of the authors (W.L.M.) has a busy urban family medicine practice, oversees a residency program, and chairs a clinical department within a large academic community hospital. The other author (B.F.C.) directs a family medicine research division and is a national research consultant. Both authors actively participate in the politics and discourse of academic biomedicine and academic social science and have experience in international health settings. The biomedical influence, with its perceived therapeutic imperative, steers toward pragmatic interventions and the desire for explicitness and coherence in information gathering and decision making and highlights the appeal of neorealist postpositivism and technology. The actual relationships that emerge within patient care reveal the uncertainty and particularity (McWhinney, 1989) of clinical praxis and turn one toward storytelling, relationship, and interpretation. The realities of power and dominant cultural hegemony are exposed in our efforts to help uninsured patients receive appropriate care, to protect the health of local habitats, to change international health policy, to get grants funded, to publish storied knowledge in biomedical journals, and to guide our departments through budget challenges and our institutions toward profitability. Growing and dying within the multiplicities of our soils, we have come to realize the relativity of all knowledge. The challenges are not epistemological but rather practical and moral. We are privileged white men holding positions of power within the belly of the beast; we are also tricksters. The conversations that we recommend for clinical research reflect these two stances.

◫ CLINICAL RESEARCH AT GROUND LEVEL

> *Fight persistently as the creeper that brings down the tree. Spread like the squash plant that overruns the garden. Gnaw in the dark and use the sun to make sugar. Weave real connections, create real nodes, build real houses. Live a life you can endure: make love that is loving.*
>
> —Continuation of Marge Piercy's "The Seven of Pentacles"

Our guiding premise is that the questions emerging from the embodied, embedded, and mindfully lived clinical experience frame conversation and determine research design (Brewer & Hunter, 1989; Diers, 1979; Miller & Crabtree, 1999b). Clinical researchers have at least six discernible research styles available: (a) experimental, (b) survey, (c) documentary–historical, (d) field (qualitative), (e) philosophical, and (f) action/participatory (Lather, 1991; see also Madison, Chapter 8, this volume). The clinical research space above ground needs to be open to all of these possible sources and types of knowledge. They all contribute to the two primary aims of clinical research at ground level. The first is to *deepen and contextualize the practical and ethical questions,* concerns, and emerging understandings for healers and their patients and policymakers. A second aim is to *trouble the waters and seek change* within the clinical research world itself. This section is organized around the following three goals: (a) *creating a space* for research that opens and celebrates qualitative and multiparadigmatic approaches to the clinical world, (b) *providing the tools and translations* necessary for discovering and witnessing clinical stories and knowledge within this space, and (c) identifying and describing the means for *telling the stories* and sharing the knowledge.

The emphasis is on the clinical text of Western biomedicine and the particular subtext of primary health care because of the authors' location in that place. Fortunately, the discussion is easily transferred to other clinical contexts such as nursing care, education, organizational management, community organizing, and international activism (see also Berg & Smith, 1988; Bogdan & Biklen, 1992; Morse & Field, 1997; Moyer, MacAllister, & Soifer, 2001; Roseland, 1998; Sapsford & Abbott, 1992; Schein, 1987; Symon & Cassell, 1998). In all of these arenas, qualitative methods are more accepted, yet the noise from policymakers is for being more evidence based and outcomes driven with generalizability and randomized designs prioritized. (See the recent "No Child Left Behind" act for an example of this in educational policy [www.ed.gov/nclb/landing.jhtml].) In education, for example, a recent "consensus" report sought to define scientific research in education and, like this chapter, argued that the methods must fit the question. Unlike this chapter, the report prioritized the value of randomized studies and expressed doubts about participatory models. The report voiced no concerns about the goal of evidence-based education (Shavelson & Towne, 2002). We offer an alternative viewpoint.

Creating a Space

The dominant biomedical world and the smaller qualitative research community both tend to maintain methodological and academic rigidity. Creating a clinical research space requires bringing both groups into the garden and developing common language. *The clinical questions are the common ground* (Taylor, 1993) for creating this space. These questions call us to rediscover the missing evidence (the people, experiences, ecology, power, and contexts) and the richness and depth of what "effectiveness" means. The clinical questions invite us to explore the human implications of rationing and cost issues, biotechnology, and genetic engineering and to enter the conflicted landscape of alternative and conventional medicine—the world between the "garden" and the "machine" (Beinfield & Korngold, 1991). The questions beg us to locate, own, aim, and share the powers inherent in clinical situations (Brody, 1992). The vulnerability exposed by the fully embedded and embodied clinical experiences that give rise to these questions also reveals the inadequacies of a neorealist epistemology (for more details, see Peräkylä, Volume 3, Chapter 11). Three core strategies for creating and entering this common ground and transforming clinical research are described. These consist of stepping carefully and strategically into the biomedical world, expanding the evidence-based medicine (EBM) space, and democratizing knowledge. Three additional strategies—using theory more explicitly, expanding cross-disciplinary collaborations, and applying the principles of critical multiplism—are also mentioned briefly. These strategies assume that change is more experience based than it is rational and that clinical participants must actively try methods if they are to adopt them. Thus, there is an emphasis on clinical participants, including patients, answering their own questions using methods appropriate for those questions.

Entering Biomedicine

Walking and working within the walls of technocratic biomedicine is exciting and daunting, and it frequently challenges intellectual and personal integrity. Thriving in this world requires understanding the biomedical cultural context while also clearly articulating a model that highlights the clinical implications of qualitative clinical research. This knowledge, if also joined by patients and other community participants, facilitates bargaining, mediation, and the formation of common language that makes possible the creation of a new research space at ground level. This is where, in languages understandable by the existing clinical world and patients, a space for more expansive imagination is created, the tools for listening and seeing are shared, and the seeds for transforming stories are sown.

The dominant biomedical paradigm is rooted in a patriarchal positivism; *control through rationality and separation is the overriding theme*. The biomedical model is typified by the following 10 basic premises: (a) scientific *rationality*, (b) an emphasis on *individual autonomy* rather than on family or community, (c) the *body as machine* with an emphasis on physicochemical data and on objective numerical measurement, (d) *mind–body separation* and dualism, (e) *diseases as entities*, (f) the *patient as object* and the resultant alienation of physician from patient, (g) an emphasis on the *visual*, (h) diagnosis and treatment from the *outside*, (i) *reductionism* and the seeking of *universals* (Davis-Floyd & St. John, 1998; Gordon, 1988), and (j) *separation from nature*. The everyday characteristics of the clinical medical world that follow from this model include (a) male centeredness, (b) physician centeredness, (c) specialist orientation, (d) an emphasis on credentials, (e) high value placed on memory, (f) a process orientation accentuating ritual with supervaluation on "science" and technology, (g) therapeutic activism with an emphasis on short-term results, (h) death seen as defeat,

(i) division of the clinical space into "front" (receptionists, billing clerks, and office managers) and "back" (doctors, nurses, and phlebotomists), (j) the definition, importance, and sanctity of "medical time," (k) an emphasis on patient satisfaction, (l) profit-driven system, (m) reverence for the privacy of the doctor–patient relationship, (n) disregard of ecological and international impacts, and (o) intolerance of other modalities (Davis-Floyd & St. John, 1998; Helman, 2000; Pfifferling, 1981; Stein, 1990). These are the common (and often tacit) assumptions, values, and beliefs that characterize the dominant voice of the medical clinic and that currently define the preferred boundaries of clinical research.

Biomedical culture is reinforced and sustained by its comfortable fit within the prevailing cultural norms of the United States and an elite globalizing corporate economy. These "normalizing ideologies" include control over the environment, rational determinism, future orientation, life as an ordered and continuous whole, and individualism with an emphasis on productivity, perseverance, self-determination, and self-reliance. They surface in public discourse as four "market myths," namely, that (a) growth benefits all; (b) freedom is market freedom; (c) we are *homo economicus, consumens, et dominans*; and (d) corporate and finance driven globalization is inevitable (Moe-Lobeda, 2002). The normalizing ideologies are also manifest in daily discourses about family, self, gender identity, and aging. Both patients and physicians refer to these ideologies and their associated discourses to help them restore order and normality to the disruptions of sickness (Becker, 1997).

This reigning voice of biomedicine has now been successfully corporatized in the United States, and its apparent goals, aside from amassing profits, are the elimination of pain, suffering, disease, and even death. The research tends to be product focused, hospital based, and disease oriented. In many ways, the current situation represents the triumph of commoditization and universalism with an emphasis on cost, customers, products, outcomes, effectiveness, standardization, and evidence. The reasons for focusing on outcomes are to inform choices (market approach), to provide accountability (regulatory approach), and to improve care (management approach). Despite the superficial appearance of hegemony and coherence, the voice of medicine, when enacted and witnessed, reveals many "hidden" multiplicities (Mol, 2002). Fortunately for qualitative researchers, these voices and actions are waiting to be heard and seen. If these voices are entered into the conversation as evidence, the clinical research space is expanded, dominant paradigms are challenged, and hope is reimagined.

Successfully entering the biomedical world as a qualitative clinical researcher requires a many-eyed *model of mediation*. Enter as eye jugglers (Frey, 1994) with multiple perspectives. This qualitative clinical model of mediation features the following 10 premises:

1. Center yourself in the *clinical world*, that is, in the eye of the storm.

2. Focus on the *questions* that dawn there.

3. Assume *both/and.* Acknowledge what is of value in biomedicine *and* highlight what is missing—what is silent, invisible, or ignored. Expand on the already existent tension between care and competence (Good & Good, 1993). Hold quantitative objectivisms in one hand and qualitative revelations in the other.

4. Follow a *natural history* path that characterized the early history of Western medicine and that is still an important aspect of primary health care (Harris, 1989).

5. Be *participatory.* Include patients and clinicians in your inquiry work.

6. Preserve and celebrate *anomaly,* that is, the discoveries and data that do not fit. Anomalies are levers for transformation.

7. Allow "truth" to be *emergent* and not preconceived, defensive, or forceful.

8. Respect the plea for *clinical action* and the perceived need for coherence voiced by nearly all participants in the clinical world.

9. Practice *humility, generosity,* and *patience.* This will enable everything else.

10. Refuse *silence* when oppression is evident or exposed. Practice testimony (Frank, 1995).

Qualitative clinical researchers bring several powerful perspectives to the clinical encounter that help surface the unseen and unheard and also add depth to what is already present. These include understanding disease as a cultural construction (Berger & Luckmann, 1967); possessing knowledge of additional medical models such as the biopsychosocial and humanistic models (Engels, 1977; Smith, 1996), the holistic model (Gordon, 1996; Weil, 1988), homeopathy (Swayne, 1998), and non-Western models that include traditional Chinese (Beinfield & Korngold, 1991), Ayurvedic (Sharma & Clark, 1998), and shamanism (Drury, 1996); and recognizing the face and importance of spirituality in human life. Qualitative researchers also perceive that the therapeutic or healing process occurs not only in the clinical moment but also in everyday life between clinical events. Thus, the study of everyday life offers additional perspectives, that is, additional voices to the research space being created at ground level. Carrying the staff of your many-eyed model of mediation, you are ready to enter the clinic.

The clinic[2] is a public sanctuary for the voicing of trouble and the dispensing of relief. Each clinic participant crafts meaning out of the "facts" and "feelings" inherent in each clinical encounter and seeks to weave a comforting cloth of *support.* Jocelyn and her family come and meet their clinician and his staff at the clinic. All of these participants' past ghosts—the emotional, physical, conceptual, sociocultural, and spiritual contingencies—and the competing demands of their presents and the hopes and fears for their futures are brought into the clinic. This is the real world of clinical practice involving intentions, meanings, intersubjectivity, values, personal knowledge, power, and ethics. Yet most published clinical research still consists of observational epidemiology (Feinstein, 1985; Kelsey, Thompson, & Evans, 1986; Sackett, 1991;

Stevens, Abrams, Brazier, Fitzpatrick, & Lilford, 2001) and clinical trial designs (Meinert, 1986; Pocock, 1983). These studies involve separating the variables of interest from their local everyday milieu, entering them into a controlled research environment, and then trying to fit the results back into the original context. For example, Jocelyn's clinician is aware of randomized controlled trials demonstrating clinical efficacy for short-term bed rest in patients with back pain (Deyo, Diehl, & Rosenthal, 1986; Wiesel et al., 1980). But the practitioner encounters difficulty in applying this information to the particular back pain and disability experienced by Jocelyn. The pieces of evidence needed to inform this encounter are many. Ideally, the clinical participants will study themselves and, thus, challenge their own situated knowledges and empower their own transformations. This requires bringing qualitative methods to the clinical experience. Let us expand the EBM research space.

Expanding Evidence-Based Medicine

EBM is the new wonder child in clinical care and clinical research. The premise is that individual clinical expertise must be integrated "with the best research evidence . . . and patient values" (Sackett, Straus, Richardson, Rosenberg, & Haynes, 2000, p. 1). Randomized clinical trials (RCTs) and meta-analyses (systematic reviews of multiple RCTs) are considered the best external evidence when asking questions about therapeutic interventions. An international group of clinicians, methodologists, and consumers has formed the Cochrane Collaboration as a means of facilitating the collection, implementation, and dissemination of such systematic reviews (Fullerton-Smith, 1995). The group has created a Cochrane Library that is available on CD, on the Internet, and in secondary publications through the *British Medical Journal*. Major initiatives are under way to ensure that all physicians, especially at the primary care level, use this evidence to guide their clinical decision making (Shaughnessy, Slawson, & Bennett, 1994; Slawson, Shaughnessy, & Bennett, 1994). The proliferation of clinical practice guidelines is one result of these initiatives. Another result is the relative reduced value of qualitative studies. But EBM actually offers qualitative clinical investigators multiple opportunities for entering, expanding, challenging, and adding variety and honesty to this space. There is so much *missing evidence*!

The double-blind (closed) RCT has high internal validity but dubious external validity and very little information about *context* or *ecological consequences* (Glasgow, Lichtenstein, & Marcus, 2003). Read any RCT report, and the only voice you hear is the cold sound of the intervention and faint echoes of the investigator's biases. The cacophonous music of patients, clinicians, insurance companies, lawyers, government regulatory bodies, consumer interest groups, animals and habitats, community agencies, office staff, corporate interests, and family turmoil is mute. Local politics and contradictory demands become the sound of thin hush. There is also little research about the *individual clinical expertise* side of the EBM equation and about the associated areas of relationship dynamics, communication, and patient preference. There is much to be learned about how patients and clinicians actually implement "best evidence." How is the evidence incorporated into patients' and communities' life stories? In addition, there are many gray zones of clinical practice where the evidence about competing clinical options is incomplete or contradictory (Naylor, 1995). What constitutes evidence, anyway (Morse et al., 2001)? Who creates it, defines it, and judges it? Trouble the waters of EBM certainty. Here are openings for clinical researchers. We can enter the EBM and RCT space and expand and challenge its vision.

We recommend replacing the metaphor of "gold standard" with a metaphor of "ancient forest standard" that needs to include qualitative methods along with the RCT. In addition to those areas already noted, qualitative methods can help to formalize the learning curve, test theory, inform hypothesis testing and future work, and enhance the transferability of the clinical trial into clinical practice. "Gold standard" suggests a singular, immutable, and universal truth, whereas "ancient forest standard" suggests diversity, dynamic complexity, and contingent multiple perspectives. We propose conceptualizing a multimethod RCT as a double-stranded helix of DNA—a *double helix trial design* (Miller, Crabtree, Duffy, Epstein, & Stange, 2003). On one strand are qualitative methods addressing issues of context, meaning, power, and complexity, and on the other strand are quantitative methods providing measurement and a focused anchor. The two strands are connected by the research questions. The qualitative and quantitative strands twist and spiral around the questions in an ongoing interaction, creating codes of understanding that get expressed in better clinical care. If the qualitative strand maintains methodological integrity and interpretive relativism and stays connected to the experiences informing the research questions, the double helix and its bonds might even experience breakage and mutation and transformation beyond postpositivism.

We hope that clinical researchers will seek out those doing clinical trials on symptom management, treatments, clinical process, and community interventions and will advocate for adding the qualitative strand. For example, if a gastroenterologist at your local hospital or academic medical center is planning or conducting an RCT concerning a new treatment option for GERD, you could offer to meet and propose adding a qualitative arm to the study with the intent of exploring any of several possible questions. How do patients understand and incorporate the diagnosis into their life stories? How do they experience the treatment? What is the impact on their quality of life, their work, their sexual activity, their family and social relations, their involvement in civic affairs, their sense of self, and their fears and desires? How does the study affect the researchers? This work will help to identify new outcomes that transpose the emphasis on individual cure and elimination of pain and disease toward care, growth, quality of life, healthier relationships, and more sustainable communities and ecosystems. Nonetheless, a double helix trial design is not adequate for assessing ecological consequences of interventions; this requires more longitudinal, mixed method, and case study designs.

Examples showing the way toward double helix trial designs already exist. Jolly, Bradley, Sharp, Smith, and Mant (1998), using RCT technology, tested a nurse-led intervention to help patients surviving heart attacks maintain a rehabilitation program and improve health habits. The quantitative RCT strand yielded statistically insignificant results; fortunately, Wiles (1998) had also conducted a qualitative depth interview study with 25 of the participants at 2 weeks and 5 months during the trial and uncovered several clinically valuable findings. At 2 weeks, most of the patients trusted the official accounts of what had happened and what needed to be done to prevent future problems. By 5 months, most of the patients had lost that trust because the official accounts had not adequately addressed the experienced random nature of heart attacks, the severity, and the level of recovery. Many of the patients perceived survival to mean that their heart attacks were mild, and because the doctors had reassured them that everything would be normal in 6 weeks, the patients assumed that they could return to their original "normal" lifestyles by that time. Another example of the double helix design for RCTs concerns smoking cessation interventions and is found in the work of Willms and Wilson at McMaster University. They learned that the meanings that patients attributed to their cigarettes were more influential in stopping smoking than were counseling and the use of nicotine gum (Willms, 1991; Willms et al., 1990; Wilson et al., 1988). Let us also join in opening the imagination inside the genome with qualitative questions and approaches (Finkler, 2000).

What are the clinically grounded questions that serve as windows for opening imagination at ground level? Clinicians and patients seeking *support* in the health care setting confront four fundamental questions of clinical praxis. First, what is going on with our *bodies?* Second, what is happening with our *lives?* Third, who has what *power?* Fourth, what are the complex *relationships* among our bodies, our lives, our ecological context, and power? These four questions also mirror the methods of numeracy, literacy, policy, and "ecolacy" (i.e., thinking ecologically) (Hardin, 1985). Each of these questions has *emotional, physical/behavioral, conceptual/attributional, cultural/social/historical,* and *spiritual/energetic* ramifications. From the story of Jocelyn, there are body questions about support. What are the emotions of living with a fear of the long-term consequences of GERD? Is Nexium more effective than lifestyle change at preventing those consequences? How will either impact family and social bodies? What is the lived experience and meaning of GERD for patients and clinicians? What is happening in the office practice as a body that helps or hinders Jocelyn's care? There are questions concerning the support of one's life or biography. Do explanatory models of GERD relate to the experience and outcome of risk? How does one's self-concept relate to GERD and response to Nexium? What are patients' and clinicians' hopes, despairs, fears, and insecurities concerning GERD? How does past experience connect to the immediate experience of GERD or participation in a clinical trial? There are questions of power about how people are supported. What is happening when patients with GERD present to clinicians in different organizational contexts of care? How is emotional distress surfaced or suppressed? What patterns exist in these different settings? Who influences whom? How is the power of the patient or clinician undermined or enhanced (Fahy & Smith, 1999)? What are the local politics? There are questions about the support of relationships. What actions in the clinical encounter enhance family relationships? How do the individuals, the families, and the clinic function as complex adaptive systems? How do the illness and its care relate to the local ecology? Many of these questions are addressed adequately only if qualitative methods enter into the clinical research space and we look toward an ancient forest standard.

This is the evidence needed! We can apply these four question categories to the critically important issues of the next decade such as the globalization of biomedicine, rationing and cost, biotechnology and genetic products, and the often conflicted landscape where alternative medicine and biomedicine meet. How does rationing affect our bodies? What are the emotional, physical, conceptual, social, and spiritual consequences? The same questions can be asked of the many new (and old) products of biotechnology. What is the impact on our lives? Where is the power, and how is it used and resisted? What are the relationships and complex systems that are affected and through which the technology is deployed? What are the unanticipated consequences? How do patients decide about therapies? How do they juggle seeing their bodies as both garden and machine? What other metaphors are used, and when and how do they change outcomes? The questions are infinite and challenging. Primary care, at its core, is a context-dependent craft. EBM lacks context in its current form; it cries out for qualitative methods and alternative paradigms. Let us get to work!

Democratizing Knowledge

Entering biomedicine and working to expand and change the EBM space also holds great risk for qualitative clinical researchers being co-opted by the dominant paradigm that they seek to transform; thus, there is a need for democratizing knowledge. The assumption is that the more everyone and everything potentially affected by any given knowledge and its associated technologies and actions has decision-making influence and involvement in the production of that knowledge, the less likely the research will be co-opted by any single power. Participatory research approaches, supported by using a participatory wheel of inquiry and its four ways of knowing, valuing variation and improvisation, applying the precautionary principle, and pursuing slow knowledge, are proposed keys to democratizing knowledge and opening the clinical research space above ground to transformational hope.

Participatory research approaches all share the characteristics of collaboration between the researcher and the researched, a reciprocal process whereby each party educates the other, and the intent to create local knowledge for improving the conditions and quality of life (Macaulay et al., 1998; Small, 1995; Thesen & Kuzel, 1999). Participatory research promotes the voices of communities in identifying health issues and helps to ensure that social, cultural, economic, and ecological conditions are included (Jason, Keys, Suarez-Balcazar, Taylor, & Davis, 2004). It also provides another entry into challenging and transforming the research space and brings us around, full circle, to the research questions. We propose that clinical researchers investigate questions emerging from the clinical experience with the clinical participants, pay attention to and reveal any underlying values and assumptions, and direct the results toward clinical participants and policymakers. This refocuses the gaze of clinical research onto the clinical experience and redefines its boundaries as the answer to three questions, namely "Whose question is it?," "Are hidden assumptions of the clinical world revealed?," and "For whom are the research results intended?" (i.e., who are the stakeholders or audiences?). Clinical researchers share ownership of the research with clinical participants, thereby undermining the patriarchal bias of the dominant paradigm and opening its assumptions to investigation. This is the situated knowledge, the "somewhere in particular" (Haraway, 1991, p. 196), where space is created to find a larger and more inclusive vision of clinical research. The opportunity is created to redefine the meaning of and responsibilities for health, to value indigenous practices and knowledge systems, to demystify science and technology, and to expand the research capacity of communities (Tandon, 1996). Patients and clinicians are invited to explore personal and/or each other's questions and concerns with whatever methods and paradigms are necessary.

Participatory approaches bring a diverse group of people and ideas and ways of knowing into a common space that challenges the traditional boundaries of science. Figure 11.1, a *participatory wheel of inquiry* derived from the work of Wilber (1996) and Schumacher (1977), represents a map for understanding and working with this diversity of traditions, experiences, and associated methods (Stange, Miller, & McWhinney, 2001), and the six research styles noted earlier. This integrative framework represents human knowledge about the natural world in four quadrants, with the horizontal axis representing inner and outer reality and the vertical axis representing individual and collective knowledge. The right-hand quadrants are the world as seen by materialist science—the view from outside. This is the domain of third-person "It" and "Its" knowledge based on detached objective observation. The left-hand quadrants are the inner or subjective aspects of reality—the domain of "I" and "We" knowledge. The left is concerned with meaning, that is, with beauty and goodness. The right is concerned with physical laws. The multiple ways of knowing and associated traditions and methods may be classified within this grid (for a similar model, see Kemmis & McTaggart, 2003). For example, both of the right-hand quadrants, knowledge of external physical and social reality, are studied using experimental and social science and epidemiological survey methods and are based primarily on the traditional biomedical paradigm and associated reductionist assumptions of materialist inquiry.

For the domains of knowledge needed for personalized, prioritized, and integrated clinical care, a more participatory and "subjective" way of knowing based on intimate involvement with self and other is required. The interior-focused quadrants on the left represent such complementary knowledge based on reflective participation. The left

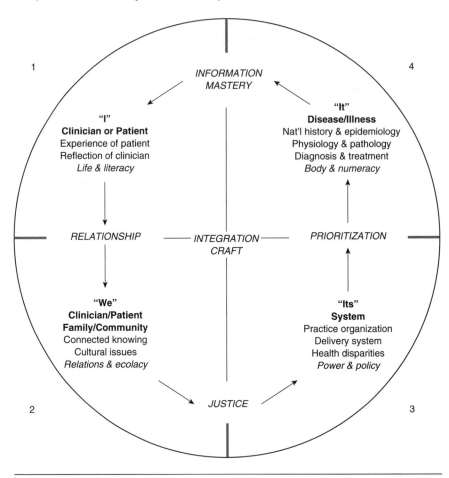

Figure 11.1. A Participatory Wheel of Inquiry

upper quadrant, "I" knowledge, refers to wisdom gained through the individual accumulation of particular experiences—reflection on clinical practice, diaries and journals, and philosophical methods. The left lower quadrant, "We" knowledge, is exemplified by the theoretical work of Lucy Candib. Candib (1995) demonstrated the connections among the developing feminist literature on ways of knowing, the general practice traditions, and the emerging literature on qualitative research and the narrative mode of thought. She argued effectively for the importance of a "connected knowing" based on personal experiences and relationships that seek to discover how the other perceives the world. Connected knowing is rooted in empathy and believability and is interested in context, relationship, and time. This way of knowing usually uses qualitative ("field" style) and participatory research strategies.

At the intersection of the four quadrants is the clinical craft or practice being informed by the multiple modes of inquiry being enacted within a participatory framework. As a means of keeping the wheel of inquiry turning and the participatory space open, it is helpful to emphasize and value *variation* and *improvisation* over standardization. Emerging understandings from complexity science and ecological science strongly suggest that "nature" and life thrive on variation and improvisation (Capra, 1996, 2002). The conventional metaphor of the "body as machine" reflects the dangers inherent in standardization. Too many voices are silenced. The participatory wheel turns within a sphere of interpretive relativism (see Peräkylä, Volume 3, Chapter 11). A more robust metaphor, one that embraces all four quadrants of human knowledge and values variation, is the "body as organism in ecological context." This metaphor contains the seeds from which a democratized knowledge and clinical practice can grow. They will not grow, however, unless the ground is fertile and not poisoned by the privatized knowledge and products of global corporations.

Much current clinical research is the hand inside the glove of corporate interests and operates on a "first act until harm proven" principle, where proven usually means establishing a direct cause-and-effect relationship. The result is the continued spread of chemical toxins, greenhouse gases, and cigarettes until such nearly impossible proof appears and convinces everyone. Older wisdom recommended "first do no harm." A current form of this wisdom, the *precautionary principle* (Raffensperger, Tickner, & Jackson, 1999), offers guidance consistent with better health and more participatory research spaces. The precautionary principle essentially states that in the presence of scientific uncertainty and the plausibility of harm, precautionary measures must be taken (Raffensperger, 2002). This principle shifts the burden of proof to those who advocate or wish to sell a potentially harmful action or product and must be open, informed, and democratic, including all potentially affected parties. Thus, it opens the research space to a more democratic process of knowledge generation and sharing. The precautionary principle obliges us to observe and foresee (as far as seven generations) before acting. This involves examination of a full range of alternatives, including no action. It begins with seeking to see the invisible, hear the unspeakable, and touch the untouchable. Learn to hear the stars and the trees and to talk to turtles, coyotes, and bears. Learn from children. Remember who you really were before the dominant culture silenced your deep awareness.

Participatory research approaches, supported by applying the participatory wheel of inquiry, valuing variation and improvisation, and adhering to the precautionary principle, all lead to *slow knowledge,* that is, knowledge that is consistent with the rhythms of life, sustainability, and appropriate scale (Orr, 2002). It assumes interdependence and uncertainty, and it acknowledges the absurdity and hubris of seeking perfection. Slow knowledge works with the complexities of reality rather than seeking to control them, and it accepts that some conflict and suffering are inevitable. Rather than trying to eliminate them, slow knowledge pursues means of comfort, care, reconciliation, resilience, and restoration that optimize the healthy embedded interrelationships of all life, one local place at a time. Slow knowledge shifts the focus from outcomes to the nurturing of life together. For Jocelyn and her heartburn, slow knowledge means deemphasizing the PPI until more is known about its multiple and ecological consequences. Instead, there is more emphasis on supporting Jocelyn and expanding her community of concern and on changing the social, economic, and lifestyle factors creating the conditions of GERD. This is more difficult and slower work; it is healing work. Slow knowledge is the result of a clinical research of love and not instrumental rationality. This is learning at the speed and scale where all of life can participate. It represents the democratization of knowledge. Imagine the possibilities for clinical research if government funding prioritized slow knowledge. Now, enter the world of biomedicine and work to expand the EBM space, but do so as a gardener with the tools of participatory approaches and a wheel of inquiry, valuing variation and improvisation and applying the precautionary principle as you tend the plants of slow knowledge. Theory, collaboration, and critical multiplism are additional strategies for helping do clinical research above ground.

Using Theory

The double helix RCT proposed earlier also creates an opportunity for clinical researchers to reintroduce theory into clinical research. Theory is frequently not explicitly stated in standard quantitative clinical studies. This often results in ungrounded a posteriori speculation. Qualitative data help to surface hidden theoretical assumptions and suggest new possibilities and connections. Theory helps to bridge dominant biomedical and other cultural worlds. Recent theoretical discussions among medical anthropologists, phenomenologists, semioticians, and sociologists concerning the *metaphor of the "body"* challenge biomedical assumptions about the human body and its boundaries and highlight the culturally and socially constructed aspects of the body that extend far beyond its corporeality (Csordas, 2002; Johnson, 1987; Kirmayer, 1992; Macnaghten & Urry, 2001; Martin, 1994; Scheper-Hughes & Locke, 1987; Shildrick, 1997; Strathern, 1996; Turner, 1992). There is an individual body, a social body, and a body politic. There are medical bodies, the earth as body, and communicative bodies. Bodies are imagined as flexible, leaky, castles, machines, gardens, or effervescent, and these imaginations both shape and are shaped by the social body, the body politic, and the world body. Arthur Frank, for example, described the use of storytelling as a means of restoring voice to the body (Frank, 1995). Bodily symptoms are understood as the infolding of cultural traumas into the body; as these bodies create history, the symptoms outfold into social space. Because of their complexity, social bodies (e.g., practice organizations) are often best characterized using metaphors such as "brains," "machines," "organisms," and "ugly faces" (Morgan, 1998). Qualitative methods become a primary source for hearing these stories and their associated metaphors, caring in relationships, and resisting the colonizing narrative of institutionalized medicine (Mattingly,

1998; Sandelowski, 2002). The study of bodies and their place in the production and expression of sickness and health becomes a core strategy for clinical research that enables the bridging of paradigms and opens the clinical research space while also resisting the standardization of the body as commodity.

Collaborating Across Disciplines

This opened clinical research space requires collaboration that emphasizes multiple linkages and different types of cross-disciplinary relationships. Linkages occur vertically where one moves up and drown through different levels or scales such as the molecular, individual, local, and regional levels. Linkages are also horizontal across different sectors at the same level of social organization such as medical practices, schools, and local businesses. Linkages also occur over time or at different times. Finally, there are multiple academic linkages, including those with the "public," with practitioners, with policymakers, and with research participants (Miller, 1994).

Critical Multiplism

Orchestrating this type of multimethod, cross-disciplinary research requires the skills and mind-set of a generalist researcher using a framework of critical multiplism (Coward, 1990; Miller, 1994). The skills and perspectives of the generalist researcher consist of negotiation, translation, theoretical pluralism, methodological pluralism, a community orientation, and comfort with and rootedness in clinical practices. These are successfully implemented through a critical multiplist framework. Critical multiplism assumes that multiple ways of knowing are necessary and that these options require critical thought and choice. "Multiplism" refers not only to multiple methods but also to multiple triangulation, multiple stakeholders, multiple studies, and multiple paradigms and perspectives. "Critical" refers to the critical selection of these options based on local history, the role of power and patterns of domination, and how the different methods complement each other. Six principles help to guide critical multiplists in their complex work:

1. Know why you choose to do something.

2. Preserve method and paradigm integrity.

3. Pay attention to units of analysis.

4. Remember the research questions.

5. Ensure that the strengths and weaknesses of each selected option complement each other.

6. Continually evaluate methodology throughout the study.

Critical multiplism is a particularly powerful framework for doing participatory clinical research and provides discipline as one moves within the participatory wheel of inquiry.

Revealing the many kinds of evidence requires entering the EBM space, developing cross-disciplinary collaborations, using multiple methods with a critical multiplist conceptualization, using bridging metaphors and theories such as "bodies," and often emphasizing participatory and advocacy approaches and democratizing knowledge. With these strategies, the clinical research space opens for the tools of the generalist clinical researcher. Qualitative researchers have seen and heard the stories and sufferings of Jocelyn and others like her, but they have often been retold in a language that patients and clinicians do not understand (e.g., Fisher, 1986; Fisher & Todd, 1983; Lazarus, 1988; Mishler, 1984; West, 1984; Williams, 1984). Neither clinicians nor patients know the language of "ethnomethodology," "hermeneutics," "phenomenology," "semiotics," or "interpretive interactionism." Much qualitative clinical research is published in a language and in places that benefit only selected researchers and not the patients and practitioners. Qualitative researchers have asked that clinicians join, listen to, and speak the "voice of the lifeworld" (Mishler, 1984). We ask clinical qualitative researchers to do the same, and we recommend the work of Carolyn Ellis and Arthur Frank as powerful examples of clear and moving text (Ellis, 1995; Frank, 1991).

▣ Providing the Tools and Translations

This section presents the tools and translations necessary for bringing qualitative methods and traditions into the clinical research space at ground level. It begins by comparing the qualitative *research process* with the clinical process. The nearly direct correspondence enables the clinical researcher to make qualitative methods transparent to clinicians and patients. This is followed by a brief overview of qualitative methods and how to create mixed method *research designs* in the clinical setting. Finally, we *put it all together* with an example of clinical research that uses some of the strategies discussed and share tips for writing, demonstrating credibility, and getting published.

Research Process

The clinical research space is created by focusing on the questions arising from the clinical experience and opens many possibilities for using the full range of qualitative data-gathering and analysis methods. Many of these qualitative approaches are presented elsewhere in the *Handbook* and are discussed in more detail in a text for primary care qualitative researchers (Crabtree & Miller, 1999). The challenge is to preserve the integrity of the questions and to translate qualitative collection and analysis methods into clear and jargon-free language without sacrificing the methods' integrity rooted in the soil of disciplinary conversations. A fundamental tenet of the proposed translation is that *the question and clinical context are primary; methods must adjust to the clinical setting and the clinical questions.* Interpretive social science traditionally has feared mixed methods because this usually meant treating qualitative as only a method subservient to the positivist paradigm or materialistic inquiry. We not only imagine a clinical research space where qualitative methods are empowered and where constructivist and critical/ecological paradigms are accepted but also note that it already exists. The key is to recognize the similarity between the qualitative research process and the clinical process, particularly as it presents itself in primary care.

Figure 11.2 diagrams an idealized relationship-centered clinical method proposed as a model for family medicine (Stewart et al., 1995; Tresolini, 1994). Notice that the overall method consists of four separate processes: exploring, understanding, finding common ground, and engaging in self-reflection. These four processes flow sequentially, but they all iterate with each other and the whole process usually cycles multiple times over time for any given illness episode. For example, chronic illness care will occur over a lifetime of visits, whereas an episode of ear infection may require only two visits (i.e., two iterations of the clinical cycle). The four clinical processes directly correspond to the four processes of qualitative research, and these parallel processes are illustrated in Figure 11.3. (The clinical equivalents are italicized in brackets above the research processes.)

The clinician begins by gathering data using purposeful or information-rich sampling. The clinician focuses his or her interviewing, observing, and touching around possible explanations related to the patient's presenting concern or opening story. The

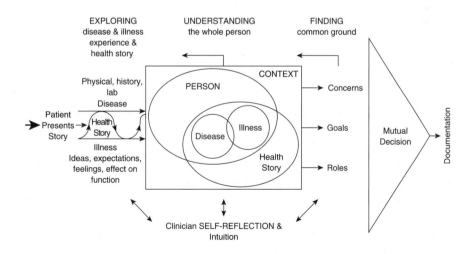

Figure 11.2.   Relationship-Centered Clinical Method

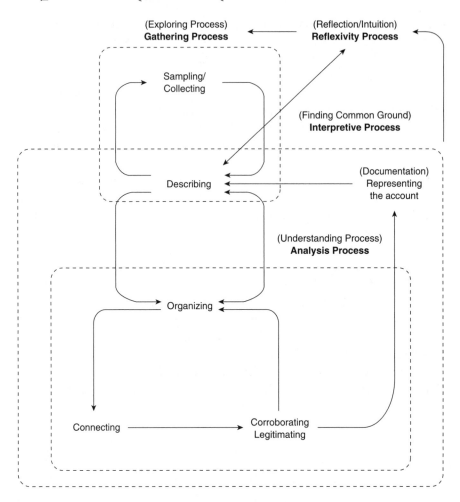

Figure 11.3.   Qualitative Research Process and Clinical Parallels

exploration seeks "disease" information following the biomedical model, but the process also searches for understanding of the patient's health story and illness experience, especially the patient's ideas, expectations, and feelings about his or her concern and its effect on everyday living. The clinician almost immediately begins to analyze the data while continuing to gather additional information. This analysis seeks to understand the patient's concern within the context of his or her lifeworld—personal, family, and community stories. This understanding is organized around sensitizing concepts, diagnostic categories, personal experience templates or scripts, and connections looked for and then corroborated against the known evidence. Using a participatory framework, the clinician periodically shares the emerging understanding with the patient (or others), and together they seek a common interpretation. Throughout this iterative process, the clinician is using self-reflection, personal feelings, and intuition to inform the gathering, analyzing, and interpreting. The visit ends when the clinician and patient agree that they have sufficient data (i.e., saturation) to implement an initial course of action. The outcome is an engaging plan for the patient and a report describing the encounter written (or dictated) by the clinician. These reports occasionally undergo peer review. This sounds like, looks like, and feels like qualitative research. However, most clinicians do not know it. Use clinical language to translate qualitative methods and standards. Let us get to work!

Finally, notice how clinical care also mirrors the double helix RCT. In both, simplified coherence for action ("disease") is in dynamic tension with personal/social/cultural complexity ("illness" and "health story") and the tension is held through the quest for care, that is, through the research questions. This is more likely when the clinical or research process is simultaneously participatory and cognizant of the power imbalances inherent in the relationships and in the greater health care system. All of the many voices must be surfaced and attention must be paid to them; we must protect the questions and prevent them from being co-opted and changed by hierarchy and the biomedical paradigm. This is the work of democratizing knowledge. Out of this fabric of relational forces, within given biocultural boundaries, are woven senses. The methods must parallel the clinical process and provide self-critique and correction. This is the intersection of doing science and reflexivity.

Research Design

Research designs in clinical research inherently require multimethod thinking and critical multiplism, with the particular combinations of data-gathering and analysis/interpretation approaches being driven by the research question and the clinical context. There are infinite possibilities for integrating qualitative and quantitative methods, with the design being created for each study and the qualitative aspects often evolving as a study progresses in response to the emerging questions. Participatory research approaches, in particular, usually involve a more emergent design process. In clinical research, research designs may be wholly qualitative (Shepherd, Hattersley, & Sparkes, 2000) or quantitative, including the use of a single method, but are increasingly combinations of these in what has been referred to as mixed methods (Borkan, 2004; Creswell, 2003; Creswell, Fetters, & Ivankova, 2004; Tashakkori & Teddlie, 1998). Clinical researchers must maintain multimethod thinking and remain free to mix and match methods as driven by particular clinically based questions.

There are many questions and contexts that require only a single method; however, single-method designs should still be considered within a multimethod context. When the investigator starts with the question and considers all possible methods before deciding that a single method is appropriate for the question, he or she is maintaining multimethod thinking. Most clinical research questions are more complex and require multiple approaches. Particular mixed method combinations of qualitative and quantitative methods are generally presented in terms of typologies of multimethod designs (Creswell, 2003; Stange, Miller, Crabtree, O'Connor, & Zyzanski, 1994). In actual practice, these typologies are too prescriptive and tend to oversimplify the complex dance of the research process. In conceptualizing a study, the clinical investigator creates a design from the full range of data collection and analysis tools, much like a child makes creations from the sticks and wheels of "Tinker Toys" or parts from a "Lego" set. There are airplanes, cars, windmills, and buildings, but they are rarely exactly alike.

One dimension of multimethod design is the longitudinal nature of the research process. Most clinical research questions are complex and multifaceted and cannot be addressed in a single study. In constructing the design, the clinical researcher is constantly balancing the desire to fully address the question with the feasibility of being able to complete the study. Narrowing the focus potentially compromises the integrity of the question, whereas trying to accomplish too much can be overwhelming and possibly not fundable. Thus, in conceptualizing study designs, the researcher may do a series of studies in a longitudinal process that fits the larger research agenda. How a design is finally put together depends on the questions and the setting. Snadden and Brown (1991) wondered how stigmatization affected adults with asthma. Answering this question required two steps. First, they identified patients with asthma who felt that they were stigmatized, and then they explored the perceived effect of that stigmatization on the patients' lives. The design solved these issues by initially using a questionnaire measuring attitudes concerning asthma to identify respondents reporting high levels of stigma. These individuals were then interviewed using interpretive interview and analysis methods.

Multiple methods can also be directly integrated within a single study in a number of ways. For example, sometimes it may be helpful to conduct two independent studies concurrently on the same study population and then to converge the results. This is the approach recommended for the double helix RCT (Wiles, 1998; Willms, 1991). Another widely used approach to designing multimethod research is to integrate multiple methods more intimately within a single research study. For example, Borkan, Quirk, and Sullivan (1991) noticed that breaking a hip was often a turning point toward death for many elderly patients. They puzzled about what distinguished those persons from others who had recovered with minimal complications. The research literature did not reveal any obvious traditional biomedical factors. They wondered whether patients' stories about the fractures had any connection with the outcomes. They used an epidemiological cross-sectional design with a sample of hospitalized elderly patients with hip fractures. Multiple biomedical indicators were measured as independent variables along with rehabilitation outcome measures as the dependent variable. There was nothing unusual here, and this design would ensure acceptance by the intended clinical audience. What distinguishes this study is that the researchers also conducted depth interviews with each patient concerning how he or she understood the hip fracture within his or her life story. Several distinguishable injury narratives emerged. These were coded and entered as another independent variable in the statistical outcome modeling. The narrative type was the most powerful predictor of rehabilitation outcome.

When discussing qualitative research design with clinicians and patients, we have simplified the jargon. The data-gathering methods are divided into interviewing, observing, and reviewing documents (including videotapes). Interviews are further subdivided into depth, focus group, and ethnographic (or key informant) (Mitchell, 1998). Participant observation is described as either short term or prolonged. Instead of using the jargon of grounded theory, phenomenology, ethnography, and hermeneutics, we frame the many traditions and techniques of analysis as a "dance of interpretation" in which three idealized organizing styles—immersion/crystallization, editing, and template (for details, see Figure 11.4 and Miller & Crabtree, 1999a)—promote the dynamic, creative, iterative, yet disciplined craft of qualitative interpretation. All three organizing styles may be used at some time during the different gathering/interpreting iterations of a particular research project.

Putting It All Together

To further demonstrate the use of a multimethod framework, we provide an overview of a longitudinal series of four federally funded studies focusing on family medicine patterns of care and change (Crabtree, Miller, Aita, Flocke, & Stange, 1998; Crabtree, Miller, & Stange, 2001; Goodwin et al., 2001; Stange et al., 1998). These studies all were funded separately by large federal grants, providing evidence of wider acceptance of the multimethod approach (for more details on funding qualitative research, see Saukko, Volume 1, Chapter 13).

The National Cancer Institute funded the Direct Observation of Primary Care (DOPC) study. The DOPC study was designed to illuminate the "black box" of clinical practice by describing patient visits to family physicians in community practices with a special emphasis on the delivery of preventive health services. This largely quantitative cross-sectional descriptive study focused on the content and context of the outpatient visit. Data were obtained through the direct observation of patient visits using a variation of the highly structured Davis Observation Code (Callahan & Bertakis, 1991) along with checklists of the patient visit, patient exit questionnaires, medical record reviews, billing data abstractions, and physician questionnaires. To supplement and enhance these quantitative data, research nurses dictated observational field notes immediately after each visit to provide richer descriptions of the variables under study. This ethnographic data were impressionistic and focused on describing the practice in terms of key features such as the practice location, office relationships, and how the practice functioned. These data eventually totaled more than 2,000 pages of

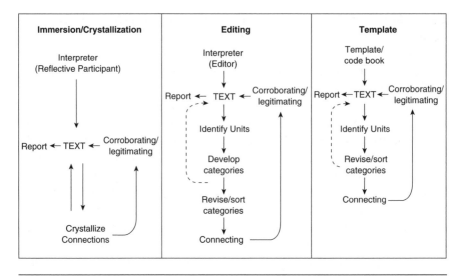

Figure 11.4. Diagrammatic Representation of Different Organizing Styles of Analysis

Source: Crabtree and Miller (1999).

field notes from observation of 138 physicians in 84 different family medicine offices. The quantitative descriptions provided valuable insights into the overall content of family medicine (Stange et al., 1998) as well as into many other facets of family medicine (see the May 1998 issue of the *Journal of Family Practice*). The qualitative field notes identified a long list of key features that appear to be important for understanding how practices operate on a day-to-day basis, particularly in the delivery of preventive services (Crabtree et al., 1998). The qualitative data were also used to formulate a new theoretical model of practice organization based on complexity theory that now provides the basis for subsequent federally funded studies (Miller, Crabtree, McDaniel, & Stange, 1998).

The Prevention and Competing Demands in Primary Care (P&CD) study was funded by the Agency for Healthcare Research and Quality as a follow-up to the DOPC study to provide a more in-depth look at how the practice and the people in the practice worked together. In the P&CD study, 18 practices were purposefully selected to include some that were doing really well in delivering preventive services and others that were doing less well. Trained observers spent weeks in each practice observing, taking detailed notes about how the organization functioned, and talking to people using key informant and depth interviews. They observed 30 encounters with each clinician and dictated field notes in the form of a chronology of what went on during the encounters. This largely qualitative study helped to refine the theoretical model developed in the DOPC study (Miller, McDaniel, Crabtree, & Stange, 2001).

The DOPC and P&CD studies directly challenged the ideology of standardization and commodification of health care. Multiple analyses elucidated the tremendous variation that exists in practice organization and clinical care. Much of this variation was beneficial along with some problematic variation. Thus, we see clinicians prioritizing care in ongoing continuous relationships with patients (Flocke, Miller, & Crabtree, 2002) and opportunistically tailoring tobacco counseling (Jaen et al., 2001) while at the same time overprescribing antibiotics for upper respiratory infections (Scott et al., 2001) or failing to manage obvious depression (Robinson et al., 2001). Practices themselves, as complex organizations, exhibited much variation, including how they hire and use staff (Aita et al., 2001) or respond to hospital ownership (Tallia et al., 2003). Using concepts from family systems (McGoldrick, Gerson, & Shellenberger, 1999), it was possible to identify different ways in which practices organize themselves and to diagram patterns of communication in a "practice genogram" (McIlvain, Crabtree, Medder, Stange, & Miller, 1998). Urban practices were very different from rural practices, which in turn were very different from suburban practices (Pol, Rouse, Zyzanski, Rasmussen, & Crabtree, 2001). The larger health care system also created variation and surprise. For example, 24% of patients in managed care had to change their physicians during a 2-year period in the DOPC study, creating discontinuity in the care of many patients (Flocke, Stange, & Zyzanski, 1997).

Based on insights from the DOPC and P&CD studies, we developed an organizational change model for tailoring interventions to the local context that incorporated characteristics of patients, clinicians, the clinical encounter, the practice, the community, and the larger health system. This model was based on our emerging understanding of complexity theory and was initially tested in a National Cancer Institute–funded clinical trial called the Study to Enhance Prevention by Understanding Practice (STEP-UP). The STEP-UP intervention randomized 80 practices in Ohio and used an initial 2- to 5-day mixed methods assessment of the practice to provide insights for tailoring feedback to the practice (an example of a double helix trial design). Based on the assessment, a facilitator would go back to the practice, show the practitioners their genogram, give them a summary report, and then negotiate a prevention-oriented intervention. The STEP-UP intervention resulted in a significant enhancement in the delivery of global preventive services in the intervention practices (as opposed to the control practices) over a 12-month period, a change that has been sustained for more than 3 years after the intervention (Goodwin et al., 2001).

An analysis of the qualitative field notes recorded during the STEP-UP intervention was used to develop a refined model of organizational change that seeks to stimulate self-reflective and ongoing learning in practices. This analysis, which focused on discovering why the intervention worked in some places and not in others, led to the National Heart, Lung, and Blood Institute (NHLBI)–funded Using Learning Teams for Reflective Adaptation (ULTRA) study. The ULTRA study is a collaborative participatory research study using a double helix design. In this study, an initial assessment of the organization by means of a 2-week multimethod assessment process (MAP) is used to stimulate a reflective adaptation process (RAP), which is an iterative team-building process combining assessment feedback with facilitation of learning teams in the practice. Patients are required as participants on these teams. The hypothesis underlying the ULTRA study is that change in overall practice processes will simultaneously affect a wide range of outcomes, including the organizational culture and clinical care such as smoking cessation counseling and the management of chronic illnesses (e.g., hyperlipidemia, hypertension, diabetes, asthma).

A research design has evolved from this series of studies that might best be characterized as an in-depth comparative case study of family medicine offices using ethnographic techniques and a multimethod participatory clinical trial using complexity theory to guide an interventional strategy. The potential for multisite, multimethod collaborative studies at ground level is demonstrated in the progression from a multimethod observational study (DOPC) to an in-depth comparative case study (P&CD), which then led to an intervention trial that is grounded in insights from the previous work (STEP-UP). This finally resulted in a participatory collaboration with practices and patients (ULTRA).

An important aspect of all of these studies is their use of a collaborative research team (Miller, 1994). The team includes physicians, nurses, epidemiologists, statisticians, psychologists, anthropologists, economists, and sociologists. We design the study together, meet frequently during the study to review the qualitative data and make adjustments to the study, and do intensive reflexivity work (Barry, Britten, Barber, Bradley, & Stevenson, 1999). This long-term collaborative teamwork has enabled the group to expand its use of qualitative methods and its operating paradigms.

Writing Strategies

There are some specific writing strategies that facilitate communication of and receptivity to qualitative clinical research (Richardson, 1990; Wolcott, 1990). The most important is *avoiding jargon* and keeping language simple and concrete. Using typologies and continua as rhetorical frames is helpful because these initially appear to be rational and measurable—qualities valued by traditional clinical researchers. Interpretive aspects can be maintained by emphasizing cultural/historical and/or inductive construction and by grounding in lived clinical experience. It is also useful to communicate either in the biomedically dominant visual mode, through the use of tables, charts, diagrams, and data matrices, or through the clinically familiar narrative mode of case reports. Narrative reports often take the form of first-person voice pathographies (Hawkins, 1993) or first-person accounts by physicians of their patient encounters (Loxterkamp, 1997; Sacks, 1984). The strategy of authoethnography, where the voice of the researcher as deeply personal subject is explicitly woven into the context of the social issues being researched, also resonates with the clinical narrative mode (Ellingson, 1998; Ellis & Bochner, 1996).

The dominant audience for clinical research perceives the issues of "validity," "reliability," and "generalizability" as scientific fundamentalist dogma resulting in heightened concerns about bias. The collaborative multimethod study of Daly and McDonald (1992) described the impact of echocardiography on patients' perceptions of self. Their story described how difficult it can be to till the soil: "The biggest problem was that physicians saw qualitative research methods as . . . prone to bias. Highly structured methods of analyzing qualitative data were effectively used . . . and are probably necessary for 'covering one's back' in multidisciplinary teams" (p. 416). They presented strategies for qualitative researchers to translate their insights and build tornado-proof hedges around their fields. The methodological guidelines for quantitative methods are not relevant for qualitative clinical researchers. The criteria for qualitative clinical research can be translated for clinical audiences in the form of telling methodologically, rhetorically, and clinically convincing stories.

Methodologically convincing stories answer the question, "How was the research designed and done?" It is important to make explicit how and why the research design, sampling strategies, and data collection and analysis techniques fit the question and research context as discussed earlier in this chapter. It is helpful to mention when the research design is cross-sectional, prospective, case–control, or similar to some other design from observational epidemiology (Ward, 1993). Specific techniques such as triangulation, member checking, and searching for disconfirming evidence should also be addressed when applicable (Malterud, 2001a, 2001b).

Relationship is essential to the clinical experience. Kahn (1993) proposed that a language of relationship be used to judge the methodological adequacy of clinical qualitative research. A methodologically convincing story addresses three different relationships: (a) the investigator's *relationship with informants*, noting how each influences the other during the research process; (b) the *relationship with the data*, particularly the circularity or iterative aspects of the research experience; and (c) the *relationship with the readers*, so that the researcher's authorial intent is clear.

One popular approach to helping primary care clinicians become "information masters" involves teaching them to recognize patient-oriented evidence that matters (POEMS) (Slawson et al., 1994). The first step is to scan an article's abstract and determine whether the results relate to outcomes that are common or important in everyday clinical practice and matter to patients and whether the results would potentially change what you currently do in practice. If the answers are yes, then the second step is to read the article and decide whether the conclusions are methodologically sound. There are simple one-page checklists for quantitative studies. The following, in an effort to enhance accessibility and quality while avoiding the checklist format that we condemned earlier, was developed by the authors and is currently being used for evaluating qualitative articles:

1. Is the method appropriate for the question?

2. Is the sampling adequate and information rich?

3. Is the research process iterative?

4. Is the interpretive process thorough and clearly described?

5. Is reflexivity addressed?

We hope that by using a question format and leaving space for interpretation, there is both sufficient flexibility for creativity and sufficient guidance for assurance of quality. A methodologically convincing story is not one that pleases a positivist or a postpositivist; rather, it is one that pleases qualitative research peers, clinicians, and patients. Thus, the use of explicit guidelines and checklists is problematic and must be tempered with a large dose of flexibility so as not to put off the doing of qualitative research (Chapple & Rogers, 1998). The preceding approach is consistent with Altheide and Johnson's (1998) idea of "validity-as-reflexive-accounting," where the researcher or team, the sense-making processes, and the question or topic are in interaction with a focus on how meanings are constructed. This is also a good description of the validity process in clinical care.

A *rhetorically convincing story* answers the question, "How believable is this text?" The readers are drawn into the story and begin imagining that the story is about them. When this occurs, the conclusions make more sense for the readers. The language and style of writing need to be familiar to the audience. Some of the quotations and observations selected to illustrate interpretations also need to reflect the readers' experience and/or values. A rhetorically convincing story assures the readers that you have "walked in their shoes." Bunge (1961) reviewed some of the features that characterize a believable story.

A *clinically convincing story* answers the questions, "Does this study make clinical sense?" and "How does this study help in the care of patients?" (Giacomini & Cook, 2000) A story is clinically convincing if it successfully addresses three features that are important in the clinical research space. The *question* must matter to clinical participants, and the results must specifically address that question. This usually means that attention is directed to the pragmatic intervention and policy focus of the clinical world. The *audience* or stakeholders are also clinical participants for whom the results matter, and this should be obvious in the text. Finally, the text reveals *assumptions* about the physical/behavioral, social/emotional, cultural/historical, and/or spiritual aspects of clinical participants' bodies, lives, and/or power. It is made clear to the readers who benefits most from the story.

A clinically convincing story is also one that enriches the possibilities for a narrative medicine (Brody, 2003; Greenhalgh & Hurwitz, 1998). In narrative-based care, the clinician views his or her primary task as partnering with the patient to create new stories from the broken ones. This involves learning the patient's language and discovering the life contexts and plans that make sense of it (Launer, 2002). This sounds like good clinical research. When possible, articulate this connection, especially in the discussion section of a manuscript. The work of Frank (1995) and his concepts of restitution, quest, and chaos narratives cited earlier are also quite relevant here.

Qualitative clinical research is convincing if the methods are appropriate for the question and the investigator's relationship with informants, data, and audience are clearly addressed; if the audience recognizes itself in the findings; and if the question and results matter to clinical participants. All of these criteria are more easily satisfied if a collaborative team does the research. When this team includes clinical participants, it creates a community of discourse where conversations at ground level can grow (Denz-Penhey & Murdoch, 1993).

Even when the writing is clear and the results are convincing, it is still a challenge to find a publishing venue. Fortunately, the options are improving. Qualitative clinical research is widely presented and published in primary care internal medicine and family medicine, nursing, social work, and educational research books and journals. Much of this success over the past two decades has been due to specific efforts to translate and introduce qualitative research in workshops within professional meetings, through newsletters, and through methods' publications emphasizing clinical usefulness. Qualitative clinical research is now appearing in clinical journals, especially in the field of primary care. *Qualitative Health Research; Culture, Medicine, and Psychiatry; Health;* and *Social Science and Medicine* serve as bridge-building publications with a nearly exclusive or significant emphasis on qualitative clinical research. All of the primary care journals have reviewers trained in qualitative research and publish qualitative studies. The *Annals of Family Medicine* provides space on its Web site to "publish" supplementary materials, thereby making it possible to condense articles into the space requirements of medical journals. The next steps are to improve ways of communicating results to the patient population and international community. The use of the Web may become a valuable means of presenting findings to patients and the broader community.

◼ CLINICAL RESEARCH BELOW GROUND

> *Connections are made slowly, sometimes they grow underground. You cannot tell always by looking what is happening. More than half a tree is spread out in the soil under your feet. Penetrate quietly as the earthworm that blows no trumpet.*
>
> —Continuation of Marge Piercy's
> "The Seven of Pentacles"

Still, the tornado approaches. When it will arrive, within our generation's lifetime or that of our grandchildren, is difficult to predict. What we believe is that the current destruction of the earth's life support systems, the widening gap between the rich and the poor, and all of the powers and structures that currently maintain this oppression of our earth community are ultimately unsustainable and self-destructive. This is, in our opinion, the most important clinical and health problem for our time. Acknowledging this, how do we, as individuals and clinical researchers, respond? We are not sure. We are not confident that the clinical research above ground is sufficient to bring about the necessary change. We are morally uncomfortable with leaving that change to others. In this section, we invite you into our conversation underground— into our own personal struggles, from positions of power, to maintain integrity and to be citizens working for the democracy and health of all life. Join with us, in solidarity as clinical researchers and as lovers of the earth, on our burrowing toward wholeness. This is "ecological identity" work—using direct experience with nature and others "as a framework for personal decisions, professional choices, political actions, and spiritual inquiry" (Thomashow, 1996, p. xiii). Our name for this pilgrimage below ground is *solidarity research.*

Clinical research above ground is opportunistic, challenging, helpful, and protective. It is public; it complicates and addresses important clinical questions and works for change. It is about career, making a living, getting published, holding positions of power, and openly challenging power. It seeks to mix methods and create new relationships, to surface the hidden, and to protect the miracle of life (Berry, 2000) where possible. These efforts at optimizing the ability to function within a dangerously broken system are critically important, and (it seems to us) they will not be enough. The research plants that bloom in the sunshine, our works above ground, are only as healthy as the roots and rhizomes that sustain us. What supports our personal integrity and wholeness, keeps our senses open to the cries of suffering and alert to hidden danger, nourishes our vision and deep interdependence, and helps us to image and experience health as membership (Berry, 2000)? We suggest that these tasks call for clinical research below ground. This could be a solidarity research that nourishes the work above ground, tenaciously grounds us to our earth community (Rasmussen, 1996), and ensures an adequate soil and seed for life before and after the tornado passes.

Solidarity research might be the proactive work building and preparing for the future. This could be our night work. Maybe this is where we join with resistance movements and new alternative structures arising around the world and, using our research skills, we work, learn, and grow with them to create a life that can emerge before and after the tornado (Perlas, 2000). This is solidarity research. The name derives from the cooperative economics in Brazil connecting local alternatives together to create networks of resistance to elite corporate globalization that is called *economia solidária,* that is, solidarity economics. We propose that solidarity research represents inquiry and learning that increase solidarity with our selves as whole persons and increase solidarity with our earth community and with other communities of resistance. It is generating better questions for our above ground research. It is story sharing. It is relationships and building community. It is mysticism—the prayer, music, and poetry that enliven community and give it spirit. It is growing love.

Foundational sources for our current understanding and development of solidarity research include the work of Paulo Freire, Ivan Illich, and Vandana Shiva. Freire (1970) emphasized the importance of words as praxis—as part of an action/reflection cycle—and of working directly with the oppressed through "dialogics" with the goals of democratizing culture and raising critical consciousness or *conscientização*. We must "learn how and what the people know." We must "learn with the oppressed the indispensable ropes of their resistance" (Freire, 1998, p. 273). Illich (1970, 1976) highlighted the importance of creating alternative local systems of mutual support to resist the current disempowering institutions of education and health care. Shiva (1994) articulated and demonstrated, with her work in India, the power of linking ecology, feminism, and social justice concerns to local resistance efforts against corporate globalization threatening their habitat and way of life.

The resistance to global corporate capitalism and the work of solidarity economics and politics is present, in some form, in nearly every nation (Notes From Nowhere, 2003). People dreaming and reweaving the power to choose and shape alternative ways of living need the skills of clinical researchers to help them name, track, and learn from the stories of their journeys. This is where we, as solidarity researchers, can join in the reclaiming and can help "to open a crack in history" (Ponce de León, 2001, p. 216).

Solidarity research, as we currently understand it, involves no new methods or grand new scheme; it is quieter than that. It does build on the core concepts related to democratizing knowledge, and it emphasizes at least three related assumptions, namely that (a) life is interdependent, diverse, always changing, and sustainable; (b) all action, including doing science, is moral activity; and (c) moral activity should sustain the common good. Common good is understood to mean those pluralistic, social, and ecological conditions and processes that seek the good of all and are arrived at through public interaction that expresses differences and seeks to include the perspectives of the more vulnerable—in other words, participatory democracy (Moe-Lobeda, 2002). Solidarity research, we propose, is about local, participatory, community-based inquiry and learning that is connected with similar activities around the globe. This work is not usually funded and often occurs after hours, but it can often be woven into existing projects and everyday activities in the workplace. It is more about how we and our families and colleagues live our lives and with whom and what we are in relationship and growing solidarity. Some of the purposes of solidarity research could be the following: (a) learning from others who are in different circumstances, (b) documenting and truth telling (the acts of testimony and witness), (c) restoring and nurturing personal and local community health, and (d) weaving connections with other communities of resistance around the globe. All four of these could inform, support, and maybe even transform the clinical research that we do above ground. So, what could solidarity research actually look like?

We suggest a three-step process: identify, connect, and create in solidarity. Solidarity research could begin by *identify*ing alternative kinds of relationships and clinical practices occurring in our own communities. Where are people already meeting their clinical needs through practices that value democratic participation, cooperation, diversity, sustainability, testimony, and direct experience with nature? Examples from our own experience include local organic farming cooperatives, domestic violence shelters, drumming circles, a conservancy group working to restore and protect a local watershed, faith-based groups working with the homeless and malnourished, and community groups helping to meet the health care needs of latchkey children and recent Hispanic immigrants. Imagine the possibilities if these groups could get connected!

The next step, after joining with identified groups, could be to *connect* them with each other and begin the process of developing relationships of mutual support. Freire's dialogic approach might be particularly helpful in facilitating learning connections that are empowering rather than paternalistic. These connections should be about building meaningful and accountable relationships from which concrete and practical exchanges, new questions and research approaches, and strategy development emerge. The work of solidarity research might be to help discover and document the interconnections between and among the groups. How does the health of the local river relate to domestic violence, homelessness, malnutrition, and healthy food sources? How does improvisational group drumming help to create community? Once local connections are established, consider connecting with similar communities and activities elsewhere in the larger region and world. We have not yet found a place where people are not working to heal the wounds and broken-ness resulting from the inherent excesses of colonialism, industrialism, and militarism and its current form as global corporate capitalism. We are in the early stages of developing connections with communities of resistance in Maine and Brazil, but the possibilities are probably unlimited. Keep expanding the circles of identification from self to local neighborhood to global commons.

It is hoped that, through the newly connected, emergent, and dynamic networks, we can begin to *create* alternative institutions and economies, new initiatives and community information systems, and refreshed imaginations. The specific role of clinical researchers would be to support all three steps by witnessing what is occurring, growing new embodied and embedded knowledge, and sharing in the empowerment of all participants. We can share the stories and use them to enhance our clinical research above ground. Just maybe, solidarity research is the small-scale, human-scale, local work interdependent with others around our earth that we do together, subversively, below ground to reclaim our homes and selves as spaces and bodies of love, healing, growth, and solidarity.

Let us imagine together. Jocelyn still works the grill at a fast-food restaurant while she takes classes at the community college for a degree in social work. She reads *Fast Food Nation* (Schlosser, 2002) and no longer eats where she works or at any other fast-food restaurants. Her family physician purchases a share in a local organic farm, and Jocelyn is able to barter for food at the same farm by agreeing to help during harvest season. The farmer also connects her by way of e-mail with an organic coffee collective in Chiapas, Mexico. That correspondence connects her with women's collectives in Chiapas whose members help to awaken Jocelyn to the relationships among her life situation, her heartburn, fast-food restaurants, the purple pill, and the threat to the livelihoods and way of life of her new friends in Mexico. A clinical researcher in the nursing department at a local university is a guest lecturer at Jocelyn's community college class, becomes interested in her story, and agrees to help Jocelyn and her family physician establish a heartburn recovery group. The researcher is now working with that group and the women's group in Chiapas to design a collaborative participatory research project. Is this a story of solidarity research? Are you connected?

◨ SUMMARY

Live as if you liked yourself, and it may happen: reach out, keep reaching out, keep bringing in. This is how we are going to live for a long time: not always, for every gardener knows that after the digging, after the planting, after the long season of tending and growth, the harvest comes.

—Concluding stanza of Marge Piercy's "The Seven of Pentacles"

There are many clinical worlds. Each of them is a place where support is sought and power is invoked. The clinical world and people's need for support occur in nursing, primary health care, specialized medical care, administration and management, education, social work, family therapy, mental health, public health, engineering, law, community organizing, and international activist work. In each of these worlds, there are questions emerging from practice. These are the questions, the settings, and the participants for doing qualitative clinical research. This is where the conversations start. Clinical research is disciplined inquiry regarding the conditions and processes that support and hinder the restoration and growth of interdependent and sustainable life.

People continue to meet in clinics, hoping to weave a comforting cloth of support, but the created relationships and patterns are now more varied, more confusing, and often too expensive. Concerns about access and cost do matter but are not adequately addressed without facing the abusive and dismembering experience of being a woman in the clinic, the pervasive delegitimation of patient experience, the clinicians' increasing sense of helpless imprisonment, and the mounting problems, discontinuities, and cultural conflicts within local communities. Knowing the probabilities is not enough and is often inappropriate. Ignoring the powerful, and often unconscious, impacts of elite corporate globalization and its ideology is morally dangerous (Comaroff & Comaroff, 2001; Ritzer, 2001). The stories, uniqueness, and context are also essential threads in the fabric. Without them, care and moral discourse remain narrowly defined, our bodies and lives remain fragmented, and power is imposed. Jocelyn remains isolated and dependent on her purple pill. She and we need the breath of qualitative research. She and we need *relationship* restored to the clinical world.

A decade has passed. Jocelyn is now a member of a community health advisory council that provides guidance for several local primary care practices and a regional health network and hospital system. They are meeting with an interdisciplinary team of researchers, clinicians, local employers, pharmaceutical industry representatives, and a fellow from the National Institutes of Health (NIH). This group is designing a new regional research initiative, jointly funded by the NIH and a local foundation, that will test a promising new approach to the care of GERD using a double helix RCT design that includes the extensive use of qualitative methods. The analysis of the qualitative data will occur independently from the RCT analysis and will be ongoing through the trial. Jocelyn is a member of the qualitative analysis team. She has authority to end the study for any reason at any time. Imagine the possibility that "Nexium" becomes a nexus for bringing people together to create *conscientização*.

Qualitative methods are needed now more than ever, but with a participatory, collaborative, narrative, and multimethod twist. Qualitative clinical researchers must engage the clinical experience and its questions and must practice humility and fidelity within a community of discourse at ground level. This is a dangerous—but exciting—conversation because it promises that no one can stay the same. Beware the idolatry of control, that is, the idolatry of measurement. If measurement is required, insist on inviting the patients and clinicians into the research process, insist on the precautionary principle, and insist on measuring suffering and love. Complicate the outcomes. Measure the dance of life's attachments and detachments, of mystery and grace, and of breathing and the rhythms of life. Measure the process of healing. Seek a healthier story. Our research needs to risk restoring relationship to the clinical world. Clinical research can heal by transforming into praxis. In time, all ideologies crumble, power shifts, and healing begins. We cannot prevent tornadoes. Thank heavens. It is much better than that. Go into the woods or beside the ocean. Join Jocelyn for the harvest at the local organic farm. *Practice solidarity research!* Do clinical research above ground that helps clinicians and patients now, and work to transform and heal. Let our clinical research also be the waters that break open fundamentalisms and flow between dualisms. At night, below ground, begin to grow a sustainable life together. When the sun rises, bloom!

▣ NOTES

1. "Patient" derives from the Latin word *patiens* ("to suffer") and from the Latin *paene* ("almost") and *penuria* ("need"). People seek clinicians because they have needs and are suffering. They are no longer complete; they lack adequate support. People come to clinicians because they do not perceive themselves as equal and/or whole. They are "patients" in need of movement toward wholeness.

2. "Clinic" derives from the Greek words *klinikos* ("of a bed") and *klinein* ("to lean, recline"). From this sense, *a clinic is a physical, emotional, conceptual, social, and spiritual place for those in need of support.* (This support can be medical, managerial, educational, legal,

economic, religious, nursing, social, or psychological.) This understanding defines clinic as a bounded text for research.

▣ REFERENCES

Aita, V., Dodendorf, D., Lebsack, J., Tallia, A., & Crabtree, B. (2001). Patient care staffing patterns and roles in community-based family practices. *Journal of Family Practice, 50,* 889.

Altheide, D. L., & Johnson, J. M. (1998). Criteria for assessing interpretive validity in qualitative research. In N. K. Denzin & Y. S. Lincoln (Eds.), *Collecting and interpreting qualitative materials* (pp. 283–312). Thousand Oaks, CA: Sage.

Baer, H. A. (1993). How critical can clinical anthropology be? *Medical Anthropology, 15,* 299–317.

Barbour, R. S. (2001). Checklists for improving rigour in qualitative research: A case of the tail wagging the dog? *British Medical Journal, 322,* 1115–1117.

Barry, C. A., Britten, N., Barber, N., Bradley, C., & Stevenson, F. (1999). Using reflexivity to optimize teamwork in qualitative research. *Qualitative Health Research, 9*(1), 26–44.

Becker, G. (1997). *Disrupted lives: How people create meaning in a chaotic world.* Berkeley: University of California Press.

Beinfield, H., & Korngold, E. (1991). *Between heaven and earth: A guide to Chinese medicine.* New York: Ballantine Books.

Berg, D. N., & Smith, K. K. (Eds.). (1988). *The self in social inquiry: Researching methods.* Newbury Park, CA: Sage.

Berger, P. L., & Luckmann, T. (1967). *The social construction of reality: A treatise in the sociology of knowledge.* Garden City, NY: Anchor.

Berry, W. (2000). *Life is a miracle.* Washington, DC: Counterpoint.

Bogdan, R. C., & Biklen, S. K. (1992). *Qualitative research for education: An introduction to theory and methods.* Boston: Allyn & Bacon.

Borkan, J. M. (2004). Mixed methods studies in primary care. *Annals of Family Medicine, 2*(1), 4–6.

Borkan, J. M., Quirk, M., & Sullivan M. (1991). Finding meaning after the fall: Injury narratives from elderly hip fracture patients. *Social Science and Medicine, 33,* 947–957.

Brewer, J., & Hunter, A. (1989). *Multimethod research: A synthesis of styles.* Newbury Park, CA: Sage.

Brody, H. (1992). *The healer's power.* New Haven, CT: Yale University Press.

Brody, H. (2003). *Stories of sickness* (2nd ed.). Oxford, UK: Oxford University Press.

Bunge, M. (1961). The weight of simplicity in the construction and assaying of scientific theories. *Philosophy of Science, 28,* 120–149.

Burawoy, M., Burton, A., Ferguson, A. A., Fox, K. J., Gamson, J., Gartrell, N., Hurst, L., Kurzman, C., Salzinger, L., Schiffman, J., & Ui, S. (1991). *Ethnography unbound: Power and resistance in the modern metropolis.* Berkeley: University of California Press.

Callahan, E. J., & Bertakis, K. D. (1991). Development and validation of the Davis Observation Code. *Family Medicine, 23,* 19–24.

Candib, L. M. (1995). *Medicine and the family: A feminist perspective.* New York: Basic Books.

Capra, F. (1996). *The web of life: A new scientific understanding of living systems.* New York: Anchor/Doubleday.

Capra, F. (2002). *The hidden connections: Integrating the biological, cognitive, and social dimensions of life into a science of sustainability.* New York: Doubleday.

Chapple, A., & Rogers, A. (1998). Explicit guidelines for qualitative research: A step in the right direction, a defence of the "soft" option, or a form of sociological imperialism? *Family Practice, 15,* 556–561.

Chrisman, N. J. (1977). The health seeking process: An approach to the natural history of illness. *Culture, Medicine, and Psychiatry, 1,* 351–377.

Chrisman, N. J., & Maretzki, T. W. (Eds.). (1982). *Clinically applied anthropology: Anthropologists in health science settings.* Boston: D. Reidel.

Chobanian, A. V., Bakris, G. L., Black, H. R., Cushman, W. C., Green, L. A., Izzo, J. L., Jr., Jones, D. W., Materson, B. J., Oparil, S., Wright, J. T., Jr., & Roccella, E. J. (2003). Report of the Joint National Committee on Prevention, Evaluation, and Treatment of High Blood Pressure (JNC 7). *Journal of the American Medical Association, 289,* 2560–2572.

Clifford, J., & Marcus, G. (Eds.). (1986). *Writing culture.* Berkeley: University of California Press.

Comaroff, J., & Comaroff, J. L. (Eds.). (2001). *Millennial capitalism and the culture of neoliberalism.* Durham, NC: Duke University Press.

Conio, M., Blanchi, S., Lapertosa, G., Ferraris, R., Sablich, R., Marchi, S., D'Onofrio, V., Lacchin, T., Iaquinto, G., Missale, G., Ravelli, P., Cestari, R., Benedetti, G., Macri, G., Fiocca, R., Munizzi, F., & Filiberti, R. (2003). Long-term endoscopic surveillance of patients with Barrett's esophagus: Incidence of dysplasia and adenocarcinoma—A prospective study. *American Journal of Gastroenterology, 98,* 1931–1939.

Coote, B. (1996). *The trade trap: Poverty and the global commodity market.* Oxford, UK: Oxfam UK & Ireland.

Coward, D. D. (1990). Critical multiplism: A research strategy for nursing science. *Image: Journal of Nursing Scholarship, 22,* 163–167.

Crabtree, B. F., & Miller, W. L. (Eds.). (1999). *Doing qualitative research* (2nd ed.). Thousand Oaks, CA: Sage.

Crabtree, B. F., Miller, W. L., Aita, V., Flocke, S. A., & Stange, K. C. (1998). Primary care practice organization and preventive services delivery: A qualitative analysis. *Journal of Family Practice, 46,* 403–409.

Crabtree, B. F., Miller, W. L., & Stange, K. (Eds.). (2001). Results from the Prevention and Competing Demands in Primary Care study. *Journal of Family Practice, 50,* 837–889.

Creswell, J. W. (2003). *Research design: Qualitative, quantitative, and mixed methods approaches* (2nd ed.). Thousand Oaks, CA: Sage.

Creswell, J. W., Fetters, M. D., & Ivankova, N. V. (2004). Designing a mixed methods study in primary care. *Annals of Family Medicine, 2*(1), 7–12.

Csordas, T. J. (2002). *Body/Meaning/Healing.* New York: Palgrave Macmillan.

Daly, J., & McDonald, I. (1992). Covering your back: Strategies for qualitative research in clinical settings. *Qualitative Health Research, 2,* 416–438.

Davis-Floyd, R., & St. John, G. (1998). *From doctor to healer: The transformative journey.* New Brunswick, NJ: Rutgers University Press.

Denz-Penhey, H., & Murdoch, J. C. (1993). Service delivery for people with chronic fatigue syndrome: A pilot action research study. *Family Practice, 10,* 14–18.

Deyo, R. A., Diehl, A. K., & Rosenthal, M. (1986). How many days of bedrest for acute low back pain? A randomized clinical trial. *New England Journal of Medicine, 315,* 1064–1070.

Diers, D. (1979). *Research in nursing practice.* Philadelphia: J. B. Lippincott.

Douthwaite, R. (1999). *The growth illusion* (rev. ed.). Gabriola Island, British Columbia: New Society Publishers.

Drury, N. (1996). *Shamanism*. Shaftesbury, UK: Element Books.

Ellingson, L. L. (1998). "Then you know how I feel": Empathy, identity, and reflexivity in field-work. *Qualitative Inquiry, 4*, 492–514.

Ellis, C. (1995). *Final negotiations: A story of love, loss, and chronic illness*. Philadelphia: Temple University Press.

Ellis, C., & Bochner, A. P. (Eds.). (1996). *Composing ethnography: Alternative forms of qualitative writing*. Walnut Creek, CA: AltaMira.

Engels, G. L. (1977). The need for a new medical model: A challenge for biomedicine. *Science, 196*, 129–136.

Fabrega, H., Jr. (1976). The function of medical care systems: A logical analysis. *Perspectives in Biology and Medicine, 20*, 108–119.

Fabrega, H., Jr. (1979). The ethnography of illness. *Social Science and Medicine, 13A*, 565–575.

Fahy, K., & Smith, P. (1999). From the sick role to subject positions: A new approach to the medical encounter. *Health, 3*(1), 71–93.

Farmer, P. (2001). *Infections and inequalities: The modern plagues* (rev. ed.). Berkeley: University of California Press.

Feinstein, A. R. (1985). *Clinical epidemiology: The architecture of clinical research*. Philadelphia: W. B. Saunders.

Finkler, K. (2000). *Experiencing the new genetics: Family and kinship on the medical frontier*. Philadelphia: University of Pennsylvania Press.

Fisher, S. (1986). *In the patient's best interest: Women and the politics of medical decisions*. New Brunswick, NJ: Rutgers University Press.

Fisher, S., & Todd, A. D. (Eds.). (1983). *The social organization of doctor–patient communication*. Washington, DC: Center for Applied Linguistics.

Flocke, S., Miller, W. L., & Crabtree, B. F. (2002). Relationships between physician practice style, patient satisfaction, and attributes of primary care. *Journal of Family Practice, 51*, 835–840.

Flocke, S., Stange, K. C., & Zyzanski, S. J. (1997). The impact of insurance type and forced discontinuity on the delivery of primary care. *Journal of Family Practice, 45*, 129–135.

Foster, G. M. (1974). Medical anthropology: Some contrasts with medical sociology. *Medical Anthropology Newsletter, 6*, 1–6.

Foster, G. M., & Anderson, B. G. (1978). *Medical anthropology*. New York: John Wiley.

Frank, A. W. (1991). *At the will of the body: Reflections on illness*. Boston: Houghton Mifflin.

Frank, A. W. (1995). *The wounded storyteller: Body, illness, and ethics*. Chicago: University of Chicago Press.

Freire, P. (1970). *Pedagogy of the oppressed* (M. B. Ramos, Trans.). New York: Continuum Publishing.

Freire, P. (1998). Pedagogy of the heart. In A. M. A. Freire & D. Macedo (Eds.), *The Paulo Freire reader* (pp. 265–282). New York: Continuum International Publishing Group.

Frey, R. (1994). *Eye juggling: Seeing the world through a looking glass and a glass pane*. Lanham, MD: University Press of America.

Freymann, J. G. (1989). The public's health care paradigm is shifting: Medicine must swing with it. *Journal of General Internal Medicine, 4*, 313–319.

Fullerton-Smith, I. (1995). How members of the Cochrane Collaboration prepare and maintain systematic reviews of the effects of health care. *Evidence-Based Medicine, 1*, 7–8.

Gardner, G. (Ed.). (2003). *State of the world 2003*. New York: Norton.

Giacomini, M. K., & Cook, D. J. (2000). Qualitative research in health care: What are the results and how do they help me care for my patients? *Journal of the American Medical Association, 284,* 478–482.

Glasgow, R. E., Lichtenstein, E., & Marcus, A. C. (2003). Why don't we see more translation of health promotion in research to practice? Rethinking the efficacy-to-effectiveness transition. *American Journal of Public Health, 93,* 1261–1267.

Good, B. J. (1994). *Medicine, rationality, and experience.* Cambridge, UK: Cambridge University Press.

Good, B. J., & Good, M. D. (1981). The meaning of symptoms: A cultural hermeneutic model for clinical practice. In L. Eisenberg & A. M. Kleinman (Eds.), *The relevance of social science for medicine* (pp. 165–196). Boston: D. Reidel.

Good, B. J., & Good, M. D. (1993). "Learning medicine": The constructing of medical knowledge at Harvard Medical School. In S. Lindenbaum & M. Lock (Eds.), *Knowledge, power, and practice: The anthropology of medicine and everyday life* (pp. 81–107). Berkeley: University of California Press.

Goodwin, M. A., Zyzanski, S. J., Zronek, S., Ruhe, M., Weyer, S. M., Konrad, N., Esola, D., & Stange, K. C. (2001). A clinical trial of tailored office systems for preventive service delivery: The Study to Enhance Prevention by Understanding Practice (STEP-UP). *American Journal of Preventive Medicine, 21,* 20–28.

Gordon, D. R. (1988). Tenacious assumptions in Western medicine. In M. Lock & D. Gordon (Eds.), *Biomedicine examined* (pp. 19–56). Boston: D. Reidel.

Gordon, J. (1996). *Manifesto for a new medicine: Your guide to healing partnerships and the wise use of alternative therapies.* Reading, MA: Addison-Wesley.

Greenhalgh, T., & Hurwitz, B. (1998). *Narrative based medicine: Dialogue and discourse in clinical practice.* London: BMJ Books.

Haraway, D. J. (1991). *Simians, cyborgs, and women: The reinvention of nature.* London: Routledge.

Haraway, D. J. (1993). The biopolitics of postmodern bodies: Determinations of self in immune system discourse. In S. Lindenbaum & M. Lock (Eds.), *Knowledge, power, and practice: The anthropology of medicine and everyday life* (pp. 364–410). Berkeley: University of California Press.

Hardin, G. (1985). *Filters against folly.* New York: Penguin Books.

Harris, C. M. (1989). Seeing sunflowers. *Journal of the Royal College of General Practitioners, 39,* 313–319.

Hawkins, A. H. (1993). *Reconstructing illness: Studies in pathography.* West Lafayette, IN: Purdue University Press.

Helman, C. G. (2000). *Culture, health, and illness* (4th ed.). Oxford, UK: Butterworth Heinemann.

Illich, I. (1970). *Deschooling society.* London: Marian Boyars.

Illich, I. (1976). *Medical nemesis: The exploration of health.* New York: Pantheon Books.

Jackson, M. (1989). *Paths toward a clearing: Radical empiricism and ethnographic inquiry.* Bloomington: Indiana University Press.

Jaen, C., McIlvain, H., Pol, L., Phillips, R., Jr., Flocke, S., & Crabtree, B. (2001). Tailoring tobacco counseling to the competing demands in the clinical encounter. *Journal of Family Practice, 50,* 859–863.

Jason, L. A., Keys, C. B., Suarez-Balcazar, Y., Taylor, R. R., & Davis, M. I. (Eds.). (2004). *Participatory community research: Theories and methods in action.* Washington, DC: American Psychological Association.

Jensen, D. (2002). *The culture of make believe.* New York: Context Books.

Johnson, D. A., Benjamin, S. B., Vakil, N. B., Goldstein, J. L., Lamet, M., Whipple, J., Damico, D., & Hamelin, B. (2001). Esomeprazole once daily for 6 months is effective therapy for maintaining healed erosive esophagitis and for controlling gastroesophageal reflux disease symptoms: A randomized, double-blind, placebo-controlled study of efficacy and safety. *American Journal of Gastroenterology, 96,* 27–34.

Johnson, M. (1987). *The body in the mind.* Chicago: University of Chicago Press.

Jolly, K., Bradley, F., Sharp, S., Smith, H., & Mant, D. (1998). Follow-up care in general practice of patients with myocardial infarction or angina pectoris: Initial results of the SHIP trial. *Family Practice, 15,* 548–555.

Kahn, D. L. (1993). Ways of discussing validity in qualitative nursing research. *Western Journal of Nursing Research, 15,* 122–126.

Kelsey, J. L., Thompson, W. D., & Evans, A. S. (1986). *Methods in observational epidemiology.* New York: Oxford University Press.

Kemmis, S., & McTaggart, R. (2003). Participatory action research. In N. K. Denzin & Y. S. Lincoln (Eds.), *Strategies of qualitative inquiry* (2nd ed., pp. 336–396). Thousand Oaks, CA: Sage.

Kim, J. Y., Millen, J. V., Irwin, A., & Gershman, J. (Eds.). (2000). *Dying for growth: Global inequality and the health of the poor.* Monroe, ME: Common Courage Press.

Kirmayer, L. J. (1992). The body's insistence on meaning: Metaphor as presentation and representation in illness experience. *Medical Anthropology Quarterly, 6,* 323–346.

Kleinman, A. M. (1988). *The illness narratives: Suffering, healing, and the human condition.* New York: Basic Books.

Kleinman, A. M. (1992). Local worlds of suffering: An interpersonal focus for ethnographies of illness experience. *Qualitative Health Research, 2,* 127–134.

Kleinman, A. M. (1995). *Writing at the margin: Discourse between anthropology and medicine.* Berkeley: University of California Press.

Kleinman, A. M., Eisenberg, L., & Good, B. (1978). Culture, illness, and care: Clinical lessons from anthropologic and cross-cultural research. *Annals of Internal Medicine, 88,* 251–258.

Lather, P. (1991). *Getting smart: Feminist research and pedagogy with/in the postmodern.* New York: Routledge.

Launer, J. (2002). *Narrative-based primary care: A practical guide.* Abingdon, UK: Radcliffe Medical Press.

Lazarus, E. S. (1988). Theoretical considerations for the study of the doctor–patient relationship: Implications of a perinatal study. *Medical Anthropology Quarterly, 2,* 34–58.

Lock, M. (1982). On revealing the hidden curriculum. *Medical Anthropology Quarterly, 14,* 19–21.

Lock, M. (1986). The anthropological study of the American medical system: Center and periphery. *Social Science and Medicine, 22,* 931–932.

Lock, M. (1993). Cultivating the body: Anthropology and epistemologies of bodily practice and knowledge. *Annual Reviews of Anthropology, 22,* 133–156.

Loxterkamp, D. (1997). *A measure of my days: The journal of a country doctor.* Hanover, NH: University Press of New England.

Macaulay, A. C., Commanda, L. E., Freeman, W. L., Gibson, N., McCabe, M. L., Robbins, C. M., & Twohig, P. L. (1998). Responsible research with communities: Participatory research in primary care [online publication of the North American Primary Care Research Group]. Retrieved October 27, 2004, from http://napcrg.org.exic.html

Macnaghten, P., & Urry, J. (Eds.). (2001). *Bodies of nature.* London: Sage.

Malterud, K. (2001a). The art and science of clinical knowledge: Evidence beyond measures and numbers. *Lancet, 358,* 397–400.

Malterud, K. (2001b). Qualitative research: Standards, challenges, and guidelines. *Lancet, 358,* 483–488.

Martin, E. (1994). *Flexible bodies: The role of immunity in American culture from the days of polio to the age of AIDS.* Boston: Beacon.

Mattingly, C. (1998). *Healing dramas and clinical plots: The narrative structure of experience.* Cambridge, UK: Cambridge University Press.

McGoldrick, M., Gerson, R., & Shellenberger, S. (1999). *Genograms: Assessment and intervention* (2nd ed.). New York: Norton.

McIlvain, H., Crabtree, B. F., Medder, J., Stange, K. C., & Miller, W. L. (1998). Using "practice genograms" to understand and describe practice configurations. *Family Medicine, 30,* 490–496.

McWhinney, I. R. (1986). Are we on the brink of a major transformation of clinical method? *Canadian Medical Association Journal, 135,* 873–878.

McWhinney, I. R. (1989). An acquaintance with particulars. *Family Medicine, 21,* 296–298.

Meinert, C. L. (1986). *Clinical trials: Design, conduct, and analysis.* New York: Oxford University Press.

Miller, W. L. (1994). Common space: Creating a collaborative research conversation. In B. F. Crabtree, W. L. Miller, R. B. Addison, V. J. Gilchrist, & A. Kuzel (Eds.), *Exploring collaborative research in primary care* (pp. 265–288). Thousand Oaks, CA: Sage.

Miller, W. L., & Crabtree, B. F. (1999a). The dance of interpretation. In B. F. Crabtree & W. L. Miller (Eds.), *Doing qualitative research* (2nd ed., pp. 127–143). Thousand Oaks, CA: Sage.

Miller, W. L., & Crabtree, B. F. (1999b). Primary care research: A multimethod typology and qualitative roadmap. In B. F. Crabtree & W. L. Miller (Eds.), *Doing qualitative research* (2nd ed., pp. 3–28). Thousand Oaks, CA: Sage.

Miller, W. L., Crabtree, B. F., Duffy, M. B., Epstein, R. M., & Stange, K. C. (2003). Research guidelines for assessing the impact of healing relationships in clinical medicine. *Alternative Therapies in Health and Medicine, 9*(3, Suppl.), 80A–95A.

Miller, W. L., Crabtree, B. F., McDaniel, R., & Stange, K. C. (1998). Understanding change in primary care practice using complexity theory. *Journal of Family Practice, 46,* 369–376.

Miller, W. L., McDaniel, R., Crabtree, B. F., & Stange, K. C. (2001). Practice jazz: Understanding variation in family practices using complexity science. *Journal of Family Practice, 50,* 872–878.

Mishler, E. G. (1984). *The discourse of medicine: Dialectics of medical interviews.* Norwood, NJ: Ablex.

Mitchell, M. L. (1998). *Employing qualitative methods in the private sector.* Thousand Oaks, CA: Sage.

Moe-Lobeda, C. D. (2002). *Healing a broken world: Globalization and god*. Minneapolis, MN: Fortress Press.

Mol, A. (2002). *The body multiple: Ontology in medical practice*. Durham, NC: Duke University Press.

Morgan, G. (1998). *Images of organization: The executive edition*. San Francisco: Berrett–Koehler.

Morrison, J. I. (2000). *Health care in the new millennium: Visions, values, and leadership*. San Francisco: Jossey–Bass.

Morse, J. M., & Field, P. A. (1997). *Principles of qualitative methods*. Thousand Oaks, CA: Sage.

Morse, J. M., Swanson, J. M., & Kuzel, A. J. (2001). *The nature of qualitative evidence*. Thousand Oaks, CA: Sage.

Morsy, S. A. (1996). Political economy in medical anthropology. In C. F. Sargent & T. M. Johnson (Eds.), *Medical anthropology: Contemporary theory and method* (rev. ed., pp. 21–40). Westport, CT: Praeger.

Moyer, B., MacAllister, J., & Soifer, S. (2001). *Doing democracy: The MAP model for organizing social movements*. Gabriola Island, British Columbia: New Society Publishers.

National Heart, Lung, and Blood Institute. (1998). *Clinical guidelines on the identification, evaluation, and treatment of overweight and obesity in adults: The evidence report* (NIH Publication 98-4083). Bethesda, MD: Author.

Naylor, C. D. (1995). Grey zones of clinical practice: Some limits to evidence-based medicine. *Lancet, 345,* 840–842.

Notes From Nowhere (Eds.). (2003). *We are everywhere: The irresistible rise of global anticapitalism*. London: Verso.

Orr, D. W. (2002). *The nature of design: Ecology, culture, and human intention*. Oxford, UK: Oxford University Press.

Pelto, P. J., & Pelto, G. H. (1978). *Anthropological research: The structure of inquiry* (2nd ed.). New York: Cambridge University Press.

Pelto, P. J., & Pelto, G. H. (1990). Field methods in medical anthropology. In T. M. Johnson & C. F. Sargent (Eds.), *Medical anthropology: Contemporary theory and method* (pp. 269–297). New York: Praeger.

Perdue, W. C., Stone, L. A., & Gostin, L. O. (2003). The built environment and its relationship to the public's health: The legal framework. *American Journal of Public Health, 93,* 1390–1394.

Perlas, N. (2000). *Shaping globalization: Civil society, cultural power, and threefolding*. Quezon City, Philippines: Center for Alternative Development Initiatives.

Pfifferling, J. H. (1981). A cultural prescription for medicocentrism. In L. Eisenberg & A. Kleinman (Eds.), *The relevance of social science for medicine* (pp. 197–222). Boston: D. Reidel.

Piercy, M. (1994). *Circles on the water: Selected poems of Marge Piercy*. New York: Alfred A. Knopf.

Pocock, S. J. (1983). *Clinical trials: A practical approach*. New York: John Wiley.

Pol, L., Rouse, J., Zyzanski, S., Rasmussen, D., & Crabtree, B. (2001). Rural, urban, and suburban comparisons of preventive services in family practice clinics. *Journal of Rural Health, 17,* 114–121.

Polgar, S. (1962). Health and human behavior: Areas of interest common to the social and medical sciences. *Current Anthropology, 3,* 159–205.

Ponce de León, J. (Ed.). (2001). *Our work is our weapon: Selected writings, subcommandante insurgente Marcos*. New York: Seven Stories Press.

Raffensperger, C. (2002). The precautionary principle: Bearing witness to and alleviating suffering. *Alternative Therapies, 8,* 111–115.

Raffensperger, C., Tickner, J., & Jackson, W. (1999). *Protecting public health and the environment: Implementing the precautionary principle*. Washington, DC: Island Press.

Rasmussen, L. L. (1996). *Earth community, earth ethics*. Maryknoll, NY: Orbis Books.

Richardson, L. (1990). *Writing strategies: Reaching diverse audiences*. Newbury Park, CA: Sage.

Ritzer, G. (2001). *Explorations in the sociology of consumption: Fast food, credit cards, and casinos*. London: Sage.

Robinson, D., Prest, L., Susman, J., Rasmussen, D., Rouse, J., & Crabtree, B. (2001). Technician, friend, detective, and healer: Family physicians' responses to emotional distress. *Journal of Family Practice, 50,* 864–870.

Roseland, M. (1998). *Toward sustainable communities: Resources for citizens and their governments*. Gabriola Island, British Columbia: New Society Publishers.

Sackett, D. L. (1991). *Clinical epidemiology: A basic science for clinical medicine* (2nd ed.). Boston: Little, Brown.

Sackett, D. L., Straus, S. E., Richardson, W. S., Rosenberg, W., & Haynes, R. (2000). *Evidence-based medicine: How to practice and teach EBM* (2nd ed.). London: Churchill Livingstone.

Sacks, O. (1984). *A leg to stand on*. New York: Summit Books.

Sandelowski, M. (2002). Reembodying qualitative inquiry. *Qualitative Health Research, 12,* 104–115.

Sapsford, R., & Abbott, P. (1992). *Research methods for nurses and the caring professions*. Bristol, PA: Open University Press.

Schein, E. H. (1987). *The clinical perspective in fieldwork*. Newbury Park, CA: Sage.

Scheper-Hughes, N., & Locke, M. (1987). The mindful body: A prolegomenon to future work in medical anthropology. *Medical Anthropology Quarterly, 1,* 6–41.

Schlosser, E. (2002). *Fast food nation: The dark side of the all-American meal*. New York: HarperCollins.

Schumacher, E. F. (1977). *A guide for the perplexed*. New York: Harper & Row.

Scott, J., Cohen, D., DiCicco-Bloom, B., Orzano, A. J., Jaen, C. R., & Crabtree, B. F. (2001). Antibiotic use in acute respiratory infections and the ways patients pressure physicians for a prescription. *Journal of Family Practice, 50,* 853–858.

Sharma, H., & Clark, C. (1998). *Contemporary ayur-veda: Medicine and research in maharishi ayur-veda*. Philadelphia: Churchill Livingstone.

Shaughnessy, A. F., Slawson, D. C., & Bennett, J. H. (1994). Becoming an information master: A guidebook to the medical information jungle. *Journal of Family Practice, 39,* 489–499.

Shavelson, R. J., & Towne, L. (Eds.). (2002). *Scientific research in education*. Washington, DC: National Academic Press.

Shepherd, M., Hattersley, A. T., & Sparkes, A. C. (2000). Predictive genetic testing in diabetes: A case study of multiple perspectives. *Qualitative Health Research, 10,* 242–259.

Shildrick, M. (1997). *Leaky bodies and boundaries: Feminism, postmodernism, and (bio)ethics*. London: Routledge.

Shiva, V. (1994). *Close to home: Women reconnect ecology, health, and development worldwide*. Gabriola Island, British Columbia: New Society Publishers.

Singer, M. (1995). Beyond the ivory tower: Critical praxis in medical anthropology. *Medical Anthropology Quarterly, 9,* 80–106.

Slawson, D. C., Shaughnessy, A. F., & Bennett, J. H. (1994). Becoming a medical information master: Feeling good about not knowing everything. *Journal of Family Practice, 38,* 505–513.

Small, S. A. (1995). Action-oriented research: Models and methods. *Journal of Marriage and the Family, 57,* 941–955.

Smith, R. C. (1996). *The patient's story: Integrated patient–doctor interviewing.* Boston: Little, Brown.

Snadden, D., & Brown, J. B. (1991). Asthma and stigma. *Family Practice, 8,* 329–335.

Stange, K. C., Miller, W. L., Crabtree, B. F., O'Connor, P. J., & Zyzanski, S. J. (1994). Multimethod research: Approaches for integrating qualitative and quantitative methods. *Journal of General Internal Medicine, 9,* 278–282.

Stange, K. C., Miller, W. L., & McWhinney, I. (2001). Developing the knowledge base of family practice. *Family Medicine, 33,* 286–297.

Stange, K. C., Zyzanskim, S. J., Jaen, C. R., Callahan, E. J., Kelly, R. B., Gillanders, W. R., Shank, J. C., Chao, J., Medalie, J. H., Miller, W. L., Crabtree, B. F., Flocke, S. A., Gilchrist, V. J., Langa, D. M., & Goodwin, M. A. (1998). Illuminating the "black box": A description of 4454 patient visits to 138 family physicians. *Journal of Family Practice, 46,* 377–389.

Stein, H. F. (1990). *American medicine as culture.* Boulder, CO: Westview.

Stevens, A., Abrams, K., Brazier, J., Fitzpatrick, R., & Lilford, R. (Eds.). (2001). *The advanced handbook of methods in evidence based healthcare.* London: Sage.

Stewart, M., Brown, J. B., Weston, W. W., McWhinney, I. R., McWilliam, C. L., & Freeman, T. R. (1995). *Patient-centered medicine: Transforming the clinical method.* Thousand Oaks, CA: Sage.

Strathern, A. J. (1996). *Body thoughts.* Ann Arbor: University of Michigan Press.

Swayne, J. (1998). *Homeopathic method: Implications for clinical practice and medical science.* London: Churchill Livingstone.

Symon, G., & Cassell, C. (Eds.). (1998). *Qualitative methods and analysis in organizational research: A practical guide.* London: Sage.

Talley, N. J., Venables, T. L., Green, J. R., Armstrong, D., O'Kane, K. P., Giaffer, M., Bardhan, K. D., Carlsson, R. G., Chen, S., & Hasselgren, G. S. (2002). Esomeprazole 40 mg and 20 mg is efficacious in the long-term management of patients with endoscopy-negative gastro-oesophageal reflux disease: A placebo-controlled trial of on-demand therapy for 6 months. *European Journal of Gastroenterology and Hepatology, 14,* 857–863.

Tallia, A., Stange, K., McDaniel R, Jr., Aita, V., Miller, W., & Crabtree, B. (2003). Understanding organizational designs of primary care practices. *Journal of Healthcare Management, 48,* 43–58.

Tandon, R. (1996). The historical roots and contemporary tendencies in participatory research: Implications for health care. In K. De Koning & M. Martin (Eds.), *Participatory research in health: Issues and experiences* (pp. 19–26). London: Zed Books.

Tashakkori, A., & Teddlie, C. (1998). *Mixed methodology: Combining qualitative and quantitative approaches.* Thousand Oaks, CA: Sage.

Taylor, B. (1993). Phenomenology: One way to understand nursing practice. *International Journal of Nursing Studies, 30,* 171–179.

Thesen, J., & Kuzel, A. (1999). Participatory inquiry. In B. F. Crabtree & W. L. Miller (Eds.), *Doing qualitative research* (2nd ed., pp. 269–290). Thousand Oaks, CA: Sage.

Thomashow, M. (1996). *Ecological identity: Becoming a reflective environmentalist.* Cambridge: MIT Press.

Tresolini, C. P. (1994). *Health professions education and relationship-centered care.* San Francisco: Pew Health Professions Commission.

Turner, B. (1992). *Regulating bodies: Essays in medical sociology.* New York: Routledge.

Waitzkin, H. (1991). *The politics of medical encounters: How patients and doctors deal with social problems.* New Haven, CT: Yale University Press.

Ward, M. M. (1993). Study design in qualitative research: A guide to assessing quality. *Journal of General Internal Medicine, 8,* 107–109.

Weil, A. (1988). *Health and healing.* Boston: Houghton Mifflin.

West, C. (1984). *Routine complications: Troubles with talk between doctors and patients.* Bloomington: Indiana University Press.

Wiesel, S. W., Cuckler, J. M., DeLuca, F., Jones, F., Zeide, M. S., & Rothman, R. H. (1980). Acute low back pain: An objective analysis of conservative therapy. *Spine, 5,* 324–330.

Wilber, K. (1996). *A brief history of everything.* Boston: Shambhala Publications.

Wiles, R. (1998). Patients' perceptions of their heart attack and recovery: The influence of epidemiological "evidence" and personal experience. *Social Science and Medicine, 46,* 1477–1486.

Williams, G. (1984). The genesis of chronic illness: Narrative re-construction. *Sociology of Health and Illness, 6,* 175–200.

Willms, D. G. (1991). A new stage, a new life: Individual success in quitting smoking. *Social Science and Medicine, 33,* 1365–1371.

Willms, D. G., Best, J. A., Taylor, D. W., Gilbert, J., Wilson, D., Lindsay, E., & Singer, J. (1990). A systematic approach for using qualitative methods in primary prevention research. *Medical Anthropology Quarterly, 4,* 391–409.

Wilson, D. M. C., Taylor, D. W., Gilbert, J. R., Best, J. A., Lindsay, E. A., Willms, D. G., & Singer, J. (1988). A randomized trial of a family physician intervention for smoking cessation. *Journal of the American Medical Association, 260,* 1570–1574.

Wolcott, H. F. (1990). *Writing up qualitative research.* Newbury Park, CA: Sage.

Young, A. (1982a). The anthropologies of illness and sickness. In B. Siegel, A. Beals, & S. Tyler (Eds.), *Annual review of anthropology 11* (pp. 257–285). Palo Alto, CA: Annual Reviews.

Young, A. (1982b). When rational men fall sick: An inquiry into some assumptions made by medical anthropologists. *Culture, Medicine, and Psychiatry, 5,* 317–335.

READER'S GUIDE

CHAPTER	SUMMARY	PRIMARY TOPICS	THEMATIC TOPICS
1.	Overview of Collection	Epistemology, Methodology	Paradigms, Resistances
2.	Money, Ethics Markets	Funds, Grants, Federal Agencies, IRBs	Review Boards, External Funding, Being Unscientific
3.	History of Performance Studies	Performance Ethnography, Culture	Critical Pedagogy, Politics of Possibility
4.	Major Case Study Forms, Triangulation	Case as Object of Study	Types: Intrinsic, Instrumental, Collective
5.	Public Ethnography, Civic Culture	Critical Ethnography, Critical Theory, Performance Ethnography	Engagement, Indigenous Political Theater
6.	Social Constructivist Approach	Interpretive Practices and Procedures	Local Culture, Civic Culture, Foucault, Discourse
7.	History of Grounded Theory	Inductive Guidelines, Social Justice	Positivism Versus Constructivism, Interpretive Criteria
8.	Critical Ethnography	Text as Performance	Human Rights, Social Justice, Performances
9.	History of *Testimonio*	Forms, Voice, Call for Justice	Political Texts, What Is Truth?
10.	Participatory Action Research History and Theories	Forms of PAR: First, Second, Third Person	Transformational Processes
11.	Clinical Methods and PAR	Experienced-Based Approach; Biomedical Models	Limits of Evidence-Based Models; Multimethods

GLOSSARY

回 A

Action ethnography: Critical ethnography involving the ethnographer in collaborative, social justice projects. See also *Critical ethnography*.

Action research: Critical research dealing with real-life problems, involving collaboration, dialogue, mutual learning, producing tangible results.

Advocacy: Arguing for action research projects that resist traditional forms of privilege, knowledge, and practice.

African American performance-based aesthetic: Using the tools of critical race consciousness to manipulate and criticize the tropes of minstrelsy that represent specific colonial racist practices.

Antifoundationalism: The refusal to adopt any permanent, unvarying, or foundational standards by which truth can be universally known.

Archaeology/genealogy: Textual and historical methods of interpretation, involving a complex set of concepts (savoir, connaissance, positivity, enunciation, discursive practice) associated with the work of Foucault; interpretive procedures showing how local practices and their subjected knowledges are brought into play, as in the history of sexuality.

Authenticity, validity as: Hallmarks of trustworthy, rigorous, valid constructivist inquiry; *Types:* fairness, ontological, educative, catalytic, tactical.

Autoethnography: Engaging ethnographical practice through personal, lived experience; writing the self into the ethnographic narrative.

Autohistory: Use of the autobiographical form to write life history or personal life stories and narratives.

Autopoiesis: A self (auto)-creation (poiesis) using the poetic and the historical to understand the current moment.

▣ B

Belmont Report: Report issued in 1978 by the U.S. Commission for the Protection of Human Subjects. This report established three principles, or moral standards (respect, beneficence, justice), for human subject research.

Biographical memory: A social process of looking back, as we find ourselves remembering our lives in terms of our experiences with others. Sociological introspection (C. Ellis) is a method for reconstructing biographical memory.

Black feminist thought: Critical race- and gender-based discourse linked to revolutionary black feminism; includes the work of June Jordan, Toni Morrison, and bell hooks.

Bricolage, bricoleur: A bricoleur is a person who uses bits and pieces and anything else to make do, to assemble a quilt, a montage, a performance, an interpretation, a bricolage, a new formation, like a jazz improvisation. The postmodern qualitative researcher is a bricoleur.

▣ C

Care, ethic of: Carol Gilligan characterizes the female moral voice as an ethic of care, involving compassion, and nurturance.

Catalytic authenticity: The ability of a given inquiry to prompt action on the part of research participants and the involvement of the researcher/evaluator in training participants in specific forms of social and political action if such training is desired by those participants.

Civic journalism: Journalism that shapes calls for a public ethnography and cultural criticism.

Cochrane Collaboration: An international group of clinicians, methodologists, and consumers formed to facilitate the collection, implementation, and dissemination of systematic reviews of multiple randomized clinical trials (RTCs).

Collaborative storytelling: An approach very similar to *testimonio,* in that it is the intention of the direct narrator (research participant) to use an interlocutor (the researcher) to bring his or her situation to the attention of an audience to which he or she would normally not have access because of his or her very condition of subalternity, which the *testimonio* bears witness.

Communitarian model of ethics: A model of ethics calling for collaborative, trusting, nonoppressive relationships between researchers and those studied. It presumes a community that is ontologically and axiologically prior to the person. This community has common moral values, and research is rooted in concepts of care, shared governance, neighborliness, love, kindness, and the moral good.

Compassionate consciousness: An embodied way of being and knowing that is a nonaccountable, nondescribable way of knowing.

Compositional studies: Contextual, relational studies that are sensitive to the fluidity of social identities and that analyze public and private institutions, groups, and lives lodged in relation to key social and economic structures.

Constructivist grounded theory: Associated with the work of Charmaz, emphasizing constructionist, not objectivist, leanings; criteria include credibility, resonance, and usefulness.

Conversational interviewing: A style of interviewing focused on encouraging subject participation. Interviews can be conducted in an informal manner, and interviewers may share more personal information about themselves than conventional interviewers.

Creative analytic practices (CAP): Writers interpret as they write, so writing is a form of inquiry, a way of making sense of the world. Laurel Richardson and Elizabeth Adams St. Pierre (Volume 3, Chapter 15) explore new writing and interpretive styles that follow from the narrative literary turn in the social sciences. They call these different forms of writing CAP (creative analytical processes) ethnography.

Critical ethnography: Critical ethnographers, drawing from critical theory and the Frankfurt school, emphasize a reflexive focus on praxis, action, experience, subjectivity, reflexivity, and dialogical understanding. See also *Action research.*

Critical humanism: An approach to inquiry that focuses on the structure of experience and its daily lived nature and that acknowledges the political and social role of all inquiry.

Critical pedagogy: The critical reflexive ways in which cultural agents resist and undermine particular hegemonic ways of understanding.

Critical Race Theory (CRT): Patricia Hill Collins (1991), Mari Matsuda (1995), Gloria Ladson-Billings (2000), and Patricia Williams (1992) have crafted Critical Race Theory to speak explicitly back to the webbed relations of history, the political economy, and everyday lives of women and men of color.

▣ D

Decolonization: Contesting colonial models of inquiry and domination, resisting hegemonic research protocols, and inventing new ways of knowing.

Diaspora identity: The identities of persons of color in the developing world who have been forced to move, to travel because of politics, economics, and other cultural forces.

Discourse analysis: The collection and analysis of spoken or written materials.

▣ E

Ethnodrama: Popular theater consisting of ethnographically derived plays located within the tradition of epic theater.

Ethnographic gaze: The classic look of the white male ethnographer and the "other."

Ethnopoetics: Ethnopoetics could be labeled investigative poetry's immediate predecessor. It is an attempt to make poetry political by merging a critique of colonialism, soft anthropology, and a poetics of witnessing. The term *ethnopoetics* was coined in 1967 by Jerome Rothenberg, Dennis Tedlock, and their colleagues.

Evidence-based research: A new methodological conservatism stressing scientifically based educational research, research using the biomedical, random, clinical trial model.

▣ F

Focus group as strategic articulation: Reconceptualizing focus groups as instruments for implementing critical pedagogy.

Freirian pedagogy: Pedagogy influenced by Paulo Freire in which the goal of education is to begin to name the world and to recognize that we are all "subjects" of our own lives and narratives, not "objects" in the stories of others.

▣ G

Gaze: Poststructuralists and postmodernists have contributed to the understanding that there is no clear window into the life of an individual. Any gaze is always filtered through the lenses of language, gender, social class, race, and ethnicity. There are no objective observations, only observations that are socially situated in the worlds of the observer and observed.

Grounded theory: A largely inductive method of developing theory through close-up contact with the empirical world.

▣ H

Habitus: Bourdieu used the concept of habitus to refer to a system of meanings and structures that generate and organize practices and representations that can be objectively adapted to their outcomes without presupposing a conscious aiming at ends or an express mastery of the operations necessary in order to attain them. Using a musical metaphor, they can be collectively orchestrated without being the product of the organizing action of a conductor.

Hip-hop movement: A gendered political, literary, and performance movement involving, in some instances, liberation work and a revolutionary call to resistance for African American and other marginalized communities. Some scholars and performers have made connections with the hip-hop generation and revolutionary black feminism.

Hybridity: Term that is characterized by literature and theory that focuses on the effects of mixture upon identity and culture.

▣ I

Indigenous pedagogy: A pedagogy that privileges the language, meanings, stories, and personal identities of indigenous persons.

Indigenous theater: Indigenous theater nurtures a critical transnational yet historically specific critical race consciousness. It uses indigenous performance as means of political representation through the reflexive use of historical restagings and masquerade. This subversive theater undermines colonial racial ideologies.

Institutional ethnography: A form of ethnography, focusing on power relations, systems of discourse, and ethnographic realities connected with the work of Dorothy Smith.

Interpretive sufficiency paradigm: Within a feminist communitarian model, paradigm seeks to open up the social world in all its dynamic dimensions. Ethnographic accounts should process sufficient depth, detail, emotionality, and nuance that will permit a critical consciousness to be formed. A discourse is authentically sufficient when it is multivocal, enhances moral discernment, and promotes social transformation.

▣ J

Justice and investigative poetics: Fight for social justice through poems calling on scholars to become more active in their communities.

▣ K

Kaupapa Māori research: In New Zealand, Māori scholars have coined a research approach as Kaupapa Māori or Dori research rather than employing the term *indigenist*. The struggle has been over the ability by Māoris as Māoris to name the world, to theorize the world. It is a particular approach that sets out to make a positive difference for Māoris, that incorporates a model of social change or transformation, and that privileges Māori knowledge and ways of being.

Knowledge economy: A term used by businesspeople to define the ways in which changes in technology such as the Internet, the removal of barriers to travel and trade, and the shift to a postindustrial economy have created conditions in which the knowledge content of all goods and services will underpin wealth creation and determine competitive advantage.

▣ L

Layered texts: A textual strategy for putting oneself into one's text and putting one's text into the literatures and traditions of social science.

Liberation theology: A school of theology, especially prevalent in the Roman Catholic Church in Latin America, that finds in the Gospel a call to free people from political, social, and material oppression, which uses *testimonio* as a way of expression.

Local understandings: Ethnographic studies tend to focus on locally crafted meanings and the settings where social interaction takes place. Such studies consider the situated content of talk in relation to local meaning-making practices.

Ludic postmodernism: Postmodernist currents associated with Derrida, Foucault, Lyotard, Ebert, and others.

▣ M

Method of instances: A method taking each instance of a phenomenon as an occurrence that evidences the operation of a set of cultural understandings currently available for use by cultural members.

Methodological fundamentalism: A return to a much discredited model of empirical inquiry wherein the "gold standard" for producing knowledge that is worthwhile is based on quantitative, experimental design studies.

Mixed-genre text: A text that crosses writing and interpretive formats (genres), including ethnography, history, fiction, poetry, prose, photography, and performance.

Moral/ethical epistemology: Epistemology that scholars of color have produced from which critical theories emerged, where groups such as African Americans, Native Americans, Latinos, and Asian Americans have the experience of a racialized and postcolonial identity.

Mystory performance: Personal cultural texts that contextualize important personal experiences and problems within the institutional settings and historical moments in which the author finds himself or herself.

▣ N

Narrative inquiry: A form of inquiry that analyzes narrative, in its many forms, and uses a narrative approach for interpretive purposes.

Naturalistic generalization: Generalizations made entirely from personal or vicarious experience.

Nonfiction, creative: A term suggesting no distinction between fiction and nonfiction because both are narrative. Thus, the difference between narrative writing and science writing is not one of fiction or nonfiction but the claim that the author makes for the text and how one's "truth claims" are evaluated.

▣ O

Online ethnography: A form of ethnography acknowledging that computer-mediated construction of self, other, and social structure constitutes a unique phenomenon of study.

Ontological authenticity: A criterion for determining a raised level of awareness by individual research participants.

Organic intellectual: Educated citizenry to participate actively in democracy, knowing enough to "read the word and the world" (Freire, 1970); helping credentialed intellectuals do the reconstructive work.

Other, as research subject: It refers to those who are studied by action-oriented and clinically oriented qualitative researchers who create spaces for those "Others" to speak and making such voices heard.

▣ P

Participatory action research: A movement in which researchers work with subordinated populations around the world to solve unique local problems with local funds of knowledge.

Patriarchal positivism: Control through rationality and separation that forms the dominant biomedical paradigm.

Performance ethnography: A critical and emancipatory discourse connecting critical pedagogy with new ways of writing and performing cultural politics in order to catalyze social change.

Performance methodology: A collectivized ensemble of precepts used by those committed to the communicative and pedagogical potential that knowledge—the process of attaining, sharing, and projecting knowing—can be accomplished through doing.

Performance of possibilities: A set of tenets offering both validity and direction for performance ethnography.

Performativity: The stylized repetition of communicative acts, linguistic and corporeal, that are socially validated and discursively established in the moment of the performance.

Poetics of place: Form of poetics in which, through the conveyance forms and content of language and story, we enter an analysis of places and the events that unfold in them.

Polyphonic interviewing: A method of interviewing in which the voices of the respondents are recorded with minimal influence from the researcher and are not collapsed together and reported as one through the interpretation of the researcher.

Postcolonial feminist thought: A mode of thought arguing that feminism takes many different forms depending on the context of contemporary nationalism. With attention to the invidious effects of "othering," it argues that Western feminist models are inappropriate for thinking of research with women in postcolonial sites.

Postmodern ethnography: Ethnography acknowledging that ethnographic practice is not apolitical or removed from ideology. Ethnographic practice hence has the capacity to be affected by or to affect social formations.

Poststructural feminism: Theory that emphasizes problems with the social text, its logic, and its inability ever to represent the world of lived experience fully. Poststructural feminists see the "communitarian dream" as politically disabling because of the suppression of gender differences and the exclusion of subaltern voices and marginalized groups whom community members are loath to engage.

▣ Q

Quality, emerging criteria: Set of understandings in which the ethical intersects both the interpersonal and the epistemological.

Queer theory: The postmodernization of sexual and gender studies bringing a radical deconstruction of all conventional categories of sexuality and gender.

Quilt maker, qualitative researcher as: Texts where many different things are going on at the same time—different voices, different perspectives, points of views, and angles of vision.

▣ R

Race, as social construction: A social constructionist conception of race refuses the notions of an essentialist or a biological ground for race, asserting, rather, that race is a linguistically and historically determined construct.

Racialized identity: Essentialized concepts of race imposed on specific individuals or groups.

Randomized clinical trial (RCT):   Clinical methodology that offers a compelling critical analysis of the biomedical paradigms and currently is considered to be the best external evidence when considering medical interventions.

Reality, hyper: It is a way of characterizing the way the consciousness interacts with "reality," when a consciousness loses its ability to distinguish reality from fantasy and when the nature of the hyperreal world is characterized by "enhancement" of reality.

Reflexivity, performative: A condition in which sociocultural groups, or their most perceptive members acting representatively, turn, bend, or reflect back on themselves (Turner, 1988).

Representation, crisis of: A moment of rupture in scholarship when texts began to become more reflexive, calling into question issues of gender, class, and race and seeking new models of trough, method, and representation.

Rhizomatic validity: A form of behaving via relay, circuit, and multiple openings that counters authority with multiple sites.

▣ S

Sacred epistemology: This epistemology places us in a noncompetitive, nonhierarchical relationship to the Earth, to nature, and to the larger world.

Safe spaces: Progressive social scientists have gained a foothold in the academy and have created safe spaces for themselves.

Scholars of color, moral epistemologies as activists: Seeking racial justice, scholars of color, using Critical Race Theory (CRT), enact critical and moral epistemologies (double consciousness, sovereignty, hybridity, postcolonialism).

Self-reflexive validity: A form of critical validity involving paying attention to one's place in the discourses and practices that are being analyzed.

Silences: Silences can reveal invisible social structures, as well as point to moral and ethical dilemmas and lack of awareness.

Social justice: A form of justice involving a moral commitment to social and economic reform and assistance to the poor; being an advocate for fairness and what is just.

Solidarity research: Research that empowers and promotes critical consciousness and acts of resistance.

Spirituality: A sense of the sacred, a sensuous and embodied form of being, including being in harmony with the universe.

Standpoint theory: Speaking and theorizing from a historically specific standpoint or position.

Subaltern: Colonized persons made to feel inferior by virtue of class, color, gender, race, and ethnicity.

Subversive theater: A theater that unsettles official versions of reality and challenges racism and white privilege.

▣ T

Testimonio: A first-person text with political content, often reporting on torture, imprisonment, and other struggles for survival.

Textualism: The study of documents and social texts as the site for the representation of lived experience. The media and popular culture are sites where history and lived experience come together. Nothing, Derrida reminds us, stands outside the text.

Transformative action: Creative, political action that changes the world.

Truth: A contested term, given different meaning within positivist, postpositivist and postmodern, and other narrative epistemologies.

▣ U

Uncertainty: The understanding that while social life is interdependent and displays regularities, the outcome of any given social event is uncertain and not fully predictable.

Unstructured interviewing: Open-ended interviewing involving an unstructured format, often used in oral history, participant observation, and PAR forms of inquiry.

Utopian performative: Performances that enact a politics of hope, liberation, and justice.

▣ V

Validity, authenticity criteria: The hallmarks of authentic, trustworthy, rigorous constructivist inquiry include fairness and four types of authenticity: ontological, educative, catalytic, and tactical.

Validity, catalytic: The extent to which research moves those it studies to understand the world and then act to change the world.

Validity, transgressive: A subversive approach to validity, connected with deconstructionism and the work of Patti Lather. There are four subtypes: ironic, paralogical, rhizomatic, and voluptuous.

Verbatim theater: A form of realistic theater or ethnodrama that uses oral history, news accounts, and verbatim reports, thereby quoting history back to itself, bringing the immediate past into the present.

Virtue ethics of care model: An ethics that goes beyond utilitarianism to include feminist notions of care, love, and communitarianism.

Voice, paradigmatic issues: Hearing the other (and the author) speak in the text, presenting the other's self in the text.

▣ W

Warranted assertion: A conclusion or assertion that is justified by a set of socially shaped reasons or judgments.

Wild places: Sacred places where meaning, self, and being dwell.

Women of color, as researcher: Women of color are urged to address, from within white patriarchy, culturally sensitive issues surrounding race, class, and gender.

Writing, as inquiry: Writing is a method of inquiry, writing is thinking, writing is analysis, and writing is a method of discovery.

Writing, performative: The kind of writing where the body and the spoken word come together. Performance writing shows and does not tell. It is writing that does what it says it is doing by doing it.

▣ X, Y, Z

Zombie research: According to Ken Plummer, a postgay humanist sociologist, in the postmodern moment, certain terms, such as *family,* and much of our research methodology language are obsolete. He calls them zombie categories. They are no longer needed. They are dead terms.

SUGGESTED READINGS

◨ CHAPTER 2

Cheek, J. (2006). The challenge of tailor made research quality: The RQF in Australia. In N. K. Denzin & M. D. Giardina (Eds.), *Qualitative inquiry and the conservative challenge: Contesting methodological fundamentalism*. Walnut Creek, CA: Left Coast Press.

Cheek, J. (in press). Qualitative inquiry, ethics and the politics of evidence: Working within these spaces rather than being worked over by them. In N. K. Denzin & M. D. Giardina (Eds.), *Ethical futures in qualitative inquiry: Decolonizing the politics of knowledge*. Walnut Creek, CA: Left Coast Press.

Cheek, J., Garnham, B., & Quan, J. (2006). What's in a number? Issues in providing evidence of impact and quality of research(ers). *Qualitative Health Research, 16*(3), 423–435.

Morse, J. (2006). The façade of scholarship. *Qualitative Health Research, 16*(7), 879–880.

◨ CHAPTER 3

Browning, B. (2005). "She attempted to take over the choreography of the sex act": Dance ethnography and the movement vocabulary of sex and labor. In D. S. Madison & J. Hamera (Eds.), *The Sage handbook of performance studies* (pp. 385–396).Thousand Oaks: Sage.

Goldman, D. (2005). Ethnography and the politics of adaptation: Leon Forrest's *Diving Dats*. In D. S. Madison & J. Hamera (Eds.), *The Sage handbook of performance studies* (pp. 366–384). Thousand Oaks, CA: Sage.

Hamera, J. (Ed.). (2006). *Opening acts: Performance in/as communication and cultural studies*. Thousand Oaks, CA: Sage.

Hamera, J. (2007). *Dancing communities: Performance, difference and connection in the global city*. Thousand Oaks, CA: Sage.

Jones, J. L. (2005). Introduction: Performance and ethnography, performing ethnography, performance ethnography. In D. S. Madison & J. Hamera (Eds.), *The Sage handbook of performance studies* (pp. 339–346). Thousand Oaks, CA: Sage.

Madison, D. S. (2005). *Critical ethnography: Method, ethics, and performance.* Thousand Oaks, CA: Sage.

Madison, D. S. (2005). Dwight Conquergood's "Rethinking ethnography." In D. S. Madison & J. Hamera (Eds.), *The Sage handbook of performance studies* (pp. 374–350). Thousand Oaks, CA: Sage.

Madison, D. S. (2005). Staging fieldwork/performing human rights. In D. S. Madison & J. Hamera (Eds.), *The Sage handbook of performance studies* (pp. 397–418). Thousand Oaks, CA: Sage.

Madison, D. S., & Hamera, J. (Eds.). (2005). *The Sage handbook of performance studies.* Thousand Oaks, CA: Sage.

Pelias, R. J. (in press). Performance ethnography. In G. Ritzer (Ed.), *Encyclopedia of sociology.* Williston, VT: Blackwell.

Performance ethnography [Special issue]. (2006). *Text and Performance Quarterly, 26*(4).

▣ CHAPTER 6

Berger, P. L., & Luckmann, T. (1966). *The social construction of reality.* New York: Doubleday.

Blumer, H. (1969). *Symbolic interactionism.* Englewood Cliffs, NJ: Prentice Hall.

Drew, P., Raymond, G., & Weinberg, D. (Eds.). (2006). *Talk and interaction in social research methods.* London: Sage.

Foucault, M. (1979). *Discipline and punish.* New York: Vintage.

Garfinkel, H. (1967). *Studies in ethnomethodology.* Englewood Cliffs, NJ: Prentice Hall.

Gubrium, J. F. (1993). For a cautious naturalism. In J. Holstein & G. Miller (Eds.), *Reconsidering social constructionism* (pp. 89–101). New York: Aldine de Gruyter.

Gubrium, J. F., & Holstein, J. A. (1997). *The new language of qualitative method.* New York: Oxford University Press.

Gubrium, J. F., & Holstein, J. A. (2008). Narrative ethnography. In Sharlene Hesse-Biber & Patricia Leavy (Eds.), *Handbook of emergent methods.* New York: Guilford.

Heritage, J. (1984). *Garfinkel and ethnomethodology.* Cambridge, UK: Polity.

Holstein, J. A. (1993). *Court–ordered insanity: Interpretive practice and involuntary commitment.* Hawthorne, NY: Aldine de Gruyter.

Holstein, J. A., & Gubrium, J. F. (2000). *The self we live by: Narrative identity in a postmodern world.* New York: Oxford University Press.

Holstein, J. A., & Gubrium, J. F. (2004). Context: Working it up, down, and across. In Clive Seale, Giampietro Gobo, Jaber F. Gubrium, and David Silverman (Eds.), *Qualitative research practice.* London: Sage.

Holstein, J. A., & Gubrium, J. F. (2008). Constructionist impulses in ethnographic fieldwork. In James A. Holstein & Jaber F. Gubrium (Eds.), *Handbook of constructionist research.* New York: Guilford.

Miller, G. (1997). *Becoming miracle workers: Language and meaning in brief therapy.* New York: Aldine de Gruyter.

Pollner, M. (1987). *Mundane reason.* Cambridge, UK: Cambridge University Press.

Sacks, H. (1992). *Lectures on conversation* (Vols. 1–2). Oxford, UK: Blackwell.

Schutz, A. (1970). *On phenomenology and social relations.* Chicago: University of Chicago Press.

Silverman, D. (Ed.). (2004). *Qualitative research.* London: Sage.
Wieder, D. L. (1988). *Language and social reality.* Washington, DC: University Press of America.

▣ CHAPTER 7

Bryant, A., & Charmaz, K. (in press). *The handbook of grounded theory.* London: Sage.
Charmaz, K. (2000). Constructivist and objectivist grounded theory. In N. K. Denzin & Y. Lincoln (Eds.), *Handbook of qualitative research* (2nd ed., pp. 509–535). Thousand Oaks, CA: Sage.
Charmaz, K. (2006). *Constructing grounded theory: A practical guide through qualitative analysis.* London: Sage.
Charmaz, K. (in press). Grounded theory. In J. A. Smith (Ed.), *Qualitative psychology: A practical guide to research methods* (2nd ed.). London: Sage.
Clarke, A. E. (2005). *Situational analysis: Grounded theory after the postmodern turn.* Thousand Oaks, CA: Sage.
Clarke, A. E. (2006). Feminisms, grounded theory, and situational analysis. In S. Hess-Biber & D. Leckenby (Eds.), *Handbook of feminist research methods* (pp. 345–370). Thousand Oaks, CA: Sage.
Dey, I. (1999). *Grounding grounded theory.* San Diego: Academic Press.
Glaser, B. G. (1978). *Theoretical sensitivity.* Mill Valley, CA: The Sociology Press.
Glaser, B. G. (1992). *Basics of grounded theory analysis.* Mill Valley, CA: The Sociology Press.
Glaser, B. G. (2001). *The grounded theory perspective: Conceptualization contrasted with description.* Mill Valley, CA: The Sociology Press.
Glaser, B. G., & Strauss, A. L. (1967). *The discovery of grounded theory.* Chicago: Aldine.
Kelle, U. (2005, May). Emergence vs. forcing: A crucial problem of "grounded theory" reconsidered [52 paragraphs]. *Forum Qualitative Sozialforschung/Forum Qualitative Sociology* [Online journal], *6*(2), Art. 27. Retrieved May 30, 2005, from http/www.qualitative-research.net/fqs.texte-2–05/05–2–27-e.htm
Strauss, A. (1987). *Qualitative analysis for social scientists.* New York: Cambridge University Press.
Strauss, A., & Corbin, J. (1998). *Basics of qualitative research: Grounded theory procedures and techniques* (2nd ed.). Thousand Oaks, CA: Sage.
Strauss, A. L. (1993). *Continual permutations of action.* New York: Aldine de Gruyter.

▣ CHAPTER 9

Bartow, J. (2006). *Subject to change: The lessons of Latin American women's testimonio for truth, fiction, and theory.* Chapel Hill: North Carolina Studies in the Romance Languages and Literatures.
Beverley, J. (2004). Testimonio. In *On the politics of truth.* Minneapolis: University of Minnesota Press.
Nance, K. (2000). *Can literature promote justice? Trauma narrative and social action in Latin American testimonio.* Nashville, TN: Vanderbilt University Press.
Sarlo, B. (2005). *Tiempo pasado: Cultura de la memoria y giro subjetivo.* Buenos Aires: Siglo veintiuno.

AUTHOR INDEX

SUBJECT INDEX

ABOUT THE EDITORS

Norman K. Denzin is Distinguished Professor of Communications, College of Communications Scholar, and Research Professor of Communications, Sociology, and Humanities at the University of Illinois at Urbana-Champaign. He is the author of numerous books, including *Interpretive Ethnography: Ethnographic Practices for the 21st Century; The Cinematic Society: The Voyeur's Gaze; Images of Postmodern Society; The Research Act: A Theoretical Introduction to Sociological Methods; Interpretive Interactionism; Hollywood Shot by Shot; The Recovering Alcoholic;* and *The Alcoholic Self,* which won the Charles Cooley Award from the Society for the Study of Symbolic Interaction in 1988. In 1997, the Society for the Study of Symbolic Interaction presented him the George Herbert Award. He is the editor of *Sociological Quarterly,* coeditor of *Qualitative Inquiry,* and editor of the book series *Cultural Studies: A Research Annual and Studies in Symbolic Interaction.*

Yvonna S. Lincoln is Ruth Harrington Chair of Educational Leadership and Distinguished Professor of Higher Education at Texas A&M University. In addition to this volume, she is coeditor of the first and second editions of the *Handbook of Qualitative Research,* the journal *Qualitative Inquiry* (with Norman K. Denzin), and the Teaching and Learning section of the *American Educational Research Journal* (with Bruce Thompson and Stephanie Knight). She is the coauthor, with Egon Guba, of *Naturalistic Inquiry, Effective Evaluation, and Fourth Generation Evaluation,* the editor of *Organizational Theory and Inquiry,* and the coeditor of several other books with William G. Tierney and with Norman Denzin. She is the recipient of numerous awards for research and has published journal articles, chapters, and conference papers on higher education, research university libraries, and alternative paradigm inquiry.

ABOUT THE
CONTRIBUTORS

Bryant Keith Alexander is Professor in the Department of Communication Studies at California State University, Los Angeles. His research is grounded in the social and performative construction of identity as related to issues of race, culture, and gender and uses qualitative, critical, and performative methodologies, including performative writing, interpretive ethnography, and autoethnography. Most recently, he has turned to cultural geography, studies in which he focuses on the spatial constitution of society through the mediating effects of culture. His essays have appeared in *Qualitative Inquiry, Theatre Annual, Theatre Topics, Callaloo*, and *Text and Performance Quarterly*, among others. He has chapters in *The Image of the Outsider; Beacon Best 2000: Best Writing of Men and Women of All Colors; Communication, Race, and Family;* and *The Future of Performance Studies.* He is coeditor of the *Performance Theories in Education: Power, Pedagogy, and the Politics of Identity* and serves as the section editor of the forthcoming *Handbook of Performance Studies* (Sage). In 2002, he was honored with the Norman K. Denzin Outstanding Qualitative Research Award from the Carl Couch Center, Department of Communication Studies, University of Northern Iowa for his essay, "(Re)Visioning the Ethnographic Site: Interpretive Ethnography as a Method of Pedagogical Reflexivity and Scholarly Production."

John Beverley is Professor and Chair of the Department of Hispanic Languages and Literatures at the University of Pittsburgh, where he has taught for 35 years. He was a founding member and co-coordinator of the Latin American Subaltern Studies Group between 1992 and 2002, the year of its demise. His recent books include *Subalternity and Representation* (1999, 2004), *From Cuba* (Ed., 2003); and *Testimonio: On the Politics of Truth* (2004). He coedits the University of Pittsburgh Press series *Illuminations: Cultural Formations of the Americas.*

Kathy Charmaz is Professor of Sociology and Coordinator of the Faculty Writing Program at Sonoma State University in Rohnert Park, California. She assists faculty in writing for publication and leads three faculty seminars on writing. She teaches in the areas of sociological theory, social psychology, qualitative methods, health and illness, and gerontology. In addition to writing numerous chapters and articles, she has written or coedited five books, including *Good Days, Bad Days: The Self in Chronic Illness and Time*, which won awards from the Pacific Sociological Association and the Society for the Study of Symbolic Interaction. Her recent publications focus on medical sociology, qualitative methods, and social psychology and include a number of articles and chapters on grounded theory. Dr. Charmaz has served as the president of the Pacific Sociological Association, vice-president of the Society for the Study of Symbolic Interaction, and editor of *Symbolic Interaction*. She is the chair-elect of the Medical Sociology Section of the American Sociological Association.

Julianne Cheek is Professor at the University of South Australia in the Division of Health Sciences in Adelaide and Director of Early Career Researcher Development. She is recognized internationally for her expertise in qualitative research in health-related areas. She has attracted funding for many qualitative research projects, with some 19 projects funded in the past four years including five consecutive Australian Research Council grants. She has also attracted large sums of funding for projects related to teaching that have qualitative principles embedded within them. Professor Cheek has published over 60 refereed book chapters and journal articles, many of which explore the application of postmodern and poststructural approaches to health care. Her latest book is *Postmodern and Poststructural Approaches to Nursing Research* (Sage, 2000).

Benjamin F. Crabtree, Ph.D., is a medical anthropologist and Professor and Director of Research in the Department of Family Medicine, UMDNJ-Robert Wood Johnson Medical School. He is also Associate Editor for the *Annals of Family Medicine*. As a full-time primary care/health services researcher in family medicine for more than 15 years, Dr. Crabtree has contributed to numerous articles and chapters on both qualitative and quantitative methods, covering topics ranging from time series analysis and log-linear models to in-depth interviews, case study research, and qualitative analysis strategies. Dr. Crabtree is coeditor (with William Miller) of *Doing Qualitative Research*, a Sage book now in its 2nd edition. He has been principal investigator on federally funded grants from the Agency for Healthcare Research and Quality, the National Cancer Institute, and the National Heart, Lung, and Blood Institute. These grants integrate qualitative methods with concepts from complexity science to better understand the differential responses primary care practices have to interventions and to design strategies for enhancing quality of patient care.

Jaber F. Gubrium is Professor and Chair of Sociology at the University of Missouri, Columbia. His research deals with the narrative organization and ethnography of personal identity, family, the life course, aging, and adaptations to illness. He is the editor of the *Journal of Aging Studies* and author of several monographs, including *Living and Dying at Murray Manor, Caretakers, Describing Care, Oldtimers and Alzheimer's, Out of Control,* and *Speaking of Life.* He has recently coedited *Qualitative Research Practice* for Sage and continues to analyze constructions of disability by stroke survivors.

James A. Holstein is Professor of Sociology in the Department of Social and Cultural Sciences at Marquette University. He is the author or editor of numerous books on qualitative research methods, social problems, deviance, and social control. In collaboration with Jaber F. Gubrium, he has published *The New Language of Qualitative Method, The Active Interview, Handbook of Interview Research, The Self We Live By,* and *Inner Lives and Social Worlds.* Holstein is currently the editor of the journal *Social Problems.*

Stephen Kemmis is Professor of Education, Charles Sturt University, Wagga Wagga, Australia. His research interests include research and evaluation methods in education and the social sciences, participatory action research, communicative evaluation, Indigenous education, university research development, and curriculum theory. His books include *Becoming Critical: Education, Knowledge, and Action Research* (with Wilfred Carr) and *The Action Research Planner* (with Robin McTaggart).

D. Soyini Madison is Associate Professor of Communication Studies in the area of performance studies at the University of North Carolina, Chapel Hill. Madison's Ph.D. from Northwestern University, under the direction of Dwight Conquergood, is one of the first scholarly examinations that focus on the intersections between performance studies and critical ethnography. She is the author of *Critical Ethnography: Methods, Ethics, and Performance* (Sage, 2005) and several articles ranging from film and performance criticism to examinations in critical race and gender studies. Madison is editor of the anthology, *The Woman That I Am: The Literature and Culture of Contemporary Women of Color.* She is a Senior Fulbright Scholar and recently completed a visiting lectureship at the University of Ghana at Legon. Her current project is an examination of staging/performing local debates surrounding human rights and traditional religious practices as these debates are influenced by the global economy and national development.

Robin McTaggart is Professor and Pro-Vice-Chancellor of Staff Development and Student Affairs at James Cook University, Townsville and Cairns, North Queensland. He is Adjunct Professor in the International Graduate School of Management of the University of South Australia. He was Executive Dean of Law and Education (1998) and Executive Dean of Education and Indigenous Studies (1999) at James Cook University. Before moving to JCU, he was Director of International Programs in the Faculty of Education at Deakin University Geelong and was Head of the School of Administration and Curriculum Studies at Deakin University from 1993 to 1995. He completed his Ph.D. at the Center for Instructional Research and Curriculum Evaluation at the University of Illinois, where he was a W. F. Connell Scholar. He has conducted evaluation and research studies of action research by educators, discipline-based arts education, arts programs for disadvantaged youth, instructional computing programs for intellectually disabled adults, coeducation and gender equity in private schooling, AIDS/HIV professional development for rural health workers, Aboriginal education in traditionally oriented remote communities, scientific literacies, and distance education provision in technical and further education. He has also conducted participatory action research and evaluation training programs for private and public sector managers, academics, technical and further education and training professionals, educators, educational consultants, and health professionals in Australia, Canada, Hong Kong, Indonesia, Malaysia, New Zealand, Singapore, Thailand, and the United States.

William L. Miller (M.D., M.A.) is a family physician anthropologist and the Leonard Parker Pool Chair of Family Medicine at Lehigh Valley Hospital and Health Network, Allentown, Pennsylvania. He is Professor of Family and Community Medicine, Pennsylvania State University College of Medicine. He is also consulting editor for the *Annals of Family Medicine.* For more than 15 years, Dr. Miller, in collaboration with Benjamin Crabtree, has been working to make qualitative research more accessible to health care researchers. He has written and contributed to book chapters and articles detailing step-by-step applications of qualitative methods and seeks to translate this work into the everyday clinical, educational, and administrative realms of health care. His research interests focus on applying the paradigm of ecological relationship-centeredness and the theory of complex adaptive systems to improving health care at the organizational, office, and encounter levels and co-creating a participatory community of practice-based research. Much of this work is shared collaboratively with Dr. Crabtree through his federally funded grants.

Robert E. Stake is Emeritus Professor of Education and Director of the Center for Instructional Research and Curriculum Evaluation at the University of Illinois. Since 1963, he has been a specialist in the evaluation of educational programs. Among the evaluative studies he directed were works in science and mathematics in elementary and secondary schools, model programs and conventional teaching of the arts in schools, development of teaching with sensitivity to gender equity, education of teachers for the deaf and for youth in transition from school to work settings, environmental education and special programs for gifted students, and the reform of urban education. Stake has authored *Quieting Reform,* a book on Charles Murray's evaluation of Cities-in-Schools; two books on methodology, *Evaluating the Arts in Education* and *The Art of Case Study Research;* and *Custom and Cherishing,* and a book with Liora Bresler and Linda Mabry on teaching the arts in ordinary elementary school classrooms in America. Recently he led a multiyear evaluation study of the Chicago Teachers Academy for Mathematics and Science. For his evaluation work, in 1988, he received the Lazarsfeld Award from the American Evaluation Association and, in 1994, an honorary doctorate from the University of Uppsala.

Barbara Tedlock is Distinguished Professor of Anthropology at the State University of New York at Buffalo. She served as editor-in-chief of the *American Anthropologist* (1993–1998). Her honors include the 1997 President's Award for distinctive leadership in forging a new vision for the flagship journal of the American Anthropological Association, the *American Anthropologist,* and for dedication and commitment to the profession of anthropology. She also received the 2002 Chancellor's Research Recognition Award for "Overall Excellence of Research in the Social Sciences," given by the Chancellor of the State University of New York. She is a former President of the Society for Humanistic Anthropology and a member of PEN (Poets-Essayists-Novelists). Her publications include six books and more than 100 articles and essays.